THE COMPLETE SERMONS OF
RALPH WALDO EMERSON

VOLUME 1

THE COMPLETE SERMONS OF RALPH WALDO EMERSON
IN FOUR VOLUMES

Chief Editor: Albert J. von Frank

Editors: Ronald A. Bosco
Andrew H. Delbanco
Wesley T. Mott
Teresa Toulouse

Contributing Editors: David M. Robinson
Wallace E. Williams

THE COMPLETE SERMONS OF
RALPH WALDO EMERSON

VOLUME 1

Edited by Albert J. von Frank
Introduction by David M. Robinson

UNIVERSITY OF MISSOURI PRESS
COLUMBIA, 1989

The publication of this volume was made possible in part by grants
from the Programs for Editions and Publications of the National
Endowment for the Humanities, an independent Federal agency.

Library of Congress Cataloging-in-Publication Data

Emerson, Ralph Waldo, 1803–1882.
  The complete sermons of Ralph Waldo Emerson.
  Includes index.
  1. Unitarian churches—Sermons. 2. Sermons, American.
I. Von Frank, Albert J. II. Title.
BX9843.E487C66   1988   252'.08   88-4834
ISBN 0-8262-0681-6 (v. 1. : alk. paper)

∞™ This paper meets the minimum requirements of
the American National Standard for Permanence of Paper
for Printed Library Materials, Z39.48, 1984.

COMMITTEE ON
SCHOLARLY EDITIONS
AN APPROVED EDITION
MODERN LANGUAGE
ASSOCIATION OF AMERICA

Preface

Most of the sermons published in this complete four-volume edition appear here in print for the first time; it is hoped that they will illuminate an obscure but formative portion of a career of acknowledged importance to the literature and culture of America. The fruit of Emerson's religious and ethical speculation until the age of thirty, the sermons represent his first sustained contact with an audience and were the basis for his earliest reputation.

An editor gratefully incurs debts of all kinds. I wish to thank Joy Graves and Jane von Frank, who assisted in the preparation of the computer transcript; Andrew Delbanco and Teresa Toulouse, who provided a second reading of the text against the manuscripts; Wallace Williams, editor of *The Early Lectures of Ralph Waldo Emerson*, for valuable advice on textual matters and for checking the text and textual notes; graduate assistants Michael Casey and Dale Hearell for their work in checking the annotations; William B. Barton, Kenneth W. Cameron, Ralph H. Orth, Joseph Slater, Eleanor M. Tilton, and Douglas E. Wilson for various kinds of help, and Joel Myerson, for generous supplies of information and encouragement from the very beginning. I would also like to thank Rick Boland and Clair Willcox of the University of Missouri Press.

The editors of all four volumes wish to express their gratitude for the work of the late Gene Irey, who compiled an extensive computer concordance to Emerson's writings, and to his friend and colleague, Mike Preston, who in the best traditions of academic cooperation has made this work available to us.

For permission to publish the sermons, I am indebted to the Ralph Waldo Emerson Memorial Association and to the Houghton Library of Harvard University. Thanks are due to William H. Bond, Rodney Dennis, Thomas F. Noonan, Jim Lewis, and the helpful and courteous staff of the Houghton Library; to Catharine Craven of the Massachusetts Historical Society; and to the staff of Holland Library at Washington State University.

For work on the present volume, the Graduate School of Washington State University generously provided a research grant-in-aid.

A.J.v.F.
January 1989

Waltham Oct. 15. 1826
Boston First Ch. Nov. 19.   I.   Script. V Thess. 58   Belknap
                                          1 Thessalonians. V. Ch. 17 Verse.   457 16
                                              Pray without Ceasing.   248

It is the duty of men to judge men only
by their actions. Our faculties furnish us with
no means of arriving at the motive, the
character, the secret self. We call the tree
good from its fruits, and the man from his
works. Because we have no power, we have no
right, to assign motives any other than those which ought in similar circumstance
to guide our own
from the most natural connexion we have
observed, in our own person, to join impulse +
action. But because we are not able to dis-
                                   to see the soul
cern the processes of thought, + can hardly
discourse with confidence after we have
passed the boundary of material seeing
— it were very ridiculous to doubt or deny
that any beings can. It is not incredible,
that, the thoughts of the mind, are the
subjects of perception to some beings, as prop-ly
ly, as the sounds of the voice, or the mo

CONTENTS

Abbreviations of Works Frequently Cited

CW   *The Complete Works of Ralph Waldo Emerson.* Edited by Joseph Slater, et al. 5 vols. to date. Cambridge: Harvard University, 1971-.

EL   *The Early Lectures of Ralph Waldo Emerson.* Edited by Stephen E. Whicher, Robert E. Spiller, and Wallace E. Williams. 3 vols. Cambridge: Harvard University Press, 1959-1972.

J   *Journals of Ralph Waldo Emerson.* Edited by Edward Waldo Emerson and Waldo Emerson Forbes. 10 vols. Boston and New York: Houghton Mifflin Co., 1909-1914.

JMN   *The Journals and Miscellaneous Notebooks of Ralph Waldo Emerson.* Edited by William H. Gilman et al. 16 vols. Cambridge: Harvard University Press, 1960-1982.

L   *The Letters of Ralph Waldo Emerson.* Edited by Ralph L. Rusk. 6 vols. New York: Columbia University Press, 1939.

Life   Ralph L. Rusk. *The Life of Ralph Waldo Emerson.* New York: Charles Scribner's Sons, 1949.

MHS   Massachusetts Historical Society. Papers of the Second Church, Boston.

OFL   *One First Love: The Letters of Ellen Louisa Tucker to Ralph Waldo Emerson.* Edited by Edith W. Gregg. Cambridge: Harvard University Press, 1962.

Pommer   Henry F. Pommer. *Emerson's First Marriage.* Carbondale and Edwardsville: Southern Illinois University Press, 1967.

W   *The Complete Works of Ralph Waldo Emerson.* Edited by Edward Waldo Emerson. Centenary Edition. 12 vols. Boston and New York: Houghton Mifflin Co., 1903-1904.

The Sermons of Ralph Waldo Emerson
An Introductory Historical Essay
by David M. Robinson

The roll of the ministers of the Second Church in Boston offers a sign of one of the most dramatic shifts in American cultural history. A reader who scanned the list would notice two names in particular: Mather and Emerson. Both Increase and Cotton Mather, representatives of different generations of Puritan Calvinism, ministered there, and these names anchor the church to its Puritan past. Emerson's brief career (1829–1832), punctuated by his well-known resignation, carries with it the weight of his future reputation. Here the course of American intellectual history changed as the American intellect left the church for the secular sphere. Emerson's ministry at the Second Church was a brief interlude of not-wholly-fulfilled promise between the brilliant career of Henry Ware, Jr., who revitalized the church, and that of Chandler Robbins, who steadily guided it for decades.[1] Few today remember Ware, fewer still, Robbins, but Emerson secured a permanent fame by moving gradually from the pulpit to the lecture platform and then on to the writing of essays and poems. His formative influence on American letters is now an accepted fact.

Later generations will inevitably be drawn to the earliest productions of a literary genius, and Emerson's sermons have been read, catalogued, commented upon, and in part published.[2] The studies that have been done, how-

I would like to acknowledge support from the American Philosophical Society and the Center for the Humanities, Oregon State University, in preparing this essay. For very helpful comments on the manuscript, I would like to thank Wesley T. Mott, Joel Myerson, Albert J. von Frank, and Conrad Wright.

1. For a history of the church, see Chandler Robbins, *A History of the Second Church, or Old North, in Boston* (Boston, 1852).

2. For the principal critical literature on the sermons, see Arthur Cushman McGiffert, Jr., ed., *Young Emerson Speaks: Unpublished Discourses on Many Subjects* (Boston, 1938); Kenneth Walter Cameron, "History and Biography in Emerson's Unpublished Sermons," *Proceedings of the American Antiquarian Society* 66 (October 1956): 103-18; A. M. Baumgartner, "'The Lyceum Is My Pulpit': Homiletics in Emerson's Early Lectures," *American Literature* 34 (January 1963): 477-86; William B. Barton, Jr., *A Calendar of the Complete Edition of the Sermons of Ralph Waldo Emerson* (Memphis, 1977); Wesley T. Mott, "Emerson and Antinomianism: The Legacy of the Sermons," *American Literature* 50 (November 1978): 369-97; David Robinson, *Apostle of Culture: Emerson as Preacher and Lecturer* (Philadelphia, 1982); Wesley T. Mott, "'Christ Crucified': Christology, Identity and Emerson's Sermon No. 5," *Emerson Centenary Essays*, ed. Joel Myerson (Carbondale, Ill., 1982), 17-40; and Teresa Toulouse, *The Art of Prophesying: New England Sermons and the Shaping of Belief* (Athens, Ga., 1987), chs. 4 and 5.

ever, have made little headway against a prevailing conviction that religion was somehow alien to Emerson's temperament; that if he began as a preacher, he left the ministry early and took a parting shot at his former profession in the Divinity School Address of 1838. "It is time that this ill-suppressed murmur of all thoughtful men against the famine of our churches; this moaning of the heart because it is bereaved of the consolation, the hope, the grandeur, that come alone out of the culture of the moral nature; should be heard through the sleep of indolence, and over the din of routine. This great and perpetual office of the preacher is not discharged" (*CW* 1:85). The popular resistance to seeing Emerson against a religious background is evident, for example, in the omission of the word *sermon* from the title of the only previous collection of Emerson's sermons, a selected edition by Arthur Cushman McGiffert: *Young Emerson Speaks: Unpublished Discourses on Many Subjects* (1938).

Because of the estrangement of modern readers from American religious culture, the spiritual and theological dimensions of Emerson's thought have been only dimly discerned. His accessibility has in part depended on a perception of his rebelliousness, and that has made it necessary to see his ministry as an unusable past that he—and we—had to discard. Emerson himself encouraged this attitude. The "ill-suppressed murmur of thoughtful men against the famine of our churches" was his own as well, a murmur indicating that secularization was henceforth to be an essential characteristic of the American cultural landscape.

To accommodate Emerson's ministerial career with the general reluctance to find much intellectual substance in churches or sermons, a model of Emerson's development arose that portrayed him as rebelling from ministerial constrictions in order to launch his real intellectual career as an independent lecturer and essayist. Certainly Emerson's working life developed by expansion, and leaving the church was an important gesture, as he explained to his brother William.

Meantime the severing of our strained cord that bound me to the church is a mutual relief. It is sorrowful to me & to them in a measure for we were both suited & hoped to be mutually useful. But though it will occasion me perhaps some, (possibly, much) temporary embarrassment yet I walk firmly toward a peace & a freedom which I plainly see before me albeit afar. Shall I pester you with half the projects that sprout & bloom in my head, of action, literature, philosophy? (*L* 1:357–58)

If, as Emerson's imagery suggests, a new birth was taking place, the gestation occurred during his ministry. Moreover, this birth was attended with some pain. In his letter of resignation he had described himself as "pained" at the circumstance of having to resign over a doctrinal issue, his administering of the Lord's Supper. He still held "the same respect" for the objects of the ministry "which, at first, led me to enter it" (*L* 1:356–57). Even allowing for the official politeness that such occasions require, the difficulty of Emerson's decision seems genuine, as his brother Charles confirmed: "And Waldo looks very sad. He would have been glad to have been well these last few months & done more for those to whom his attachment seems the stronger when the bonds of it are just snapped." Charles also noted the reluctance of the parish to accept the resignation: "They part from their pastor, whom many of them tenderly love, & all respect, with heavy hearts" (L 1:356, n. 45). This is charitable rebellion, if indeed it is rebellion at all. The comments of Charles and of other witnesses and participants point up the emotional complications that attended not only Emerson's resignation, but his entire ministry. The difficulty with the model of an Emerson who burst out of his ministerial bands into literary fame is that it sets in opposition two phases of Emerson's life that are more accurately seen as a single fabric.3

An understanding of Emerson's sermons begins with an understanding of the religious culture that helped to form them, the liberal religion of Boston and eastern Massachusetts that came to be known as Unitarianism.4 The history of that movement can be traced ultimately to the Calvinism of the New England Puritans, a theology rich with tensions and dilemmas. In reaction against the Great Awakening of the 1740s, a liberal party emerged in the Puritan churches and attempted to accommodate the prevailing orthodoxy to the pressures of change. The liberals, Arminian in their theology, found certain aspects of Puritan Calvinism repugnant, especially the doctrine of God's determining omnipotence and its conflict with a belief in the freedom of the human will. The Calvinist stress on human depravity combined in a frightful way with the image of an absolute God whose will had determined that depravity and whose purity demanded that it be punished. Calvinism was a vital and changing theology with an unquestionable capacity to nurture a fervent piety. Emerson's Calvinist aunt Mary Moody Emerson stood as a constant reminder to him of what the drift of modern liberalism stood to lose. And as Phyllis Cole has reminded us, Mary Moody Emerson delivered to her nephew a family inheritance of deep pietistic devotion that remained intact in his sensibility even during this period of enormous theological change.5 Calvinism could be preached with either a moving charity or a cold and frightening rigidity. The generations of eastern Massachusetts clergymen preceding Emerson increasingly found those elements of what came to be known as "orthodox" Calvinism a hin-

---

3. For a discerning discussion of Emerson's relation to the pulpit after his resignation from the Second Church, see Conrad Wright, "Emerson, Barzillai Frost, and the Divinity School Address," *Harvard Theological Review* 49 (January 1956): 19–43; rpt. in Wright, ed., *The Liberal Christians: Essays on American Unitarian History* (Boston, 1959), 41–61.

4. See Conrad Wright, *The Beginnings of Unitarianism in America* (Boston, 1955); Wright, ed., *A Stream of Light: A Sesquicentennial History of American Unitarianism* (Boston, 1975); and David Robinson, *The Unitarians and the Universalists* (Westport, Conn., 1985).

5. Cole, "From the Edwardses to the Emersons: Four Generations of Evangelical Family Culture," *College English Association Critic* 49 (1986–1987): 70–78.

drance to their intellectual development and their capacity to worship and to foster worship in their parishes. In a process of gradual evolution, they left it behind.

This dissent culminated in the biblical scholarship of Joseph Stevens Buckminster and Andrews Norton, and in the moral philosophy of William Ellery Channing and Henry Ware, Jr. One measure of the vitality of this new intellectual stimulus was its capacity to nurture a number of thinkers whose culture was deep enough to go beyond it. Emerson was prominent among these younger figures. The liberals distinguished themselves with a positive doctrine of human nature, but their distinction between human capacity and human virtue was important. They did not reject the fact of evil or of limitation, or overlook the grimmer aspects of life. But they argued that life was best seen as a trial, or probation, in which certain intrinsic powers of human nature were given the chance to develop and thrive. Life was a testing ground, or an arena of discipline, whose end was the culture of the soul, a development toward moral perfection that would continue both in this life and in the life to come. The core of liberal preaching was this vision of trial and a corresponding call for self-culture through discipline as a necessary response.

The doctrine of probation was brought forward in response to the doctrine of depravity, which, according to the liberals, portrayed God unjustly, sold human ability short, and ultimately discouraged moral development. Channing's "Unitarian Christianity" (1819), one of the fundamental documents of the liberal movement, was a withering attack on the Calvinist portrayal of God.

According to its old and genuine form, [Calvinism] teaches, that God brings us into life wholly depraved, so that under the innocent features of our childhood is hidden a nature averse to all good and propense to all evil, a nature which exposes us to God's displeasure and wrath, even before we have acquired power to understand our duties, or to reflect upon our actions.[6]

Innate depravity, when combined with the doctrine of election, formed what Channing portrayed as a monstrous vision of life.

This system also teaches, that God selects from this corrupt mass a number to be saved, plucks them, by a special influence, from the common ruin; that the rest of mankind, though left without that special grace which their conversion requires, are commanded to repent, under penalty of aggravated woe; and that forgiveness is promised them, on terms which their very constitution infallibly disposes them to reject, and in rejecting which they awfully enhance the punishments of hell.[7]

6. *William Ellery Channing: Selected Writings*, ed. David Robinson (New York and Mahwah, N.J., 1985), 89. See also Conrad Wright, *Three Prophets of Religious Liberalism: Channing—Emerson—Parker* (Boston, 1961), 5–19.

7. Channing, *Selected Writings*, 89.

The Calvinists insisted that this depiction was unfair, and in fact many of them were in the process of modifying their own dogma. But the liberals developed their central doctrine of probation against this perception of Calvinism. The Unitarians did not seek to revise Calvinism by envisioning human nature and human life in uniformly positive terms, even though they felt that the stakes against humanity had been grotesquely unfair in the Calvinist system.

By 1823 it was depressingly clear to the Calvinist leader Lyman Beecher that much of Boston and eastern Massachusetts had been lost, at least temporarily, to the liberals. In Channing they had found a leader around whom to rally, and his "Unitarian Christianity" had cemented the group's purpose. The liberals developed a faculty of theology at Harvard to counter Andover Seminary, founded by the Orthodox in 1808. In 1825 they formed the American Unitarian Association and in 1826 completed Divinity Hall at Harvard.[8] Beecher's 1823 sermon "The Faith Once Delivered to the Saints" was an important response to these events, an attempt to hold the line against the liberal advance by demonstrating that the pure flame of Calvinism was being successfully passed to a new generation.[9] As Beecher's title suggests, the Orthodox party argued that its position was the pure flame of Christianity itself, which the liberals were abandoning. Such an implication pressed the liberals for a response. In 1825 Henry Ware, Jr., at the height of his ministry at the Second Church in Boston, answered Beecher's sermon with a liberal statement bearing the same title.[10] Ware's response virtually summarizes the religious culture in which Emerson matured.

From the fundamental idea of "One Infinite and Eternal Being" who was "without equal, rival, or partner," Ware expounded the doctrine of God's "moral government over his creatures." As "subject" of God, the human being "is treated as a free moral agent, capable of choosing between right and wrong, and accountable for his choice." These superficially bland postulates mask Ware's strategy of framing his doctrine of probation in direct contradiction to election. "In this world [the human being] is placed in a state of trial and probation, for the purpose of forming and bringing out his character, in preparation for a final allotment of condition in conformity with his character" (2:229–30). The doctrine offered a clear alternative to Calvinist election and provided a practical focus of character formation for the spiritual energies it generated. This reversal of assumptions regarding God and human nature translated the question of salvation into one of character development. The Unitarians thus made the cultivation of the soul the essence of religion.

Ware characterized life as a "state of preparatory discipline," in which an

8. Unitarian influence in eastern Massachusetts was also augmented by a legal decision involving the parish in Dedham, Massachusetts. See Earl Morse Wilbur, *A History of Unitarianism in Transylvania, England, and America* (Cambridge, Mass., 1952), 431.

9. "The Faith Once Delivered to the Saints," in *The Works of The Rev. Lyman Beecher* (Boston and Cleveland, 1852–1853), 2:243–300.

10. *The Works of Henry Ware, Jr., D.D.* (Boston, 1846–1847), 2:229–50. Page and volume numbers for quotations will be cited parenthetically.

individual who is "neither virtuous nor vicious; neither holy nor sinful" attempts to develop certain powers, namely, "reason and conscience," in order "to exalt and purify his spiritual nature, and deliver it from subjection to the sensual" (2:230). Life is a trial of character, the purpose of which is to strengthen and develop the spiritual nature of the individual and thereby bring him closer to the character of God. In another sermon on "The Doctrine of Probation," Ware emphasized that the world was not meant as a scene of happiness or retribution, but was rather "a place of preparation, of duty, of trial" (3:410). In speaking of life as a preparation, Ware invoked a long tradition of Puritan thought, which had developed doctrines of "preparation for grace" as a means of accommodating the human will to the doctrines of election.[11] For Ware, however, the soul was empowered to develop its spiritual identity. To the Unitarians this was an important distinction. One of their favorite arguments against Calvinism was that its view of both God and human nature tended to discourage the active development of the spiritual powers. In Channing's words:

[Calvinism] tends to discourage the timid, to give excuses to the bad, to feed the vanity of the fanatical, and to offer shelter to the bad feelings of the malignant. By shocking, as it does, the fundamental principles of morality, and by exhibiting a severe and partial Deity, it tends strongly to pervert the moral faculty, to form a gloomy, forbidding, and servile religion, and to lead men to substitute censoriousness, bitterness, and persecution, for a tender and impartial charity.[12]

In contrast, the liberals imagined a fairer, more benevolent God and constructed a new sense of the moral life. The doctrine of probation was essential to this vision. Their thinking constantly returned to the theme that life was a moral or spiritual proving ground.

The centrality of this aspect of Unitarian thinking is particularly important to remember in light of the historical reputation of Unitarianism as a rational religion. They accepted, indeed ardently promoted, their identity as a rational religion but recognized that the label carried the suggestion of coolness and reserve. How could this reasonableness, however attractive on one level, accord with the fervent piety of the Protestant tradition, and especially with the conspicuous example of that fervency in their Puritan (and Calvinist) ancestors? "The Faith Once Delivered to the Saints" was a troubling concept to the Unitarians because it suggested that liberalism was a declension from certain original Christian values. The cutting of one theological bond to the past, their rejection of Calvinism, made it all the more important to maintain a connection with the moral and pietistic tradition that Puritanism represented.

11. See Perry Miller, "'Preparation for Salvation' in Seventeenth Century New England," in *Nature's Nation* (Cambridge, Mass., 1977), 50–77, and Norman Pettit, *The Heart Prepared: Grace and Conversion in Puritan Spiritual Life* (New Haven, Conn., 1966).

12. Channing, *Selected Writings*, 90.

Channing found the resources for reformulating that moral tradition in the concept of "disinterestedness," which he derived from the Scottish moralist Francis Hutcheson (1694–1746). By defining virtue as the increasing capacity to act against individual self-interest, Channing articulated an important counter to the emphasis on the self that was more than implied in his doctrine of self-culture.[13] The growth of the self consisted ultimately in the development of the "moral sense," an amorphous but crucially important concept that the Unitarians had inherited primarily from the Scottish common sense philosophers Thomas Reid (1710–1796) and Dugald Stewart (1753–1828). This concept had a particularly strong appeal for the young Emerson. The demands for pious dedication, fervent belief, and continual self-sacrifice that this mode of thought produced could well rival anything devised by the Puritans. Thus the New England Conscience survived the greatest shift in the history of American religious thought.

* * *

The pietism of nineteenth-century Unitarianism was not well understood until Daniel Walker Howe's description of it in 1970. Howe demonstrated that the cultivation of the religious affections was an imperative among the Unitarians and that they developed a "very special type of emotional sensitivity, a combination of religious affection and moral taste."[14] Ware's influential devotional manual, *The Formation of the Christian Character* (1831), brought together the concept of probation with the desire to cultivate religious emotion by showing that the nurturing of a deeply felt piety was the central response to the trial of life. For Ware the "primary characteristic [of religion] is a certain state of mind and affections. It is not the external conduct, not the observance of the moral law alone, which constitutes a religious man; but the principles from which he acts, the motives by which he is governed, the state of his heart" (4:292). While Ware intended that this "state of the heart" should refer to the mind as well as to the affections and while he would argue vigorously that moral action flows out of such a state, it is evident that he viewed religion primarily as an emotional phenomenon. Religion for Ware was an attitude of service, devotion, gratitude, and humility, which the term *piety* comes closest to capturing. This piety was also in part an attitude of vigilance or a "watchfulness and self-discipline" that "belong to all times and occasions" (4:375). Thus no thought, act, or feeling of the self was without religious significance. The trial of life and the responding discipline that it called out extended to the most ordinary and trivial events; both the trial and the discipline were unceasing.

It is as a product of this religious culture that we first confront Emerson. Nurtured in a dynamic and evolving liberalism, he was particularly influenced by a pietistic strand of it. The assertion of his first sermon (1826) was that "we

13. David Robinson, "The Legacy of Channing: Culture as a Religious Category in New England Thought," *Harvard Theological Review* 74 (April 1981): 221–39.
14. Howe, *The Unitarian Conscience: Harvard Moral Philosophy, 1805–1861* (Cambridge, Mass., 1970), 153.

pray without ceasing. Every secret wish is a prayer. Every house is a church, the corner of every street is a closet of devotion." Emerson was a magnet for intellectual influences, but as his early work shows, our historical understanding of him must begin with the pietism of the early Unitarian movement. We must, that is, begin where he did. His father, William Emerson, was a minister of markedly liberal tendencies. Joseph Stevens Buckminster, who preached William's funeral sermon, left an example of cultivation and piety that held Boston culture in thrall for decades after his death at the age of twenty-eight in 1812.[15] The great William Ellery Channing, Emerson's tutor in theology, preached with the sort of "moral imagination" that inspired the vocationally drifting young man to feel that he might perhaps succeed in the ministry. Ware preceded him in his first pastorate at the Second Church and presented a formidable pastoral example. Modern thinking in the middle of the nineteenth century veered away from these men, and thus they remain in comparative historical obscurity. But the generational turn toward modernism that Emerson represents was far from a complete break with the past. In expanding circles of significance, Emerson would continue to see life as a process of ceaseless prayer and devotion, in which the religious impulse would come to inhabit "the corner of every street."

*   *   *

Emerson graduated from Harvard in 1821 and began a difficult period of transition in which he inched toward the ministry. His father, minister of Boston's First Church, had died a decade earlier, leaving his family nearly destitute. Emerson was obliged to assist in financing his younger brothers' education and so took up schoolkeeping for several years in the early 1820s. It was a chore that, on the whole, he did not enjoy, but it bought him time as he considered the possibility of entering the ministry. Literary and oratorical ambitions and a deep religious sensibility pulled him toward it, but he balked before an oppressive sense of the demands of the calling. In April 1824, a month before his twenty-first birthday, he made a personal dedication of "my time, my talents, & my hopes to the Church" (*JMN* 2:237). In recording his decision to enter the ministry, he confessed his "passionate love for the strains of eloquence" and added, "What we ardently love we learn to imitate" (*JMN* 2:239). He began to meet with Francis Cunningham and William Ellery Channing "for the sake of saying I am studying divinity, & not to have 3 years of poortith when school deserts me" (*L* 1:146). The serious tone of the journal entry juxtaposed with the jocular tone of the letter suggests how his genuine desire for the calling of the ministry was mixed with a mild reluctance. That he had gone to Channing for guidance is not surprising, and to the extent that he had entered the ministry with enthusiasm and expectation, Channing was the reason. About six months before his dedication to the church, he wrote his Aunt Mary about Channing's

15. See Lawrence Buell, "Joseph Stevens Buckminster: The Making of a New England Saint," *Canadian Review of American Studies* 10 (Spring 1979): 1–29.

"preaching sublime sermons every Sunday morning in Federal St.," mentioning his "Evidences of Christianity" in particular (*L* 1:138). He later singled out Channing's Dudleian lecture of 1821, *The Evidences of Revealed Religion*, as a specific model of the kind of preaching to which he aspired. Channing's tutelage was principally one of example. He gave Emerson a list of books to read, but apparently no close supervision, and left him in charge of ordering his own studies.[16] In late 1824 Emerson expressed some frustration with his own inability to take charge of his studies, hoping for "an Order introduced into the mass of reading that occupies or impends over me" (*JMN* 2:300). His situation, however, was not unusual. The New England ministry trained through a very loose apprentice system, in which students gleaned what guidance they could from established ministers but generally shifted for themselves in their preparation. The rise of the theological seminary—Andover in 1808 and then Harvard—was beginning to change this situation in the 1820s.[17] But though Emerson enrolled for divinity studies at Harvard in 1825, the course of his haphazard theological education would change little. Soon after his arrival at Divinity Hall, his health began to deteriorate, and although he attended what lectures he could, he was not required to do any specified work. He left without graduating and admittedly ill-prepared as a theologian. Oliver Wendell Holmes reported his saying, "If they had examined me, they probably would not have let me preach at all."[18]

By 1825 his family's financial situation had improved enough to allow him to cease schoolkeeping. Still, his own prospects seemed dim. His journal for January begins with a reflection about his change of direction: "I have closed my school. I have begun a new year. I have begun my studies." These studies represented to him a sort of withdrawal. "I turn now to my lamp & my tomes. I have nothing to do with society" (*JMN* 2:309). But almost immediately, Emerson's escape was cut short by a swelling and inflammation of the eye, which impaired his vision and made prolonged study impossible. As Evelyn Barish has shown, this was one of the symptoms of the tuberculosis that seriously endangered Emerson's life as he began his ministerial career.[19] He had to abandon study, seek recuperation on a relative's farm, and briefly return to schoolkeeping. His

16. For the list of books and authors which Channing gave to Emerson, see Kenneth Walter Cameron, "Dr. Channing's Two Reading Lists," in *The Transcendentalists and Minerva* (Hartford, Conn., 1958), 3:1010-22. Among the dozen names on the list, those which seem to have influenced Emerson the most were the natural theologian William Paley and the devotional writer Henry Scougal. For further details on Emerson's reading, see Cameron, *Ralph Waldo Emerson's Reading* (Raleigh, N.C., 1941); *Emerson the Essayist*, 2 vols. (Raleigh, N.C., 1945); and Walter Harding, *Emerson's Library* (Charlottesville, Va., 1967).

17. See Conrad Wright, "The Early Period (1811-1840)," in *The Harvard Divinity School: Its Place in Harvard University and in American Culture*, ed. George Huntston Williams (Boston, 1954), 21-77.

18. "Ralph Waldo Emerson," in *The Writings of Oliver Wendell Holmes*, Riverside Edition (Boston and New York, 1906), 11:41.

19. Barish, "The Moonless Night: Emerson's Crisis of Health, 1825-1827," *Emerson Centenary Essays*, ed. Joel Myerson (Carbondale, Ill., 1982), 8.

impaired vision was gradually restored through operations, but these miseries with his eyes were complicated by a severe attack of rheumatism (also related to his tuberculosis) in the winter of 1826 and then by symptoms of pleurisy, a "stricture" in his chest which was aggravated by prolonged public speaking.[20] Emerson continued his studies as best he could in 1825 and 1826, and in apparent response to his Uncle Samuel Ripley's invitation to fill his Waltham pulpit, he was licensed to preach on October 10, 1826. It was apparent by then, however, that his consumption had to be treated, and with his uncle's financial assistance, he undertook a recuperative voyage to Charleston and St. Augustine for the winter of 1826–1827.

Thus, when Emerson preached his first sermon in the fall of 1826, his future was much in doubt. Even a year after his stay in Florida, he still felt the verdict on his health was not determined: "I am living cautiously yea treading on eggs to strengthen my constitution. It is a long battle this of mine betwixt life & death & tis wholly uncertain to whom the game belongs" (L 1:227). This struggle for health made his already difficult entry into ministerial training even more trying and his later emergence as an influential preacher and lecturer more surprising. Barish has made the severity of Emerson's tubercular condition clear, demonstrating "how he emerged from the crisis stronger and healthier in many ways than before."[21] The ways in which Emerson differed from his brilliant brother Edward are instructive—Edward could not slow down and thus broke himself, suffering a nervous collapse and later dying of tuberculosis. Emerson willfully made himself an idler for several years and gradually regained his health.

Although Emerson was a long time in overcoming his disease, his winter retreat was a turning point. The record of his preaching engagements shows an almost steady round of supply preaching beginning in the spring of 1827 on his return from Florida. Back in Cambridge, he began to avail himself of the pulpit opportunities that his family ties gave him. He preached eight different Sundays in the summer of 1827 at his father's old church, the First or Chauncy Place Church. In July he preached in Concord for his step-grandfather Ezra Ripley and also in his uncle's pulpit in Waltham. By late August he had expanded his field, preaching at the Federal Street pulpit occupied by Channing and Ezra Stiles Gannett, and later supplying pulpits in Northampton, Greenfield, Deerfield, New Bedford, Harvard, Watertown, and Concord, New Hampshire (where he met his wife Ellen).[22] From the summer of 1827 through 1828, Emer-

20. Barish, "The Moonless Night," 3–11.
21. Barish, "The Moonless Night," 2. Barish supports with extensive medical detail the general thesis of Emerson's emergence propounded in Stephen E. Whicher's *Freedom and Fate: An Inner Life of Ralph Waldo Emerson* (Philadelphia, 1953). Her essay is an important corrective to Jonathan Bishop's implication that Emerson's bouts of bad health were strongly related to his dread of entering the ministry: see *Emerson on the Soul* (Cambridge, Mass., 1964), 167–71.
22. Emerson's preaching record, among his manuscripts at Houghton Library, Harvard University, contains the record he kept of his preaching engagements. An adaptation of this record is published in Kenneth Walter Cameron, *Index-Concordance to Emerson's Sermons, With Homiletical Papers* (Hartford, Conn., 1963), 2:695–703.

son was almost constantly employed as a supply preacher. He was building an inventory of sermons and carefully protecting himself from what he by then recognized as a potentially fatal tendency to overexertion.[23]

It is significant that Emerson continued in this pattern of supply preaching longer than he might have. There were opportunities for permanent settlement, but he chose not to pursue them.[24] Health considerations partly account for this delay, but they were reinforced by a selectivity about the place of settlement and a desire for further intellectual and practical preparation before undertaking the rigorous work of a New England parish minister. Emerson shared the still-prevalent expectation that settlement in a parish was for life. Though this tradition was beginning to weaken in the early nineteenth century, accepting a call to preach as a candidate for a church was a serious undertaking, and Emerson shied away from it.[25] His letters show that what he hoped for was a series of Sunday engagements that would not require too much disruptive travel and would keep his weeks largely free for study.

One thing is clear. Despite his haphazard training and his extremely delicate health, despite the constant financial worries and the repeated interruptions of his study, he was a very effective preacher. Frederic Henry Hedge, who first observed Emerson in 1828, noted that while both his younger brothers, Edward and Charles, showed more promise, Waldo still possessed "a refinement of thought and a selectness in the use of language which gave promise of an interesting preacher to cultivated hearers."[26] Although this may indicate an important aspect of Emerson's capacity, the evidence suggests that there was more, a force of emotional appeal that transcended Hedge's cold evocation of linguistic refinement and cultivation. Emerson explained in a letter to William that in preaching "I aspire always to the production of present effect thinking that if I succeed in that, I succeed wholly. For a strong present effect is a permanent impression" (*L* 1:211). This is hardly the confession of an exclusively literary preacher. In July 1828 he offered some revealing oratorical advice to his younger brother Charles, whose valedictory oration he had heard at Harvard. Though full of praise for Charles's talents, he criticized him for a certain aloofness from his audience, calling his effort "a fine show at which we look, instead of an agent that moves us." In Emerson's view, "Though he uttered the words, *he did not appeal* to the audience," primarily because "he felt that he was an object of attention to the audience" rather than the audience's being "an object of attention from him" (*L* 1:238–39; Emerson's emphasis). This is more than an inculcation of humility; it is shrewd pragmatic advice that helps to

23. He wrote William on August 31, 1827, asking for sermon topics or even model sermons, noting that "I am not so well but that the cold may make another Southern winter expedient. I hope not" (*L* 1:211).

24. See Emerson's letter to William of April 30, 1828, on his motives for refusing pastoral settlement (*L* 1:234).

25. Donald M. Scott, *From Office to Profession: The New England Ministry, 1750–1850* (Philadelphia, 1978), 1–17.

26. James Elliot Cabot, *A Memoir of Ralph Waldo Emerson* (Boston, 1887), 1:138–39.

account for Emerson's considerable effectiveness as a preacher and later as a lecturer.

Emerson was garnering his new pulpit assignments from a number of sources. Family ties were important at first, but eventually several leaders of the Unitarian movement, including Ezra Stiles Gannett and Henry Ware, Jr., began to call on his services.[27] Gannett, as secretary of the recently formed American Unitarian Association, became a conduit for information about vacant Unitarian pulpits and available preachers, and a leader in the Unitarian missionary effort that coincided with the building of Divinity Hall and the founding of the A.U.A.[28] Emerson had refused the A.U.A.'s offer of a missionary assignment in Western Massachusetts in July 1827 (*L* 1:203), and in August preached at Federal Street, Gannett's pulpit. Soon after came the opportunities in Northampton, Greenfield, Deerfield, New Bedford, and Concord. Obviously, he was effectively learning and practicing his craft in these years, as is suggested by a letter to Gannett from William Kent of Concord, New Hampshire (Emerson's future brother-in-law), asking to have Emerson back for a return engagement: "We want a man of force & popular address, as our society is at this moment in a situation the most critical & important. . . . Such a man was Mr Emerson, the society was constantly increasing while he was here, & our meetings fully attended, his leaving will operate to our disadvantage unless he can be prevailed upon to return or his place supplied by someone possessing qualities somewhat resembling" (*L* 1:222, n. 135).[29] Kent's reference to Emerson as a "man of force & popular address" helps confirm that Emerson was an effective orator for a large class of people and not a preacher with a narrow literary appeal.

*   *   *

In 1828 Emerson tried to limit his engagements to pulpits within easier commuting distance from Divinity Hall, protecting his health, which still worried him, and making time for his studies. In April he noted that he was avoiding any invitations "that may lead to permanent engagements," considering himself "dependent for my degree of health on my lounging capricious unfettered mode of life." Even so, "I slowly multiply my sermons for a day I hope of firmer health & solid power" (*L* 1:229–30).

Two events would change this pattern of waiting. On Christmas Day 1827, while in Concord, New Hampshire to preach, he met Ellen Tucker and began to fall in love. The relationship grew during return visits in May and June 1828, and after a final visit in December, they were engaged to be married. Emerson seems to have been genuinely smitten by Ellen; "purblind these lovers be," said

27. To Gannett were due the invitations to Greenfield, Deerfield, Northampton (*L* 1:212), and Concord, New Hampshire (*L* 1:222), and to one of the Henry Wares (probably the younger) the invitation to New Bedford (*L* 1:213).

28. On the formation of the American Unitarian Association and Gannett's role in it see William Channing Gannett, *Ezra Stiles Gannett: Unitarian Minister in Boston, 1824–1871* (Boston, 1875); Charles C. Forman, "Elected Now By Time," in *A Stream of Light*, ed. Wright; and Robinson, *The Unitarians and the Universalists*, 25–46.

29. See also *Life*, 129.

his brother Charles.[30] Certainly the engagement and marriage were a sign of Emerson's continually improving health.

The second decisive event was quite apart from the first. Traveling home from a preaching engagement in Northampton on June 2, 1828, Henry Ware, Jr., collapsed, exhausted, with a severe inflammation of the lungs. Ware remained gravely ill for several weeks. In October he suffered a relapse and was soon forced into seclusion in Brighton. Emerson was called to supply his pulpit at the Second Church.[31] "Mr. Ware is ill again, & all good men are sorry," Emerson wrote William in October. "You see what lies before your brother for his mortal lot. To be a good minister & healthy is not given" (*L* 1:249). Ware was one of the best preachers among the Unitarians and the clear leader in the work of pastoral care. That he excelled in so many endeavors no doubt contributed to his collapse, as the worried Emerson must have sensed. In July he began to supply Ware's pulpit and was drawn uncomfortably close to the front lines of pastoral duty. Ware's illness "will probably confine me where I am for the winter," he told William. "It has some obvious advantages over any other service but involves more labor" (*L* 1:249). These events pushed Emerson into a quicker pace than he had been keeping. From July through November 1828 he often preached three Sundays a month at the Second Church, filling out his schedule with engagements at other churches. Though he was not responsible for pastoral duties, he was forced to expand his stock of sermons and was no doubt drawn more deeply into parish affairs than he would otherwise have been. He also knew that there were plans to create a professorship for Ware at Harvard and thus that the Second Church pulpit might well come open.

Emerson was in a delicate situation. Clearly he was a prospective pastor, and the longer he preached there, the clearer that seemed. But he had doubts about settling permanently, which were complicated by Ellen's delicate health. Moreover, the Second Church, while approving of Emerson, had no wish to part with Ware. They had won something of a battle to keep him when he had turned down a promising offer to move to New York, and he was undoubtedly a pastor deeply loved by his parish. When it became obvious to Ware that he could not resume his duties, he submitted a letter of resignation (December 27, 1828), telling his church, "You need an active pastor." Replying, "We are not yet willing to give Mr. Ware up," the parish refused the resignation and proposed instead a colleague "to assist him in the discharge of his duties." Ware accepted the proposal on January 9, 1829, and two days later the church asked Emerson to assist in the ministry.[32]

Emerson noted the sudden changes in his life in a journal entry. "My history has had its important days within a brief period. Whilst I enjoy the luxury of an

30. See Rusk's discussion in *Life* and the quotation from Charles on 142. See also *OFL* and Henry F. Pommer, *Emerson's First Marriage* (Carbondale, Ill., 1967).

31. John Ware, *Memoir of the Life of Henry Ware, Jr.* (Boston, 1890), 1:233–37, 2:5–9.

32. Ware, *Memoir*, 2:12–17.

unmeasured affection for an object so deserving of it all & who requites it all,—I am called by an ancient & respectable church to become its pastor." The tone of the entry is one of humble gratitude, but with an edge of concern. "I feel my total dependance. O God direct & guard & bless me, & those, & especially *her*, in whom I am blessed" (*JMN* 3:149–50). The reason for the concern was Ellen's health. On January 28 he wrote William that "she has raised blood a week ago," one of the most serious danger signs of tuberculosis. "I have abstained in much hesitation & perplexity from giving any answer to the call at the Old North. thinking that perhaps the doctors might tell Ellen she ought to go away" (*L* 1:259). When he finally decided to accept, there was more humility and hesitation in his answer than such an occasion might demand. "If my own feelings could have been consulted," he confessed to the church, "I should have desired to postpone, at least, for several months, my entrance into this solemn office." Under the circumstances, he described himself as coming to the church "in weakness, and not in strength" (*L* 1:261). Weakness and uncertainty notwithstanding, Emerson was launched on his pastorate. He joked darkly that his approaching ordination in March would be his "execution day" (*L* 1:264), but it seems to have been no ordeal.

Ellen's temporary recovery and his own building confidence helped to open what we must now come to regard, given the evidence of the sermons and journals, as a period of great intellectual expansion. Insofar as Emerson's later resignation of his pastorate has been the focus of historical inquiry, the inevitable view has been that his ministry was an enchainment to the past that he had to escape. Such a view will be difficult to sustain in the light of the complete record of the sermons. Emerson found in his pastorate, despite his apprehensions, an opportunity for expression that was vital to his development. That he eventually left his ministry is in some respects a measure of how much he was able to grow there.

The church of which Emerson took charge had undergone a major transition and revival under Ware. John Lathrop, Ware's predecessor, had a tenure of forty-eight years, and the church was in need of rejuvenation by the end of his pastorate. Moreover, shifting economic patterns in the city had made the North End an "unfashionable" district, rendering the Second Church somewhat less prestigious than certain others in Boston.[33] The arrival of the energetic Ware in 1817, however, ushered in a "golden age" for the church.[34] Emerson's relations with the formidable Ware were generally quite cordial, but the situation was fraught with potential for discomfort. In December 1828 Emerson wrote to Ware defending himself from Ware's charge that he lacked sufficient scriptural reference in one of his sermons. "I have affected generally a mode of illustration rather bolder than the usage of our preaching warrants," Emerson explained, "on the principle that our religion is nothing limited or partial" (*L* 1:257). This

33. Gay Wilson Allen, *Waldo Emerson* (New York, 1981), 129.
34. Robbins, *Second Church*, 132.

high ground would be hard for Ware to object to, as the canny young preacher must have known, but even so, Emerson took a conciliatory tone and promised to avail himself of Ware's advice when he repeated the sermon. The exchange apparently did no damage to the relationship. As he began a European voyage in the spring of 1829, Ware wrote to his brother, "My colleague has begun his work in the best possible spirit, and with just the promise I like." Apparently, the congregation agreed. "The few, who talked of leaving the Society, are won to remain," Ware noted, "and it is as flourishing as ever."[35] Soon thereafter he wrote Emerson a warm letter of congratulation on his start, including, of course, some advice on how to proceed. Still officially the pastor, but knowing that he would probably move to Harvard eventually, he expressed some decidedly mixed emotions about leaving the Second Church. "I do not know what time and absence may do to diminish my interest in this Society; but I feel at present, as if it could never be lost, and that I shall watch its welfare with as great anxiety as ever. But I am henceforth separated from all active concern, and shall feel no right to intrude myself into its affairs."[36] And indeed, Ware's connection with the church did remain close. He filled Emerson's pulpit in the weeks after Ellen's death and later preached the ordination sermon for Emerson's successor, Chandler Robbins.

Although there was no unusual strain between the two men, it was a challenging professional situation for Emerson. Ordained on March 11, 1829, as junior pastor to the ailing Ware, Emerson in fact had sole charge of the church. He was confronted with difficult demands in what he felt were the two potentially conflicting roles of the minister, preaching and pastoral care. In two successive sermons on the duties of the Christian minister (Sermons XXVIII and XXIX) preached immediately after his ordination, Emerson urged his congregation to recognize that "there is an expectation that will operate unfavorably on my inexperience arising from the very signal merits which have created among you so warm a sympathy in your minister" (Sermon XXIX). Looking back after one year in the pulpit, he defended his elevation of private study aimed at sermon preparation over the duties of pastoral calling. The duties of the "preacher and pastor," he noted, were "often in some measure incompatible" (Sermon LXIX).[37]

* * *

Emerson was responsible for conducting two worship services every Sunday, each of which included a sermon, prayers, scripture readings, and hymns. He also presented occasional lectures and was responsible for baptisms, marriages, funerals, and pastoral calls on his parishioners. There were also other duties connected with his work, such as distributing Church funds for the poor, administering church affairs, and attending ministerial association meetings. The public responsibilities of a New England clergyman also had to be met, so

35. Ware, *Memoir*, 2:24.
36. Ware, *Memoir*, 2:33.
37. See the detailed discussion of this issue in Robinson, *Apostle of Culture*, 40–47.

he served on the school committee in Boston and as Chaplain of the Massachusetts Senate.[38]

Emerson apparently found acceptable ways of handling these varying responsibilities. Cabot reported Emerson's confession that he did not "excel" at pastoral calling and noted several instances of awkwardness or shyness in the performance of some duties, but these do not appear to have damaged his pastorate.[39] Indeed, Emerson seems to have succeeded admirably by concentrating his energies on his preaching. His expounding a religion of direct moral relevance to his hearers may well have compensated for any reticence in his personal intercourse. Ware's move to Harvard became a reality in 1830, and Emerson thereafter assumed sole official charge of the church at a salary of $1,800 per year—as much as Ware made and more than Chandler Robbins would be paid to start. He maintained the reputation for effective preaching that he had earned as a young supply preacher, eventually perfecting a pulpit style notable for its directness, clarity, and moral relevance. Cabot noted the "absence of rhetoric" in the sermons, suggesting the avoidance of artifice in favor of plain dialogue with his auditors. He referred to one of Emerson's parishioners who recalled "the reality given to the things of religion" by the sermons.[40] James Freeman Clarke agreed that Emerson made his impression on hearers without the use of bombast or forced rhetoric. He told of going with Margaret Fuller to hear Emerson preach "in the old church at the North End. I recollect that we were both impressed by the calm, sweet, and pure strain of thought which pervaded the discourse."[41] Fuller's testimony in a letter to Harriet Martineau was typical of the impact that Emerson had throughout the 1830s and 1840s on the young intellectuals who came to be known as the Transcendentalists: "You question me as to the nature of the benefits conferred upon me by Mr. E's preaching. I answer, that his influence has been more beneficial to me than that of any American, and that from him I first learned what is meant by an inward life."[42] Emerson was molding through his weekly sermons the liberalism that he inherited from Channing and Ware with a new and intense devotional intuitionism which had remarkable religious and literary force.

Ellen's death in February 1831 left him stunned with grief but had no immediate adverse effect on his pastorate. In fact, he plunged into a series of Tuesday night lectures for the youth of the parish and seems not to have had any thoughts of leaving the church before the anniversary of his wife's death. Relations with his parishioners continued to be satisfactory. Even the congregation's

---

38. For details, see *Life*, 137–41 and Allen, 129–37. I am grateful to Albert J. von Frank for information on Emerson's pastoral duties.

39. Cabot, *Memoir*, 1:169–70.

40. Cabot, *Memoir*, 1:151.

41. Clarke, "Memoir of Ralph Waldo Emerson," *Proceedings of the Massachusetts Historical Society* 18 (June 1885): 108.

42. *Memoirs of Margaret Fuller Ossoli*, ed. William Henry Channing, James Freeman Clarke, and Ralph Waldo Emerson (Boston, 1852), 1:194–95.

reaction to Emerson's reluctance about administering the Lord's Supper, the issue that precipitated his resignation in September 1832, shows that he had a considerable reservoir of support. Although his letter of June 1832 to the church is lost, he apparently asked either to observe the supper only as a "commemoration," dropping the "elements" of wine and bread or "to be relieved of his own responsibility as administrant of the rite."[43] The church, working principally through a committee of seven, refused the demand but took pains to avoid making the issue one that would cost them Emerson's services. Both sides won a reprieve from the final decision when the church closed for repairs for several weeks at the end of June and again when illness prevented Emerson from resuming his preaching in August. The weeks of postponement confirmed Emerson's decision not to compromise on the issue, and he delivered his sermon on the Lord's Supper (Sermon CLXII) on September 9, 1832. His resignation followed immediately.

Did a reluctance to administer this sacrament alone end Emerson's ministry? Although he probably would have continued on for a time had the church accepted his proposal, the general scholarly consensus that the disagreement over the sacrament was symbolic of deeper discontent is surely true. There were examples later in the century of Unitarian ministers who led their congregations in new and experimental directions. James Freeman Clarke's Church of the Disciples in Boston, William J. Potter's ministry in New Bedford, and O. B. Frothingham's ministry in New York all come to mind in this context.[44] And as William Hutchison has shown, the impulse toward church reform was a fundamental energy of Transcendentalism.[45] Conceivably Emerson might have accomplished something of the same with enough patience and the right kind of persuasion. But his struggle was less to change institutions than to free himself and others from them. The essence of his gesture had already been articulated in his journal the January before his resignation:

It is the best part of the man, I sometimes think, that revolts most against his being the minister. His good revolts from official goodness. . . . The difficulty is that we do not make a world of our own but fall into institutions already made & have to accomodate ourselves to them to be useful at all. & this accommodation is, I say, a loss of so much integrity & of course of so much power. (*JMN* 3:318–319)

Powerful as this statement is, Emerson added to it a paragraph of afterthought in which he admitted that the world would have difficulty getting along "if all its *beaux esprits*" quit its "approved forms & accepted institutions." As he put it, "The double refiners would produce at the other end the double damned" (*JMN* 3:319). Thus the decision to resign, though consistent with his

43. Cabot, *Memoir*, 155, and *Life*, 160.
44. For details, see Robinson, *The Unitarians and the Universalists*, 101–6, 234–35, 262, 308–9.
45. Hutchison, *The Transcendentalist Ministers: Church Reform in the New England Renaissance* (New Haven, Conn., 1959).

innermost sense of integrity, was difficult. He was saddened to leave his parishioners and concerned about his responsibility toward them. His family worried that he was making a mistake. But however real, these obstacles could not
contain the pressure of the inner logic of change that had been building in him.
He remained a preacher but ended his pastorate at the Second Church in the fall
of 1832.[46]

*   *   *

Emerson prepared for the ministry during the Second Great Awakening
(1800–1830), a period of major crisis in American religious culture. To this
Awakening we can trace the decline of Calvinism, under attack from both the
Boston liberals and the evangelical movement; the emergence of the denomina-
tional shape of American religion, including the pervasiveness and persistence
of its evangelical character; the termination of tax support for established
churches in New England; and the codification of a public consensus about a
special American destiny and identity.[47] Given the essentially evangelical and
revivalistic character of the Awakening, the impact of these changes on New
England Unitarianism is often overlooked, but as Howe has argued, the Unitarians "were more than participants in the Second Great Awakening; they were
among its pioneers."[48] The revivalists' powerful methods of invigorating
religious experience could be met only in part by rationalist scorn; liberals came
to realize that they had to demonstrate the emotional power of their enlightened
theology as well and prove that their theological advancement had not come at
the cost of the piety of their Puritan ancestors. To evoke emotional fervor while
resisting the perceived excesses of revivalism was the task that devolved to the
Unitarian ministry when Emerson began to prepare for it.

A long process of change in ministerial authority also culminated during the
Awakening, when the ministry ceased to be an "office," invested with peculiar
influence in the social structure of the New England town, and began to be a
"profession," with real but circumscribed power deriving from specialized
knowledge in an increasingly complex social structure.[49] The fading expec-
tancy of lifetime tenure in a parish, the growth of professional ministerial orga-
nizations outside the church, and the evolution of the theological seminary were
signs of this transformation. The changes meant that ministerial authority had
increasingly to be generated through social persuasion. The ministry found
itself with growing sources of competition for intellectual and moral authority
in a more complex social order. A minister could no longer easily assume that

46. Emerson later preached regularly at the Unitarian church in East Lexington, later known as
the Follen Church, from 1835 to 1837. He was responsible only for preaching there or for securing
someone to fill the pulpit in his absence. See Douglas Percy Brayton, *The History of the Follen
Church* (n.p., 1939), 7–8.

47. William G. McLoughlin, *Revivals, Awakenings, and Reform: An Essay on Religion and
Social Change in America, 1607–1977* (Chicago and London, 1978), 103. McLoughlin credits
R. H. Gabriel with original use of the phrase "Second Great Awakening."

48. Howe, *Unitarian Conscience*, 161.

49. Scott, *From Office to Profession*, 1–17, 52–75.

his power was somehow in the order of things; he could no longer hold it as permanent.

In 1824 when William Ellery Channing preached the ordination sermon for Ezra Stiles Gannett, his younger colleague at the Federal Street Church, he outlined "The Demands of the Age on the Ministry."[50] Channing's influence on Emerson was surely augmented by this sermon, which came while Emerson was struggling with an unsuccessful attempt at schoolkeeping and moving nearer to his decision to enter the ministry.[51] If we recall the defiant orator who indicted the ministry for its lifeless preaching in his Divinity School Address some fourteen years later, the appeal of Channing's sense of the challenge of the modern ministry will be clear. It was, as Channing saw it, "an age of earnestness and excitement," in which "men feel and think . . . with more energy than formerly." The signs were in the political revolutions of the day, which "sprung from a new and deep working of the human soul." They could also be found in "the bold and earnest spirit of the literature of our times," an indication that "men want and demand a more thrilling note, a poetry which pierces beneath the exterior of life to the depths of the soul" (272). The spirit of this new Romantic age also pervaded religion, Channing felt, making novel and challenging demands on the minister.

To suit such an age, a minister must communicate religion—not only as a result of reasoning but as a matter of experience—with that inexpressible character of reality, that life and power which accompany truths drawn from a man's own soul. We ought to speak of religion as something which we ourselves know. (273)

Channing's vision was simultaneously inspiring and daunting. Its effect on a young man considering the ministry can well be imagined—it would encourage a kind of intense introspection about self-worth while it would fire the imagination with visions of the "life and power" of felt religion. Anyone who has negotiated the emotional ups and downs of Emerson's early journals, with their amalgam of ambitious self-confidence and despairing self-reproach, will recognize the fuel that Channing's sermon would have added to this inner fire.

One of Channing's most impressive themes was the necessity of preaching from genuine experience:

He [the minister] should speak of God, of Christ, of the dignity and loveliness of Christian virtue, of heaven and redemption, not as of traditions and historical records about which he has only read, but as of realities which he understands, and feels in the very depths of his soul. (273)

50. *The Works of William E. Channing, D.D.*, (Boston, 1875), 269–78. Quotations from this sermon and the Divinity Hall sermon discussed subsequently will be cited parenthetically.
51. Emerson mentions the sermon in a letter to his brother William of July 8–10, 1824: "Gannett is ordained Colleague of Dr Channing & the Dr's Ordination Sermon is expected from the press with unmeasured applause" (L 1:146).

It is no very long step from this to Emerson's remarks about the "dry bones of the past" in *Nature* or his attack on historical Christianity in the Divinity School Address. The immediate context of Channing's remarks was revealed in his explicit reference to the situation of Unitarian preaching. In an age in which individuals "listen impatiently to great subjects treated with apathy" and "want a religion which will take a strong hold upon them," religious systems can survive only by "awakening a real and deep interest in the soul." This is the challenge that the liberals had to face, as Channing recognized: "It is objected to Unitarian Christianity that it does not possess this heart-stirring energy; and if so, it will, and still more, it ought, to fall; for it does not suit the spirit of our times, nor the essential and abiding spirit of human nature" (273).

These are strong words under any conditions, but from Channing they had special impact. Revivalistic preaching, which used highly emotional means to restructure the psyche and life, challenged the liberal preachers of the day to present a rationally viable but emotionally satisfying alternative. It was the latter of these demands that in many cases weighed most heavily.

At the dedication of Divinity Hall in 1826, Channing again took up these issues in dedicating the school "to the training of ministers, whose word, like their Master's, shall be 'with power'" (257). In stressing "power" as the central aspect of preaching, Channing obliquely raised the issue of the changing, perhaps dwindling, authority of the preacher. Such authority must not, he warned, be won back with the tactics of the opposition. "We would not train here, if we could, agents of terror to shake weak nerves, to disease the imagination, to lay a spell on men's faculties, to guard a creed by fires more consuming than those which burned on Sinai" (259). The revivalists' power was force gone astray, working at cross-purposes with the ultimate end of the ministry, "the strong action of the understanding, conscience, and heart, on moral and religious truth, through which the preacher is quickened and qualified to awaken the same strong action in others" (257-58). Establishing a middle ground between hellfire ranting and scornful intellectualism, Channing had again placed the emphasis on a deeply felt religious experience communicable to the hearers. The power of the minister derived from his own experience. Its sanction was the honesty and depth of that experience in the preacher himself. Emerson's growing conviction that all moral standards were grounded in the self thus had the additional confirmation—and the additional burden—of a ministerial authority which was ultimately self-derived.

Emerson recognized "how great a revolution" had taken place "in the character and position of the clergy in this country." In a late sermon he noted that they were no longer "shepherds of a flock" (Sermon CLXXI). The minister now "solicits your attention to truths which engage him and therefore should engage you." Most significantly, "he drops all shadow of a claim of authority over you." The change, he admitted, "may sometimes give rise to regret in both parts," but ultimately Emerson had seen its benefit: "I am inclined to think that nothing is worth defending which rests upon a false basis." Yet the dilemma remained—to move his hearers without resorting to the practices of the revivalists.

* * *

Millennialism was one of the cornerstones of the Second Great Awakening. The concept of progress toward a perfect future could be a powerful tool in the pulpit, fusing both religious fervor and social expectations. It has been seen principally as an aspect of the revivalist mind, and its centrality to American evangelicalism is clear. The success of the revivals was, to the evangelicals, empirical evidence of the coming millennium. But millennialism had its liberal version as well, as we find in Emerson's preaching, and was an important part of the Unitarian response to "the demands of the age."

In 1827 Emerson depicted the widespread acceptance of a God of benevolence as part of a religious progress that betokened the approaching millennium. "It has been thought that Christianity is preparing its own triumphs, that a purer age shall come, when God shall be worshipped in spirit and in truth" (Sermon VIII). That age would, Emerson argued, spell the end of "civil laws, that are now found necessary to coerce the peace of society"; it would be an age in which "Knowledge shall cease to be the property of the few, but shall be sought by all men with that eagerness with which they now seek wealth"; it would be an age in which "men shall feel as a community." Religious progress was by Emerson's definition the move away from Calvinist theology toward a purified liberal Christianity. But the sense of an impending utopian era, signaled by the rising religious fervor of the present time, is similar in the liberal and revivalist versions. "Welcome then this approaching era of human bliss!" Emerson urged his hearers. "God speed this pure Millennium."

Emerson's millennial optimism eventually became channeled into the non-institutional spirit of Transcendentalism, and his own enthusiasm for the liberal cause, as it was identified with Unitarianism, became dim with time, even dimmer in memory. Here is a college conversation which he recalled over thirty years later and recorded in his journal:

When I was a senior in College, I think,—Samuel Barrett whom I had known in Concord was about to be ordained in the Chamber-street Church and I called upon him in his room in College. . . . We talked about the vices and calamities of the time,—I don't recall what the grim shadows were, or how we came on them,—but when I rose to go, & asked him what was the relief & cure of all this? he replied with cheerful ardor, "Nothing but Unitarianism." From my remembrance of how this answer struck me, I am sure that this antidote must have looked as thin & poor & pale to me then, as now. I was never for a moment the victim of "Enlightenment," or "Progress of the Species," or the "Diffusion-of-Knowledge-Society." (JMN 15:81)

As some important moments in the sermons themselves suggest, the progress of liberal religion had not seemed so "thin & poor & pale" to him as he recalled. The hopes that he had invested in the progress of religion were central to the message he preached. This millennial enthusiasm sets the tone of Sermon CLXV, which Emerson preached to the Second Church after returning from his European journey. He referred to Christianity as "the most emphatic affirmation of spiritual nature" but added, in the spirit of his growing Transcendentalism, "It is not the only nor the last affirmation. There shall be a thousand more." Emerson had by now relegated Christianity to the status of *a* rather than *the* revelation, without altering his millennial optimism.

The dawn is reddening around us, but the day has not come. The teacher is teaching but has not finished his word. That word never will be finished. It was before the heavens and shall be after them. But a part of this message is spoken this day and every day. There are truths now being revealed. There is a revolution of religious opinion now taking effect around us.

The "progress of religion" in the 1820s had quickened into a "revolution of religious opinion" by the middle 1830s. Both descriptions reflect Emerson's sense of the accelerating religious pulse of his time and his projection of the golden age to come. His prophetic sense of the dawning of a new age reminds us that these sermons are part of a larger context of American millennial optimism, which lent much fervor to the emerging Transcendentalist movement.[52]

*   *   *

In one important area, however, Emerson's response to the cultural changes of the day led him—and the liberal movement in general—in a much different direction from the evangelicals. In the words of Lawrence Buell, "The sense of a bond between religion and art became an important theme in Unitarian thought during the two decades before Emerson's emergence as a writer and finally reached a culmination in his idea of the poet-priest."[53] This bond between religion and art reminds us that the sermons were crafted productions presented in a religious setting in which there was a growing sensitivity to other aesthetic concerns. Buell is careful to note that there were clear distinctions between sermon writing and secular writing, but the thrust of his research was to demonstrate the enormous literary consequences of changes in the way Unitarians wrote sermons. Of course, Emerson brought an acute aesthetic sensibility to the pulpit; indeed, literary and artistic concerns—and especially a love of oratory—played a large role in attracting him to the pulpit in the first place.

The close link of the emotions with aesthetic experience helps to account for the Unitarian interest in the arts. The raw emotion of revivalism was to some

52. The millennial aspects of the sermons suggest that in some respects they were part of the powerful cultural consensus formed by the interplay of millennial optimism, social and economic development, and the Puritan jeremiad tradition. See Sacvan Bercovitch, *The American Jeremiad* (Madison, Wis., 1978).

53. Lawrence Buell, "Unitarian Aesthetics and Emerson's Poet-Priest," *American Quarterly* 20 (Spring 1968): 3. See also his important study *Literary Transcendentalism: Style and Vision in the American Renaissance* (Ithaca, N.Y., 1973).

extent countered in Unitarian preaching by the intellectual, emotional, and aesthetic complexities of the well-wrought sermon. Such sermons could thus satisfy some (if not all) of the emotional needs which the congregation brought to the worship service. In one of his earliest publications, a review of F. W. P. Greenwood's *Collection of Psalms and Hymns for Christian Worship*, Emerson had an opportunity to express his poetic taste. Several months later he again indulged his interest in sacred music by preaching on church hymns (Sermon CXXXI).[54] There one can find the rudiments of his later theories of the poet-priest, or divinely inspired bard, that were important themes in *Nature*, the Divinity School Address, and "The Poet."

The sermons themselves are also aesthetic productions, although our full understanding of them as such will depend on future analyses of their dependence on and departures from structural formulas, their clusters of imagery and metaphoric patterns, their sacred and secular allusions, the interplay of biblical and modern phraseology in them, and their oratorical and conversational rhetoric. An awareness of the aesthetic qualities of these theological productions, combined with an improved understanding of the religious basis of Emerson's later writing, will sharpen our realization that, despite a general cultural trend toward secular styles and values, religious and literary concerns continued to be mutually implicated in nineteenth-century New England.

*   *   *

As these sermons reveal, Emerson was neither a theological controversialist nor a dogmatist. Although he did, as his duties or inclinations dictated, take an occasional swipe at Calvinism or praise certain tendencies in the liberal movement, these are for the most part isolated, even uncharacteristic, gestures. His principal concern was to communicate religious experience and to inculcate a pietistic state of mind that resulted in moral action. In 1828 he reduced Christianity to its simplest terms:

It asks no struggles with nature . . . nor heaps a mountain of difficulties in your path to be encountered at once. *It only requires that in a single moment you do a single thing right. This* is the whole of religion . . . . To do this, is to be a Christian. (Sermon XVIII)

The life of devotion could thus be translated into an unending series of moral actions. Unceasing prayer and unending moral choice were complementary aspects of the same moral outlook. Of necessity these actions included the mundane as well as the dramatic, but each of them was a test of sorts, a fresh measure of the ability of the soul to act out its best qualities.

Emerson accepted the doctrine of probation as a fundamental premise and centered much of his preaching around it, though he rarely set out to produce

54. See Kenneth Walter Cameron, "An Early Prose Work of Emerson," *American Literature* 22 (November 1950): 332–38, which reprints with commentary Emerson's review from the *Christian Examiner* 10 (March 1831): 30–34. The review and sermon were part of Emerson's effort to have the Second Church replace its hymnals, which he felt contained objectionable doctrine.

doctrinal pronouncements as Ware and Channing did. He had admitted to himself early on that his talent did not lie in rigorous or systematic theology. "My reasoning faculty is proportionately weak," he frankly concluded in 1824, "nor can I ever hope to write a Butler's Analogy or an Essay of Hume." But this lack would not prevent him, he felt, from pursuing "the highest species of reasoning upon divine subjects, [which] is rather the fruit of a sort of moral imagination." This, he felt, was the mode of Channing (*JMN* 2:238). Such a resolve at the outset of his religious studies freed Emerson as a minister to focus on the moral implications of his community's received doctrine and to translate the theology of the liberal movement into the daily lives of his parishioners.

In 1828 Emerson preached one of his few sectarian sermons, arguing that the recent progress of religion had consisted in overcoming the Calvinist denigration of human potential (Sermon XIV). In an allusion to the decades of Unitarian controversy in the immediate past, he admitted, "The noise and sometimes the bitterness of controversy is the price we pay for freedom of conscience and enlightened views of religion." But his rejection of Calvinism was forceful: "We have not so learned the lessons of Christ as to think that the sin of Adam had poisoned the blood of all the race of man; had called down the wrath of the Almighty upon them all without reference to their character; had turned their good to evil, their prayers to blasphemies, their hope to horror." Emerson counterpointed his attack on the "baleful doctrine" of election with a description of the Scripture's "cheering revelation that our souls are immortal; that this world is a state of discipline, a school of preparation to train us up for endless being." This understanding of life as discipline placed "character" at the center of religious culture, so "all that we do goes to make up our character, and . . . on our character, our happiness wholly depends." The formation of character, the liberal version of salvation, thus explained the entire biblical revelation.

"In every human heart, conscience, if we listen, is heard to say, that never have we done enough," Emerson preached in 1830 (Sermon LXXXIII). The working of this moral sense is perennial, unceasing. Emerson's call for self-improvement thus arose from "the undiminishing standard that everywhere exists in the human breast," an intuited power that made the distinction of right and wrong possible. This standard, the moral sense, was one of his most deeply held beliefs.[55] As he explained, the moral sense was never known "to rank itself even with the practice but always somewhat higher." It is not a static and unchanging standard: "The more it is observed the higher it rises." This internal standard accounted for both the hope and the painful duality of life, the "immeasurable difference between what we are and what we are capable of being." Later he

55. For commentary on Emerson's doctrine of the moral sense, see Merrell R. Davis, "Emerson's 'Reason' and the Scottish Philosophers," *New England Quarterly* 17 (June 1944): 209–28; Wallace E. Williams, "Emerson and the Moral Law," (Ph.D. diss., University of California, Berkeley, 1963); Bishop, *Emerson on the Soul*, 66–72; Joel Porte, *Emerson and Thoreau: Transcendentalists in Conflict* (Middletown, Ct., 1966), 68–92; and Robinson, *Apostle of Culture*, 50–55.

would identify this disjunction between the ideal and the actual, the "double consciousness," as the great burden of life. But in 1830 he depicted this moral discrepancy as a means of inspiration, as an occasion for asking "whether we are systematically aiming to answer the ends of our being."

What this effort at self-culture meant in practical terms would vary over the years for Emerson. He stressed intellectual development as a part of it, but like Ware he also saw religion as a matter of the heart. In 1828 he described the affections as the distinguishing element of the religious character. Religion requires that you "give your affections to God" in a continuing act of pietistic devotion (Sermon XXVI). As in the theology of Jonathan Edwards, these insatiable affections are a manifestation of the moral sense: they "seek always entire goodness and truth." He stressed that "these affections can be *cultivated; that they grow by their own exercise.*" Public religious exercises can contribute to this growth, but its mainspring is "that devotional frame of mind which at all times and in all places judges itself by secret reference to the Divine Will."

The Christian, Emerson preached, "believes he is here merely to be trained—here at school to learn how to act and suffer" (Sermon XLI). The austerity of such images of self-culture is confirmed by Emerson's grounding of it in discipline, in a kind of renunciation and self-sacrifice that he recognized as often in Stoic philosophers as in early Christian martyrs. It is true that there was a new burst of self-affirmation in the Unitarian dissent and that this affirmation burned even more intensely in the Transcendentalist movement. But it is often overlooked that Emerson anchored even his buoyantly transcendental *Nature* with a chapter on "Discipline." There persisted among the Unitarians, despite their rejection of innate depravity, a healthy respect for the dangers of the self. This suspicion of antinomian self-indulgence was a significant element in Andrews Norton's later attack on Transcendentalism as a form of infidelity. The self, he felt, simply could not bear the spiritual weight that Emerson and his followers were placing on it.[56] Emerson himself felt the need to provide some brake to the antinomian implications of his early preaching, and his response was to emphasize self-sacrifice. "We are to give in every moment living sacrifices" (Sermon LXXXVII). Self-love was possible "only as we are parts and manifestations" of God (Sermon XCVI). In 1831 he brought the whole of the doctrine of self-culture to a remarkable summation.

In short all the cultivation of our moral and intellectual powers is teaching us to say 'Thy will be done'; that our will, as far as it is separate from the will of God, is evil and pernicious, and as the soul comes to breathe that sentiment, the presence and perfection of God is felt. (Sermon CXXI)

The paradox of the doctrine of self-culture—or one of them at least—was that

---

56. See Robinson, *The Unitarians and the Universalists*, 80.

the growth of the soul was at bottom a process of the abnegation of the will. The expansive soul was in important ways a retreat from the self.

This paradox has its basis in the close relation of the doctrines of the moral sense and of the God within. These have long been recognized as essential themes in Emerson's thought, and the sermons confirm how pervasive they were from the very beginning of his career. In 1827 Emerson noted that "the main, central, prominent power of the soul is the *moral sentiment*—the Conscience, the distinguisher of right and wrong" (Sermon IX). Emerson was molded in fundamental and lasting ways by the Unitarian conception of the moral sense, and even that interesting foil to the Unitarian movement, Hopkinsian Calvinism, made its contribution to this discourse.[57] In Sermon XLV Emerson labeled as an "extravagance" Samuel Hopkins's theory of a "disinterested love of God," a love so strong that it could content the soul "to perish forever" for God's glory and the benefit of the universe. Yet the idea of utter self-abnegation as the ultimate moral act had an attraction for Emerson. "There is something so generous and sublime in [the theory's] absurdity," he wrote, "that good men will forgive it." The world was constituted, in its doubts and instabilities, so that "something very like disinterested benevolence may be nourished in it."

In his fullest sermonic rendering of the moral sense, Emerson depicted cognizance of duty as "the most remarkable property of our human nature" (Sermon CLIV). For him that capacity was integral to the very functioning of the mind: "There never was a man of sane mind who did not know the distinction of right and wrong." As the sermon develops, the sentiment of duty, or the moral sense, is depicted as the soul itself or the medium by which the soul reveals and expresses itself. The moral sense is first "a regulator in the human constitution," a force which provides stability amid both external and internal changes. For Emerson, "the simple principles of right action" cut through all theological dispute.

These are the first foundations of all religion, and run under all the forms in which man ever worshipped. It is strange that men do not see that there is more of God and religion in them than in doubtful and obscure questions of faith, though they should be discussed and cleared up by the tongues of angels.

Modern commentators have come increasingly to see in Emerson a doubting, struggling, irony-laden figure. That picture of him, for the most part true enough, does not tally with the public voice we hear in this moment as he holds hard to the surest foundation he can find. That foundation is not Scripture, the Christian revelation, or even a sure sense of a transcendent Creator. Everything depends on the moral sense. But to understand a thinker's foundation is also to

57. It has been argued that Hopkins was influential on Channing's development of the doctrine of disinterestedness, but as Conrad Wright has shown, other thinkers were of much greater importance, and Channing was never a Hopkinsian. See "The Rediscovery of Channing," in *The Liberal Christians*, 22–28.

understand his vulnerability, that point at which the entrance of doubt or skepticism is the most threatening. The most profoundly disturbing moments of thought for Emerson are those in which the moral value of human actions is questioned—especially, as in "Circles," when his own premises lead him to suspect that there is "an equivalence and indifferency of all actions." He labeled this form of skepticism "Pyrrhonism" and struggled with it repeatedly in the 1840s (*CW* 2:188).

The experiential fact of the moral sense led Emerson to the larger question of its origin. In one remarkable passage we find how deeply, even by 1828, he had explored religious skepticism and pure naturalism and what he had weighed skepticism against.

I may believe that the stars have burned in their courses forever—that no hand hurled them into their eternal paths, but that they have walked in those circles from a frightful infinity *without a cause*. I may believe when I daily see the ocean evaporate its clouds, that this precious burden is lifted by heat, and borne by the winds, and poured again over the land—*by accident*. I may believe that all the processes of vegetation originated *without thought* and go forward *without being promoted by any regard to the wants of animal life;*—yes, I may believe all this but I can never believe that the Conscience of man came to him without an author, or reason, or end. I hear the voice which it alway utters, 'There is a God.' (Sermon XXI)[58]

One sees how little Emerson based his religion on biblical revelation, even from the outset of his career. His grounding in the moral sense did not here dictate any hostility to revealed Christianity, but the passage shows how the gradual eclipse of biblical revelation, with its Christology, miracles, and doctrine of atonement, could leave Emerson so unperturbed.

The inner voice of conscience, a continual reminder of God, thus was closely connected to the idea of the God within. Emerson was conversant not only with the rationalistic tradition of the moral sense theory, but also with an emotionally rich tradition of Christian devotionalist thinking. He held that, to the individual possessed of the idea of God, "it is not any longer an idea, a theory, a sentiment; it is in itself a living soul; it is a life within life" (Sermon LXXXV). This soul within, which the individual must strive to nurture and cultivate, suggests that the moral sense was, for him, very far from a rational or calculating faculty. Merrell R. Davis has shown how Emerson's moral sense doctrine anticipated his later immersion in the idea of "Reason" that he adopted from Coleridge, and there are affinities between Emerson's idea of the moral sense and the Romantic concept of the imagination.[59] But however Romantic its direction, this vital inner force had foundations in devotional writing which predated Romanticism. "It is, as it has been truly called, the life of God in the

58. Cf. *JMN* 3:135-36.
59. Davis, "Emerson's 'Reason.'" See also Robinson, *Apostle of Culture*, 51-52.

soul of man," Emerson noted (Sermon LXXXV), linking the concept directly
to Henry Scougal's 1677 devotional work.[60]

In 1831 Emerson argued that because "God is with us and in us" we should
"hold [our] own nature in a reverential awe" (Sermon LXXXVIII). Moreover, in
keeping with the conception of life as a state of probation, the individual should
see that "to build up his own being on this eternal foundation is his work in the
world, consisting in a continual selection and separation of that which is sinful
from that which is divine." None of this is inconsistent with the commitment to
revealed religion shared by all the denominations of the day; indeed, the predominant view of the Unitarians was that the process of culture was based on
that revelation. But an important complication arises from statements such as
this from the same sermon: "I say to a thoroughly good man, if such an one
there were, it is only so far as you find Christianity within your soul that I
recommend it." The remark predates in public discourse a journal entry of
1832: "You must be humble because Christ says, 'Be humble'. 'But why must I
obey Christ?' 'Because God sent him.' But how do I know God sent him?
'Because your own heart teaches the same thing he taught.' Why then shall I not
go to my own heart at first?" (*JMN* 4:45).

Thus, Emerson's conception of the moral sense and its link to the God within
eventually led him to an increasing emphasis on the self as normative in
religion. This was no linear development; the trail is fraught with inconsisten-
cies and backtracking. In 1832, late in his ministry at the Second Church, he had
been pressed to make an important distinction to his congregation: "It is not
our soul that is God, but God is in our soul" (Sermon CLX). That distinction
preserved the transcendence of God and prevented the idolatry of the self that
opponents of the doctrine feared. "There is something in us that is higher and
better than we. There is something in us that never consents to any wrong."
That he could call humans "in our fabric God-believing God-worshipping creatures" (Sermon CXXXVII) emphasized that the process of self-culture was a
following out of our nature, an organic development of an existent potential.

Themes of probation and discipline and self-culture provide a continuity of
thought that explains Emerson's connection to his immediate past and takes
him well into his post-ministerial Transcendental period. A perception of that
continuity in turn provides a focus for other key issues that were in a state of
transition not only for Emerson but for his generation. Those questions center
principally on the supernatural aspects of Christian belief: the nature of Jesus
and the truth of the biblical miracles.

Emerson rejected supernaturalism implicitly in *Nature* and explicitly in the
Divinity School Address. These dramatic gestures of rebellion account for
much of his principal appeal to literary and intellectual historians. But the heat
of old controversies has obscured the fact that Emerson's rebellion was in
important senses an extension of what he originally possessed. In fact, the

---

60. Scougal, *The Life of God in the Soul of Man* (London, 1677).

changes in intellectual doctrine that later achieved dramatic intensity were being worked out, indeed had almost been resolved, in the sermons. The move against supernaturalism was neither sudden nor linear, but it was unmistakable. We see it most persuasively in his Christology.

Emerson's rejection of the miracles as a basis for the religious authority of Jesus was begun and essentially completed during his ministry at the Second Church. Insofar as this position may be taken as indicative of Transcendentalism, Emerson was a Transcendentalist by 1832. Andrews Norton, who would have defined the issues that way, was thus six years late in his attack.[61] Emerson was refashioning the legacy of Christ to suit his religious sensibility, finding the uses to which a new concept of the "Saviour" could be put in the process of culture.[62] In this transition Emerson was following the general drift of the German Higher Criticism in a rejection of a supernatural interpretation of the Bible. Barbara Packer's discerning study of Emerson's lectures on the New Testament has confirmed that his acquaintance with the Higher Criticism gave additional impetus to his anti-supernatural inclinations.[63] He had absorbed at least some of the Higher Criticism from his brother William, who had written home during his theological studies in Germany.[64] Certainly by 1831 his sermons had begun to show a quickening in the process of theological liberalization that he underwent in the ministry. His professional and intellectual confidence developed simultaneously. The result was a wariness about the specific supernatural claims of Christianity and a renewed commitment to its moral truths.

In his careful reconstruction of the intellectual background of Emerson's Sermon V, Wesley T. Mott demonstrated how deeply Emerson meditated upon the nature of Christ in the period just before he entered the ministry. Even in this overtly Christological sermon, Mott found that Emerson departed significantly from standard beliefs about the supernatural mission of Christ. For Emerson, Jesus is "not perhaps a savior in the conventional sense," but rather "the great model of moral growth."[65] That distinction is crucial, for it shows how the contours of Christology could be adapted to this new model of the self.

The sermon does not, however, reject the supernatural nature of Christ. "He sits at the right hand of God," Emerson said, and "he shall acknowledge you before his Father in Heaven." Statements such as these are reminders that it was not the conception of the nature of Christ which was essential, but the uses to

---

61. In fact, the miracles issue was tied to the general shift away from empiricist epistemology, which was the deeper background of the controversy.

62. McGiffert noted that there were "eight sermons devoted primarily to an exposition of the person and work of Christ, which were preached fifty-one times" (*Young Emerson Speaks*, 233).

63. Packer, "Origin and Authority: Emerson and the Higher Criticism," in *Reconstructing American Literary History*, ed. Sacvan Bercovitch (Cambridge, Mass., 1986), 76–82. See also Kenneth Walter Cameron, *The Vestry Lectures and a Rare Sermon* (Hartford, Conn., 1984); and Karen Kalinevitch, "Turning from the Orthodox: Emerson's Gospel Lectures," in *Studies in the American Renaissance: 1986*, ed. Joel Myerson (Charlottesville, Va., 1986), 69–112.

64. William studied under Johann Gottfried Eichhorn; see *Life*, 115, 152.

65. Mott, "Christ Crucified," 29.

which that concept might be put. In Sermon LXXVI, which Emerson revised in 1832 to make his position on Jesus clearer, he made a distinction crucial to his demythologizing of Christ. "It was the value of this truth that gave him his spiritual empire. Do not think that he owed to the curiosity and reverence that followed one possessed of miraculous power the weight of his lesson."[66] This made Jesus the product of his message; it placed priority in the idea and not in the man. In this Christological Copernican Revolution, Jesus' devotion to a form of truth—that truth revealed to the individual through the moral sense—proved his authority. The radically humanizing tendency of this thinking was evident in 1830 when Emerson preached that "the truth is dawning on the world that Jesus Christ was the express image of [God's] person only inasmuch [as] he was a better man than any other" (Sermon LXXXIX). Jesus was not a savior from the human condition, but an exemplar of what the human condition could be. His personality reinforced the imperative for self-culture.

Because the ground of authority had shifted from the supernatural to the exemplary, the whole question of biblical miracles had to be reassessed. Appended to one of the drafts of Sermon LXXVI is this telling notation: "I am disposed to think with Coleridge about the Miracle." Coleridge's idealism was a potent influence, as scholars have long known, in part because Emerson was already thinking of Jesus as a moral example rather than a figure of miraculous authority. Emerson thus developed a Christology that was nearly opposite to that which his later nemesis Andrews Norton was developing as the cornerstone of his theology. Norton had staked the entire validity of the Christian message on the empirical evidence of the supernatural miracles as witnessed historically. But in 1831 Emerson preached that the "decisive" proof of the miracles was that their fraudulence would be "utterly incompatible" with "those who declared them and lived by them." "There is nothing in the teaching of Jesus or of his apostles that would encourage what is called pious frauds but all that abhors them" (Sermon CIII). That is to say, the moral character of Jesus established the supernatural quality of the miracles, rather than vice-versa.

This line of thinking called for a new conception of religious revelation, as the ultimate authority of the Bible faded. Generations of Unitarians before Emerson had struggled with this question more deeply than he had, but as Sydney Ahlstrom has argued, many Unitarians continued to believe that "the Bible was the very word of God."[67] In the 1829 ordination sermon, he affirmed the scriptures as "the direct voice of the most High—the reason of God speaking to the reason of man" (Sermon XXVIII). But this is only a point of departure for changing attitudes, changes that came with far less struggle than those

66. The sermon manuscripts, with their evidence of revision, suggest that Emerson took special care to formulate his position on this issue. Sermon LXXVI is an important text for understanding his intellectual development.

67. Sydney Ahlstrom and Jonathan S. Carey, eds., *An American Reformation: A Documentary History of Unitarian Christianity* (Middletown, Conn., 1986), 33.

concerning Christ or the miracles. He preached in 1830 on the biblical doctrine
of the last judgment but made it clear that the truth of the Bible was meta-
phorical. Forms of religion will pass away, as will "the imagery . . . in which
religious truth has been contained," such as "the idea of heaven as a kingdom;
of God as a king; of hell as a pit of fire; of Jesus as a judge upon a bench." In
Emerson's own simile, "These images are like the leaves on which the Scriptures are written": they will perish while "the truth of which they are the vehicle" will remain eternally (Sermon XCV). One parenthetical remark in a
sermon of 1831 made the issue clear: "It is not a Revelation that makes man
religious. He is of a religious nature" (Sermon CXI). As the human soul
increasingly came to be the locus of religious value for Emerson, the importance
of the Bible faded. One might well be "a Christian without knowing it," he
preached in 1831, because of "the original edition of [the Bible] in his heart"
(Sermon CXXXVII).

Thus, Emerson continued to move away from supernaturalism toward a natural religion, a pattern that defined his entire intellectual career and created one
of his chief cultural legacies. He gradually came to articulate a newer vision of a
natural and secular faith, "a quiet yet sublime religion . . . whose temple shall
be the household hearth" (*EL* 3:315). He acknowledged in 1860 what historians
have since recognized, that "we live in a transition period, when the old faiths
which comforted nations, and not only so but made nations, seem to have spent
their force" (*W* 6:207). Emerson's sermons show how he worked during that
period of transition to preserve a form of faith on new grounds by adopting and
then expanding the idea of a religious culture of the soul.

What will it mean to view Emerson through this new lens of the complete
texts of his sermons? It will now be clearer to us that he was molded by the
religious culture of New England Unitarianism and that he was given much of
his intellectual impetus by the definitive aspects of that culture, especially by the
doctrine of self-culture. The Romantic movement's rejection of its immediate
past and its corresponding claims to absolute originality have often been
accepted uncritically as historical fact by modern readers. As a result there
exists only an obscure sense of these important roots of New England Transcendentalism. Some familiar boundaries in literary history may thus be altered
by a renewed sense of the seamlessness of early nineteenth-century American
cultural history as these texts reveal it. Any recognition of the centrality of
preaching as a mode of discourse in Transcendentalism makes it unlikely that
future assessments will be made on purely literary or philosophical grounds.
The body of work that Emerson's sermons represent—and they represent, of
course, but a fraction of Transcendentalist preaching—will locate the movement more securely as a subject of intellectual and interdisciplinary historiogra-
phy. Literary achievement has, of course, been the Transcendentalists' principal
avenue of influence, but the reorientation of studies of the movement will not
mean a diminution in its stature. In fact, the overwhelming evidence of the
religious origins and achievements of the Transcendentalists will clarify their

purposes, allowing them to be judged on their own terms. Emerson described the period from 1820 to 1840 as a time when "the mind had become aware of itself" (*W* 10:326). The Transcendentalists found this new and liberating self-consciousness through the theological categories they inherited. Through those same categories we will recover the richness of their achievement.

TEXTUAL INTRODUCTION

With the exception of a portion of one sermon that is privately owned, the manuscripts of all 178 of Emerson's surviving sermons are deposited in the Houghton Library of Harvard University. A few sermons toward the end of the series are fragmentary, but in only two instances (sermons LXIV and CLXVII) have the manuscripts disappeared altogether.

The manuscripts are in the form of fascicles, generally consisting of four or five sheets of the standard letter paper of the day folded once and nested in a single gathering. The fascicle was most often sewn through the center fold, though occasionally the separate folios were stacked and sewn through the margin. Most sermons contain inserted leaves or smaller sheets and strips of paper affixed some time after the sewing with red or black sealing wax. The threads in several manuscripts have deteriorated or disappeared entirely, but in no instance has the ordering of the leaves been in doubt. The continuity of the inscription, pinhole evidence, and a pencilled numbering of the leaves (done by William H. Bond when the sermons were acquired by the Houghton Library) have been sufficient in all cases to assure a correct ordering. The manuscript of each sermon is described in the Textual and Manuscript Notes at the back of the volume.

Emerson never supplied titles for his sermons, but instead followed the ministerial practice of his day by identifying them for his own reference with Roman numerals, almost invariably centered at the top of the first page. Some confusion on this point has arisen as a result of Arthur McGiffert's decision to supply titles (usually in square brackets) for the sermons in his selected edition, *Young Emerson Speaks* (1938). Although the convenience of such titles is considerable, they have been rejected here as inappropriate to a critical edition, both because they are unauthorized by Emerson and because they are demonstrably interpretive and frequently misleading. The temptation to reproduce Emerson's numbering system in Arabic numerals has likewise been resisted (as indeed has all modernizing of the text), despite the precedent that McGiffert offers. It is interesting to note that although Emerson referred to his sermons solely by Roman numerals in his Preaching Record during the period of his most active ministry, he began listing them in Arabic numerals after he resigned his Second Church pastorate.

Copy-Text

The copy-text for the sermons is, of course, the manuscripts themselves. Emerson committed none of his sermons to print during his lifetime, and there is indeed some indirect evidence that he did not wish them published at all. While the manuscripts show varying amounts of revision, it is clear that no sermon was brought to a state that its author would have found satisfactory for publication. They were written out fully (he did not preach, just as he did not lecture, from notes), but written out with a care for oral delivery rather than for the requirements of an editor or compositor. The punctuation and orthography are therefore extremely casual.

The fact, however, that oral delivery is itself a form of publication deserves to be carefully considered by any editor of sermons or lectures. Emerson's sermons were "published" in the obvious sense that he made them available to a public, but also in the less obvious sense that in the act of reading he removed all evidence of revision and produced a text more or less polished. Emerson's earliest reputation rested on a series of such performances, or performed texts, about which the manuscripts can be said in the strictest truth to offer good but always imperfect evidence. Even setting aside the probability that Emerson occasionally departed from his text in the oral delivery, it is usually impossible for an editor to tell precisely when the author made a particular manuscript revision: whether before the first delivery, for example, or between the sixth and seventh. A text, therefore, that simply incorporates all manuscript alterations is more likely to approach the latest than the earliest oral form of the sermon; by the same token, a text that rejects all manuscript alterations will approach the earliest oral form, though often at the cost of preserving many errors that Emerson must certainly have corrected at once. Indeed, it is clear that a great many of the revisions evident in the manuscripts—including but not limited to false starts, corrections of eye-skip errors, and overwritings in continuous passages—were made before the first delivery, so it is more accurate to say that a text without any manuscript alterations would correspond to no delivered state of the sermon, but would represent something like an intermediate draft.

There are reasons for preferring the earliest delivered version and other reasons, just as cogent, for preferring the latest version.[1] The main reason for preferring the early version has to do with the ordering of the sermons. Composed as they were in a definite and ascertainable sequence, they are presented here chronologically. It would obviously be unfortunate if this order were obscured by the fact that Emerson might at a later date have heavily revised one sermon but left another, originally written a week later, relatively unrevised. The sequence of the sermons is that of their composition, which is also to say that the ordering of the sermons in any edition is logically consistent only with the presentation of their first versions.

1. It should be noted that the total difference that Emerson's revisions make will be reckoned considerable or inconsiderable by different readers. Editors have debated whether and under what circumstances the presence of multiple revisions must imply a multiplicity of texts or versions. The fact that Emerson may have delivered a particular sermon a dozen or more times makes the concept of "versions" more discretely meaningful.

The reason for preferring the later versions, on the other hand, is that they make in several respects the better texts. An editor can reconstruct the last version with far more confidence than he can any earlier version for the simple reason that when Emerson stopped delivering sermons (as late as 1839), he stopped revising them. But the later texts are also better in another sense. There can be no doubt that Emerson's revisions are consistent improvements of thought and style; they correct grammatical and syntactic errors, clarify obscurities, prune oratorical excesses, give greater depth to hastily sketched ideas, and in general add to the cogency and appeal of the oral argument. No editor is or should be immune from "literary" considerations, even though such matters cannot themselves determine editorial decisions, which must flow from clear and generally applicable textual principles and not from particular and idiosyncratic literary preferences. Considerations of literary value should, in other words, play a role in the editor's conception of the "best text" that he is bound to deliver; they should play a role in his largest and earliest decisions about textual principles so that they will not contaminate the proffered text later by affecting particular decisions about accepting or rejecting this or that variant reading.

The principal editorial issue in planning the present edition, therefore, was the extent to which it was feasible and desirable to reconstruct the form of the first delivery. In practice, such a goal meant the rejection of all authorial emendations made after the sermon was delivered for the first time. Unless the editors adopted the unwarranted assumption that Emerson first read from a perfect fair copy, we should have to distinguish between corrections and additions made before the first delivery and those made afterward. Except in the few instances in which an inserted sentence or passage refers to an event that can be historically associated with a particular later delivery, there is simply no way to make such a discrimination.

The dilemma is largely resolved when it is observed that the twenty-one sermons delivered only once by Emerson show, on average, almost as much manuscript revision as the others. This is perhaps fair warrant for an assumption to which the editors are forced in any event: that the preponderance of revision was worked out at or very near the time of first delivery. No doubt some revision occurred later, but these instances continuing to be unidentifiable, it was thought best, on balance, to accept all of Emerson's revisions except those few that could be shown to have been made subsequent to the first delivery, with some degree of confidence that the resulting text would not be far removed from the version first heard by Emerson's auditors.

Each sermon was edited, therefore, on the presumed likelihood that a large majority of the revisions were made before the first delivery. This presumption, supported by the evidence of those sermons delivered only once, is least appropriately applied to sermons for which more than one manuscript survives. In the present volume, for example, sermons XXXV and XXXVII are each represented in two complete manuscript versions, one heavily revised and the other a fair copy that underwent some slight further revision. It is evident that some state of each manuscript corresponds to one or more actual deliveries. Once again, however, it is impossible, in examining the earlier manuscript, to distinguish emendations made before the first delivery from those that Emerson made after the first delivery with the specific intent of producing a revised fair copy. Clearly, any revision appearing on the earlier manuscript made for the sake of producing the second manuscript relates to deliveries associated only with the later manuscript, and therefore ought not to be incorporated into any text based on the first manuscript. The solution arrived at is a pragmatic one involving a slight but necessary compromise with consistency: in each instance where more than a single manuscript exists, the second is chosen as copy-text, and the entire text of the first manuscript is reproduced in the Textual and Manuscript Notes.

One other editorial decision requires comment. Given the nature of the manuscript materials, the editors faced a choice between presenting the sermons in genetic form or in clear text. The genetic form, adopted in the Harvard edition of Emerson's *Journals and Miscellaneous Notebooks*, for example, is generally held to be appropriate for private documents not intended by their author for publication. This form of presentation requires that all authorial alteration of the manuscript, all additions, deletions, variants, transpositions, and so forth, be recorded by the use of special editorial symbols in the text itself rather than presented as textual notes in the back matter. As the term "genetic" implies, this method of presentation emphasizes the compositional process at the expense (relatively speaking) of an accessible finished product and is of most immediate use to a rather small audience of academic specialists. The clear text presentation is generally held to be appropriate for public documents—those previously published or intended by their author for a public audience. Here the text is "clear" of editorial symbols; the author's emendations are followed in the text (treating the manuscript, as it were, like a set of directions), while the fact and actual appearance of emendation are recorded in a set of appended textual notes. This is the form of presentation adopted in the Harvard edition of Emerson's *Early Lectures*, which has been a general model for the present edition of the sermons. A main rationale in both instances for selecting this method of presentation is that the documents, though not previously published in the usual sense, were indeed public and performed rather than private. Some users of the present edition would no doubt have preferred a genetic text, but given the necessity of choosing, it has seemed the better course to select the clear text, not only because it is favored by generally agreed upon principles of textual editing, but also because the significance of the sermons lies rather more in the picture they give us of Emerson's contact with the moral and theological content of Unitarianism than in what they tell us of his compositional practices. Neither of these matters is unimportant, and neither kind of edition fails to do justice to both of them, but given that clear and genetic presentations do inherently emphasize different aspects of a text, it is reasonable that the emphasis fall on the relatively more important feature.[2]

Textual Notes

The textual notes give the manuscript reading in every case of authorial insertion, deletion, substitution, transposition, and variant reading. With the exception of the categories of silent emendation listed below, the notes also record every instance in which a word or part of a word has been editorially supplied or deleted (for example, to correct Emerson's accidental doubling of words), or in which punctuation has been altered for clarity. No editorial emendations, silent or otherwise, occur in the textual notes, the purpose of which in each instance is to give the manuscript form using such standard symbols as are necessary to describe the situation.[3] Thus, a textual note might take this form:

our ⟨beliefs⟩ ↑Xty↓.

The symbols indicate that Emerson canceled "beliefs" and inserted "Xty". Although abbreviations in the edited text are regularly and silently expanded (the clear text would in this instance read "our Christianity."), the textual note is always bound to reproduce the manuscript form. Because the expansion of abbreviations is treated in this edition as a *silent* emendation (see the list below), no textual note is provided when Emerson uses "Xty" or any other abbreviation in the course of a sentence he did not revise. Put another way, the occasion for the textual note in the example above is not the abbreviation, but Emerson's substitution of one word for another.

Silent Emendations

Regularizing has been kept to a minimum, though the editors have been aware that in certain respects the manuscript form and the orally delivered form would not have corresponded (as in the case of abbreviations, for example) and have taken this fact as partial justification for such silent emendations as the following:

1. Citations for biblical texts at the head of each sermon are given in regularized form, spelling out the book of the Bible, which Emerson often abbreviates, and giving chapter and verse in Arabic numbers, which Emerson does not consistently use. Emerson often quotes the Bible, as indeed he quotes other sources, from memory; inexact quotations are not corrected.

2. The following abbreviations are expanded: altho' (although), amt. (amount), & (and), bro't (brought), Xt (Christ), Xdom (Christendom), Xty (Christianity), ch. (church), cd. (could), eveg. (evening), gov^t. (government),

---

2. For further discussion of these issues, see Albert J. von Frank, "Genetic Versus Clear Texts: Reading and Writing Emerson," *Documentary Editing* 9 (December 1987): 5–9.

3. A key to these symbols appears at the head of the Textual and Manuscript Notes.

hereaf. (hereafter), hist. (history), incor. (incorrect), mt. (might), m.f. (my friends), nt. (not), pd. (paid), relig. (religious), Rev. (Revelation), sd. (said), servt (servant), shd. (should), y^e (the), y^{r}s (there's), tho't (thought), Wm (William), wd. (would), yrself (yourself).

3. Numbers and numerical terms are spelled out: e.g., 1 (one), 3^d (third).

4. Missing punctuation is supplied when undoubtedly called for, as periods at the ends of sentences, commas or semicolons in series, commas or colons to introduce quotations, and question marks at the ends of rhetorical questions (silently emended from a period when necessary). Emerson's use of single and double quotation marks is preserved without imposing uniformity, but omitted marks in a pair are supplied. Apostrophes have been supplied where necessary; if there is any doubt whether singular or plural possessive is intended, the manuscript form is given in a textual note.

5. Words beginning a sentence (following Emerson's period) have been capitalized; capitalized words following Emerson's semicolons (but not his colons) have been reduced to lowercase.

6. Terminal punctuation consisting of a period followed by a dash has been retained within paragraphs when it seems to have the force of a semicolon. The dash is silently omitted when it falls at the end of a paragraph.

7. Emerson's usual practice is to put commas and periods inside his quotation marks. Contrary instances in the manuscript seem to be the result of haste and carelessness, and are therefore silently regularized.

Variants, Transpositions, and Other Reported Emendations

1. Emerson occasionally inserts an alternate word or phrase above the uncanceled corresponding word or phrase in his initial inscription. This situation is always reported in the textual notes, where it takes the form /first/ second/. The clear text regularly adopts the second inscription in a pair of variants unless doing so results in a reading that is objectionable on the grounds of grammar or sense.

2. Emerson's usual method of indicating transposition is to label the relevant sentences, phrases, or words with subscript numbers 1 and 2 (or, more rarely, a and b) and to mark off the material to be transposed with square brackets. In a few instances, three elements are designated for transposition. The clear text reflects the transposed order; the original order is given (with Emerson's numbers or letters represented as superscript) in a textual note.

3. Misspelled words are corrected and the misspellings reported in the textual notes. Inconsistency in the use of British and American forms is not regularized. No attempt has been made to revise odd spellings (e.g., "swoln" or "herse") when such spellings occur in dictionaries of the period or when contemporary authority has been found in the *Oxford English Dictionary*.

4. Emerson's erratic punctuation has been altered in the few instances when the original punctuation is likely to cause confusion. All such instances are

recorded in the textual notes. All ambiguous instances in which *missing* punctuation has been supplied are recorded in the textual notes.

5. Words that Emerson accidentally omitted, or that are illegible or lost through damage to the manuscript are supplied without brackets in the clear text and the situation indicated in the textual notes. Accidentally doubled words (as well as a few deliberately used catchwords) are corrected and reported in the textual notes.

6. Notes by Emerson—either footnotes or parenthetical notes—that briefly indicate the source of a quotation are given in the editor's explanatory footnotes, where they are identified as Emerson's; they do not otherwise appear in the text or textual notes. Emerson's notation of hymn and scripture selections, often appearing at the top of the first manuscript page, will be reported in tabular form as an appendix in the final volume of this edition. Emerson's notations concerning the date and place of delivery, irregularly given on the last manuscript page, are incorporated in the information supplied in the first explanatory footnote for each sermon as well as in the Chronology; they do not otherwise appear in the text or textual notes.

It has been the practice of recent editors of Emerson's works to keep a record of silent emendations and to deposit a copy of that record in one or more libraries for the convenience of interested scholars. Since the present edition was prepared with the use of a computer, the editors have elected to make available computer records of earlier stages of the text: specifically a genetic text version done according to the principles exemplified in the Harvard edition of *The Journals and Miscellaneous Notebooks*. These records will be deposited at the Holland Library at Washington State University and will be available to scholars for a nominal fee.

Editorial Annotations

Editorial annotations, which appear as footnotes to the text, have been kept to a minimum. For each sermon the unnumbered first note supplies what is known about its composition and, drawing on Emerson's manuscript Preaching Record and notations on the sermon manuscript itself, information about when and where it was delivered. If substantial draft passages relating to the sermon exist in the *Journals and Miscellaneous Notebooks*, that fact is given in the first note; otherwise, the existence of briefer draft passages is indicated in the appropriate place in subsequent notes. Biblical and other allusions are identified, as are Emerson's uses of sermon material in lectures and other later compositions.

Emerson's repetitions of the main Bible text in each sermon are not annotated. Phrases of common occurrence in the King James Version of the Bible, such as "tender mercies," "children of God," and "sackcloth and ashes," for example, belong to Emerson's generally biblical rhetoric in the sermons and are not annotated.

An Emerson Chronology

January 1826 to July 1829

Note: When two sermons are listed as having been preached on a particular day, the first is the morning sermon, the second the afternoon sermon. A third sermon indicates a special Sunday evening service. It should be kept in mind that Emerson's preaching was not entirely confined to the Sabbath: he also delivered sermons for Thursday (or other weekday) lectures, Fast Days, Thanksgiving, and Christmas.

While Emerson (and others) often referred to Boston's Second Church as the "North Church" or the "Old North Church," it is here always identified as the Second Church. It should not be confused with another "Old North," the Anglican church associated with Paul Revere's ride; that church, which Emerson referred to as the "New North," was at this time led by Francis Parkman, father of the historian. Similarly, Nathaniel Frothingham's First Church was popularly known as "Chauncy (or Chauncey) Place"; to avoid confusion, it is regularly identified in the following Chronology as the First Church.

1826

Jan.–Mar. 28	Conducts school in Roxbury.
c. Apr. 1	Opens school in Cambridge.
Apr. 6	Complains of rheumatism (*L* 1:168).
June 11	Begins I (*JMN* 3:28).
July 25	Completes I.
July 28	Begins II (*JMN* 3:28–29).
Aug. 1	Writing sermons (*L* 1:170).
Aug. 2	Hears Webster's oration in honor of Adams and Jefferson (*JMN* 3:29).
Early Sept.	Reads *Observations on the Growth of the Mind* by Samson Reed (*L* 1:173).
Sept. 29	Complains of difficulties with his lungs (*L* 1:176–77).
Oct. 10	Preaches I before Middlesex Association. Is approbated (licensed) to preach.
Oct. 15	Preaches I and II (Waltham, for Samuel Ripley).
Late Oct.	Lung trouble continues; closes school in Cambridge (*L* 1:178, n. 35).

Nov. 12	Preaches I (First Church).
Nov. 24–Dec. 7	Voyages to Charleston, S.C.
After Dec. 7	Preaches I (Charleston).
Dec. 13	"I have for a fortnight past writ nothing" (*JMN* 2:389).

1827

Jan. 6	Writes draft of V (*JMN* 3:62–64).
Jan. 10	Departs Charleston for St. Augustine in the sloop "William" (*L* 1:185, n. 10).
Feb. 4	Writes draft of opening to VI (*JMN* 3:72–73).
Mar. 11	Preaches I (St. Augustine).
Mar. 28	Sails for Charleston with Achille Murat.
Apr. 6	Arrives in Charleston (*L* 1:193).
Apr. 7	"I have not written a sermon since I left home" (*L* 1:194).
Apr. 15	Preaches II (Charleston, for Samuel Gilman) (*L* 1:196).
Apr. 28	Arrives in Alexandria, having first gone to Baltimore (*L* 1:196).
May 13	Preaches I (Washington, for Robert Little) (*L* 1:197, n. 42).
May 21	Writes draft passage for III (*JMN* 3:81–83).
May 27	Preaches I and II (Philadelphia, for William Henry Furness).
June 1	In New York writes draft passage for III (*JMN* 3:90–91).
June 3	Preaches I and II (New York, Second Unitarian Church).
June 10	Preaches III (Concord, Mass., for Ezra Ripley).
June 17	Preaches III and IV (First Church).
June 19	In Concord writes draft passage for V (*JMN* 3:91–92).
June 24	Preaches V and II (First Church). Has been staying at Concord, but engages a room at Divinity Hall (*L* 1:201).
June 28	Preaches V, Thursday Lecture (Concord).
July 1	Preaches V (Waltham, for Samuel Ripley).
July 8	Preaches VI (First Church).
July 15	Preaches VII (First Church).
July 22	Preaches VII and VI (Concord, Mass., for Ezra Ripley).
July 29	Preaches VIII (First Church). Declines offer to missionary in western Mass.: "I believe I better consult my health by remaining in the country, & preaching only half days in Boston" (*L* 1:203).
Aug. 5	Preaches IX (First Church).
Aug. 12	Preaches X (First Church).
Aug. 17	"I preach half of every Sunday. When I attended church on the other half of a Sunday & the image in the pulpit was all of clay & not of tuneable metal I said to myself, that if men would avoid that general language & general manner in which they strive to hide all that is peculiar and would say

only what was uppermost in their own minds after their own individual manner, every man would be interesting" (*L* 1:207).

Aug. 19   Preaches X (Federal Street, for William Ellery Channing).

Aug. 22   "My eyes are not so strong as to let me be learned. I am curious to know what the Scriptures do in very deed say about that exalted person who died on Calvary, but I do think it at this distance of time & in the confusion of languages to be a work of weighing of phrases & hunting in dictionaries" (*L* 1:208).

Aug. 26   Preaches XI (First Church).

Aug. 29   Takes M.A. degree.

Aug. 31   "I am going to preach at Northampton, in the service of the Unitarian Assoc., for Mr. Hall, a few weeks, whilst he goes into the adjoining towns to missionize. His church is a small one, & I shall be able to preach all day I suppose without inconvenience. Afterward I am at liberty to do the same for Mr Willard of Deerfield & send him on the same errand. . . . Meantime be pleased to rejoice, that I have in my trunk eleven entire sermons all which I have preached at First Ch. Mr Frothingham has come home in excellent health & spirits . . . . Prithee, dear William send me some topics for sermons or if it please you better the whole model 'wrought to the nail.' For much of my time is lost in choosing a subject & much more in wishing to write. Everett in his early discourses used great plainness & simplicty. I have by me seven of them in MSS. I aspire always to the production of present effect thinking that if I succeed in that, I succeed wholly. For a strong present effect is a permanent impression" (*L* 1:210–11).

Sept. 2   Preaches V (Stone Chapel).

Sept. 9   Preaches X and V (Northampton, for Edward B. Hall); stays with family of Joseph Lyman (*L* 1:203, n. 63; 1:211).

Sept. 16   Preaches VII and V (Greenfield, at the Courthouse, for Winthrop Bailey) (*L* 1:213).

Sept. 23   Preaches VII and X (Deerfield, for Samuel Willard).

Sept. 25   Preaches I (to Franklin Evangelical Association meeting in Northampton) (*L* 1:212).

Sept. 30   Preaches III and X (Greenfield, for Winthrop Bailey).

Oct. 7   Preaches VI and V (Deerfield, for Samuel Willard). "Mr. Henry Ware wrote to me lately to engage me to supply Mr [Orville] Dewey's pulpit during the three first weeks in November" (*L* 1:213).

Oct. 9   Reports on his activities to Ezra Stiles Gannett: "I have offered my services to preach lectures in the week but circumstances have made it inexpedient in towns where it was proposed. The clergymen are very glad to see me, having feared that the mission was indefinitely postponed. . . . I have been much disappointed in being obliged to lead so vagrant a life, as you know I came hither with different expectations and hoped for leisure & retirement for study which I needed much. But it would not do for a missionary to be stiffnecked, and so I have been a shuttle" (George W. Cooke, *Unitarianism in America* [1902], 151).

Oct. 14	Preaches VI and III (Northampton, for Edward B. Hall).
Oct. 21	Preaches VII and VIII (Northampton, for Edward B. Hall).
Oct. 25	Preaches unidentified sermon in evening at Lenox (*L* 1:217).
Oct. 27	Returns to Northampton (*L* 1:217).
Oct. 28	Preaches IX and II (Northampton, for Edward B. Hall).
Oct. 31	Returns to Concord (*L* 1:216).
Nov. 1	Travels to New Bedford (*L* 1:218).
Nov. 4	Preaches X and V (New Bedford, for Orville Dewey) (Preaching Record erroneously gives Nov. 6).
Nov. 11	Preaches VI and VIII (New Bedford, for Orville Dewey) (Preaching Record erroneously gives Nov. 13).
Nov. 18	Preaches I and III (New Bedford, for Orville Dewey) (Preaching Record erroneously gives Nov. 20).
Nov. 25	Preaches X and VI (Harvard) (Preaching Record erroneously gives Nov. 27).
Nov. 29	Thanksgiving; preaches XII (Waltham, for Samuel Ripley).
Dec. 7	Writes "Sonnet, Written in Sickness" (*JMN* 3:87) at 14 Divinity Hall, to which he had recently moved.
Dec. 9	Preaches X and VI (Watertown, for Convers Francis).
c. Dec. 15	Two days after agreeing to go to Concord, N.H., "a gentleman came to me from Brighton to engage me to go there. I was sadly sorry he had not come before as it was precisely such an engagement as I desired, since it would permit me to reside wholly at Cambridge" (*L* 1:222).
Dec. 16	Preaches VIII (Purchase Street, for George Ripley).
Dec. 23	Preaches X and III (Concord, N.H., Courthouse); stays with family of Stephen P. Breed.
Dec. 25	Christmas; preaches XIII in Concord, N.H., and there meets sixteen-year-old Ellen Tucker for first time (*L* 1:222, n. 135).
Dec. 30	Preaches VIII and VI (Concord, N.H.).
Dec. 31	"I preached a sermon last evening upon the close of the year. Mr [Jonathan] Farr spent the Sabbath in town & preached in the afternoon. The people were anxious to have an evening service which always attracts the members

of the other societies, so I adapted one of my sermons to the occasion as well as I could. On Christmas day I preached a new sermon which I wrote on Monday & Tuesday" (*L* 1:221–22).

1828

Jan. 6	Preaches I and IV (Concord, N.H.).
Jan. 9	Writes draft passage for XXXVI (*JMN* 3:100–101).
Jan. 13	Preaches III (Brattle Street, for John Gorham Palfrey).
Jan. 17	Preaches III, Thursday Lecture (First Church).
Jan. 27	Preaches VI (Federal Street, for William Ellery Channing).
Feb. 8	"I am writing sermons. I am living cautiously yea treading on eggs to strengthen my constitution. It is a long battle this of mine betwixt life & death & tis wholly uncertain to whom the game belongs. So I never write when I can walk or especially when I can laugh" (*L* 1:227).
Feb. 10	Preaches X and VI (Waltham, for Samuel Ripley).
Feb. 17	Preaches X and V (Carlisle).
Feb. 24	Preaches X (Concord, Mass., for Ezra Ripley).
Mar. 2	Preaches X and III (Dedham, for "Mr. White").
Mar. 9	Preaches VII and III (Waltham, for Samuel Ripley).
Mar. 16	Preaches X and III (Lexington).
Mar. 23	Preaches X and III (Medford).
c. Mar. 27	"A text is the hat of a sermon. Who buys a hat before a head is made?" (*JMN* 3:122).
Mar. 30	Preaches X and V (Lechmere Point, for Warren Burton) (*L* 1:227).
Apr. 3	Fast Day; preaches XVII and I (Lexington). "I am just returned hither this evening from preaching all (Fast) day at Lexington, where I fill the pulpit till the return of Mr Briggs from the South where he has wintered. . . . I was agreeably disappointed (for so it was) in escaping all engagements at the New Church in Boston. I am embarrassed at present whenever any application is made to me that may lead to permanent engagements. For I fancy myself dependent for my degree of health upon my lounging capricious unfettered mode of life & I keep myself & I slowly multiply my sermons for a day I hope of firmer health & solid power" (*L* 1:229–30).
Apr. 6	Preaches VII and VI (Lexington).
Apr. 13	Preaches XV and XVI (New South, for Alexander Young).
Apr. 14	Ezra Ripley leaves Concord to attend an ordination in Baltimore (*L* 1:231).

Apr. 20	Preaches XV and I (Concord, Mass., for Ezra Ripley).
Apr. 27	Preaches XVI and XVIII (Concord, Mass., for Ezra Ripley).
Apr. 30	"Why here am I [in Concord] lounging on a system for these many months writing something less than a sermon a month . . . . I have just refused an invitation to preach as candidate at Brighton One should preach Bucolics there. It is the third No to which I have treated the Church Applicant or Vacant. Myself & some of mine advisers exhort me to wait a great while—2 or 3 years—for sound head & wind & limb & sermonbarrelfull before I settle. . . . I have written 18 sermons" (L 1:233–35).
May 1	Preaches XVIII, Thursday Lecture (Waltham, for Samuel Ripley).
May 4	Preaches XVI and XVIII (Lexington).
May 9	Preaches VIII, Friday Lecture (Concord, Mass., for Ezra Ripley).
May 11	Preaches XIX and XVIII (Brattle Street, for John Gorham Palfrey).
May 18	Preaches XIX and XV (Federal Street, for William Ellery Channing).
May 25	Preaches XVI and XVIII (Concord, N.H.).
June 1	Preaches XIX and XIV (Concord, Mass., for Ezra Ripley).
June 8	Preaches X and XVIII (Shirley).
June 15	Preaches XIX, XV, and XIV (Concord, N.H.).
June 22	Preaches VII and XX (Concord, N.H.).
June 29	Preaches X and XVIII (Charlestown, Second Church, for James Walker).
June 30	"Henry Ware is very ill & I fear from the last accounts no good ground of hope exists for a real restoration. However, his friends do not think so yet.—I have engaged to supply his pulpit but shall probably relinquish it" (L 1:236). His brother Edward becomes deranged.
July 2	Takes his brother to McLean Asylum.
July 6	Preaches XVIII and XX (Lechmere Point, for Warren Burton).
July 13	Preaches X and XVIII (Second Church).
July 20	Preaches XIX and XVI (Second Church).
July 27	Preaches V and II (Second Church) and XIX (Purchase Street, for George Ripley).
Aug. 3	Preaches XX and XIX (Waltham, for Samuel Ripley).
Aug. 7	Receipt of this date for "Sixty dollars being for the supply of Rev^d Mr Ware's pulpit four Sabbaths including & ending July 20th" (MHS; see L 1:237, n. 49).
Aug. 10	Preaches XX and VI (Second Church).

Aug. 17	Preaches XV (South Congregational Church, for Mellish Motte) and XXI (Second Church).
Aug. 24	Preaches XV and III (Second Church).
Aug. 31	Preaches XXI and X (Waltham, for "Mr Whitman").
Sept. 5	Preaches XVIII, Lecture (Medford). Receipt for $30 "for supply of Rev^d Mr Ware's Pulpit to the 4th August" made out to Emerson, endorsed by Charles C. Emerson (MHS).
Sept. 7	Preaches XIV (Second Church) and XXI (First Church).
Sept. 14	Preaches XXII and VIII (Second Church).
Sept. 21	Preaches X and XVIII (West Cambridge, for F. H. Hedge).
Sept. 28	Preaches XXIII (Federal Street, for William Ellery Channing) and XI (Second Church).
Oct. 5	Preaches XXI (Brattle Street, for John Gorham Palfrey) and XXIII (Second Church).
Oct. 10	Recently declined request to supply church at Concord, N.H.: "I shall probably be expected to supply Mr Wares pulpit, till December" (*L* 1:248).
Oct. 12	Preaches XXIV (Second Church and New North Church, for Francis Parkman).
Oct. 17	"Mr Ware is ill again & all good men are sorry. You see what lies before your brother for his mortal lot. To be a good minister & healthy is not given. This event will probably confine me where I am for the winter. It has some obvious advantages over any other service but involves more labor. . . . I am now going to Dover N.H. for two Sundays by an exchange" (*L* 1:249–50).
Oct. 19	Preaches X, XVIII, and XIV (Dover, N.H.).
Oct. 26	Preaches XXI, XIX, and XX (Dover, N.H.).
Nov. 2	Preaches XIX (Harvard College Chapel) and XXV (Second Church).
Nov. 9	Preaches XXII (Harvard College Chapel) and I (Second Church).
Nov. 11	Drafts portions of XXVII (*JMN* 3:142–43).
Nov. 13	Receipt for $75 "for supply of Rev^d Mr Ware's Pulpit to the eighth of September" (MHS).
Nov. 16	Preaches XXVI (Second Church) and XXI (Hollis Street, for John Pierpont).
Nov. 23	Preaches XXVI (New South, for Alexander Young) and XXVII (Second Church).
Nov. 25	Receipt for $105 "for supply of Rev^d Mr. Ware's Pulpit to the twenty-seventh of October" (MHS).
Nov. 27	Thanksgiving; preaches XII (Second Church).
Nov. 30	Preaches XX and XXV (Concord, Mass., for Ezra Ripley).

Dec. 4   "Edward is quite well—it seems. He is going with me day
                after tomorrow to Concord N.H. to spend three Sundays
                . . . . I have preached a good while at Mr. Ware's. I was on
                no definite agreement as to time. It is well understood Mr
                Ware wd. shortly resign & go to Cambridge. I did not
                think it very delicate to hang on longer; if the parish was to
                be regarded as open for candidates I was monopolizing. So
                having spoken to Dr Ripley I told them I wd. come away at
                the end of November. They made a fuss & sent me word
                that if they heard candidates there wd. be a division &
                therefore the best people in the society wanted me by all
                means to stay. I told them if there was a chance they wd like
                any body better than I, t'was a reason why I should leave
                them forthwith, for if I am settled, I choose it should be on
                my own merits & not because I have kept a better man
                from being heard" (L 1:252).

Dec. 7   Preaches XXI and XXII (Concord, N.H.).
Dec. 14   Preaches XXIV and XXVII (Concord, N.H.).
Dec. 17   Engaged to Ellen L. Tucker.
Dec. 21   Preaches XXV, XXIII, and XXVI (Concord, N.H.).
Dec. 24   "I am preparing today to go to Waltham & preach a
                Christmas sermon tomorrow Mother Grandfather & all
                will be there" (L 1:256).
Dec. 25   Christmas; preaches XIII (Waltham, for Samuel Ripley).
Dec. 28   Preaches XIII (Second Church and West Church, for
                Charles Lowell).
Dec. 30   Acknowledges Ware's criticism of his reliance on secular
                illustrations: "I can readily suppose I have erred in the way
                you mention, of failing to add to my positions the authority
                of scripture quotation—& am very much obliged to you
                for the particular improvement you have suggested, which I
                shall not fail to avail myself of, when I shall have occasion
                to repeat that sermon" (L 1:257).

                                    1829

Jan. 4   Preaches X and XXI (Groton).
Jan. 11   Preaches XXV (First Church) and XXII (New South, for
                Alexander Young). Second Church votes to offer the posi-
                tion of colleague pastor to Emerson at a salary of $1200 per
                year, paid quarterly; vote was 74 for Emerson, 3 for Charles
                Follen, 1 for Samuel K. Lathrop, and 4 ballots returned
                blank. In event of Ware's departure, Emerson was to
                become pastor at a salary of $1800 (L 1:260 and n. 4).

Jan. 16	Receipt for $67.50 "for the supply of Rev^d Mr. Ware's Pulpit for the month of Nov. 1828 with the exception of one Sabbath & including thanksgiving day" (MHS).
Jan. 18	Preaches XIX and XXI (First Church of Salem, for Charles W. Upham).
Jan. 19	Ellen Tucker is "attacked with a bleeding at the lungs" (Pommer, 12).
Jan. 22	Writes to Second Church Committee, postponing his decision.
Jan. 25	Preaches XX (Federal Street, for William Ellery Channing).
Jan. 28	"I have abstained in much hesitation & perplexity from giving any answer to the call at the Old North, thinking that perhaps the doctors might tell Ellen she ought to go away. . . . But now that I have talked with Dr Jackson & talked with the committee men I believe next Sunday I shall say Yes. As to going to New York in the Spring, I believe not. I shall probably be ordained the second or third week in March & until that time I must find supply for the pulpit which I do by exchanges" (*L* 1:259).
Jan. 30	Accepts Second Church call (MHS; *L* 1:260–61).
Feb. 1	Preaches XX and XXI (West Cambridge, for F. H. Hedge).
Feb. 3	"Mr Ware is not expected to remain senior pastor more y^n a few months—so I am to look for no efficient aid from him" (*L* 1:263).
Feb. 8	Preaches X and XX (Stowbridge). Officially joins (or rather, by vote of Proprietors, is accepted into) Second Church, having previously been a member of First Church, where his father ministered (MHS).
Feb. 15	Preaches XV and XXVII (Waltham, for Samuel Ripley).
Feb. 19	Receipt for $15 "for supply of Rev^d Mr. Ware's Pulpit one Sabbath in Nov. last" (MHS).
Feb. 22	Preaches XXVII (Brattle Street, for John Gorham Palfrey).
Mar. 8	Preaches XV and XIX (Medford).
Mar. 11	Ordained junior pastor, Second Church. Dr. Peirce (Brookline) gave the Introductory Prayer; Samuel Ripley (Waltham), Sermon from the text "Preaching peace by Jesus Christ"; Francis Parkman (New North), the Ordaining Prayer; Ezra Ripley (Concord), the Charge; N. L. Frothingham (First Church of Boston), the Right Hand of Fellowship; Ezra Stiles Gannett (Federal Street), an Address to the Society; and Charles Upham (Salem), the concluding prayer. Ordination was preceded by an Ecclesiastical Council representing some thirty Unitarian

churches and followed by a banquet at Hancock School-house Hall. Church records indicate that "The day was fine, the assembly great, & all things done happily, decently, & in order" (MHS; see also the broadside "Order of Services" and *L* 1:265 for Edward B. Emerson's description of the events of the day).

Mar. 13	Completes XXIX. Now living in North Allen Street.
Mar. 15	Preaches XXVIII and XXIX (Second Church). Performs his first marriage, that of Minot Pratt to Maria J. Bridge. There would be seven more during the year, and a total of 44 during Emerson's pastorate (MHS).
Mar. 21	Completes XXX.
Mar. 22	Preaches XXX and VII (Second Church). "I have been exceedingly busy the last week in making my introductory visits in the parish. It is a new labor & I feel it in every bone of my body. I have made somewhat more than fifty pastoral visits and am yet but in the ends & frontiers of my society. ¶ This day I have preached at home all day & married a couple & baptized a child & assisted in the administration of the supper. I fear nothing now except the preparation of sermons. The prospect of one each week, for an indefinite time to come is almost terrifick" (*L* 1:267).
Mar. 26	Completes XXXI.
Mar. 29	Preaches XXXI and II (Second Church).
Apr. 3	Completes XXXII. Now living at Chardon Street.
Apr. 4	Receipt for $253.85 "in full for my salary to April 1, 1829" (MHS).
Apr. 5	Preaches XXXII (Second Church) and XXXI (Purchase Street, for George Ripley).
Apr. 9	Fast Day; preaches XVII (New North Church, for Francis Parkman, and Second Church).
Apr. 12	Preaches XXIV and XXXI (Waltham, for Samuel Ripley).
Apr. 15	Ware again complains of Emerson's secular illustrations (*L* 1:257, n. 122).
Apr. 19	Preaches XXXIII (Second Church).
Apr. 24	Preaches XVIII, Friday Lecture (Second Church).
Apr. 26	Preaches XXXIV (Second Church) and XXXI (West Church, for Charles Lowell).
Apr. 30	Preaches XXXIII, Thursday Lecture (Federal Street, for William Ellery Channing).
May 3	Preaches XXXV and IX (Second Church).
May 9	Completes XXXVI.
May 10	Preaches XXXVI (Second Church) and XXXI (First Church).

May 13	Receipt for $20 "on a/c of my salary" (MHS).
May 14	Participates in an ordination, giving Right Hand of Fellowship (*L* 1:270).
May 17	Preaches XXXI and XXXIII (First Church of Salem, for Charles Upham).
May 23	Completes XXXVII.
May 24	Preaches XXXVII and IV (Second Church).
May 30	Completes XXXVIII.
May 31	Preaches XXXVIII (Second Church) and XIX (Stone Chapel).
late May	Elected to Chaplaincy of State Senate (*L* 1:270; *OFL*, 44–45).
June 7	Preaches XXXI and XXXIII (Concord, Mass., for Ezra Ripley).
June 13	Completes XXXIX.
June 14	Preaches XL and XXXIX (Second Church). The morning sermon, a report on the Evangelical Treasury that included a plea for charitable contributions, resulted in donations of $85 (MHS).
June 15	Second Church raises donation of $300 for financially beleaguered Unitarian church in Washington, D.C. (MHS). Charles Emerson writes that "Waldo goes to Concord N.H. tomorrow to see the seasons, he says (he preached yesterday a sermon about the beauty of the seasons & the lessons to be learned of them) but we know there are fairer flowers than those of the field" (*L* 1:271, n. 46).
June 16	Goes to Concord, N.H., and stays with Kents, Ellen's family.
June 18	Ellen's tubercular symptoms recur (*L* 1:271).
June 21	Preaches XXXI, XXXIII, and XXXII (Concord, N.H.).
June 28	Preaches XXXVIII and XXXIV (Concord, N.H.) (Preaching Record erroneously gives June 27).
June 29	Returns to Boston, leaving Ellen in Concord, N.H., to recuperate (*L* 1:271, n. 46).
July 1	Ware's salary from Second Church terminated; Emerson's salary increased to $1800 (*L* 1:267, n. 28). Responds to further criticism from Ware, who continues to doubt the importance of scripture in Emerson's views (*L* 1:273).
July 2	Completes XLI.
July 4	Completes XLII.
July 5	Preaches XLII and XLI (Second Church).

THE SERMONS

I _____

Pray without ceasing.

I Thessalonians 5:17

It is the duty of men to judge men only by their actions. Our faculties furnish us with no means of arriving at the motive, the character, the secret self. We call the tree good from its fruits, and the man, from his works.[1] Since we have no power, we have no right,[2] to assign for the actions of our neighbor any other than those motives which ought in similar circumstances to guide our own. But because *we* are not able to discern the processes of thought, to see the soul—it were very ridiculous to doubt or deny that any beings can. It is not incredible, that, the thoughts of the mind are the subjects of perception to some beings, as properly, as the sounds of the voice, or the motions of the hand are to us. Indeed, every man's feeling may be appealed to on this question, whether the idea, that other beings can read his thoughts, has not appeared so natural and probable, that he has checked sometimes a train of thoughts that seemed too daring or indecent, for any unknown beholders to be trusted with.

It ought to be distinctly felt by us that we stand in the midst of two worlds, the world of matter and the world of spirit. Our bodies belong to one; our thoughts to the other. It has been one of the best uses of the Christian religion to teach, that the world of spirits is more certain and stable than the material universe. Every thoughtful man has felt, that there was a more awful reality to thought and feeling, than to the infinite panorama of nature around him. The world he has found indeed consistent and uniform enough throughout the mixed sensations of thirty or forty years, but it seems to him at times, when the intellect is invigorated, to ebb from him, like a sea, and to leave nothing permanent but thought. Nevertheless it is a truth not easily nor early acquired, and the prejudice that assigns greater fixture and certainty to the material world is a

---

Completed and dated July 25, 1826. Preached fourteen times: October 10, 1826, before the Middlesex Association of Ministers; October 15 in Waltham; November 12 at the First Church, Boston; sometime in December in Charleston, S.C.; March 11, 1827, in St. Augustine, Fla.; May 13 in Washington, D.C.; May 27 in Philadelphia; June 3 in New York; Sept. 25 before the Franklin Evangelical Association in Northampton; November 20 in New Bedford; January 6, 1828, in Concord, N.H.; April 3 in Lexington (Fast Day); April 20 in Concord, Mass.; and November 9, 1828, at the Second Church, Boston. The subject and text were apparently suggested by a Methodist laborer named Tarbox, who worked on the farm of Emerson's uncle John Ladd in Newton. Emerson spent some time at the Ladd farm in the summer of 1825 (see *J* 2:98, n. 1).

1. Cf. Matthew 7:16–20.
2. "It is the duty . . . right": see *JMN* 3:28.

source of great practical error. I need hardly remind you of the great points of this error. I need not ask you if the objects that every day are the cause of the greatest number of steps taken, of the greatest industry of the hands and the feet, the heart and the head, are the perishable things of sense, or the imperishable things of the soul; whether all this stir from day to day, from hour to hour of all this mighty multitude, is to ascertain some question dear to the understanding concerning the nature of God, the true Constitution and destination of the human soul, the proper balance of the faculties and the proper office of each; or (what of immortal thought comes nearer to practical value) whether all men are eagerly intent to study the best systems of education for themselves and their children? Is it not rather the great wonder of all who think enough to wonder that almost all that sits near the heart, all that colours the countenance, and engrosses conversation at the family board are these humble things of mortal date, and in the history of the universe absolutely insignificant? Is it not outside shews, the pleasures of appetite, or at best of pride; is it not bread and wine and dress, and our houses, and our furniture, that give the law to the great mass of actions and words? This is the great error which the strong feeling of the reality of things unseen must correct. It is time greater force should be given to the statement of this doctrine; it is time men should be instructed that their inward is more valuable than their outward estate; that thoughts and passions, even those to which no language is ever given, are not fugitive undefined shadows, born in a moment, and in a moment blotted from the soul, but are so many parts of the imperishable universe of morals; they should be taught that they do not think *alone;* that when they retreat from the public eye and hide themselves to conceal in solitude guilty recollections or guilty wishes, the great congregation of moral natures, the spirits of just men made perfect;[3] angels and archangels; the Son of God, and the Father everlasting, open their eyes upon them and speculate on these clandestine meditations.

I. The necessary inference from these reflexions, is the fact which gives them all their importance, and is the doctrine I am chiefly anxious to inculcate. It is not only when we audibly and in form, address our petitions to the Deity, that we pray. We pray without ceasing. Every secret wish is a prayer. Every house is a church, the corner of every street is a closet of devotion. There is no rhetoric, let none deceive himself; there is no rhetoric in this. There *is* delusion of the most miserable kind, in that fiction on which the understanding pleads to itself its own excuse, when it knows not God and is thoughtless of him. I mean that outward respect, that is paid to the name and worship of God, whilst the thoughts and the actions are enlisted in the service of sin. 'I will not swear by God's name,' says the wary delinquent; 'I will not ask him to lend his aid to my fraud, to my lewdness, to my revenge; nor will I even give discountenance to the laws I do not myself observe. I will not unmask my villany to the world, that I should stand in the way of others, more scrupulous, nay, better than I.'

And is it by this paltry counterfeit of ignorance that you would disguise from

3. Hebrews 12:23. For the preceding phrase, see *JMN* 2:123.

yourselves the truth? And will you really endeavour to persuade yourself, that, God is such an one as you yourself, and will be amused by professions, and may, by fraudulent language, be kept out of the truth? Is it possible, that men of discretion in common affairs, can think so grossly? Do you not know that the knowledge of God is perfect and immense;[4] that it breaks down the fences of presumption, and the arts of hypocrisy; that night, and artifice, and time, and the grave, are naked before it; that the deep gives up its dead, that the gulfs of Chaos are disembowelled before him; that the minds of men are not so much independent existences, as they are ideas present to the mind of God; that he is not so much the observer of your actions, as he is the potent principle by which they are bound together; not so much the reader of your thoughts, as the active Creator by whom they are aided into being; and, casting away the deceptive subterfuges of language, and speaking with strict philosophical truth, that every faculty is but a mode of his action; that your reason is God, your virtue is God, and nothing but your liberty, can you call securely and absolutely your own?

Since, then, we are thus, by the inevitable law of our being, surrendered unreservedly to the unsleeping observation of the Divinity, we cannot shut our eyes to the conclusion, that, *every desire of the human mind, is a prayer uttered to God and registered in heaven.*

II. The next fact of sovereign importance in this connexion is, that *our prayers are granted.* Upon the account I have given of prayer, this ulterior fact is a faithful consequence. What then! if I pray that fire shall fall from heaven to consume mine enemies, will the lightning come down?[5] If I pray that the wealth of India may be piled in my coffers, shall I straightway become rich? If I covet my neighbor's beauty, or wit, or honourable celebrity,—will these desirable advantages be at once transferred from being the sources of his happiness, to become the sources of mine? It is plain there is a sense in which this is not true. But it is equally undeniable that in the sense in which I have explained the nature of prayer, and which seems the only proper sense, the position is universally true. For those are not prayers, which begin with the ordinary appellatives of the Deity and end with his son's name, and a ceremonial word—those are not prayers, if they utter no one wish of our hearts, no one real and earnest affection, but are formal repetitions of sentiments taken at second hand, in words the supple memory has learned of fashion; O my friends, these are not prayers, but mockeries of prayers. But the true prayers are the daily, hourly, momentary desires, that come without impediment, without fear, into the soul, and bear testimony at each instant to its shifting character. And these prayers are granted.

For is it not clear that what we strongly and earnestly desire we shall make every effort to obtain; and has not God so furnished us with powers of body

4. Cf. Job 36:4, 37:16.
5. II Kings 1:10 and Luke 9:54.

and of mind that we can acquire whatsoever we seriously and unceasingly strive after?

For it is the very root and rudiment of the relation of man to this world, that we are in a condition of wants which have their appropriate gratifications *within our reach;* and that we have faculties which can bring us to our ends; that we are full of capacities that are near neighbors to their objects, and our free agency consists in this, that we are able to reach those sources of gratification, on which our election falls. And if this be so, will not he who thinks lightly of all other things in comparison with riches; who thinks little of the poor man's virtue, or the slave's misery as they cross his path in life, because his observant eye is fixed on the rich man's manners and is searching in the lines of his countenance, with a sort of covetousness, the tokens of a pleased contemplation of the goods he has in store, and the consideration that, on this account, is conceded to him in society; will not such an one, if his thoughts daily point towards this single hope, if no exertion is grateful to him which has not this for its aim; if the bread is bitter to him that removes his riches one day farther from his hand, and the friends barren of comfort to him that are not aiding to this dishonourable ambition;—will not such an one arrive at the goal, such as it is, of his expectation and find, sooner or later, a way to the heaven where he has garnered up his heart? Assuredly he will.

And will not the votary of other lusts, the lover of animal delight, who is profuse of the joys of sense, who loveth meats and drinks, soft raiment and the wine when it moveth itself aright, and giveth its colour in the cup;[6] or the more offensive libertine who has no relish left for any sweet in moral life, but only waits opportunity to surrender himself over to the last damning debauchery; will not these petitioners who have knocked so loudly at heaven's doors, receive what they have so importunately desired? Assuredly they will. There is a commission to nature, there is a charge to the elements made out in the name of the Author of events, whereby they shall help the purposes of man, a pre-existent harmony between thoughts and things whereby prayers shall become effects, and these warm imaginations settle down into events.

And if there be, in this scene of things, any spirit of a different complexion, who has felt, in the recesses of his soul, "how awful goodness is, and virtue in her own shape how lovely,"[7] who has admired the excellence of others, and set himself by precepts of the wise, and by imitation, which, a wise man said, is 'a globe of precepts,'[8] to assimilate himself to the model, or to surpass the uncertain limit of human virtue, and found no model in the Universe, beneath God, level with his venerated idea of virtue; who looks with scorn at the cheap admiration of crowds, and loves the applause of good men, but values more his own; and has so far outstripped humanity, that he can appreciate the love of the

6. Proverbs 23:31.
7. Milton, *Paradise Lost*, IV, 847–48.
8. "Of Great Place," in *The Works of Francis Bacon*, ed. James Spedding et al. (London, 1857–1874), 6:399.

Supreme; if he aspire to do signal service to mankind, by the rich gift of a good example, and by unceasing and sober efforts to instruct and benefit men; will this man wholly fail, and waste his requests on the wind? Assuredly he will not. His prayers, in a certain sense, are like the will of the Supreme Being:

> "His word leaps forth to its effect at once,
> He calls for things that are not, and they come."[9]

His prayers are granted; all prayers are granted. Unceasing endeavours always attend true prayers, and, by the law of the Universe, unceasing endeavours do not fail of their end.

Let me not be misunderstood as thinking lightly of the positive duty of stated seasons of prayer. That solemn service of man to his maker is a duty of too high authority and too manifest importance to excuse any indifference to its claims. It is because that privilege is abused, because men in making prayers forget the purpose of prayer, forget that praying is to make them leave off sinning, that I urge it in its larger extent when it enters into daily life.

I have attempted to establish two simple positions, that, we are always praying, and that it is the order of Providence in the world, that our prayers should be granted. If exceptions can be quoted to me out of the book of common life, to the universality of either of these doctrines, I shall admit them in their full force, nor shall I now detain you by any inquiry into the abstract metaphysical nature of that happiness human beings are permitted to derive from what are called possessions, and how far it belongs to the imagination. I shall content myself, at present, with having stated the general doctrine and with adverting to its value as a practical principle.

And certainly, my friends, it is not a small thing that we have learned. If we have distinctly apprehended the fact which I have attempted to set in its true light, it cannot fail to elevate very much our conception of our relations and our duties. Weep no more for human frailty, weep no more, for what there may be of sorrow in the past or of despondency in the present hour. Spend no more unavailing regrets for the goods of which God in his Providence has deprived you. Cast away this sickly despair that eats into the soul debarred from high events and noble gratification. Beware of easy assent to false opinion, to low employment, to small vices, out of a reptile reverence to men of consideration in society. Beware, (if it teach nothing else let it teach this) beware of indolence, the suicide of the soul, that lets the immortal faculties, each in their orbit of light, wax dim and feeble, and star by star expire.—These considerations let our doctrine enforce. Weep not for man's frailty—for if the might of Omnipotence has made the elements obedient to the fervency of his daily prayers, he is no puny sufferer tottering, ill at ease, in the Universe, but a being of giant

---

9. Quoted without attribution in Thomas Brown, *Inquiry into the Relation of Cause and Effect* (Andover, 1822), 63. See *JMN* 2:47.

energies, architect of his fortunes, master of his eternity. Weep not for the past; for this is duration over which the secret virtue of prayer is powerless, over which the Omnipotence of God is powerless; send no voice of unprofitable wailing back into the depths of time; for prayer can reverse in the future the events of the past. Weep not for your wasted possessions, for the immeasurable future is before you and the wealth of the Universe invites your industry. Nor despair that your present daily lot is lowly, nor succumb to the shallow understanding or ill example of men whose worldly lot is higher. Be not deceived; for what is the Past? It is nothing worth. Its value, except as means of wisdom, is, in the nature of things actually nothing. And what is the imposing present? what are the great men and great things that surround you? All that they can do for you is dust, and less than dust to what you can do for yourself. They are like you stretching forward to an infinite hope, the citizens in trust of a future world. They think little of the present; though they seem satisfied, they are not satisfied but repine and endeavour after greater good. They, like you, are born to live when the sun has gone down in darkness and the moon is turned to blood.[10]

My friends, in the remarks that have just been made I have already in part anticipated the third great branch of our subject, which is that *our prayers are written in Heaven.*[11]

III. The great moral doctrines we have attempted to teach would be of limited worth if there were no farther consideration in this series of thought. You are pleased with the acquisition of property; you pray without ceasing to become rich. You lay no tax of conscience on the means. You desire to become rich by dint of virtue or of vice; of force or of fraud. And in virtue of the order of things that prevails in the world, as I have stated, you come to your ends. Is this all? Is the design of Providence complete? Is there no conclusion to this train of events, thus far conducted?

The wicked has flourished up to his hope. He has ground the faces of the poor.[12] He has the tears of the widow and the curse of the fatherless but they lie light on his habitation; for he has builded his house where these cannot come, in the midst of his broad lands, on a pleasant countryside, sheltered by deep ornamental woods, and the voices of the harp and the viol tinkle in his saloons;[13] the gay and the grave, the rich and the fair swarm to him in crowds and though they salute him and smile often upon him they do not utter one syllable of reproach nor repeat one imprecation of the poor. But far away, too far to be any impediment to his enjoyment, the wretches he has cruelly stripped of their last decent comforts, and the well-saved means with which sinking poverty yet strives to bear up, and make a respectable appearance in society,— are now, in small unaccommodated tenements, eating a morsel of bread, and uttering in unvisited, unremembered solitude, the name of the oppressor. And

10. Cf. Joel 2:31, Acts 2:20, and Revelation 6:12. See also *JMN* 2:45.
11. Cf. Hebrews 12:23.
12. Isaiah 3:15.
13. Isaiah 5:12.

have we seen all, my friends, and is poor struggling worth to be rewarded only with worth, and be poor and vile beside, and is Vice to go triumphing on to the grave? Aye; to the grave. Hitherto, shalt thou go, and no farther, and here shall thy proud waves be staid.[14] My friends, there is another world. After death there is life. After death in another state, revives your capacity of pleasure and of pain, the evil memory of evil actions, revives yourself, the man within the breast,[15] the gratified petitioner in the exact condition to which his fulfilled desires have, by the inevitable force of things, contracted or expanded his character. There is another world; a world of remuneration; a world to which you and I are going and which it deeply behoves us to survey and scrutinize as faithfully as we can, as it lies before us, "though shadows, clouds, and darkness rest upon it." It is plain that *as* we die in this world, we shall be born into that. It is plain, that, it is, if it be any thing, a world of spirits; that body, and the pleasures and pains appertaining to body can have no exercise, no mansion there; that it can be the appropriate home only of high thought and noble virtue. Hence it must happen, that, if a soul can have access to that ethereal society, fleshed over with bodily appetites, in which no love has grown up of thought and moral beauty, and no sympathy and worship of virtue, but in their place gnawing lusts have coiled themselves with a serpent's trail into the place of every noble affection that God set up in the recesses of the soul when he balanced the parts and modulated the harmony of the whole. And these pampered appetites that grew in the soil of this world, find no aliment for them in heaven, no gaudy vanities of dress, no riotous excitement of song and dances, no filthy gluttony of meats and drinks, no unclean enjoyments, finding none of all this, it must happen, that these appetites will turn upon their master, in the shape of direst tormentors; and if the economy of the universe provide no natural issue, whereby these mortal impurities can be purged with fire out of the texture of the soul, they must continue from hour to hour, from age to age, to arm the principles of his nature against the happiness of man.

Of this mysterious eternity, about to open upon us, of the nature of its employments and our relation to it, we know little. But of one thing be certain, that if the analogies of time can teach aught of eternity, if the moral laws taking place in this world, have relation to those of the next, and even the forecasting sagacity of the Pagan philosopher taught him that the Laws below were sisters of the Laws above,[16]—then the riches of the future are dealt out on a system of compensations. That great class of human beings who in every age turned aside from temptation to pursue the bent of moral nature shall now have *their* interests consulted. They have cast their bread on the waters, (for the choice lay

14. Job 38:11.

15. For "the man within the breast," see Adam Smith, *The Theory of the Moral Sentiments* (London, 1853), 185. Used in *L* 1:174, *JMN* 2:263, and "Heroism," *CW* 2:146. See also Sermon II, n. 12; Sermon IV, n. 6; Sermon XXI, n. 2; and Sermon XXXVIII, n. 6.

16. Emerson alludes to this Socratic belief in "Plato: New Readings," in *Representative Men*, *CW* 4:47; and in "Progress of Culture," *W* 8:223. See also *JMN* 6:32.

often between virtue and their bread), trusting that after many days a solemn retribution of good should be rendered to them in the face of the world.[17] Insult and sorrow, rags and beggary they have borne; they have kept the faith though they dwelled in the dust, and now, the pledge of God that supported them in the trial must be redeemed, and shall be, to the wonder of themselves, through the furthest periods of their undying existence.

Their joy and triumph is that revelation of the gospel which is most emphatically enforced by images borrowed from whatever was most grand and splendid in the imaginations of men; but crowns and thrones of judgment, and purple robes are but poor shadows of that moral magnificence, with which in the company of souls disembodied, Virtue asserts its majesty, and becomes the home and fountain of unlimited happiness.

Nothing remains but the obligation there is on each of us to make what use we can of this momentous doctrine. Is it to another condition than yours, to some removed mode of life, to the vices of some other class of society that this preaching, with strict propriety, belongs? No, my friends, if you are of the great household of God; if you are distinguishers of good and evil; if you believe in your own eternity; if you are tempted by what you feel to be evil attractions; if you are mortal,—it belongs to you. If you have ever felt a desire for what Conscience, God's vicegerent, enthroned within you, condemned; if impelled by that desire, and wilfully deaf to that condemnation, you swerved towards the gratification, and obtained the object, and stifled the monitor—then it is you, and not another; then you have uttered these unseemly prayers; the prayer is granted and is written in heaven; and at this moment, though men are not privy to all the passages of your life, and will salute you respectfully, and though it may be your own violated memory has ceased to treasure heedfully the number of your offences—yet every individual transgression has stamped its impress on your character, and moral beings in all the wide tracts of God's dominion and God over all fasten their undeceived eyes on this spectacle of moral ruin. To you therefore it belongs, to every one who now hears me, to look anxiously to his ways; to look less at his outward demeanour, his general plausible action, but *to cleanse his thoughts*. The heart, the heart is pure or impure, and out of it, are the issues of life and of DEATH.

17. Ecclesiastes 11:1.

II

I have learned in whatsoever state I am, therewith to be content.

PHILIPPIANS 4:11

One of the first observations we make on life is to notice the inequality of human condition. The next, is to listen to the voice of universal discontent. The ear is pained with the great dirge resounding on every side, which announces the inconsolable affliction of all mankind. But the calamity has none of that lightness and tolerable sorrow that belongs to a general affliction,—to an evil, shared by many, and fatal to none; like the grief of a nation, bereaved of its lawgiver, where all are sorry, but none is sad, and a funeral ostentation is offered without any tears; but this grief is homefelt, particular, and permanent. In the dawn of the faculties it spreads its light clouds over the soul, and thickens, as the day of life advances, until it settles into a fixed eclipse casting into darkness all the parts of life. Whatever may be the first inferences, the fact cannot be doubted.

In all the diversity of condition that is contained in this assembly, is there an individual ready to stand up, and declare himself at peace with himself and all men, and happy? No matter what others may think of you, there is not one here; there is not one in the world. 'A single house,' said a Roman poet, 'will shew all that is done and suffered in the world.'¹ The walls of a single church, will certainly afford a fuller collection of human character. But there is no man happy here; there is no man in the world.

There is nothing in nature, certainly nothing in human nature, without a reason. It is the mark of the superior wisdom of this age to admit in its full force, the incontrovertible evidence that is in man, of design and of God. To what end, then, this strange incongruity?—A being come from the author of all good with a machinery of faculties in him which, being put in operation, go in discord, and the result is unhappiness. The old question of Epicurus called the

---

Preached eight times: October 15, 1826, in Waltham; April 15, 1827, in Charleston, S.C.; May 27 in Philadelphia; June 3 in New York; June 24 at the First Church, Boston; October 28 in Northampton; July 27, 1828, at the Second Church, Boston; and March 29, 1829, again at the Second Church.

1. Juvenal, *Satires*, XIII, 159–60; quoted by Samuel Johnson in *The Rambler*, No. 161. Used in "Ethics," *EL* 2:144; cf. *JMN* 3:120, 6:220.

Unanswerable question will be triumphantly repeated. "If there be a God, is he willing to prevent evil, but not able? then is he impotent. Is he able, but not willing? then is he malevolent. Is he both able and willing? Whence then is evil?"[2] And all the frightful inferences which in the East and West, in ancient and modern times have perplexed the student of God and man, will arise in their dark conclusions to dismay the Understanding. The question need not appal us. There are no doubt questions of speculation on which the competence of our understanding may be disputed, and a wise man will be as temperate in what he admits as in what he objects. All the reasons of what we see are not shewn us. They are in the illimitable universe. They are reserved for eternity. Some of them come not into the scope of finite faculties but belong to vaster relations and disencumbered minds. But the course of events all along discloses something of their secret frame, enough to suggest to those who watch for these intimations, a pious curiosity for more manifestations of the same unapproachable hand. Why then has He who is supposed to desire the happiness of men, made men unhappy? We answer—in order to their happiness.

What is Happiness? Let us bring to the inquiry the best experience we have been able to acquire in our acquaintance with things, for we shall be met at the outset by an ancient cavil which demands why we were not made *originally* happy. It is because as far as our reason enables us to judge, it is contrary to the nature of things. What is Happiness? Shall we say of the clod because it suffers nothing and the sun shines down warm upon it, that it is happy? Shall we say of the sluggish animal, that is next to a clod, whose frame was never disturbed by the commotion of thought, and never by the scourging of pain, that it is happy? Shall we suppose a being created like ourselves in all points save one,—the capacity of pain; a being endowed with the power only of contemplating good; his eye closed to suffering, his heart fortified against the assault of fear, fortified against the inroad of desire; his blood rolling regularly in the channels of health, his mind without change, his knowledge without curiosity, his sky without cloud, his life without death? His unbroken hours sliding softly by in the interminable monotony of peace, the passive witnesses of whatever knowledge, the sight of innocence and peace could furnish out of hours, years, and ages, from half an universe—and shall we call him happy? He is happy, if sleep is better than waking, if absence of virtue is better than virtue, if satiety is better than desire, if death is better than life. Is sluggish unmeaning peace, bare consciousness illuminated by the light of life, happiness? Then let us forsake the pledges we have put in the state, the hostages we have given to fortune,[3] the hopes we have nourished with such dear anxiety, the exertions we have, from year to year, prolonged and redoubled. You have scorned the degradation of being satisfied with a mere subsistence, your bread, and wine, and raiment; it

2. Quoted from David Hume; see *Dialogues Concerning Natural Religion*, ed. Henry D. Aiken (New York, 1955), 66, and *JMN* 2:419.

3. "Of Marriage and Single Life," in *The Works of Francis Bacon*, ed. James Spedding et al. (London, 1857–1874), 6:391. See *JMN* 1:316.

could have been long ago secured. You have gone toiling on, to get means of allying yourself in holy marriage, of providing education for your children; means of educating yourself in the import and use of the institutions of God and man; and into a better fulfilment of the duties of citizenship; means of earning a goodwill from your neighbors, and a good reputation in the community. But it seems you have been mistaken all this time; let us forsake all these, and abandon this cold and rugged land of our forefathers, and make haste to depart for some more bountiful clime, where the torrid sun ripens without cultivation the fat weeds of the soil into sustenance for man; where the bark of trees is sufficient clothing, and the mild firmament a sufficient tent to dwell in; let us go throw ourselves down and sleep out life in those quiet fields, despising knowledge that must be procured with toil, and virtue that must be got through suffering, affections that may be deceived, and honour that must be deserved. Is this happiness? or will it prove to be misery? Is not happiness rather to be found in temptation overcome, in gratified expectations, in difficulties subdued by per-severance, in relieved pain, in heroic effort, in painful thought, in militant and conquering virtue? Is there, I beseech you, any quality in moral nature to be represented by the word, if it be not this? But how can there be ease, when there was never unrest; or expectations be gratified, that never disturbed the soul; or knowledge please, that was preceded by no curiosity, or difficulties be encoun-tered, that never came; or victories delight that never were desired? Is not hap-piness built on action? Is not pleasure the fruit of pain? Then are not all these uneasy impulses given us to bring us to the knowledge of good, which in no other way we can conceive to be known? Evils, then, are impulses. Trial is education. Pains are teachers.

The natural condition of man, is a condition of want, and it is the great peculiarity of this condition, and one upon which our faculties have no means of making any judgement whether it be an imperfection or not, that all that is valuable grows out of the necessities and imperfections of his being. It is the common history of every day, that we are stimulated by a want to procure a gratification. The new satisfaction opens to view new wants, of which we were not conscious before, which again excite us to vigorous exertion. By every one of these labours, the labourer is strengthened. By all the efforts he makes in the pursuit, he is himself becoming a being of more powerful nature. What is there of great value in the world which did not come from this stock? The good affections which make up virtue, have nothing equivocal in their creation. The natural history of the soul has been explored, by diligent study, to as good purpose, as the natural history of the body, and it is found, that, our necessities are our instructors; that, it is what we do, that makes us what we are; that the dependance of our condition, which obliged us to repair frequently for assistance to those next us,—created in us, this benevolence,—this dear love of parents and friends, and, in its larger applications, Patriotism, and phi-lanthropy,—that inspiring principle, of which we are apt to grow proud, as if it were a badge of our surpassing and angelic nature. Out of our necessities, out

of the frailty of the frail, grew this ardent zeal to learn what the creator (felt to
be our great natural Protector) had left to be learned of himself. Out of the same
humble origin came the imposing institutions of civil empire, now grown to so
forgetful a greatness,—out of man's dread of the wolf and the bear, and his
fellow creature who was to him a wolf; out of this, came his desire of leaguing
himself to the host of his kind, and being no longer a weak solitary agent, but a
feared member of a huge confederacy. Hence too his ambition to rule in them,
as a representative of the wisdom and power of the whole, and all those virtues,
graces, resources, that as being means to this end, come within the scope of this
ambition, and make such vast distinction between the highest and lowest of
mankind.

It becomes plain then that Happiness, as far as our reason or our experience
can inform us, is not a flood of unmixed useless enjoyment, for no such thing
can be, but is if it be any thing a series of reliefs, a change from worse to better.
Nor is God chargeable with having made us voluntarily the victims of pain, for
the nature and the uses of unhappiness are also evident. It is an uneasiness, a
useful uneasiness in the body or mind, prompting to the attainment of some
good agreeable to its nature; that is to say, All unhappiness tends to happiness.[4]

It was said that our unhappiness is designed for our good, a lesser evil for a
greater benefit. If this representation be just it would be certainly not only very
unreasonable to complain of these partial evils by which we are all borne down,
but there would not be room for the exercise of that state of mind, which our
text recommends. We ought not certainly to be contented with an evil condition
which was given us expressly to make us dissatisfied, and so to prompt us to
exertions to amend it. And I hesitate not to say, that in this construction, discontent is a duty, discontent with your sin, discontent with your sorrow, discontent
with your ignorance. For can you think any ordinance of revealed religion is so
positive as to contravene the nature of man and the Law of God written in the
lines and elements of his condition, and to which the Christian dispensation is a
subordinate instrument? No man who was ever brought to mature understanding could find himself born to insignificance, to a ragged poverty, to an evil
name, to the inheritance of an evil example, and by his side the unfolding
faculties of a powerful understanding as the implements of his deliverance from
the ignominy of his lot, without perceiving also that there lay on him, the charge
to attempt and accomplish his deliverance. In like manner, in the same degree as
any individual suffers from the want of any good which it lies in his power to
attain, to the same extent is he bound, by moral law, to a discontent with the
deficiency, and an exertion to supply it. Herein lies the excuse of ambition, not
of that ignoble kind which hates what is good, in the love of what is great, which
aspires to place and not to merit and courts the crowd instead of the good, but
that ambition which explores with sincere sorrow the distance between its own
virtue and knowledge and the virtue and knowledge of other men; and explores

---

4. "It becomes . . . happiness": see *JMN* 3:28–29.

it in order to repair it; which counts deficiency a fault; and thinks every moment and every power and every opportunity are not its own, but *lent*, on a great usury which must be paid; which thinks meanly of thrones and public trusts as objects of desire, for it measures what is worthy by a grander scale than princes. For the genuine objects of human ambition will not descend into comparison with the tinsel ornaments by which Kings and Conquerors are deluded into a perilous responsibility which they poorly sustain. The pure ambition aspires after moral power whose elements are knowledge and goodness. These are attributes of a majesty which time and change cannot impair; these attributes which it covets it distinctly sees to lie within the scope of human capacity and to be those natural ends, which are common to itself with every member of God's moral universe, with the innumerable generations of men past, present, and to come; the angels and archangels, the seraphim and cherubim, these are not the august spectators but the competitors and partakers in this progress from greatness to greatness, from glory to glory. This is the ambition which nature and providence excuse, the just ambition for which we were made.

Far be it from us then, my brethren, to sit down in sluggish indolence and disregard those goods which God has set before us. Let us not contemn the virtues which we want or hold in slight estimation the talents and the knowledge we ought to acquire and say I have learned to be content. It is not the part of magnanimity to lay a lazy hand on the generous bequests of Providence without regard to the giver or endeavours to deserve the gift. We are required to be up and doing, to walk with circumspection, to work with diligence, to forget the things behind, and to press forward toward those which are before.[5]

But if it was the design of God that these imperfections in our condition should exist, what motive or what law binds us to the cultivation of a mind resigned to the dispensations of God with regard to us and keep down and pacify those bitter repinings that would otherwise rankle in the heart and exasperate it to despair? And what contentment is it that the apostle in our text would enforce by his own example? There is obviously a distinction to be made in the nature of events. It is our duty to amend what is alterable and to be content with what is unalterable. The events of which I have spoken belong to the great class of events over which we have power. There is another great part of our condition which is unalterable.[6] The sun, we cannot pluck down from heaven, though he dazzle our eyes with his light or scorch us with his heat. The moon will wax and wane, careless of our pleasure or displeasure, our occupation or our fortune. Summer and Winter, seedtime and harvest, the rivers and the storms, diseases and changes, belong to the prodigious constitution of the universe, and hold on their steadfast succession, deaf to the prayers of any of its atoms. With regard to all these objects therefore that are called the order of nature or of human life, a perfect submission, a perfect contentment is the only

5. Philippians 3:13–14. Cf. *JMN* 3:29.
6. *JMN* 3:28.

humour proper to a wise man. It may be the day of our planet is too long or too short to suit our whim. We run of a conceit that we can descry imperfections in the properties and arrangements of the atmosphere or the soil, and find a pleasure in accusing the deficiencies of nature as if it betrayed a certain grandeur of spirit; or it may be we murmur that the storm has shattered our ships on the sea or our edifices on the shore; or it may be we gnash our teeth at the untimely death of lover and friend; of him that was dearest and next us. But the absurdity and the presumption of this inexcusable railing at the order God has established in his works, (and all these events and these interests are more his than ours,) is felt in the statement. No man ever indulged this impatience without feeling its folly even whilst the passion impelled the complaint.

But let us not forget that there are sufferers in the world, who are not disposed to do a foolish or presumptuous thing and who cannot accuse their own negligence for the adverse lot with which they have been obliged to struggle, but whose fortunes have been darkened in the morning of their days, and who seem to be left naked to their enemies.[7] Misfortune is a sacred thing. It would be worse than vain to tell the man of sorrows that it is ridiculous to repine,[8] that he must steel himself with a little philosophy against the accumulated griefs that have crushed him to the ground. Some answer is due to that man to whom misery has not been matter of speculation, or of sympathy or of distant wonder, but has come into his doors, interrupted the hope and labour of an honest livelihood, bereaved him of his health and left him dumb when his children asked him for bread; his children, it may be, in their promising youth falling victims to violence and disease, his name, it may be, by human injustice consigned to grinning infamy amidst that very circle of kinsfolk and acquaintance wherein his last hopes of compassion and subsistence staid,—if such an one, from his lowly dying bed, yield to a desire to go hence and be here no more,[9] and would search the religion of Christ if it indeed have consolation, and can teach contentment in these perilous extremes,—it needs a grave and considerate answer. My friends, suffering and grief are no new names, and death has been long a dweller in the earth. Old things are past away,[10] but these materials have never departed out of the texture of man's life and departed ages utter to us the same voice of solemn tribulation that we are uttering to posterity. But the weighty experience of so many ages has disclosed to our eyes the sources of consolation. They that have been sorely tried and have endured to the end, have found their loss to be unspeakable gain.[11] The doctrine which we have maintained respecting the uses of unhappiness, is amply borne out by the oft told story of human affliction. It is the tribute of acknowledgement from those who have passed through its stern and painful school that the proud and callous

7. Cf. Shakespeare, *Henry VIII*, III, ii, 457.
8. Cf. Isaiah 53:3.
9. Cf. Psalms 39:13.
10. II Corinthians 5:17.
11. Cf. Matthew 10:22.

heart of man is there trained to humility and gentleness. In compensation for an unstable external good they have been ennobled by the rich retribution of internal virtue, and whilst their holdings in this life have been lopped away, the character, the eternal man within the breast,[12] has been dignified in the scale of moral beings. In cells of poverty, in prisons of persecution, in dens of refuge, and on beds of torture, the hero and the martyr have been educated to that perfect stature of greatness which overcame the fear of death, which endured the cross and despised the shame.[13]

It should also be remembered, though the time will allow me only to name it, that our virtue is example; that God contemplates a social as well as a selfish good in his dispensations to each of us; that he instructs other men by the lesson of your magnanimity or your effeminate repining.

Let us consider a moment the just inference from those truths to which we have directed our minds. In the crowd of inconveniences and petty evils which embarrass every step of our advancing life, we are to find the seeds of goodness and virtue. These are the teachers of our ignorance, the guideboards God has set up on all the roads of time to show the direction in which Heaven lies. Poverty is the blessed nurse who by hard habits braces the nerve of manhood to athletic strength; brushes aside from the manly limb the clinging cobwebs of sloth; scours off the rust of sensuality and sends out the soul inured to rugged thought, and dangerous event, and ripe for immortality. The ignorance which pains us with a sense of inferiority—it will excite us to become wise. The press of care, which prevents you from the enjoyment of those very earthly goods you have obtained—it sharpens your understanding, makes you fruitful in resources, it calls your thoughts to another world of pleasure and of peace. Is sickness unmixed evil? Does it not give an insight as from a vantage ground into the vanity of life? It is the poorest reception then we can give to those parts of life we are accustomed to count our misfortunes, to sit down and repine. They are much our friends, they are an earnest and a passport to better things. Welcome be then the infirmities, the interruptions, the disasters with which it is our lot to wrestle; welcome these heralds come from our father in Heaven, to assure us we have another home. Welcome these stern correctors whose reward is with them.[14] Welcome these momentary sorrows so that we have grace enough to turn them to their proper use. And when they surpass the ordinary measures of fortitude and bow down the sinking strength of sorrowing humanity to the dust, there is still the pure hope that God on high is the Author, the Witness, and the judge, and the gracious promise enforced by the reasoning and experience of all the departed children of God, that though weeping may endure for a night, yet Joy cometh in the morning.[15]

12. See Sermon I, n. 15.
13. Hebrews 12:2.
14. Cf. Isaiah 40:10, 62:11, and Revelation 22:12.
15. Psalms 30:5.

III

But be thou an example of the believers,
in word, in conversation, in charity,
in spirit, in faith, in purity.

I TIMOTHY 4:12

The ordinary admonitions of the Christian moralist are addressed to man as the creature of God. Without regard to any other relations in which we may stand it is thought to be a sufficient foundation for our virtue that we are sinful beings in intimate dependance on the almighty Being. And when the mind is matured in virtue, when the mind has been long accustomed to the contemplation of God, it is both pleasant and sublime to conceive the soul as divorced from all other society, and finding its heaven in its state of free and perfect communion with the Divine Mind. It is certainly the first and should be a sufficient motive to human virtue that it has been enjoined by God on each of us as the condition of his favour and of our happiness. But, my friends, at our best estate we are imperfect and frail. An immediate connexion and dependance upon God is too lofty a motive to sustain and console our virtue in the daily warfare of the world. It is high, we cannot attain unto it. We want something else nearer. We are made of clay too coarse to be affected by all those finer influences which act upon us from the spiritual world. Our clouded eyes cannot always see God walking at our side. We do not feel the everlasting arm that led us up into life and holds us here.[1] We need the support of what we can see and feel. We must lean on the objects of sense. We must do as others do. In short we are virtuous and vicious as social beings, in obedience very much to the example of those who surround us. The increased moral obligation, which arises out of this source of society has been, I am well aware, often and carefully measured and cannot be expected to afford any ground for original remarks. But it is a subject of such weighty importance as to deserve our most anxious consideration. I am anxious to dwell upon it and I shall willingly incur the risk of

Preached thirteen times: June 10, 1827, in Concord, Mass.; June 17 at the First Church, Boston; September 30 in Greenfield; October 14 in Northampton; November 20 in New Bedford; December 23 in Concord, N.H.; January 13, 1828, at the Brattle Street Church; January 17 (Thursday Lecture) at the First Church, Boston; March 2 in Dedham; March 9 in Waltham; March 16 in Lexington; March 23 in Medford; and August 24 at the Second Church, Boston.
   1. See Luke 24:15–16 and Deuteronomy 33:27.

repeating old and well known truth in the humble hope of giving new force to the great practical maxims which it involves.²

It is almost unnecessary to call your attention to those great features in our life which mark us as social. We are surrounded on every side by this blessed influence. Our pleasure and our pain, our knowledge, our property, our projects, our hopes, our actions are social. All that the eye sees and the ear hears has relation to the social life of man. When we came up this morning to the house of God, did we come in savage solitude each from his lonely house, a congregation of hermits to whom their meeting together is unwelcome? and when the hour of prayer is past are we to separate again to sunder at once these sympathies of devotion which we have reluctantly indulged? Is our only joy in private meditation, when our house is empty and our door is barred? in an unpartaken pursuit each of his own surly interest? Must we eat our bread alone and spread our table in secret? We rejoice before God that it is not thus we live. Nothing can be more alien to our nature than this ungrateful picture. We dwell in families. We have taken sweet counsel together. We came up to the house of God in company.³ We do not live for ourselves. We do not rejoice, we do not weep alone. Our lives are bound up in others. Our blood does not roll in selfish flow through our lazy veins. It beats in our breasts pulse for pulse with a true accord to the honour and the shame of a hundred other hearts to which God has united us in family or in friendship.⁴ It reaches farther, this mighty sympathy, this golden hoop that binds our brothers in, and does not embrace only our kindred and acquaintance. It runs round the whole land in which we live and agitates our bosoms with words that are uttered or actions that are done at the distance of a thousand miles from our peaceful homes. The prosperity of your nation is felt to be your prosperity, its honor confers honor on you. And if the foot of an invader defiled at this moment any sod on our soil I need hardly ask you standing where I stand (in Concord) if your blood would keep its even and temperate flow, for the voice would cry to me from the graves of your fathers. No, our souls delight to spend their thoughts on the welfare of others. Not a wind can blow its tidings from any corner of the world however distant or barbarous but it awakens some of us to an interest in the fate of others, which weans us for a time from the nearer concerns of ourselves and our neighbor.

Such and so intimate is the connexion in which God has created us, and for purposes which are as clear as they are grand. The meanest understanding may see what a prodigious addition is made to the force and to the happiness of man from the existence of society. Compare the effects produced in God's lower works, in the brute and insect creation, by those animals that are solitary and those that are social; compare the wondrous dwellings of the beaver and the bee, with the unprovided rock of the eagle and the lion. And then add reason to the workman and compare the powers of man when he is alone, with the

2. "The ordinary admonitions . . . involves": see *JMN* 3:82–83.
3. Psalms 55:14.
4. "All that the eye sees . . . friendship": see *JMN* 3:91.

powers of man in society. In solitude he is weak; in society he is strong. In solitude his mind and body decay; his mind languishes in stupid ignorance; his body is famished for the want of bread; the wolf and the bear are his dreaded enemies; his sickness is not nursed; his sorrows are not consoled. In society, his mind is expanded in its efforts to accommodate itself to the large minds which every hour brings before him; he has a command over objects that are on the other side of the earth; the dangers that once beset him, he fears no more, for all men are his protectors; even mortal pain is less an evil, for the arts that all are cultivating can relieve it; and death is less dreadful, for he is sustained in its downward march by the sympathy and service of his friends. Consider, I beseech you, one moment the face of the world around you and tell me what it is that has wrought upon it this wonderful effect. Three hundred years ago the country you inhabit was dwelt in by men living alone, not joining themselves in society, by laws, institutions, or arts. The country was then a silent wilderness. What is it that has sprinkled its hills and valleys with towns; what is it that has felled its forests, that has chalked the continent with roads and furrowed it with canals and reduced its noble streams into the servitude of man, that has filled its enormous regions with rejoicing nations, subdued them with laws, enriched them with arts, and consecrated them with temples to the living God, and multiplied innumerable blessings for which the voice of thanksgiving ascends from them all this day in a mingled incense to heaven? What is it under God but the joint human exertion; the cooperation of men in society?

These are the great and obvious advantages of our social condition in the improvement of our physical powers, and the creation of happiness that arises out of them. But this condition has another influence vastly more important to which I am chiefly anxious to call your attention. This world is not our home. We are on earth to prepare for heaven. Our social relations are full of helps and full of perils also to our virtue and our happiness. Our pleasures are doubled by the cheerful sympathy that extends them to our friends, and our griefs are divided by the same sympathy and made light and tolerable. It is incredible also how much we are stimulated to virtue by the virtue of those we love and how much our moral character is built on the hope of their approbation. God has placed us in such intimate relations with our fellow men that the influence of others upon our character can hardly be appreciated. We learn virtue almost as we learn our native tongue, by imitating the tones and actions of others, and we learn with the more fatal facility the example of vice. It is not a revelation, which first instructed each of us in our duties and our hopes. It was not books and sages, it was not even conscience that taught us the rudiments of our religion. Almost before even that immortal monitor began to be heard in our infant breasts, we uttered the great name of God on a mother's lap. We copied in the dawn of the faculties from other countenances, the expression of human passions. Perchance in that pliant hour our moulding character took a bias from those about us which it will forever retain. Who of us has seen a child busy at its little games and beheld that little imitator of all the motions and sounds about it, prompt to copy the slightest action of its parent, without feeling how burden-some a responsibility rested on them to whose care God had committed its introduction into life?

And now, my friends, let me call your attention to the great object to which all these views of our social condition point, to the immense importance which belongs to your conduct when it is considered as *example*. Since you cannot hide your deeds, since you are environed by a cloud of witnesses,[5] since your smallest action and idlest word is thus a conspicuous mark for the study and imitation of all with whom your example has weight, let me beseech you to make that example the perfect model it ought to be. There is no man who has not much influence, and if your life is faultless the whole of that influence is cast into the right scale. But if any part of your character is defective—if you obey many Commandments, but are guilty in one, then the whole of your virtue is made use of to sanction that vice to which you have yielded.[6] All those who find themselves tempted to the same offence will quote triumphantly your name and merits and plead that they may surely do what one so good and so honoured has done before.

Moreover the contagion of vice is so swift, it is so much easier to copy a fault than a merit that the danger to others is certain when you swerve by one hair's breadth from the straight and narrow way.[7] If in the transaction of your affairs you talk of one purpose whilst the sharpened eye of your friend detects another lurking in your thoughts, it is strongly probable that he will meet your decep-tion with his deception. Dissimulation invites dissimulation.

Every hour of your life, every word you utter is infinitely important. You are one of those members who make up society. It depends on you as much as on any other, whether the standard of religion in society shall be high or low, whether others shall be countenanced in their vices by your authority, or shall be shamed out of their intended indulgence by the spectacle of your purity. Men are looking to you. Youth is looking to you and it may depend on your deter-mination at any moment whether the young man in the strength of his passions shall have the ardour of his virtue chilled, and an evil bias given to the whole tenor of his unfolding life, or whether he shall be encouraged to spurn the tempter and unite himself to the sons of God. But be assured whichever influ-ence you exert it will not, cannot end with the individual who has thus adopted your course. For his influence you also will be accountable and for the issues of those whom his influence has guided. It reaches on, this perilous effect, through all the mighty ages of the time to come.

It is impossible for you to determine the effect of any one action. It is impossi-ble for you to say at any time—'I shall safely sin. None can be injured but myself by what I am doing. I am not regarded by others and the action itself is obscure.' You judge not wisely in this matter. It is one of the most remarkable

5. Hebrews 12:1.
6. Cf. James 2:10.
7. Cf. Matthew 7:14.

things in the order of Providence to see how short an arm man extends at any time to aid the great revolution of events, to observe how little matter kindles so great a fire.[8] It is like the infant's hand which plays with the pin of an engine till he has ignorantly set in motion wheels that astonish him with their activity and deafen him with their thunder. So do men habitually begin actions which in their influence have immortal duration and immeasurable magnitude. We daily behold consequences proceeding to a greatness out of all proportion to the insignificancy of the things that gave them birth. Kings and counsellors whom oceans part,[9] will league together in the prosecution of magnificent schemes which after a parade of embassies and panegyric which send its fame everywhere end in smoke. At the same moment in an obscure corner a peasant, a beggar, raises his finger from the dust, or in the neverending train of thought an idea darts into his soul, which action or thought is the parent impulse which numbers ages and nations among its coadjutors, and all the after history of mankind as its effect. And no man can reach that foresight which shall say to this event, Prosper, and to another, Go in vain. You cannot discriminate the seed that shall perish in the soil from that which shall multiply itself a thousand fold. The present moment is in your power; but the Past is unalterable, the future is inscrutable. Nor do you know when you give utterance to an idle or an evil word whether its poison is to be lost in instant oblivion, or whether it is to be the accursed occasion of prodigious and eternal calamities.[10] Your own moral character is of immense importance to yourself alone. But its importance to others is still greater. Nor can we doubt a moment that this was *intended* by God. Your example is one of the great means he employs in the education of others and it is certainly a worthy ambition by which we may thus be excited to cooperate with God in the salvation of men by making our lives a perfect pattern such as he may approve for the instruction of our fellow men. Why has that portion of your life which has flowed from good principles failed of this effect and who is it that undo the good which you sometimes do? It is yourselves. It is yourselves. Your good lost its effect, your good example went for nothing, because those who would have relied on it saw that it was only an irregular, occasional virtue, a capricious ebullition of a character not trustworthy.

Take the advice of the Apostle to Timothy. Be thou an example of the believers. Aye, and be thou an example of the unbelievers also that the strong persuasion of your virtue may bring them also to the foot of the cross and to the worship of God.

My friends, I do not, for I believe I cannot, ascribe a greater importance to this subject than it deserves. I lament my own feebleness. It ought to command our earnest and humble reverence. If we were wise, we should soon forget to plume ourselves upon our knowledge; our talents; our wealth; we should

---

8. James 3:5.
9. Cf. Job 3:14.
10. "It is one of . . . calamities": see *JMN* 2:323-24.

escape that strange delusion of valuing ourselves above our neighbor because our religious opinions were more exclusive and our faith more orthodox. Human opinions are dust and vanity in the comparison with human actions. If we were wise we should discover how pitiful was this angry altercation about words and creeds and exchange this sinful emulation of human passions, miscalled religion, for that high and genuine emulation wherein the angels and archangels of God are partakers, the emulation of good deeds. It is in vain that we put solemn words in our mouth or even good intentions in our minds so that they bear no fruit in action. It is not prayer that saves, but practice. He that sets a good example is the true saint. He that sets a good example is the benefactor of mankind. He is the true hero before whose honest fame the sounding titles of this world's greatness sink into contempt. He that amid the defilement and temptation of the world uplifts the image of a good example is like the glorious vision of the king of Babylon "a form like unto the Son of God, walking in the midst of the fire."[11]

Before I conclude the subject permit me to suppose a strong case to illustrate the force of example. Suppose then an eloquence which I would to God were mine had moved the spirits of this congregation and had awakened their imaginations—let me rather say their slumbering understanding—to a discernment of the prodigious effect they were capable of producing; and that under this impression an hundred, fifty, or even ten, had sternly resolved to break away once and forever from the insidious seductions of sloth, of depraved customs, of open and of secret vice and scorning the tame indolence which dallies away life in doing neither good nor evil should give themselves up to a manly, unfeigned, uncompromising ardor for virtue; should sever themselves with that omnipotent force which God confers on virtue alone from the deeds, the words, and the appetites of vice, and, plighting their pure hands to heaven and each other, should lead lives void of offence before God and before man,[12] what, let me ask you, would be too much, what would be enough, to expect in its full effect from the determination of this inviolate brotherhood? In honest homage before them, the mask would fall from the face of the hypocrite. The sneer would die on the lip of the sophist—Virtue would prove too awful for the argument of the infidel. The emulous flush would mantle in the cheek of youth as he marked how the great things and great men of the world dwindled down by their side— by the side of these august assertors of the honor of God and the honor of man. They would infuse new blood, I borrow the language, they would infuse new blood into the aged veins of the world. The honor that heretofore has attached to the pomp of wealth and earthly grandeur would forsake the palace and the camp; the laurels of victors would wilt under this meridian light. The glory, the romance in which youthful imagination delights would separate itself from the bad passion to decorate the good. A new epoch would open in our history. Men would be enamoured of the beauty of virtue.[13] They would recognize at last the

11. Daniel 3:24–25.
12. Acts 24:16.
13. "Before I conclude . . . virtue": see *JMN* 3:81–82.

perfect beauty of that venerable example which eighteen hundred years ago the Son of God disclosed to the world but of which the world was not worthy.[14] It has wrought on men with a slow and purifying effect; it has reformed the face of the world and now in these latter days by the blessing of God on these his chosen servants his true disciples might cover the earth as the waters cover the sea.[15] Such should be the high office and success of these martyrs to the world. And though they disdained the fading echoes of vulgar fame, would age on age as they revolved in the periods of heaven, would the farthest duration, think you, impair their powers or detract from their renown? or God assign any date of praise to this high, this venerable, this celestial ambition?

And now, my brethren, in conclusion let us take to ourselves our own part in those duties which so obviously grow out of these views of our condition. We have seen that God has placed us in a most remarkable connexion and interdependence on each other, that certain mighty purposes are answered thereby, that our power and our happiness are incalculably augmented, that this social connexion has an inevitable influence upon our virtue and our vice, and that hence our obligation to cease to do evil and to learn to do well is wonderfully increased, that much of the future is in our hands, and that we are able by a strenuous perseverance in a religious life to give a great impulse that may act on all the future character of mankind, but if we will foolishly yield to the whispers of these rebel passions that war against the soul, if we will forget the great objects for which we live, forget the life and the death of Christ, forget the presence of God and the hope of Heaven, that we shall throw all our weight into the scale of iniquity and after our dust is festering in the soil the evil influence of our example shall be running on in ceaseless activity to the ruin of unborn generations. God forbid it should be so. God forbid that we, my friends, should hesitate a moment in the course that lies before us. We will give ourselves up to that course which shall remove the corrupt condition of the world. Fear not how few and feeble you may be in your great undertaking. Power does not depend on the number but on the energy of those that embark in a cause. Fear not, my brethren, though you are few. Fear not, my brother, though you are but one. You are not alone—for God is on your side.

His spirit is upon you. His angels aid you in this your labor of love.[16] The spirits of just men made perfect, the unseen assembly of all the good,[17] are your approving coadjutors. When your strength fails your children shall rise up and call you blessed and carry forward the holy cause,[18] and when God shall call you to Himself, you shall hear a voice on high, Well done, good and faithful servant, enter into the joy of thy Lord.[19]

14. Hebrews 11:38.
15. Cf. Isaiah 11:9 and Habakkuk 2:14.
16. "Fear not how few . . . love": see *JMN* 3:90–91.
17. Cf. Hebrews 12:23.
18. Proverbs 31:28.
19. Matthew 25:21.

Be not deceived; God is not mocked; for whatsoever a man soweth, that shall he also reap.

GALATIANS 6:7

The influence of wealth upon society is so great and constant that it is presented to our mind, as an object of near or remote interest in every hour of our intercourse with the world. And this is so not by our choice or our fault but by the ordination of God. We cannot help desiring to acquire property. We hunger and thirst and must be fed, we are naked and must be clothed, the air is cold and the night is dark and our bodies are exhausted with toil and we must be sheltered by houses and refreshed by sleep. Moreover we were born into connexions with other men and those connexions multiply as we grow up into life. It is more than a necessity, it is our pleasure and our pride that we should have food and raiment and a dwelling for many more than ourselves—for brothers and sisters, for children and friends. Such are the first reasons which lead to the acquisition of property. These make all the value of wealth in the beginning of society. But as civilization advances, wealth, that is to say, an abundance of these means of satisfying the animal wants, becomes of vastly greater importance and a principle of wonderful effect on the fortunes of man.

It is found that it confers power. Civil society produces a very unequal distribution of goods, and he that holds in his hands the bread of many can controul the actions of many, and a thousand men are thus made to minister to the happiness of one. It will buy also a thousand refinements. The good desire the power it confers in the ambition of a wider beneficence. The bad wish to become formidable and secure. That portion of it which each individual needs for subsistence is still sought with all the eagerness which the instinctive love of life and the gratification of the appetites teaches. The rest, the surplus, is pursued with almost equal ardor. The good desire it that they may do more good, the bad that they may gratify their appetites or their spite. The world is shaken with the incessant striving of all the interests and passions engaged in this pursuit. But if the world is disturbed by it, it is also enriched by it. If life is agitated by this fierce controversy, it has given new value to life. It has gathered

---

Preached four times: June 17, 1827, at the First Church, Boston; January 6, 1828, in Concord, N.H.; May 24, 1829, at the Second Church, Boston; and February 25, 1838, in East Lexington.

men in cities, it has brought the arts to perfection, it has brought what were once the privileges of a few within reach of all. It has smoothed the rugged way of this world with unnumbered comforts.

This diligent desire of becoming rich has sharpened the faculties and added to the accomplishments of men, has taken man out of the woods where he hunted and slumbered in savage want and brought him into communities where he is an active, forecasting, social, benevolent being.

This state of things has vast importance in its aspect on our moral character. We are not exposed to this engrossing pursuit of animal comforts without the hourly danger of involving our virtue also in the pursuit. And what an amount of crime, what selfishness, what hardness of heart, what curdling malignity, what thirst for human blood has grown out of the excess of the laudable pursuit I need not remind you. It has been the theme of the moralist in every age. It has provoked the denunciation of the good and wise and the solemn and memorable warnings of the Son of God. My friends, I am not the accuser or apologist of the rich. I respect this institution of Property as one of the most efficient principles which God has established in the world to excite our powers and our virtues, and it is in the feeling of this, its importance as a part of the great scheme in which we stand, that I am led at this time to offer to your consideration some remarks upon truths in relation to it that seem to me of much moment.

I believe it is not considered as much as it deserves how much the good and evil of this life is dealt out on a system of Compensations. All things are double one against another.[1] What is taken from a man in one way is made up to him in another. Nothing is given or taken without an equivalent.[2] Since the Christian Revelation has made known another life, all moral reasonings refer, as is well known, to man's whole existence, to a vaster system of things than is here disclosed, and there can be no doubt that in the whole existence, here and hereafter, perfect justice is done to all. But I am disposed to think that there are strong presumptions here exhibited to lead us to believe that in many cases *in this world* perfect compensations do prevail; that very much is done in this world to adjust the uneven balance of condition and character.

There are certain great and obvious illustrations of this doctrine which lie on the outside of life and have therefore been always noted. That prodigality makes haste to want; that riot introduces disease; that fearful crimes are hunted by fearful remorse; that the love of money is punished by the care of money; that honest indigence is cheerful; that in fertile climates the air breathes pestilence and in healthy zones there is an iron soil; that whilst the mind is in ignorant infancy the body is supple and strong, when the mind is informed and powerful the body decays. These and similar remarkable compensations and all which we see lie at the foundation of our faith in God's being and attributes.

---

1. Ecclesiasticus 42:24. See *JMN* 2:340, 6:143; used in "Ethics," *EL* 2:153, and "Compensation," *CW* 2:64.
2. Cf. *JMN* 3:79.

And it makes the great value of this class of facts, the testimony they bear to the existence of a controlling Providence amid the affairs of men. No man who follows out these inquiries to their result but has felt the conviction stealing on his soul that other eyes than men's behold his affairs and control the issues of them.

But this subject is very embarrassing from its extent. In the hope of being definite and intelligible and directing your attention to such views as involve conclusions of great practical value I shall confine myself at present to observations upon this great law as it affects the ordinary dealings of men in their pursuit of wealth.

I believe that if facts were truly seen it would be felt that sin is ignorance, that the thief steals from himself,[3] that he who practises fraud is himself the dupe of the fraud he practises; that whoso borrows runs in his own debt;[4] and whoso gives to another benefits himself to the same amount. This it will be admitted is a system of perfect compensation. Let us see whether it will hold.

There are two ways in which the good or evil, and the riches or poverty of a man is to be measured, as it exists in the view of *self* and of *society*, and we would examine our doctrine in these two respects.

I. Let us then leave out of view the existence of other men and in the view of individual unconnected character, as a moral being having duties to fulfil and a character to earn in the sight of God, am I impoverished in my own just estimation that I have given my goods to feed the poor, that I have hazarded half my estate in the hands of my friend, in yielding to calls of moral sentiment which made a part of my highest nature? In my own secret judgment am I the richer that I have unjustly taken or withheld from my fellow man his good name, his rights, or his property? Am I the richer that I have tied up my own purse and borrowed for my needs of the treasure of my friend? Shall I count myself the richer that I have received a hundred favours and rendered none?[5] Myself, the man within the breast,[6] am the sole judge of this question and there is no appeal from the decisive negative. The daily mistake of thousands and tens of thousands who jump to make any pitiful advantage of their neighbour must not be quoted against this tribunal. For they err by taking the representative for the principal, the picture for the substance, the false for the true. It is not the true estimate of a man's actual value that is made from the balance of figures that stands in his favor on his ledger. This is to be corrected from the book of life within him, by an appeal to his sense of the manner in which the property was obtained. If it was acquired by clandestine fraud, which has yet escaped disclosure, it is clearly a false estimate. If it was obtained by arts at which the eye of the law connives, but which still are in substance frauds, it is clearly a false estimate. If it is the reward of honest industry, and skill, to which, said the

---

3. *JMN* 2:343, 6:215. Used in "Compensation," *CW* 2:66.
4. Used in "Compensation," *CW* 2:65.
5. Used in "Compensation," *CW* 2:65.
6. See Sermon I, n. 15.

ancient philosopher, the gods have sold all things,[7] his estimate is correct,—his doings are respected in heaven and in earth. Each man knows—whatever language his neighbours or his journals may speak—knows what is his just standing,—whether he is indebted or whether he has rendered to men as much as he has received of them, and has made others rich and happy. We mistake in assuming the outward property, the mass of plate and stamped paper that men can shew, for their real possessions. These are but representatives of real value, and where real value is not these may often be fraudulently retained. But I think it must be apparent to us all that in the aspect of self, as far as our own consciousness is concerned, the doctrine that nothing in the intercourse of men *can be given* is sound. That our own judgment is faithful and will not call that ours which was not righteously acquired.

II. The doctrine is no less true, no less important, in its respect to our social nature, i.e., the judgement of society is always right in the end. If a man steals, is it not known? If he borrows, is it not known? If he receive gifts, is it not known? If I accept important benefits from another in secret or in public, there arises of course from the deed a secret acknowledgement of benefit on his part and of debt on mine or, in other words, of superiority and inferiority. Of course whatever may be the extent of a man's obligations or the number of his connexions, the record of each transaction is faithfully transcribed in the bosom of himself and his brother man. And it matters not though he should strive to hide his obligations to other men and make none privy to his dependance. The impression that is stamped on one mind of any character is readily transferred with exactness to other minds, and he who is conscious of uncommon liberality or who expects returns that are not rendered is seldom slow to speak of the tardiness of gratitude. He is stupid who has succeeded in obtaining many loans which he knows his inability to pay, and imagines his credit to stand firm. It does not stand firm. He has got the ill reputation of a borrower and he will soon learn that the reputation will defeat the ends for which it was borne. Or further; suppose a man on the expectation that his frauds will be unknown to all; perchance on the distrust of the Providence of God, takes a clandestine advantage of his neighbour and repeats the crime on others and guards the fact with such scrupulous and profound deception that mortal wit cannot uncover his iniquity. Perhaps we are supposing an impossible case; for mortal wit can undo what mortal wit can do. The ingenuity of honesty can devise no cipher, can engrave no plate, which the ingenuity of dishonesty cannot counterfeit. The system that has been combined can be analyzed by an equal understanding. In short, the history of the world may testify that whatever truth the wit of man

7. Cf. Epicharmus, "The gods demand of us toil as the price of all good things," quoted in Xenophon, *Memorabilia*, II, i, 20, and paraphrased ("the *Gods* sell us all the Goods they give us") in *Essays of Michael Seigneur de Montaigne* . . . , trans. Charles Cotton (London, 1693), 2:555. See *JMN* 2:344, 3:266, 3:343, and Charles L. Young, *Emerson's Montaigne* (New York, 1941), 97. For another occurrence, see Sermon XIV, n. 1.

has ever been sufficient to shroud the wit of man has been found sufficient to reveal.

But granting this were possible and that the particular crime that had been perpetrated were concealed, is there any reasonable man who can fear that such an offender will long maintain the standing that upright principles give in society? Whoso labors under such apprehensions mistakes strangely his own nature, and has scanned with but incurious eyes the enginery of the moral universe. My friends, the sin of man cannot be hid.[8] My friends, he that has committed a sin has done himself a fatal injury, and though the disorder that is in his soul may be concealed a moment, it will break out somewhere without delay. When I have swallowed arsenic I have not only tasted a bitter drug, I have done a fatal mischief to my constitution, and time will soon betray not what potion or what quantity I have swallowed, but that I have poisoned myself. In like manner he that has got loose from the checks of religion, he will soon make it felt that his moral health has been assailed and disordered. The insidious sin will infect every avenue of life, every hope, every affection, every thought.[9]

He that has committed a fraud has not merely made himself so much the richer and his neighbor so much poorer, in secret. He has done more. He has ceased to be an honest man. He thought, poor deceived offender, that he had made himself amenable to a distant retribution, to what he had heard in church of Heaven and Hell. Alas, he did not see that in the moment he reached out his hand to that evil act that moment his transgression was visited upon him. He was forsaken by his own innocence, which was a wall of defence about him. The barrier which was built between him and destruction is broken down and he is free to walk in the broad road of Ruin.[10] Alas, my friends, a deep, a dire compensation is made for every transgression, for every unjust advantage that man can take of man. The compensation is this, that the strong checks of religion have lost their force and though he believes he shall not sin again, unless God avert the mischief he shall sin again, he will prosecute his downward course till it is plain to man as to the angels of God that he is fallen. For every offence he will be exactly so much the more degraded being in the view of others. In this respect therefore, i.e., in the view of society, no man gains any thing without an equivalent.

These are the laws by which our pursuit of the lawful goods which this world offers us have been regulated by the interference of a Providence, an interference which is so wonderful in the view of this exact system of checks and balances that I know not who will be so hardy as to deny. I consider these views to be of great importance to us because we all have the same wants and it is of much consequence to us that we believe what is said so often, that the means of happiness are not happiness unless the mind consents.

It is undeniable that riches lawfully gotten are a blessing from heaven and

8. Cf. I Timothy 5:25.
9. For a draft of the preceding nine paragraphs, "I believe . . . thought," see *JMN* 2:340, 2:343–46, 2:349.
10. Cf. Matthew 7:13.

add wonderful means of comfort to man. Our community is full of instances of wealth accumulated by honest and liberal hands, got with a blessing and spent with a blessing, wealth held on the conditions which Christianity appoints, held by its possessors as stewards not as proprietors.[11] And this reward of virtue the mind always beholds with unmixed satisfaction. But it is as undeniable that gotten at too great a sacrifice they are more than worthless. I have seen, all men in the common circumstances of life may see now and then, instances of this, the men who are rich without being happy, victims marked and stamped as with the curse of Cain going up and down in the world, whom no external splendour can adorn, no comfort can soften, no riches satisfy;[12] men who have fixed their hopes in rank earth and are late in learning their miserable mistake. Descriptions of this last are apt, I know, to fall coldly and unregarded on the ear, but it is because they are so much the commonplace of life that they have been quoted out of it and become the commonplace of the moralist. Who has not seen the thrift, coldblooded and hard-hearted thrift, that has wrought out for itself its own reward. Men and women that set out to be rich, that sold their body, its strength, its grace, its health, its sleep, yea and sold their soul, its peace, its affections, its time, its education, its religion, its eternity, for gold. They have paid the price and by the laws of Providence they have received their purchase. But by the laws of Providence they shall receive nothing more. They have not bought any immunity from bodily pain, any grace from the elements, any courtesy from the diseases; they made no mention with their dealers of gentle affections and asked no more of the Intellectual Principle than how to cast their drivelling balances of loss and gain. Health, knowledge, friendship, God, these were no partners to their contract, no guarantees against disaster. These were defrauded of the just debt which each human being owes them in order to scrape together the means by which wealth was to be bought. But these are creditors that will not let them pass unchallenged. They have asked no protection against the evils of life and God has left them naked to them. There is not a corner in the earth that does not swarm with enemies to our peace of body or of mind, and it is the proper object of our study in this life to teach us how some may be overcome, some may be neutralized, how to contemn some, and to encounter some on equal ground. But these have neglected the designs of their Maker. Ignorance is theirs with a brutal understanding which is wrapt up in itself and is denied the consolation of perceiving and enjoying the advancement and happiness of others. And whilst the great body of the good and wise are advancing on every side, the power of man adding to his knowledge and his beneficence, these who profess the means of so mightily aiding in the cause, are alone and forlorn. Unmindful of these consolatory triumphs, cold to these hopes, they sit by their firesides in chambers which many climates have contributed to adorn and prate to each other their stale gossip smelling of corruption

11. Among several relevant passages, see I Peter 4:10.
12. Genesis 4:15.

and folly, and feel the sad inefficacy of things without, to mend the error and deficiency within.[13]

My friends, I have attempted to establish the position that a system of Compensations prevails by God's will amid all the dealings of men in common life and that in virtue of this law, no man can enrich himself by doing wrong, or impoverish himself by doing right; because no man can long impose a false estimate of himself either upon himself or upon society. Let it console you under your griefs that grow out of your worldly estate. You have lost your hard earned substance by inevitable misfortunes or by the fraud of others and you say you have no equivalent. Many a one by losing the means of luxury has gained health of body and health of mind. Let him ask himself if he will render back what he has acquired to receive again what he has lost? But consider again, my brother, is there none? Peradventure you have a more contented mind. You have a softened heart. Affliction is indispensable in our training for Heaven. You have acquired Holiness in consequence of your misfortunes without which no man shall see the Lord.[14]

But, my friends, I should do great injustice to my own views of this subject were I to leave it here without reminding you that I conceive this system of Compensation to have a wider—a vaster—application than that which we have noticed. I believe it to be vast beyond our idea, that it not only touches the giving and receiving of property, but governs all the pleasures and pains, the action and suffering of man, that it is but the expression of the Justice of God running through the Universe, that every defect in one manner is made up in another, that every suffering is rewarded, every sacrifice is made up; every debt is paid. It points us also to further and more perfect Compensation. It points to a life to come. This world is but the porch through which we enter into another. Let us be assured that what is done here is not forgotten there. Let us distinctly understand how much God has made us the masters of our own eternity, that whatsoever a man soweth, that shall he also reap, that if we pour our abundance into the bosom of the poor, if we are the instructors of the ignorant, the firm friends in good report and in bad report of God, of good men, and of our country,[15] if we spend our strength and our soul in urging the great cause of human virtue, if our life like the life of our Master in Heaven is held ready to be offered a spotless sacrifice—be assured that your whole devotion from feeblest exertion to the sigh you have breathed to heaven shall in no wise lose its reward.[16] And oh, my friends, let it deter you from every secret sin you have meditated from the most secure and unseen indulgence of passion, the strong conviction that the everlasting laws that God has set to watch in the universe will fasten on their victim in the moment of his offence, will implant in his bosom the seeds of vengeance which will grow rank and ripe to his ruin.

13. "I have seen . . . within": see *JMN* 2:341–42.
14. Hebrews 12:14.
15. Cf. II Corinthians 6:8.
16. Matthew 10:42 and Mark 9:41.

Let us not pass idly on our ways but see the consequences that besiege every road wherein we walk. Let us beware what we do, seeing we do nothing in vain;[17] seeing that we are beginning trains of thought and action that never end; that every hour we are sending messengers before us, that will acquit or accuse us before the angels of God. Be not deceived; God is not mocked; for whatsoever a man soweth, that shall he also reap.

17. Possibly a reminiscence of Arisotle (*Politics*, I, 2): "οὐθὲν γαρ, ὡς φαμέν, μάτην ἡ φύσις ποιεῖ," given as "Natura nihil agit frustra" by Sir Thomas Browne in *Religio Medici*, I, 15, and as "Nature does nothing in vain" by Bacon in *The Advancement of Learning*, in *The Works of Francis Bacon*, ed. James Spedding et al. (London, 1857–1874), 4:365. The phrase is also to be found in Aristotle, "Of the Soul," III, 12. See *JMN* 3:10 and 3:22; used in *English Traits*, W 5:148.

V

We preach Christ crucified.

I CORINTHIANS 1:23

It is better, said Solomon, to go to the house of mourning than to the house of feasting.[1] There is something more safe and salutary to our virtue in the influences of sorrow, than in the enticing splendor of scenes of joy. Man does not stand firm in a high and giddy prosperity. The tender eye of the mind is dazzled by excessive sunshine. 'We are purified by pity and terror.'[2] By these passions our attention is arrested, our faculties are startled from their sleep into strenuous exertion. Our pride is prostrate, and vanity is sick, and the love of pleasure sleeps, and anger dies, when God darkens the chambers of the soul with grievous affliction and the voice of Reason begins to be heard amid the silence of the passions. It is good when we are not afflicted, to consider affliction. It is good in health, to remember sickness. It is good when blessings are heaped upon our heads, to estimate the dear price of them which others paid. There is little danger of our carrying these gloomy entertainments of the soul to any kind of excess. For the animal spirits are not to be long repressed. Love and interest, the meeting of friends, the social board, the joys of conversation and the festive cup are every hour tempting us back to ease and hilarity. The religious service of this day seldom has too morose an influence on the rest of the week. That danger departed with a former age. I shall be excused, I hope, in attempting to engage your attention to a grave and mournful theme. There is a great abundance of smooth and pleasant speculation on the agreeable topics. We hear from day to day in every form the congratulations that are cheerfully exchanged from every quarter on the distinguished advancement of the age. Men are rejoicing in what they have lately learned and done. The philanthropist exults in the progress of public opinion. He is glad because the strongholds of error are broken down. The Christian points to the power with which the kingdom of God is extending

---

Preached eleven times: June 24, 1827, at the First Church, Boston; June 28 (Thursday Lecture) in Concord, Mass.; July 1 in Waltham; September 2 at the Stone Chapel; September 9 in Northampton; September 16 in Greenfield; October 7 in Deerfield; November 4 in New Bedford; February 17, 1828, in Carlisle; March 30 in Lechmere Point; and July 27 at the Second Church, Boston.

    1. Ecclesiastes 7:2.

    2. Aristotle, *Poetics*, VI, 2. Quoted in *JMN* 3:25, 4:55, 4:56, 6:184; used in "Society," *EL* 2:110. "It is better . . . terror": see *JMN* 3:91–92.

in the world; he rejoices that, at last unsatisfied with affecting the outward face and manners of society, it begins to penetrate to the core, and is at the same time reaching out its powerful arm to civilize and purify the children of men in the farthest Indian isles. Leave them to their joy. It is just and blameless. But the heir who calls his friends to rejoice with him in his newfound riches, will sometimes pause in the flow of festivity and breathe a sigh to the memory of that benefactor whose abstemious industry hoarded and whose affectionate solicitude bequeathed to him his ample possessions. And it is a natural and reasonable gratitude on our part which sometimes carries us back in devout recollection to the founder of our spiritual privileges,[3] to the suffering author of our religion— to him whose blood was shed for the healing of the nations.[4] Come then let us leave awhile our heritage and the pleasant places in which our lives have fallen and go out into a distant land and a darker time. I bid you to no summer holiday, to no field of joyful ceremony. I bid you to the sad Aceldama, to the field of blood, to a ghastly and atrocious spectacle, to the hill of Calvary and the passion of Christ.[5]

It is good to refresh our virtues by the example of perfect innocence, to invigorate our fortitude to meet the trial and temptation of the world by remembering the sorrows of Him who was tempted in all points like as we are yet without sin.[6]

I would go back to that most affecting page of human history which portrayed in living lines the personal character and the death of Jesus Christ, a being whose character has taken such strong hold of the mind as to divide the opinions of men as to his nature and office more than did ever any question, one so great as to leave foundation for the opinion that he was a portion of the Deity and in the opinions least reverent that he was first of men—a being who would be called renowned did not fame and what men call glory sink before the majesty of his character into things offensive and ridiculous; one whose effect on the fortunes of human society, taking out of account what may be called supernatural influence, has been far the most powerful impulse of those that ever wore the human form, and yet whose influence on the world is now, I had almost said, but *beginning* to be felt; a being whose life was so pure and whose death was so sublime as if no consequences had followed would of themselves have attracted the greatest admiration.[7]

The remark is not new yet must not be omitted here, that the weak side of our nature is always inclining us to lavish our admiration on all that comes to us decorated with the signs of outward splendor, and to withhold it from any pretentions which are not supported by these appearances. From necessary

---

3. "There is little . . . privileges": see *JMN* 3:92.
4. Revelation 22:2.
5. "Aceldama," or "the field of blood," was the name given to the potter's field bought with the blood money relinquished by Judas Iscariot (see Matthew 27:6–8 and Acts 1:19).
6. Hebrews 4:15.
7. Compare this paragraph with *JMN* 3:55.

causes it happens that no man is wholly uninfluenced by the pomp of wealth and power and most men conceive men and things to be respectable, just in that degree that they are related to wealth and power. If an opinion is patronized by the great, men say that opinion deserves consideration. If it is known only to the obscure, it does not concern them. But we judge in this matter according to the flesh and in the manner in which it pleased God to establish in the world the Christian religion it seems to have been designed to correct this ancient error. He chose the weak things of the world to confound the mighty.[8] He would teach us not an intellectual truth but a moral lesson of high and eternal importance. He would teach us that not in plenty, not in ease, not in luxury and gay prosperity is the true glory and strength of human nature to be found, the great prizes of existence to be won, but that they grow in the dark soil of affliction, that trial is wholesome to us, and success is dangerous, that security enervates, that Danger ennobles us. The emblem of our faith is not a crown but a cross. "We are baptized into suffering," 'and our sacrament is the symbol of Christ's death and passion.'[9] Who of us has not compared the way of God when he magnified his servant in his great dispensation to the way of men, when they would magnify theirs?

My friends, let us remember what was the manner in which this august Instructor, this highly authorized Commissioner, appeared in the world. Was he like the other men that have given the law to nations? Was he one of the men of mire and blood? Was he born in the lap of grandeur, the child of the Caesars, cushioned on the soft embroidery of a palace amid kneeling nations and nourished safely up to an effeminate manhood amid incense and luxury, amid music and gold like the petulent progeny of an earthly king? Or was he indicated to men by military fame, by the splendor of victories and the horror of his desolations like the renowned conquerors, the men of iron who reaped their laurels in the grim front of the fight walking betwixt the living and the dead whose triumphal march is made not through the gates of towns but through the ragged overhanging breach which their artillery have opened?[10] whose entertainment in life is the torture of wounded men, whose music the groans of the dying? These and such as these are they who in old and in later times have attracted the wonder of the world and have been saluted in their lives by all titles of adulation and gone down to their tombs attended by the voice of panegyric and the ostentation of funeral pageant. O, my friends, it was none of these whom God put into the world in the high capacity of Saviour of men but a despised Hebrew; among men reputed a carpenter's son; born in a manger; a

8. I Corinthians 1:27.

9. J. T. [Emerson's note]. See Jeremy Taylor, *Twenty-Seven Sermons Preached at Golden Grove*, Sermon IX, in *The Whole Works of the Right Rev. Jeremy Taylor, D.D.* (London, 1828), 5:536.

10. "men of iron . . . opened?": see *JMN* 6:27, where the language is quoted from an unidentified work of Georges de Scudery.

man of sorrows and acquainted with grief, the associate of humble men and one who had not where to lay his head[11]—

> The man who was crowned with thorns
> The man who on Calvary died
> The man who bore scourging and scorns
> Whom sinners agreed to deride.[12]

All that was simple and unpretending in his circumstances was made to show in stronger relief the majesty of his life; all that was distressing and terrible in his lot to disclose more manifestly the purity and sublimity of his virtue. It was designed to set the greatness of the world at nought. It was designed to give us a perfect pattern of obedience to God at the same time that a confirmation was added by a holy life as well as wonderful works to the authenticity of his mission, and the truth of his tidings.

Pilate had washed his trembling hands.[13] Herod and his men of war had led out their lowly victim. They had platted a crown of thorns and covered him with a purple robe. They knew how keenly a proud spirit is alive to contempt when it runs fiercely into the face of danger. But they were unable to comprehend in their pitiful ferocity that there is a greatness of soul to which evil fortune and good, to which the honor and dishonour of men, are accidents, a magnanimity so high and serene that mockery and scorn cannot touch its composure. It sleeps to them. It sleeps to the things of this world in a vision of divine contemplations, an elevation of the soul too sublime to waste itself in idle vaunts and bravade. It is clothed in humility. It walks with God.

Let us repair to the mount of Crucifixion. Let us see if his death bore out the testimony of his life. Death which sets the seal to mortal character and leaves them unalterable. And his was a death of pain and ignominy. It has been said, "none can aspire to act greatly but they who are of force greatly to suffer."[14] And he was called to drink of a cup that is not mingled for many.

They were skilful hands that sketched in our Scriptures the tragic events of that memorable day. They have told with sad fidelity the story of his sufferings, the insane vindictiveness with which his countrymen thirsted for his blood, the fear that fell on them, his chosen followers, who forsook him in his agony and fled.[15] Let it be remembered however for the consolation of human nature in the view of that hour of its deep depravity, that Jesus Christ in that dreadful

---

11. Isaiah 53:3, Matthew 8:20, and Luke 9:58.

12. *JMN* 3:64.

13. This detail is given only in Matthew 27:24, though in the account that follows Emerson draws on all four gospels.

14. Edmund Burke, *Letters on a Regicide Peace*, Letter 1, in *The Works of the Right Honorable Edmund Burke* (Boston, 1866), 5:250–51. See *JMN* 6:32, 6:156; also quoted in a letter to Mary Moody Emerson, June 15, 1826 (*J* 2:104).

15. Cf. Matthew 26:56, 27:25, and Mark 14:50.

occasion was not wholly abandoned by the sympathies and admiration of men. It is recorded by the Evangelist St. Luke that as the mob moved towards Calvary there followed him a great company of people and of women which bewailed and lamented him. The blessed martyr forgot the death he was to die, forgot the terrors of his ghastly cross in the impulse of his benevolence. He turned to them and said, Daughters of Jerusalem weep not for me but weep for yourselves and your children.[16] His eye went forward to the future. He thought of the bitter retribution which this generation should reap when the armies of the Roman Empire should visit upon them their grievous transgression. He saw the havock that war and famine and pestilence would bring to their doors; when, in their despair, heedless of the enemy without, they should rend each other in extreme rage; when blood should be poured as water in their streets; and the foundations of the city should be turned up with the plough, when the mothers of Judaea, in the strong necessity of hunger, should forget the law of nature and slay for food the babe at the breast. These things his merciful spirit contemplated and he said, Weep not for me daughters of Jerusalem but weep for yourselves!

But ignorant of the future and blinded by passion even to the present, his cruel enemies kept on their way. My friends—there is a majesty in every step taken up that disastrous mountain, when the mind enters into the thoughts and purposes of him that walked thereon. The arm, in which was lodged the miraculous virtue which nature acknowledged through all her works, hung unnerved by his side, and the tongue, which had spoken peace to the stormy sea,[17] and life to the dead, was dumb. His thoughts went back to the painful picture of all the past, to the thick darkness which sin had created in the world, and which all the taper lights of philosophy had been unable to dispel.[18] Man had not found out his immortality, had not found out the God who made him. But he has been commissioned from on high to bring this message from our Father in heaven to teach us to all generations his will and the purposes to which we exist. He has borne his affectionate testimony, He has done the work which God gave him to do.[19] To add to his works of wonder the last testimony he brings his life to bear witness that his doctrine is true. And now he offers himself a silent victim and feels that he is accomplishing a mighty destiny. There as he walks amid that raging multitude, he lost the dizzy spectacle around him. His eye passes into the future and grieves at the painful progress which the doctrine of the Resurrection has yet to make through the superstition and sin of the world. His searching eye passes by the weary centuries wherein his name is taken by unholy lips and his doctrine perverted to an unhallowed use of power and pride. Through the unfolding mist of ages his calm eye rests on a few, it rests on the faithful who in this latter day shall consecrate themselves with pious self devotion to the

16. Luke 23:27–28.
17. Mark 4:39.
18. "My friends . . . dispel": see *JMN* 3:63.
19. John 17:4.

cause in which he is about to offer up his life. It rests on you, my friends, it rests on you and appeals to you with a passion which you will not misapprehend. It invites you by all the memory of his life, by the love of God his father and our father and by the immeasurable hopes which he has disclosed to your immortal minds, it invites, it implores you, to love yourselves as he has loved you, to take up your cross and be his faithful disciples, to make not vain the labour, the agony, and the death which he is finishing, but to show men at last how they may overcome the body in seeking the welfare of the soul. It looks to that tremendous load of moral depravity by which the head of humanity has been so long borne down to the earth. It beseeches you, in your day and generation, in imitation of him, to lift that weary head towards God and Heaven. It bids you despise the sufferings of the body, in the expectation of the glorious reward. It bids you welcome to immortal life.

These things, these awful hopes, are present to him that stands up mute and uncomplaining on the top of Calvary. But it was not the hour for meditation; it was the hour of blood. The cry of Crucify him! Crucify him! burst from the savage lips of that enormous multitude and the hills of Judaea rang with the ominous echoes.[20] Then the cross was planted in the earth; and He,—the man who came from God,—was hung thereon.

Then was heard the scoffing of the priest and the Levite, of the sadducee and the pharisee and the dismal shouting of that bloody crowd. Come down, come down to us, Son of God, from the Cross, they cried in daring irony.[21] They wagged their heads whilst the bitter pangs of death were passing, but as the darkened world, in which his benevolent spirit had found so stormy a home, faded from his closing eye, the words that he said, were, Father, forgive them, for they know not what they do.[22]

It is finished.[23] He hath given up the ghost, the land was darkened, and the vail of the temple was rent in twain.[24] He—the pure and holy one whose radiant innocence had contracted no blemish, no taint of mortality,—He is at peace, his sufferings are ended, his warfare is accomplished. Henceforth is laid up for him a crown of glory.[25] Weep not, my friends, weep not for him. But weep for them. These evil men whom God had abandoned to their own depravity, whose garments were rolled in his blood, who had made a covenant with death and with hell, they were at agreement, their faces are stricken with blackness and God turned them back the way they came.

It is a memorable answer and exhibits to us a most significant commentary on the story they have told, which is recorded by the Evangelists as having been made by Pilate on the following day. A fearful company of priests and Pharisees

20. Mark 15:13–14 and Luke 23:21.
21. Mark 15:30–32.
22. "And now he offers . . . do": see *JMN* 3:63–64. "Then was heard . . . do": see Matthew 27:39–40 and Luke 23:34.
23. John 19:30.
24. Matthew 27:51, Mark 15:38, and Luke 23:45.
25. II Timothy 4:8.

came together unto Pilate, saying, Sir, we remember that deceiver said whilst he was yet alive, After three days I will rise again. Command therefore that the sepulchre be made sure until this third day lest his disciples come by night and steal him away and say unto the people, he is risen from the dead (so the last error shall be worse than the first). Pilate said unto them, Ye have a watch; go your way, Make it as sure as ye can.[26] Alas, poor pigmy actors in this scene of madness and crime, Make it as sure as you can! Make fast the sepulchre, and set a watch, and seal the stone, and bind down the dead in his linen shroud, when the Almighty hath said—Let him arise. Lift your rebel fingers from the dust against the Everlasting arm that set yonder sun in the heavens, and not the less brought into the world his holy child Jesus, whom you with sinful hands have crucified and slain, and now will baffle you in your folly, and raise him from the dead. He has burst the bonds of death. He has put on the garments of glory for a putrid shroud. Ministering angels rolled away the stone from the door of the sepulchre: the soldiers that watched became as dead men.[27] He has appeared unto men. He has ascended to his Father in Heaven.

My friends, it has been an opinion entertained in all ages by the wise and good, that when death has interrupted our communion with our friends, that communion is not wholly broken. There is nothing in nature or in revelation to forbid the belief that when those are removed from us who were wont by their example and their approbation to encourage our virtue they are still permitted to observe our actions and, though unseen themselves, to approve every triumph which we gain over our evil propensities. It seems reasonable to believe that we are ever environed with the unseen society of our departed friends to witness our trials and our victories, that perchance they sometimes suggest to our secret soul motives of encouragement or reasons of consolation. Shall we then who bear the name of Christ be chargeable with any extravagance of opinion if we presume to hope that wherever in the earth his faithful disciples are found, there is his spirit by their side, to animate them in action, to protect them in peril? We yet hear his voice first heard after the Resurrection on the Mountains of Galilee—"Lo! I am with you alway, even unto the end of the world."[28] Listen to his words and this day he fulfils the prediction. He sits at the right hand of God.[29] He visits the children of men. You can enter into a sublime sympathy with him. You also can go about doing good. As He suffered for us, leaving us an example that we should follow in his steps.[30] Whensoever you breathe a pure affection to heaven, when you forget yourself to spend your strength in promoting the happiness of others, in every blessed moment that

26. Matthew 27:62–65.
27. Matthew 28:2–4.
28. Matthew 28:20.
29. Mark 16:19.
30. I Peter 2:21.

you resist and overcome the temptations of the world in the pure hope of
becoming more like to our Master, more acceptable in the eye of God,—in that
moment be assured, his heart goes with you, his gentle spirit commends you; he
sees that you acknowledge him on earth and he shall acknowledge you before
his Father in Heaven.[31]

31. Matthew 10:32 and Luke 12:8.

VI

Believe in the Lord your God
so shalt you be established.

II Chronicles 20:20

We are the changing inhabitants of a changing world. The night and the day, the ebbing and flowing of the tide, the round of the seasons, the waxing and waning moon, the flux and reflux of the arts and of the civilization of nations, and the swift and sad succession of human generations—these are the monitors among which we live. The lands that are now tilled by man, were once the bed of the sea and regions that formerly were covered with the harvests and the cities of men are lost under the waters of the ocean. The world that looks so fair and substantial to the eye is found to be unsubstantial. The ground on which we stand is passing away under our feet. Decay, decay is written on every leaf of the forest, on every mountain, on every monument of art. Every wind that passes is loaded with the solemn sound. All things perish,—all are the partakers of this general doom—but man is the chief victim, the prominent mark, at which all arrows are aimed. In the lines of his countenance it is written that he is dying, in a language, which we can all understand. Alas, my friends, we have but to look each other in the face and observe the rapid alterations which a year, a month, yea, one hour has wrought there to see how fast these animal juices are drying up, these blood vessels failing, the nerves paralyzed, that gave activity to the functions of the frame. Beautiful youth does not see in itself how it should grow grisly and old. But ye who have youth and beauty, are older since you came to the Church and must learn that the fruit of man, like the fruit of the ground, withers as it ripens. Love and vanity may flatter you that your eye has lost none of its light, that your skin retains its vermilion tint, but love and vanity cannot flatter long. You who suspect these dull admonitions when you feel the blood

---

Draft notes in *JMN* 3:72 and 3:78 show that the sermon was begun as early as February 4, 1827, at which time Emerson had a different text in mind (Psalms 112:7). Preached thirteen times: July 8, 1827, at the First Church, Boston; July 22 in Concord, Mass.; October 7 in Deerfield; October 14 in Northampton; November 11 in New Bedford (the Preaching Record erroneously gives November 13); November 25 in Harvard, Mass. (the Preaching Record erroneously gives November 27); December 9 in Watertown; December 30 in Concord, N.H.; January 27, 1828, at the Federal Street Church; February 10 in Waltham; April 6 in Lexington; August 10 at the Second Church, Boston; and April 11, 1830, again at the Second Church.

leaping joyfully in the vessels of life—alas! you have soon to learn that the destiny of man is given to sterner commissioners than vanity and love. It is a vain task to strive against this universal fate. It sweeps us on, young and old, pure and impure, the well known and the unknown; it sweeps us on—day by day and hour by hour into the land of silence. There is no remorse, no exception, no reprieve. A few months more and it will be the turn of the first and last of us. We regret when each of our successive birthdays arrive, the manhood we are losing, the youth we have lost. We dislike to be numbered among those to whom we have hitherto turned our eyes with a feeling of self congratulation in the superiority of our fortune. It was an advantage acknowledged that we were young. It is gone. You were in the last ranks of the procession of the living; all the ground was yet before you; and the example of ten thousand predecessors might teach you to perform your march with a decency and dignity which they had never exhibited. But the host moves on; it never halts; already, new thousands behind you, are treading on your steps; you are in the midst, you are in the foreground of the host; you will soon stand at the gates into which enter all the travellers of that innumerable caravan—the gates of the tomb.[1]

Is there any limit fixed to this unceasing fluctuation, to this unintermitting decay? Hope is ardent in the bosom of man in youth, in middle age, and we well know there is no bound to the schemes which we have laid out, the outlines we have traced, on the broad and lighted sky of the future. But has the hope of any of us dared to overpass the everlasting lines of human destiny? Will not the future be as the past? Are we chartered with any exemption from the evils of life? Have we brought in our hands any safe conduct to show to Pain and Death, our ghastly enemies? Shall we not, my brethren, be *sufferers*, as all our fathers were? shall not we be sick? shall we not die? Consider a moment the changes that may, that must, be made by any assignable period of coming time. What vicissitudes will mark the course of the next twenty years? It is not much time whilst it passes, or when it is remembered; but it is much of life. And he who shall come up to this church, as we have come this day, to pay his duty to the unchangeable God, when that period of time shall have elapsed, believe me, my friends, he will find few of us here. He shall look round in vain for the elder part of this congregation; he shall look in vain for most of those who are in middle life, for most of those who are young. Twenty years will have brought children to manhood, dismissed them from the paternal roof, and sent them out in all the paths of adventure on the land and the sea and in different regions of the globe; will have changed the smooth cheek of youth to the careful complexion of men and matrons; will have wiped out of their memories those images that now are familiar and delightful; will have taken its enchantment from the dance and the song; will have undeceived a thousand hopes; will have undone a thousand advantages; to some of the young it will break the cloud that now hangs

1. "We are the changing . . . tomb": see *JMN* 3:72–74. For "innumerable caravan," see William Cullen Bryant, "Thanatopsis," line 74.

over their prospects; it will give friends, and health, and prosperity, and esteem; and some of them it will bereave of health, and friends, and prosperity, and esteem, and life. Some of us who are already mature, twenty years will make old. It will make some that are poor rich, and make rich men poor. It will have cooled our friendships; it will have taken from us those who are sitting by our side, our parents and equals; it will change their countenances and send them away. Twenty years will have fixed characters that now are forming, and will have blasted characters that are established. That time will have wrought strange and unlooked for and all undesired alterations on ourselves. Those who now have come up to this house, in the easy enjoyment of health and vigor— their senses acute, their understandings powerful, their prospects pleasing or proud, who rise up now, and go whithersoever they would, behold! the time cometh, when they shall stretch forth their hands, and another shall lead them, and carry them whither they would not.[2] Each of those years shall do upon us its appointed office of change and injury; one shall furrow the countenance; another dim the eye; another shut the ears; another break the spirits; another stretch you helpless and hopeless on your bed, to be visited with wasting pains; to count the weary days and the loitering months which pass over you, and bring no joy upon their wings. These are the outward changes that this period will effect. But o! my friends, there are greater changes than these. He that shall come up and visit our places when so many years are gone, will miss many of us who are not to be found in other churches, or on foreign lands, or yet on restless beds of pain in their own houses, but whose bodies have been laid at rest in their lonely shrouds, and who have left this world forever. Twenty years, my brethren, will carry *many* of us,—it may be, the *most*,—very possibly, *all* of us into the world of souls, and to the throne of God, will bear us to what bewildering scenes! will disclose to us what overpowering magnificence of moral and intellectual nature! will show what eye hath not seen nor the highest imagination dared yet to whisper to mortal ears,[3] will explain the dark parable of human existence, the reasons of our afflictions and the mysteries of Providence.

Or if any of us whose days are numbered are conscious that we have listened in the past and that at present we listen to the whispers of a sordid interest, of merciless selfishness, of appetites which ought to be governed, of sloth, and pride, wo, wo unto us, my brethren, for the tremendous discoveries that are before us. Twenty years shall teach us that awful and everlasting connexion which the Most High has formed between misery and vice; shall turn those secret fears which we desperately defied to sad and fatal realities of suffering.

But we are pursuing too far this train of thought. It leads us away from our design. The vicissitudes that have now been alluded to are such as touch only ourselves. The same inexorable law is extended to all the inhabitants of our country, to the whole generation of which we are a part. It reaches to all the

2. John 21:18.
3. Cf. I Corinthians 2:9.

works of man. It reaches to all the works of God. The stars that were known and counted by the elder Astronomer are not now found in their place. Change and decay found them out in their far and silent steeps, and they have fallen through the abysses of night. In short, wherever there is matter, there is mutation. One alteration begets another, and man, the observer of all, feels himself afflicted with the same evil he laments. It is a question which arises with great force in our minds whenever we turn our thoughts to these melancholy images of progressive ruin, whither we shall go for refuge, what rock, what rampart is left, behind which we may retire, and feel safe? What is the natural relief which man possesses to keep him from growing giddy whilst he gazes on these turning wheels of nature?

There is obviously but one immoveable support, but one consolation to our fear, and that is in the idea of God, in the belief of an overruling Providence. It was feelingly said by the Psalmist in the view of the good man at ease whilst others were tormented by fears of change, whilst he listened to the report coming from all the objects in the world: He shall not be afraid of evil tidings; his heart is fixed, trusting in the Lord.[4] The firm conviction founded on the study of the works and the word of God, that there is above us a Being of immutable perfections, who made us for purposes of infinite benevolence and by whose everlasting law these changes of nature that disturb us subsist—this conviction lays the tempest in the breast and soothes the soul into a holy calm and confidence. But the belief in God and his Providence does not end here. He that has learned this will learn more. He will learn that if there be a God who made us, who upholds this system of things in which we stand, he has not forsaken his fair creation; He has not retreated into some pavilion of glory, some distant heaven of majesty on high, whence he beholds *from afar*, the doings and the fortunes of his creatures, but that he is at hand; that he is, at every moment, the present source of life and action, that in him, in literal truth, his children live, move, and have their being;[5] that without him, we should perish; that we do not lift our hands without his imparted strength; that he orders this vicissitude of things; that in the wildest commotion, in the swiftest decay, his sovereign will controls the active elements and sets bounds to their overflowing force, which they cannot pass. My friends, this position is not rashly taken. Despite the crude and unconvincing sophistry that has sometimes imposed on studious men of a doubting temper, the signatures of the Author of nature are too strongly stamped on his workmanship to be overlooked. Leave men to themselves and they always return to this wonderful idea of a God. Teach them, especially, to be good, which is bringing them near to God, and be assured they will not be long in discerning the Divinity. However we may turn our faces against him, somewhere in the Universe is its maker. Somewhere in the Universe, we must meet the truth, though now we may deny or defy it. Some

4. Psalms 112:7.
5. Acts 17:28.

account there must be of your existence, the existence of the soul in this state of discipline; some account of this well adjusted balance of good and evil; some foundation to this prodigious mixed empire of virtue, reason, and the passions over the general mind of man. Here or elsewhere, in some corner of the immensity of space in some one memory, in some bright intelligence is chronicled the annals of man; some history of the origin, and preservation of society; some knowledge of the destiny, which in the immense future, impends over it; some significant inscription of the name and character of Him, who led us up here into life, to see his works and inquire of his name. Somewhere we shall meet a Being who, though high and omnipotent, is yet our near companion on the way of existence, who protects us by his power and imparts of his power to us the ability to do right or to do wrong.

And now in reference to the idea of God let this distinction be strongly made, that the changes which we have been remarking belong but to one part of our nature, belong to matter, and not to mind. Our bodies were made of the dust of the ground, but our minds were made in the likeness of God.[6] All that is material is dissolved. The Sun himself shall grow old and dim, the face of the earth is changed, but what is related to God, our mind, our moral nature, does not grow old. God, my brethren, does not grow old and our minds which were made in his image do not grow old. Thoughts never lose their immortal youth. Moral truth does not grow old. The gospel of Jesus Christ has gathered no decrepitude from the weight of ages. I appeal to those who have gone in the hour of deep affliction to its venerable oracles; who have stood over the grave of virtue and piety, and have yielded themselves to the religious associations of the place; I appeal to them whether they found the remembered conversations of the Lord powerless and cold? or whether in the view of his meek but sublime character, the world, to which they were returning, did not lose somewhat of its imposing shew? Humility, temperance, love, faith, purity, lose none of their force to please and to purify by the lapse of years, because time does not touch the soul or what belongs to the soul. The soul was made in a higher element. It breathes already the air of eternity. Faith in God, my friends, will not suffer by time. "Believe in the Lord your God, so shall you be established." Let me beseech you, then, to withdraw your affections from the fading objects of this world, which, as we have seen, do hourly waste and decay, and which shall involve in their destruction the destruction of your happiness which was united to them, (for where your treasure is there will your heart be also) and turn to that which is indestructible.[7]

"Choose you this day whom you will serve";[8] whether you will prefer this slippery hope and attach your affections, your exertions, your being, to the pursuit of riches and pleasures, to dust and ashes, or whether you will ascend above these shadows and join yourself to the high and infinite and imperishable

6. Genesis 2:7, 1:26.
7. Matthew 6:20-21 and Luke 12:33-34.
8. Joshua 24:15.

and almighty, form an acquaintance with spiritual things, acquire love of truth
and love of duty. Then, shall you look down from a serene height on the storm
and commotion of the world below; with pity, on men in the bondage of passion; with courage, on the changes which menace your mortal part. Then shall
you stand fast though the mountain be removed. Then shall you go in peace,
down the vale of years, yes and walk unappalled through the valley of the
shadow of death, unhurt and immortal.[9] For you shall have united yourself by a
purifying faith to the Divinity; you have walked on earth with God in sublime
companionship; and death, which releases the spirit from its prison of clay,
shall only render more intimate that blessed connexion.

A celebrated English preacher whose praise is in our churches closed his
discourse with a bold appeal which the fervour of his eloquence permitted to
the passions and imagination of his hearers.[10] He pointed their mind's eyes to
the Recording angel who waited on the wing in the midst of the assembly to
write down some name of all that multitude in his book of Life. "And shall he
wait in vain?" he said, "and will you let him take his departure for heaven
without making him the witness of a single soul converted from his sins?" My
friends, we know that his sentiment was but a flight of oratory, natural enough
to a fervid spirit, and which the urgency of the occasion might excuse. My
friends, no Recording Angel that we know of, hovers over our assembly, but a
greater than an angel is here. There is One in the midst of *us*, though our eyes
see him not, who is not a fictitious or imaginary being, but who is too great and
too glorious for our eyes to bear. There is One here imparting to us the life and
sense we at this moment exercise, whose tremendous power heaved on high the
rolling globes of the Universe and upholds them and us. You cannot discern him
with the gross orbs of sight, but can you not feel the weight of His presence
sinking on your heart? Does no conscious feeling stir in your bosoms under the
eye of your Author, under the eye of God, who is here? He, who is everywhere
present, He, without whose unceasing aid we should drop at once from life and
motion, shall He walk unhonoured amid the congregation of his worshippers?
Let us feel his presence, let us hasten to acknowledge the Almighty mind. He
searches the hearts of his servants.[11] He seeth in secret,[12] and must be worshipped in spirit and in truth. He reads the thoughts and purposes with which
we came up here to his temple. He detects the first rising resolution that points
toward virtue. He hears the first faint sigh of penitent recollection. My friends,
what doth he see here? Does the eye of the Divinity fall on hearts cold as
marble to the influences of his spirit? on selfish and worldly minds which hear
his name as a customary word without disturbing a moment's ease; without

9. Psalms 46:2 and 23:4.
10. Perhaps Philip Doddridge (1702–1751), the author of *The Rise and Progress of Religion in
the Soul* (London, 1745). See *JMN* 1:324.
11. "A celebrated English preacher . . . servants": see *JMN* 2:303–4. Compare the last sentence
with I Chronicles 28:9 and Romans 8:27.
12. Cf. Matthew 6:4, 6:6, 6:18.

shaking one evil intention; without kindling one solitary hope that his mercy will save us from our sins and open heaven to our dying eyes?[13] Standing here in His awful Presence, as the Ambassador of his goodness and the disciple of his Son, let me beseech you to let your lives exhibit your belief on his name and to show this living faith that shall teach men whose we are, and on whom we trust; that shall guide us innocent through the strong temptations of the world, and present us holy and unblameable at the bar of judgment.

13. Cf. Shakespeare, *I Henry VI*, III, iii, 48.

VII

The Sabbath was made for man.

MARK 2:27

We are assembled, my brethren, on another of the Lord's days to worship Him in his house. We solemnize no new holy day, we set up no new institution. We celebrate an ancient festival. We are renewing time-hallowed rites which our forefathers paid in the land, and their fathers in elder countries from which they came. Nor are we alone in what we do. Our countrymen in a hundred cities, in a thousand villages, through all the wide tracts of American civilization from the shores of the Ocean back to the borders of the forest, with one accord are repairing to the church with like intent as ourselves. I need not remind you how much wider the same institution is spread. This day wheresoever the sun in his course visits the children of civilization even to the farthest islands, the people have rested from their labours and the priest is lifting his hands towards heaven. Even the sailor on the barren seas by the custom of nations rests from unnecessary toil. It is, (with all the deductions which the state of the world requires to be made,) in some sort, the jubilee of our globe.

But, my friends, there are circumstances well known to us all in the state of society among us that often force on the mind of the preacher an unwelcome doubt as to the justness and truth of the views entertained on this subject by his Christian brethren. Of the great primary fact on which this worship and all religion depends, that there is a God to whom we stand in the relation of creatures—there is no ignorance. No, the great name of God is upon every tongue. Not a nation, not a tribe in the desert or amid savage mountains, but have found out his name, not a heart in all the barbarous ages but had attained the conception of Deity and Providence. But whilst men know his name, they sometimes know no more. There is an astonishing reluctance to the labor of thought. They take the received ideas of God and finding a form existing in society appropriated to his worship, they quietly slide into the track which is laid already and plead to themselves, that they have satisfied all the demands of duty. They do not, therefore, feel as they ought the personal obligation which

Preached nine times: July 15, 1827, at the First Church, Boston; July 22, in Concord, Mass.; September 16 in Greenfield; September 23 in Deerfield; October 21 in Northampton; March 9, 1828, in Waltham; April 6 in Lexington; June 22 in Concord, N.H.; and March 22, 1829, at the Second Church, Boston.

should bind men (let me say) to the *punctilious* observance of the Lord's day. They are satisfied with a general respect, but leave undone without remorse, the duty of meditation and prayer, and, with slight apology, the attendance on church.

It is important that we hold right views of the obligation of the observance of the Sabbath. An institution so prominent as this is over all the civilized world and answering so powerfully as it does the ends it was designed to promote—I mean the preservation of religion in the world—certainly deserves our attention. And then it is to some men the day from which all that is good and great in their existence dates; the day on whose tidings, eternity depends; the day which gives its colour to all other days, or, if not, all other days seem, in a measure, to be lost. I trust then we shall not lose the time which is devoted to an examination of the moral obligation that binds us to regard the Lord's day. It may be defended as a ceremonial institution; but not entering at present this discussion I conceive that if its cause were faithfully pleaded, only on the ground of expediency, no man could escape the sovereign voice with which conscience would command him to pay regard to the religious duties of the day. I beg your attention to the subject not now as involving the honor of God, or any question of obedience to his written Law, but I speak as to good men, desirous to consult the welfare of man, the prosperity of the State, the wellbeing of your children. I desire to offer to your notice a few of those particulars in which, according to the language of our benevolent master, the Sabbath was made for Man.

I. The Sabbath was made for Man, firstly, as a *day of rest.* A day of rest, for the body and the mind. When the decree had gone forth "thou shalt eat thy bread in the sweat of thy brow, all the days of thy life,"[1] there needed this beneficent institution, this relief to the children of toil and sorrow, of one day of repose in seven. It is too obvious to need to be discussed, the advantage of the Sabbath in this respect; it will need no recommendation to those whose lot has made the six days, days of labor, and whom an unseasonable covetousness and ill judged industry has not led to invade with new cares this season of rest. Indeed even in the view of a minute economy, the vigour and refreshment gained to man and to beast by this repose, is found to make the subtraction thus made from time of profitable occupation no loss but an advantage. I pass, at once, to the second consideration.

II. The Sabbath was made for man as an *opportunity for moral and intellectual improvement.* From the condition of our nature, it happens that the great majority of men are immersed in daily labor for daily bread. But when these wants are supplied is the measure of duty and existence full? Or have we not been told in the books of religion, or in the secret whispers of our own consciousness that we are *moral* beings; that this animal frame, whose appetites we so studiously consult, is only the clothing, the minister of a soul which is the nobler nature, and whose benefit all the order of things in God's creation does

1. Cf. Genesis 3:19.

chiefly seem to regard. Obviously, then, something more is necessary than this daily diligence in our vocation—for the training a human soul to a fitness for heaven. If no respite were afforded from this returning drudgery, where should the spirit feel her freedom? where acquire her relish for immortal thoughts? where be excited to that love of knowledge, that impatient thirst for improvement, that ardent looking for the infinite and eternal, which it needs to prepare it for its future affinity with disembodied minds? Its present narrowed walk will not educate him to this. I know it may be said, and justly, that such is the nature of moral goodness that its greatest triumphs may be and not unfrequently are disclosed on the humblest theatre; that the sublimest virtue sometimes glows in cottages; that all the charities of life may be shewn in the shop and the workyard as well as in temples and senates; that all the rules and offices of religion are as applicable to an humble and obscure life as to one of greatest employment. It is true, and chiefly true because of the beneficent influence of the Christian Sabbath. But if this gift of God should fall into neglect, if it were taken away from the use of men, I fear it would soon be felt that there was a want of its natural element in which the virtuous affections could expand. Unrespited bodily labour would become peevish and melancholy. There would be little seen of the aspiring spirit in the poor drudge bending over his exacted task. These dreary labors were a strange preparation for heaven. It were like chaining a slave to the oar to train him for a statesman. Without such an institution as the sabbath, it is true, they who had wealth and lettered leisure, might still cultivate those arts and studies which are the glory of men, but the great bulk of the community would waste and corrupt in their bondage of ignorance. Their increasing moral inferiority in society would beget a dangerous malignity toward the other classes in the state. They would become

> "A savage horde among the civilized,
> A servile band among the lordly free."[2]

It is not easy to estimate too highly the value of the Sabbath in this respect. In bringing together the highest and the lowest citizen, in making the latter feel the sublimity of the distinctions which Religion enforces, in the view of which the gradations of human society are wholly effaced; but above all in the soothing, reforming, elevating efficacy of the Religion itself, which is here explained, which teaches men how to live and how to die, and which insists on repentance from sin, and purity of life as the sole conditions of everlasting happiness.

III. The Sabbath was made as an *interruption and a diversion from the business of the week*. It is a peculiarity of our nature very well known to you and which your daily experience may attest that whatever object the mind pursues without intermission, it has a continual tendency to magnify. Whatever that object may be, whether great or small, whether worthy or unworthy, as a

2. William Wordsworth, "The Excursion," IX, 309-10.

favourite science, a peculiar view of religion, a person beloved, riches, music, or a political party, the eye of the mind makes it the central point of the picture of life, and learns to consider all other things merely in relation to this idol of the affections, merely as helping or hurting the effect or the interest of this. That recurring idea becomes the sole principle of association, the thread on which all others are strung, and very soon assumes in our imagination a disproportioned magnitude by whose side all other pretensions dwindle into disregard. When, from any nobleness of nature in the individual, or from happy education, it happens, that the object pursued is really great, and such as to justify any degree of devotion, we entirely approve his enthusiasm. Thus nothing is greater in just sentiment than St. Paul's dedication of himself to the Gospel of Christ. Nothing do men regard with more complacence as respectable and beautiful than a patriot surrendering himself body and soul to the achievement of the deliverance or the exaltation of his country. Nothing more respectable than the entire self-devotion of a Wilberforce to the cause of African liberty.[3]

But when this oneness of purpose is disgraced by the object, when the object is a low appetite or passion, as eating or drinking or gain or sleep, then this very disposition of our nature we are treating becomes, like all other perverted goods, an instrument of dishonor and mischief. We then feel pity and disgust for the man of only one design, for the glutton, for the drunkard, for the miser, and the sluggard. Even when the object is not dishonourable, but simply not elevated, we feel that there is an inequality, a deformity in the mind capable of an absorbing regard to one pursuit. It strikes the eye as a species of insanity—as Timothy Alden exploring the Continent for Epitaphs.[4] Now, my friends, to beings like us who are set in this world merely for a moral discipline, merely that we may be educated as in a school for the pursuits and events of our *after-existence*, the great, the immeasurable eternity which awaits us,—in beings with these hopes, it does appear a species of insanity, the contracting our thoughts and efforts within any sordid and selfish round; the devoting to the getting of meats and drinks, powers which can comprehend the laws of nature; the circumscribing within the narrow compass of one professional pursuit, or the sphere of one little neighbourhood of cares, anxieties, and expectations,— affections which were made with a force and a reach sufficient to embrace the whole human family, the unseen agents of the invisible world, and God our Father in Heaven. That this is a danger which growing out of the constitution of the mind itself infests every day the walks of life; which is likely to hamper the mind of each of us in those particular pursuits which belong to each, there can be no doubt. We have commented on this folly in others. We may find the rudiments of this evil in ourselves.

Now what is the antidote provided against this endemic disorder by him who

3. William Wilberforce (1759-1833); "Mr Wilberforce never speaks in Brit. Parliament but for Slaves" (*JMN* 2:400).

4. Timothy Alden (1771-1839), author of *A Collection of American Epitaphs and Inscriptions*, 5 vols. (New York, 1814).

foresaw all the exigences of the race he had planted in the earth? It is the Sabbath. A day subtracted from busy life, regularly returning at short intervals, and sacred to services widely different from our secular concerns. It is a break in that series of thoughts apt to run with immoderate strength in a single direction. It found the mind on duty amid grovelling earthborn cares; it summoned it off to services agreeable to its highest nature, calling thereby into exercise those sovereign parts of the soul that are apt to lie sluggish and passive in the lower labours of six days. It called us away from our various callings to furnish us with an idea proper and worthy to absorb the soul. The mind has then answered its grand and full design when it loses itself in the contemplation of God.

It was not merely an interruption but a diversion also, and likely to be more powerful just in proportion to the strength of each man's mind. It demands attention to glorious and commanding objects. It leads men up out of the low ground in which they have been dwelling, to a high moral elevation,—to a point of observation like the Mountain of Pisgah of the ancient prophet, from whence they may behold undisturbed the wide-lying landscape of the past and the future, may measure what has been done and what remains to do, may look forward to that shadowy valley wherein terminate all the roads of life, and descry beyond the dim and solemn magnificence of other worlds towering in the distance.5

I trust that my words find some echo in your breasts. My brethren, I trust that we have all at some time experienced this wholesome effect. Has that propitious hour never illuminated your life, when you found your spirit under the strong persuasion of God's word in his holy sanctuary rejecting with inward delight the unsatisfying labours and pleasures which it abandoned on this day for better thoughts? When your faculties have been here awakened to the study of that purpose to life which you had well nigh forgotten in the bustle of daily care, when God has disclosed himself to you in the thoughts of the mind,—has not the perishing world, and all that it contains, seemed to ebb away from the constant soul;—mortal things to withdraw themselves as a curtain from the immortal things which they had intercepted? has not virtue stood manifest in immutable beauty? has not the memory found a new home in the life and lessons of Jesus Christ? Has not conscience called you to a life of unblameable integrity? Has not hope opened to your vision the everlasting heavens?

In short have you not been enlightened, consoled, purified by this diversion of your thoughts? Has not this world appeared less imposing? its pursuits, your daily care, have they not shrunk from that gigantic aspect they wore but yesterday, and revealed themselves to you in the true proportions which they hold in the view of wise and pious men, in the view of angels, in the view of God, *means* and not *ends*, appearing a small and insignificant part of human life, and not the absorbing centre, the main design?

5. "a point of observation . . . distance": see *JMN* 3:9. For Pisgah, see Deuteronomy 34:1.

These are some of the more striking respects in which the Sabbath was made for man. Its perfect adaptation to his wants is strongly evinced by that firm hold it has kept on society in all the fluctuations of human opinion.

Reason, as it was miscalled, has had her reign. The insane voice of Atheism has been heard in the world, and yet, blessed be God, on this day we still hear the sweet sound of the Sabbath bells. They do not now deafen to men the voice of feeling and philanthropy nor stun the ear that hears them with the austere knell of supernatural malice and dread. It is now many centuries that they have impelled every Sabbath morn the train of solemn associations in the minds of all civilized men. It is a blessed office they have done. It was a useful service even when they summoned men to the gloomy chapels of ascetic penance and to the accusing eloquence of the Genevan Church. In ages when 'the voice of the laws could not be heard for the din of arms,'[6] and public opinion was diffident or misguided, under the leading of dissolute feudal captains, vice was admonished by the knell from the tower of the monastery. It recalled to men's minds the terrible images of a dark theology. It has been thought that the rude and super-stitious views of religion held in the darker ages were better suited to the general ignorance, more fitted to repress crime than juster views would have been. Juster views could not then have been generally taken. Men who were unable to understand the religious feelings of Fénelon, of Newton, and of Locke would yet be alarmed by the preaching of St. Bernard, of St. Dominic, and of Calvin, of Knox, and Melanchthon.[7] It was then a rude remedy for a rude disorder. With all the instruments sacred in man's associations, these too have changed their tone to be the organ of his altered feelings. Their peal is not now terrible; today their sound is sweet in the ears of men, and it is no disagreeable intrusion that interrupts the business of life with the dear and solemn hope of better worlds. I pray Heaven they may never be hushed; that the impatience of prejudices and the mad pride of heart that lurks under the laudable love of knowledge may never assail the venerable institutions of Christianity; that Civilization may not shoot out into conceit and in overstrained taste, and a refinement beyond nature, sacrifice or risque in any reprobate day, that pure creative principle to which the triumphs of Reason owe themselves,—Man's hope of salvation. Then those bells which have been the music of Revelation through centuries, in their final notes, shall bewail the downfal of the last hope of humanity, and seem to warn the world of impending ruin when the great safeguards of human society, the love and fear and worship of God, are broken down and removed.

God forbid, my friends, that such a crisis should impend over us; God in his mercy avert so dark a calamity from our country which he has signalized by

6. Caius Marius [Emerson's note]; i.e., Gaius Marius (157–86 B.C.). Quoted in Plutarch's "Life of Gaius Marius," in *The Lives*, ed. John and William Langhorne (New York, 1822), 3:157.

7. François de Salignac de la Mothe-Fénelon (1651–1715), Archbishop of Cambray and author of *Télémaque;* Sir Isaac Newton (1642–1727); John Locke (1632–1704); St. Bernard of Clairvaux (1091–1153), opponent of Peter Abelard and founder of the Cistercian order; St. Dominic (1170–1221), founder of the Dominican order; John Calvin (1509–1564); John Knox (1505–1572); Philip Melanchthon (1497–1560), associate of Martin Luther.

glorious virtue and glorious fortune. Not in this land let the Sabbath be dishonoured; not here whither his pure servants, the great men of God in another age, fled for his sake, for the Sabbath's sake, to found an empire in the primitive forest where they might keep their sacred hours in the beauty of Holiness.[8] The men from whom it is our well grounded boast that we descend were men of no fading renown, of no easy ambition, but stern self-denying Christians who knew that they bore the future destinies of men in their righteous hands, who braved the ocean and the desart and the savage and famine for conscience' sake confiding in the blessing of Heaven on their cause, confiding that the Fathers' God would visit in mercy the children to the third and fourth generation,[9] that a little one would become a thousand and a handful a great nation. They despised, they feared, the degenerate effeminacy which excuses healthy men from the duties of the altar because the day is cold or the streets are wet, because the east wind blows or the hour of prayer is unseasonable. They called the Sabbath a delight, the holy of the Lord, honourable, and did not their own works, and sought not their own pleasure nor followed their own thoughts.[10] These were the venerable auspices in which the foundations of our civil institutions were laid and a pious eye, my friends, will see in this history the causes of that all unrivalled prosperity with which Providence has visited their children's children. Here, then, my friends, it should lose no portion of its honour. You owe it to all those who in all the past have given their strength to the support of these religious institutions, the direct effect of which has been that degree of public and private morality from which you now derive the most sensible advantages. You owe it to them to contribute the solemn sanction of all your influence to the holy keeping of the Sabbath day. You owe it to the good of all ages and nations that you should signify your approval of what they have done and suffered in the cause of virtue by bearing your part also in your day and generation. You owe it to your fathers who purchased at so dear a price the unexampled advantages of your condition. You owe it to your children not to defraud them of happiness in this world and an immortal hope in the world to come. You owe it to yourselves to use this golden talent aright as you would be accepted when you render up your account hereafter.[11]

8. Cf. I Chronicles 16:29 and Psalms 29:2.
9. Cf. Exodus 20:5, 34:7.
10. Isaiah 58:13.
11. Cf. the parable of the talents, Matthew 25.

VIII

God is love.

I JOHN 4:16

It has been well remarked that Christianity is a progressive religion. It seems to have been but imperfectly understood in the first ages of the Church, being seen by the Jews with Jewish eyes, and by the other converts with those prejudices which belonged to their several conditions before they embraced the new faith. It was only darkly seen in those ignorant Middle Ages so emphatically known as the night of the world. And when Europe recovered from her stupor, and threw back in the astonishment of her first resurrection the graveclothes of superstition wherein she had lain bound, Christianity only grew brighter as the dogmas and institutes under which men had disguised it were one after another stripped off and consumed. And, ever since, whilst men in the progress of civilization have been outgrowing the barbarous usages that encumbered the early advancement of the human mind, Christianity has all along kept pace with or kept in advance of its course. The application of a clearer sighted reason to the religion of Christ, has only recommended it the more to the love and admiration of wise and thoughtful men.

But whilst we acknowledge in this fact a valuable signature of its divine Author, we have to lament a disadvantage under which we labour compared with the primitive believers; namely, the circumstance that we derive our religion through the impure channels of less enlightened ages, and it comes to us tainted and discoloured by the soil through which it has flowed. The language of theology, that important part of language in which man's relations and duties are expressed, partakes of the times from whence it has descended; it is gross and erroneous; it is human and bigoted. It slowly accommodates itself to the needs of the times, and does most sadly and unworthily misrepresent the noble truths of which it is the organ. It has cast a mist of deformity around the beautiful image of truth, which, could men see, they would be struck at once with reverence and love. It has shrouded in terrible clouds the benign majesty of God. It charged his government with decrees that shock our inborn sense of

Preached eight times: July 29, 1827, at the First Church, Boston; October 21 in Northampton; November 13 in New Bedford; December 16 at the Purchase Street Church; December 30 in Concord, N.H.; May 9, 1828 (Friday Lecture), in Concord, Mass.; September 14 at the Second Church, Boston; and November 22, 1829, again at the Second Church.

right. It clothed the heavenly heroism, the lowly obedience, of Christ in a garb of wild fable, that if it could command belief would unsettle the understanding. Every page of the history of the Church is full of these melancholy errors.

I believe, my friends, that religion has suffered great violence from popular misapprehension. I speak not of what has occurred in any remote age or nation but of this day and this hour. It is a cause of regret that it wears a repulsive aspect in the eye of men. I believe that when men sin they know not what they do. I believe if it were seen how full of beauty and delight a religious life really is, it would not be necessary to charge it on men as a burdensome duty, it would only be necessary to open the doors of the Christian Church, and they would come in. (It is the divine property of moral truth that it continually opens new revelations to the eye. No man gives himself to a virtuous life but finds new pleasures in his course and wonders that another can be blind to their beauty.) It is not new to you this sentiment of regret that men should reject what appears so attractive. The cause of it is to be explored in the incorrect views of religion and mainly in the incorrect views of God that prevail in the world.

It seems to me that the idea of God, which grows up so naturally in the human mind in every condition,—that this idea has lost its original brightness in the common mind.[1] There is a kind of irrelevance, or (let me speak out,) a kind of impertinence felt in introducing the name of God and our relations to God in mixed conversation. It arrests at once, and this among good men, the genial flow of social entertainment. It creates an uneasiness in many breasts as if a rebuke had been intended, or as if the speaker were a pharisee who would assume some arrogance of spiritual pride. It would seem that men are afraid of God; that they are daunted, as if some enemy had been unseasonably named in the hour of joy. It has also happened that some classes of Christians observing this phenomenon have too hastily drawn from it a pernicious inference that there is naturally in the human mind a hostility to the Author of its being. Whatever account is to be given of the appearance, this ominous doctrine, at least, cannot stand. It is surely easier to believe that we are the production of a blind chance than it is to represent to reason the Deity, a being of infinite wisdom, sitting in the Heavens and combining the sublime elements and powers of a human mind and finishing his work by imprinting an indwelling and invincible aversion to himself in the immortal agent.

Now with regard to the fact, it must be plain that if right views of God should ever become popular views men would be ashamed and astonished at these feelings. It needs only that men should duly consider what must be the character of that Being who did not only make us with beneficent designs, but made us what we are, gave us this power of receiving delight from the eye and the ear and all the senses, and supplied the senses, those eager searchers after happiness, with abundant gratification. It was not accident, nor education, it was nature, it was God, that taught our minds how to receive pleasure from the

1. Milton, *Paradise Lost*, I, 592.

gentle play of the social affections; from daily and domestic charities; from the exercise of the fancy and the wit; that opened our taste to the beauty of fine conversation; that imparted this delicate discrimination to detect the latent charm of masterpieces in the arts; who attuned the ear to music and to eloquence. Now is it not just to judge this Artist by his works? He that made the eye shall he not see?[2] He that made us cheerful and hopeful is he a vindictive and melancholy Potentate brooding in the solitude over the immeasurable vengeance his red right arm can inflict?[3] He who made the heart of childhood overflow with laughter; who consoled the breast of youth under the intellectual and mechanical toil so necessary for the development of the youthful moral agent; who consoled this toil by the flow of inexhaustible spirits so that its refreshing presence should every where be felt as a stimulus to the exhausted, a tonic to the paralyzed affections—Is He, the Giver of all, indeed a dread and dangerous Being towards whom our gratitude must ever take a tinge of terror?

Again. Consider under what character is he disclosed to us in the distribution and composition of the forms of unintelligent matter? Who is it that moulded the globe in his hollow hand?[4] Who is it that gave the Sun his commandment and adjusted the stupendous forces of the planets to that delicate law which keeps the Seasons in their mighty round decorating the green earth with the blooms of spring; renovating life with the atmosphere, the heat, and the fruits of summer; calling man with the almost articulate voice of the autumn winds, to pensive meditation; and curbing the too exhausted expenditure of the forces of the soil and of the cultivator by the cold of winter, and leaving the ground fallow under its crust of snow? Who is it that sends out the morning in such festal pomp, and pours the day spring over lake and field and river, glittering under the sunbeam until the eye of the pious beholder is dazzled, and his heart overflowed with the glorious beauty? Who is it that arched the storm with his coloured bow? that hung the mountains with their magnificent drapery of cloud? Who is it that sends down the night in its beauty and takes off the bright veil of the garish day from the glowing, adoring firmament?

Did the Being who has done all this design that men, for whom he has done it, should dread or should love him?

Or if we consider him in the light wherein revelation exhibits him, as full of pity for the sinfulness of his human family when groping for the walk of duty with the glimmering lamp of reason, He sent into the world a herald of his love in a modest guise befitting the Divinity whose sovereign care is Mind.

Not enveloped in clouds of thunder and flame, not charioted by troops of angry cherubim from the abodes of his Father's majesty, but born in peace and humility in the manger of an inn. Thus even from his cradle in Bethlehem is taught that lesson of such vital importance to their welfare that though man

2. Psalms 94:9.
3. Cf. Henry Kirke White, "The Lord our God is Lord of all," line 15, and Milton, *Paradise Lost*, II, 174.
4. Cf. Isaiah 40:12.

regards the body, the outward circumstance, God only regards the purpose and the mind. This in fact was the very message which the Son of Man brought into the world, which was thus intimated in the advent. He came to point out to men the capital error of human nature, namely that shortsightedness that mistakes the nearest for the greatest object, and conceives that to be good on the whole which is seen to offer a particular good.

But do these marks of deep interest in our fate betray any character in God but benignant love? Is there any thing in the tender mercy of this dispensation to warrant that dark blasphemy that in another age bore the name of theology and whose spirit I am sorry to say is not yet wholly departed and which called the earth—"the Scaffold of the Divine Vengeance"?[5] ("Perfect love casteth out fear.")[6] Is it not manifestly the same hand that works in these *moral* contrivances that we had owned before expanding ourselves to the gratifications of the *material* world, and feeding with omnipotent energy the channels of life, and the sources of joy?

Such, my friends, is the character of God, and such must be the character of Religion, which is God's law. Pure religion and undefiled consists, according to the Scripture, in doing good.[7] It does not consist in ceremony or in grimace. It does not consist in making fasts or prayers or penances or in giving the body to be burned.[8] It does not consist in going scrupulously to Church many times in a week, in being the well known member of all religious societies of prayer and contribution. These are good and laudable means but it is a fatal mistake which esteems them the ends of faith. But it does consist in accommodating the life of man to his destiny. We have been informed by a message from God that though after a few years a change will take place in our condition yet that we shall never perish but are always to be connected with an order of things in which temporal distinctions are nothing and moral distinctions are everything. Every word, therefore, every action that is in harmony with this immortal hope is religious and every one that is in discord with these expectations is the reverse. Religion, then, is not an austere, macerating, monkish observance, befitting the gloom of cloisters and the solitude of desarts. It is cheerful, social, masculine, generous. It is inquisitive of the ways of man, inquisitive of the works of God. It walks about doing good in the streets of cities. It scorns appearances. It uncovers the vestures of fortune to get at the heart. Its whole business everywhere and at all times is to add to the amount of happiness. St. John in the Wilderness is less its representative than St. Paul in

5. The phrase, quoted to Emerson in a letter of January 1824 from Mary Moody Emerson, is attributed to Jacques Saurin (1677–1730), a French Protestant preacher. See *JMN* 2:225, 2:307, 4:9; used in "The Individual," *EL* 2:184, and "Historic Notes of Life and Letters in New England," *W* 10:336.

6. I John 4:18.

7. Cf. James 1:27.

8. I Corinthians 13:3.

the Areopagus.[9] What were for ages called in Europe the *religious orders*, Religion, my friends, does not acknowledge. They said Lord, Lord, but did not the works of active virtue.[10] But all that is noble in the eye of men, all that ever attracted the general praise of society is religious. Whatsoever traits of recorded heroism have come down to us; whatsoever anecdotes of ancient or modern fame have transmitted the memory of selfdevotion, of valor, of abstinence, of wisdom, of sacrifice,—all that is excellent in them is in strict coincidence with religion. All that is amiable in the world is religious. The spirit of a gentleman and the spirit of a Christian, which have been divorced by vulgar opinion, are one. Religion demands the same courtesy, the same bounty, the same benevolence, the same independence, the same grace and spirit of demeanour, that elegant taste demands. Only it cries shame upon any motive lower than the highest that shall dictate the pursuit of these accomplishments. One is satisfied to be seen of men, the other stands in the Eye of Heaven and desires all the perfection it can attain. Be not deceived, true religion does not ask less than false religion, it asks more. It demands observances and prayers and charities and demands the whole heart beside. It asks all that can ennoble man. God is Love and religion is the law of love. The doing of good, of all good, is its whole end.

But it must have occurred to us all that to one who regards the real relations of man and what should be the dominion of religion in the world it does now fall very far short of full success. It is not to be supposed that it has satisfied the divine purpose. It is not to be supposed that Christ died in vain, that his kingdom in the world will always be straitened. We must regard the purposes of Providence here on the earth to be yet incomplete, to be yet in the rudiments of what they shall become.

I wish it might be deeply considered by us what would be the full effect of the prevalence of just views of God and of religion. It is an experiment that has not been tried within the periods of certain history. There was in fable a golden age; there was in history an iron age; there has been, Heaven knows, a superstitious age; but there has never been a religious age. Such an epoch has been predicted in the mighty prophecies of old and has been prepared by the tendencies of the present time, in the secret amelioration wrought by Christianity in the bosom of society. There is, we trust, room for this soaring hope in the aspect of the world. I have not forgotten, I remember with grief, that numberless population in the barbarous East that lie in the bondage of pagan ignorance; I remember the corruptions that blemish religion even in the heart of Christendom; I know and I lament that so large a class of good men, here among us do yet entertain those disastrous views of religion that go so far to pervert men and dishonour God; and which are only mitigated by that redeeming character in religious

---

9. John the Baptist was the voice "crying in the wilderness" (cf. Isaiah 40:3 and Matthew 3:3). For Paul in the Areopagus of Athens, see Acts 17:19.

10. Luke 6:46.

feeling which will not let the mistakes of the understanding wholly deprave the heart. With all these deductions, wise and pious men have thought that there has been a slow but progressive amendment in the manners and morals of society, that the standard of public virtue has been raised, and as it is the tendency of all good to beget good, no less than of evil to produce evil, that this effect is increasing.

It has been thought that Christianity is preparing its own triumphs, that a purer age shall come, when God shall be worshipped in spirit and in truth; an age, when the civil laws, that are now found necessary to coerce the peace of society, shall wither to a dead letter before the prevailing energy of a virtuous public feeling; when the absence of fraud shall do away the bloody code of prevention; when, from that expansion of the mind derived from religion, knowledge shall cease to be the property of the few, but shall be sought by all men with that eagerness with which now they seek wealth. When men shall feel as a community; when the stormy spirit of faction shall sleep in the reverence of brotherly love; when the strong shall aid the weak, and men shall be penetrated with the conviction that then is the greatest aggregate of virtue and enjoyment; when each spends himself in behalf of the whole.

Let me not be told to dissolve this pleasing vision, that such an ascendency of religion is dangerous to the state, as some dark periods of ecclesiastical history can testify, for I answer that religion disowns that influence which assumed her name to pollute it with crimes of so deep a dye. Would such an age, think you, break down the barriers that fence the security of property? It would back their strength with the divine command. Will it relax the bands of international faith? Its own law bids men love their neighbor as themselves.[11] Will it invade the institutions of learning or even cripple the exertions of genius in the elegant arts? It will breathe into them a life they never knew and cause them to react on their cultivators. Will it sour the intercourse of society and dispense with the decent forms that keep that intercourse under necessary check? No. It will guard them with a sensitiveness derived from purity that fashion never could feel.

Welcome then this approaching era of human bliss! God speed this pure Millennium; this more than fulfilment of the reasonings of wise, and the hopes of pious, men; this inspired vision of the Hebrew bards, this long foreseen, this deeply projected result, that buoyed up the soul of the great Martyr of Calvary, and for which hope he gave up the ghost. And how is it to be accelerated? and where are the apostles of this desirable day? It is to be accomplished as every great thing the world has seen, by individual effort. It is to be done by each of us, with God to our aid. Every word, every action, the least, the humblest,—to a cup of cold water given in the sincere spirit of devotion, is a contribution to this holy work. 'Never was a sincere word utterly lost,'[12] and every moral agent,

11. Matthew 19:19.
12. Mme. de Staël, *Germany* (London, 1813), 3:401. See *JMN* 6:61, 6:157; used in "Religion," *EL* 2:95 and "Spiritual Laws," *CW* 2:92.

from the Angel to the child, who gives his strength, much or little, to the service of God and man, is an anointed apostle of the cause. To do good to the utmost of your ability, is required of you. To do good is the very office appointed you in the world. It is the employment that lies before you, if God accept you, through the ages of eternity.

What is man, that thou art mindful of him?

PSALMS 8:4

Some thousands of years have passed since King David put this question in his pious ascription. He stopped as he praised on his harp the glory of the heavens and noted in the innumerable host of stars the little planet whereon man is lodged; he exclaimed, What is man? The royal minstrel after a few years was gathered to his fathers; a palsy crept upon the cunning of his hand and the strings of his divine harp were snapped with time. But the question he had asked was not answered. His son, the prosperous favourite of Heaven and accounted the wisest of men, examined all the parts of human fortune but proved all unable to read the mystery or make known the interpretation.[1] His royal line is perished. His mighty city, the glory of the East, has been razed to the ground. His nation has long fulfilled the tremendous doom which the awful voice of prophecy had for ages portended. Far and wide from their promised land the children of Israel and Judah have gone out into all the nations to be a shaking of the head and a byeword among men.[2] The prodigious revolution of human affairs has swept into ruin not the generations of men alone but all the cities, the nations, and the very names that were then strong and honourable. Other empires have been founded and overthrown by the waters of Jordan. Tracts then unexplored have been filled with men. New continents have been disclosed and new nations born. And in all this passage of time and all this unmeasured multiplication of human life the question *what is Man?* has not lost any of its interest although much has been done towards furnishing an answer.

It is a question, my brethren, that cannot be indifferent to any of us. There is not one here so gay or so gloomy or so busy that he has not sometimes found this anxious inquiry in his mind. It involves all we can hope or fear. It involves the whole of life and, what is of much more consequence to us, the whole of what is to follow. It is a question directly of what agency interests man, beyond and above his own. What is man, is in fact wholly dependent on the question What is God?

Preached three times: August 5, 1827, at the First Church, Boston; October 28 in Northampton; and May 3, 1829, at the Second Church, Boston.

1. David, musician in the court of Saul and traditionally the author of the Psalms, was succeeded by his son, Solomon, as King of Israel in Jerusalem.
2. Deuteronomy 28:37.

It is of little consequence that we discuss the nature and value of a single duty if we have no clear understanding of the character and condition of Man, the being who owes them, or fix with accuracy the perfections and dispensations of God before we have learned what is our interest in him, our relation to him.

It will aid us, it is probable, to form just views of our duty to refresh within us good resolutions from their just sources, to review rapidly as the time requires the false answers and the true which have been suggested to the interrogation of the King of Israel.

Man, said the pagan proverb, is the son of the earth, and the grandson of nothing. Man, said the pagan philosopher, is the unpremeditated result of a blind necessity and the same necessity will reduce him presently to dust. He is the offspring, said another, of mere chance and 'tis ridiculous to inquire why he is what he is, or whither he is tending for all his constitution and all his destiny is subject to the same tossing incalculable chance. He is vanity, said Solomon, he is vanity and vexation of spirit.[3] He is an animal one degree higher than the brute, said Epicurus, created in the sport of the Gods, who have left him to himself and do not disturb their own felicity by any superintendence of his race.[4] Man, said the gloomy scoffer, go visit him in his shroud. Look where he lies in a dreamless sleep in his narrow house. There's no colour in his cheek, no beating at the heart. He shall talk, think, and act never again. His soaring affections are dissipated at last, his faculties, his schemes, are broken, his unbounded wishes—here is all that is left. No matter how high his lot. "The heart and life of a great emperor is the breakfast of a little worm."[5]

These are the answers which a vain philosophy or a vainer conceit furnished in another age to that grave inquiry in which all the inquirers felt that they had the deepest stake. But God did not permit that men should remain in this pernicious ignorance of their own hopes and his goodness. He sent his son into the world to solve the great enigma that had baffled the mighty and disconcerted the wise. He scattered the doubts of men by revealing the doctrine of immortality and of a moral government of the universe. And now in the spirit of his religion let us attempt to answer the question as well as our better lights of experience and revelation will enable us. It appears, then, that each of us has been set here on the earth by our common Father who is an infinitely powerful and good Being. God has put you in the earth that he may add an unit to the amount of happiness by endowing you with life and then with immortal powers. He has set us down each in such circumstances as he, for reasons not yet known to us, saw in his wisdom to be best for each. He has created us poor and destitute. Naked we came into the world, not of raiment alone but of all the equipment of powers, the affections, the accomplishments, that make our

---

3. Solomon's refrain in Ecclesiastes; see 1:14, for example.

4. No comparison between men and animals has been found in the writings of Epicurus. The description of the relation of the gods to men is Emerson's roughly accurate paraphrase.

5. "Apology for Raimond de Sebonde," in *Essays of Michael Seigneur de Montaigne . . .* , trans. Charles Cotton (London, 1693), 2:207. See also *JMN* 6:12.

crown of immortality.[6] Nothing but the folded up seminal principle of all this aftergrowth did we possess. We are compelled ourselves to bring them out of darkness to their powerful maturity by an obedience to those necessities, which call them out on every side. The same Providence that first designed still presides over the infant's development. Follow out the history of a single child and mark how God is continually shifting and enlarging the field of its intellectual vision. As the scholar proceeds to a more advanced treatise from an elementary one, so from the busy mind of that little trifler God withdraws in succession one motive, one desire, one group of objects, as fast as their several ends are answered. Whilst it is still a babe and has not learned the first properties of matter nor the use of its limbs there is imparted to it an incessant restlessness, an unlearned curiosity, that have no intermission in the waking hours. When the years increase, and the body has been moulded to answer the purposes, to be the minister of the soul, this inconvenient excess of inquisitiveness and bodily uneasiness subsides, and the same power that gave these means of knowledge now begins to furnish new and larger opportunities, new and manlier and more cogent motives. And now in its more advanced education, we begin to recognize tendencies and powers that intimate its true destiny. It begins to be seen that God is designing us for higher and better things, that the child of clay is the heir of immortality. Within the bosom of man, affections expand that he is conscious may feed him with immeasurable joy. My brethren, I do not think we accustom ourselves enough to consider the wonderful properties of our nature. We are apt to forget the great qualities that exist in things familiar to us. Man is a common sight. We are surrounded by tens of thousands of our fellow beings and do not stop to ponder on the greatness of their fate. We disregard in their multitude, that which would amaze us, if it stood alone. The bosom of this being so frail, so weak, subject to contagion and destruction from so many forms of disease, begins to dilate with lofty thoughts that speak to him of a more desirable creation. Within that wasting form, a mind abides that contains that masterwork of Deity, the memory, the capacious house of thought, where the innumerable ideas of a whole life, the persons, the places, the traditions, the studies, the very color and shades of all things, live again for our use unconfused and immortal. By this faculty, this feeble agent who can walk but a span at a time along the ground, sends back his soul with a speed that mocks the whirlwind to other places and times, and hath a kind of property in all the past. By his reason, by his hope, by his imagination he surveys, he masters, all the present, and runs forward into the tardy ages of the future. I need not finish the enumeration of powers, since it only needs, my friends, that each of you should explore that standing miracle, your own soul—to see how miserably short of the truth is any description. I must only add that over all these collected energies and the main, central, prominent power of the soul is the *moral sentiment*—the Conscience, the distinguisher of right and wrong, that

6. Job 1:21.

gives to all these powers the unity of one moral being; that adds its sentence of censure or approval to every act of the agent; that in every moment of temptation points as with a silent finger to something, it says not what, that is to come. Do these things, these wonderful faculties, smell of corruption? Do you think these can perish as a body can perish, and this divine instinct of the future can corrupt and moulder with the earth it animated? Or do they not vindicate to themselves another birthright as creatures of God made in his image?

To these beings thus constituted God has revealed his character and will, has commanded their obedience to his moral law and sanctioned it with happiness and misery. Hear the words of the apostle who preached the righteous judgement of God, who will render unto every man according to his deeds; to them who by patient continuance in well doing seek for glory, honour and immortality, eternal life; but unto them that are contentious and do not obey the truth, but obey unrighteousness, indignation and wrath, tribulation and anguish upon every soul of man that doeth evil.[7]

And, furthermore, my friends, a pious mind will draw from these observations the inference which reason and religion do abundantly sanction, that the account of his existence which each of us must render to himself, the reason of all the persons and things with which we have been associated is this, that God is unrolling the universe before each of us for our instruction, is placing us in successive series of circumstances, is bringing into the neighborhood of each, now one and now another mind or group of minds in exact accommodation to what are seen to be our peculiar exigences at the moment, until by just degrees we shall be fitted in each immortal fibre for the scenes of action and thought that are presently to be disclosed.[8]

My brethren, let us be careful that these considerations lead us to proper feelings. I dwell on these noble parts of our nature not that it may excite pride in our breasts, it is the last feeling it ought to awaken, but that seeing what endowments and opportunities we have—comparing the greatness of our maker's design with the lowness of our performance, comparing what we might be with what we are, it may make us humble, may make us contrite, may make us better.

And for what purpose does this education go on; and why so vast an arena of preparation; and to what theatre of action do such difficult exercises invigorate us? That is to say, to what world are we transferred, when our bodies sleep the sleep of death? Is it imagined, by any of us, that when life draws to its close we have done our work; that if our imperfect obedience has found favor with God, our toils are over; our crown is ready; our minds are to become channels through which happiness is to flow as a stream, and flow forever? Are we to be laid up, much as children imagine of Eastern Kings, in magnificence and joy, in abodes of beauty, in the instantaneous gratification of every wish amid armies

---

7. Rom II [Emerson's note]: i.e., Romans 2:5–9.
8. "God is unrolling . . . disclosed": cf. Emerson's letter to Mary Moody Emerson, April 10, 1827, in *J* 2:184.

of bright beings who fulfil with every act the measure of our sovereign felicity? These are but rude ideas of heaven and not many degrees removed from the absurdity of that faith which promises the believer all sensual luxury. No, my friends, not such an intimation of God's purpose is gotten from what is done here. Is it an idle Paradise, an eternity of dreams, a long and pleasant sloth? Are we to sit sluggish as if our science were full, our virtues perfect, and this poor earth had been the triumphal field that witnessed our ultimate success in moral and intellectual action? Alas! my friends, what have we done and where are the mighty virtues we have exhibited that we should think so meanly of what is expected from us by our Maker and of the employments of the future time? No, the earth is rather the porch, the threshold, of the mighty temple wherein our exertions are appointed, the antechamber where we prove our strength and provide ourselves with the instruments of labor. Let us judge of heaven by earth; judge of happiness to come by happiness that is past. Consider what are the purest enjoyments of which your nature has yet partaken and believe it will be capable of the same and better when it drops its vestment of flesh. As the tree falleth so shall it lie.[9] As you die in this world, you shall be born into that. You'll enter that world with the character with which you left this. I beg you, then, to reflect if in your life any enjoyment has been so pure in its beginning, its progress, and its consequence, as the doing of good. It had no end. That enjoyment was ever the parent of new enjoyments. Let me ask again whether your experience has determined that sloth and indulgence of passion, and voluptuousness did not, when their consequences were also seen, lose their seeming beauty in loathsome deformity? And whether the greatest pleasure was not found to consist in overcoming pleasure?[10]

No, my friends, I cannot but think we beguile ourselves with very incompetent notions of the future. Eye hath not seen nor ear heard nor the heart imagined the glory that shall be revealed, saith the Scripture.[11] Will heaven then fall short of our feeble conceptions? And yet our own minds condemn the representation of a scene of passive enjoyment. We do injustice to the Deity, we do injustice to our own convictions by such a belief. It is a scene of magnificent action, of ever enlarging diligence and labor, of great beneficent achievement, of which at present our straining conceptions can shadow out but a poor and inadequate idea.

But I should do injustice to my subject did I leave it here. There is yet another element that enters into the composition of man. He is a tempted being and prone to sin. The design was to rear us to virtue. And the only way in which virtue is acquired is by resistance to evil. But alas, he has yielded to the pleasures of vice which are but for a season and slighted the boundless good which lay in

---

9. Ecclesiastes 11:3.

10. In *The Rule and Exercise of Holy Living*, Jeremy Taylor quotes St. Cyprian: "For to overcome pleasure is the greatest pleasure" (*The Whole Works of the Right Rev. Jeremy Taylor, D. D.* [London, 1828], 4:74). See *JMN* 6:43.

11. Cf. I Corinthians 2:9–10.

store for his integrity. And lo, my friends, what widespread consequences avenge the guilt. Sin which was admitted a little thing to the heart of each, now bloated and terrible, walks abroad like a pestilence consuming the health and the happiness of the world; it is in every place, in courts; in cottages; in action; in speech; and nestles in the heart.

And what remedy is provided to stay the plague? What balsam is in Gilead to heal this poison of the atmosphere we breathe?[12] What is the last crowning gift to man that makes him what he is, and more—glorifies him to what he may become? Religion, my brethren, the religion of Jesus Christ, that will renovate the dying man of sin with the new man of the spirit and blows the trump of resurrection over the sheeted dead.

It is an old fable that has appeared in some form amid the fictions of different nations and which seems to be therefore an idea agreeable to the human mind that there existed enchantments for the restoration of exhausted nature, that there were powerful persons to whom an art was known by which youth and health could be recovered to the old and decrepit, and fair proportions to the crooked and deformed. I need hardly represent to you, if such a magician should appear among us, with what alacrity we should unburden ourselves of disease and decrepitude. Who would not think his swiftest haste was loitering who prepared to get rid of a chronic and loathsome disease which disturbed the operation of all his senses, which made his life a burden to his friends and a burden to him, which made all the joys of life lose their character when he partook of them and only filled his bosom with the sharpest mortification? Yet this, my friends, is but a faint delineation of the evil of sin, which is the sickness of the soul; for one but kills the body, and ends in death; but the other kills the soul. But what the ancients only feigned of the cure of the body, to us is come to pass, is more than realized in the cure of the soul. A way of health, a divine panacea, is freely offered us for the healing of this pest that has broken out and is consuming our immortal parts. Religion is this best restorative, this real enchantment that straightens the distorted mind, that infuses new hope into the self-abandoned heart, the ardour of benevolence into the contracted soul, shedding the love of truth like sunlight into the darkened and noisome chambers of the understanding, impels like a torrent the feeble circulations of the thoughts and purposes, and sends out the being that crept before in a selfish, small, and despised round of petty ends, renewed, invigorated, to be a ministering angel in the world, to teach the ignorant, to aid the weak, to go about the earth, like his Divine Master, doing good.

My friends, let these considerations have their weight with us. We are of this ancient erring highly destined human race. Let our lives furnish the best answer to the question, What is man? We are the creatures of the Almighty, the candidates for heaven. We are tempted by our passions. We are frail and sinful. We need this antidote to bear about us as a medicine to our disease, as a solace to our griefs, as the ornament of our life, and as an earnest of heaven.

12. Cf. Jeremiah 8:22.

X

Let them learn first to show piety at home.

I TIMOTHY 5:4

It is a very common mistake to regard the eminence of men in forming our estimate of virtue. A king's virtues never suffered in the telling. Those who stand high in society are thought to derive from that circumstance some degree of licence to vice and there is therefore something gratuitous and deserving of more praise in their goodness. Hence it happens that we ourselves desire conspicuous occasions for the exhibition of our own moral principle, wish that we had our neighbor's immense possessions to edify men with our charity, or the gifted mind of our friend that we might plead with a most devoted eloquence the cause of the afflicted, oppressed, and poor. When therefore we consider our own characters we are very apt to take to ourselves credit for what we think we should do in any case of extraordinary trial. We omit the examination of what we are and what we do and please ourselves with the contemplation of our possible virtues in possible cases.

"But the main part of life is made up of small incidents and petty occurrences."[1] It is the duty of but very few of us to command armies or rule or counsel nations. If we therefore keep our virtue in store till it find a field which we shall think worthy of its action, it will wait long, or rather it will never exist, for virtue exists only in action.

In the next place let it be remembered that no virtue can be properly called small. A great end makes the means great. We read with the utmost interest the most insignificant particulars that relate to the life and actions of a genuine hero because we esteem them, however slight themselves, to be all of them steps to some high national end, which was then uppermost in the actor's soul. The

---

Preached twenty-seven times: August 12, 1827, at the First Church, Boston; August 19 at the Federal Street Church; September 9 in Northampton; September 23 in Deerfield; September 30 in Greenfield; November 6 in New Bedford; November 27 in Harvard, Mass.; December 9 in Watertown; December 23 in Concord, N.H.; February 10, 1828, in Waltham; February 17 in Carlisle; February 24 in Concord, Mass.; March 2 in Dedham; March 16 in Lexington; March 23 in Medford; March 30 in Lechmere Point; June 8 in Shirley; June 29 at the Second Church, Charlestown; July 13 at the Second Church, Boston; August 31 in Waltham; September 21 in West Cambridge; October 19 in Dover, N.H.; January 4, 1829, in Groton; February 8 in Stowbridge; November 29 at the Second Church, Boston; November 28, 1830, at the Friend Street Chapel; and June 5, 1831, in Burlington, Vt.

    1. Not located.

same thing determines our opinion of all action, not the movement itself but its tendency and end. If to pluck a rose or to snap the finger had been made a concerted signal of a man's resolution to die for a particular cause, there would then be grandeur in that frivolous action.[2] If it were possible for us to go back and see the person and actions of our Lord precisely as they were seen in Nazareth and Galilee 1800 years ago, would any trait of his demeanour, do you imagine, appear to you small and indifferent? Knowing the sublime purpose that glowed within his bosom as he sat in benevolent discourse with his twelve observant friends, would a glance of his eye, would the lifting of his hand, escape our notice? Would not his least motion seem to us fraught with extreme and tender interest? Now the case is precisely the same with whatever conduct is prompted by high principle. It dignifies the act, be it ever so minute. You need not endow a hospital to be very good. You may be greatly virtuous, even though, through the blessing of God, you do not live in times when you must give your body to be burned or to be sawn asunder for your faith. Less imposing duties are great enough and sometimes more than enough for our languid obedience. The narrow confines of Home are a field of preparation large enough for all the glories of Heaven. Our religion teaches us that whatsoever the strict adherence to truth at all risks, the denial of an indulgence at the table, the suppression of a merry or petulant remark likely to wound the feelings of another—even the charity of an encouraging word or smile given to humble worth—the least of these, done out of a solemn sense of duty, done in the Eye of God, is great and venerable.[3]

Since it is in our houses that we spend the greatest part of life, since we can never be great if we are not reverenced there, and nowhere be good if we are vicious at home, I shall need no apology for asking your attention to the duty of domestic piety, for the main regard of religion must be to make us good at home.

It seems to be thought, as has been intimated, that our virtue demands for its strenuous exertion a great occasion, an active life, and something removed from the quiet dulness of home. But who made this distinction between times and seasons and occupations? Did God, my friends, limit virtue by rule or line or distinctions? Did he command us to love and fear him only in one place or another, at noon or night, or yield us permission of following our inclinations twice, if we did his bidding once? Do you find any compromise in his word that you may give your winter to sin if you will give your summer to God? or doth he ask or will he accept any thing less than the whole? Provided that you are scrupulously upright in business in the street, does he sell you the privilege of vicious indulgence in your own house? Must you not love God with your whole heart and mind and strength?[4] The household hours are hours of life. The household hours carry their accusing or approving testimony on high, and they

2. See *JMN* 6:49.
3. Matthew 25:40.
4. Cf. Mark 12:30.

have a weightier evidence than others because they contain in them the sincere expression of the heart; for no man is a hypocrite at home.

"Let them first learn to show piety at home," said the affectionate apostle to his friend. For he knew how prone men are to commit fatal mistakes, to deceive themselves by pushing forward any substitute in the place of vital piety, to shroud an immoral life behind the best professions or the strictest creed; behind a virtuous carriage before the great; behind good humour and a liberal mind before the world. But let them show piety at home. That shall be the test of the character. There is many a man who goes out into the world gaily drest in smiles and kindness, who is full of grace and bounty abroad, of correct views and pleasing conversation. But when he returns home, when the doors are shut and the curtains drawn, and the hours pass without event, he says, 'there is no need to shine, these are of necessity my friends; by blood, or by dependance.' He takes off his goodness like a cumbersome garment and grows silent and splenetic; he has got rid of the preposessing elegance of his address, that buoyant alacrity in the offices of politeness that won your praise. He is intemperate at his table; he is a sluggard in his bed; he is slothful and useless in his chair; he is sour or false in conversation. He breaks the commandments because he is at home. A strange reason, surely, for licence and vice! Will the curtains of his windows shroud him from the Omniscient Eye? When we need the stimulus of a great occasion and many observers to excite our virtue, what is it in effect but to say that we fear men more than God, and respect men more than we respect ourselves?

That virtue must needs be the most acceptable tribute of obedience which is practised before few persons and on humble occasions. If a man is good before a king or a sage it is possible that his goodness springs from a calculating prudence; if he is pure before a child or a beggar, it is manifest he loves virtue for virtue's sake. And hence the high value we set on piety at home.

Let it be remembered that it is not ourselves so much as Providence that appoints our situation in life, that appoints us to great or to humble occasions of usefulness. But our virtue is in all cases determined by ourselves. It is ours to say whether we will rise in our daily life to the dignity of angels, or whether we will creep nameless and worthless through infamous years of selfishness and sin to a dishonourable old age of shame and sorrow. One who contemplates the beauty of a life that is nobly led under the unerring guidance of religious principle is sometimes astonished how there should be hesitation upon its advantage, that all men do not run to render the homage of their obedience to the law of God. It is a beautiful but monitory thought that not an hour of our waking time after we have learned to distinguish good and evil—that not an hour of the longest life but may be signalized by a virtuous action, by some sacrifice though small and unknown to another's wish, or of our own inclination to our duty, and as it is the consequence of all goodness to increase the power of him that has it, that one of us, my brethren, by a rigid study of himself may every hour become a richer and mightier moral agent; may tomorrow be happier than today; may rake together with each flying moment the bright atoms of knowledge and goodness5 until he ceases to count his days by the wretched marks of passing time, by his returning pleasures of the table, by his periodical augmentations of property, or yet by the furrows of his brow, but numbers them on the golden dial of his own soul by the acquisitions he has made and the good deeds he has done. He sees in the virtues of his children with joy the genuine fruit of his own; he beholds in the beggar at his door the living record of his charitable years.

And let me ask which of all those much magnified goods which others pursue so fondly, of which we are all apt to think so much, delicate food, a gay dress, personal beauty, the regard of people in higher rank, friends, flattering prospects, or whatsoever accidental advantages, ought so much as to be named in comparison with the value of one wellspent hour? I beg that this may not be understood as mere declamatory praise of virtue, proper enough to this place and of no imperative interest, but that it is true to the letter, and every one in his house shall one day feel its force—that a wellspent hour in the life of a man is, when he comes to die and see things in their true dimensions, felt to be a solid advantage by the side of which opinions and conditions, earthly pleasures and advantages become extremely contemptible. One well spent hour is the proper seed of heaven and eternity. For he who has opened his heart for a time to all the influences of religion, who has devoted himself for a time to the service of conscience and fulfilled its dictates to the letter, will go back to that hour with pure and justifiable delight. That time will be laid up in his mind and become the pleasant place of the memory. Good will come out of it whenever it is reviewed. (It will be like the embalmed body of the mighty—the fragrance of Arabian myrrh and spikenard shall steal from it when it is visited.) It will strongly incite in his breast the desire to copy its beauty into the yet unwritten page of this day and the morrow.

II. Again. Let them first learn to show piety at home, for there our piety can do some good. That is the place where we are best known, and where, if we are religious, some one will have the good of it by benefit from us, or at least by our example. Our ways of thinking, talking, and acting there will exercise a stronger influence than ever we can hope to create elsewhere. Did you never wish you were of more importance among your fellow citizens? Did you never covet the influence of a great man? Have you never coveted a more extensive influence than you possess? Have you never sighed to be born a king? never looked with a greedy eye on that augmented power that the rich necessarily hold in their hands and excused your ambition by asserting that you should put that power to so much better use? In his parlour every man has power. There can be no question of the force with which your influence acts upon the inmates of your dwelling. Let us try your capacity to be ruler over many things by your

5. "may rake . . . goodness": cf. Emerson's letter to Mary Moody Emerson, April 10, 1827, in J 2:184.

faithfulness over a few things.[6] If you have learned to show piety at home; if you kept the purity of that sanctuary from contamination; if you have made it the holy fountain of generous and honourable habits; if prayer has been offered on the altar of God, morning and evening; if its secret history could be opened to the world without regret or dishonour; then, fear not but God in the boundless future shall more than recompense your honest stewardship. Fear not but in the earth also, your reward shall be reaped. The same moral force that has dignified your character at home will surely give you standing and reverence abroad. The competence of a man is known to his neighbors. Your children will rise up and call you blessed.[7] And God and man will provide you opportunity to do good to the farthest of your ability. But if, alas! you are afraid to give the account to be given of your abode, if it has been the hiding place of folly and sin, if those that have grown up in it betray by the too certain sign of their life what pernicious lessons they learned in its precincts, then you have done what in you lay to combat the great cause which God created you to promote; you have abused all that power which he put in your keeping, and it is surely with an ill grace you ask for more with all this ground to believe that if you had more you would do worse.

III. God gave us our social affections not as instruments of pain, not as fetters to enslave us, but as bands of strength wherewith we might better bear our burden by sharing it; to be sources of delight, to furnish new motives to industry in multiplying the powers of the body and the mind. By drawing us to each other by the strong cords of friendship and love, he invested the fireside with its sacred delights, appointing therein to man the place to be born and the place to die, and surrounding the name of home with its sweet and solemn associations. Our gratitude to him should teach us its use and honor; should write his name on the best of his gifts. If his name is to be honoured any where let it be among our brothers and sisters, our parents and friends. Let us not hide our hopes and duties *there*, in dumb ingratitude. Let us bear one another's burdens.[8] Let us aid each other in our difficult emergencies. When fortune has thrown us into foreign lands, when the tokens of affection we receive from afar, make the eye wet and the heart yearn to that distant home, let its beautiful remembrance come over the soul with the force of religious recollection, animating us to duty, deterring us from sin. It will seem to us a new revelation sent to us from Heaven. My friends, these ties are soon to be severed, for such is the lot of man, and it may aid us to form a just judgement upon the value to the character of these virtues if we consider what it is, when death has stricken us, that gives the best consolation to the bereaved. Inquire of those who mourn what they have found in the memory of the dead that was able to supply any comfort to the desolate heart. Was it the advantages of external prosperity, of advancing rank

6. Matthew 25:21.
7. Proverbs 31:28.
8. Galatians 6:2.

in society, of mortal beauty or success that saved the cherished image from being a source of hopeless sorrow? No! they are gone forever, and left no wreck behind.[9] Was it the triumphs of genius? Alas! they gave but keener edge to disappointment. But was it not the remembrance of the private virtues of those we deplore, "the daily beauty of their life" in that home of which they were the pride and honor,[10] is it not these recollections that slowly abate the poignancy of grief because we believe that the character of which these were the graces could not die and yet shines with the same in the purer light of a spiritual world?

My friends, let *us* learn to show piety at home. It will aid us in that work to keep always in view the difficulties that stand in the way. It is the want of a definite point to which we should direct our efforts. What is the history of every Sabbath? Men come to church and struck with the force of some divine truth which is here presented, their consciences also bearing it witness, they make on the spot a good resolution and mean to keep it. But the service is done; they go home and the old and accustomed rooms suggest old and accustomed feelings; they are put off their guard, and when the temptation comes their altered purpose has been forgotten and they break their vow. This danger is to be met by a correspondent care. Now make your purpose something less. Let us contract our purpose, that we may concentrate our strength. Let us aim to spend a single hour of perfect purity and call God to our witness and aid. Let us aim to spend *one single hour* of every day without spot or blemish, without an error even in thought, and give ourselves with our might to the performance. God will bless the purpose. If it be sincerely attempted doubt not of success. Though you may labour with mortal infirmity, though you may fail once and again, you shall be backed by Omnipotence and shall not fail in the end. That hour you shall find the auspicious season that shall send out its good influences on every portion of your life and fortune, and when the clock strikes and tolls out its departure, and you consider that the seal of your own praise is set to it, that one virtuous hour is safe beyond the reach of accident, and it is gone to bear its unalterable witness to your character on high, it shall fill your breast with solemn gladness, it shall infuse the good contagion of its own virtue into the other hours of the day, it shall be blessed in your memory to the last hour of your life.

My friends, I should esteem myself most happy and successful if the doctrine I have attempted to recommend might weigh with any of you to set yourselves to this experiment, to make this small venture for your everlasting welfare. You will believe me, it will not subtract one moment of real enjoyment from the life it is to glorify, one individual pleasure that deserves the name from the home where it is tried. It will make that life worthy of the name. It will make that home you love, no matter how poor and unfurnished, no matter though the wind blows, the venerable home of all virtue and good hope where angels shall

9. Cf. Shakespeare, *Tempest*, IV, i, 156.
10. Cf. Shakespeare, *Othello*, V, i, 19.

visit, and the glory of the Almighty shall overshadow it with his wings.[11] And when that day which comes to all shall come to you, of sickness and death, it shall bereave it of its pang and translate you to the resplendent home of all the good, of the innumerable armies of martyrs, of saints and angels and of God, the Judge of all.[12]

11. The image occurs frequently in the Psalms.
12. Hebrews 12:23.

XI

Happy is the man that findeth wisdom.

PROVERBS 3:13

There is a daily complaint which we have all at some time heard or uttered that life was barren of interest. It is not barely an idle saying of those who would say something or even of the melancholy or of the sick in soul or in body. It has been made the excuse of intemperance and of squandered time. It has been made the excuse of vices to which men resort, as they say, for excitement with the wretched pretence that they are so constituted that the time which is not marked by new events, is of itself an insupportable burden. They speak as if their days should be each freshened by new pleasures or embittered by unexpected distress. One who heard them would imagine that in them the ordinary feelings of man were reversed, that they fear from afar the coming of a quiet hour and count no greater calamity than an innocent day. It seems to argue some signal incompetency in the means and objects of human action to occupy the powers employed upon them and charges on Providence the faults of man. And this in the face of all that immense treasury of knowledge which lies before men unexplored whilst life is too short for the understanding of all the mighty works of man and infinitely too short for us to compass the works of God.

But there is quite another explanation to be given of this evil by those who narrowly examine the fact. Let it be compared with a closely parallel case. He who reads a book in a language unknown to him, or he who shuffles the draughtsmen in a game he does not understand may easily tire of his employment and complain of its insupportable dulness. But in the first instance the practised eye that traces the well-known characters of his native tongue receives from those mute signs (these black strokes on paper) the inspiration of thought. By that dumb page his understanding is enlarged, his passions startled from their sleep, he is moved with wonder, he is stung with remorse. In the other instance the player watches with equal anxiety the chips of carved wood with which he plays his game, and the petty alterations of place on a checquered board which move the scorn of the beholder have to him sometimes an intense interest passing that of words, a fatal eloquence often which intoxicates his spirit and overcomes his virtue. It is almost needless to explain the appositeness

Preached three times: August 26, 1827, at the First Church, Boston; September 28, 1828, at the Second Church, Boston; and May 16, 1830, again at the Second Church.

of these illustrations. Ignorance is the cause whence life as well as the book and the game appear worthless and dull. We rest in the objects of sight without extending our regard to the consequences which they involve. We examine the particulars, we examine letters and baubles which are in themselves unmeaning, and give no heed to the train of real events of which they are made arbitrary signs.

The cause of this (so common, that it is, in some measure, known to every one of us,) is ignorance. But whence this ignorance? and how may it be remedied? It is not like sin a malady contracted on the earth, nor is it an incidental defect foreign to the purposes of our existence, but it is an original want with which we were created and which it is a chief business of life to supply. As hunger stimulates us to procure the food appointed for the sustenance of life, ignorance is but an appetite which God set us in the beginning to gratify. And if it be contrary to nature to deny our bodies food, it is contrary to a higher nature,—it violates the order of Providence to let the mind lie torpid, and refuse to procure that knowledge which is its vital principle. Sloth is sinful and this neglect is punished by loss and ruin to the mind that permits it. So apparent is the duty of expelling our natural ignorance, of using our faculties of chasing from the mind this great darkness by the light of intellectual truth, that the wise pagan represented wicked men as involuntary offenders, as doing what seemed to them right and profitable in the thick mist which hid from their eyes their real interests. In all languages also this easy and natural metaphor from knowledge to light and from ignorance to darkness hath gone into common use.[1]

The remedy for the evils, the unhappiness of life, is wisdom. "Happy is the man that findeth wisdom." I need hardly remind you of that just and unmeasured eulogy which the wise son of David has bestowed upon it, when he declared in the language of strong persuasion that her ways were ways of pleasantness, and her paths peace.[2] Wisdom, he said, is the principal thing; keep her, for she is thy life.[3]

But where shall this wisdom be acquired? What are the topics to be preferred? Where are the teachers to guide and the facilities to aid us? My friends, I cannot think that we need go far to be satisfied in this point. In the age in which we live, our senses may be our instructors. A man with an inquisitive eye only needs to look around him to find abundant exercise for his sluggish faculties. Let us consider then for a moment in succession the different walks wherein wisdom may be sought, not alone to relieve the irksomeness of life but with the nobler end of supplying an immortal mind with immortal happiness. Let us look first at the objects that surround us in life and see if they be wholly wretched and worthless, and afterward at moral nature.

I. It is a great and moving scene that the world offers us. The noble and unexpected trains of events, the simple and untiring grandeur of the great globe

1. A draft of the first three paragraphs occurs in *JMN* 2:295–96.
2. Proverbs 3:17.
3. Proverbs 4:6–7.

on which they pass, the number and character of the agents, their forms and qualities, the apparent minuteness of their means in comparison with the ends they bring about, and the religious sentiments which men entertain touching the invisible spectators of their action, combine together to make a very attractive spectacle. These are all things precisely adapted to exercise our minds by the study of them and to fill the void of which we complain. The sciences, as they are called, or the classes of facts which human investigation into the laws of nature has laid open, have attained by the patient collection of so many generations of inquirers a maturity and magnitude sufficient to occupy alone the best part of a man's years and to deserve a great expense of time. The arts are at this day so numerous and have made the dominion of man over nature so considerable as to add very greatly to the worth and beauty of the spectacle. Not content with the satisfaction of his first wants—to be wholesomely fed and warmly clothed and lodged and making it his sole philosophy to reduce the number of his wants and wisely despising the imaginary greatness of that primitive state of society "when wild in woods the noble savage ran,"[4] man has invented new wants for the sake of providing new gratifications. He has emerged from the woods where he shivered under the storm and the cold. The sheep is sheared, the loom is contrived, and mines, vegetables, and fishes lend to his raiment their splendid dye. Granite and marble are quarried for his structures. He descends to the margin of the sea and launches his little bark into its unfathomable waters.

These are but units in the catalogue of his arts. The manufacture of books is the art of arts, that has impelled thought and information like a torrent over the globe; the art by means of which he that sits recluse and obscure over a midnight lamp is able to speak in thunder to societies and nations and in the exercise of a higher power leave behind him the impotent prerogatives of kings. It is the device by which the subtile creations of the intellectual power which come and go in the vision of genius but leave no trace when the soul that entertained them is extinct are invested with the permanent attributes of matter, and made to speak to all countries and times. But I desist from any attempt to enumerate his endless inventions. The world is shaken by the enginery which man's wit has confided to his industry. It ploughs the deep; it lays bare the river beds or arches them with stone; it perforates mountains or climbs on their precipices into the kingdom of eternal cold and builds observatories amid Alpine avalanches and compares the purity of upland and lowland air and the altitude of hills. (When the summits of Andes have been surmounted indefatigable art descends into the valleys and searches the bosom of the earth and ransacks the subterranean chambers of nature for gems and gold, for iron, and silver, and coal. A thousand feet below the surface in chasms whence the sun and the moon and the face of the Universe were never beheld, man is immured

4. John Dryden, *The Conquest of Granada*, Part I, I, i, 209, quoted by Samuel Johnson in the *Life of Dryden* (*Lives of the English Poets*, ed. G. B. Hill [Oxford, 1905], 1:461). See also *JMN* 2:273.

and wears out his cheerless years in the streets of salt mines.) In short Art is every where seen. Art dives into the sea and traverses land. Art arms man against man with chemical forces that can hardly be computed and joins men together with facilities for joint useful action which separates taught from untaught man by an almost infinite interval.[5]

But what are these arts and sciences? They are only the use and effect of those faculties which God gave man in their right operation and in all their beautiful triumphs; a pious eye, my friends, will discern no cause for pride, but much for meditation, and much for thanksgiving. These sketches are taken with a design of shewing that the scene which the world offers us is not wholly void of interest and worth; and that a spectator, who turns his attention only to the occupations of men, need not deplore the total unprofitableness of leisure devoted to these occupations. It is intended to suggest, that, to minds so constituted as ours, such a scrutiny into the works of man, as is proposed, can be made to lighten the intolerable burden of vacant time, and enliven it by exciting a curiosity to be gratified. I honour the discretion that assigns a large portion of youth to the pursuit of these inquiries. I respect that ardour which is not quenched by mature years. But I will not disguise the fact that these also may fail of their end, and that the man who is best acquainted with what is known and done, will sometimes sigh at the vanity of his acquisitions, and the barrenness of life. The eye is dazzled at first, and tires at last of the magnificence with which it has become familiar. When this has exhausted its power to please, we have yet a capacity and an appetite which it fails to fill and satisfy. Shall we then recede from our first position that our unhappiness is caused by our ignorance, and our ignorance is our fault? Not in the least; we are only to look elsewhere for its food.[6]

II. There is another class of facts, there is another world of thought, that is open to the diligence of the Mind. There is the moral universe—the native land, the final home of the soul. There are the endless and wonderful contrivances by which God has adjusted the soul to its objects in life, and to the society of all other souls. There is the strange and awful history of the divine compensations; the strict measure of retribution for every deed of good and evil to every being in the world. There is the great array of confederated causes, the manifestations of design whereby we get the evidence of the being and perfections of God. There is the idea of God himself—the stream without a source, the age without an infancy, the glory, the energy that fills the universe without beginning and without ending—the idea so graven in the human heart that wherever society exists, there is religion, and yet the most towering soul that yet has lived was all unable to compass the infinite idea, and last of all—the mysteries of man who investigates them all, the soul, the human soul, that indefatigable inquirer, that wonderful stranger, the citizen of another. Who has uncovered its history? Unseen it

5. A draft of the two preceding paragraphs occurs in *JMN* 2:296-98; used in part in Sermon XII: see n. 8.
6. "These sketches . . . food": see *JMN* 2:298-99.

came, uncomprehended it acts alone, and unbeheld it departs—these may furnish occupation and entertainment to the most ardent and insatiable curiosity.

Is there no occasion worthy of your effort in the study which these things offer to your mind, in the study of those mighty final causes which testify the existence of God; for example, in that curious and admirable disposition of moral forces by which the general advantage is inseparably linked to particular, the social to the selfish, so that whatsoever effort is anywhere made for the most confined personal betterment, the same effort, to its whole extent, ameliorates the condition of mankind,[7] or in watching the unerring progress of God's retribution in public and private affairs, wherein a man, that has lived sixty or seventy years in the world, is able to discern sometimes in a long line of events, the fire, which was smothered at one point, stealing secretly along until it broke out at a distant interval and made amends to destruction for its delay. Or, can you not find most profitable occupation in pondering the gracious revelation of Deity to man, by that exalted person in whose external fortunes God was pleased to rebuke the pride and prejudice of the world by appointing him for our sin to sorrow and poverty, a cup of vinegar and a crown of thorns, to birth in a manger, and to death on a cross?

These are studies which ennoble the character of the student and really possess for those who have entered them, that absorbing interest which throws things that are seen and present very much into the shade. Yes, before these, which are the glory of the unseen world, all other things do fade and die.[8] What, I pray you, are the arts that decorate our dwellings, that clothe our bodies, that increase the conveniences of travelling by land and by water, that please the eye, that pamper pride, when compared with the divine art that formed in secret the soul of man, that established in the Universe the firm boundaries of good and evil? What, though grand, are the material laws that keep the planets in their orbits, to the laws that hold the passions in their awful places, and ordered the faculties, and balanced Reason and Desire in the mind of man?

III. But there yet remains another part of wisdom to which none can plead the want of power or time. "Behold, the fear of the Lord that is wisdom and to depart from evil is understanding."[9] An operative wisdom, a wisdom of good works, it is this, which is the end and perfection of the character. It is this which demands the whole effort of the first archangel and the incipient energies of the little child. The highest speculations, the most rapt devotion, the collected conclusions of all philosophy, the retentive memory that stores up all the libraries of learning and science, are all a dead letter, are worthless rubbish by the side of the living principle, which, in the word of the Scripture, makes men *wise to eternal life*.[10] It is this alone, which can cope with the untried extent of the

7. "so that whatsoever . . . mankind": see *JMN* 2:304.
8. Cf. II Corinthians 4:18.
9. Job 28:28.
10. II Timothy 3:15.

powers of the mind, and which can last as long as life lasts in the soul. For whether there be prophecies, they shall fail, whether there be tongues, they shall cease, whether there be knowledge, it shall vanish away, but charity never faileth.[11] And what is charity but wisdom of good works? Let it not disparage the high duties of meditation and the study of the word and works of God that we lay such high emphasis on this wisdom for these are the best preparation for exalted usefulness. Good works are the fruit which grow best and most naturally from this honorable stock.

It is the peculiar nature of this wisdom, that it needs not schools and manuscripts to teach it. It may be learned and professed and exhibited in shops and warehouses, in our house and on the way. It will never be unseasonable; it will never, like some kinds of knowledge that give men the conceit of wisdom, grow out of use and profit. It will prepare us for heaven; it will lead us there. My friends, let us be exhorted to the attainment of this heavenly wisdom whose fruit is happiness. Let us be assured we shall not, when every day bears witness to this wisdom of our life, complain of life that it is barren and weary and curse the day when we were born.[12] I will not say it shall deliver you from all the sufferings to which flesh is heir,[13] but it shall enable you to bear them without shame or loss.

> "The good man wears disaster as the angel wears
> His wings to elevate and glorify."[14]

It shall elect and appoint you to immortal life. "Happy is the man that findeth wisdom." Happier in the life that now is, than the most favoured child of unsanctified prosperity and happy beyond what eye hath seen or the heart of man conceived in the life which is to come.[15]

11. Cf. I Corinthians 13:8.
12. Job 3:1–3.
13. Cf. Shakespeare, *Hamlet*, III, i, 62–63.
14. Samor. [Emerson's note]. See Henry Hart Milman, *Samor, Lord of the Bright City: An Heroic Poem* (London, 1818), 15.
15. Cf. Isaiah 64:4 and I Corinthians 2:9.

XII

It is a good thing to give thanks unto the Lord.

PSALMS 92:1

We are assembled, my friends, at the return of this ancient anniversary, to express our gratitude to our Almighty Benefactor. There is a suitableness which has not escaped your attention in the season of the service. When Autumn hath yielded up her yellow stores, when the husbandman has gathered in the fruit of the ground,—in all countries and times, it hath appeared to the moral feeling of man, the suitable occasion to render thanks. In the earliest ages, the Assyrian, the Greek, the Roman, paid these joyful rites; and our voice of praise, this day, is but a little verse of the harvest hymn of centuries, which has ever since the beginning ascended from earth to heaven.

But the measure of blessings which has ever prompted the voice of thanksgiving has been very unequal. The plenty which another season has brought us, is one of the least of our advantages. If we are met to thank God for his goodness, it seems to me, that, men have seldom had more occasion for gratitude. We are encompassed with benefits. But the feeling of gratitude is not by any means correspondent to the obligation. It is not those who live in the abundant light of the middle zone of our globe, who most prize the gift of the sun, but it is the poor Greenlander, and Laplander,—those who dwell in the dark and cold extremities of the ball, who, in the long six months' night, remember his glory, and expect his coming, and climb their frozen hills, to watch when the twilight shall reappear; and when, at last, the first gleam of the returning orb flames on their mountain tops, welcome the beam, with rapture, which we can hardly conceive, and celebrate a solemn thanksgiving to their gods. In like manner, it is not commonly those who, in peaceful days, enjoy the advantages of healthy climate; civilized life; equal laws; good education; whose table is bountifully spread; whose cup is filled; whose spirits are regular, and whose health is sound, and whose sleep is sweet,—it is not commonly these, who are most prompt and frequent in the office of thanks: but those who have been bred in the austere house of affliction, those who are used to privation, who come

---

This Thanksgiving sermon was preached in whole or in part on as many as four occasions: November 29, 1827, in Waltham; November 27, 1828, at the Second Church, Boston; November 28, 1833, in New Bedford (the Preaching Record merely indicates "Thanksgiving Sermon" under this date); and December 1, 1836, in East Lexington, when, according to the Preaching Record, Emerson supplemented Sermon XCVII with two pages from Sermon XII.

hardly by their bread, who know the bitterness of persecution, and of sorrow, and of dependance, who, in the language of the ancient exile, "know how salt is the taste of the bread of others, and how hard the way is, going up and down the stairs of others;"[1] who have learned, in the abundance of present evil, to ask if there be not some bright reversion of good in the future; 'tis these who are swift to acknowledge the hand of Providence, in unexpected good fortune; in recovery; in rest; in deliverance; in prosperity. The restored paralytic; the childless widow, whose son was revived; the delivered martyrs in the fiery furnace;[2] the exhausted mariner when the west wind disperses the tempest; our fathers—the famous sea-worn pilgrims, disembarked, at last, on an inhospitable coast;— these, who have suffered much, rejoice more in a partial relief, than those who live in luxury and are loaded with blessings. Others have received little and are grateful, but we have received much. Ours is indeed an unexampled prosperity. It doth not appear that God hath lavished on any other age or people, that degree of good, upon which, here in our land, the eyes of the world have long been turned with admiration and desire.

But, my friends, it is not safe to live in too rash a prosperity. The order of things, in the world, does not consent to unmixed success. We were not sent hither to be pampered with joy, to be sheltered, under the soft wing of affection, from every rude wind of the world; to lie soft in sloth, aloof from oppression, impertinence, and pain, whilst we dream this dream of life. No, we were put hither to be disciplined; to form virtues to strength by exercise, to be educated, like those for whom great destinies are in store, by toil, privation, and exposure; ignorant, to be trained to sages; helpless, to be invigorated to potentates of heaven; men, to be educated to angels. We are not called darlings, but children of God; not minions, but well provided dependants on Providence. It is written in the Scripture that whom God loveth, he chasteneth.[3] It would follow, that, he prospers, often, those whom he doth not approve, and whom the ministers of vengeance have marked. Unmixed felicity is seen to breed the seeds of disease in the mind of man; for he was born for adversity;[4] as the hardy alpine plant corrupts and dies, when transplanted from its bleak glacier, to a richer soil and a southern sun. It is not when the sky is thick with mist, and the morning gloomy with cold and rain, that the planter in the sugar islands apprehends the approach of hurricanes, but when the day goes forth in unclouded beauty, when there is no spot in the firmament to mitigate the dangerous splendour of the morning sun, and the earth sends up her fragrance, unbroken by a breath of air, it is after such a season, that the noon arrives, piled high with thunder clouds, and all things full of omens of alarm. There is in all human happiness, a pro-

---

1. Dante, *Paradiso*, XVII, 57–60, quoted from Ugo Foscolo, "Dante," *The Edinburgh Review*, 30 (Sept. 1818): 351. See *JMN* 6:46.

2. For the paralytic, see Matthew 2:4-12 and Luke 7:11-15; for the widow, see II Kings 4; for the martyrs, see Daniel 3.

3. Cf. Proverbs 13:24 and Hebrews 12:6.

4. Cf. Job 5:7.

pensity to a pause, and a reverse. There are two urns by the throne of Jupiter, said the ancient moralist, one of sweet, and one of bitter waters, and he mixes them both in the cup of every mortal.[5] This is but an expression of what our own experience teaches us of God's Providence. It is this fact, that dashes our best fortune with grief, that the brightest prosperity brings with it, no earnest of continuance, and rather inspires a suspicion of insecurity.

But it will be asked—what is the inference from these reflexions? Ought our prosperity to give us uneasiness? Is good-fortune to be reckoned a misfortune? There is a time to weep, and a time to rejoice.[6] But is it a time to distrust, and form dismal forebodings of the future, now, on this appointed jubilee, when we are met with the express design of indulging our sympathies of joy? No, my brethren, that religion whose cause we plead, was never the foe of human felicity. It exists to add to the amount of happiness. But it would teach us how to enjoy; it would mend this defect in our lot, and put an end to this disastrous uncertainty. It annexes a condition to the mercy of God. It teaches us that the way to be safe is *to be thankful*. It warns us, that we are indolent in our gratitude; that though we should think it shameful and base, to receive the most important benefits at the hand of one of our friends, and repay them with offences and affronts, yet we are apt to receive God's goodness with cold and skeptical indifference; to turn on the hand that holds us, and in breaking the laws, and grieving the spirit of infinite benevolence, to become the Enemy of our best Friend, our Father in Heaven. Is not this a reason why these blessings should cease to descend? But, it is said, it is impossible that our gratitude should avail Him, and there is nothing which such atoms as we are can render to God. What shall we do?—*Be thankful*. Accept the favour he bestows. Do not let it fall into your hands, as a thing of course, but go out to meet the mercy, and acknowledge it as such. There is something in gratitude which, if I may so speak, diminishes the debt, and, where nothing but gratitude can be offered, goes, in a moral view, to square the account. Here there can be no return. From man to God no gift can pass, for all was God's before. But gratitude is a free will effort, on the part of a moral agent, which God is pleased to regard, as an equivalent for his goodness. It elevates the soul towards Himself, and serves his purposes in the Universe, by adding to the amount of moral good, to the sum of happiness. A grateful man is a fellow-worker with God. My brethren, by these representations of what is both our duty and our interest, I desire only to awaken the feeling. I will not presume to prescribe what forms, what results it shall take in action. It is altogether unnecessary. It will work out its own. It will come to glorious issues. A grateful man, I shall cheerfully engage, will be a benevolent man. There is an eternal brotherhood, a perfect affinity between the virtues, that will never fail. The sun may break his bands of attraction, may fail to rise tomorrow; the moon may forget her orbit in the sky; but the human

5. Homer, *Iliad*, XXIV, 663-68 (see *The Iliad of Homer*, trans. Alexander Pope, ed. Maynard Mack [London and New Haven, 1967] 564-65).
6. Cf. Ecclesiastes 3:4.

heart that has once been deeply penetrated with a sense of God's unmerited goodness, will not fail in the law of love to man, will not forget to exercise the tender mercies it has experienced.

And what has convened us, my brethren, in these solemnities of praise? Has some small mercy been measured out to us in the multitude of public and private afflictions? Has the land been darkened with sorrow and a ray of hope broke in? Other states appoint a day of thanks when the pestilence which had unpeopled towns, had spent its poison, and health returns; or when the war, which forced the strength and youth of all the country, the stay of age, the helpful laborer, into its merciless embattled lines, has consumed the strength of the combatants, and a victory or a famine restores peace. And some lands hold a religious festival for a single blessing, as when a river swelled by mountain rains overflows its banks and gives the promise of a fruitful year to tracts that would else be parched to dust by the winds of the desert. And on our own soil, our fathers came up to the house of God in cautious bands with the musket at their shoulder, to thank God that they and their children had escaped one night more from the arrow and the axe, and, in after generations, to rejoice in the temporary success of their arms, in the battles of the revolution.

But it is not so with us. We have not been punished with the plague, or ravaged by war, or threatened by famine, or by the savage. We walk in peace in our ample domain, with none to molest or to make us afraid. We have come in compliance with a venerable custom sanctioned by the usage of near two centuries (and sanctioned too, by our own hearts) whereby our fathers were accustomed to commemorate their sense of that signal Providence which had given to human nature an asylum in the west from the evils which in the old world it had brought upon itself. We come to quote, with emphasis, the language of David in the presence of the Most High,—"He hath not dealt so with any nation."[7] The husbandman has come to rejoice in the abundance of his harvest; the merchant in the safety and thrift of his commerce; the mechanic in the skill of his hands, in the demand of his labour and the ease of subsistence. Age has come to compare the prosperity of the present with the political disasters it can remember when life was new. Manhood to be thankful for strength and freedom and success; and Youth is come to contemplate the felicity which colours with hope and beauty the prospects of life; and Childhood catches, with prompt imitation, from all around, the countenance and language of gladness. We are marked above our brethren of the human race as favoured of heaven. In the history of mankind, there is not a single race, not one period recorded that can compare with our own in the amount of national prosperity. It has always been easy to find a plenty of national miseries. In this country, with all the clamour of our party spirit, it is not easy to put the finger upon one, which comes home to the door of the citizen. That state has been said to be happy, in which the laws are higher than any citizen. Ours are those reverend and sov-

7. Psalms 147:20.

ereign laws. I need hardly enumerate, those remarkable distinctions that call on us so loudly for praise. Within us those mighty faculties are already unfolded, the memory, the reason, the imagination, by which we are made capable of infinite progress.

It seems almost superfluous to point you to those shining advantages of our condition which have given such lustre to this country in the view of all mankind, to that equality which places the son of the poor laborer and the opulent proprietor, on even ground, and invites them both to the first honors and powers in the gift of society, to that cheapness of the means of knowledge which is pouring the copious streams of refinement and information into all the avenues of society, into the farmhouse and the workshop, or to those which belong to us in common with others—to that advancement and multiplication of all the arts of life that lightens labor and increases pleasures and brings solace and luxury to the fireside of the poor and the rich. We have abundant cause to be grateful for the progress of man; for the immense facilities of knowledge and enjoyment which the slow accumulation of so many centuries of improvements has furnished us. The Arts have arrived in our day at that perfection and have made the dominion of man over nature so considerable as to deserve admiration. Man has emerged from the woods where once he shivered under the storm and the cold. The sheep is sheared, and the loom is contrived and mines, vegetables, and fishes lend to his raiment their splendid dye. Granite and marble are quarried for his structures. He descends to the margin of the sea, and launches his little bark into its unfathomable waters. A bauble, a particle on the interminable waste, I see it mount the ridges and sink into the vallies of the Ocean; but the understanding of him that guides it, which was the gift of God, sits sovereign of its course. Its curious furniture of helm and sail and compass lead the little adventurer on in safety and though the whirlwind from heaven sweep across his path, and the tempest tear his canvass, as in sport, it contends with the elements and rides out the storm; and comes at last over nearly a straight line of thousands of leagues of water, to visit the farthest corners of the world. When the message of another nation has been delivered here, and the fruits of the tropics bartered for those of the pole, when the character, language, and country have been scrutinized by the eyes of the stranger, he sets his sail anew, and flees over the deep, to enrich the science of his own land with his strange tidings and its wealth with those gifts of Providence which are denied to its soil. These are but units in the catalogue of his arts. The manufacture of books, is the art of arts that has impelled thought and information like a torrent, over the globe; the art, by means of which he that sits recluse and obscure over a midnight lamp is able to speak in thunder to societies and nations, and, in the exercise of a higher power, to leave behind him the impotent prerogatives of kings. It is the device by which the subtile creations of the intellectual power that come and go in the vision of genius and leave no trace when the soul that entertained them is extinct, are invested with the permanent attributes of matter, and made to speak to all countries and times. The world is shaken with the enginery which man's wit has confided to his industry. It ploughs the deep. It lays bare the river beds; or arches them with stone; it perforates mountains, or climbs on their precipices into the kingdom of eternal cold; and builds observatories amid Alpine avalanches. When the summits of Andes have been surmounted, indefatigable Art descends into the valleys and searches the bosom of the earth and ransacks the subterranean chambers of nature for gems and gold, for iron, silver, and coal. A thousand feet below the surface, in chasms whence the sun and the moon and the face of the Universe were never beheld, man is immured, and wears out his cheerless years in the streets of salt mines. In short Art is every where seen; Art dives into the sea; and traverses the land; and joins men together with facilities for joint useful action which separate taught from untaught men by an almost infinite interval.[8] And is there nothing in all this to prompt our hearts to praise?

But, my friends, when we have enumerated our civil distinctions, the advantages of education, the advantages of a healthy climate and a fruitful soil and the enjoyments derived from the progress of the arts of life, we have not yet touched the highest sources of our happiness and reasons of our gratitude. The profligacy of another generation may assail and demolish the noble institutions of our liberty and laws. Your soil may yield its fruit to a foreign master or be trampled by the bloodhounds of domestic anarchy. Your fleets may rot on the margin of the main whose wastes they now traverse as the highway of the world. The day may come when a palsy shall wither the arm of Art; when the looms, the presses, and the forges of New England shall stand still; when this strong population which is marching to the west over mountains and lakes shall halt and disappear; when this mighty continent shall be swept clean of its rejoicing nations and become once more the hunting field of an Indian tribe. Or, it may be, those revolutions, that have taken place in the globe itself, may return. The ocean may be poured over these fair states, and the long sea grass grow over our cities. All this may impend, and not touch our greatest blessings. The country we now love with the fondest affection, may flourish or may fall,— but to us it cannot long be a country. It must grow cold—this warm thrill of patriotism—before more deep and solemn feelings. It is really to us of *trifling* importance what events await it; for we are citizens of another country. Let us bless God, my friends, that all the greatness and glory of the world is but dust in the balance to the eternal weight of glory to which it hath pleased him to invite us.[9] Within the breast of each of us now resides a power that shall live in immortal youth when the earth shall pass away and the heavens be no more.[10] Within us those affections are already expanded which knit themselves to your children and friends as they gather around you in the social circle and which suggest to us the heaven that must arise from their pure and unbounded exercise. We have not been left in ignorance of our hopes and our duties. To us a Son

8. "The Arts . . . interval": see *JMN* 2:297–98 and Sermon XI, n. 5.
9. Cf. Isaiah 40:15.
10. Cf. Revelation 21:1.

of God is born; to us a Saviour is given;[11] to us immortality is brought to light, and we have been instructed how by patient continuance in ways of well doing we may seek for glory, honour, and eternal life.[12] These are the true occasions of joy and praise.

There are those among us, it may be, upon whose ear, the topics of public and social rejoicing fall with a cold and unaffecting sound. This day may remind some among us, rather of what they have lost, than of what they have received: but upon these occasions of *spiritual* thanksgiving, there can be no difference of sentiment. There is a piety that sings anthems of praise as it sits amid the ruins of its earthly hopes. The connexion of our minds with God our Maker, and the hope of heaven remain. These shall stand fast to us though the passing afflictions of time press heavy on our lot. Although the figtree shall not blossom, neither fruit be in the vines; the labor of the olive fail and the fields yield no meat; the flock be cut off from the fold and there be no herd in the stalls; yet we will rejoice in the Lord, we will joy in the God of our Salvation.[13]

In addition to the substantial enjoyment which this progress of art has effected and to the still more valuable faculty which it has called out in so many ingenious and able laborers, the myriads whom it feeds in the densely peopled lands of Christendom contrasted with the thin and starved population of a hunting or a pastoral tribe of savages, the superior moral condition of the civilized man is not to be forgotten. The savage state is not the virtuous state. If refinement has its own crimes the aggregate of crime is less and its character milder. It is a blessed conclusion of political economy that the moral character of a community is mended or relaxed with the greater or less security of property and that on the same security of property civilization depends.[14]

Permit me in conclusion to suggest one more view of the subject. It has been said that our blessings are insecure. Our past experience has a thousand voices to proclaim the fact. But, my friends, let it admonish us to wisdom. There is a wise and excellent institution well known to you in all commercial communities by which the profits of industry are secured to the possessor and put out of danger from the common contingencies of fire and storm; so that the merchant can hear the tempest rage without apprehension for his cargoes on the deep, and the sleep of the proprietor is not broken by fear of danger to his warehouses from the fires of a capital. Now, my brethren, let me beseech you to take a lesson yourselves from this wisdom of the world. You are, at this moment, in possession of numberless blessings for which we are met to thank God today. *Insure* these blessings. Secure them now so that if they be taken from you, you also may receive an equivalent. Do you ask how this may be done and what equivalent is in store? Comply with the conditions on which they are promised. Hold them as a steward and not as a proprietor. Devote them, devote your-

11. Cf. Isaiah 9:6.
12. Romans 2:7.
13. Habakkuk 3:17-18.
14. "It is a . . . depends": see *JMN* 2:288.

selves, to the sovereign uses which Heaven approves to the doing of good. Feed the hungry, clothe the naked, and then, happen what may, fear not, my brother, you shall be safe. If it please God to take away his gifts, he will leave with you a heart softened and fitted for heaven: he will give you his favor which is eternal life. We bring you the claims of those whom it has pleased God to exclude from an equal share in those blessings for which we give thanks. We supplicate you to spread out the hand of charity to those whom God has made your pensioners. We bid you pay a premium of insurance on the prosperity you enjoy, that God may continue to smile on your industry, on your homes, on your virtues, on your hopes, and when your dust shall sleep in the ground, the trumpet of the angel of the Resurrection may call you to *give thanks* amid the ten thousands of his saints.[15]

15. Jude 1:14.

XIII

Unto you is born this day in the city of David a Saviour who is Christ the Lord.

LUKE 2:11

We are met, my friends, on the anniversary of that day which for many ages has been set apart by the great majority of Christians to celebrate the nativity of the Founder of our faith. It is hardly necessary to urge upon you the propriety of giving some extraordinary notice to the day. Our own ancestors did indeed account it superstitious and were averse to give the sanction of their countenance to the multiplication of the holidays of the church. But we who know how bitter were their feelings of dislike to the church of England out of which they came, and how harsh and cruel a stepmother she had been to the Puritans, can easily understand how their aversion to its abuses should sometimes betray them into unjust prejudices against its best institutions. But with us there exists no reason for similar apprehensions. Two centuries have strangely changed the aspect of affairs. The day has long gone by since men in this country learned to look with terror at the forms and rites or at the ambition of that ancient Church. Our civil freedom or our freedom of conscience cannot now be endangered by the surplice or the mitre so offensive to our fathers and we may copy whatever is favorable to devotion in her solemnities without peril from the usurping influence of bishops. Moreover we have the authority of the apostolic command, Whatsoever things are true, just, honest, lovely, and of good report, wherein there is virtue and wherein there is praise, these things think upon and practise.[1] And do we think it just and becoming to celebrate with all the forms of honor and congratulation the jubilee of our Independence? Do we delight to repair to the rock of Plymouth to indulge our sympathies of joy in the unexampled prosperity of New England, and shall we not feel and admit the far higher and holier claim upon our gratitude that comes to us out of mourning and desolate Judah, from the little town of Bethlehem where the Son of Man was born who brought life and immortality to light? Were it not absurd to be overjoyed at events that affect our worldly prosperity, our freedom and civil

---

Emerson preached this Christmas sermon four times: December 25, 1827, in Concord, N.H.; December 25, 1828, in Waltham; and December 28, 1828, at the Second Church, Boston in the morning, and in West Boston in the afternoon.

1. Philippians 4:8.

privileges during the few years we live in the world, and at the same time to turn coldly away from contemplating an event that revealed to us all that we live for, all that we hope, our relations to God, to the universe of moral beings, and to Eternity? Through the darkness and sin of two thousand years I see the light of the shepherds' star and am refreshed. Over that vast and dreary space of time I hear distinct above the jargon of sects, above the fearful noise of human passions, I hear the song of the angels. I hear and must listen to the sound. I should accuse myself if I could repress my joy. Yes, my friends, apart from all consideration of the propriety of these recollections, apart from all comparison between this and other seasons of general joy, this occasion has in itself a beautiful solemnity and is necessarily agreeable to the human mind. It will not harm us to give ourselves up to the feelings it has so powerful a tendency to excite. It will not encroach upon our time. Can we not watch with our master in his cradle an hour?[2] There is no lack among us of worldly prudence and care, there is quite an abundance of common festivity and common griefs. It cannot be said they have not their share of our attention and our time. But come, let us break away from them all; they can spare us one hour of inviolate joy. The voice that spake peace and good will to men let it speak peace to our minds and let us proclaim therein a solemn festival;[3] a little breathing space; the sabbath of an hour to thoughts of God, of his holy child Jesus, and of our own connexion with him, which outlives our connexion with this perishing world.

In all other occasions of gladness, such is the imperfection of our condition, there is generally something to lament. When we exult in the successful achievement of our independance we glory in what was once an occasion of bereavement to ten thousand families. The gain of the whole is purchased by the grief of the many. In order to a triumph there must be victims. But we signalize a jubilee which is single in the Universe. Ours is a joy without reproach or deduction, a spotless, a holy commemoration, a conquest of good over evil: a conquest of souls to God: a blessed revelation to man of unheard of happiness: of pardon to sin: and of infinite progress in knowledge and enjoyment through the never-ending ages of the future.

Suffer me then, my friends, to call your serious attention to some considerations upon the peculiar circumstances and the value of that event this season commemorates. You all know the remarkable fact that there appears to have been about the time of the Advent, a general expectation, a looking for in the world of some manifestation of the will of Heaven beyond the ordinary course of Providence. Among the Jews it arose very naturally from the strong and fervent predictions of their ancient prophets, which continually returned from their denunciation of retribution on the crimes of their own generation, to the bright and beautiful vision of the Conqueror to come, of the child to be born, of the dayspring from on high that was to illuminate the world, that should scatter the darkness that had gathered about the Divine perfections, that should reveal

2. Cf. Matthew 26:40.
3. Luke 2:14.

him to men not as their Law had revealed him, a stern and jealous Deity encompassed in darkness and thunder, with the ministers of vengeance by the side of his throne, but should declare his true and eternal character, should declare to men that God is Love,[4] that he is our Father, who sends us a message of mercy from on high, to show us the way to heaven.

But not among the Jews alone, it would appear, this hope existed. As sometimes the occurrence of great events in the world has been preceded by unaccountable rumors which have been justified by what followed, so it would seem that the communication from God to man was waited for in expectant silence by the nations of the earth.[5] There is a singular passage in one of the Dialogues of Plato, which, it must be remembered, were written 400 years before the birth of Christ, in which Alcibiades converses with Socrates on the proper objects of Prayer, and Socrates asks him if it does not seem likely that God would send into the world some teacher who should inform us what we ought to pray for and they agree that it will be wise to wait for the instructions of that messenger.[6] If such expectations were entertained by the wisest in Greece it would appear also that in Rome the ancient books which were kept in their temples and called the Sybilline prophecies, had intimated also the approach of a better and clearer dispensation. The famous pastoral of Virgil inscribed to Pollio has been often compared to the prophecies of Isaiah, so similar is the language in which he foretells the coming of a more virtuous and peaceful age.[7] The shutting also of the doors of the temple of Janus for the first time for some hundred years, which were never closed but in time of universal peace, had prepared men to expect some auspicious and unknown events.[8] To all this St. Paul evidently alludes when he writes to the Romans, For the earnest expectation of the whole creation is waiting for the manifestation of the sons of God[9]—and afterward—that the Creation should be delivered from the bondage of corruption into the glorious liberty of the Sons of God.[10] This was the state of human feeling. Man wondered in the world why he that had framed this stupendous Creation had left himself without witness therein.

Man felt, whilst God was not clearly made known, what all men now feel when they live without acknowledgment of God,—a strange disproportion between his desires and his condition, between what he is and what he seems made for: so noble in his powers and so lowly in his necessities that there

---

4. I John 4:8, 4:16.

5. Emerson had recorded this idea in his journal in December 1824; see *JMN* 2:307.

6. "The Second Alcibiades," in *The Works of Plato*, trans. Thomas Taylor (London, 1804), 4:612. This is an apocryphal work composed in the second or third century B.C.; see W. R. M. Lamb, *Plato* (New York and London, 1927), 226.

7. Vergil, Eclogue IV. St. Augustine was the first to remark on the presence of Christian prophecy in the poem; see Robert Coleman, ed., *Vergil: Eclogues* (London, 1977), 52–54. For Emerson's knowledge of the Sibylline prophecies, see *JMN* 1:43, n. 17.

8. Octavian closed the doors of the Temple of Janus after returning from the battle of Actium in 31 B.C. See Suetonius, *The Twelve Caesars*, II, 22.

9. VIII Rom. 19 [Emerson's note].

10. Romans 8:21.

needed another world to explain the difficulties of this. My brethren, this feeling must have arisen in your own minds in every hour of uncertainty. I have before had occasion to allude to it more at large. You will forgive me for dwelling upon it a moment in this connexion.

Though the Earth we inhabit is nobly furnished, though the heavens are arched gloriously over our heads, yet when morning breaks in the east and the sun rises, man steps forth from his little dwelling into this swelling scene to labour, to eat, to drink, to laugh, to talk, to sin, and to sleep again. He heeds it not, this wondrous majesty wherewith the great house of nature is adorned. Let the sun go up the sky and the moon shine, and innumerable stars move before him in orbits so vast that centuries shall not fulfil them, though the seasons roll and the winter cover his fields with coat of dazzling snow and the summer pour out upon them her horn of plenty, he does not care, he does not know; he is creeping in a little path of his own; he is following a few appetites; is peering round for a little bread; is devising some minute arts to get an atom from his neighbor's heap and add it to his own; he is laying stratagems in petty things for the admiration of his fellows; he is bewailing small inconveniences; he is pouting at the cold or the heat; he is absorbed in the apprehension or the suffering of his diseases.

Man felt the *absurd*, if I may so call it, of his condition. He lifted up to the heavens an eye of despair and asked to what purpose was all this prodigal magnificence if the only fact that could aid and stablish him, namely the Being of God to whom he stood in relations of dependance, had no support from all. He walked on earth but there was no voice of God. He explored the stars but they were silent in their courses. He waited in Rome, in Greece, in Egypt, impatient for light to break that should show him why he was made and what was to become of him in the immense future before him. He waited not in vain. In the sky of the East a star arose. On the midnight heaven the silver accents were heard of the heavenly host praising God and saying, Glory to God in the highest. On Earth peace, goodwill to men.[11] This day is born in the city of David a Saviour who is Christ the Lord.

I cannot but regard the manner in which it pleased God that his chosen messenger should appear in the world as peculiarly consistent with his character and office. I rejoice also in the fact as a strong incidental evidence to the authenticity of the evangelists, that they have not made any attempt to colour or conceal the humble place and circumstances of his birth, which to men of their expectations and prejudices as Jews must have appeared strangely unsuitable to the character of the Messiah which he claimed. We rejoice that he was not born in the lap of majesty and ostentation. We feel the sublimity of his houseless and unfriended lot. We feel how the artificial distinctions of life, the poverty and riches, rank and lowliness, sink into dust before the greatness of Him that sent him and the dignity of the office he was appointed to bear.

And now, my friends, I would invite your meditations to the excellence of the

11. Luke 2:13–14.

divine gift. I would not affix a superstitious regard to what has real claim enough of its own upon our gratitude and love. I would not take—I dare not take—from that awful reverence which is due to God alone and bestow it on his son who so often and so expressly denied his title to be more than the servant and messenger of the Most High, who delighted, in his humility, to represent himself as nothing;—that the words that he spoke were not his; that the works which he did were not his, brought no glory to him, but to his father in whose name and by whose power they were said and done.[12] But I would seriously consider the genuine divinity of the gift to ignorant and sinful men. My friends, when you have gone into your closets and shut your door, when you have knelt in secret before God and felt that you were in the immediate presence of the majesty of Heaven and Earth and have attempted strongly to conceive of the Being you addressed, have you not sometimes found it a difficult and bewildering effort?[13] In the weakness and ignorance of our nature the human mind must often struggle ineffectually to compass the great idea of an infinite Being everywhere present in whom we live, move, and have our being.[14] Unless the thoughts are very powerfully concentrated they are prone to wander. The heart must be wound up to devotion. It must be warmed by the sense of some signal mercy, or, which is the great injunction of Christianity, the feelings must be trained by long use of habitual reference to the divine Presence or the affections will grow cold toward God. If this difficulty disturb our acts of devotion, and the best and wisest men have often complained of it, how much more hard was it for those who lived before the Christian Revelation to acquire and preserve in their daily life just conceptions of the character of God and of their duties to him? The idea of Deity oppresses the imagination. It is very easy for us to understand how men were led into idol worship. They had within them, as all men have, a religious feeling, a notion of God, of some being or beings greater in nature than man, and who made and governed men. The idea of God—It encumbered them. It struggled to find expression. It tempered their joy. It authorized their hope. It added horror to fear. It armed their sorrow for sin with a scorpion sting. In obedience to this strong feeling they strove to express it and to do it honor by building idols and temples and paying it a visible and costly service, and devised a thousand ceremonies to keep alive their sense of this presence of the Gods among men and this gave the mind a temporary consolation and ease. But God by outward revelation to the Jews and by inward revelation to the minds of the wisest of the heathens taught them their error. But the rude mind of the people still found doubt and fatigue in a spiritual service. It might do for Cherubim, for the stupendous intellects that waited with sleepless eye about his Throne to see him unveiled.[15] But not so with dust and ashes. Man must put something between God and his own nothingness.

They worshipped therefore in Greece and Rome imaginary gods who were

12. John 14:10.
13. Cf. Matthew 6:6.
14. Acts 17:28.
15. Revelation 4:8.

personifications of the divine perfections. Minerva was his wisdom; Apollo was his light and eternal youth. The Fates were his eternal decrees. And in the Dark Ages, as we emphatically call them, when the Christian religion, grossly misunderstood, was confounded with these ancient superstitions, nations knelt before the shrines of the Virgin. Even this superstition was a wonderful improvement on the pagan worship. There is something in a high degree religious and beautiful in the affection with which the Catholic regards the Holy Virgin, which is every way preferable to the pagan conception of Diana, of Venus and Juno, and which may serve to show that a corrupted form of Christianity is better than the finish of paganism. Her votary calls her the stainless benevolent; he supplicates with that confidence he would feel towards a mother her intercession for his sake, and the countenance which the genius of the Italian painters has delineated for the virgin has an angelic sweetness far different from, and far more attractive than, the stern beauty of the ancient goddesses.

But this was the continual tendency of human weakness feeling the necessity of supernatural protection and of some bright example by which life might be guided to run into the worship of false Gods; to tremble before the true. But it pleased God in his infinite mercy to reveal his character distinctly to men. The great internal distinction, I believe you will agree with me, of this Revelation we receive is, that it is the only account that has disclosed a character of God agreeable to the human mind. All former theologies, by whatever genius developed, by whatever sublimity elevated, distorted the Deity with monstrous features. Something wild and prodigious for which the soul saw no reason was always added to the power and knowledge of the infinite mind. But in the Christian Religion, God is made known to us as the God of Man. It is made clear to us that we are made in his moral image,[16] and that to find out him we must explore ourselves, that these high faculties of ours, the Reason and the Affections of man, of which the elements exist in the humblest outcast that wears the form—when carried out to their perfection do compose a mind that fills and quickens and governs the Universe.

We are not simply told that there is a God, but God is really revealed to our minds.

We learn to regard this as the most interesting relation of man, that in the lowest cabin of the squalid savage, in the unwholesome caverns of the mine, wherever man appears, there goes one capable of seeing and loving God, capable of the most towering thought and uncompromising virtue.

We are made to enter into a sublime sympathy with our maker; to speak to him day by day; to watch his eye as it always rests on us; to perform or to forbear actions in obedience to it; to act from him, and with him; and finally we are sent forward on a great and neverending progress to greatness in the effort to bring ourselves into his majestic likeness.

16. Cf. Genesis 1:27.

There is still one more view kindred to this which I wish to take of the subject. To show himself not the severe abstraction of Justice and Power, he sent a being among men to teach and in a manner to exemplify his character, one that could sympathize with men, could, like men, pursue knowledge and glory, glory in its highest forms, that of sufferance, one to be born at Bethlehem; to be hungry and tempted in the wilderness; to weep at Bethany; to be oppressed during life by the awful consciousness of his fate; to be insulted with hideous aggravation; to die on Calvary the death of a malefactor.

For these reasons we rejoice and are glad because he not only taught us that we are heirs of eternal life but because he taught us the paternal character of God; because he exhibited in his life a model for ours; taught us how a man in scrupulous obedience to the commandments of God might resist temptation and keep himself unspotted from the world;[17] and exhibited in this way an image of the Divine nature reduced within the compass of our understanding and love. Therefore we delight to remember his nativity. Beautiful is the name of Bethlehem through all ages. Dear to human nature is the name and venerable idea of its blessed and glorified instructor. A healthful example, a cheering encouragement, a bright beacon lit up in the darkness of the old world and sending out its pure and hospitable light into all the future history of man. My brethren, when I consider the consequences of that joyful night, when I attempt to measure the good that has accrued to the world from the Christian Dispensation, the commanding check it has for ages kept upon the dangerous passions of men, how it has rivetted the social bonds and brought forward so many noble spirits to the help of suffering humanity: when I look at the early history of an institution, these great and blessed mysteries which have hoarded comfort from age to age for human suffering—the august Founder, the twelve selfdenying heroes of a pious renown, distancing in moral sublimity all those primeval benefactors which ancient gratitude deified; the apostles whose desiring eyes saw little lustre on earth and no consolation but in extending the victories, the moral victories, of the cross; the martyrs who had found after so many sensual ages in a faith for things unseen,[18] in a moral intellection, more than a compensation for the lust of the world and the pride of life; and after all these and better even than all these, the boundless aggregate of hearts and deeds which the genius of Christianity touched and inspired, the violence of fiery natures to which it has whispered peace, the antidote it has administered to remorse and despair, the Samaritan oil it has poured into wounded hearts,[19] the costly sacrifices and unpurchaseable devotion to the cause of God and man it has now for eighteen centuries inspired. When I consider all this, the sum of what is most precious on earth, and trace it back in its long progress to the humble manger of a Jewish inn, I am overawed by the manifest interposition of the hand of God in behalf of his sinful children, and I echo the solemn anthem that announces glad

17. James 1:27.
18. Cf. Hebrews 11:1.
19. Luke 10:33–34.

tidings of great joy to us and to all men. Glory to God, peace and goodwill to men.[20]

Finally, my friends, let us deeply consider each of us in the silence of our own hearts what is our share in the joy of this day. True it is that everlasting life has been made known to men, that Jesus Christ the saviour who was born this day did exhibit amid the extremes of sorrow and poverty and ingratitude and persecution a radiant, a perfect, a godlike character, and taught us how we might obtain the favor of God by an obedience like his own. And have we complied with the condition? Has our daily life been led, like his, in an uniform progress from duty to duty, from faith to faith, from trial to trial, never surprized into sin by temptation, never cast down from our integrity by difficulty or opposition? If it be so, rejoice and be glad for by the word of him that this day was born, great is your reward in heaven.[21] But if the exceeding great and precious promises which he brought, have been slighted by you, if your days have been made dark by sin, if the immortal faculties that slumber in your breast have been neglected or abused, alas! my brother, alas! what is it to you that squadrons of angels announced his birth, what matters it though the Almighty clothed him in power to bear witness to the truth of his mighty commission, what is it to you that death could not destroy him, that the tomb rendered back its trust, that he forsook it and arose? or yet that he ascended to his Father and ever liveth to make intercession for his faithful disciples? What is it to you but another weight of sin which will be laid to your charge, inasmuch as you have sinned against this marvellous light?[22] You have seen what prophets and kings desired but were not able, and have averted your eyes.[23] The prevailing eloquence of his life, the wonders of his hand, have failed to move you. The great tragedy of his death and the interposition of the Almighty for his Resurrection have failed to move you; then is this day an occasion of sorrow and danger, for the light of this day shall be remembered against you as an opportunity which you have slighted, as a warning which you defied. But no, I trust in God it shall not be so with us. Let us remember that life is short, and neglected opportunities will never return; that Christ will not again appear, till he comes to sit in judgment. Let him that in body was born in Bethlehem, in spirit be born in our hearts. Let us celebrate his nativity there. Let his temper grow up in our souls. Let his laws controul our actions; and govern our minds; and when he shall come to judge the earth in righteousness, we shall appear with him in glory.[24]

20. Luke 2:10, 14.
21. Matthew 5:12.
22. Cf. I Peter 2:9.
23. Cf. Matthew 13:17 and Luke 10:24.
24. Cf. Acts 17:31 and Colossians 3:4.

Wherefore we receiving a kingdom which cannot be moved, let us have grace, whereby we may serve God acceptably.

HEBREWS 12:28

In every age of the world men have been divided into parties in government, and sects in religion. Great good and great evil have undoubtedly arisen from this division of opinion, and the disposition to espouse with heat the defence of one system of doctrines. The *evil* has been the excitement of bad passions in the controversy; the indulgence of ill will against those who differed from us on abstract questions until it was embittered to exasperation and revenge. The *good* that has flowed from the same source is not less great and indisputable. It is, the development of truth which is always the result of free discussion. As soon as men are inflamed to dispute they seize immediately upon the weakest point of their opponent. Whatever falsehood, whatever error, whatever vice can be detected in the precept or practice of the obnoxious system is sure to be exposed. The attack is repeated and repeated till at last it is successful and that post is abandoned. Thus, upon each side of every great question, one error after another is abandoned forever by its defenders, and the world is the gainer.

But does the good or evil preponderate? This question is the same as to ask whether the iron despotism of the East, where every citizen's life and property, his wife, his children, his projects and enterprizes are at the absolute disposal of a single man, a foolish passionate despot, whether this government, which secures profound peace from age to age, the peace of ignorance, fear, poverty, and superstition, without art, without commerce, without virtue or hope, be not better than the limited government of such a state as England or France agitated by its turbulent parties and goaded always by the indignant cries of half a nation out of every course of impolicy and dishonor. Or as the question affects religious sects, it is to ask whether the Inquisition of Spain which takes the life of him who doubts the infallibility of the Pope and the divine purity of the holy

---

According to a notation at the end of the manuscript, this sermon was completed in Cambridge on February 1, 1828. Preached five times: June 1, 1828, in Concord, Mass.; June 15 in Concord, N.H.; September 7 at the Second Church, Boston; October 19 in Dover, N.H.; and November 8, 1829, at the Second Church, Boston.

Catholic Church, whether the silent acquiescence produced by terror in all the absurdities of a most foolish superstition be not more desirable than the keen and incessant altercation of the different denominations of New England in the defence of their own and the attack of opposite doctrines—in the course of which so much critical learning of the Scriptures has been acquired and displayed; so many ancient errors exploded and such deep and vigilant interest awakened amongst all classes in the great religious inquiries themselves.

It is the order of Providence in this world that every good thing should be bought with a price.[1] In our civil institutions the inconvenience of party spirit is the price we pay for liberty. And, in the church, the noise and sometimes the bitterness of controversy is the price we pay for freedom of conscience and enlightened views of religion. And the good and wise, my brethren, have thought these blessings worth all and more than all the purchase.

It is not therefore a thing to be deplored as an unmitigated evil—the existence of religious controversy. It may be abused and carried to the extravagance of persecution and civil war: but as long as it retains its milder form of temperate though ardent discussion; as long as it is directed to the honest and laborious investigation of the scriptures, and of all the stores of sacred learning, so long, it is a sign of good: a sure token that public opinion is advancing in the right way, in the way to truth.

In our day, my friends, our attention is continually called to the efforts that are made to preserve or to carry forward the progress of religious improvement. We build churches to the recovered faith of the apostles and primitive believers. The land is filled with sermons and tracts that plead with men on every point of faith and of practice. Every good man is glad. It is a genuine subject of congratulation. And in view of all this I am led to offer you some remarks on the progress of religious opinion and the duties and the hopes of which it reminds us.

I. Our attention is called to the progress of religious opinion. And there can be no more genuine cause for sincere pleasure. My friends, if you should take a savage out of the woods, and it were possible for you, in the course of one short hour to illuminate his mind with all that Newton knew,—I do not know that we can at all conceive the tumult of joy and astonishment that would awaken in his soul. When he compared the newly acquired power of his mind to range through the universe; its deep research into the secrets of nature; its familiar acquaintance with all her infinite wonders; his new conceptions of the power and perfections of God the Author of nature; when he considered this immense leap of his mind, and compared it with his former condition; his squalid ignorance; his petty skill in a few wretched arts whereby he supported, from day to day, his worthless life:—would he not feel that he had become another being? Would he not feel that he had mounted in the scale of existence, and arrived as it were at the powers and happiness of an angel? And would he not value, as life itself, his new advancement? Would he exchange, would all sensual felicity

1. See Sermon IV, n. 7.

tempt him to exchange the truth he had gained for the prejudice he had lost? And now, my friends, is it less a cause of joy to us, is it a change less real, or less valuable,—the fact that the Christian community, in which we live, have made a progress in their knowledge of God, and human duty, and human hopes,—a progress upon the knowledge of other ages, and other nations, as marked and sublime as that we have just supposed, of the most profound and instructed philosopher over the savage that roams our forest? Is the change less real and glorious, because it has been the slow work of ages; the work of martyrs and just men; the work of thousands of toiling minds, and not momentary and miraculous? I know not why we should appoint days of thanksgiving to make a public expression of our gratitude to God for the common blessings of the year, for the beneficent order of the seasons, the abundance of the harvest, the prosperity of our civil institutions, and all things that have chief regard to our bodily good, and take no note when it pleases God, the author of the mind, to visit with his sovereign influences the mind, to unloose it from the bondage of ages and bid it arise and go forth. Shall we suppose that the good Being we worship, the Father of our spirits, looks with less complacence on the blessing he has conferred when he has succoured a soul that was blinded by ignorance and diseased by prejudice with the divine light of truth and brought it into healthful action than when he has given bodily sight to the blind and recovery to the sick? No, my brethren, whenever one error is exploded, whenever one step is gained in our approach to truth in the knowledge of God and duty, the church universal on earth, that is to say the great company of wise and good men throughout the world of whatever name or tongue or kindred, rejoice in that progress. The angels who have joy in heaven over one sinner that repenteth rejoice also in one error that is reformed, and God, over all, approves it.[2]

It is hardly necessary that I should attempt to mark the stages of this revolution in human opinion. Indeed it is hardly possible I should, for, it grows out of high and distant causes and the kingdom of God comes not by observation.[3] Its progress is not less certain because it is insensible. You cannot see the movement of the sun on the arch of heaven, but we can discern from hour to hour what progress he has made to the meridian. You cannot detect the effect of true religion upon the character of our own community during the past month or the past year but we can measure the immense interval that separates us as Christians from the unnumbered millions of the barbarous East, from the Hindoo parent who propitiates his bloody gods by mutilating his form or follows with gloomy countenance the red track of the chariot of that tremendous idol whose name excites terror and disgust in all Christian lands.[4] But not to insist on the

2. Luke 15:7, 15:10.
3. Luke 17:20.
4. The Jagannath (or Juggernaut), an idol of Krishna in Puri; devotees would throw themselves under the wheels of its chariot at the time of its annual procession. Emerson's early interest in Hindu religions has been treated by Kenneth W. Cameron in *Indian Superstition* (Hanover, N.H., 1954) and *Emerson's "Indian Superstition": With Studies in His Poetry, Bibliography, and Early Orientalism* (Hartford, Conn., 1977). See also *JMN* 2:195.

superiority of our religion to these extremes of delusion, we are easily able to measure the progress that has been made from time to time in the understanding and practice of our own Christian faith. We can measure the great advance made on the corruptions of the Romish Church by the early reformers, by Wicliffe and Erasmus and Luther. We can estimate the progress made by our fathers, the Puritans, on the English reformed Church. And now, our hearts and our understandings can approve the simplicity and beauty of that purified Christianity, which a better understanding of the scriptures and of the character of God have taught us, over some of the dark superstitions which our fathers received.

My brethren, in our minds God is restored to the supremacy of the Universe—to that undivided and eternal authority which the infinite Creator claims for himself, and which we dare not withhold. In our minds his government is acquitted of those high charges of which sinful man in ignorance, (on which God will have mercy) had accused it. We have not so learned the lessons of Christ as to think that the sin of Adam had poisoned the blood of all the race of man; had called down the wrath of the Almighty upon them all without reference to their character; had turned their good to evil, their prayers to blasphemies, their hope to horror. We cannot find in our bibles, cannot in our hearts admit, that baleful doctrine, that, God from eternity elected some of his children to happiness and some to misery, without regard also to character. We have learned that the scriptures teach none of these things, but that the purpose of the scripture is to reveal to us the will of God, to give us the cheering revelation that our souls are immortal; that this world is a state of discipline, a school of preparation to train us up for endless being; that all that we do goes to make up our character, and that on our character, our happiness wholly depends; inasmuch as we are good, we shall be happy, and inasmuch as we are bad, we shall be miserable. For this, we believe, the Son of God came into the world—to teach us these truths, and to give us in *his* life, a model for ours. To prove that he came from God, he did wonderful works, such as none could do, unless God were with him. For this, he died and rose again.—We think it a sure mark of truth in the better views of religion which begin to prevail amongst us the more pure and elevated views of the character of God; that we are taught to regard him as our Father and our best Friend; as a pure and benevolent spirit who made all things for good.

Having these views of the reality and the value of the progress of religious opinion we have a word to say:

II. Secondly, on the duties of which it reminds us. This progress that has been made in religious opinions it belongs to us to make our own, to maintain and to continue. And let us not think lightly of the duty. Do not, I beseech you, confound it yourselves with worldly interest or sinful pride; and give no occasion to others to imagine for a moment that it is the pride of opinion, or a bigoted attachment to a creed, or the frantic spirit of party—that these poor motives are all or any of the principles that urge us to use our might in asserting our faith; but a higher and holier feeling, a deep instinct of the mind belonging to its life, and immortal within us by which it cleaves to truth with a strong delight. Truth is the object God made it to pursue, and all within us charges us to keep holy and inviolate the Gift of God.

But the main duty, my brethren, which arises out of the possession of religious knowledge (and all that makes the subject of any practical value) is to use that knowledge as the guide of our own conduct. Indeed, my friends, unless this is the end of inquiry all our zeal to find the truth and all our exaltation in the possession is solemn trifling. It is a small thing that we know; we must practise also. That we know, will only add to our condemnation, if we do not according to our knowledge. It will not serve you, my brother, that you accurately interpret the Gospel, the Fathers, the Catechisms and Creeds; that you know all that Augustin expounded and Calvin decided and Erasmus denied; that you can explain every text, and trace the history of every corruption. This is not Christianity. But to copy the life of Christ into your heart and history, to show your brethren of other persuasions that you have a purer law by exhibiting a purer life: yes, to translate the light that you see, into the good which you do; the knowledge of your mind, into the holy works of your hands:—this is Christianity, and this the duty of which all that we say of the prevalence of liberal Christianity should hourly admonish us. Moreover this is the way in which we shall best promote, carry steadily forward, the march of religious truth. We do not think we have come to the end. We count not ourselves to have apprehended or to be already perfect, but forgetting the things which are behind, we press toward those which are before.[5] But the advancement of religious knowledge in ourselves or in others is to be effected chiefly by a good life. The best reformers, the most infallible teachers, are justice, temperance, and charity. 'If ye will do the will of my Father,' said our Lord, "if ye will do the will of my Father, ye shall know of the doctrines."[6] It is a just and sound conclusion that all men form, in the view of an unspotted character, that the principles which govern it must be such as God will approve;

> "For modes of faith let graceless zealots fight,
> "He can't be wrong, whose life is in the right."[7]

The virtues of those who profess a pure faith will thus answer the twofold purpose of increasing their own spiritual light, and of drawing to their opinions the goodwill and candid examination of all the good of whatever name.

These are the duties which devolve on those to whom the mercy of God has given in unusual measure the light of religious knowledge. It becomes us anxiously to remember and discharge them. Let us beware that we be not deluded by a vain conceit of superiority because we perceive our opinions on the spec-

5. Philippians 3:13.
6. John 7:16–17.
7. Alexander Pope, *An Essay on Man*, III, 305–6.

ulative points are truer than those of others. Let not our imperfections, I pray you, cause the truth to be blasphemed. Let it not be said that liberal opinions tend in the smallest degree to relax and unbind the eternal obligations of morality. Perhaps you were trained in another creed, and rejoice now in the more rational opinion you have embraced. Because we have found out that God is not that fearful Being clothed only in terrors that he has been represented, let us not make him such by our own sins. Because you have altered your opinions God has not withdrawn his eye. Because you have found out that he is paternal, he has not ceased to be just. If this delusion should have crept into your minds the error that you have admitted is tenfold more dangerous than the error you have escaped. Especially let us not imagine that because we have associated ourselves to men of enlightened religious views and do not believe the articles of the English or Genevan church, that therefore our views are enlightened and our faith is sound. Do you love the Lord your God with all your heart?[8] do you keep the life of your Saviour in your thoughts as the example of your own? do you show piety at home?[9] These are the only safe tests of right opinions, for if you do these things ye shall never fall.[10]

III. Finally, my brethren, what has been done in the reformation of error and the establishment of truth is valuable for the hopes it sets before us. We believe there is a force, an indwelling might, in the religion we acknowledge, which will carry it on to victory over all the prejudices and falsehoods of the world to the end of time. We believe nothing can stay its course. We believe it came from God and will lead men to God. We are not impatient because its progress is slow. Falsehood grows up rapidly and has its old age and dies. Truth grows and spreads slowly, but it never grows old. No matter though generations, though ages elapse, and do not behold its triumph; its triumph is sure. We, my friends, shall watch it one hour.[11] We shall spend our strength in its support (God grant we may!) and then sleep in death. But the cause shall live, when we die, and every aid we gave it, shall rejoice our spirits in the morning of the Resurrection. Though now it numbers among its advocates but a small minority, but a handful of hearts, the hour is coming when it shall multiply blessings to all the family of man; when it shall break the captive's chain; and visit the cottage of the wretched and forsaken; overcome the passions, ennoble the desires, and strengthen the faculties of all men. It shall give to all in all the periods of coming time, the sublime hope it now gives us, that, every exertion, however humble, to do good and to resist evil, will be accepted of God, and tends to increase our happiness forever.

8. Matthew 22:37 and Mark 12:30.
9. I Timothy 5:4.
10. II Peter 1:10.
11. Cf. Matthew 26:40 and Mark 14:37.

So teach us to number our days, that we may apply our hearts unto wisdom.

PSALMS 90:12

We are assembled once more, my brethren, for religious worship. The light of another Sabbath has brought us up to the Sanctuary to meditate on our hopes as the children of God; to take note of our duties and our sins; to consider the past, and to lay out our work for the future.

We are come to take note of the passage of time. We have dismissed another week of our short life into the eternity of the past. Again we are beginning, as we are always beginning, to live. These holy walls remind us of the ends of life which we are apt to forget. Here we are out of the world; and here, I doubt not, you have felt those hallowing influences come over your souls that become this place. We have seen enough of the vices of the world. We have already obeyed its temptations too long. Here let us make a final stand. Much of life is gone; let us consult how to make a wise use of the remainder. All our duties are included in this one, the improvement of time.

What is Time? Who is this mighty power that doth so much and is desired so much and is never seen; whose name is in every mouth, the proverbs of his value and of the impossibility of recovering him when once he has escaped: him, whose painted image, with the solemn symbols of the hourglass and scythe, the child admires, and the man approves with a sigh: him, whom all desire when he is gone, and slight when he is at hand? Is he a capricious stranger who goes to one door and passes by another? Are his gifts dealt out penuriously and partially like wealth and favour? Or does he confer different gifts on different men, here a blessing, and there a curse, that he causes some to smile, and others to weep, as he takes his flight? No: he comes to all, he is prodigal to all, and his gift to all, is one—*opportunity;* and they may use or refuse it as they please. This possession which we call time heaven has given equally. Some of us are born to

---

Completed in Cambridge on February 13, 1828. Preached twelve times: April 13, 1828, at the New South Church, Boston; April 20 in Concord, Mass.; May 18 at the Federal Street Church; June 15 in Concord, N.H.; August 17 at the South Congregational Church, Boston; August 24 at the Second Church, Boston; February 15, 1829, in Waltham; March 8 in Medford; August 23 at the Second Church, Boston; January 3, 1830, in Cambridgeport; January 1, 1832, at the New North Church; and October 2, 1836, in East Lexington.

wealth and some to poverty; some in free and Christian communities and some are born the children of slaves; but all are born to an equal share of this great and common inheritance. And having this, our wanting or abounding in the others is much the same. Our command over time is unlimited; and in this, consists the main power of man. For time will put the mightiest and the meanest energies very much on a level. What the greatest can accomplish suddenly, the feeblest can do, with time. It is a well-known principle of mechanics that any force, how little soever, may be made to overcome the greatest, the difference of force being compensated by time.[1] The hand that can only lift a basket of earth in time can remove a mountain. The principle is equally just when applied to morals. The height of virtue and the depth of vice are not suddenly attained. A long series of humble efforts will surmount the rudest obstacles, will achieve great actions, will obtain victories over passion, will establish heroic habits, as the incessant dropping of a rivulet, on a mountain side, will carve a channel in its granite floor. This is a great and stable law of God's Providence whose practice we witness in every day's events and in all parts of life. It is this which makes its value and gives it so great claim on our serious consideration.

But let us leave the general view of a subject of such embarrassing extent, and apply it more particularly. We hear a great deal said about the difference of human lot. There goes a man on whom all eyes are fastened as he passes along the public street: he is on his way to the Senate-house: though born in the ranks of humble industry, he moves the state by his commanding opinions. Every careless word he drops is blown by every wind to the ear of all his countrymen and his standing is watched and his power felt in the legislative operations of distant nations. And here, in his very path, is one, created with the same passions, with as keen a relish as his for distinction, and as quick a sense of dishonour; as well-born, as well nurtured,—but whose opinions, in the eye of the partial world, are wholly insignificant; one whose name is obscure, who was never gratified with praise, who has found that his friends forget his face, and when death has once overtaken him, is never again remembered by those who have hurried home from his funeral. Is not this unjust? is it not proper occasion for complaint? Who is it that made this mighty difference between brethren? It was themselves. It was none other. And wherein did that difference consist? Simply, in the unlike use they made of time. The main difference betwixt man and man is the different use they make of time.[2] "Every man," said the Roman maxim, "is the architect of his own fortune."[3] He whom you call the favourite of heaven and enriched by its lavish and undeserved bounty is not so. You mistake. He is only reaping his own harvest. It is now many years that he has been husbanding his time with exactest parsimony. He has made his years long

1. "It is a . . . time": see *JMN* 6:21.

2. "The main difference . . . time": see *JMN* 3:101.

3. In Sallust's "Speech to Caesar" the maxim is attributed to Appius Claudius Caecus; see *Sallust*, trans. J. C. Rolfe (Cambridge, Mass., 1947), 445.

and his days long and his hours long. He has crowded them full with business and study. He has grudged himself sleep. He has not spared himself time at the table with his friends; he has contrived to push the pith of many lives into the short term of his own.

The other man loved his ease. He was one who would not be pestered with care. What was not easy to be done today he postponed till tomorrow. When business pressed on his quiet, he was drowsy and must yield to slumber, or was sad and must seek recreation. He forgot that just opinions of men and business cannot be formed, without a painful scrutiny into public and private affairs; without the toil of the hands and the head; without early and late study of books, and a long discipline in generous arts. He forgot that time was passing, and that the little that remained was not long enough for his sorrow. What if I have quoted to you only one class of laborious men, those who aim at mere political power? It is the same with those who follow honor, wealth, or fame. The cases I have put are surely common. They represent two great classes of men familiar to our experience: One of them has *lived;* the other has *spent so much time.* It is a difference, my friends, that I fear we do not sufficiently consider, the distinction betwixt time and life. Time, duration, what is measured by so much motion of the heavenly bodies, or by so many beatings of the pulse, or so many vibrations of the pendulum—what is it? it is emptiness, it is nothing. The whole conception, its substance and value are in the events it contains.

If action, if the action of my mind be suspended, what is it to me though suns rise and set, though moons wax and wane, though ages and revolutions of ages go by—it is all but one moment. I do not live. And in like manner he who is conscious of its passage, if his mind lie torpid even though his body be in health and motion, though he breathe the air till his limbs that were supple and strong are bent down and his head grows white under the hand of age, he does not, for all this, grow old, grow mature. All his years are only so much time, so much running of the sand, so many tickings of the clock. This is time; but life is something more. Life is the being of a soul, of an intelligent, remembering, reasoning, forecasting man; it is the succession of thoughts that run round the universe, 'that wander through eternity';[4] it is the collection of actions, of virtues, of generosity, of devotion; the indefatigable pursuit of knowledge and glory; the career of a moral being from its education to its reward; the ardour of hope; the acquaintance of good and evil; the choice of pursuits; the choice of religions; the exercise of free agency; the time to serve the Lord. This is life and not time. This it is which prompted the wise sentiment of Solomon, "Honourable age is not that which standeth in length of time, nor that is measured by number of years; but wisdom is the grey hair unto men, and an unspotted life is old age."[5]

---

4. Milton, *Paradise Lost*, II, 148.
5. Wisdom of Solomon 4:8. See *JMN* 4:310-11.

But whilst these lessons are sounded in our ears, whilst books teach us and experience admonishes and conscience charges us, still we waste our time; we refuse to number our days that we may apply our hearts to wisdom. We spend our substance, we fret our souls to explore new ways of murdering time.[6] Now, my friends, I am not going to inveigh against theatres, balls, and festive clubs; against holidays and public amusements; for I hope there are checks enough upon the excess of public pleasures. Your own prudence, your care of your own reputation, your desire not to be accounted dissolute or untrustworthy, your regard for your own family, your unwillingness to defraud them of their just claims on your estate by a too profuse expense—all these, I will suppose, are strong guards enough and will commonly keep you safe from a pernicious waste of life in these amusements.—Besides, in the life of common men these enjoyments are only occasional, holidays that seldom occur and cannot therefore be expected to do great harm. No, my friends, it is not these that are so much to be feared. It is small vices, domestic evils, not the *public* but the *private* waste of time,—our deportment among our friends, our deportment when alone—'tis these evils that run up to such frightful accumulation and undermine the power and happiness of man.

If we bring the question to a point, and review the last day we yet have lived: I believe, my brethren, that if we will any of us go faithfully to the consideration how yesterday was spent, we shall find that we did not *fill* that day, that there were many chasms in it which might have been supplied with good actions, with charities, or at least with good thoughts. It seems to me, my friends, that this comparison of what was required with what has been performed is one that must probe the consciences of us all. Have we ever thought what *are* these days that go over us in such profuse succession, and ring no alarm in our ears as they pass to tell their office or their end? Have we forgot that they are watchful witnesses who utter no voice but keep their record for the ear of God? What is a day? Is it not a curious vessel made with such divine art that its bulk can be expanded to any dimensions at the pleasure of the owner? so that the more you put into it the more it will hold. Is it not to be valued as a ship, not for itself but for its costly cargo; or as a purse, for the coin of gold and silver it contains? With this distinction, that no art, no industry can fill it to its entire capacity. Is it not like the muscles of the body which the more they are strained by use, the greater burden they will bear, or is it not a mine of unfathomed wealth which seems to the rude eye a barren rock, but yields ingots and diamonds, precisely in proportion to the labor? My friends, I use these figures of speech but it is only to make more evident the plain duty that bids us most carefully to number these days of ours. Is there within these walls that holy man who bears in his memory a single day which he lived as he ought; one in which he wasted no moment, in which there was no unlawful act, no selfishness, no sensual indulgence, no sinful desire? I say, Blessed, for his sake, is this house and this people! For such

6. Cf. *JMN* 3:101.

virtue, where it exists, is not singular in its acts. If he has known the glory of one day like this, one has not been able to satisfy him. He will add to their number, he will perfect their beauty and crowd them with virtues. His hours go up to heaven commended by secret prayers, and the intervals of occupation were filled by a cement of virtuous thoughts. Think, I pray you, on the peace which reigns in his breast, when he goes to his bed at night. The day is past; another period of his virtues is numbered and finished; another bright herald charged with his duty has departed to heaven. The sun has traversed the firmament, the moon and the stars have completed their diurnal round,—but he has made that day illustrious with a *moral light*, before which their ancient fires are dim. My brethren, the apostle Paul declared to the Ephesians that "whatsoever good a man doeth, the same he shall receive of the Lord."[7] Shall we not liken this man, then, as he witnesses the departure of the day, to a merchant standing on a foreign shore who has launched another ship deep freighted with his wealth to the land to which he is shortly bound? He has done his duty; he has performed his part, and fearless of the future, he looks to heaven with pious confidence.

Will it be asked what is the design of these representations? Will it be said that they point to a degree of moral greatness, to an use of time, that is plainly impossible to our frail and tempted nature? Do you ask what is the just improvement of time? How shall it be ascertained how much of social pleasure I must forego; at what point the care of my worldly estate becomes excessive and how deep are the demands of God and duty upon my time? These questions are easy to be answered; there needs no nice casuistry to determine them. *Whenever we are acting with the perfect approbation of our conscience, we are improving the time.* No matter how small or frivolous the employment, with what low associates, or in what obscure resorts, if it have the full consent of our understanding, then, we do not live in vain. We have only to remember the true end of life; to bear in mind that we were not sent into this world to make a fortune, or to lead a party, or to be famous, or to sleep, or to be merry or proud; but that we are permitted to pursue all honest occupations in such a manner as not to interfere with our first occupation, which is to become wiser and better. I know it is common to allege that the necessary care of our bodies and especially sickness, the great and small disorders of our system, call for so much attention as very much to diminish our disposable hours. But I believe if we narrowly look we shall find that for one hour that sickness takes out of our lives, our pleasures, our passions, commonly take ten. Besides, time can be redeemed from sickness. The greatest enterprizes have been concerted and executed from the bed of languishing disease. The soul in good men often keeps its vigour and disdains to sink under the weakness of the body. It is recorded of the emperor Vespasian that after he was seized with a mortal complaint he persisted in discharging his duties and directing the public affairs with the same assiduity as before: and when his Physicians attempted to dissuade him from this incessant

7. Ephesians 6:8.

attention as being full of danger to himself,—"an emperor," he replied, "should die standing."[8] It was a noble sentiment and worthy of a Christian heroism. I pass by a nobler example, familiar to us all, of one who in the extreme moments of mortal suffering discharged the last offices of human kindness and of divine magnanimity. And how many saints, how many wise and good men, when they came to die, have been elevated by pure religion above the thought of pain—and steadfastly set themselves to do the work of him that sent them on the earth, even when the hand of death was sealing up their eyelids, when the pulse was ceasing, and the clay was growing cold. Yes, time may be redeemed from sickness, may be redeemed out of the jaws of death, but cannot be redeemed from pleasure, from appetite, from passion. These are hard masters who clench their gains with an iron grasp. Ambition, Avarice, Luxury, Evil speaking, these no less than Indolence are our dangerous enemies; for, time misemployed is as much wasted as time unemployed. But all the Virtues are our faithful friends. Temperance is an improver of time; which both saves the hours which luxury wastes at his riotous board, and is alert for vigorous action in those when luxury is stupefied by drowsiness and indigestion of his surfeit. Truth is an economist of time, because it has no steps to retrace, and needs no frauds to patch up the flaws and leaks of former frauds, no apologies, and no repentance. Honour improves the hour; because it has not a broken reputation to mend and the unpopularity of vices to counteract; it has no suspicions to lull asleep, no festering wrongs to salve over. Humility saves it, who does not offend her instructors, and has no high bars of prejudice to overleap; and Charity saves it, who has no hatreds to reconcile, who suffers long, and is not provoked, and seeketh not her own.[9]

But why should we spend more time in considering what it behoves us to do with it? Our way lies plain before us. And now what hinders that we, my brethren, should here resolve by the grace of God to redeem the days that remain to us on the earth. They will be few at the most. They are but a span to that duration which God has made to depend upon them. This day is not yet spent. Its irrevocable record of good or evil is not yet registered on the everlasting tablets. Yonder sun yet hangs waiting in the firmament for your resolution. What hinders that we bind ourselves by an inward vow this day at least to consult the welfare of our souls; this day sacredly to abstain from all that causes us to offend. Let him not go down to his rest before we have searched our hearts and implored strength from on high to assist us and especially let him not rise on the morrow before a solemn deliberation upon our duty shall have prepared us for what awaits us. So shall we best obey the commandments of God and of his Son, and turn the trials of this life into the peace and glory of the next.

8. "Against Idleness," in *Essays of Michael Seigneur de Montaigne . . .* , trans. Charles Cotton (London, 1693), 2:559. See *JMN* 6:18, 6:156.

9. I Corinthians 13:4–5.

XVI

Blessed are the poor in spirit;
for theirs is the kingdom of heaven.

MATTHEW 5:7

And who are the poor in spirit on whom this great gift is conferred? For these are words of the highest authority; this text at least is not controverted; the language is explicit, and the reading is sure. In the hearing of this voice why should not the warfare of sects and parties be suspended? for, all that they can pretend to contend for, the most comprehensive of all rewards—the *kingdom of heaven itself*—is here offered, not to a sect—not to the abettors of any speculative opinion—but to all the cultivators of a certain disposition of mind. And who are these whom the Saviour calls the poor in spirit? What happy race? what angelic company? What are their numbers? where is their abode? Do these distinguished children of God dwell among their fellowmen or sequestered and apart? Surely all who are aiming at goodness and glory must feel an anxious curiosity to discover those happy and honoured beings to whom not a promise is made but a victory is declared: not that they shall see God—but, that theirs *is* the kingdom of heaven.

My brethren, I fear that the number of these highly distinguished servants of God is very small. My brethren, if we search up and down in society for the lowly of heart we shall often return from an unavailing pursuit. There be that are called gods many in human power and lords many of intellect of public opinion:[1] but they view themselves as others view them: they have placed their happiness in the loftiness of their station. And if you go lower in the ranks of the community you shall find men ashamed of the character you seek. You shall find some who pretend to it and some who think they have it: but, still, as you look nearer, you shall find under a quiet brow and a sordid dress, a restless and swelling mind. Under every roof, whether laid with marble, or thatched with straw, you shall see the inhabitant jealous of disrespect; eager to call your notice to those advantages of his condition which he thinks ought to raise him in your opinion; and commending this Christian grace to all men and by all ways,

---

Manuscript dated March 25, 1828. Related journal notes on the subject of pride are dated March 28, 1828 (see *JMN* 3:124). Preached six times: April 13, 1828, at the New South Church; April 27 in Concord, Mass.; May 4 in Lexington; May 25 in Concord, N.H.; July 20 at the Second Church, Boston; and September 6, 1829, again at the Second Church.

1. I Corinthians 8:5.

except by example. I am afraid wherever human nature is found, this defect will be found. *Pride*, pride is the universal and unsharing distemper. And our Saviour had regard to this universal passion and knew how rare and singular was this grace when he pronounced upon it that unmeasured benediction, "Blessed are the poor in spirit; for theirs is the kingdom of Heaven."

My friends, I suppose it needs no learned commentary to ascertain the meaning of our Saviour. Whether we are sensible that we deserve any of the good to be given to the poor in spirit, or not, we are all of us able to understand pretty clearly what is the temper that is recommended. The meaning is not that which those who love not our Lord Jesus Christ would fix upon it. The *poor in spirit* are not those whom the world calls *poor spirited*. The poor in spirit whom Jesus blessed are not those who fail to assert their pretensions in the world because they want courage but because they are uplifted by desires of something higher: not because they want enterprize and energy to win their way to wealth and honour but because they have no admiration of those things, now that they have obtained a glimpse of God, and have been struck with a sense of their own deficiencies.

The poor in spirit whom Christ had in view are *the humble*. If there be any one virtue which more than all others is distinguished in the lessons of the gospel and approved in the example of the Founder it is Humility. Christianity was preached to the poor. The Messiah took upon him "the condition of a servant and a life of poverty and a death of disgrace."[2] All his sentiments and actions were at war with pride.

In dwelling upon this benediction of our Lord I think we shall not lose the time in considering how well our own daily observation upon the nature and evil of pride coincide with that regard which he paid to the opposite virtue.

Pride assumes a thousand forms. You will not think I have chosen an unprofitable topic and that to preach against pride we must preach only to the rich and splendid. It is the most common sin. It lurks under rags as well as flaunts in purple. It is not, it is true, of the same malignant festering nature as the more odious vices, and does not, like them, shoot out into tremendous crimes; but it is always at our elbow, with a little temptation, and makes up in mischievous industry what it wants in enormity, and so works its full share in the main mischief, I mean, the perverting our moral character. And then the vice has this aggravation, that *it is its own apology*, that it so blinds the eye that its victims value themselves on that very thing which is their bane and disease; they caress the corruptor; they are proud of their pride. We have already seen that it is inconsistent with Christian doctrine, and *now*, now, my friends, I shall try to show you concerning this vice three things: 1. that it is a disposition of mind the most unbecoming to such beings as we are; 2. that it is always a token of littleness and imperfection; 3. that it always stands in the way of every man's advancement who indulges it.

I. Pride is a disposition of mind the most unbecoming to such a being as man.

---

2. Not located.

A being so frail and exposed to so many accidents and a slave to so many low necessities should not be proud. Does nature teach him pride? when she arrays her elements and he shudders at their strength? when the thunder threatens him and the ocean tosses his frigate to shivers and drowns a hundred men under one heaving wave? when a grain of gunpowder or the feeble form of a poor worm has force enough to destroy the life of one man, and a gas underground may inflame and the yawning earth shake down a mighty Capital and slay and bury a hundred thousand: when an eastern mist may break up the health of a whole nation and send an epidemic that shall burst all the distinctions of society as bubbles in a few short weeks and leave not enough alive, a thin and timid remainder when the plague is spent, to bury the dead. Alas! my brethren, since the moment that life parts, down go all the fabrics of pride. What have *we* to do with it? What more absurd than that a man encompassed as he is by the immeasurable eternity behind and before him; bowed also almost to the ground by sin; with God on high, and his soul within, and the Universe around him calling him to his solemn duty as a moral being, that he should parade into light these little insect distinctions that mark one mote from another and be uplifted because forsooth he says that his blood is better than your blood, his wit keener than your wit, or his gold more than your gold! One would think that the sorrows that afflict him would suppress this silly conceit; that the dismaying darkness that rests on the future would draw him away from it; that the great work he has to do would absorb his attention and detach him from it.

II. In the next place, *it always betrays a littleness and imperfection.* For all pride is founded on a mistake; upon ignorance. We imagine things to be worth much, which are worthless. We mistake pebbles for diamonds. A little boy is proud of his trinket buttons: as he grows bigger, he is ashamed of the same ornaments; and a nobleman is vain of distinctions that are as ridiculous in the eyes of a truly enlightened mind. Every body plumes himself on some point,— upon property, or learning, or person, or manners, or connexions,—and on one or more of these accounts, tosses his head a little, or leads the conversation into allusions to these particulars. Now the very first index by which we detect our own increase of wisdom is our discovery of the folly of these pretensions. We valued them because we thought them valuable; as our knowledge increases, we find that there are better things, and then our regard for the first at once disappears.

Again. It is an ancient maxim, *Reverence thyself.*[3] The good man reveres himself, reveres his conscience, and would rather suffer any calamity than lower himself in his own esteem. This is righteous human dignity of which pride is a

3. See *JMN* 3:142, 4:342, 4:357; used in "Ethics," *EL* 2:152. Emerson's source may have been the "Aureum Pythagoreum Carmen," line 12: "sed maxime omnium verere te ipsum"; see Friedrich W. A. Mullach, ed., *Fragmenta Philosophorum Graecorum* (1860; rpt. Darmstadt, 1968), 193; other possibilities are Francis Bacon, "Colours of Good and Evil": "Maxime omnium teipsum reverere"; and *The Advancement of Learning:* "It is a precept, that a man should above all things reverence himself"; see *The Works of Francis Bacon*, ed. James Spedding et al. (London, 1857–1874), 4:468 and 7:80.

foolish counterfeit. Now he that makes his pride in any thing that is not himself, certainly betrays a low opinion of himself. If things whose value we know, such as money, or dress, or fashion, stand so high in that man's estimation, if they seem to him to enhance very much his value, it is very clear that his value must seem to him, and must be, very small; that his soul, *himself*, must be a pitiful matter under all this idle parade. There is always a well grounded suspicion that there is something wrong, something to be ashamed of, when a man affects haughtiness. For why does he make pretensions unless because he fears he cannot support them? If a man is unquestionably the greatest general, the ablest speaker, the richest merchant, he makes no bustle to assert his claims; he is not anxious to establish what nobody thinks of denying. Besides, it is apt to be the case that a lofty look is only the mask of a servile soul. A little observation will show that those who wear the proudest demeanour—when some occasion occurs that makes it their interest to conciliate an inferior—are ready to take off their pride, and are not ashamed to stoop and to shuffle with a base condescension, till they have gained their point,—and then, they lose their humility.

No; Pride doth not accomplish its aim. It is a foolish suicide. It defeats its own end. For does it not aim to make us think that this man is better and greater than other men? But, in reality, it betrays that he is less. It discovers what he would fain conceal, that his views are limited, and his motives low; that he is near-sighted: that he is occupied with the straws and chips in the corner where he stands, for want of power to see the objects of grandeur that rise around him, that he has never yet attained one glimpse at the Universe, at the true nature of God, and angels, and men, which, once seen, is never forgotten; which dispels forever the delusion which our senses practise upon us, and brings down arrogant shadows to their original insignificance. An Arab of the desert, or an inhabitant of the Low Countries, may easily maintain that a little hillock in his level land is one of the highest elevations of the globe, and as long as he compares the hillock with the plain, it may not be easy to convince him of error; but once transport him to a mountain country; carry him to the steep summit of the Alps; astonish his eye with one single glance at the mighty map outspread in vast tranquillity below him,—and he is forever undeceived, and will never extol his hillock again. Is it not so with the proud man? If you can once open his eye to what he doth not really see, to the prodigious greatness of his own destiny as a man, he too shall be undeceived and will be poor in spirit.

III. In the next place *a man's pride is always an obstacle in the way of his own advancement to goodness and greatness.* It was the observation of a truly wise man that "No man ever had a point of pride that was not injurious to him."[4] Every body is the friend of the humble man: but a haughty deportment is always felt by those who witness it, to be an insult to themselves, and naturally

4. Burke. Letter to Barry. [Emerson's note]. The letter to James Barry is quoted in Sir James Prior, *Memoir of the Life and Character of the Rt. Hon. Edmund Burke* (Philadelphia, 1825), 124. Used in "Politics," *EL* 2:71, "Ethics," *EL* 2:153, and "Compensation," *CW* 2:64; see also *JMN* 6:157.

provokes ill will and injury. Pride is a real obstruction in the way of a man's becoming wiser. I know not how I can better illustrate this remark than by calling your attention to a contrast of characters which has probably fallen under your frequent observation. Two men went into society to converse. Both were animated by an equal desire to get knowledge, but with an unequal regard to the opinion of others. In one a wellbred dignity of manners upon which he values himself puts a constant restraint upon the spirit of inquiry and free conversation; whilst the other, forgetting all but the subject of discussion, rushes to his mark, with a thorough disdain of the barriers of ceremony. One has perhaps inferior parts, but he has no pride; is eager to learn the sentiments of the company upon points of interest to him: he runs every risk, and has no ambition to say good things, or to be admired as a gentleman; but shows a generous disregard of appearances in the satisfaction of a curiosity, which, he is, however, ready to justify. And this man, though he break down the cobweb fences of artificial politeness—you shall find he wins apace upon the confidence and love of all with whom he converses, by the manifest honesty and benevolence of his disposition, and as confidence invites confidence, he is continually increasing his knowledge, for the heart is laid open to him. The other cannot bring himself to violate an elegant decorum or to express any thought until he have first considered whether the language may not be slovenly or whether the argument be worthy of his reputation. He is continually distressed by fear lest he should make a sorry figure in the conversation, and must not, on any consideration, be embarrassed in the support of his opinion, before the eyes of these witnesses. The consequence is that his conversation is powerless and cold; that his good sense lies latent and unprofitable; that he does not attach the heart to him; and always stands in the way of his own advancement in the study of man. Is not the case familiar? It may be found in almost every parlour.

Moreover Pride is the parent of Contention: it is the fruitful author of innumerable falsehoods and is punished with the absurd mortification of constant detection. It is a hypocrisy which deceives no one. And it is strange that those who use it do not see how ineffectual it is. We see through every body's lie but our own. We put on our face the very mask that made us laugh when others tried to deceive us with it, and solemnly try to deceive them.

Thus I have attempted to establish 1. the unsuitableness of pride to the condition of human nature; 2. that it is also, in all cases, a discovery of weakness; 3. that it is always an injury to us. But in making this commentary on this pernicious passion, we make the strongest recommendation of the Christian grace which our Saviour in the text approves. For all that can be said against pride is so much said in favour of humility.

My brethren, let these considerations have their weight with us. Especially let us regard the emphatic praise which our Lord bestowed upon this virtue in his doctrine and in his life. "Learn of me," he said, to his disciples, "I am meek and lowly of heart": and to imprint the precept, he girded himself with a towel, and washed their feet.⁵ I am afraid we are not sufficiently aware how prone we all are to offend in this respect. We are apt to call pride a local and partial vice which lives only in high places. But how gross an error this is, we shall be convinced, if we reflect that the occasions of pride are the inequalities of condition, as the source of it is our ignorance, and in whatever particular we excel or imagine that we excel our neighbour there is great danger that there it will take root in our weakness and spring up unforbidden. There is a pride of opinion as well as of wealth; a pride of talents as well as of blood; and what is strangest and worst of all a *religious pride:* but to be proud of our religion, is to cease to be religious. We are impatient of contradiction and therein betray our pride. We would have men pay us some deference; we would impress them with the idea that our honor is very nice and all our opinions are sound, and herein we discover pride. But let us be ashamed of an attempt to put a poor deception on others, and feel that the best way to *seem* great and good is to *be* great and good; and that if we would accomplish the great objects for which God sent us into the world; if we would enter into the kingdom of heaven, we must be too great to be proud; we must forever abandon our arrogant pretensions knowing that a proud look and a lying tongue are an abomination to the Lord;⁶ and must be clothed with simplicity and meekness; must come in the spirit of a little child.⁷ Blessed are the poor in spirit for theirs is the kingdom of Heaven.

5. Matthew 11:29 and John 13:4–12.
6. Proverbs 6:16–17.
7. Mark 10:15 and Luke 18:17.

Sanctify a fast.

JOEL 1:14

We are assembled in conformity to an immemorial usage of our ancestors and of the Christian Church upon a day set apart to the duties of penitence. It is an occasion which has divided the opinions of men concerning its use and propriety. I cannot but think it a most reasonable institution—most suitable to human habits and condition. I do not think that it is a fault of men to distress themselves immoderately in the consideration of their imperfection, or in remorse for their sins. Temptation never ceases. Our passions never relax their hold. Our appetites are never satisfied. Pleasure never forgets to swing her baits before our eyes. But the stern duties of self examination and self accusation are of another complexion, are gladly remitted and forgotten. I see in society many men that are lovers of pleasure—crowds of men and women that never swerve from following their interest, that pay every tittle of duty, mint, anise, and cummin, to the world;[1]—but, it has never been my fortune to see one man who erred grievously in the opposite extreme; who made his life miserable by the excess of his compunction, by any habits of savage heroism such as we have heard of in monks and hermits for the mortification of the flesh; by keeping a perpetual fast; by scourging the body with whips; by exhausting the mind with prayers of despair. I do not regret the fact. I rejoice that these extravagances have disappeared,—which are as hostile to religion, as they are to humanity. I only notice the fact, to show that the tendency of our times is certainly not to a superstitious performance of these duties, but rather to their neglect. Now Penitence is assuredly a duty of the first importance. Whatever may be your views of the nature and character of God, and your opinions of Christianity, no man of correct perceptions can doubt the necessity of a humble penitence to beings whose virtue is so infirm as ours. The voice that went before Christianity—"Repent! for the kingdom of heaven is at hand,"[2] still goes before it, and goes with it into every heart. The duty is proper to individuals: and the

---

The manuscript indicates that this Fast Day sermon was completed on April 2, 1828, in Concord. Preached three times: April 3, 1828, in Lexington, and April 9, 1829, at the New North Church in the morning, and at the Second Church in the afternoon.

1. Matthew 23:23.
2. Matthew 3:2, 4:17.

duty is proper to nations, that all men may call to mind the public sins, and consider how much it is in the power of each citizen to restore health and purity to the public morals.

In our own case, I cannot but think the duty more than usually binding. If this nation had been undergoing a long period of commercial distress, or of great political disadvantage, of any sort, its temper might perhaps have been more steadily turned towards the acknowledgment of the Divine Providence. But we have not had the lesson of adversity. We are, on the contrary, daily called to consider the peculiar happiness of our political condition. Through the goodness of God, our prosperity is so unmixed, has been so stationary, a whole generation having grown up since it began, that we have almost ceased to think it extraordinary. The great convulsions under which other nations suffer, which have broken up the peace of communities in former periods for a hundred years at a time, that have changed towns into camps, the family of man into a military host—are so far from us, are so little apprehended by us as calamities to which we may be liable, that mere fables, the works of fiction which the press is daily producing, are read with far greater interest than the record of these facts. So strange a prosperity has attended us that it is no uncommon complaint—the very triteness of the topic as a subject of discourse. One who regarded the most favourable aspect would think that in this new world a new order of things had opened. That the old plagues of mankind, war, famine, pestilence, were really by-gone things; that their causes were taken away, and that henceforward events would follow smoothly, without violent and frightful evils.

But are these expectations well grounded? Is that government which under God's blessing our Fathers framed so perfect in its provisions, so nice in its finish as to admit all good and exclude all evil? Has its beneficent influence been so decided as to alter the character of the human race as soon as they came within its ample household? Or if this be not so, and our political system partake of the imperfection of all human institutions, yet has not God appointed new and straiter laws to those physical events that in the old times were the ministers of his wrath? Are the sources of natural evil sealed by his grace in this happy country? Are the winds commanded that they shall not breathe poison, and the locust and the caterpillar that they shall not eat our harvests?[3]

I am sorry, my brethren, that we have not any sort of foundation for these pleasing expectations. Pleasing indeed it would be to believe that the banners of War should be no more uplifted; that the earth had already rung with the last volley of musketry guilty of human blood; that henceforth unstained ages should roll rich with improvement and mankind lie at agreement side by side, nation with nation, a vast society of peace. But, no; these good days lie in wait, God alone knows how far off—For, consider, what have been the causes of

---

3. "We are, on the contrary . . . harvests?": see *JMN* 3:121.

war?—Human passions. But are they removed? When our fathers shook off the dust of the old world from their feet did they shake off all its pollutions?[4] Was theirs an emigration from the Passions, and from sin as well as from violent priests and a corrupted nation? When amid prayers and tears they burst the bands of nature and forsook their native land and came forth from the persecuting roar and hiss of crowded cities, into the desolate sea;—as these sounds of the old world died on the wind, did they lose also that whisper of Temptation which is always softly sounding in human ears? Like the Pilgrim, in the simple story of Bunyan, as they went up the steep mountain of Difficulty did the burden of vice fall forever from their shoulders? If so—then why this solemn rite? Why did they leave us this dismal tradition, appointing us with each returning Spring, a day of Fasting, Humiliation and Prayer? No, my brethren, human nature does not change with change of place and change of circumstances. Fifty or sixty centuries have spent upon man the storms of their wrath and the sunshine of their bounty; he has met with all events; he has acted all the parts in the round of character—but here he stands, the same being God made in the garden; he has not lost one passion, nor parted with one frailty.[5] If you provoke him, he will resent it. If you put up a bait to his avarice he will hazard much, something of honesty, something of benevolence, and all his quiet in the pursuit of it. And hence the seed of quarrels in families, and of wars in nations. Yes; Man is the same, and if the course of events has been different—if a course of events of a milder complexion has attended that colony of the human race which has grown up here, it is not that he has been less liable here to danger, but is owing to particular manifestations of the mercy of God. We lie exposed as much as heretofore to the calamities that afflict mankind. For the elements have not been abridged of their force: poison, fever, famine, earthquake, inundation, that have been weapons in the armoury of divine justice, keep every whit of their tremendous energy unabated.[6] If such should be the order of God's providence—think you there will be any lack of power in the sun in one sultry summer to parch the surface of your fruitful fields into a heap of sand? or may not your waving harvests be sometimes at the mercy of a little worm scarcely perceptible at the roots of the corn he has broken down—whose habits elude your art and rob you of your bread? Or have the winds, in these latter ages, lost their ancient fury; or the storm its irresistible artillery? Or have we purified the chambers of the mine, of their dangerous vapours beneath our feet? Far down, in their eternal treasuries, are gases accumulated from age to age that the entrance of air or a spark of fire might explode with a force that would burst the planet.[7] Or what shall hinder that God *now*, as afore time,—and here, as in the old world, should heap up the sea from its bed, and pour a vast innundation over the territory and the cities and the memory of a sinful people? It is now

4. Cf. Matthew 10:14, Mark 6:11, and Luke 9:5.
5. "For, consider . . . frailty": see *JMN* 3:121–22.
6. "Man is the same . . . unabated": see *JMN* 3:122.
7. Cf. *JMN* 3:122.

only four centuries since the sea came in upon the city of Dort in Holland and drowned 100,000 persons in the swallowing tide. And even now, the sailor in the Belgic waters in calm weather can sometimes descry beneath his ship, the broken towers and ruins, covered with sea-grass, of that ancient town.[8] Or what shall hinder that God should fan the cinders of a volcano in the bosom of these now silent and pastoral hills?

I see no reason why these frightful calamities should not be regarded as admonitions and punishments. I see no superstition in taking such a notice of them. I bow to this hint of Eternal Providence, this expression of omnipotence.

Man exists under the same liabilities now, as at any former time, and the means of afflicting the human race have never lost their force, though God has forborne to use them. Let us consider, then, what is our condition? Let us see if we walk in a safe way.[9] Is this nation so pure, is public virtue so sound among us, as to give no hint of degeneracy and decline? My friends, I certainly am not disposed to behold the aspect of our beloved country in a sad and unfavourable light. I do devoutly acknowledge that high Providence of Almighty God in the series of astonishing events which at so late and so happy a time disclosed this western world and laid so broad and deep the foundations of our prosperity. When compared with other nations I see in our history a history of virtue,—the exhibition of a highly moral and religious character;—not individuals only, but whole communities, full of probity and full of patriotism. Our annals bear no records of that horrid social profligacy, when a whole nation was through every faculty and in every part a dark malefactor; when the whole head was sick and the whole heart was rotten. Nevertheless—though we have to thank God, that our country is not yet plunged into that hopeless degeneracy which has overtaken other states—it cannot be disguised, that prosperity has begun to have upon us, its common effect; has made us wanton and secure and worldly. Good men have begun to feel sad forebodings concerning us. There is something ungrateful in the malignity of our parties; something fatal to religion in the license of our press; something impious in the slippery levity of our obligations to the state;[10] something unpardonable in the fury of religious controversy, something threatening in the steady growth of vices,—in the spread of intemperance, of unchastity, of fraud, from the centre to the circumference of our land.

Hence arises the imperative duty which we meet this day to fulfil and, God grant, with a sincere and single mind. For these reasons we are called on to fast, to adopt whatever rites shall impress on ourselves the magnitude and solemnity of the occasion. For these reasons we bow humbly in sorrow and penitence; for these we pray for mercy and deliverance.[11]

And is this all our duty? Does the obligation end with the office of penitence?

---

8. For the inundation of Dort, see *JMN* 3:73 (cf. *JMN* 6:99).
9. "I see no reason . . . way": see *JMN* 3:122.
10. "records of that horrid . . . state": *JMN* 3:122–23.
11. Cf. *JMN* 3:123.

If we shall fulfil, with religious exactness, the ceremonial and the moral duties that belong to this day,—when the sun goes down, shall our obligations have an end and perish with it? If it be so, to you then is the language of the Lord addressed by his holy prophet, "Ye shall not fast as ye do this day, to make your voice to be heard on high."[12] No, my brethren; fully to apprehend our public duty—our duties as citizens—we must feel this plain and inevitable truth, that, the fate of the community depends on its virtue, and the virtue of the community, on the virtue of its members.[13] This great and leading fact which lies at the foundation of all patriotism, is not appreciated, I fear, as it ought to be. The sins of the nation are *our* sins. If any man laments the vices of the times—it is a fair question to ask whether he himself is faultless. If he is not, he is daily adding weights to that burden which he affects to lament. It is we ourselves and we alone who can cure that evil which we bewail. On a former occasion I took an opportunity to invite the attention of this congregation to the immense importance of their conduct when considered as *example*.[14] That consideration returns upon our minds with all its force in this connexion. For how does any man acquire the boldness to break any commandment, but that when he is tempted to the sin and weighs the pleasure and convenience of the commission against the dangers of it, he remembers that other men have done and are daily doing the same; that you, his fellow men, will not severely judge him, because you are conscious of a similar weakness in your own characters. That weakness, then, in *your* character is accountable for the crimes that have ruined *his*. For is it not apparent that, if each man in the community,—if each one of us— had done his duty wholly and strictly (in the sight of God and of man) the severe purity of that community would have stared him in the face when he meditated his sin, would have looked it down, and shewed him the offence in its true colours till it grew to an abomination in his own eyes? To *us*, then, my brethren (for I am led by truth I cannot help to this gloomy and unavoidable conclusion,) to us is owing that degree of guilt, that lowered tone of public sentiment, that cries so loudly to man for penitence, and to God for judgment.

Come, then, my friends, let us make this day something more than an unmeaning ceremony. Let us, since there is such tremendous reason, give a better answer to our conscience and to God, when they ask us *why we fast?* than to say, 'because our ancestors fasted a hundred years ago.' Let us awaken our spirits to a real and effectual contrition. Let us gird on sorrow as sackcloth, and a hatred of sin as ashes.[15] Let us mourn for the sin of the land, as *our sin*, and go sternly to the work of reformation. Do not complain that the business of redeeming a nation is too mighty for your hands. Does your heart fail you and your spirits sink unequal to the task? Be strong; fear not: your whole duty lies in a narrow compass—is one practicable thing—that is to *reform yourself*, to

12. Isaiah 58:4.
13. "the fate . . . members": see *JMN* 3:123.
14. In Sermon III, delivered in Lexington, March 16, 1828.
15. Cf. Isaiah 58:5.

bring up to the perfect mark of Christian perfection, one single man. We have already observed that in all the lapse of his history man had lost not one passion, not one vice. But, be it remembered, he has not lost one virtuous disposition, one motive to the love of God and the compliance with his commands. He has gained encouragement to goodness by observing all the evidence which the passage of ages, the rise and fall of so many empires, in short the fortunes of the human race in the wide diversity of circumstances, have borne to the overruling Providence of God.[16] He has all the encouragement which God intended to afford to virtue in that great Revelation of his will to man by Jesus Christ. In this thorny path of virtue which he would travel he has the noblest encouragements, sublime consolations. Let him consider that every good deed he does on earth is written down in heaven. Let him show that he was born for the blessing of his country. Let him consider that what he does, he does for mankind. Let him consider that future generations shall reap the fruit of his virtues, and all the countless ages of the future shall come to him loaded with his reward.

16. Cf. *JMN* 3:123.

My yoke is easy, and my burden is light.

MATTHEW 11:30

In the land of Judea, in view of the burdensome practice of the Mosaic ritual, in view of the insufferable impositions of the Pharisees, and of the patience of the people under their oppression,—Jesus says, "My yoke is easy and my burden is light."

But the language of the Saviour, as was usual with him, had a wider application than those who heard it could conceive. He stood by the little town of Capernaum, but the world was present to his mind. He spoke to a handful of Jewish villagers, but he addressed through them the human race. Harken, my brethren, for he saith unto us, and to all men, "Come unto me, all ye that labour and are heavy laden, and I will give you rest: Take my yoke upon you, and learn of me, for, my yoke is easy and my burden is light."

Is it not strange that the experience of ages has shewn that this peculiarity of his religion should be the greatest objection to it? Is it not strange that this very simplicity of the gospel, this freedom from all harsh and sanguinary demands, this easy law, should be the main stumbling block that has stood in the way of the Jew and the Greek, of the infidel and the bigot, of the servants of passion and of pride, from bringing to Christianity the offering of their obedience?[1]

Let us consider the extent of the meaning of our Saviour. His yoke is easy compared with those dominions which oppose his own, compared with that of passion, of opinion, of false religion, compared with those under which men bring themselves.

1. In the first place, the yoke of the passions is harder to be borne. Our passions will always be either servants or masters. If we do not govern them, they will govern us. There's no middle way. They are artful tempters. They do not reveal to us their strength, when they first invite us to comply with them. They plead that they are weak, and if we do not like the gratification they offer us we can refuse to be guided by them again. They sit in ambush to catch the

Completed on April 26, 1828, in Concord, Mass. Preached fourteen times: April 27, 1828, in Concord, Mass.; May 1 (Thursday Lecture) in Waltham; May 4 in Lexington; May 11 at the Brattle Street Church; May 25 in Concord, N.H.; June 8 in Shirley; June 29 at the Second Church, Charlestown; July 6 in Lechmere Point; July 13 at the Second Church, Boston; September 5 in Medford; September 21 in West Cambridge; October 19 in Dover, N.H.; April 24, 1829, at the Second Church, Boston; and on the evening of March 20, 1831, at the Friend Street Chapel.

1. Cf. I Corinthians 1:23.

man when he lies at ease, and unguarded, and persuade him that the vice to which they would lead him is only a virtue pushed to its extreme. But when he has once yielded, he is bound hand and foot:—he does not see his fetters; he does not hear the clank of his chains, but the rivets are fast, you may see him going in the very path which he tells you he shudders to tread. Need I repeat this oft told tale? Need I tell you the struggles, and the sorrows, and the misery of that man who is the slave of his passions?

How often has it been remarked when we have seen notorious malefactors come to a bad end, what a thorough mistake they had made; that they had exhausted the most diligent industry, the most inventive ingenuity—days and months of contrivance—for what? to roll in pleasure? to dwell in palaces? no, but to procure mere freedom from punishment, to preserve a squalid and degraded life in forlorn and frightful places, in caves of the woods, or in some infamous corners or dark cellars of a metropolis; whilst half the talent and energy they had exhibited with this wretched success, if well directed, would surely have given them honest wealth and respectability and high standing in the community.

But those whom the laws have branded with ignominy are but a small part of the victims of passion who have forgotten that there is an easier yoke, a lighter burden.

2. The yoke of religion is easier to be borne than that of human opinions. The gospel that Christ brought us is plain and reasonable. He insisted on *principles:* But men all over the world insist on *opinions.* He laid the stress upon the moral character, upon the virtues of the heart, but men have disguised the gentle spirit of his gospel under their traditions and have sat in judgment on the notions of the head. He said, 'Blessed are the meek, the poor in spirit, the pure in heart, the peacemakers.'[2] But man said, 'Cursed are all they who do not believe as I believe.' And assuming this authority, they have added to the gospel a mass of creeds and dogmas which violate its spirit and withdraw men from truth.

3. Again; the yoke of Christ is easier to be borne than the burden of the forms of false religion. It is only necessary to remind you of what has been so often shown: the contrast between the stern and bloody religions of the eastern world, Indostan, of Mexico, of the Asiatic islands, and the mildness of the Divine revelation. There is no abomination so dark and dreadful in spirit and in practice, but sometime or somewhere man has accepted it as a law of God. Every cruel rule that has usurped the name of religion, that has enjoined an infinite multiplication of empty forms; that has commanded men to abstain from every social joy, to fast, or to whip, torture, slay themselves, or to burn or drown their children, in the name of God and for the sake of their souls, has been sure of success. It had no lack of votaries, and its votaries had no lack of zeal. Each has taken up in turn the axe of persecution, and hunted down its victims, among the good and the wise.

So oppressive is the sense of transgression in our nature that wherever man

2. Cf. Matthew 5:5-9.

has sinned, he seeks for some relief, some expiation. Any thing he will endure or perform but the simple demands of the Divine law. One would imagine that an obedience to this true Religion was the most formidable and impracticable thing in the world; and now let us accurately consider what it really requires.

The true religion which Christ came to reveal—or rather to reveal its sanctions and hopes, for, the religion existed and exists throughout eternity past and to come, the same to angels and to men—the true religion hath none of these obstacles or hard demands. Think what it requires of you when strictly considered. It asks no struggles with nature, nor throws dangers in the way at which courage itself turns pale, nor heaps a mountain of difficulties in your path to be encountered at once. *It only requires that in a single moment you do a single thing right. This* is the whole of Religion—the whole of that law by which God guides every moral being to his happiness—one single duty in one single moment. To do this, is to be a Christian.

Do not imagine, my brethren, that I am doing any disparagement to this high and momentous law. I am very far from wishing to diminish, by one jot, the importance or the interest of the cause I plead. I only desire to set the ease and the difficulty of obedience in its proper light. Consider then that every moment of your life brings with it an alternative: offers you an opportunity to do right or to do wrong. This moment you are in God's house: it is in your power to fix your attention upon those meditations that belong to this day and this place or to give loose to your roving thoughts. Would you fulfil God's law? You have but one thing to do. Tomorrow, the labours of life return. At one season, you will be transacting affairs of trade. The opportunity will present itself of taking some small advantage of your neighbor. At one instant the duty of truth and the crime of deception will offer themselves to your mind. There is but one thing to be done.

At another season, you shall supply the waste of nature by food. When the wants of hunger are satisfied, the temptation remains, to pamper the palate. In a particular moment, you will be sensible of the temptation and be sensible of the duty of temperance. There is but one thing to be done.

At another, you shall lay plans for the coming year or for the employment of life. In every deliberation, there shall be a best side and a worst. You shall see this to be of present sordid advantage, and that to be conducive to your final good. In every moment, there is something to be adopted or to be rejected. Still there is but one thing to be done.

And so we may go through all possible events, and crowd life as much as we may, the whole demand of Religion will never amount to more than this. There will always be a choice between a temptation and a duty, and you will always be directed, if you desire it, *how* you shall choose; for Conscience will always point with her silent finger.

Such then is the simplicity of our religion when stripped of the disguises with which the sin and folly of men have deformed it. Let it be remembered, however, that divine property of our nature that every virtue paves the way to virtue, that every sacrifice makes the next sacrifice easier, until a holy life ceases to be an effort and becomes a habit of happiness. At every step the yoke becomes easier and the burden lighter.

And is it then so hard and painful a thing to be a Christian? Is it really beyond our power to compass the small effort that is necessary in one moment to discharge its appointed portion of duty? Can we not watch with our Lord one hour?[3] Can we not watch with him one moment? We murmur at the difficulty of so great a work. It is because we err in contemplating as a mass what is really a multitude of separate objects. God has divided the work of life into little parts, as life itself is divided into years and hours.

I will not disguise, whilst I make these representations, that there is a difficulty—serious difficulty—in beginning a religious life. But the difficulty is wholly in the beginning, in breaking the ice of evil habit. Once resolutely embarked it is easy to persevere and with every advance more pleasant till all sense of effort is lost in the delight of doing well.

I know not how these views can be better illustrated and imprinted than by calling to your recollection the substance of an ancient narrative familiar to us all.[4] In the time when the kingdom of Syria was powerful, and Benhadad the king had established himself by his victories on the throne of his ancestors, the general of his armies became his favourite and he made him the minister of his empire. His minister was wise and great. He had prospered in all his purposes: he leaned on the throne which his battles had defended, and no man resisted his will.

Then his heart was filled with pride, and he said, Lo, I am great in the eyes of this nation. Who shall hurt me?

Then was the minister of the king of Syria stricken with a loathsome disease and his body covered over with sores of leprosy, so that all men departed from him with fear and he tore off his purple robe and sat down on the ground and bemoaned himself. Then the king his master heard that there lived in Palestine a man of God of whom the rumour went that he had received power from heaven to call armies of angels to his side; to give sight to the blind, and to strike with blindness them who saw; to stop the rain and to cause rain to fall.

So he sent his minister to the king of Samaria with letters and gifts; and the king sent him to the village, where the great Prophet dwelt. And when he and his servants and his chariots stood before the prophet's door, the man of God sent out a messenger, directing him to wash himself in the little river that ran below the town and he should be cured.

But the sick man who expected to command reverence by the magnificence of his retinue and the renown of his name was disgusted at this apparent indifference. He, the favorite of the great king—for whose welfare nations offered vows—is he such an one that this Jew does not think it worth his while to come

3. Cf. Matthew 26:40.
4. II Kings 5:1–14.

to his door to see him, but sends a boy with his careless message? I thought he would come down, he said, and invoke his gods with solemn sacrifice and lay his own hand with prayer upon my flesh, and heal the disease.—And so I am to go alone to this jewish stream! And for this I have made this tedious journey. Are not the rivers in my own land, the waters of Damascus, as pure and as holy as these waters of Israel? And he refused to go and turned back on his way in a rage. But his servants came nigh unto him and said, "My father! if the prophet had bid thee do *some great thing*, wouldst not thou have done it? how much more, when he saith unto thee, 'Wash and be clean.'" At these words, he perceived his folly and obeyed the direction of the man of God. But as soon as he entered the river his disease departed and his flesh became as the flesh of a child.

This is the story of Naaman. It was the fashion of a former age to find in all the persons and events recorded in the Old Testament so many types of that more perfect system of moral government which is revealed in the new. I am far from wishing to fix any superstitious value upon this or any similar narrative. But I believe we may find in this story an useful mirror of our own disposition. There are a great many Naamans in the world. It is as if we had read the history of ourselves.

True it is, my friends, that the leprosy is not known among us. It is a plague which does not visit these parts of the world. We shudder at this loathsome evil only in the painting of travellers. But that moral evil of which it was but the shadow, the taint of sin—the leprosy of the mind—we share in common with the Syrian and the Jew. This is the pest which does not spend itself with time; which Quarantines cannot keep aloof; which seas or climates cannot bound; it spreads its active infection alike among the old and the young; alike under polar cold and tropical heat.

Here whilst we suffer under this general contagion, God has sent his messenger to us to give us directions how we may be healed. What is the command? not that we offer a hecatomb in sacrifice or pour out rivers of oil, not that we spend our substance, or maim our limbs, or slay our children.[5] No nothing of all this, but simply, Wash and be clean: Cease to do evil: learn to do well. Let the sense of duty to God enable us in each moment to discharge the duty of the moment.

But because God has given to history the message of his will for our ears, because he doth not burst the silence of his heavens and speak to us in thunder and by miracle, we slight the benevolent command; we submit to the yoke of our own passions, and go on our own evil way. If *some great thing* had been enjoined on us, if any accumulation of rites or penances had been demanded of us as a substitute for a meek and quiet temper, for simple obedience to the command of Conscience, there is no doubt we should have thought our salvation cheaply purchased by any weight of external observances.

My brethren, let reason be allowed to whisper to us that sensible expostula-

5. Cf. Micah 6:7.

tion of the servants of Naaman. At least let not our stormy passions prevent us from giving a fair trial to this divine medicine, this revelation which promises so much.

It bids us form habits of virtue. If the first efforts be hard, let us remember that the object is great; if the first efforts are hard, yet the next shall be easy; and God shall crown every sincere exertion with his favor which is life.

XIX

For as many as are led by the spirit of God, they are the Sons of God.

ROMANS 8:14

Every year is diffusing among men a more just idea of the Christian religion. Every new inquiry ascertains that the errors it has been made to teach do not belong to it but have been added to it by the ignorance or wickedness of men. It is now purifying itself. It speaks a language worthy of its Author. We now discover that the beauty of the gospel—the sovereign distinction—the seal of Heaven stamped upon it is—the catholic benignant spirit which it breathes. We find that it is churches and counsels—it is human littleness—that has been exclusive and damnatory: the gospel breathes now and breathed always peace and good will. 'I perceive,' said the Apostle Peter, in the first age of its declaration, 'I perceive that in every nation, he who feareth God, and worketh righteousness is accepted of him.'[1]

The uniform effect of all the progress of men in the knowledge of the Divine revelation has been—a more spiritual faith. The more the mind is enlightened, the less it values forms and observances, and the more it prizes virtue. It is the heart which Christianity aims to affect. If it can conquer this, it is sure the life will be right. It is the great, the main conclusion of religion that in the eye of God not the *actions* but the *principles* of moral beings are regarded. It is to some remarks in illustration of this doctrine, that principles are important, that actions have no other importance than that derived from the principle, that I wish now to invite your attention.

My brethren, I am afraid this distinction is not perceived as it ought to be; and yet it affects all we say and do. Men are perpetually appealing, when you blame them for a fault, to the insignificance of the matter. 'If,' say they, 'this little deception of benevolence or of politeness, I have used, were some great fraud, or

---

Completed on May 7, 1828, in Concord, Mass. Preached fifteen times: May 11, 1828, at the Brattle Street Church; May 18 at the Federal Street Church; June 1 in Concord, Mass.; June 15 in Concord, N.H.; July 20 at the Second Church, Boston; July 27 at the Purchase Street Church; August 3 in Waltham; October 26 in Dover, N.H.; November 2 at the Harvard College Chapel; January 18, 1829, at the First Church, Salem; March 8 in Medford; May 31 at the Stone Chapel; July 26 at the Second Church, Boston; January 10, 1830, at the New North Church, and finally September 18, 1836, in East Lexington. A draft of most of this sermon occurs in *JMN* 3:126–30.

1. Acts 10:34–35.

affected the peace of society, there might be cause for your solemn censure. You say, I have told a lie, but in this little affair, the truth was a trifle, the falsehood is a trifle, and there is no need to look so grave.' But, my friends, who does not see, that, the greatness or smallness of the action is really no consideration at all? All that is important, all that we were sent into the world for, is, that we might be trained to certain *principles*. Let us consider this a little in detail, in application to the several virtues we are commanded to cultivate.

The consequences of Charity are of more immediate effect and are more easily followed out than of the other virtues. But the good that you do to the children of poverty by an act of charity, how pitiful it is! When you give a dollar to a starving beggar, what good have you done? You have appeased his hunger for a little hour, and given bread to himself and his famished child, until the evening;—perhaps you have lit the fire on his frosty hearth, or covered the straw on which he lies from the cold. But with the morning sun, his misery returns, and again, for pity's sake, he is begging, from door to door, for a crust. To him, your kindness has done little; it is to *yourself* the good was done. As long as you exist, you shall be the better for that action. The performance of that action has given a portion of strength to the noblest fibre in your moral frame; has done something to increase a disposition that is essential to your eternal well being. This is Charity. Now with respect to Truth. It is good for your neighbour that you do not deceive him. It is good for your neighbour that you do not slander him. But it is not very important. If he is good, he will live down calumny, and, in any event, our happiness depends more on what we think of ourselves, than on what others think of us. And it is possible that you may tell a thousand fables, as true, that will really do very little harm, if they should be written in history, and believed to the end of the world. It is of very little consequence whether Asaraddon or Tigranes was the name of the fiftieth king of Syria, but if you, knowing it to be Asaraddon, say it was Tigranes, you have done a great and indefinite evil. To whom?—to the world? no, but to yourself. You have violated a solemn law within you, which you are sensible ought never to have been violated. If with an intention to deceive, you have uttered a falsehood,—you have rebelled against yourself, you have begun to unsettle all the foundations of goodness in your nature.

Extend the view from Truth to Honesty, which is nothing but Truth applied to affairs, instead of words. You are driving a bargain with your wealthy neighbour, compared with whose accumulations, your means are a pittance. 'Of what manner of consequence,' you ask, 'can it be to him if by any oversight or negligence of his, which you have just detected in the settlement of your account, he has paid twice its value for an acre of land or a bale of merchandize?' This is the way you reason, when Conscience accuses you. Though they see the wrong—though they cannot help feeling the reproach of duplicity, yet men choose to exculpate themselves, and prevaricate. I tell you if you have dishonestly obtained from your neighbour so much as a crumb of bread, you have done an outrage to your nature that must be atoned for or punished. You have taken one step towards all that is dark and tremendous, in the system of things.

So it is with Temperance. The injury done you by one offence, by one instance of intoxication, although of uncertain danger, may be very little to your now vigorous constitution. The sensual habit is all. The shameful slavery of your moral being to your animal being. The base subjection of your soul to your body. You have given up your life, the direction of your advancing destiny to a base appetite. You are quenching the immortal spark under the grossest propensities and it is this self degradation, this ruin of a man, which is to be deplored.

So is it with Humility; with Prudence; with Industry; with every virtue, and every grace. It is not the effect of the particular action they dictate, that we are to value, but only that the principle has found a vent, has been developed, has become a part of our character.

There are illustrious examples of this fact in our civil history. When your fathers associated themselves throughout the country in a refusal to pay another penny in the pound for tea, and, for their refusal, abode all the horrors of a political Revolution,—was that poor penny uppermost in their thoughts, and guilty of all this blood? It was the *principle of Freedom*, for which they contended.

My friends, I dwell the longer upon these illustrations, because the practical error is so common and so pernicious, which I wish to expose. We are very apt to overrate the importance of our actions. I am very anxious not to be misunderstood. I do not mean to deny that our actions are of great importance, for they surely are of the greatest; but I wish it to be felt in what manner they are important; that it is only as they are expressions of principles, and not for themselves and their effects on the world. The same motive—the love of justice—for example, may prompt two different men, to precisely opposite conduct. Two jurors may come to unlike conclusions respecting the innocence of a prisoner, and one may give his word to kill and one to spare. In a moral view the action, the word of acquittal or of conviction, is indifferent: the motive in both cases is reverend. Men of a very religious turn of mind are prone to think (at least their language gives this impression,) that the designs of God in the world are very much affected, if not dependant upon what shall be done or determined by themselves, or their society, or their country. They speak as if they thought that God and good angels were watching their conduct with a degree of apprehension lest the divine will should not be fulfilled for want of their cooperation. They exhort you to devote yourself, or to give your contribution to this or that cause, without delay,—not for the true reason, not because you have no right to delay the doing a good action, but, because they would have you think that you put the cause of Christianity or of mankind in jeopardy—which are to be promoted by your activity. We lose ourselves in the details of this prejudice till we become blind to the absurdity that we are making the everlasting progress of the Universe hang upon the by-laws of a Missionary Society or a Sunday School.

Let us think of ourselves more humbly. The just way to consider things is this. Truth says to us, Give yourself no manner of anxiety about events, about the consequences of actions. They are really of no importance to you. They have another Director, Controller, Source: The whole object of the moral and material creation to you is the formation of your character. Do not suffer yourself to be blinded by an overweening conceit. Consider how feeble and insufficient you are to your own safety and do not think that God needs your aid. To that Providence who can accomplish the vastest purposes with a power and a speed that affrights the imagination it is surely of no concern for its affairs, whether you live or die. It is for another reason, for your own happiness, for your education to moral greatness, that he permits you to exercise your little agency in his cause. If you imagine you were called into being for the purpose of taking a leading part in the administration of the world—in order to guard one province of the moral creation from ruin, and that its salvation hangs on the success of your single arm—you have wholly mistaken your business. Creep into your grave, for the Universe hath no need of you. Alas for thy foolish presumption! For what hast thou which thou didst not receive;[2] and cannot He, who gave you this power, commit it to another, or use it Himself?

The proper antidote for all false and narrow estimates of actions is to be found in a habitual regard to the great relations we bear to God and to Eternity. In view of our whole existence, the events of this life cease to appear important. It seems to us now a question of very material interest, whether we shall be poor or rich; what profession in life we shall enter; what connexions we shall form; how long we shall live; and even much inferiour considerations, as what is our personal appearance; or in what town, or what street we shall reside? Which of us does not remember that these are points which he has debated with heat and determined with difficulty and had no doubt that their magnitude was as great as it seemed? But which of you has lived forty years, thirty years, twenty years, and has not outlived some of his opinions on these particulars? Already they have lessened in your eye. Already you have doubted whether these external circumstances really made the difference which to an unpractised eye they seem to make in human happiness. But how, think you, they will seem, when, in the revolution of time, you look back at the distance of a thousand ages hence, on the morning of your existence?

When this planet we now inhabit shall have been swept from its system, and its system is no longer reckoned in the astronomy of the Universe; when the fires that now roll in these heavens above us, have combined in new constellations, or obey new laws; or when, by that dread will which peopled eternal space with their burning hosts, they shall disappear; when God shall be all in

2. I Corinthians 4:7.

all;[3] when you shall be nourishing the powers of an angel's intellect, and exploring the height and the depth and the length and the breadth of the wisdom and the knowledge of God,—then, when you look back a moment at the scenes of your infancy and this poor earth which was your cradle,—will it really seem to you of consequence, whether you were dressed in silk or in mats; whether you lived on one side or another of the globe; or whether you staid there, one or two summers more or less?

Or will you remember with the same vanity, as now, all that your hands performed; the house that you built; the money that you earned; the honours which you attained; the pages which you wrote; your extensive influence, your charitable acts? No; these will pass away and be insignificant—these will depart into utter oblivion; but the principles which these actions brought into exercise will survive this unmeasured duration—in immortal youth. The principle which led you, when a child, to disobey your parent; when a man, to resist or elude the laws, will harm you then. The principle which prevailed with you, when a boy, to brave the displeasure of your companions for truth's sake; and, when a man, to cleave to your opinions, though your bread or your life was the forfeit, shall ennoble you then, in the society of disembodied minds,—shall endear you to the Deity in that far distant and awful hour. It is the object of Christianity to put men under the government of principles; to exalt the soul and depress the body. It does not ask of you forms or sacrifices. "As many as are led by the spirit of God they are the Sons of God."

My brethren, I believe I need not insist upon the importance of these views to our everlasting interests. I believe I have an advocate in your breasts, that is more persuasive than any language. For I am urging the cause of a truth which God has written upon every mind. It has been obscured by false religion, and it is apt to be darkened in our own hearts. It is good to bring it out into day. It is good amid the vanities of life, amid all the perishing trifles, that, hour by hour, attract the attention, and try the temper, and waste the time, to take hold on imperishable principles. There is something elevated and beautiful in being guided, not by every idle gale of accident from without, but by heaven-born principles within: in having the chart of our own course within ourselves: there is something grand in linking our existence to the existence of the Deity, by obeying the laws which he observes. I find a kindling excitement in the thought that the sentiment which prompts a child to an act of generosity is the same which guides an archangel to his awful duties; that into the humblest transaction in which we can engage, we can introduce the authority of those majestic laws which make the sovereignty of the Creation, the character of God. It seems to me in obeying them, in squaring my conduct by them, I part with the weakness of humanity, I exchange the rags of my nature for a portion of my maker's majesty. I hear an approving voice from the Universe of beings. I lean on Omnipotence. To be governed by our passions, is to be governed by objects of

3. I Corinthians 15:28.

sense, for it is those things that the passions pursue; but to be governed by principles is to be directed by influences from the unseen and eternal world. Let us remember that God looks upon actions with other eyes than men; that with him the greatness of the occasion or the number of the actors are of no esteem. He explores the heart and the motive. Let us remember that no place is so obscure but it may be made glorious by goodness; no circumstances so abject but religion will make them venerable; that no duty can ever be mean, and that no hour of life elapses, without giving opportunity for the exercise of eternal principles.

Speak evil of no man.

Titus 3:2

I am about to offer to your consideration, my Christian friends, some plain remarks upon a vice which is very common, and almost universal among us, a vice to which we are daily tempted, and which—I am afraid—a great many of us daily indulge. I mean Calumny—the practice of speaking evil of our neighbour. I believe you will all admit that it is one of the crying sins of the times and one which, though of the most pernicious consequence to public and private peace and virtue, is the hardest to repress or to control. The law of the land can reach and punish the bold libel that is scattered abroad in daylight; what has been said on the housetops can be publicly refuted, and the evil in some degree remedied, but the slander that is dropped at the fireside in familiar conversation, that is suggested by one and magnified by another, that is imprinted and circulated by looks and gestures—this though it may often spread as widely and work as actively as the first, it is impossible to counteract. "The tongue," saith the Apostle James, "can no man tame."[1] Let us apply to it then a higher force. Let us teach it subordination to the laws of God.

There are some considerations, which, it seems to me, must always have weight to check this evil propensity in us, if we only admit them.

And chiefly the value of character. The worth of every word and deed is estimated, wherever we are known, less by itself than by the worth of the person by whom it is said or done. One man makes a great exertion, or utters a wise sentiment which falls to the ground. Another man does not lift his hand unobserved. For we judge those whom we know, not by what they do *now*, but by all that we remember of them. We keep in our minds with respect to each individual an impression which is the general result of all his actions which have come to our knowledge. This general result is what we call *Character*. Now this is the great engine by which the world is moved. All the effect of each of us upon society, depends upon this; upon the degree and kind of impression which the united mass of our actions have left. When this is good, it is our chief treasure.

Preached ten times: June 22, 1828, in Concord, N.H.; July 6 in Lechmere Point; August 3 in Waltham; August 10 at the Second Church, Boston; October 26 in Dover, N.H.; November 30 in Concord, Mass.; January 25, 1829, at the Federal Street Church; February 1 in West Cambridge; February 8 in Stowbridge; and September 20 at the Second Church, Boston.

1. James 3:8.

It is our strength. It goes before us as our recommendation in all the societies of men, and gives meaning to our speech, and might to our hands. This it is which calumny assails. This moral power over men it can deprive us of. It cannot touch the moral property itself; but it can destroy its influence upon others. It can rifle us of what is to most men dearer than houses and lands, than wife and children, or than life itself. It is this value of character that makes or that ought to make its sacredness. It is this consideration that should make us wary of the abuse of the tongue. I speak now of course of the value of character to the possessor. There are not many men of such hardened ill nature, but if their attention were called at the moment when they are tempted to give currency to an idle suspicion, to consider the pain it will inflict upon him who is the object of it—they would relent, would pause ere it passed their lips. You can renew the merriment of your company by relating as a fact a wanton sarcasm upon the motives of your friend. Stop and ponder one moment, the good and the evil likely to ensue. To check that pulse of momentary mirth let the image of the good man rise to your memory before you wound him. Remember at how high a rate—higher than his prosperity or his life—he holds his good name. Consider that although it may be in him human weakness, it has been for years the delight of his heart—that deserved esteem in which his acquaintance hold him, which he fondly trusts will go down like an inheritance to his sons. But the heedless scandal you are tempted to relate will presently circulate and come to his ears. You can strew his pillow with thorns and banish sleep from his eyes. You can turn to poison what was once his pleasure and can plant the sting of sorrow in every heart of that happy house. A word will do it; a word from you will destroy their peace. Choose now whether you will speak or whether you will forbear.[2]

In speaking thus of the value of a good name to the possessor I do not wish to exaggerate its worth. There is danger, if we are not guided by elevated motives, that we should value reputation at too high a rate, and as we are all at all times exposed to calumny it is important we think justly upon it. I do not conceive that the injury to a well balanced mind can be very great when its deeds or motives are slandered. The real injury is of course nothing. The mind remains as good as it was before. But the pain it will be made to feel from being the victim of unruly tongues, will be acute or trifling, according to its strength. A strong mind, above all a mind having a firm trust in God, will see clearly that the world's opinion is no tribunal for it; that the world's opinion is a king of snow; that to its own master—the Lord of the Universe—it standeth or falleth.[3] The reputation which your virtues gave you among men, was a reward which men gave and can take away; but not so with your goodness itself. It was nobly said by Demetrius (Phalereus), the benefactor of Athens, when the Athenians threw down his statues in their city, "that they could not overthrow the virtues

2. "There are not . . . forbear": see *JMN* 3:131.
3. Romans 14:4.

for which they were erected."[4] This sentiment should console us when the shafts of slander are aimed at us. You may be calumniated for those very things which you know deserve praise. Your intentions may be misconstrued, your good actions misrepresented because you adhere to a purer cause in religion or in politics than others. Then there is a good word of encouragement spoken to you from your Lord, Rejoice and be exceeding glad for great is your reward in heaven, so persecuted they the prophets that were before you.[5] And it may be that it is some real fault in your character which your enemy exaggerates and exposes; then, you may make good out of evil. When men speak evil of you, let it be a warning to flee those vices of which you are accused. When Plato was told that his enemies traduced him, "It is no matter," he replied, "I will live so that nobody shall believe them."[6]

We have been speaking of the value of character in the eye of the possessor. But Character has another value, still more important. I mean its value to others. I beg your attention to this subject a moment, to that value which a good name that has been dearly bought by a life of goodness has, as a lesson to the community—and how easy it is to deface it. If you could go into every cottage, to every low solitary farmhouse, where the name of God is known and reverenced, you should find the poor man this day gathering his little family about him and dealing out to them, according to his skill, the laws of his Creator and quoting to them in illustration of his doctrine the names of here and there a man in his neighborhood who has obeyed the commandments and has prospered. He vindicates, by this simple logic, the ways of Providence to man.[7] The little circle store up that name in their memories as an encouragement to their virtues. If you blast that name in the heedlessness of foolish gossip, you pluck away a pillar from their faith; you rob goodness of a powerful motive; you take from the soul a consolation.

I regard this consideration as one of great importance and I wish to dwell upon it a moment longer. I appeal to the best feelings of all who hear me, and ask, after our own conscience what property is more really valuable to us, than the character of our friends? We always feel hurt, and justly, when we hear those malignant sophisms which always mark a shallow reasoner—which found all virtue upon a creeping calculating selfishness and accuse all mankind as hypocrites. We feel a just indignation. Besides being contradicted by the experience of our best hours, we see it belies those whom we know to be good, and whose virtue we have always felt to be important in its example to us, and to the world. In moments when sorrow has almost undone us; when our own faith wavers; when we are disturbed with doubts—whither then does the mind repair for

4. William de Britaine, *Human Prudence; Or the Art by which a Man and a Woman May Be Advanced to Fortune, to Permanent Honor, and to Real Grandeur*, ed. Herman Mann (Dedham, Mass., 1806), 75. See *JMN* 6:67.

5. Matthew 5:12.

6. "Upon Some Verses of Virgil," in *Essays of Michael Seigneur de Montaigne* . . . , trans. Charles Cotton (London, 1693), 3:98. See *JMN* 6:77.

7. Cf. Milton, *Paradise Lost*, I, 25–26.

unfailing encouragement, but to that little and honoured company of good men and women among our friends, whose probity, whose selfrespect, whose charity, whose piety, are an anchor to our faith; friends who, like a squadron of angels, gather on a mount before us, and send out from their seraph faces, courage and light into our hearts. When the Minister of destruction was sent against Sodom ten good men would have saved the city;[8] and five or six good men whose virtues we best know—are commonly our examples, our evidences, our defenders against the assaults of temptation and the props on which we lean. We quote them as strong instances in our conversation and the faithful memory brings up their images in all their silent eloquence to approve us when we do right, to accuse us when we have done wrong.[9]

Such being the value of character, firstly to the possessor, as being his greatest pleasure, and greatest means of good, and secondly to others, as the muniment of virtue, it is easy to feel the heinousness of that criminal who tampers with it and ruins it. Yet this mischief is daily done with a facility that is shocking, and by people who in other respects it may be regard the law of love. Perhaps we ourselves, my brethren, may find that we have lent our aid to add to this sore evil of the world. It is frightful to see how much conversation among good mild Christian people turns upon the defects of their acquaintance, and how lightly this is done. You drop a word of disparagement in society upon an honoured name. You do it in thoughtless consent to the humour you find prevailing in the room. You think perhaps that you are safe; for your friends are well bred, and they will understand you to banter, and not to mean all you say. But consider that this part of your conversation is best remembered of all. All your wit, all your learning, is speedily forgotten by the careless ear that heard them—but every word that was pointed against your friend, is treasured and will be repeated by every one to whose ear it comes.

Then it is so natural,—nay—without the steadiest vigilance—so unavoidable, this free and unmerciful discussion of character. For want of a general cultivation of the mind to any high degree, the common places of conversation have not sufficient savour to dissipate our languor. Men and women cannot find excitement enough in the superficial talk they use upon subjects they have never explored and fly for refuge from insipidity to scandal.[10] Another cause no doubt of this vice is our love of superiority, which, when it fails to excite *us* to become better, hath a diseased pleasure in finding wherein others are worse.

But if the temptation to evil speaking is so strong, the more is the merit of resistance. And there is always something that betrays elevation of mind in the readiness to assign good motives for actions of unknown motive. It is the vulgar way to suggest an ill motive for whatever an ill motive will explain; and it marks malignity and a consciousness of acting from low motives. I know it is hard to forbear, and therefore he is a sublime spirit who does forbear calumny. Who

8. Genesis 18:32.
9. "I appeal . . . wrong": see *JMN* 3:131–32.
10. "Then it is . . . scandal": see *JMN* 3:131.

can mix with society and wholly refrain? But who can yield to it without losing his own self-respect? What a sermon upon slander is contained in the feeling with which a good man rises up from a conversation in which he has been led into that offence! He feels disgraced. He feels that he has played a base part, and catered for the wickedness of low minds: also that he has injured himself, in the esteem of those with whom he conversed; has thrown himself upon the mercy of those who have no mercy upon character; and has made himself answerable to those who have been reviled in his presence.

But it will be urged that there are limits to that forbearance which duty recommends to us. Some will say, I know a man whom I can never see without feeling an apprehension for the public or private mischief he may cause. I have a conviction which I cannot escape, and cannot silence, that he is dangerous. He is a candidate for public office, he is courting the acquaintance of my friends; and must I not do all in my power to put the public or my friends upon their guard by making known my views of his corrupt habits and character? To this question I think the answer is plain. Certainly if it is in the power of none but you to expose the public or private danger, it is your right and duty to do so. But this is a case which can hardly ever occur. In the present imperfect state of the world you may safely leave the office of stigmatizing bad men to the public eye and tongue. If there be in any man a weak or vicious point, doubt not it will be exposed with a full cry of Calumny. Ample justice, I doubt not, will be done to every defect, to every crime, by those who in the eager resorts of business are collecting and repeating the news of the hour and giving good and bad fame to public men. Here is the sore side of our nature. It was an old and keen observer of man who said, Men's failings live in brass, we write their virtues in water.[11] No, my brethren, there is little danger that injury will arise from the want of your activity in aspersing the character of any man.

On the contrary there is danger lest you deceive yourself, and under colour of serving the cause of truth, magnify venial faults into grave charges, and serve your own evil passions. Were it not better, since the world is shaken by this clamour of calumny, which surely will not let the faults of any one escape, that you should seal your lips in endless silence upon the frailties of your friends? It is honest to be still. And when this injurious gossip goes on around you—let your silence be felt as its proper rebuke. There are times when the silence of a good man is more impressive than any harangue.[12] Perhaps it will be in your power to do much more than simply to discountenance this pernicious ribaldry. I have heard of the success of a good man who restored peace to a jarring neighborhood simply by extorting from each of his neighbors and repeating again to each what good word or action one could remember of another. It was an honourable employment to circulate anecdotes of kindness, to excite an emulation of charity, of humility and truth. This was to be a benefactor of men.

11. Misquoted from Shakespeare, *Henry VIII*, IV, ii, 45–46. See *JMN* 2:273, 6:166.
12. Cf. *JMN* 3:132.

But to live a calumniator—to live to hinder the happiness of others—this is base and dreadful. To go up and down in society a malicious whisperer; the living register of the faults of others; the faithful chronicle of every crime; the magnifier of small vices; the executioner of reputations; the distributor of infamy!

But mark also how the arm of heaven's retribution overtakes the offender. If he has made bitter the cup of happiness to others, he has poisoned the fountains of his own. If the hand of Ishmael is against every man, every man is armed against him.[13]

Thus we have seen the threefold evil of this abuse of the tongue; that Calumny injures the person calumniated; injures society; and injures the Calumniator. Therefore, brethren, I exhort you in the words of the apostle, "Speak evil of no man." Let us remember the solemn warning of our Saviour, "By thy words thou shalt be justified, and by thy words thou shalt be condemned."[14] Let us feel how low and unworthy of our calling, of our Duties and our hopes as disciples of the Lord Jesus and as children of God—is a whisper of detraction. The day is coming to us all, when the voice of passion and of party spirit and of private interest and resentment shall be hushed, when the trumpet of fame shall be mute; when admiration and desire and success shall lie down in marble slumber and nothing survive to judgment but the character we have formed on earth. Then Blessed shall be the lips that were never sullied with a lie; that being reviled, reviled not again;[15] that never uttered an accent of slander; and never breathed other words than those of truth, of Charity, and of Peace.

13. Genesis 16:12. Compare the two preceding paragraphs with *JMN* 3:132.
14. Matthew 12:37.
15. I Peter 2:23.

These . . . are a law unto themselves; which show the work of the law written in their hearts.
ROMANS 2:14–15

In proposing these words of the apostle as the subject of our meditations it is my purpose to invite your attention to some remarks upon the nature and office of Conscience to which the text relates; to consider its remarkable power; and its final cause; and lastly to consider the very striking proof it furnishes, of the existence and government of God.

At the outset of these inquiries there has been much discussion concerning the nature of what we call the Conscience. The question whether it is a separate faculty like the sight or the touch; or whether it is only the operation of the understanding upon a peculiar class of ideas is obviously one of no practical bearing and is vain because it can never be decided. It is a question of more importance whether it is capable of improvement by education.

There is no need of curious metaphysics here. We are men. We all know the meaning of right and wrong. We do not remember the time in the early dawn of our faculties when we first learned the alphabet of moral distinctions. The perception of good and evil we feel is intwisted with life. We may almost say, we exist to make that distinction. It makes a part of every idea. That distinction was writ by the Eternal on the mind that is to live eternally. If there be any thing which can be said to be the object of our being, it is to make this choice between good and evil. Life is a never ending succession of these alternatives; and the sentiment which approves one and condemns the other is the Conscience. It is not a simple perception that one action is good and another evil and ending there,—as the eye perceives that one leaf is green and another red, or that one is longer and another less, and no more—but the distinction of the sentiment we call the Conscience, is, that it *includes a command to adopt or to reject;*—to perform one action, and to forbear another.

Completed and dated at Divinity Hall, Cambridge, Mass., July 30, 1828. Preached fourteen times: August 17, 1828, at the Second Church, Boston; August 31 in Waltham; September 7 at the First Church, Boston; October 5 at the Brattle Street Church; October 26 in Dover, N.H.; November 16 at the Hollis Street Church; December 7 in Concord, N.H.; January 4, 1829, in Groton; January 18 at the First Church, Salem; February 1 in West Cambridge; October 18 at the Second Church, Boston; January 24, 1830, at the Federal Street Church; August 8 at the First Church, Charlestown; and January 8, 1837, in East Lexington.

With regard to the question, whether the Conscience is capable of improvement, or, whether, like an instinct, it is perfect from the first, there can be no doubt, that a man is a better judge of duty than a child. In the child, the decision is as prompt and as peremptory when the case is fully understood, when all the circumstances are known. But the child is embarrassed by his ignorance. There is an obvious connexion between the intellect and morals which makes our knowledge of the last correspond with the development of the mind. Though the principle of every duty is simple, yet its expression in action is complicated by numberless considerations, and of these the infant mind has no experience. It is in precisely the same position with regard to actions generally, that we are when called to judge of a particular action, of which we do not know the causes or the parties. The child does as we do,—judges at random or suspends his judgment. If I see a man take a purse of gold from another, there are many things of which I must be informed, before I can determine whether this were a violent, a knavish, or an honest action; and many more to enable me to judge of the precise degree of virtue or vice that belongs to the transaction. But of actions within the sphere of his knowledge, the child's perception is as clear as the man's. The little child refuses to pollute his lips with a lie, with the same conviction in the rectitude of his purpose that the archangel feels when he holds his allegiance to the Most High in defiance of the wiles or the force of evil angels.[1]

There was a wise citizen of Athens—the wisest certainly of all the pagans that preceded our Saviour—I mean Socrates—who taught his countrymen that he was always attended by an invisible Genius or Daemon by whose advice, he said, he governed all his actions. This daemon, he told them, never urged him to the performance of any action, but if at any time he proposed to do any thing that was not for his good, it warned him, by a customary signal, to forbear. He said, he was accustomed to obey these signals, as if they were the voice of God. This man was hunted by an atrocious conspiracy in his native city and most unjustly doomed to die. In pleading his cause, he told his judges that although they bid him be silent, yet God had bid him teach from day to day the youth of his country. When his friends bribed his jailor, and furnished him with the means of escape, a little before the sentence was to be executed, he refused to fly; for, the Daemon, to whom he always listened, forbade him, suggesting to him, that it was not becoming in him, who for seventy years had lived under the protection of the Laws of Athens, to dishonour those Laws when they aimed a blow at him. The last hours of his life he spent in explaining to his friends his own grounds for believing that the soul was immortal and when the time was come, drank the poison with cheerful determination.

In this manner it would appear that Socrates designed to describe by a lively image that man within the breast which we call Conscience;[2] and there is some

1. "The little child . . . angels": see *JMN* 2:49.
2. "There was a wise . . . Conscience": see *JMN* 3:106–7. For "the man within the breast," see Sermon I, n. 15.

reason for the distinction made, inasmuch as we can all feel we are rather commanded what not to do than urged to any performance. But in all our ordinary use of this word we understand something more; we speak of the whole power, of which this is a part; we imply its highest functions of *reward* to good and evil, as well as command to do and to forbear. I cite this instance only to show that the force of this principle was as familiar to the pagan and as fully understood by them as by us.

Now this power, this sentiment, this process of the mind, whatever opinions or language we may adopt concerning its nature—this Conscience is an idea about which there can be no ignorance, no misconception among us. It is familiar to you and to me and to all men. It is the oldest power in the world. Its force is attested in the primeval records of the race. "It came to pass when Adam heard the voice of the Lord God, in the garden, that he hid himself."[3] And ever since that evil hour, in all the lapse of time, in all the numbers and fortunes of his posterity, this principle has kept every whit of its strength in human breasts to bless and to curse. It has observed its unalterable laws. In the history of the world, there is not mention made of one man who found his goodness exclusive or unhandsome; or who wished to make it less, or to undo his virtues, because they hindered his peace of mind: but there have been multitudes who have struggled and writhed under the pressure of their vices; who have longed to unsay their falsehoods; to unswear their broken oaths; who have beseeched the mountain to be merciful and cover them forever from the staring spectre of a guilty deed.[4] It met them in the house; it met them on the way, it drew the curtains of their sick bed; it dogged them down to the very grave; and they feared, in the morning of the resurrection, it would rise, as well as they.

My friends, it is a matter of strange and terrible contemplation, the power of Conscience to punish human transgression, the manner in which God has secured the sanction of his laws. No precarious or tardy retribution, no imperfect judgment, as in human affairs, halts like a cripple after the daring offender, or wreaks its uncertain wrath upon the feeble accomplice, and lets the great criminal go; but a prompt, and unerring, and mighty power, which never falters, and never is deceived, treads on the steps of human offence. Is there one of us, my brethren, is there one of our race,—the hardiest infidel—who is minded to strive with his fate, and shake himself free of this subserviency to moral obligations? one who in the face of mankind will break the commandment and say, 'I will maintain what I have done; it is good and not evil; and blame and the silly terrors of superstition, I defy.' Poor tiny bravo! who seest not, to use words of the ancient, that "the wise gods laugh at us, whilst we strut to our undoing";[5] who art presently to learn that whilst you defy blame from *abroad*, it is nearer than the nearest,—it is fastening its fangs on the memory,

---

3. Cf. Genesis 3:8.
4. Hosea 10:8 and Luke 23:30. Cf. *JMN* 6:21.
5. Misquoted from Shakespeare, *Antony and Cleopatra*, III, xiii, 111–14. Used in "Shakspear [Second Lecture]," *EL* 1:314.

not of your patron, nor your neighbour, nor your brother, but on your own. By the force of an invisible and all uncontrollable event, that started out of darkness in the moment of your evil deed,—yourself are made the inflictor of vengeance, yourself is the victim.

Let the culprit, because his nerves were firm, let him try, if he can, to salve the sore. Let him put on a determined face, and stand out against this spectral remorse. He says it is unmanly and unreal;—let him try to reason it down. When he is alone in his chamber, it comes and sits by his side. Let him rise up, and quicken his sluggish spirits in the chosen haunts of pleasure, among youthful and blooming faces, to whom the morning brings health on his wings, and the gift of bounding spirits, and who hurry the night away in lighted halls, with music and wine. What ails him that his brow is so dark amid these tempting viands, this sparkling wine, this unrepressed good humour, this happy wit? Ask him not—for Oh his heart is heavier than his looks. Vex him not with kind importunity; do not look in his face or his stammering tongue will betray its secret. The accuser Conscience is curdling his blood here in these pleasant chambers. Which way soever he looks he is scared by grisly visions. The sleepless remembrance of his crime pursues him and all the medicines of the world will not soothe him to repose.

It is related by the ancients of Bessus, an inhabitant of Poeonia, that he slew his own father, and lived many years unsuspected of the crime. But going one day to sup at the house of one of his friends, he stopped as he was passing a porch and pierced a swallow's nest with the point of his staff and killed the young. Those who stood by inquired of him how he could amuse himself with such an action for which there appeared no cause. "No cause!" exclaimed Bessus, "does not this swallow always cry to me and falsely say that I have killed my father?" These words were eagerly caught up by the bystanders, and soon reported to the king. And an inquiry being made, the crime was proved on him, and he suffered death for parricide.[6] The annals of society are full of these anecdotes; the records of our courts are full of these painful stories of unexpected disclosures of guilt. They have passed into proverbs and make a part of the belief of mankind that though hand join with hand, though tongue with tongue conspire to hide, yet Conscience will be stronger than all, and in despite of all will publish to infamy the darkest passages of outrageous crime.

But there is a purpose to be answered by this mechanism which is always so curious and sometimes so terrible. There is surely some origin, some final cause, for this uneasy monitor that now burns and now whitens the cheek, against our will; that hinders a man of his sleep; takes away his appetite; unsettles his eye; fills his ear with ugly sounds; sits heavy at his heart, when he sits alone, and makes him afraid of others, when he is in company. Though he is wise, and well mannered, he trips in his talk, and is violent in his speech. Has he

6. The story is in "Of Conscience," in *Essays of Michael Seigneur de Montaigne* . . . , trans. Charles Cotton (London, 1693), 2:57.

not the same memory, the same prudence, and like inclinations? Is not his health as firm, as it was yesterday; and doth he not set an equal price on a good name? Whence then this changing colour on the cheek, this unsteady step, this cowering face? If he have done wrong, and does not wish the disgrace, why does he take all these means to betray what he should studiously conceal? Alas, my brethren, it is not his work; it is the work of another. To this transaction another party breaks in. Man is overmastered. It is the work and the power of God.

Let us consider for a moment the end answered by these provisions, for I believe there is nothing within the compass of human observation that has such commanding claims on our admiration. It is, I believe, the master work of Deity, as far as our knowledge goes. The end to be answered is, the moral government of the Universe, without what we should call the continual interference of the Deity. The peace of the Creation is to be kept, without making it needful that God should visit an offender with instant and signal misfortune or should strike the blasphemer with thunder. To do this he hath opened in every mind the Conscience,—this swift perception of approval or censure on all that is done or left undone. This law, so sure, so inevitable, is the gravitation of the moral world. This Praise and this Blame are the two forces that keep moral beings to their orbit. You will observe—it is not mere perception of right and wrong, of accord and discord; it is more, it is a new element: after transgression, it is stern, unrelenting, envenomed pain, increasing with the crime, and tending directly to the point at which moral government aims, viz., an irresistible Compunction which ends in Reformation. Thus Conscience is the police of the Universe;[7] from which there is no escape, no hope of concealment, connecting every human soul with God its maker, and making it impossible to any to elude for a moment his irresistible dominion.

It is matter of lamentation and offence to many in the fact that the more enlightened views of Christianity that prevail among us have thrown into the shade the strong oriental language in which in the Scriptures the punishment of sin is described. But I apprehend that he who has once maturely considered the infinite force of Conscience to inflict pain and the invariable steadiness with which it follows up transgression can never bring himself to doubt the reality of future retribution. He needs not a revelation,—it is written in his nature that sin shall suffer—he will feel that the figurative language of darkness and fire and the undying worm are but faint representations of the real evils that wait on iniquity.[8]

Such is the power and such the use of the Conscience. It seems to me an overpowering proof of the Being and government of God. When I consider its infinite force; how inconsiderable are all other perceptions by the side of this perception; that this alone makes the distinctions of happiness and misery; that it will breathe the air of heaven into the deepest dungeon on earth, or will make

7. "There is surely . . . Universe": see *JMN* 3:134–35.
8. Cf. Isaiah 66:24 and Mark 9:44, 9:48.

a hideous gehenna out of the sweetest paradise; when I observe its unbroken uniformity through all ages and races; its unfailing sovereignty over the human mind, wherever it has acted or suffered;—my doubts of a Providence fade and disappear. I cannot coax down the astounding conviction. I have read of those who doubted, I am told there are those who doubt the Being of God. But there is no fable so extravagant that I cannot more easily admit than the possibility that this moral government is uncaused. I may believe that the stars have burned in their courses forever—that no hand hurled them into their eternal paths, but that they have walked in those circles from a frightful infinity *without a cause*. I may believe when I daily see the ocean evaporate its clouds, that this precious burden is lifted by heat, and borne by the winds, and poured again over the land—*by accident*. I may believe that all the processes of vegetation originated *without thought* and go forward *without being promoted by any regard to the wants of animal life*;—yes, I may believe all this but I can never believe that the Conscience of man came to him without an author, or reason, or end.[9] I hear the voice which it alway utters, 'There is a God.'

My brethren; God, who wrote this eldest revelation of himself and his law after this manner on our hearts, has seconded its testimony by a messenger from heaven. By the voice of our Saviour, and by the works of his hands, he has opened to us the great purpose of all this moral machinery we have now considered, namely, that he has created us for an immortal progress. This office existed before to the Gentile and the Jew. Men were made "a law unto themselves, having the work of the law written on their hearts." But though wise and good men, in view of this power, were struck with wonder and eagerly believed that death could not be an eternal sleep, yet Christianity first brought immortality to light, and so explained the value of this undying monitor within us. There are some questions of which every man must judge wholly from his own experience, and thus judging I for one am satisfied that in this life only, in the long run, to use a familiar expression, every man is happy precisely in proportion to the fidelity with which he conforms his conduct to his Conscience.

My brethren, this divine Director belongs to each of us. It will prove, as we use it, our good or our evil angel. It will scatter light or darkness in our path through this world. It will go with us when we go out of the world and make for us the bliss of heaven or the pains of hell. Let us feel that it is a law, if we use it rightly, not of general provisions and occasional use, but of application to every moment of time and every the meanest deed or thought of life. Let us feel that it is our friend and that all, that resist its will, are our enemies. Let us obey its laws; let us hearken to its feeblest whisper; let us follow its guidance through evil report and good report;[10] through temptation and the fear of death; through painful duties, and through humble duties; assured that it will lead us to everlasting Peace.

9. "I may believe that the stars . . . end": see *JMN* 3:135–36.
10. II Corinthians 6:8.

Stand, therefore, having your loins girt about with truth.

EPHESIANS 6:14

I quote from the powerful exhortation of the apostle this figurative expression with the hope of fixing your attention upon the great and commanding doctrine it contains. At first view it may seem an unnecessary labour studiously to represent the advantages of truth, to say that a lie is pernicious, and that to be always true is to be always noble; for who does not know and say the same thing? But it must also be well known to you that there is a vast deal of falsehood in the world, false theories of life; false valuations by men of themselves, and other men, and of virtue, and vice. All men assent readily enough to the proposition, that, truth is good, but it is but too evident that they apply it to their own conduct feebly and partially, and do not practically feel, that, it is, in all possible cases, their interest to observe it. And it seems to me, that, no effort however low and feeble can wholly fail that has for its object to dignify truth in the eyes of men.

The supreme Being is chiefly represented to our minds as the God of Truth; as One who perceives all things as they are, and therefore infinitely elevated above passion and error.

And Man is constituted to delight in truth. Truth is the natural object of the human mind, to which it ever points and tends; its great and vital perception— to distinguish between what is and what is not. All truth is beautiful in its eye; it is always restless amid falsehoods. Wherever the mind perceives that truth is violated, it is indignant. Wherever there is an intention to deceive, there all minds are revolted by the attempt, and unite, by common sympathy, to put it down. Who is not swift to expose a lie? Is there any place where dissimulation is not odious, or any, where affectation is pleasing? This love of truth is as constant, as the instinct of animals, which guides them to their proper food, and makes them avoid poison; and implanted with the same regard to the welfare of the moral being. For all falsehood of opinion is injurious to the intellect, and all falsehood of action is injurious to the morals.

Preached five times: September 14, 1828, at the Second Church, Boston; November 9 at the Harvard College Chapel; December 7 in Concord, N.H.; January 11, 1829, at the New South Church; and October 11 at the Second Church, Boston.

Truth is great and brave; falsehood is always ignoble and mean. Truth loves the light; falsehood lurks in holes, or seeks to raise a cloud between it and the observer's eye. The face of truth is open, and affectionate, and dauntless; that of falsehood is retiring, and uncertain, and afraid. Do not all men understand with instant sympathy the signs of fraud in the countenance? Confront the accuser and the accused, and let us judge between the true man and the traitor. Let the lie be fenced with what guards it may, and maintained by whatever probabilities—its ingenuity, its audacity, are vain. You shall presently see one of the parties agitated with unnecessary heat, and then checked by sudden cold-ness. You shall see him change his ground of defence or attack, and forget himself in strange contradictions. The other party meets the deep diplomacy of fraud with simple denial. He too, perhaps, shall discover indignation and anx-iety and contempt. But there is a force in his expression of these feelings, that was wanting in the other; for, unerring nature colours his countenance, and speaks with his tongue. All the windings of subtlety, all the masks of dissimula-tion, are confounded and exposed by that tranquil eye, and those unembar-rassed words, and the truth shall be so clear, that a child may be a judge between them.

It is the exclusive prerogative of truth to be without fear, and without reproach. He that is above fear, he that cannot tremble at the consequences of actions, will never disguise what he has done. It is the badge of noble minds. It is one of the most pleasing and beautiful distinctions in the forms of the English government which excuses a peer, when he sits in judgment, from the ceremony of swearing, and accepts his affirmation, as equivalent to an oath; as if men, in a rank so honoured, could not stoop their advantages so low as to the guilt of falsehood.

This principle is the rule and measure of human goodness. No art can make amends for its want. None can weave a lie so well, that it shall long be mistaken for the spotless and unshrinking texture of truth. There is no subterfuge or equivocation so skilful, but inquiry will always worry you out of it. In your daily intercourse, try to put off an urgent petition with a false pretence, and see how quickly you shall be driven from your ground. In truth alone, can you stand unshaken. I do not deny that deception may for a time succeed; oh no; for the world is full of falsehoods; but, I say that their triumph and their reign is short. Your haughty manners, your unfounded pretensions, your parade of wealth, or of consequence to which you have no title, may serve your turn to make you stared at by many a vacant eye. The idle crowd will go by, "and wonder with a foolish face of praise";[1] but every now and then you must meet a man whom God has instructed to distinguish between true and false. You will have to encounter an eye, that takes pretension for nothing, and vanity for nothing, and looks on evasion as a flimsy veil, which cannot hide littleness and folly. Are you sure your hollow artifices will bear the majestic regards of truth?

---

1. Alexander Pope, "Epistle to Dr. Arbuthnot," line 212. Quoted in *JMN* 2:239, 2:365.

or will you not pay dear for your little hour of triumph, in the shame and rage of detection?

But the power and value of truth is not particular and local, but absolute and universal. When it is accurately considered, it will be found, that, the deviation from truth is the cause of all the moral disorder in society; that all wars between nations, and quarrels between individuals arise out of false views of their relations and interests; that truth is, therefore, the proper peacemaker of the world; the producer of all good; the real reformer and benefactor of men. For all the virtues are only particular examples of an obedience to the truth of things. Thus, it is true to nature to eat and drink what nature requires: and this is Temperance.

Truth fulfils its engagements both public and private, whether trifling or dangerous, whether to itself or to others. And this certainty of action makes the virtues of Honesty, Perseverance, Fortitude. All *fraud* is founded in false views, as if the enjoyment of wealth were inseparable from wealth itself instead of being dependent entirely upon the state of mind of the possessor. And pride is a falsehood; and selfishness and envy arise out of false views of our nature and interest. And with regard to all animal pleasure—does not experience every day tell inexperience the same thing, that when it looks back it finds each individual instance of unlawful gratification to have been a mistake, that it seemed to be good but it was found to be evil, that the soul of man is put back, is put down on the scale of being, by every moral delinquincy, continually losing ground which it may never recover;—a loss that is the more frightful, because as the soul departs from right, it seems to lose the sense of its own departure.

My brethren, let it be seriously considered by us how far the best men swerve from this implicit adherence to truth, and with what advantage a greater reverence for it would be introduced into our own lives. Consider how much it would take from the bitterness of life. It would save flattery to the young, and reproach to the unfortunate, and slander to the good. It would seal up unclean and blasphemous lips. It would save years of life which now we spend in unlearning error. It would check the excess of pleasure, and the fury of revenge, and the calculations of selfishness. If the breast could have a window, which revealed its secret thoughts to every observer, let us ask ourselves if we should not think and act differently? Let us examine ourselves and let us scorn to owe any thing of our reputation to the difficulty which others find in determining our real merits.

Have you accepted of praise which you knew you did not deserve? Have you excited hopes which you never meant to gratify? Have you awakened in the young a confidence in their abilities, which their abilities did not warrant, and which therefore had the effect to cover them with late and bitter mortification? Have you pretended, in the presence of the inexperienced, to a rigour of principle which is much beyond your mark, so that when afterwards they found you lax in your morals, it went far to unsettle their own convictions? Have you oppressed with the shew of kindness a man whom, when his back was turned, you have loaded with ridicule and reproaches? Or have you been the victim of ridicule, and sacrificed to the fear of derision, the honest expression of your opinions, disowned your convictions of right, forborne your purposes of duty, and given up to the jest of some assuming scorner, your faith and your hope and your virtue,—in the face of your own accusing conscience, in the face of men and angels, of the encompassing cloud of invisible witnesses, and of God the judge of all?[2]

It is good to erect in our own minds the Idea of right, that we may feel its advantage in contrast with the painful deformities of error. We should compare the man of the world with the perfect beauty of a life that in all points was square to the truth. I would lead you to a man whose lips were never polluted by falsehood; whose heart was never fooled by images of false delight; whose eyes never roved, whose feet never walked in ways which his judgment disapproved; who will not honour with supple gesture and salute a man whom his virtuous soul abhorred; nor follow with pretended wonder a spectacle, because the world is gone after it, which he does not value at a straw; who does not express intemperate admiration for a popular man, whose character he knows and condemns, nor intemperate abuse of another man, whom the fickle public does not like today; who does not borrow his opinions every hour, from those with whom he converses, and contradict with extravagant assertions today, the extravagant assertions which only yesterday he made. No; he is not of such a temper: these are the habits of men and women that can everywhere be found, who live without plan, or motive, or profit, or pleasure,—blown about by every wind of interest or doctrine.[3] But the man of whom I speak—oh, how seldom is he seen! You shall meet a thousand in the streets, and he is not among them. You shall walk long amidst farms and forests, without encountering him. He is one whose mind is poised on itself; who thinks that there was a purpose, for which he was sent into being; who thinks that no actions are without consequences; no words fall to the ground; no thoughts are insignificant; who holds nothing too great, and nothing too small for the exercise of his understanding; who does not reckon authorities, and, in each question of duty or of speculation, appeals not to the great names who have sided on one or the other part, but appeals to his own eye, and his own conscience, with meekness, but with courage; who, in the hour of trial, listens only to himself; who does not judge of actions, by their effects, but by their principle; nor of men, by their fortunes, but by their fruits. This is a man whose theory of duty and whose practice are the same; whose manners are the simple expressions of his feelings; a man who derives no respect from his remoteness from observation, and who is better loved and honoured the closer he is seen. Other men have their secrets and suspicions. He is always open. As his master is not the opinion of the world, but Truth itself, he can never go out of its dominion. His actions therefore are the same in his

---

2. Cf. Hebrews 12:1, 12:23.
3. Cf. Ephesians 4:14.

chamber as in the aisles of the church or the open street. He has no privacy. It is related of the virtuous Agesilaus, king of Sparta, that whenever he made an excursion from his capital, he lodged in the temples most renowned for sanctity; "and whereas," says his Biographer, "upon many occasions, we do not choose that men should overlook our conduct, he was desirous to have the gods themselves inspectors and witnesses of his actions."[4] Let us derive instruction from so sublime a frankness. In every effort that we make, to bring our life into consistence with truth, we approximate to the Divine Character,—we necessarily gain the approbation of God.

It is an important consideration by which experience should win us to what the reason cannot fail to approve, that all disguise of character is commonly attempted in vain. We may flatter ourselves that we hug our vices in secret, but—we are all known, my brethren. Vice as well as virtue hath, if I may so speak, a most *divulgatory* nature; it cannot be hid: the act may be concealed, but the effects will peep out. It has been said, in allusion to the swift communication of intelligence in modern society, that great men live in glass houses: All men live in glass houses. The roof is taken off from the closet of our retirement and our innermost solitude revealed to the world. In the language of our Saviour, 'For there is nothing covered that shall not be revealed, neither hid which shall not be known.'[5] For although a large part of our actions is performed in private, yet every individual action has its specific effect upon our character; and this is exhibited in public. There is therefore no such thing as a successful hypocrisy, and he that is not in his secret soul the servant of truth, will not have from men, any more than from God, that honour which nothing but genuine integrity can obtain.

My brethren, let us consider that life is short, that even on the supposition that we could veil our vices and reap from fraud and hypocrisy the fruits of truth, yet the day is coming of retribution and discovery, when the world shall pass away from our eyes and all its deception come to an end, when nothing shall abide before the face of God but the Truth which he loves.

Let us, as the servants of the true God, and the disciples of his Son, who brought us the assurance of everlasting life, let us be guided by him into all truth. There is one pure being in human history whose life was truth, whose lips pure. If his life in man's eye was sorrowful, in God's eye it was glorious. Let us consider what a glorious era would open on the world, if all men would consent to be governed by this divine law. Let us do something towards such an event, by obeying this law ourselves. Let us form habits of truth. Let us abstain from affecting what we do not feel. Let us not speak without consideration; and what we have once said, however insignificant the matter, let us make good with our actions. Let our faith be kept sacred in trifles, and then it may be trusted in grave affairs. Let us carry this principle farther than a mere regard to the gov-

4. Plutarch, "Life of Agesilaus," in *The Lives*, ed. John and William Langhorne (New York, 1822) 5:48. See *JMN* 3:97.
5. Luke X.2 [Emerson's note]; i.e., Luke 12:2.

ernment of the tongue; let us bring all our actions into agreement—not with the fashion of the time, or the moderate demands that the decency of society makes upon its members,—but with the eternal laws of God. Let us follow the truth and it shall lead us to God. The way is plain; the reward is sure; every effort is accepted; and by every effort our strength is increased. "Stand, therefore, having your loins girt about with truth."

XXIII

*For the invisible things of him, from the
creation of the world, are clearly seen,
being understood by the things that are made,
even his eternal Power and Godhead.*

ROMANS 1:20

The most remarkable fact that concerns ourselves, with which we are acquainted, is the existence in all human minds of the idea of Deity. A large part
of mankind are daily engaged in humble occupations. A very small part have
leisure and curiosity for lofty speculations, but the most towering thoughts of
sages beguile only a small portion of their time, and send them speedily back to
the low care of providing for the wants of the body. Though the earth, we
inhabit, is nobly furnished, though the heavens are arched gloriously over our
heads,—yet when the morning breaks in the east, and the sun rises,—man steps
forth from his little dwelling into this swelling scene, to labour, to eat, to drink,
to laugh, to talk, to sin, and to sleep again. He heeds it not, this wondrous
majesty wherewith the great House of nature is adorned. Let the sun go up the
sky, and the moon shine, and innumerable stars move before him in orbits so
vast that centuries shall not fulfil them; let the seasons go round, and winter
cover his fields with coats of dazzling snow and the summer pour out upon
them her horn of plenty—he does not care—he does not know—he is creeping
in a little path of his own; he is following a few appetites; is peering round for a
little bread; is devising some little arts to get an atom from his neighbour's heap
and add it to his own; he is laying stratagems in petty things for the admiration
of his fellows; he is bewailing small inconveniences; he is pouting at the cold or
the heat; he is absorbed in the apprehension or the suffering of his diseases. And
is this the state of man? What then avails him the mighty mind which belongs to
his race, but which so few have leisure or desire to educate and use? What is
there to save them from lapsing both heart and mind into deepest darkness, and
carrying down this ambitious race to the level of the brutes? There is much,

---

Manuscript dated September 24, 1828. Preached five times: September 28, 1828, at the Federal
Street Church; October 5 at the Second Church, Boston; December 21 in Concord, N.H.;
November 15, 1829, at the Second Church, Boston; and March 5, 1837, in East Lexington. In the
first paragraph, Emerson borrows a passage from Sermon XIII (see p. 144).

there is all to save them, they can not fall so far. On the other side there is this one saving fact, the existence in all human minds of the idea of Deity. For the knowledge of God is in their minds and it is a species of knowledge that one way or another will work out great effects. The lowness of their lot cannot drag them down, for they are ever lifted upward by the majesty of this living belief. Wide as the institutions of Christianity extend, and blessed as is their effect, they cover but a scanty portion of the globe—but do they mark the limits of the knowledge of God? And do all the millions, that occupy the major part of the earth's surface, out of the pale, and out of the census of civilization, go without it? The voice of Sinai they have not heard, the seventh or the first day of the week, they do not keep holy, they pursue their labour in this morning's light, and go to the forest for game, to the river for fish, and to the earth for bread, as they did yesterday. The seventh day, they do not observe—*but they have a sabbath of their own.* The church bell is unheard on the sides of Thibet, or the woods of Patagonia; the name of the Cross beyond the Caucasus is an unknown sound; but, deep in the mind of each individual of all those families, and hordes, and empires of men, abides this thought, that abides in us. Wherever man is found—in the decorated abodes of eastern softness; or wading out from his smoky cellar into the snow drifts of the polar circle—there exists and reigns over him this strange conception. Go where you will,—follow man in whatever coast you find him—his steps will soon lead you to the symbols, by which he has expressed this thought, or to the spots which it has consecrated. He will go to a costly sanctuary on which his architecture has spent its skill; or to a rude enclosure whose idle fence of basket work is awful in his eyes, and sacred from his intrusion; or to a grove of trees; or to an upright pillar of stone; to some type or place or ceremony by which his mind has striven to do reverence to that idea which oppresses it.

In speaking of the universality of the notion of God in the mind of the human race (to which fact, I believe, there are no well attested exceptions,) I do not pretend to say that the idea is uniform. In this respect, I believe, there is the widest difference, and, that, perhaps, very few individuals of the human race entertain very pure conceptions of God, and every one possibly a different opinion. But it seems to me a very imposing and very important consideration that in all breasts the first simple belief of a superior intelligence exists; that, every where, in whatever depths of ignorance or suffering, man is upheld by this redeeming faith—which contains in itself the seed of all improvement.

Let us devote a few moments to the notice of the proper foundations of this universal consent. Let us consider how simple and accessible are the steps by which the unperverted mind arrives at the conviction of the Divine Being and Providence. I do not ask your attention to these views because I think men are prone to atheism, but I believe we cannot recur to the great inscriptions of his name, which God has written on the face of the world, without being touched and instructed, the moral is so plain.

In strict reason to account for what we see, on every side, we are obliged to resort to the immediate agency of God. We put God away from us, by calling his operation, his *laws*. What keeps the earth without deviation in its appointed orbit? 'The power of gravity,' replies the astronomer. But if you ask—Who gave it gravity?—and what is gravity?—he must answer—the present and immediate agency of God.[1] When he heaved it, at first, from the hollow of his hand,[2]—we know not how many ages ago, he gave it this force, this orbit, and this law; and a moment since he gave it; and now he gives it.

If a man were solitary in the universe, if no beings were sufficiently like him to permit of being compared, there were still enough in his wonderful frame— its powers of thought; its beautiful mechanism; the harmony of the ear and the voice; of the hand and the eye; to move all his admiration and suggest the power of the secret cause. But how happened this meeting—this consent of an hundred worshippers? Why are we not so differently constituted that each should think and act for himself in a wild unsocial habit? How is it that so many have come up together; that our hearts beat as one heart; that we are touched with the same emotion; are struck with the same truth; and pray with one prayer?—that so many individuals—each exhibiting in his own organization, in the adapta- tion of part to part, a world of wonders, should all be wound up also,—if I may use the expression,—to the same tune; should be thoroughly intelligible to each other? The fellow feeling, the common understanding, runs through the race. These harmonious sympathies connect in strict alliance all tribes and complex- ions and tongues. Is there an event of uncommon sorrow or of tremendous crime that has occurred in one solitary spot; seas cannot hide it; obscurity cannot disguise it; unknown languages speak it to languages that are known. It travels on all the winds; till every cottage, in every clime, is made to breathe the same sigh of pity, or clamour of indignation. What is the cause of all this? We are brethren, and have one Father, who is God.

One of the best cures for Atheism may be found in the examination of its argument. There is but one alternative offered to the human mind to account for what it is, and what it knows. Either the world came by *design*, that is, by God; or, it came *without design*, that is, by chance. Now if a man can bring himself to believe that this great Order which he beholds at any one moment, exists in that moment, by chance, yet I do not see how he can hold his opinion, when he sees that although there is a perpetual flux and change, yet the same order lasts to the next moment, to the next day, for years, for centuries. The idea of Chance involves disorder, violent change, and excludes the possibility of permanence. Yet see what is recorded of the human race. The history of man reaches through five or six thousand years. How is it that in all the casualties of so long a time, under all the varying causes to whose action they have been exposed,—men have not only kept their form but have never lost or gained one passion, or one sense; that still they laugh and weep, that the eye has not lost its adaptation to the Sun, nor the ear forgotten the pleasure of sweet sounds; that

1. Cf. *JMN* 2:47.
2. Isaiah 40:12.

the form of Youth is yet comely; that the lineaments of age are venerable; that life hath all its attraction, and death is yet dreadful to human apprehension?

And what is yet more strange, the moral constitution of our minds—from which we get our first perceptions of the being and character of God—remains the same. There is one uniform moral sense giving through all ages the same venerable unaltered testimony to the being of a Rewarder of moral character. If there is any where a man outwardly formed like ourselves, to whose healthy mind right and wrong are the same; if there be any, to whom, in his midnight thoughts, the memory of his fraud is delightful; if ever the guilt of murder was washed out from the conscience, and crime had no punishment of painful thoughts; then, indeed, our argument is weak, and virtue may be an empty name. But no: centuries revolve: nations are rooted out: customs change: but the custom of virtue does not change. Truth is the same it was before the Flood. Remorse has not lost its tooth; shame is as strong, and fear as pale, and hope as undaunted, as they were a thousand years ago: the motives of good and evil stand the same as of old; and the beam of the balance trembles with the same weights of pleasure and of pain. Is there any chance in this? Be it so, if you will. We will not quarrel about a name. But a chance that never wavers from century to century; a chance that is uniform in all countries and conditions; that never falters or varies in distributing pleasure to virtue, and pain to vice; is a chance that encourages calculation, and suggests an obstinate suspicion that it will outlast my body, and meet me again in the world of spirits.

My brethren, I believe it is from these simple observations, and not from abstruse reasonings that the best argument for the Divine being and government is obtained. It is because God is within us; it is because we are so formed that all things declare him to us, that we find it so hard to escape the conclusion. Day unto Day, night unto night bear witness to him; and every wise purpose, every happy thought, every beautiful feature, every good deed, is an argument to establish the being of God. These all plead more convincingly than the voice of thunder, the earthquake, the explosion of comets, for these last might chance in a chaos, but those can never *chance*.

The idea of God is the foundation of all religion, not of the hope of future retribution alone, but of the obligations that respect virtue and vice. If this fails, all things fail. It is this idea which explains the Revelation, and it is the best testimony to the revelation, that it perfectly falls in with this. We ought therefore to have a reason of this faith that is in us. But, my brethren, do not imagine that these evidences are to be found by painful study, for neglecting which, you may plead the want of time and preparation. Study may teach that the elaborate objections of Skepticism are vain. But the eyes may ache, all night, over folios, and fail to find the argument. No, you are masters of the question, whether learned or unlearned. It is the heart, which is the seat of the evidence. The kingdom of God is within you.[3] And there its evidence is best explored.

The proper sequel to these reflections is to consider the place which this idea

3. Luke 17:21.

holds in the human soul. That consideration involves the great moral of our doctrine. We shall find, that, the soul is in confusion, unless this idea exists therein; and that, its power and happiness depend úpon the truth, with which this appears, that it introduces order and harmony, into the chaos of the mind; that it gives a satisfactory theory to human life, and, that, the moment it is imparted, and felt,—all that seeming disproportion which struck us, at first, between man's condition and powers, and his humble necessities, vanishes: because, whilst his soul is illuminated by this infinite thought, no employments can be servile, no greatness or lowness of fortune can be of any account. But the time will not admit of our following farther, at present, these important reflex-ions.

My brethren, since we are thus admonished by all without, and all within us, that God is, and that he is the Rewarder of such as seek him, let us feel the duties it imposes.4 Let us reflect—we can not too often, or too deeply,—upon the nature of God. Let us feel that we are never concealed; for the eye of the Highest seeth us. Let us feel that we are never forsaken, for, by Him, we live;5 never helpless, for, Omnipotence hears, and brings to pass our good desires; never unrewarded, for He is at hand to execute his laws. Let us offer him the incense of prayer, of faith, of patience, of love, and of good works.

4. Hebrews 11:6.
5. Acts 17:28.

XXIV

We should live soberly, righteously, and godly, in this present world.

TITUS 2:12

By our assembly in this house, my Christian friends, we have declared our willingness to learn of God, our duty. There is an anxiety which every moral being sometimes feels, to know what is expected of him, by the great Being who made him. I say *sometimes;* for I well know how dangerous are the cares and pleasures of the world; how rudely they come in upon our best feelings, and holiest hours, and are always drawing us astray. But this anxiety, this apprehension of God's displeasure, this humble desire to secure his favor, will return. It is in our nature; and God in his mercy has given it force, by surrounding us with a thousand monitors, that are always calling to us, as we hurry onward, and bidding us stop, and consider. The voices of these monitors, we all have heard.

We have all met with disappointments; and these are monitors. We have fallen into the company of holy men, and God sent them to us, though we perchance did not discern it, and slighted their errand. A good word of divine truth has beamed from a book we took up in an idle hour. We have passed by the grave-yards, and have not always been listless to the awful lessons on their simple stones. As you spelled out, on their worn surfaces, the old inscription, which, in all countries and all languages, tells one thing, that here lie the bones of man, have you not felt how few months should pass before the clay that moved warm with life above should lie cold and insensible below? Or you have languished under premature infirmity, and wasting sickness, and as you counted the lonely watches of the night, you heard loud warnings, that your days were numbered. Or perhaps you have been out upon the deep, and have been overtaken by the storm, and as your ship was tossed as a little shell, upon the mountains of water, there was a voice in the tempest that told you, you could not fly from the presence of God.[1] But we need not go so far to seek what conscience has found

---

Preached five times: October 12, 1828, at the Second Church, Boston; October 12 at the New North Church; December 14 in Concord, N.H.; April 12, 1829, in Waltham; and January 31, 1830, at the Second Church, Boston. The significance of the sermon text may have been suggested to Emerson by a reading of Samuel Johnson's *Diary* (see *JMN* 6:65) or Jeremy Taylor, *The Rule and Exercise of Holy Living*, in *The Whole Works of the Right Rev. Jeremy Taylor, D. D.* (London, 1828), 4:56. Sermon XXVII is a sequel.

    1. Cf. Jonah 1:3–4.

in every hour's events. The morning sun, the sabbath bell, the remorse of a fault, the voice of sermons, and the word of God—these are monitors which have called us, times without number, to the solemn consideration of ourselves. It is a duty which we deeply owe to our Almighty Benefactor. We have come up this day to his house; let us discharge it here. Let us go reverently to his word, to the gospel of his son, and inquire what it becomes us to suffer, and to perform.

I know not, my brethren, where we can find a better scheme of human duty than in the remarkable passage, of which the text is a part. It may serve as a compend of the whole duty of Man. "For the grace of God," says Paul, (I solicit your attention to the whole passage,) "that bringeth salvation, hath appeared unto men; teaching us, that denying ungodliness, and worldly lusts, we should live soberly, righteously, and godly, in this present world, looking for that blessed hope and the glorious appearing of the great God, and our saviour Jesus Christ, who gave himself for us, that he might redeem us from all iniquity, and purify unto himself a peculiar people, zealous of good works."

Herein is our duty declared in all its relations; its foundation indicated; and the great hope which God has connected with its performance, made known. The object is moreover declared for which Christ lived and labored and suffered.

We should live soberly, righteously, and godly. It is thought that all human duties are comprized under this precept. To live soberly is to perform our duties to ourselves; to live righteously, our duties to others; and to live godly, our duties to God. I design to ask your attention to some remarks upon each of these classes. In the present discourse we shall confine our attention to the first.

I. We should live *Soberly*. In the large sense in which this word is used by the apostle it seems, as we have said, to imply all the personal duties. It is equivalent to the old precept, Bear and Forbear;[2] and has obviously two respects—one, of action, enterprize, industry—or, in a word, of *Self direction;* the other, and not the least difficult of performance—of abstinence, of vigilance, of checks, in one word, of *Self Command*.

I. In the first and most extended sense of this command, it directs to the pursuit of all the good that appertains to a rational being. A truly *sober* examination of ourselves will never excuse in us a life of religious inaction. We shall not have done our duty to ourselves, when we have refrained from intemperance and gross crime. We shall not have done our duty to ourselves until we have carried all our powers to the highest perfection those powers can reach. If there is any learning, or property, or influence, or virtue, which we can acquire, and, by such acquisition, become mightier moral agents, mightier in the cause of God and goodness, this law enjoins every just exertion for its attainment. It frowns upon all sensual indulgence, that interferes with your progress in goodness. It frowns upon sloth. Diligence is the first of its precepts, for this soberness, whilst it is a cheerful, is a laborious spirit. It keeps good hours. It does not

2. Vicesimus Knox, *Elegant Extracts . . . in Prose*, 7th ed. (London, 1797), 2:1027. See *JMN* 6:156.

loll all day in easy chairs, nor covet a morning sleep, when the sun has gone up the sky, and the human family are come forth to their labour. Fortitude is another duty proper to it. There is a constitutional firmness, which makes the exercise of this virtue more natural and easy to some minds than to others. But in all men God has so balanced the soul in reference to temptation and danger, that by strong effort it can man itself, to meet every evil, and death itself, without disgrace. The disobedient colour of the cheek may come and go, the nerves may shrink, the flesh may be weak, but the spirit shall be strong[3]—and I appeal to you, my friends, whether you do not think the feeblest spirit among us can bring itself to that immoveable determination that no disaster or torment or terror can alarm.

Another duty comprised in this law is Humility. The more we increase in knowledge and goodness, the wider prospect we attain of our wants, imperfection. It is the ignorant and the foolish man who is proud. The sober man is humble.

In fine, the generous principle of Christian soberness, whilst it looks to things unseen by the bodily eye, doth honour and seek every accomplishment, every grace that man can have. It loves what is great but it does not scorn what is small, and whilst it aims to become master of all that can dignify it in its own eyes, it is lowly and gentle and thinks meanly of what it has attained in comparison with what it wants.

II. That we should live soberly implies the difficult duty of self command. The word in the original text ($\sigma\omega\phi\rho\acute{o}\nu\omega\varsigma$) peculiarly imports temperance and self restraint; that we should have all our appetites and passions under controul. God will neither accept the raptures of devotion nor the inefficiency of good intentions, in the room of a chastised and well ordered life. And, my friends, do you think he asks too much? Is it hard to require that your passions should be under subjection to your reason? It was the very end, my brethren, which he designed in giving you life, to educate you to virtue, by giving you passions, whose use would lead to good ends, whose abuse to evil ends, at the same time that he gave you power to bring them into subjection by creating in you a sense of right. And how would you live? Riotously? Would you steep your senses in swimming excess, and carry out every pleasure to its highest relish, to the point where it verges on pain? Does it seem pleasant to you to go hand in hand with the reeling voluptuary; to bind your head with roses; to call around you the merryhearted; to drink deeply of old wine until your reason is unsettled, and memory is gone? I hope it does not. Riot punishes itself. It is easier to abhor than to define this unmanning intemperance. The body of the drunkard is the tomb of a soul. Can nature speak out more strongly? Can God utter more significant admonition than comes from that dismal object? God's upright image stretched along the ground in a swinish sleep; those beautiful and aspiring faculties overmastered and down; those pure affections that embrace God

---

3. Cf. Matthew 26:41.

and man—how has their expression faded out of that bloated and loathsome countenance!

Or if you had no taste for this perilous crime which opens the door to all the rest, perhaps you find the law of soberness too strait for you to walk in, and choose to indulge in elegant liberties, in milder forms of vice. As far as you can go in the indulgence of your appetites, without danger to your health, you think it good to go. You have come to the conclusion that you have been denying yourself, to no good purpose, a great deal of real happiness. 'I have crippled my powers,' you say, 'by unreasonably withholding my hand from the good nature has provided me. I will sit no longer in this ungenerous temperance of sackcloth and ashes. To be sure, I have health for my reward, and a cool judgment; but I will not go so far in the course I propose to enter, as to put these in jeopardy. At least I will make the experiment, and if I do not like the event, I will resume with firmer confidence my old habits.' But before you begin, let me tell you the objections to such an adventure. You will never stop at that limit you propose. And when the hour of repentance comes, as it surely will, though slow and late, when surrounded by the ruins of your fortunes and your character, you bitterly regret this first departure and wring your hands, and look back to the virtues you forsook—you shall not be able to return to them. For in indulging this hope, you mistake the nature of man. In that nature there is not a middle condition between virtue and vice. If you renounce the government you must take the yoke of your passions.

Do not suppose then that this choice of more or less indulgence, is only a question about the degree of pleasure. By no means. It is a question about all your character, all your intellect, and all your influence; for, all these are involved in your decision. For, are we born with a character? did you inherit your mind stored and expanded? Was your influence the same in your cradle? Do these things come to us entire, and remain to us entire? Are they not all things of *growth*, and subject to the education we receive first from others, and then, from ourselves? Do you suppose that any power or accomplishment inheres immoveably in your nature, defying the action of moral causes? Is genius a property which you can stupefy in vulgar sensuality, in the madness of passion, in persevering frivolity for twenty years, and then repair its drooping head, and bid its beautiful powers shine out again, unimpaired? Is purity a convenient robe which you can throw aside when it interferes with your freedom, and having done so, and having given yourself up for a season to every abomination, till even depravity turns to disgust, can you then, in compliance with a momentary humor, assume again that stainless robe? Can charity shut its liberal hand and bury its treasures in the ground and stalk around them with the stealthy pace of the sleepless starving miser, for a time, and then suddenly dispense blessings as bountifully as before? Or can Industry relax his labours, and lie soft, and sleep long, and forget his proverbs of prudence, and form himself to indulgences of indolence,—and then, snap asunder the iron habits of years, and leap to his labours before the dawn, with his old alacrity? No; this is not the way with us, or our virtues. What we are depends on what we do. The moment purity departs, licentiousness comes in. The loss of intelligence is the thing with dulness. When you cease to be active you begin to be idle. All our powers, all our virtues, all our vices—are progressive. And he that plays the fool today, from wantonness, tomorrow shall do the same, because he cannot help it. We can not afford to tamper with ourselves. It is too dangerous ground, and is most unseasonable. The humor that we only affect at present, in a few weeks will make a part of our character.

Now if these things are so, if our character is in our own hands, if such things are at stake, and levity involves so much danger,—there is no duty for which we have such imperious need as Self Command. We are to live soberly. We are to be masters of ourselves. And all our hopes for the future are wrapped up in our obedience to the injunction of the apostle.

This duty may well deserve our careful consideration. He that ruleth his spirit, said Solomon, is better than he that taketh a city:4 and it was an ancient maxim, that, no one is fit to command others, who has not first learned to command himself. Every hour will give occasion for the exercise of this master virtue. The distinctions of society are very great, and in those who seem to suffer by them, are apt to provoke a repining, perhaps a malignant disposition: and to keep this spirit down, needs strong self command. The temptations to the misuse of the tongue, to slander, to falsehood, to profanity, lie ever in wait around us, and teach us our need of this wary protector. "If any man," saith St. James, "offend not in word, the same is a perfect man."5 To every man is his own infirmity, his own besetting sin. His private retirement, his daily business, the social board, the care of his family, his intercourse with the world—will give ample scope to his exertions for the acquisition of the full and unintermitted dominion over himself, that shall subject the law of his members to the law of his mind.

There is such force of interest ever urging us on the side of duty, that when the advantage of compliance and the advantage of resistance to temptation are both considered with perfect coolness, it is not easy to silence or disregard the voice of reason. The great danger to our virtue lies in our want of preparation for the assault. Passion takes us at unawares; carries us by surprize—in a moment, and then we sit hours and years deploring the consequences of obeying an extravagant impulse. Now herein consists the value of self command. Let us learn to master ourselves for that brief interval—to keep the rebel eye and hand and tongue, as under bars of steel for one important moment, till reason shall have time to decide. Thus to live soberly, is a golden rule of life. He that has got this principle for a habit need not sigh for the ruby of Ormus, nor the gold of Ophir.6 That man is sufficient unto himself. He needs not friends to back

4. Proverbs 16:32.
5. James 3:2.
6. Ormus (or Hormuz), a city situated on an island in the Persian Gulf, was noted for its opulent trade with India. Marco Polo described it, and both Milton (*Paradise Lost*, II, 2) and Marvell ("Bermudas," line 20) refer to it. Ophir is mentioned several times in the Old Testament as a source of gold.

him; nor patrons to take him by the hand, and say, 'Come up hither'; nor splendid genius; nor inexhaustible wealth: these are but means of strength, and he is strong himself.

When we are come to that self possession that no sensual softness can bend us, no danger shake, no importunity mislead us; no luxury quicken our regulated appetites; no fear of offence disarm us of the power of saying No, to the tempter,—when we cannot be brought to sanction with a smile, or the least implication of assent, the sentiment which combats our sense of right, then, my friends, we shall have answered the purposes of life. We shall have made our use of temptation, and opportunity, and pleasure, and pain; of the instruction of events; of the revelation of God; of the example of Christ; of the hope of heaven; then, we may look with pious confidence to Him from whom we received our being, saying, "Lord, now lettest thou thy servant depart in peace."[7]

7. Luke 2:29.

XXV

We should live soberly, righteously, *and godly, in this present world.*

TITUS 2:12

In a former discourse upon these words, I offered to your consideration some remarks upon the duty of 'living soberly.' It was observed, that the passage from which the text is taken, is a summary of the Christian religion; that the text itself is a compend of human duty, since to live soberly, righteously, and godly, is to discharge our duties to ourselves, to others, and to God. It was then attempted to exhibit the reasonableness and the advantage of complying with the first part of the apostolic injunction. In the present discourse let us consider the full import of the command that we should live *righteously*.

To live righteously, is to live in a manner not to violate the rights of others. A very obvious and important application of this duty, is its respect to the *property* of others. A man honest in his dealings, is called a righteous man. And we will direct our attention first to the consideration of righteousness in this restricted sense.

It ought never to be forgotten in our homeliest reasonings, that, our faith, as Christians, teaches us, that, this life is a state of discipline; that, this world is our school, and, therefore, we must regard all things in it, not as valuable in *themselves*, but only in their *utility to our character*. Now Property is the most remarkable and important instrument, when viewed in this light, that exists in the world. We are instructed by its gain; we are instructed by its possession; we are instructed by its loss. In every exertion that it prompts, in every feeling it inspires, it is a constant exercise, an education, to the affections and to the active powers. I suppose it is sufficiently plain that it belongs only to this bodily state; that we all want property only because we are now tenants of a body which eats, drinks, is cold, and sick. With our worldly life we all lay it down. We carry no dollar of all our accumulations, no reversion of all our investments into the spiritual world. He who owns a county can only occupy six feet of the soil, and not long ere nature, who wastes nothing, will change his clay into new forms to bloom in flowers or to move with animal life. Let us learn then habitu-

---

Preached six times: November 2, 1828, at the Second Church, Boston; November 30 in Concord, Mass.; December 21 in Concord, N.H.; January 11, 1829, at the First Church, Boston; February 21, 1830, at the Second Church, Boston; and July 16, 1837, in East Lexington.

ally to regard it as only a temporary institution and feel that to our eternal self,—it has no value at all except as a means of instruction. In those schools where the young are trained to gymnastic exercises, where the object is to bring every muscle to its greatest perfection of form and vigor, the frames and bars of wood and iron which are commonly found there and employed in various exercises, have no worth in themselves in the eye of those who are trained there; they are mere blocks of wood or iron; but in this *use* have great value, as being admirably adapted to strengthen the arm, or to open the chest. Now we should think in the same manner of Property, as having in itself no real value, but as being of the most important use to the soul, as the framework, on which the exercise of righteousness is to be learned. By and by, this world will pass away; then the institution of Property will cease. Whilst it lasts, let us make our use of it, according to the commandment. That is, 'let us live righteously' by it.

My friends, I do not imagine that there is any one who has now come up to this holy place, with hands unclean with theft. Robbery and naked fraud are the extremes of unrighteousness, where the evil principle is so clearly seen, that it is universally hated. It hardly needs that the laws should punish what public opinion punishes with open execration. And it surely needs no lesson from the pulpit to give new force to your own convictions of the enormity of this vice. But there are modes of dishonesty which public opinion does not brand with infamy, but which are not less heinous in the eye of that law whose authority we urge. There are ways in which men that would be shocked at the idea of stealing do really steal the property of their neighbour. There is many a man who would instantly risk his life in vindicating his honour from the charge of having robbed the rich, who will pilfer from the poor. That is, he will incur a debt to those who live by daily labour and forget the obligation entirely or postpone to a period of cruel length, the payment of a debt which is bread and raiment to those from whom it is withheld.

Whence arise those disasters in trade, which are occurring every month, whereby the commercial embarrassment of one man, is made to bring down an untimely poverty upon ten or twenty families beside. I know there are casualties, not under our control, by which the ruin of property is sometimes made. The worm may crop the harvest; the most judicious calculations may be defeated by a political crisis; a fire may consume your factories; a storm may sink your cargo in the deep, after prudence had done all to keep what industry had done all to acquire. But these great misfortunes are not the ordinary occasions of this mischief. It is not in the worm, or the fire, or the storm, that the main cause of these evils lies. It lies in man. Man does not live righteously. A want of a steady and delicate attention to the feeling of justice; a making haste to be rich, and a little carelessness about the means, are the usual sources, it is to be feared, of these calamities. Men are dazzled by the near prospect of sudden wealth, and run unjustifiable risks, where want of success will deeply injure those who have confided in them. Or, it may be, you spend profusely; you cannot deny your vanity, the gratification of fine dress, fine house, and fine furniture, when your credit can procure them, although you are uncertain that you are now master of the means of meeting the expense you so freely incur. I am not a lover of parsimony. I honour the liberal hand which freely expends what it has freely acquired. I rejoice in that splendour, as well as in that competence, which, in all our maritime towns, gives evidence of the triumphs of industry and art. But true religion will never have attained its just ascendancy in our land, until it is felt that it is a grave crime, which ought not to be excused or palliated, when the ostentation of wealth is indulged by one man, at the risk of the smallest amount of property belonging to another. No matter though your schemes are visited (in God's anger perhaps,) with unexpected and undeserved success, and the hazard you made of your neighbor's purse, should never be known, the guilt is not diminished in the eye of God, and its effects exist, and will appear in yourself. You have made a mistake, the great, the common mistake with regard to riches, esteeming them the end, and not the means. Instead of using them to become righteous, you have become unrighteous to use them.

My brethren, we ought to feel that too great importance cannot be attached to an exact fidelity to the discharge of pecuniary obligations. No economy, no parsimony, that is made necessary by this object, can ever be ridiculous. Men whose fortunes are not equal to their own necessities are solicited to give their names to this subscription for a new book, or a public work, or for some scheme of social enjoyment. They are pushed on to expenses they cannot meet by the fear of being esteemed mean spirited, when they ought to feel that it is a meanness of spirit which prevents them from saying No. And sometimes there appears a greater apology for unlawful expense when a demand is made upon your charity. But consider that you have no right to be charitable whilst your just obligations are not redeemed. For in yielding to what you call an impulse of generosity you are giving away the bread of another. The merit of all charity must be commensurate with the sacrifice,[1] but you sacrifice what is not your own. Nor can too much care be given to impress on the young the principle, that they have no right to that which is not their own. It is related by Dr. Priestley in his own Memoirs, that he never lost the impression of a lesson received in his early childhood from his mother, who, finding that he had brought away a pin from a neighbouring house, sent him back to return it.[2] It may be in the power of us all to impart the same lesson with most salutary and lasting effect.

But there are other rights beside that of Property, which we are bound by religion to respect. This right, (and alas! that I cannot say in our country, that of personal liberty) is maintained by the laws of the land. Those laws are satisfied if a citizen does not defraud his fellow, and call him righteous if he does not break his oath or his plighted word, even though his exactness in demanding his own dues amounts to severity. But the righteousness we teach is more than this.

---

1. "The merit . . . sacrifice": see *JMN* 3:65.
2. *Memoirs of Dr. Joseph Priestley* (London, 1806), 2–3.

It governs the conversation, the manners, the whole life; it does not stop short with justice but adds mercy. It does not rest content with abstaining from wrong, it owns the generous impulse to do good. It scorns its own accommodation. It lives for friends, for society, for country, for man. I hope that in the remarks that were just now made I have not been misunderstood as in the smallest degree aiming to weaken the spirit of benevolence. Those remarks are strictly limited to cases where the will outruns the means. But, I consider that in its fullest extent the law of righteousness enjoins benefits, generosity, sacrifices. The righteous man will not only give to the poor but he will freely contribute his part to keep up the good action and enterprize of society; will feel the claim of useful and of elegant institutions upon his countenance and aid. Besides, there are innumerable occasions in daily life and conversation that cannot be specified where yet the duty is imperative. There are innumerable applications of this principle which clearly cannot be touched by the coarse hand of human law, but which we feel to be enforced by the divine. Thus, if you consider what a sacrifice of the time and interests of others, a want of punctuality in one man in the course of a long life, will occasion, you will feel that other men have a *right* to your diligence in this particular. If you meet a wretched beggar dying of hunger in the public way, do you not feel that he has a most imperious *right* to your care and your bounty? If you see a man of acute feelings and humble pretension mortified and oppressed in conversation by one of better condition, but of a selfish, brutal, and overbearing temper, do you not feel that he has a right to the kindness of that oppressor and of yourself? If you consider the duration and the degree of the effect which your example will have upon your children, your dependants, your equals, do you not feel that they have a right to your utmost circumspection in word and deed? Yet the laws are silent on all these points. A higher law enjoins them, which is written in your hearts.[3]

Yes, my friends, that punctuality which fulfils even trivial engagements; and that politeness which pays the most cautious deference to the feelings of others, are parts of righteousness; and charity and mercy are no less essential to it than honesty and truth.

To find the whole import and extent of the duty, we have only to consider the connexion in which we stand to other beings, and to make our whole conduct suitable to that connexion. If God had appointed each of us to a solitary existence, with no being but Himself to whom we should have any relation, our duties had been few and simple. But other duties are assigned us, and a greater scope of life appointed. Our natural home is society. We are limbs of a body. We belong to families, to parties, to nations, to mankind. And we find that God has distinguished this virtue with an appropriate reward: we are made good and happy, precisely in proportion as we postpone our own advantage, to the promotion of the advantage of others. We are able by our experience to discover that beautiful law of the social system that the spending of self enriches not impoverishes the agent, that he becomes every day, a stronger power on whom

3. Cf. Romans 2:15.

is poured the beneficence he had bestowed on others, as the planets throw back their light upon the sun. Herein is the greatest perfection to which humanity attains, when it ceases to live for itself that it may live for others. It has been remarked of some of the best men that ever adorned our race, that they appeared to lose themselves in the great actions they performed; they put their whole being into them. They seemed to live in the life of the cause to which they dedicated their powers. Its reverses were their sickness; its prosperity was their health. Low minds are busy in contriving, from afar, some trivial advantage for self. They are jealous lest another should obtain some petty accommodation they covet for their own. But great souls, souls touched with the love of God, and the desire of righteousness, abhor these unmanly calculations. They see too far, they know the value of life too well, to lose it in pitiful bickerings for objects, which, an hour after they are gained, are worthless and forgotten.

My brethren, let us never mistake a false spirit for that true obedience to the social law, the true charity, which is the glory of our nature. Our virtues are imperfect and unequal. Men will occasionally give themselves up to a generous fervour, will perform an act of charity or patriotism, and think they have made amends for thoughtless prodigality or deliberate fraud; that an occasional eleva- tion of sentiment has compensated for habitual neglect of private and petty duties. Let it be deeply fixed in our minds, that nothing in the power of man to give, neither sacrifice, nor prayers, acts of munificence, nor strains of genius, nor achievements of valour, can ever atone for the want of habitual right- eousness; that the humblest servant of this sacred law, is more respectable, in the scale of being, than the laurelled conqueror. And when the distinctions of this world shall pass away, and the film of its ignorance fall from our eyes, we shall perceive that the distinctions of virtue are real and eternal; those of human condition accidental and momentary. Have patience a moment with the inequalities of the world, if they disturb your faith, have patience a moment— and they shall be done away. But, then, 'he that is righteous, shall be righteous still.'[4]

Let us keep in our minds the example of our Lord, who rendered unto Caesar, the things of Caesar, and to God the things of God.[5] Let us carry this principle of a strict respect to the rights of others, into its least, as well as its largest applications. Let us observe in ourselves the smallest omissions. Let us not trespass on the time or the feelings or the pleasures or the characters of men, any more than upon their property. Let it keep our lips from calumny, and from strife. Let it teach us to pay respect to the aged, and consideration to the unfor- tunate, and kindness to the poor, and care to the young; tribute to whom tribute is due; honour, to whom honour.[6] Let us make our life, in all its parts, square with the eternal laws by which the Universe is governed, and humbly look to God, for the reward of the righteous.

4. Revelation 22:11.
5. Matthew 22:21, Mark 12:17, and Luke 20:25.
6. Romans 13:7.

XXVI

We should live soberly, righteously, and godly, *in this present world.*

TITUS 2:12

We have, in two former discourses upon this text, considered our personal and our social duties. It remains, according to our plan, to consider what duties our relation to God prescribes. This relation, we have found it difficult, if not impossible, to exclude from the partial views of human duty, which we have already taken. Nevertheless, upon the foundation of self respect alone, and without the aid of this great idea, some moralists have attempted to build a perfect system of duty. But it is at first sight an inferior and imperfect theory of life that poorly limits the eye of the actor to his own advantage, even though this is magnified, by being on the greatest scale, and for duration without end.

Neither have we attained a complete system, when we have added to the personal obligations, the laws of social duty. The duties we owe to others may be discharged alike by those who feel and by those who do not feel their obligation. A man without one generous sentiment of love, it is possible, (though no wise likely to happen,) may discharge every office, to the last tittle, of the social law. An enlightened self interest may guide him, a cold icy approbation of right, on the part of his understanding, whilst the heart, whose part in actions gives them all their life and value, keeps aloof. Decency and calculation may be proxies for self devotion and love.

But in adding *godliness* the religion of Christ puts the keystone on the arch; to perfect the theory of life; to apply the last check; the sovereign rule which shall exclude all falsehood, all possibility of abuse, from the government we would erect over the soul of man.

We should live godly. How shall this be done? It is clear that mere forms of service cannot satisfy God who sees the mind. It is trifling with Him, to walk to church to do him honour, whilst you go with the deliberate purpose of meditating there upon some frivolous or some criminal pleasure, or of adjusting in your

Manuscript dated November 13, 1828. Preached ten times: November 16, 1828, at the Second Church, Boston; November 23 at the New South Church; December 21 in Concord, N.H.; March 7, 1830, at the Second Church and again the same evening in Charlestown; March 14 in Hartford; March 21 in Philadelphia; April 18 in Concord, Mass.; November 1, 1835, in East Lexington; and October 30, 1836, in Wayland. Emerson returned to this subject in Sermon XXXV.

mind the terms of a bargain. True words and outwardly righteous acts will serve the purpose of living 'soberly' and 'righteously,' but something more is needed for pleasing God. 'What remains to be done?' says a man whose whole life is dedicated to the ambition of adding more acres to his farm, or new sums to his investments in trade. I am not dissipated; I am not profane; I say my prayers as I learned them from our Lord. I teach my children to say them. I set my dependants a good example; I am punctual at Church; all men observe the regularity of my Christian walk. I contribute my portion to the stated quarterly and annual charities. What lack I yet? What is to be given, that man can give to his maker, if words and actions will not suffice? Religion answers to him, and to all, Manifestly nothing else but the affections. 'To live godly,' in the language of the apostle, is *to give your affections to God*.

The *affections*. Now, my brethren, I desire to detain your attention, for a little while, upon this wonderful part of our nature. I need not explain what they are. The name of *affection* is eloquent. You know that moralists make a distinction in man's nature between reason and sentiment. We make it ourselves in daily conversation, in some form. We speak of acting from judgment, and acting from feeling; or of a man of enthusiasm and a man of calculation. You can imagine a man who pays a very careful attention to the support and comfortable condition of an aged parent whom he does not love and whose happiness he does not desire: for, he says, it is well that every one should subsist; and no one will take care of this superannuated person, if I do not; and I find people are very severe in their reflections upon ungrateful children; and I shall be much praised for my filial piety. And here is a man, who cares nothing for the laws and nothing for opinion, but strains his slender means to give ease and luxury to the pillow of her who gave him life,—led to this care by the strong love which makes him feel the sufferings of that parent, as his own.

I. Now this sentiment, or feeling, or affection, by whatever name we call it, this principle which does not reason, which does not hesitate, which does not count the cost of action, and weigh the advantage of duty in the scales of self interest, but leaps to duty and goodness, wherever they appear,—is the noblest part of our nature. Suppose there was a world where there were not affections:—can any thing be imagined more dull and repelling than the habits of beings whose thoughts never travelled beyond themselves? But now let love enter,—and life, interest, and grandeur come in. If you should chance to surprize a man of grave and respectable appearance in the performance of a servile office, it would seem to you unhandsome and disagreeable: but, if you learn that in so doing he is performing a necessary service to another man, who is his dearest friend, who is sick, or poor, or imprisoned,—then, the same act (which was mean before) becomes elevated and honourable in your eyes. Wherever the affections appear, down in the bottom of society, in the hovels of squalid wretchedness, they dignify the being whom they animate. The beggar in the dirt who draws his own rags over his child to keep out the north wind from his shrinking limbs, doth an action which the highest mind cannot see with indifference. We may carry this sympathy much farther. For in the brute creation, man feels the strongest interest in the mutual benevolence of animals. And that passage in the voyage of an old navigator, is never read without emotion, which offers to the imagination, the spectacle of a white bear on the ice fields of the polar circle, licking and bemoaning her wounded young, careless of her own danger till the sailors put an end to her life from a feeling of pity. So the fable of the pelican is beautiful to us, which represents that bird as pecking her breast and nourishing her young with the blood of her own veins. I quote these instances to make more apparent the fact, that, the affections nowhere appear, without giving beauty and interest to all that they touch.

II. I beg you, in the next place, to remark their wonderful power. Consider the fervor with which they move the whole man; how a strong passion will seem to give organization and harmony to the rudest mind, and bring into action, with wondrous effect, powers whose existence was not suspected before. Social life abounds with striking proofs of this force. Observe this man, a stranger in the crowded city, oppressed by fortune, hindered by sickness,—he meets in his affairs a thousand obstacles; yet I see him applying to them an invincible energy, losing no portion of heart or hope; night and day he labours;—for what cause? What supports him through all his toil? He hath no companion or comforter; I see that he laughs and he weeps alone. What are the cords that draw him in these solitary ways? Now hear the simple solution. On the other side of the world, are two or three persons whom he loves. The arms of their affection reach him, across the mighty waters, and intervening lands. To add to their comfort, he came to this foreign coast, and the love of them beguiles his banishment. They draw him to them, by that mighty tie, and influence his actions from hour to hour.

Having thus spoken of the *excellence* and of the *strength* of the affections of the soul, I come now to the consideration of their *objects*.

III. Every one of us is joined to some others whose society we seek with unconquerable desire: whose loss, by the stroke of death, is contemplated as making a chasm in our happiness which nothing but the Christian hope that they are only removed and have not perished, and that we shall see them again, saves from being remediless. We *must* love. The man does not live who has no fellow being whose happiness he enjoys and sometimes proposes as an end of his own exertions. Now, what is it, that you love? Is it the body, or the soul of your friend? Is it skin deep beauty, a little form, or colour, or motion? No, surely; for, if your friend should retain precisely the same bodily appearance, but should undergo the most entire change in his character; if, instead of acts of kindness, he should startle you with acts of malignity; if the same voice, whose tones of tenderness dwelt in your memory, should now utter nothing but sarcasms of hatred; black falsehoods; calumnies; and blasphemies; if he should lie down to devise mischief, and rise up to work it; should do all abominable deeds, and exult in the afflictions he occasioned; if you found, in short, that, with the semblance of an angel, you had loved a devil, would your love remain?

It would change to aversion and horror. No, my brethren, it is not the body, the proportion of external features, which we love, but the spiritual properties of which these are the vehicle, or the expression.

And now I beg you to remark what seems to me a very important truth, which is, that, the affections seek always entire goodness and truth, that perfect goodness is their natural object, and that though they do not find it on earth, yet they always require perfection.

What is the meaning, else, of that language, applied to young men and women, that *they have placed their affections unworthily?* Whence all these warnings that experience addresses to youth upon the importance of caution in this particular, and which are so often neglected, and afterwards remembered with a late and fruitless acknowledgment of their wisdom? What is the meaning of the remark that such a mother, or such a wife, *is blinded by her affections?* Why this blindness, why this disappointment, if not, that the affections require virtues, suppose virtues, in their objects, and when they find vices, suffer the deepest chagrin, or strive to keep up the delusion that existed at first? The reason why affection grows cold, is because the being whom it believed fault-less, it now finds to have faults; it loved the perfection it thought it saw; it recoils from the imperfection, as soon as it is manifest.

In saying that we expect a perfect moral character in those whom we ardently love, I speak of the natural tendency of the affections; I speak of the affections, as they exist in youth, and not of the regard we give, in after life, when a slow experience has corrected our hopes, and taught us that qualities deserving attachment may be found coupled with others deserving aversion.

But now to establish this great fact that perfect goodness is the natural object which the affections seek, and to push our analysis one step further,—I will suppose, my brethren, that one of you, who has been taught by experience not to expect unmixed goodness in men, has formed a sincere regard for another man, who has been thrown into his way on the paths of life. Though you have learned to eye mortal merits with distrust, let me ask, if it will give you pain, to find him far worthier than you thought him? Suppose, on a longer and closer acquaintance, you find in your friend a soul incapable of fear; an integrity, which the Universe cannot bribe, a charity that seeks your good, and the good of all men, with a contempt of its own; you discover, in him, a mind teeming with the most wonderful amount of knowledge; a penetration into human character, that no art can baffle, no splendour mislead; and, withal, the utmost energy in combining means to effect the noblest ends: Now, when your growing intimacy with your friend, surprized you daily with the disclosure of these properties in him, would not your heart leap with delight, in the glory of its acquisition, in the possession of the affections of such a being; and would not your main happiness arise from your devotedness to this attachment?

Now, let us enlarge these excellent powers and properties, on every side, taking from them what remained of human infirmity, until you make a *divine friend.* Let it be supposed, that, God had chosen this mode of leading you to himself; that after enjoying the love and admiration that spring from an inter-course with the glorious, that you now discover that you have been conversing with the shrouded perfections of an Infinite Mind; that, God, instead of being that stern and awful Lord of creation that he had been represented to your imagination, was a friend thus infinitely lovely and grateful to the mind, and thus apt to excite the most energetic affection. If this had been, my brother, would you not kneel down and adore? Would not the eye of Faith be satisfied? Would not a holy joy awaken in your affections, that, they had found and rested in their great and final good? Would not the objects of the world, the evils of life, the pleasures of sense, be contemned in the desire of that communion which your spirit had learned to hold with your God?

My friends, do you think I have put a far fetched and extravagant case? Do you say, that, it might be so, that we should thus surrender ourselves to the divine love, if God had chosen such a mode of making himself known? Well, now, I beg you to consider, if he have not chosen such a mode? I have put this case, because, it seemed to me similar to the real facts of God's Providence. You have not indeed known this one sublime associate in whom all the excellences of moral and intellectual character were clustered and concentrated. But have you not been acquainted with this perfect character, *in parcels?* Have you not known many individuals, your own companions on the ways of the world—in each of whom you recognize some feature of this divine beauty; in one man, purity; in another, incorruptible honour; in another, a boundless charity; in another, simplicity; in another, a towering mind? Consider that every good man, every good thing, every good action, word, and thought that you love, is only a *fragment of the divine Nature.* Thus does our Father make himself known to his children. This is the hourly revelation by which our minds are instructed in his goodness. Thus this world, the beautiful order of nature, and all the persons with whom you converse and all the events and (as you call it) the *fortunes* of your whole life, are only a systematic series of lessons by which God is training you to the knowledge, and so, to the love and enjoyment of Himself.

Whilst the time admonishes me to conclude I see well that I have only opened the great duty of which I proposed to treat. It expands before us as we go on. For the duty of godliness is vast both in contemplation and in action; involving, as it does, the manner in which the affections are to be trained to their great object, the manner in which the soul unites itself to God.

But what is the inference from these reflexions? What but this, that we are to learn the love of God by cultivating with religious care our reverence for virtue, wherever it appears, knowing that this is his nature and the law of his being, and knowing (according to the consenting experience of all good men—) that pre-cisely in proportion as our regard to goodness increases—so will the idea of God reveal itself to the mind.

Here then is the great practical truth at which we arrive as a point of rest from which we proceed to duty, namely; that these affections can be *cultivated;* that they grow by their own exercise; and that precisely as we would obtain the regard of a good man by doing those things which would be agreeable to him, we are to obtain the love of God, by doing those things which we know he will approve.

God, who thus makes himself known to us in the course of events, or, by what is called Natural Religion, has added, to these imperfect intimations, the direct revelation of Jesus Christ. Therein he has removed our uncertainties and corroborated the daring hopes which the mind had formed. Why our affections sought a perfect good, and rejected an imperfect good,—is now made clear. They sought Him, among his creatures; for it was Himself alone which could satisfy them. He hath given us rules for our conduct in this world, and hopes to guide us to another. He hath bade us to live soberly and righteously. Let us fulfill the duties we owe to ourselves and to our fellow-beings. He has finished this law by directing, by permitting, us to love Him. Let us obey this commandment also. My friends, the Apostle Paul saith, love is the fulfilling of the law:[1] if we will discharge this highest duty you cannot fail in duty to yourselves and to men: it includes them all. Let us look to him in all events. Let us rejoice and be exceeding glad.[2] For what are trials and temptations to us? what is sickness, or poverty, or reproach, or the loss of friends, or the hour of death? For a voice comes out of heaven to our ears,—"Set your affections on things above, and not on things on the earth."[3] Fear not; temptation cannot harm you, nor sorrow, nor the evil that is permitted to be in the earth; you shall pass in purity and joy through the light afflictions of mortal life, till the God whom you have learned to love, shall make you perfect by uniting you to Himself.

1. Romans 13:10.
2. Matthew 5:12.
3. Colossians 3:2.

XXVII

Therefore, let no man glory in men;
for all things are yours.

I CORINTHIANS 3:21

The Apostle Paul, in his first epistle to the Corinthians, reproves them for their levity and party-spirit, inasmuch as they had already begun to overlook the blessings offered to them in the Christian religion, in a foolish desire of each convert to exaggerate the merits of his peculiar teacher. One was jealous of Cephas, because himself had learned of Paul. But the affectionate apostle calls back their attention from the workmen, to the work. He suggests to them, that, the truths which were taught them, make these dissensions insignificant. 'Let none,' he saith, 'be disturbed with a pitiful controversy about a man, an instrument; for, all things are yours; whether Paul, or Apollos, or Cephas, or the world, or life, or death, or things present, or things to come."[1]

My brethren, I wish to adopt the lofty sentiment of Paul: to pursue into some details the idea to which he has given so bold and general expression.

Doth the Apostle say, 'All things are ours;' come then, let us rejoice in life.

Life is only valuable to us in proportion to our enjoyments. Perhaps some of you can remember a time when your wants were so many and your possessions so few and so precarious, or, when some lingering bodily illness, bereaving the day of its beauty, and the night of its peace, made life appear so worthless, that some danger which threatened to put an end to it, was contemplated, by you, with perfect indifference. But if there are those, who remember this feeling, if, since, your affairs have thriven, your property is enlarged, your bonds to society have multiplied, by adding to simple self love, the interest of friends, of wife, and children; the care of a reputation, or, of institutions which you warmly befriend; have you not found your attachment to life growing stronger, precisely in the same proportion?

When an army is to be formed, who are they that throng to the drum of the

Manuscript dated November 21, 1828. Preached six times: November 23, 1828, at the Second Church, Boston; December 14 in Concord, N.H.; February 15, 1829, in Waltham; February 22 at the Brattle Street Church; April 25, 1830, at the Second Church, Boston; and August 6, 1837, in East Lexington. Notes and draft passages for this sermon occur in *JMN* 3:141–44. On the first page of the manuscript is Emerson's notation: "This discourse is intended as a sequel to the XXIV."

1. Cf. I Corinthians 3:21–22.

recruiting officer? Is it the substantial proprietor, the merchant, the parent, the man of office, the man of genius, those who have a stake in society, and much to lose; or, is it the friendless, the houseless, the vagabond, the forlorn, who have no character and no hope, to whom life offers little good, and who are therefore tempted by a few dollars to put it on hazard?

There are two sorts of life: the life of the body and the life of the soul. Though there are some who value the first lightly, there are more who underrate the second. The great majority of men are very careful of the bodily life. How many words, how many actions, how many anxieties, are daily directed to the care of the pulmonary, the bilious, the nervous system; to keep a little spark in this perishing clay! But the life of the soul, they regard often with indifference. But when they do so, it is from precisely the same cause, viz., that their soul has no possessions.

The gospel of Jesus Christ has added an infinite worth to the spiritual life, by the objects it proposes. It shows eternity to depend on time. It found men dwelling in the dust, in which they were born; their souls, contracted by a little ambition, and engrossed by little pursuits. It says to the soul, 'Arise! put on thy beautiful strength, oh virgin daughter of God! behold the work that is given thee to do,—to resist temptation; to inform thine ignorance; to cleanse thee from defilement; to aspire to the perfection for which thou wert formed; and to walk in the light and in the love of God, forever. Be of good cheer, for all things are yours.'

But men do not hear its divine encouragement. They do not appreciate the value of themselves. Their bodily life, their limbs, their goods,—they are prompt enough to esteem and to defend. But their spiritual life, their character, their moral power, they hold cheap. We see men daily who have no consciousness of their immortal gifts. They are full of superstitions about fortune, or the power of circumstances, or the laws of destiny, of which they think themselves the victims, (and so they are, if so they think themselves,) and overlook the secret power of the human mind over circumstances, and its ability to make its own fate.

As the business of life, is, to perform well our own part, to make the best use we can of all the powers committed to us, it becomes an imperative duty to explore our own strength. In the early ages of the world, before yet the light of Christianity had been imparted, the sentence 'Know thyself,' was thought the hardest and highest precept of human duty. It was written over the porch of the most sacred temple in the ancient world.[2] And it would be strange, if with all the additional value that Christianity has given to this knowledge, it should be dishonoured by us.

In pursuing these reflections, I wish to invite your attention to two points of consideration; *first;* that the proper object of all knowledge is to make us

2. The inscription in the temple at Delphi is mentioned by a number of Greek writers, including Pausanias in *Description of Greece*, trans. W. H. S. Jones (London, 1935), 4:507, and Plato in "The First Alcibiades," in *The Works of Plato*, trans. Thomas Taylor (London, 1804), 1:81.

acquainted with ourselves. *Secondly;* that the fruit of that knowledge, is, the conviction, that, we are masters of our own condition, that, all things are ours.

I. My brethren, it is not enough considered by us how much it is the proper business of life to learn *ourselves.* We may read history, but this is what we learn there, or we learn nothing. All wise men agree in advising the young to make themselves acquainted with the records of our race, in past ages. But let us ask ourselves—what are the persons who figure on their page? what is Caesar, or Cromwell, or Washington, or Buonaparte, to me?—what is Socrates or St. Paul or Howard,[3] but beings of like capacities and infirmities to mine, by whose story, I may learn how I might act and suffer? And there is not a single heroic action in the annals of man, that may not just as well be unknown as known to you, unless it speaks to a kindred sentiment within yourselves; unless it reveals to you some power, some feeling within your own mind, which had not been excited before. Other men, whether seen in society, or sought in history, are only diagrams on which we study, with more leisure and convenience, our own nature, or instruments whereon to exercise our own virtues. When I am disgusted by the bloody annals of despotism and hideous profligacy, I learn, with alarm, to what depths of depravity, my passions will lead me, if I surrender myself to their solicitations. When I read the story of the martyrs of religion and liberty, I see how God has proportioned the strength of the body and the mind; and that my mind may be trained to such firmness of virtue, as to be superior to all torment which the body can bear and live.[4]

The same reasoning may be applied to all the pursuits of man. We may explore all the sciences, but they are naught, if they do not end in being aids to this supreme science. For the sciences and arts are nothing else but the relations of different objects in the Universe to the human mind. When you examine the principles of architecture, and discover that there is a beauty in the proportion of a column, that does not exist when that proportion is altered, what do you more than ascertain one of the laws of your own mind? Because, do you not see, that if your mind were differently constituted, that proportion would not appear? For if there were no mind in the whole universe, what would it signify, what were the forms of matter?

So it is with all we do. We may engage in professions; we may manage affairs; till farms; buy land; make fortunes; build houses; navigate ships; enact laws; these are all but various ways appointed by the order of Providence in the world to teach us the same lesson, to make us acquainted with the powers of our own minds, and the affections of our own hearts.

II. Secondly; it should be felt by us that we are the arbiters of our condition in

---

3. John Howard (1726–1790), English philanthropist and prison reformer.

4. "I think there is some reason for questioning whether the body and mind are not so proportioned, that the one can bear all which can be inflicted on the other, whether virtue cannot stand its ground as long as life, and whether a soul well principled will not be separated sooner than subdued" (Samuel Johnson, *Rambler*, No. 32 in *The Works of Samuel Johnson* [New Haven, 1969], 3:178). Quoted in *JMN* 2:397, 6:51.

life. It is a great truth that makes men wise, when once they practically feel it, that every man carries about with him, favour or disgrace. All men are solicitous of the good will of their fellowmen; but we are apt to impute the reception which we meet in society, to the disposition of others, and forget that we ourselves alone determine what that reception shall be. Men fear one another; they timidly wish that they may receive more notice; you anticipate with a faint heart the neglect you will suffer, at the meeting of business or pleasure, you prepare to attend. Consider, I pray you, that this very fear cannot help producing that neglect. You may stop at the doorstone of the house you are entering, and learn the welcome that awaits you within, by consulting your own mind. It will render you a true and faithful reply. Do you find it sustained by your own self respect? You shall be sure of the respect of others. Doth it shrink with unseemly sense of incompetence and unworthiness? You shall see, with what prompt fidelity, your friends shall echo its judgment. Society seems to be severe upon faults. It is merely a mirror, reflecting back your own sentence upon yourself. You have spent an evening at a social entertainment, and have come home chagrined. Do not imagine that the disturbance of your spirits is occasioned by the haughty deportment of one of the company, or the impertinence of another, or the frivolity of all. If you really seek the truth, you shall find the cause in yourself. You went thither, in ill humour; or you went with false expectations; to gratify a vanity which was mortified; you went thither, knowing you had passed an idle or a vicious day; your mind was unbent; you had no vantage-ground of virtuous deeds on which a good conscience could fortify itself; and now do you wonder, that you were not reverenced? Do you wonder that, being unsound, you were found to be unsound? Have you not learned, what all events teach you, that, nothing can save you from the ill issues of your own acts?

Instead of feeling this responsibility, men surrender themselves without a struggle to the action of every outward event. They lean upon those who stand next them. They grope their way through life, stretching forth their idle sloven hands, in a suppliant or repining spirit. They go from day to day wondering what shall befal them in a certain place, or at a future day, instead of deciding what they will have befal them, that is, what they will do. You shall see in society, numbers of discontented men, who complain that the doors of preferment are closed upon them; that prejudices stand in their way; that a hard measure is dealt to them; that with equal merit as others, they meet an unequal difficulty. And they imagine perhaps that they can at any time quit their own neighborhood or their own country and in another part of the world where they are unknown there is no impediment to the most brilliant success. Be not deceived. You carry your fortunes in your own hand. Change of place will not touch the disease which change of character must cure. You will weave the same web in England, in the Indies, as at home if your hands have only learned to make a single texture.

I believe, my friends, that these views may be carried much farther, and admit of a very much greater variety of illustration than I have attempted to employ: I will only inquire if there be not in your own experience ground to think that no events, prosperous or adverse, befall us, of which we cannot find a reason in the inward history of ourselves. It may be the time will come to each of us when we shall clearly discern, that the order of God's Providences *without* us, was delicately adapted to the spiritual exigences *within* us; when we shall see that if every misfortune was not a misconduct of our own, that every honour was not a desert, yet every pain or pleasure was needed by us in the then state of our mind, that every affront was a folly of ours; when we shall learn to acquit other men of the injuries we suffer, and trace them out to be the inevitable issues of our own conduct, or the necessary discipline by which God guides us to our wellbeing.

The practical value of these truths, it seems to me, is very great. "All things are yours." You are the Universe to yourself. We are not feeble, we are not pitiful, any more than we are vicious, except by our own fault. We are very powerful beings. We can, as we choose, be trained into angels or deformed into fiends.

We should learn then, my brethren, to fear and honour ourselves. It is a great rule which will make us wise unto eternal life.[5] Here is a man of plausible manners who knows what is right and is good as long as you are by, and manifests great regard for your good opinion. You found him saying what he thought it would be agreeable to you to have him say. He borrows the key of his conversation implicitly from those whom he thinks better than himself and obviously curbs the expression of bad feelings out of regard to them. When you see this, you are afraid to trust him alone. You can feel no security that he will not be uncivil and tyrannical to those of whom he does not stand in awe, to his inferior, to his dependant. Now what is the natural remedy for this? Do you not see, that if you can only inspire him with the fear of himself instead of others, you would provide him with an inseparable keeper that would never let him go wrong? Do you not see that the same is true for yourself? that there is no one on earth whose regard you have such urgent reason to cultivate, as your own; no other, whose approbation will be so dear, or whose reproaches so intolerable? Consider that innocence alone is safe; that, no secrecy can make vice secure from surprize and observation; and that the only way to insure an inviolable respectability, is, never to offend your own eye.

And when we shall have established this great rule of conduct, then let us go on, with humility, but with courage, to further deductions from the cheering declaration of St. Paul. For all things are yours. Let not this truth excite presumption and arrogance. These are the last feelings it should awaken. Let us celebrate in our minds a holy thanksgiving to God who hath been pleased so richly to endow us in his own likeness, and let us with solemn selfexamination and prayer entreat Him for light and counsel that we may faithfully administer this great charge that is given us, and sustain, as we ought, this oppressive responsibility. Let it inspire us to the greatest efforts. There is nothing really

5. Cf. Timothy 3:15.

desirable to us that wisdom and perseverance cannot attain. Let us choose great objects, with a just and generous ambition, and relax no nerve and spare no energy in the indefatigable pursuit. Be assured with a perfect assurance, that you shall be the better for all the knowledge and all the virtue that you add to yourself, exactly to the fulness of its amount, and no more, that no particle of the spiritual *man* can ever be lost. As God has made you a law unto yourself,[6] fulfil that law to its whole extent, and God shall be responsible for the event and the reward. Time is short, but it shall be yours; and the world unsatisfying, but it is yours; and life, and death, and things present and also the world to come.

6. Romans 2:14.

I am not ashamed of the gospel of Christ:
for, it is the power of God unto salvation
to every one that believeth.

ROMANS 1:16

I am not ashamed of the gospel of Christ, said the Apostle Paul; it was the declaration of a valiant heart. In him, it was no superfluous tender of adhesion to a cause already strong enough, nor arrogance of courage where no danger was. It was a challenge that a martyr gives to all terror of pain. It bid calamity do its worst—his part was taken—his soul was fixed. It was the pledge of mortifications to be borne; of advantages bravely given up; of infamy to be suffered in the place of renown; of indefatigable toils; of anxious days; of sleepless nights; of hourly exposure to death which would come at last in some hideous form. It was not alone, that he undertook to be the patron of an opinion new and unknown, the brother of a low obscure sect, the friend of the friendless, the lover of what men called vulgar and vile. Oh no, the world whose pride he insulted by his aversion and his doctrine was not to be appeased by a verdict of silent contempt. The Jew and the Pagan cried Blood! against the execrated schismatic, the lean beasts of the amphitheatre were unchained and let slip on him, and where he went, he heard the hisses of the world.

"Odio humani generis" is the expression of Tacitus upon the Christians in speaking of the occasion when St. Paul is supposed to have suffered martyrdom.[1]

The Apostle of the Gentiles made good his words with his life. He bore all. He overcame evil with good. He endured to the end.[2] He came off more than conqueror from the field of his battle.

Paul of Tarsus died triumphing at Rome, his head being severed from his body by the command of Nero. My friends, I do not recall the memory of this sad life and this celebrated murder with any view of awakening in you an

---

Preached once, at the Second Church, Boston, on the morning of March 15, 1829, the first Sunday after Emerson's ordination. Here and in Sermon XXIX (given in the afternoon of the same day) Emerson discusses his conception of the duties of a Christian minister.

1. *Tacitus: The Histories; The Annals*, trans. John Jackson, (Cambridge, Mass., 1951), 4:284.
2. Cf. Matthew 24:13 and Mark 13:13.

useless sympathy, a departed indignation. You look upon this story as I do. We do not count it any marvel that Paul was not ashamed of his faith. In our minds the association is familiar of seeming wretchedness with real glory. We know by heart from God's word what is the style of God's Providence. The mind leaps at once from the sufferings of virtue to its eternal reward. Why was not Paul ashamed of the gospel of Christ? Let us hear his answer—"Because it is the power of God unto salvation," or in other words, "because it hath a divine power for the salvation of every believer."

My brethren, if we can conceive the feeling that animated Paul, it is easy to adopt the language of Paul. I am well aware that it is one thing for me at this day, here in the bosom of my friends and the friends of Christianity, to say I am not ashamed of the gospel, and quite another thing for Paul to say so amidst timid friends and fanatic foes, and before the ragged front of Roman persecution. But for other reasons than the fear of danger, and for reasons more cogent than fear in their action upon a well constituted mind—I take these words to myself. I believe that after eighteen hundred years of exposition and diffusion and influence the effects of the gospel are small and feeble; that is, small and feeble, considered in relation to the source from which it came, and the power that is in it. Christianity is the decent and reverend religion of our land, and therefore we support it. We are Christians by the same title as we are New England men,³ that herein we were born and reared. I know that men who do not love the gospel do not know what it is; and I believe that many religious men do not derive from it all the comfort they could. I see the grossest ignorance and the most injurious prejudices existing in regard to that which I love and honour. I grieve to see men esteem as tyranny what I feel to be a law of love. I am pained to remark a secret fear or dislike of what is full of beauty and full of glory. And now that the occasion to which all the years of my education have looked forward has come to me of bearing my testimony to the value of my faith—I wish to take up again these ancient words. I rejoice to perceive and to affirm that eighteen centuries justify the sentiment. What Paul said to the great and powerful of this world—I will say to the wise of this world—I am not ashamed of the gospel of Christ, for it is the power of God unto salvation.

By the public services of the last week, my Christian brethren, a very interesting relation was established. You have called me to the Pastoral office. I have accepted the charge. You have summoned the fathers and brethren of the churches to ordain me—by the ancient and simple rites of prayer and the imposition of hands—to the sacred work. I have been admonished of my responsibility and counselled in my course. The hand of the fellowship of the churches has been given me and I have been sent forth on my way with God's blessing invoked upon my head by the good and the wise.⁴

3. This is Emerson's adaptation of a sentence from Montaigne's "Apology for Raimond de Sebonde." See *JMN* 6:30, 6:156.

4. At the ordination ceremony on March 11, Samuel Ripley of Waltham, Emerson's uncle, gave a sermon entitled "Preaching Peace by Christ." This was followed by the Ordaining Prayer given

I have attempted to weigh in the balance of an even judgment the advantages and the difficulties of this office, and I embrace with alacrity this occasion of complying with a most reasonable usage which expects of the newly installed pastor some statement of his views of the duties which his engagements impose upon him.

The first and obvious distribution of the duties of a Christian minister, is into the two classes of public ministrations and of pastoral visits. I wish to speak to both these points.

The principal public performances of a minister are prayer and preaching.

Of the nature and reasonableness and of what constitutes a successful performance of the first of these offices, there is but one opinion among good men. How rarely the gift of prayer is possessed in any high degree of excellence, I am well aware. It is a fruit of a frame of mind. It is to be sought in the affections and not in the intellect; to be compassed by the love of God rather than by the study of books. Most of you, my friends, have probably experienced at some time the power of a fervent prayer upon your mind. If you have, you know it to be singular in its excellence: it doth soothe and refresh and edify the soul as no other exercises can.

But it is not so much by efforts to make good prayers that the minister is to succeed in producing the blessed effect at which he aims as by leading a good life. That man who studies to act always with a secret reference to God—who finds God on his left hand and on his right in every place and in every event, who feels that when he muses in the silence of his own soul, God is there—can hardly fail to call his Father by names which he will acknowledge, and in tones and sentiments that shall find their echo in every pious heart.

The second public duty of a Christian minister is *preaching*,—a high and difficult office. In prayer he is only the voice of the congregation, he merely utters the petitions which all feel. In preaching he undertakes to instruct the congregation, himself an erring man, to deal out to his brethren the laws of the Almighty, to carry the conviction of duty home to their hearts, to encourage the faint hearted, to persuade the reluctant, to melt the obdurate, and to shake the sinner. That man has very low and humble views of this office who satisfies his conscience with uttering the commonplaces of religion for twenty or thirty minutes, reciting a lazy miscellany of quotations from scripture and then dismisses his unfed, unedified audience, hugging himself that he has not spoken an offensive syllable, and that he has come off so cheaply from his Sabbath work.

Even with this slovenly performance of his part, I know, many hearts will reap their own advantage from his words, because they are already in that

by Francis Parkman, the Charge by Ezra Ripley of Concord (Emerson's step-grandfather), the Right Hand of Fellowship by N. L. Frothingham (successor to Emerson's father at the First Church, Boston), an Address by Ezra Stiles Gannett, junior pastor of the Federal Street Church, and a concluding prayer by Charles W. Upham of Salem. The ministers of more than thirty churches attended. According to the Second Church records, "The day was fine, the assembly great, & all things done happily, decently, & in order" (MHS).

devout frame that any holy text is sufficient to raise and fix their thoughts on heaven. But the preacher has not the less been unfaithful to his charge. He has done much to exhaust the charity of the charitable, he has disgusted the intelligent, he has furnished an apology to the indifferent and a triumph to the scoffer. But it is not so much the evil he has done as the good he has failed to do, that I regard. He has missed an opportunity of perfecting good purposes that were ripening already; there were temptations that his breath might have blown away, there were apprehensions which he might have soothed, and doubts which he might have cleared. The mightiest engine which God has put into the hands of man to move man is eloquence. I believe there is not one of us, my brethren, whose opportunities have been so abridged, living in this free state, as never to have witnessed its prodigious effects. When great sentiments call it out from a great mind, and especially when it rises to topics of eternal interest, it is glorious to see how it masters the mind, how it bows the independence of a thousand to the reason of one; how it goes on with electrical swiftness from unobserved beginnings, lifting him that speaks and them that hear, above the dust and smoke of life—searching out every noble purpose, every sublime hope that lurks in the soul. Then is that sympathy lofty and pure; then the speaker and the hearer become the pipes on which a higher power speaketh. It is like the breath of the Almighty moving on the deep.[5]

Now different men have the gifts essential to this divine art in very different measure. Yet in every man the principles of it lie, and every man who gives himself wholly up to a just sentiment which he lives to inculcate, will be eloquent. But the careless preacher leaves this weapon of matchless force to sleep in sloth and disuse. God keep me from this frigid indifference.

Brethren, when I consider the true nature and dignity of the office I have sought, whilst I am oppressed by the perception of my own incompetence, I am animated to exertion by all the motives that can invigorate and gratify hope. There have been times and places where the name of a priest was opprobrious. The office must always have honour or shame from the manner in which it is borne. But the office of the priesthood was never made for contempt. To my eye, when its duties are ably discharged, it is the most august station which man can fill. But to be worthily filled—to be a preacher equal to the demands of the times, and to the hope of the times—preaching must be manly and flexible and free beyond all the example of the times before us.

The reason why Christianity has found so many open enemies and so many lukewarm friends is not a defect in Christianity itself but a defect in its teaching. Christianity is true. What is true can never be ridiculous; it is falsehood and mistake that are ridiculous and mean. If Christianity were taught always in a manner as simple, absolute and universal as its truth is, nobody could look down upon it. In itself, no man can look down upon it. It is not the Christian faith but a vain imagination of his own, which the skeptic sees and rejects,—a

---

5. Cf. Genesis 1:2.

poor distorted copy which the ignorance of men has formed and which unfaithful teachers have confirmed. The world was wrong and the pulpit has not set it right. It seems to me that our usage of preaching is too straitened. It does not apply itself to all the good and evil that is in the human bosom. It walks in a narrow round; it harps on a few and ancient strings. It is much addicted to a few words: it holds on to phrases when the lapse of time has changed their meaning. Men imagine that the end and use of preaching is to expound a text and to unfold the divisions and subdivisions of meaning of *Grace*, of *Justification*, of *Atonement*, of *Sanctification*, and are permitted to forget that Christianity is an infinite and universal law which touches all action, all passion, all rational being; that it is the revelation of a Deity whose being the soul cannot reject without denying itself; that it is a rule of action that teaches us to attain the highest good of intelligent nature; a rule which penetrates into every moment, and into the smallest duty, that it is always seasonable; that it is our support, our comfort; that it is our spiritual home; Yes, Religion is the *home of the mind*, from which man may wander, but he wanders unhappy, and bewails at every new departure his inability to return.

These views of Christianity should always be present to the mind of him who would preach as becomes those who bring the oracles of God.

I shall labour then, brethren, as far as my poor abilities will reach, to use a freedom in my preaching befitting the greatness of the Gospel and its universal application to all human concerns. I shall not be so much afraid of innovation as to scruple about introducing new forms of address, new modes of illustration, and varied allusions into the pulpit, when I believe they can be introduced with advantage. I shall not certainly reject them simply because they are new. I must not be crippled in the exercise of my profession. If there is any talent, any learning, any resource, any accomplishment, which I can use and convert to the service of this gospel, whose servant I am, I shall without hesitation avail myself of it. As there is not a grain of sand nor a wretched weed quaking in the wind, but contributes its part, an essential part, to the gravity of the globe, and the equipoise of the system; so all the facts in the Universe, rightly seen, attest the truth of Religion. If to me were given that starlike vision which could see and make report how they all bear evidence to it, I cheerfully would. But I cannot. I am humbled at my ignorance. I see a few and dim parts. It would be silly to shut myself voluntarily within a yet narrower circle, and only use a part of my pittance of truth.

I have spoken thus at length upon this important part of clerical duty which more than any other marks and characterizes the minister because I was anxious to meet on the threshold an objection that I thought would lie in the minds of many cautious Christians against modes of preaching which I may think it prudent and they may think it bold to adopt. I am well aware that no apology, however satisfactory, can ever make bad preaching useful, and that good preaching of whatever cast will carry its own vindication. Still I am willing to fortify by the highest authority my opinions, if any one hereafter should object to me the want of sanctity in my style, and the want of solemnity in my illustrations. I shall remind him, that the language and the images of Scripture which his ear requires, derive all their dignity from their association with divine truth; that they belonged once to what was low and familiar; that our Lord in his discourses condescended to explain himself by allusions to every homely fact, to the boys in the market, to the persons dropping into the custom offices; to the food on the board, to the civilities shown him by the hospitality of his entertainer; and would he not, let me ask, if he addressed himself to the men of this age and of this country, appeal with equal frequency to those arts and objects by which we are surrounded, to the printing press and the loom, to the phenomena of steam and of gas, to the magnificence of towns, to free institutions, and a petulent and vain nation?

It may be easily inferred that my views of my duty as a Christian teacher impose on me the necessity of giving to my own mind the highest cultivation, and that of every kind my manner of life will permit. *It imperiously demands the critical knowledge of the Christian Scriptures, which are to be considered the direct voice of the most High—the reason of God speaking to the reason of man.* But does it less demand the contemplation of his benevolence and his might in his works? It demands a discipline of the intellect, but more than all it demands a training of the affections. Whatever else can be spared, this is essential. Any defects can be excused but the defect of a pure heart and a good life.

Having thus expressed my views of what preaching should be, the same views must regulate my expectation of its fruits. The success must be of the same kind as the exertion. I do not plant a vine and gather corn. But as I plant, I hope to reap.[6] It is a sad and meagre commendation of a Christian minister, when the departing congregation whisper to each other the praises of his manner, his language, and his voice, and congratulate themselves on a skilful emphasis, or a musical period, and then go away and remember the service no more. Believe me, brethren, if this is the top of my success, I have miserably failed of my end. Far be it from me both now and hereafter—that wretched vanity which sits down contented with the serenade of friendly praises on no better foundation than these accidental advantages. But if I can add any distinctness to your idea of God, any beauty to your notion of virtue; if I can represent the life of Christ in such vivid and true colours as to exalt your love; if I can persuade one young man to check the running tide of sensual pleasure by the force of moral obligation; if I can prevail with one old man to forgive an injury that has rankled in his breast till hatred has grown into habit, out of regard to the example of Jesus and his law of love; if I can arrest one angry sarcasm of wounded pride in the moment of irritation, one syllable of slander as it trembles on the tongue, by the memory of the motives I have called to your

6. Cf. Galatians 6:7.

aid; if a sermon of mine shall be remembered as a solace in the chamber of sorrow; if, when the eye of one of you is closing forever on this world, your spirit, as it passes, shall thank me for one triumphant hope,—then, my brethren, it is praise enough; then I shall bless God that I have not been wholly wanting to his cause, that, by me, one mite is added to the sum of happiness.

XXIX

But we preach not ourselves, but Christ Jesus the Lord; and ourselves your servants for Jesus' sake.

II Corinthians 4:5

In the former part of this discourse I considered the two leading public offices of the Christian minister. There remain for our consideration his performance of the sacraments of matrimony, of baptism, and of the Lord's Supper, and his duties as a Pastor. I shall then request your candour to some brief remarks upon the expectations a minister may form, founded on a faithful discharge of his own duties, of sympathy and cooperation in his purposes from the people of his charge.

He is called to bear a part in the most important and solemn occasions that belong to human life. It is his to tie the bands of wedlock, to bind on the part of heaven the league of affections between man and wife necessary to the existence and order of society, to turn the water of a civil, into the wine of a holy, union.[1]

It is his to sprinkle the new-born man with water, to mark the acquisition of one more intelligent being into the great family of the Father of the Universe. There is nothing trifling, nothing insignificant in this event, and baptism is the application of our faith to it. The account that we give of the existence of the human race is the *benevolence* of the Deity who doth not sit in the solitude of his own perfections but rejoices in adding continually and infinitely to the amount of happiness and pouring forth around him the profusion of being and of joy. And surely nothing can be more suitable and right than to mix a religious feeling with the parent's gladness, to consecrate to God this his last creation, to set His name and his Son's name on the forehead of the new moral agent now in the morning of the immeasurable day of his action and virtue.

Of a very different character and interest is the other rite of Christian usage. The Lord's Supper is usually regarded, and I think not with sufficient reason, as a melancholy memorial. It commemorates, we say, the *dying love* of Christ. Yes, but he has conquered death, and he, the Head of the Church who bends over us as we sit at his board, is now our Friend and Intercessor at his Father's throne. But with whatever associations we come, it commemorates his love and so

---

Completed March 13, 1829, at Emerson's home in North Allen Street. Preached once, at the Second Church, Boston, on the afternoon of March 15, 1829. It is the sequel to Sermon XXVIII.

1. Cf. John 2:3–9

comes with an aspect that to most minds the other injunctions of religion do not wear. This is the symbol of a holy affection. And so it opens the doors of the heart. He, therefore, who adventures to break the bread and pour out the waters of life should be himself susceptible of emotion. The minister should be a man of feeling, or I fear he will vainly endeavour to excite movements in other souls that have no archetypes in his own.

But, brethren, you have not called me only to read and unfold to you, according to my ability, the oracles of God, and to discharge the customary public functions of marriage, of baptism, and breaking of bread in the name of Christ; you have called me to affectionate and *domestic* relations as your pastor.

This day is in all things to me a day of hope. Whilst I am permitted to speak of myself, I am rather describing to you my hopes than my expectations. I can easily conceive a perfection in the performance of a minister's duties which far exceeds the low limit of my powers. But we must aim high to secure any good. It is better to fail in our efforts in a good cause, than not to have striven in it. Suffer me then whilst I run over with curiosity and hope the scene that opens before me.

In order to be of any use to you as a pastor I must be regarded in a just light.

It is fatal to that success which a good pastor can look for when he is eyed as an austere zealot whose severe eye is always wary to pick flaws in your practice and error in your doctrine, who is always eager to bring you to the confessional, who strikes prattling childhood dumb with awe and disgusts light hearted youth; a man whose mouth is full of menace; who is the tyrant of sick beds; and the tormentor of the dying. He forgets that he is the messenger of the Prince of Peace; the Herald of glad tidings of great joy, that whilst he knows the terrors of the law he should *persuade* men.

Nor less when he is regarded as a man aloof from other men, a peculiar officer, important when his own occasions come, but out of place where health and enterprize and friendship meet; whose form is contemned in the sunshine of ease and only grateful in the shade of a cloud.

Not thus must the pastor be esteemed, who can hope to serve you in Jesus Christ, but as the mild and blameless friend who would win you to a life of purity by the shining example of his own; who does not affect to hate the good and the glory of this world, but has been led by the very lustre and harmony of things below, to the belief in something better; who sees with an affectionate eye your prosperity, and seeing it harmonize with his views of a Providence always secretly directing the succession of human affairs, desires to come and tell you so and bid you thank God and not your own right hand: who sees with emotion your affliction, and seeing by his own experience how it can be made to redound to your good, how, when a little time has passed, you may be made to bless God that it came to you, comes in, with sorrow as a man, for your pain, but with triumph as a Christian, in that clear and strong hope which conquers calamity and conquers death.

But the condition of man has one hour further of yet more solemn interest than the affliction that strikes nearest to us. The hour will come to yourself to die. It will come to each of us. It belongs to God's order—which we call nature—as much as hunger or sleep. Here, under the canopy of heaven, we grow up, we ripen to manhood, and we decay. In a few years or months or days the symptoms of that change will appear in you. The alarm will sound in the ear of your mind, that you have done with men, and men have done with you. You will be withdrawn by a weakness you cannot stimulate, from the living crowd that fill the street. In your various places of resort, you shall be sought but you shall not be found.[2] In the shop, along the wharves, in the bank, on the exchange, in the courts, in social parties, in the church—you shall be missed. You have retreated to your chamber to a solitude which the world cannot relieve. I say you are alone; it is true you are nursed by the cares and assured of the sympathies of your friends. They knock at your door and they offer you— what men can. But alas, my brother, is that solitude less? When the system is convulsed with its last throbs, when all the aids of nature and art have been exhausted in vain—is not he alone who sees the shades of the last night shutting down over his senses, though the whole world environed his bed, and armies of friends cry out at his side? What would it avail? Can they hold him back? Ah, my brethren, at that hour wealth and poverty, genius, power and wretchedness, are all alike; even friendship bewails its weakness, and the dearest affection— what can it do? One medicine there is, one solace, one hope. Into that solitude the man of God shall introduce a sweeter society than the merriment of health has ever made; into that darkness of this world the good pastor shall let in the light of another. Yes, brethren, when God enables him to reach the ends of his blameless ambition, the good pastor may illuminate with glory the gloom of the chamber of death. In that hour, at least, when trifles are neglected and cere- mony is forgot, I hope to be understood and esteemed as an effectual friend, that the tidings which I bring, that the cause in whose strength I come, will give power to my weakness. I that am your fellow in the same fate by God appointed will endeavour to quicken your faith by the same motives that sustain my own. We will talk of the Resurrection from the Dead. We will call to mind the words of the Friend of the human race to his elder disciples, 'Yet a little while and ye shall see me.'[3] We will think of the love he bore us. We will comfort one another by the thought of the benevolence of God which having encompassed us with so many blessings here, may surely be trusted with our future welfare. We will talk of the new heavens and the new Earth,[4] till the earth shall fade before the magnificence of the growing vision. Across the darkness so long dreaded of the valley of death,[5] we will behold the Mount of our Hope lifting its everlasting summits into light. And though our flesh fail and our heart fail, we will rejoice in the Lord, we will glory in the God of our Salvation.[6]

I dwell on this capital duty of the Pastor because it is the reason why pastors

2. Cf. John 7:34.
3. John 16:16.
4. II Peter 3:13.
5. Cf. Psalms 23:4.
6. Cf. Psalms 73:26 and Habakkuk 3:18.

are made. For the hour of death all other hours prepare. Why are we here? What else is the motive of all this apparatus of a clergy and worship; why do the sabbath bells sound, and whence is the interest so bright and so tremendous of this Book? If we did not die, there were no need of religious monitors to prick us on to duty. If we did not die, life in its long course would be sermon and monitor enough; the moral laws of God would assert themselves by their effects: virtue would be seen to produce happiness, and the want of virtue to inflict woe, as undeniably as the sun produces light and the absence of the sun produces darkness. But life is short and we hardly get over its illusions before it is time to put on our shroud. God calls and eternity presses on us whilst we lose our time in the ancient mistake, pursuing seeming for solid good.

Hence the need of loud alarms of bibles, of tracts, of prayers, of churches, of ministers, of afflictions, of pains.

These, brethren, are the scenes and occasions of pastoral duty. And it is a consideration of much importance that the habits of the pastor are essential to a faithful and successful preacher. Human nature is so much the same in all its forms that a man who draws with any accuracy his pictures of virtue and vice from such a range of acquaintance as most men possess, will continually present traits and dispositions which you recognize as familiar to your own experience. When he drew the character of his friend, it tallied with the character of yours. Still the preaching of a stranger must always be cold and unaffecting in comparison with the preaching of the pastor. For he sees only the outside of the people. He has no light to guide him in the selection of topics. Many of his exhortations must be aimed at random, and when he has reached the heart, he is ignorant of his success, and again is ignorant that he has gone wide of the mark. But when he has come into your acquaintance, when he has sat by your fire and established relations of friendship and confidence with you, when he knows the story of your lives, what you suffer and what you hope, your reputation in the town and the prospects of your children, then he possesses a key to your hearts, he knows the good man's urgent motive, he knows the sinner's vulnerable side, he knows the doubt that perplexes you, what secret satisfaction you nourish, and to what virtues you most incline. He will find the subjects of his exhortation in your sick chambers, and bereaved houses, in your parlour, and in the societies to which you belong. Besides, when he comes into the pulpit, he comes into the midst of his friends; and he knows their goodwill has prepared a welcome for his message, a kind interpretation to his remarks. He is sure of being understood. They are familiar with his modes of thought and will not complain of a vague and uncertain impression because they know he is to return from the pulpit to their fireside, and is always ready to explain in the parlour what was obscure in the desk. It is abundantly plain what additional force and effect his preaching must derive from these facts.

It is usual on occasions like the present for the new pastor to disclose to his people his views of their duty in relation to himself. I have spoken so long upon my own duties that I have left myself little time to remind you of yours. It can be the more easily excused because (to use that ancient and hallowed metaphor) I do not come to reclaim sheep that wander in the wilderness without a shepherd[7]—but I come to do in weakness what has been done in strength, to help, as I can, the spiritual progress of those who have loved their spiritual guide as he deserved to be loved, and have never been wanting to him.[8] I doubt not, brethren, of your readiness to extend to me every reasonable indulgence and all cordial cooperation in every good word and work. Still there is an expectation that will operate unfavorably on my inexperience, arising from the very signal merits which have created among you so warm a sympathy in your minister. I cannot leave this allusion without one remark. I am not permitted at this hour to indulge myself in dwelling on the virtues of my elder brother. It is well. They need no praise. I am permitted to congratulate you and myself that his counsel and sympathy are not withdrawn; to believe that whilst he exists his heart is here, his prayers and his hopes shall be blended with ours. But I must beseech you, brethren, to consider that no man can suddenly be a good pastor. It is an office in which experience is more necessary than any gifts. You must overlook many mistakes. You must forgive many seeming neglects. You must forgive many real omissions. You must impute a good purpose where you can, and the moment that even charity cannot find a palliation for an action of mine, you must frankly come and tell me my fault. Confidence invites confidence, and I earnestly desire that between you and me no strangeness or reserve should ever exist. I hope to be received on the footing of familiar acquaintance in your houses, and to be sought without ceremony in mine.

Let it be considered by you, brethren, how essential it is to every hope of making me useful to you that the freest intercourse should subsist between us. If then the young have any project, any purpose which I can aid, let them be deterred by no mistimed scruples from coming to me as to a brother who is anxious to serve them. If those who have reached mature age, if those who are grown old, have any counsel to impart, have any anxiety, any doubt, any coldness of faith, let them in kindness inform me, assured that my diligence shall not be wanting to them.

In fine, brethren, give me your countenance, your sympathy, your counsels, and your prayers. And forget the imperfections of the workman in your interest in his work, remembering that we are ambassadors for Christ, as though God did beseech you, by us; that we pray you in Christ's stead, Be ye reconciled to God.[9]

And now, brethren, I enter on my duties with all good hope, but without levity and without presumption. I feel the force of the vows that are on me, to work the work of him that sends me, in prosperity and in adversity, in honour

7. The source of the metaphor is the parable of the good shepherd in John 10. Cf. Matthew 9:36 and Mark 6:34.

8. The Rev. Henry Ware, Jr., Emerson's senior pastor at the Second Church.

9. II Corinthians 5:20. As the manuscript indicates, this verse was Emerson's first choice as sermon text, but he canceled it in favor of II Corinthians 4:5.

and in reproach, by speech and by action, from year to year, as long as God shall endue me with strength and opportunity. I feel the encouragements, I hear the warnings that come to me, as I approach, a youth and a stranger to this ancient temple. I seem to tread on holy ground. I raise this day a feeble voice in walls that have echoed the voices of the elder saints and holy fathers of the New England Church.[10] Do we err, brethren, in deeming that their glorified spirits encompass our assembly, and delight in the places whence the incense of their prayers ascended? They call on you, they call on me, to make clean and holy the hands that are to lift up, in our day and generation, the ark of their testimony. They call to us, to aspire to the glory they now partake, by the same steps on which they mounted, by faith, by obedience, by prayer, and by love.

10. The Second Church was gathered in 1650; Increase and Cotton Mather were among its first ministers.

XXX

While we look not at the things which are seen, but at the things which are not seen, for the things which are seen, are temporal, but the things which are not seen, are eternal.

II CORINTHIANS 4:18

In the beginning of life we are wholly occupied with what is perceived by the senses. The light of day, our food, the faces that surround us, and the nearest objects absorb the whole attention of the infant. As the apprentice to a mechanical craft must first learn how to use his implements, so it is with us. Though the infinite work of thought and duty be our main business, yet the world of matter in which we live, objects of sense, are our tools of art and our materials, and so, 'tis every way proper that the first thing we should be taught is their use; just as the child, who is learning to read, studies pages of unmeaning combinations of letters, that themselves are nothing, but are by and by to enable him to read what is of utility. What we see, taste, touch, hear, and smell, is for some time all we know. All that is bright dazzles; all that is loud, commands our notice. A coral bauble, a bright bead, is happiness enough. A child values a red apple above a kingdom.[1] As we advance however into life and the kingdom within us begins more and more to appear, we begin to catch the pleasant hint that there's something else in the world beside colour and bodies, that more is meant than meets the ear.[2] We begin to find that the objects of sense are rather the occasions and materials of thought than the ends to which we think—that is, to which we live.

We begin to exist in the great world of ideas, of recollections, of purposes, of knowledge, and to perceive that the external world is only hands and feet to the internal world. The Spirit that is native of an infinite creation begins to grow impatient of a finite scene. The affections open and the intellect toils.

As our minds expand by knowledge, we necessarily discern beyond each object itself, its bearings and relations to other objects, and we come to value

---

Manuscript dated March 21, 1829, at North Allen Street. Preached twice: March 22, 1829, and May 30, 1830, on both occasions at the Second Church, Boston.

1. *JMN* 6:80.
2. Milton, "Il Penseroso," line 120.

244

things, not for themselves, but according to their powers. Every object, besides that it is large, or soft, or of one or another color or taste, we find is a symbol of something else. In looking at a watch, the child delights in the chased and polished case, in the seals and rings and moving wheels; the man only esteems what is the result of all, the precision with which he ascertains the passage of time. And not only does one eye rest on the type, and another on the thing typified; but, the same object will suggest very different thoughts to different minds, according to their unequal elevation and unlike habits. Take a piece of coin, a silver dollar, and show it to ten persons and what a strange difference there will be in the thoughts it will excite in their breasts. One man will be reminded by it of that which was his last necessity of a piece of furniture or an article of dress he would procure; another thinks of some trifling sensual accommodation which his palate chances to crave; another remembers a book which he means to possess. Another imagines how the eye of his poor depen- dant would beam with gratitude for comforts which this trifling gift would secure, and last of all is one, that unhappy madman, the miser, who thinks of nothing farther than what his eye sees; who thinks of no symbol, of no unseen world, who sees a round piece of silver and no more, and desires that thing for its own worthless sake. Now this single illustration may serve to show how little the thoughts of any one are confined simply to what the eye beholds, for, though the object is the same to all in all the instances except the last, the mind leaps from what is present to what is absent, and in every direction.

Indeed when it is well considered it may be truly said that, in some sense, all men live very much more in the unseen world than in the visible—that is, derive more pain and more pleasure from their recollection of what is past and their anticipation of what is to come, than from what is now before them. Hence the power of all familiar things. Go into a room in which once you lived, but which for years you have not visited, and without any conversation, without any action, the bare sight of certain articles of furniture, a picture, a certain colour of the walls, will move you more than the deepest tragedy that genius ever drew. It is not what is present but what is absent, that so stirs the blood. For precisely the same scene will be surveyed by a stranger with entire indifference.

There are innumerable illustrations of this fact of the immense difference in the amount of meaning which the same spectacle suggests to the instructed eye and to another. In every large body of men how many interests are collected not obvious to any mind that is not acquainted with all. When lately I had occasion in this place to allude to the advantage which the pastor of a society has over a stranger in the flock,[3] I could not help thinking of the difference of the same spectacle to the eye of your elder pastor and to mine. As he looked along these pews, which I saw only with curiosity, every face was a history to him. In each well known family, he remembered years of desires and of efforts,—how many hopes accomplished and defeated! how many chasms he marked where once he knew the forms on which hope and beauty dwelt, and which were lighted by the

3. See Sermon XXIX.

expression that is in the face of man, of everlasting hope. And here and there what chasms he apprehended, knowing what changes and dangers await and what death watches for you. The biography of families is full of fate. The history of a parish contains the same evidence of God's Providence as the history of an empire. And the longer and more intimate the acquaintance with it, the more deeply interesting is the moral it unfolds.

Now the fact to which I wish to direct your attention is, that, the best part of our being, the only part of our condition worth living for, is the *unseen part;* not the chamber but its associated events, not the clock but the knowledge of time, not the face of man but the character, not the chemical atoms of the world but the harmony and the design—and benevolent design—which they are made to discover.

I have said that in some sense all men live more in the invisible world than in the visible. For the most abandoned sensualist strives to be happy in the contemplation of absent pleasures. But it is needless to say that the meaning of the apostle in our text is restricted to the highest sense of unseen things, to the contemplation of what is perceived by the soul and cannot be perceived by the senses.

The higher you ascend in the scale of being the more is the influence felt of unseen things. God is a pure spirit and acts spiritually, and the richest blessings he imparts are spiritual gifts.

Of consequence, all true greatness consists in emancipation from the dominion of objects of sense and in living in the unseen world. We never do any thing noble except by a strong predominance of thought over sensible objects. All that ever kindles a generous glow in the countenance is the sacrifice of the seen to the unseen, of the dead matter to the living spirit. The hero who boldly meets the bayonet and bullet doth thus by fixing a stronger regard upon thoughts than upon things, upon the ideas of his country and his own honour than upon all the advantages which life can offer him. The martyr beholds heaven in his soul and gives his body to the faggot; and there is greater in honour than he; for the flames of his torture are a bed of glory, in the eye of a stricken, admiring and remembering populace. But there are sufferers sustained by the same hope in yet severer trials. There is many a pious daughter of sorrow in hovels and almshouses who nurses the fretful and unpleasing bed of age and who wastes her years in a long and *unpraised* martyrdom, without one murmur, without one petulant syllable, though summers pass without fruit or joy to her, and winters without the social face of friends. Why doth she thus? She does it for God's sake, she does it for the sake of the unseen world, to which she looks, to which she aspires, wherein she finds and shall find her reward. Many a son of adversity is condemned to eat the bitter bread of dependance and yet keeps the soul erect.

There was an ancient hero who on hearing the king of Persia called the Great King inquired, "How is he greater than I, if he is not more just?"4 This was

4. Emerson may have found this anecdote in Plutarch's *Morals*, ed. William W. Goodwin

looking to the things unseen.

Therefore always the scientific man who explores the unseen relations of things seen; the scholar whose acquaintance is with the sentiments and learning of departed men; the philosopher who leaves the appearance to find the causes of action; and the Christian who acts as under the eye of a cloud of invisible witnesses, and of God the judge of all,[5] therefore are all these respectable, as so far removed, on the one side, from the childhood of being, from the state of infants and of brutes, and as so far approximated, on the other side, to spirits, and to God.

In short, it may be said, that, just in proportion as we abstract ourselves from things seen, and study things unseen, in precisely the same ratio, we grow great and good, by advancing to the ends of our being. The grovelling voluptuary is one who looks no farther than the present gratification. As he seeks his pleasures with more regard to consequences, he becomes a refined epicurean. As he takes into view still more and farther considerations, he becomes a philosopher; when he includes eternity in his scheme of action he becomes a Christian.

Now the great doctrine which we teach, the sum of the gospel of Christ and the Resurrection from the dead, is that men ought to live as looking not at the things that are seen but at the things that are not seen, for the things which are seen perish, but the things which are not seen are everlasting. It adds an immense importance to every action we perform by lifting the veil of the future, and showing it linked to consequences multiplying and magnifying without diminution and without end. It encompasses every solitude with an everliving society. It alters the face of all action, belittling what is done in crowds and in day, and crowning with dignity and beauty what is done by the obscure in obscure places, deeds of the right hand which the left hand did not know.[6] In the decay of nature it comes to man in his last hour and strangely transforms the signs of suffering to symbols of joy, clothes with ethereal strength that fainting form, turns the last hour of this world to the first hour, the bursting youth of infinite being. This is that great doctrine of Faith preached to the Gentiles by the Apostle Paul, the Faith that enters within the vail,[7] purifies the heart, that worketh by love, by which we are justified, and by which we are saved.

Hence too the whole value of the Christian ordinances. It is this way of viewing things that gives all its sacredness and all its tenderness to the rite of our Lord's Supper. What we see is the type of what we know. We eat bread and drink wine in memory of one whom mortal eyes cannot behold, and if there were nothing but what we see how vain and frivolous a ceremony were this. But the Christian faith quickens the dead body of a rite with a living soul. It awakens all the affectionate and reverential recollections that attach to our Saviour's name and life and death. It invokes his presence. It asks for his inter-

---

(Boston, 1870), 1:219, 1:371, 2:319, 2:455, or in Plutarch's "Life of Agesilaus." See *JMN* 4:50, 4:342; used in "George Fox," *EL* 1:167 and in "Politics," *EL* 2:70.

5. Hebrews 12:1, 12:23.
6. Matthew 6:3.
7. Hebrews 6:19.

cession. It smites us with the memory of our own guilt. It exhorts us to penitence, to reformation, to virtue, to hope, to triumphant faith. Not unworthily,
not in vain then shall we have partaken in this simple memorial, if, when we
arise to go out from the ordinance we depart with truer sorrow for our imperfection and better purposes for the future than we brought in hither.

Therefore, brethren, let me exhort you to look not at the things that are seen,
but at the things which are not seen. Consider that all elevation of character
consists in a steadfast regard to the mind, to the motive, to the moral colour of
actions, and not to their outside. Consider that the objects which are seen, the
garments you wear, the house you inhabit, and the house of your own flesh, the
limbs of your strength, the form and the face, of whose comeliness you are so
vain, and for whose support and delight you so curiously and daintily provide,
must very shortly perish, or if they last a little while yet they are not *yourself*,
they are but the shell in which now you abide and which you must presently
leave forever. You must die and go—where? Into another condition of visible
things? into another city of pleasant accommodations? to wake up again in
other worlds, the chase of appetites, the pursuit of flying pleasures? once more
to follow worldly gain? once more to be poor or rich, as you have or as you want
land and gold? Oh no! God forbid it. We are going into the world of unseen and
eternal things. We are going where nothing exists, but moral distinctions, to a
condition which he cannot now conceive, whose thoughts are chained to flesh
and sense; to a spiritual house, to the enjoyment of the love of God, to the
perception of his wisdom, and to the emulous imitation of his infinite perfections. Do you not see hence what is the best preparation for the place to which
we pass? That he who is yet in the bondage of the flesh, who thinks of the relish
of certain meats and the flavor of certain drinks, of base heightenings which he
calls refinements of luxury—must be dark and miserable where these gross
pleasures cease? but he who dwells in a pure atmosphere considering things that
can neither be eaten or drunken or touched or seen, upon whose soul the
Universe is pouring already its calm and full glory, upon whose soul the presence of God is felt as the society of a friend, though awful, yet pleasing, is now
prepared for that other life.

My brethren, I wish I might prevail with you to carry into every hour this
spiritual sight. It should teach a contempt of trifles; it should teach a hatred of
sin. It is of little moment how you look. It is of vast consequence how you feel.
By only opening the eye of your mind to a consciousness of the presence of that
Being who never shuts His eye on you, you shall learn to raise your practice to
your duty. You shall find that those actions are not the best, for which you are
praised the most but it shall cheer you in the persevering performance of many a
humble exertion, (if need be) of many a menial office, many a forgotten and
thankless benefit, knowing that the spirit of love and duty in which it is done, is
a conquering ennobling principle, which, by the necessity of moral nature

uplifts you continually among the children of God. The doors of Heaven are always open to you. You may enter on its felicities before you have passed out of mortal life, if only you will unite yourself to your Maker by doing his will, by lightly esteeming the delusions of sense, and sacredly watching the intimations of the soul.

XXXI

Whatsoever thy hand findeth to do, do it with thy might.

ECCLESIASTES 9:10

You must often have remarked, my Christian friends, the strange disagreement in the descriptions given by men of human life. Solomon bitterly calls it vanity and vexation of spirit,[1] and the sacred writers generally, paint it with a gloomy pencil that loves the shades. Men stricken with misfortune, bereaved and poor and disheartened, are very apt, in the gloom of indigence, to cast the blame on a partial Providence, to forget to look for the causes of their trouble into themselves, and indeed to charge the evil on the Order of things with the more acrimony that it may not be suspected that they deserved the disasters they have met. The world they say is a great hospital—what you call its pleasures—they are only alleviations, it is full of all forms of disease; in its spaciousest walks you shall detect indisputable marks of severe suffering hard by, and at every turn terror and famine and madness peep out and alarm you. So says repining age, so says unsanctified affliction.

But to other eyes it wears another face. Human life is described by the young and hopeful, by those who have much and who hope much, who are at ease, whose stomach is full of meat, whose sleep is sound and whose heart is light, as a place of pleasure, one delightful dream in which whatsoever we want doth straightway appear. Man is painted as the prospered child of Heaven which had clothed him with beauty, and armed him with strength. How fair, they said, was the morning of his youth, how bright the promise of his powers, opening under the sunshine of favour and hope. How excellent the affections which glowed in his cheek and gave grace to his manners and whispered to his heart a cheerful promise of pleasure and praise.

And then when the maturity of his manhood arrived and he stood up in the face of heaven, the master of all its gifts, accomplished with so many divine

---

Completed March 26, 1829, at Emerson's home in North Allen Street. Preached ten times: March 29, 1829, at the Second Church, Boston; April 5 at the Purchase Street Church; April 12 in Waltham; April 26 in West Cambridge; May 10 at the First Church, Boston; May 17 at the First Church, Salem; June 21 in Concord, N.H.; July 19 in Roxbury; September 13 in Springfield; and June 20, 1830, at the Second Church, Boston.

1. Solomon's refrain in Ecclesiastes; see 1:14, for example.

faculties, the true Image of God, Behold, they said, his arts! See, how the winds are his wings and the sea his path from nation to nation of his mighty race. And the idle powers of nature no more shall waste their energies, the fire, the steam, the waterfall, the spring of steel are become his day laborers. See how he changes the face of the earth and channels the land with artificial rivers and builds out his cities like wharves into the deep.

See how nobly he is provided! the arch of heaven vaulted over his head and the green earth lighted by the sun and the moon, spread as a garden out to the horizon.

But I need not, my friends, describe to you the good and evil of man. I speak to men. In stronger lines than I can draw, the picture lies already in the memory of each individual. You know what Death and Pleasure mean. Yourselves have tasted the mixture of the cup, you have known what men loved and what they hated in the world.

These descriptions answer rather to different hours in every experience, to different moods of the same mind, than to any radical dissimilarity in the perceptions of men. And at least we may hope that to what extent soever this difference of thinking with respect to our external condition may go, we can unite in our sentiments concerning the object of our being placed here.

Men say, grant that you have described the house well, but what is it for? We will take the most favourable picture, but the Universe was not made for recreation. Life was not given without some sufficient end. If the mansion is so grand, the grander is the purpose. When talents are imparted, an usury is to be paid. When a labourer is hired he is hired for a work. Life is serious and was given in stern earnest.[2] Something is to be done. What is this work? What is to be done?

These are grave and momentous questions which it behoves us all to put and to which all theology aims to reply. There certainly does not appear that unanimity of sentiment at the first sight which every sound mind would suppose should exist in men on a question of this commanding interest. It should affect the whole race as one man. Yet I believe the difference of opinion is more seeming than real. With great show of irreconcileable contradiction in their language, with a painful number of sects and heresies, after all is seen and all is sifted—their meaning is one.

Our passions so readily blend themselves with our opinions that we can hardly help exaggerating the importance of any truth we receive which others do not receive. And I know well that large classes of Christians at different times and even in our times have included in their statement of essential goodness certain views wholly speculative of the Divine nature and of the human soul which other classes of Christians reject with dislike. But goodness is of no sect. And if you bring together two good men who copy the life of Christ into their life, with whatever diversity of sentiment, when actions are compared and language is explained, you shall always find in them a wonderful consent.

2. Cf. *JMN* 6:87.

Now the true end and proper object of life must be one that reconciles all differences of lot and meets the approbation of every sound mind. As a good man who was menaced with the dangers of the sea, said, "the way to heaven is as short by water as by land,"[3] so, whatever is the true end of life must be one that can be equally attained in every condition and every employment. Now here are two men who dwell side by side with hardly any resemblance in their life. One of them is wholly occupied from sunrise to sunset in mechanical toil; he has no leisure for books, scarcely any for recreation; he goes from his farm or his shop to his meals and to his bed. Thus he does day by day for thirty or forty years. The other man surrounds himself with books; he never lays his hand upon the chisel or the axe but spends his whole time in literary or scientific speculations. What is true of these individuals is true of vast numbers.

Now here are two classes of the same race, two occupations, how unlike! of the same immortal reason. And the question immediately rises, Is any thing common to both? or, if the first is fitting for heaven, how can the second be also?

Now this case (which comes under every inquirer's daily observation) when coupled with false views of religion, has made some people doubt of religion, and then it is sometimes set up in apology by those who seem to suffer by it, by the poor and the busy, and especially by those whose business excuse themselves from a personal interest in the truths of Religion, from knowing its forms, from doing its works, by pleading this very want of time. Now this plea of want of time, so often made—nay, under which we try to shroud from ourselves our own sense of delinquency,—the gospel of Christ and the laws of moral nature do make of none effect. There are places where our fellow men are found and therefore where you might have been placed, where such a plea might have some colour. The ships of our commerce are continually visiting a country larger than the United States and filled with a population nearly five times as numerous, where the positive laws on which the people are taught their salvation hangs, demand of them an intolerable multitude of the silliest ceremonies. The poor Hindoo shall not rise from his bed until he has uttered six several prayers. He is directed on pain of eternal torment what postures he shall assume in his prayer, in his labor, in taking his food. He shall not wash his hand nor his lips without appropriate ceremonies, the most insignificant act cannot be done, until the wearisome folly of sacred postures and sacred words is gone over, and if he comply with his laws the greatest part of life is consumed in these wretched follies.

Now, my brethren, it is not so with us. Our religion which came down from Heaven does not lay this burden on human shoulders. Our religion has one command, one aim, one end; and that is, *Duty*. The business of life to us, to all

3. Originally the words of Friar Elstowe when threatened with drowning by Henry VIII and the Earl of Essex; recorded in John Stow, *The Chronicles of England* (London, 1580), 562. The sentiment was more popularly known as the last words of Sir Humphrey Gilbert, lost with his ship in 1583; see Richard Hakluyt, *The Principal Navigations* (London, 1598–1600), 3:159.

intelligent beings, is not prayer, or psalm, or ceremony, but simply Duty. This is the theory that accounts for every difficulty, that reconciles every seeming incompatibility. This is the answer we offer to the objection just now stated that some occupations preclude the attainments of a religious life inasmuch as they leave no time for them. There is no such occupation. There never was since the world was made the least injunction of religion omitted from want of time. My brethren, the very wonder and excellence of Religion is that it lays claim to all the life without embarrassing one moment of it, that it goes alike with its glorious and cheerful face into the shop and the college and on the sea and into mines and into senates and into lazar-houses, that it never was unseasonable, nowhere an incumbrance, that such is the mode and nature of the preparation we make for heaven that it is made at recreation as well as at prayer, in the corners of streets as on our dying bed. *It is the man that is to be mended*, and not a catechism that he must learn. In obedience to my own convictions, I can never too much insist upon the right view of religious ordinances, that they are only means and not ends. It is not being religious—that you are baptized in the name of God; it is not, that you go to meeting; it is not, that you join the church, that you pray, that you preach; but, only, that your character is good, that your eye is God-ward, that your heart is full of love to man, that your life is a temple full of Christian graces. Pure Religion and undefiled, consists, according to the scripture, in doing good.[4]

There is nothing done but it may be done with this frame of mind. As there is no place where God is not present, so there can be no work which he will not bless, if his blessing is desired. By the performance of duty, by the exact obedience in every action to the dictate of conscience, the mind is brought into the natural, the healthy state; the state of truth; the state in which every mind would wish to be, when it passes out of this into another world. And to gain this state of mind is our business, and not to become learned, or rich, or famous.

What then is the great inference we draw from the view we have just taken? It is briefly told in the words of our text;—*Whatsoever thy hand findeth to do, do it with thy might.* This is the conclusion in which all reasoners of whatever complexion will agree, the melancholy Solomon, and the ardent Paul. This is out of the debateable land of warring sects, within the barrier of mighty truth. This doctrine shines through all the precept and all the practice of Jesus Christ. Whatsoever your hands find to do, do it. Not in solving a doctrine of abstruse sense, not in remote and difficult ways, not in strange lands, not in distant years,—but there, where you stand; there, in your own house, with your brothers and sisters around you, in that employment by which you live, in that spot, in the present hour, your duty, your religion, your salvation lies. There is your place of trial prepared. There, though perhaps you do not yet see it to be so, the witnesses attend; the actions are recorded; and the Judge decides. There, in many a fleeting moment, which in their sum make months and years, by many a

4. Cf. James 1:27.

little unnoticed word and thought, a character is forming, full of peace or full of woe. There if you sin, you fail, and the judgment of God shall follow, and there you may endow yourself with virtues that shall recommend you to the love of all minds. No room is left you, brethren, for repining at your lot. All lots, all conditions, in the eye of heaven, and for the purpose of life, are the same. God will have you stand in a low place without shame, and in a high place without pride. He appoints our degree, by imparting the advantages of parentage, talents, wealth, country, and so on, upon which, what is called success in life depends. But that cannot be success in life, whatever men say of it, by how much soever it may be envied, which fails of life's great end. The grave will shortly cover with its clods the glitter of wealth, the parade of names, and all memory of the distinctions that now rise like mountains between man and man. But then the naked merits of faithful obedience shall survive. O my friends, learn to look at life with God's eye, and not with man's, and remembering that life is short and death is nigh, learn whatsoever your hands find to do, do it with your might.

Forgive us our debts.

MATTHEW 6:12

The difference of opinion between men on all speculative questions is so great that that opinion must have a great share of truth in it which all admit. It is cheering to have a great consent to a great sentiment. If only one man, of all the race, had reasoned out the being of God, and no man acquiesced in the stupendous conclusion; if no sympathy of conviction kindled in the soul, when it saw the features of its Father's face uncovered, still, there could not fail to mingle something of astonishment and something of reverence with our skepticism, when the great Dream was told us. We could not but feel that there was a glory in that dreamer's delusion, that was wanting to the solid vanities on which the thoughts of other men rested.

But if a hermit who, in a lonely desart, untaught by revelation, unacquainted with men, with the glorious face of nature for his book, the seasons, the rivers, and mountains, the beasts of the field, and the birds of the air, for his arguments; and above all, with himself, at once the explorer and the explored, as the materials of his reasoning—if such an one had arrived at a just view of the Divine Mind, and, while his soul was glowing with the revelation, hastened forth to join the congregation of his race, and impart the news to the nations—when he found his opinion to be as old as the human soul, his solitary faith shared and substantiated by the unvarying conviction of all people, would it not seem to him a fortune worthy of the idea, would not this homage of a world, seem to him a celebration every way suitable to the dignity and loveliness of the thought?

There is this universal consent to the existence of God. So far there is unanimity and there it almost stops.

In every nation the degree of civilization affects the character of its worship; the accidents of climate, of language, of manners, of national descent, all contribute their influence to mould and colour the Idea that is entertained of the Father of the Universe. To every mind also is an individuality of religion. A new mind is a new temple, built to the worship of God, with one purpose as all

---

According to a manuscript notation, this sermon was completed on April 3, 1829, at the house on Chardon Street. Preached twice: on April 5, 1829, at the Second Church, Boston, and on June 21 in Concord, N.H. The sermon elaborates a journal entry for December 30, 1828 (*JMN* 3:149).

others, but of different proportions and in the use of differing modes. Every mind worships God after its own predominant humour. The affectionate man pours forth declarations of unlimited love to the supreme object of all affection. The student of nature, the botanist, the chemist, the physician, dwells with delight on the boundless wisdom which builded the world, and looks to a nearer connexion with God as to what promises him a vast enlargement of knowledge. A humble man speaks ever the language of adoration, and says, Lord be merciful to me.[1] The melancholy man fears his power; the injured awaits his justice, the prosperous thanks him for his bounty. But there is one prayer in which all lips unite, all countries, all languages, all classes, all souls, one view of God's relation to us which has the same evidence as his being, this universal and perfect consent. This observation is the knowledge of our imperfection and error; this prayer is *Forgive us our sins*.

It is important that we hold just views concerning the meaning of this universal prayer, and I beg your attention whilst I attempt in a plain manner an analysis of the petition.

Our object is to consider the laws which regulate forgiveness. It is proper first to say that I distinguish between forgiveness as it is expressed in action— which abstains from doing injury and does good to the offender—a duty which is enjoined upon us by the Christian faith—and forgiveness as it is a state of mind from which the other comes, averse to the doing an injury to the offender because it perceives in him an altered mind, and a benevolence to us. This last is the proper and perfect forgiveness. The good action may be done without, but it is then the offspring of a high magnanimity, it is a forced virtue, but the last brings the heart into the matter and then the actions flow naturally and of course.

If a man who has injured you comes to you and entreats your forgiveness, what are the feelings that arise in your mind? Your thoughts run back to the mischief he has done you. He has betrayed the trust which you reposed in him. It may be by a blameable delinquency, after you had laid him under great obligations, he has wasted your estate, broken your credit and beggared your family; or perhaps he has wounded you in your honour, or the honour of your house, by a personal insult; or he has aimed at your character one of those poisoned words that are never forgotten; and now you are called to revolve in your own mind whether you will forgive him, that is, whether you will cease to bear him ill will and can bear him good will instead, and will seek his good, as you seek the good of those you love, by the performance of all friendly offices.

Now the moment you come to this consideration, does not this one fact at once appear to you evident, that whilst the *actions* it enjoins, are in your power, the abstaining from all attempts to injure him, the state of mind is not in your power, *forgiveness must always depend on the state of mind of the offender, and not of the offended?*

---

1. Psalms 41:4.

The natural relation of two minds is of course that of mutual kindness. If two strangers are introduced in society they encounter each other with smiles and readily endeavour to do each other good offices. If two savages meet in the woods, their first impulse is to associate and not to quarrel. So if you are of a sound mind you would be friendly to this offender, if he were not unfriendly to you. But he has discovered by his actions an enmity towards you, that has naturally provoked your resentment. And now his submission and request for your pardon are an indication, surely, that he sees that he is wrong, and you are right; and just so far as these are evidences of the real state of his mind, so far they must have on you an irresistible effect.

For let the injury that was done you, be of the cruelest kind, and wholly irreparable, yet if now his mind is wholly reconciled to you, so that he remembers the action with poignant remorse, and now anxiously seeks to promote your good by all the means in his power, if he finds his own happiness in promoting yours, do you not see that this benevolence on his part, will disarm your vengeance; that this alteration in his mind cannot fail to effect an alteration in yours, that minds are so constituted that you cannot help forgiving him?

It is no matter how dreadful was the outrage done you, because it is not the injury we punish, but the state of mind it discovers. A man has struck you with such violence that the blow has broken one of your limbs. You cannot repress the violence of your anger. If a tree or a stone had fallen upon you and broken the limb, you would not feel any resentment, though the harm is the same; it is only the malignity that excites your anger, that is, only the state of mind, but if the state of mind is changed, so must be the feeling it causes.

Now put yourself in the case of the offender. You are conscious by your own act of wanton ill-nature of having wounded your brother's peace of mind; but time and reflection have placed your action in a new and odious light. In the garden of your shame you hear the voice of God: your conscience upbraids you:[2] you feel in your own mind, every pang that he feels with yet more acuteness. You desire to make every reparation in your power.

You ask his forgiveness with these feelings, and yet observe in him an extreme reserve and suspicion. He meets your heat with coldness, your affection with some remains of fear or contempt. At the same time, there is nothing in yourself which can warrant this distrust. And you feel that this set of feelings in him relates to a past state of mind and is wholly unjust; and you ask, Why he should retain a feeling so improper to the relation between you? The answer is plain, Not that he wishes, or is able to return love with hate, but that he doubts whether your new regard for him is sincere, whether the kind offices you do him are not a mask to hide your soul from him, because you apprehend the effects of his displeasure.

If the man whose forgiveness you entreat could read your thoughts, as you read them, do you not see, he could have no more disposition to injure you, than you have to injure yourself?

2. Cf. Genesis 3:3–10.

Now, my brethren, with this view of the matter, in which I believe we shall all acquiesce, let us carry our inquiry one step farther, and consider the petition when it is made to God. The natural relation of the mind to God, its Parent, the Mind from which it came with all its gifts, is, of course, in the highest degree, intimate and friendly. And the manner in which his love to us is sought and cultivated by us is closely analogous to the way in which we seek the regard of each other, by doing that which we suppose agreeable to him, by yielding up our own will and adopting his, as the rule of our action. But you have done injustice to the relation that subsists between you and this heavenly friend. You have done what you knew to be every way disagreeable to him, and you come now to ask his forgiveness. You say, Forgive us our sins. Now what is the main difference between this supposition and the case that we have just considered, when you craved forgiveness of your fellow? What but this, that here is no disguise, no darkness; that God sees your heart, as you see it. Consider then, my brethren, what is the irresistible conclusion to which we are brought. Here lies the truth, on whose account I have asked your attention to this subject.—Do you not see, that the fact to which just now we were led, returns upon us with overwhelming force, that forgiveness of sin must depend on the state of mind of the offender, not of the offended, that it is not in the power of God to forgive you until with all your heart you desire forgiveness. And therefore that no man ever uttered or ever shall utter the Saviour's prayer, Forgive us our sins, without knowing at the moment of utterance, precisely how far his prayer is granted.

If in the hour when you kneel down and say it, you do truly repent of your sins, if you feel the same disapprobation of vice that is felt by the Deity, and truly resolve to offend no more, then God hears you, then the influences of his Spirit are falling upon you, and you shall arise and depart a better, a purer being.— But if while you say these words the memory of sin is pleasant and it seems to you the old temptation will have its old power, why do you say forgive my sins? It is in vain.

Brethren, I deal in solemn truths. I have no ambition to startle you with sounding paradoxes and therefore I wish your credit and consideration to this doctrine no whit farther than it forces itself on your own conviction. It is built on the nature of man and the revelation of Christ. You may say that when you ask God's forgiveness, you mean you wish to be saved from the consequences of sin already committed. You have deserved, you think, to lose many earthly blessings which yet remain to you and which it may please God to continue. But consider that the main consequences of sin are in the soul that sinned, that all good things may be continued to you, and if the soul is perverted, the relish, the power of enjoyment of all is lost; consider that in the soul itself shall be the Paradise of God,[3] or the abodes of the spirits of hell.

So therefore let it be considered by you, how vain it is to utter a prayer of words, that is not the genuine breathing of your mind. O do not cease to make that prayer, for heaven is in it, but make it with your soul, before you make it

---

3. Cf. Revelation 2:7.

with your lips. Subdue your passions; govern your actions; do what Christ has charged upon you as the condition of your prayer: abstain from injuring men, love other men as yourself,[4] and thus look to it that your heart, as you see it, and as God sees it, is wholly at peace with God, that you do deeply regret your transgression, and love him fervently;—then you shall make that petition with a sublime serenity, and God shall grant it in his mercy ere it has passed your lips.

4. Cf. Leviticus 19:18 and Matthew 19:19.

XXXIII

The wisdom which is from above, is gentle.

JAMES 3:17

I propose to offer to your consideration at this time some remarks upon the value of the duty of gentleness. I would urge this virtue with that moderation which becomes the subject. It is the last subject on which exaggeration or overstatement might be allowed. Still it is a grace of such daily and hourly use in action, in conversation, in manners; in praise, in censure, in opposition, in beneficence, even,—in great actions, in small affairs—that it deserves a good deal of regard. It seems to belong to the state of man. As soon as we come to consider our true condition, how short is the longest life, how feeble and dependant we are, how many faults we have, how little merit, how very likely we are to be in the wrong even when we have measured our way with great circumspection, and how certain we are to be in the wrong if we are positive and angry, we shall see the reasonableness of being gentle. Thus much we shall see by only casting our eyes round the little neighbourhood of things and faces amidst which we live. But if we lift up our eyes to a wider and higher view of being, if we look at the immeasurable existence that lies before us, the vastness of knowledge and the glory of virtue, till we feel the insignificancy of our attainments; and then turn our eyes upon the great Author of all who fills the universe with his goodness and love; who made us fruits and examples of his benevolence; whose tender Providence notices the fall of a sparrow, and numbers the hairs of our head,[1] and who teaches us that the way to serve him is with the heart, then our hearts will warm to each other, and we shall perceive the meaning of the apostle who declared, that, "the wisdom which cometh down from above, is gentle."

Yet, brethren, I need not tell you that this grace of a meek and quiet spirit is not the way of the world. The ignorant eye is caught by pomp and pretension. A

Preached eleven times: April 19, 1829, at the Second Church, Boston; April 30 at the Federal Street Church; May 17 at the First Church, Salem; June 7 in Concord, Mass.; June 21 in Concord, N.H.; July 19 in Roxbury; July 23, 1830, at the Second Church, Boston (Friday Evening Lecture); August 8 in Charlestown; September 26 at the Twelfth Church, Boston; August 21, 1831, in West Cambridge; and March 16, 1834, in New Bedford. Lydia Jackson is said to have first seen Emerson when he preached at the Twelfth Church; the record shows that he conducted services there only once, on September 26, 1830.

1. Matthew 10:29-30 and Luke 12:6-7.

child esteems a swaggering soldier above all the sages on earth. And he that is childish in thought, though grey with years, will be impressed and swayed by violence of words and actions rather than by their reason. Nevertheless there is a power in gentleness that generally makes itself felt and it is rather in our own actions that I would complain of the want of it than of any want in the capacity of men generally to appreciate its value when it is exhibited by others.

In recommending this virtue I would not represent those who want it as wanting all goodness, for I know there have been and there are men who are not gentle and yet are truly great; but I say they would be greater, if they were gentle. Splendid virtues no doubt appear, and shine through all ages, into which gentleness did not enter. Peter, the ardent friend and follower of our Lord—the rebuked yet honoured disciple, though of an infirm and uncertain spirit, yet marked above his brethren as the rock on which the Church should be built, was not gentle.[2] And Luther, who overthrew the power of the church which abused the prophecy to Peter, and confronted for truth's and conscience' sake, all the wrath of the civil and ecclesiastical arm that had crushed the elder reformers,—was not gentle. Yet no one can deny sublime merit to both of these moral heroes. Now it has happened that in view of these and similar characters that have figured in history, the admiration of men has sometimes misled their moral judgments; and when it was seen that they were deficient in this virtue, rather than censure their favourites, men have agreed to contemn the virtue. You will, therefore, sometimes find the remark in histories that in difficult and disastrous times, minds are born suitable to the times—of a sharp and stern character such as danger braces and not shakes, and it is supposed that the mild virtues would unfit them for the emergencies, on which they are called to act. To the conflicts in which they are to engage, the kind feelings would be unseasonable: their language is rough, their manners are savage, their virtue is ferocious. The Puritans who laid the axe to the root of the English tyranny in Church and State, and who established civilization and Christianity in America, were men of this stamp.

To all this glozing of human imperfection I wish to express my hearty dissent. I do not believe that the graces of the Christian character are ever incompatible with its most robust strength and highest majesty. I believe its strength is infirm, and its majesty incomplete, without them. Virtue is consistent with virtue. To say that the delicacy of feeling which is Christian gentleness would disqualify men for heroic action, is to say that the wisdom which cometh down from above is sometimes out of place, that in the little knots of human affairs matters are often pending of such prodigious import that the eternal laws of the moral universe are for the time suspended, that virtue ceases to be virtue, and that which was great becomes mean.

Let us not be deceived. This were a strange misapprehension of the divine laws that govern and make the perfection of human character. They never

2. Cf. Matthew 16:18.

diminish nor accommodate nor alter. They are the same yesterday, today, and forever.[3]

There is no character in which the want of gentleness is not a defect. Power becomes tyranny wherever its exercise is not tempered by kindness. You all know the famous sentence uttered by Luther when his friends endeavoured to dissuade him from going to the Diet of the States, at Worms, when summoned thither on the charge of heresy, by representing the manifest danger of his life. He replied in language so harsh as could not be repeated, but for the heroism of the sentiment: "I will go to Worms, though there be as many devils on the road, as there be tiles on the houses of that city."[4] Now I ask if there would not have been more sublimity in the action, if, with the same resolution, he had forborne this ungentle expression. Does it not indicate a greater man to perform great actions with the same ease as if they were trifles than to do them with parade and the sound of trumpet?[5] It is written in the book of Judges, of Samson, that he slew a lion on his way, and passed on and told neither father nor mother of it.[6] It is written in the epistle of Jude that "Michael the Archangel, contending with the Adversary, durst not bring against him a railing accusation, but said, The Lord rebuke thee."[7] But if you would know the whole beauty and power of the grace the gospel teaches, you shall read it in all the life and in the death of our Lord, a man in whom the benevolence of the Father beamed, who took the children in his arms, who when he was reviled, reviled not again, and when all that hatred and wrath of man could do was done on Calvary, said, as he hung amidst his murderers, Father forgive them.[8] And in allusion to his character as well as to his sufferings he is called the *Lamb* of God.[9]

There are two reasons why we should cultivate this virtue, first, because it will be of great service to us in all our intercourse with men; and, secondly, because it is enjoined on us by God's law as an essential part of the religious character. (I say two reasons—whilst perhaps it would be more just to resolve them into one.)

Gentleness is of the greatest service to us in all our intercourse with men. It is safe to be gentle. He that walks modestly will not be likely to be overturned by a rude encounter. And you will never be ashamed of having been gentle.

What should chiefly recommend it is that it is one of these *house-virtues*, not one of the ostentatious ornaments kept for great days and public places, but always wanted, always in use to make happy hours at home. All endowments are poor without it. There is no house so spacious, no advantages of condition

---

3. Cf. Hebrews 13:8.
4. Emerson may have encountered this frequently quoted remark (from a letter of March 5, 1522) in John Frederick William Tischer, *The Life, Deeds and Opinions of Dr. Martin Luther*, trans. John Kortz (Hudson, N.Y., 1818), 32–33. Used in "Martin Luther," *EL* 1:125.
5. Cf. Matthew 6:2.
6. Judges 14:5–6.
7. Jude 1:9.
8. I Peter 2:23 and Luke 23:34.
9. John 1:29.

so signal but the little worm of ill nature will eat out the pith and heart of all their sweetness. Beauty is good, but the charm of gentleness will outlast the charm of beauty; and genius is precious, but those who dwell under the same roof, will often hold genius cheap when it fails in this grace. There is a continual tendency in man to the exaggeration of himself, and to foolish desire that all others should fall down and worship the manners, the opinions, the actions, which he has set up. Now gentleness is the proper preservative and antidote that throws all things into the safe mean, and secures men from that towering and quarrelsome confidence which is at once the cause and the omen of overthrow. Minds of unlike and averse inclination, that without it should perpetually thwart and pain each other, may put on this grace and live side by side. It is the oil that is poured in to prevent friction in the machinery of society.

And yet after all that reason and religion can say, you may go into many a family and see men who move about, the spoilers of peace, the hinderers of happiness under their own roof,—stern, irritable, peevish people, whom every trivial inconvenience, every petty domestic delay, goads into rage, who are ambitious to be hated,—the tyrants of their family board, and the friends and the children of their own blood sit around in unsocial chagrin—scared into silence. Alas for that man who is so jealous of his own importance, as to meet every observation, every sally of pleasantry, with a fierce rebuff; who erects the standard of contradiction in every conversation in which he engages. He does not see that he is an object of surprize and pity to every one that comes within his doors; that we wonder how he can contrive to make so many people unhappy. And what if those who indulge this most unhappy habit of mind, enjoy in their turn, starts of good humour, have holiday hours, and bursts of merriment; it is no atonement, and very poor dependance.

A joyful event, the acquisition of a great blessing, will fill the ill tempered man with kindness which overflows on all around him. But 'tis only an April day of good humour. What is the value of good fortune and the divine bounty to him whose best complacence is a tower of cards which a breath can bring down, when so small an accident as the delay of a meal, or the violent shutting of a door will introduce a tempest of passion into his immortal mind? The cloud shuts down over his soul, and hides from his view his own dignity and his own duty, the love of man and the fear of God.

There is yet another case which I think is much more common than the last, in which ungentleness appears as a sin of Conversation, and which is equally rebuked by common sense and by the Christian faith. It is apt to appear among members of the same family, among young men and women who do not feel any important interest in cultivating each other's regard. When they are abroad under the eye of society they are kept from impertinence and bickering by the fear of offending others; but they foolishly put off that restraint at home, and are apt, in every petty question that turns up, to fly to the argument *ad-hominem*, as it is called in books, that is, to a personal charge. They cavil and contradict, reddening as they go, deeper and deeper into abusive dispute; and sour looks, and long periods of sulkiness, follow sometimes for weeks, in consequence of a little difference of information about an insignificant fact. "A soft answer turneth away wrath," said Solomon,[10] and oh, what deep contrition, what long unavailing remorse would the seasonable remembrance of this easy lesson have saved to those who have mourned over disappointed affections, over families divided by a succession of little affronts, of pitiful altercations, of disgraceful obstinacies in trifles! All the strength of the social principle, which God made the bliss of life, is thus turned by the perversity of man into his bane, for to its full amount, it is here a source of chagrin.

There is no manner of life where this grace will not prove to you a rich blessing. As has been intimated before, it will not weaken the character it adorns. The greatest gentleness is consistent with the greatest firmness of character. It is related of a distinguished English statesman in the court of King James I, that he was gentle almost to effeminacy in his manners, but when some older courtiers attempted to put affronts on him, they found his courtesy was only a mask over the most terrible determination that ever lived in man.[11] The gentleness we teach goes deeper than this, and affects the heart as well as the manners. It teaches a patience that conquers suffering and the forgiveness of injuries. But it leaves all the sinews of the character in their original strength, and adds to them the might of a divine principle, to make them equal to the whole work of Duty.

(Now, brethren, whilst I earnestly commend this grace I do not speak of gentleness as in itself a great virtue, as always implying great merit, but I say it is an essential part of virtue—an essential part of a perfect character and is a peerless ornament. It does not imply great merit for it is often constitutional and then is a felicity not a merit. But if your neighbour has received at his birth an ample estate and you have received an even temper, your blessing is greater than his. But it is in no man so richly native that it does not need his constant care that the crosses of life shall not ruffle it. Virtues are not bequeathed to us "*in tail*"—so that they cannot be alienated. None is so firmly ours as not to need the careful attention of every day to its existence.)

Now, brethren, the apostle in our text declares that the wisdom which cometh down from above is gentle. In our exertions, therefore, to attain the heavenly wisdom, let us first array ourselves in this white garment. God has commanded us to strive to make ourselves perfect, and we, with the example of our master before us, are aiming, I hope, to be so. Let us then carefully keep this commandment which grows out of the law of the love of our neighbour. Let us keep the rein on pride; and guard our actions; and oh, let charity stand sentinel over our tongue. Words, rash proud angry words, are the mischief makers, whose activity gentleness will check. And the best way of restraining

10. Proverbs 15:1.

11. This sentence is used in "Manners," *EL* 2:138, where the statesman is identified as George Villiers, first Duke of Buckingham (1592–1628), the leading courtier and personal favorite of James I. Used also in "Race," in *English Traits*, W 5:68.

them, and to teach ourselves Gentleness, is the habit of Consideration. And if you will let me offer a rule to aid your progress in this grace it will be this, accustom yourself to ponder safe things before you utter them, and that shall induce the habit of pondering unsafe things, and so leave you the power to forbear to speak what once having spoken you cannot recall. Consider, wherever you act, that God is present, and you can scarcely be rude or ill-tempered. Remember you are set here to fit yourself for heaven, and the wisdom that cometh thence and leadeth thither is *gentle*.

XXXIV

If in this life only we have hope in Christ,
we are of all men most miserable.

I Corinthians 15:19

It is often said by those who look with severity on human life that men make a great ado about nothing. Each of us knows something of the private history of two or three hundred persons. What each man calls his knowledge of the world is his acquaintance with the language, the business, the habits, and the success of this limited number of people. You have a vague hearsay knowledge of the occupation of two or three thousand more. And if you study your recollections of this company with whom you have walked in the world, it is true a good many instances will probably occur to you of great promise and poor performance. You will think of young men who set out in life with the reputation of excellent habits or of great acquirements or of fine genius, who deceived this expectation by an ill life or by an early death. You will remember those who have been elevated by a sudden fame of prodigious skill in some valuable art, but the quiet passage of time has shown that they have added nothing to the length of life or to your comfort or your power. You have heard of wonderful schools that were very bad schools. You have heard of inventions and discoveries that were to change the aspect of the manufacturing interests, but no change followed. You have heard marvellous stories so circumstantial and so authenticated as to put the facts beyond doubt and found them presently to be totally false.

Churches have sprung up, founded on new interpretations of Scripture, and all prophecy and all argument, we were told, confirmed the promise of their speedy and universal extension, and the time was come and the world called aloud for it, but in one or two summers the churches vanished away. All round you there is a bickering of mighty passions; what long foresight, what patience under privation, what hard-hearted competition, what untiring activity, to get a subsistence, and an abundance, which when it is got, there is no insurance office provided, which can warrant you the enjoyment of it one poor day. Then there are struggles for office which strain up for one high place by all studies, by

Composed at the Chardon Street house and dated April 26, 1829. Preached four times: April 26, 1829, at the Second Church, Boston; June 27 in Concord, N.H.; July 12 at the Pine Street Church, Boston; and June 20, 1830, at the Second Church, Boston.

all contrivances, by all actions, for ten or fifteen years, and when it is gained, what else is gained but discomfiture and calumny and mortification?

You lose your office, you lose your property, you lose your good name, you fail in your projects, you are disappointed in your affections, you are balked of your honours, and it is too late to begin again with richer experience and firmer purposes, for your bed is made in the ground and the night is come and you must go.

It is written in dark characters on all we see, "Man that is born of woman, is of a few days."[1] Yes, brethren, if in this life only we have hope, our happiness is very deceitful and imperfect. Our situation may not call us to lead those brave lives in the face of all persecution and contempt to which St. Paul alludes, when he addressed his fellow sufferers of the early church.[2] But as long as the eye rests on this life there is plenty of disappointment in your own history, there are many drawbacks on your present enjoyments, there is a grief sitting heavy at the heart of each of us, and oh there is an afflicting uncertainty that darkens all our hopes.

It is not at all worth while to exaggerate the evils of life. They are quite bad enough for the argument; quite bad enough to suggest to the inquisitive reason to grope round for something better. The eye of the infant turns to the light, the soul of man thirsts for immortality.

The expectation which is the common bond of human nature, that unites all feelings, the golden hoop that holds society staunch, and gives effect to human laws, is the doctrine of the resurrection of the dead. There is no man of sober mind who thinks wisely of the human condition to whom this hope is not more dear, infinitely, than any earthly good. Being is dear to us though in privation and pain, and if it were proposed to their choice, some, I am persuaded, would prefer the experiment of a new existence, though certain of suffering, to lying down under the heavy clods of an everlasting grave.

On this account all the phenomena of the spiritual world have the highest interest for us; yet men and women within the memory of the present generation have turned pale at the apprehension of seeing ghosts. It was for ages believed that the souls of departed men revisited the earth in frightful forms, and even now I do not know that all its superstition has departed from the shroud. Before the influence of the press, that mighty diffusion of knowledge, these idle fears have well nigh vanished. And men have consented to be convinced that what has no material body cannot without miracle be perceived by material organs. But the reason of my alluding to this faith, is, to remark how strange it is that ever this belief was entertained with fear and strong repugnance of its objects,—that it should have been so universally connected with low and disagreeable images. One would think it should have been in the highest degree grateful to the mind.

1. Job 14:1.
2. I Corinthians 4:12.

Granting the re-appearance of the departed were possible, I cannot but think that a serious man would eagerly give all he had or laboured for on earth, all acquirements, all possessions, for the conviction that should be wholly satisfactory to himself and to other sound minds, that he had had intercourse with a disembodied man. It would be an awful season, but one of unmeasured joy. For he would have that certainty which it has pleased God to withhold from us and which no evidence however strong can ever supply, the testimony of his own observation that consciousness may return when the body is perished. The moment in which the mind was satisfied that it was communicating with the soul of a departed friend, would be to it like the first moment of consciousness that follows death. To some men I am sure it would be a rapture of thrilling delight. The mind would start up with all her faculties into intense and reverent attention, to hail this first assurance of its own eternal nature. It would be the first gleam of the light of heaven seen through the chinks of the soul's dark and noisome mansion—the body.[3] It would be assurance of the prisoner himself come out from his narrow cell into the glory of day, assurance that the pent up inhabitant of this poor clay, suffering from its low necessities and its unclean diseases, would come forth to take the free air, to be a citizen of the Universe, to grow up in its powers to the colossal measure of its desires and its virtues.

It is not my design at present to go into the grounds on which we build our hope of our own immortality. I reserve the discussion a little longer, for one would not enter lightly upon the great topic to which all the energies of the greatest minds have ever been directed and whose leading evidences are familiar to you. I only have had in view at this time to look at the first aspects of the question, to remind you of its desirableness and of its reasonableness, and to express my views of the place it holds in the Christian revelation. Though I think the argument from nature is strong, we must yet depend on Revelation for our chief evidence. We cannot afford to do without. The matter is too important to us, to let it lack any light we can get.

Before Revelation the great fact on which the consolation of man is founded is its perfect reasonableness. It is strange and of very deep importance to these speculations, the fact, that *we are able to look into a future moment.* We have done so, we have done so a thousand times, and when the moment that was future became present, when the time arrived, we found our anticipations true. All of us are conscious of having had some foreknowledge of the present hour, some intention of coming to church on this day, and some idea of the services that now you find yourselves engaged in. We all know with a good degree of certainty what we shall be doing for the week to come. Tomorrow and the next day you will detect yourself doing what now you anticipate, and you shall remember it was once future.

Now what prevents our looking twenty years ahead? or a hundred? or on into the bosom of infinite time? What shall hinder me now from forming some

3. Cf. Edmund Waller, "Of the Last Verses in the Book," lines 13–14; quoted in *JMN* 2:101.

idea, though faint, of the feelings of an hour that I shall spend when a thousand years are come and gone, and which idea that hour, when it comes, shall verify? That I have no experience and therefore can have no knowledge of the mode of existence of the soul out of the flesh is of no importance, since I have ideas of things that belong to me which flesh or place or time or death do not affect. Clearly do I see that there are thoughts in the soul which are independent of the changes of matter; that there are some feelings agreeable to the child and to the man that cannot change if I should endure to endless duration. Thus we have all within ourselves more or less degrees of love of our neighbour. Now suppose that, prompted by this feeling and in reference to that remote hour, you now repress a strong purpose of revenge and determine instead to do a good office to one who has wronged you. Now I say consult yourself, and you shall find that you are as certain, granting the being of the mind, that, at that hour the memory of this indulgence of benevolent feeling will seem to you to have been good and not bad, as you are now that you are sitting in this Church.

Well now the reason why, without revelation, you cannot predict your existence with absolute assurance, is the obvious one that we see our own bodies and all other matter continually decaying, passing into new forms. But you can't help discerning that you are of a twofold nature, of matter and of spirit, and you cannot fail to see that there are things which are spiritual that do as really, and distinctly exist, as brass or stone, and which are moreover eternal, as brass and stone are not; because they are what time cannot change, cannot touch. Do you not see that truth is good and falsehood evil as surely as honey is sweet, or the water of the sea is salt? Water and honey may change their nature, may be governed by new laws without absurdity, but moral truth, moral being, cannot. Truth and falsehood will never alter, they are of unchangeable nature. There is therefore nothing unnatural in the expectation that the soul will be thus thinking at that remote hour, whilst it is unnatural to expect such continuance to the body. Consider, then, brethren, if this perception of the eternity of certain feelings which we partake doth not afford strong presumption that we who feel them shall be eternal also.

Now brethren, I rejoice in this perfect reasonableness of the doctrine of the future state that opens the way into the human mind for the revelation of Christ and teaches us its value, and gives weight to its evidence, and enjoins upon us an obedience to its laws.

The doctrine of the immortality of the human soul is the main doctrine that makes all the value of Christianity. This is a position that it is surprizing it should ever have been disputed by any reasonable man. I do not know why any man who weighs his professions should call himself a Christian except out of gratitude to Christianity for this doctrine. Every thing else which a revelation could disclose is utterly worthless until this great truth is told. All we wanted to know was whether we decease from being when we die, or whether we enter upon larger existence. Before this fact is known, when I stand tottering upon the brink of everlasting annihilation, of what manner of consequence is it to me, who is he that reigns in nature, or whether there be any who reigns at all?

If this faith fail all things fail. All effort, all virtuous desire, would be taken away, for they stand on the same foundations as this faith. All resignation to a humble lot would be taken away. What matters it to any of us whether we are great or small here, in the world, so that the great hope of all souls is sure? For who can doubt but that in the ages that lie before us, of intercourse with spirits of every degree of grandeur, be it of thought or of virtue, he can fail to find his own level or fear to be robbed of his just fame? But strike down this blessed doctrine of the Resurrection, towards which the wise and good, the countless generations of men, as they scanned, in their little day, the impending future, have darted their desiring eyes,—to which every conclusion of the intellectual power, and every effort of the moral power have pointed from the first glimmering of human history,—and you have done more for ruin, than if you had shaken down the stars in their courses.[4] And after this downfal, all things here below, or there above, are so insignificant to us, who are to be connected with them but a moment, that one could hardly bring himself to consider any thing seriously.

What a moment is fifty or seventy years, the life of man, when measured on that illimitable time wherein we look backward into its silent waste and no monument, no footstep of our own is there, and forward into its immeasureable solitudes, and no hope for us, no cheerful voice of man or angel greets us from the gloom? If this handbreadth of life is my all, I cannot stop to consider, I must hasten to act. I shall take up the words of the poor pagan skeptic, "let us make haste to live, for we shall all be fables presently."[5] As we hurry to reap all the delight we can from our brief and insecure possession, we never should stop—it would not be worth knowing, unless for amusement, what was law, what was truth, much less what were the opinions about law and truth, the froth and scum of men of words.[6] Take out of man the hope and the belief of everlasting life and the world would run riot with strange excess. The sentinel conscience would come down from his watch tower. The frame of society would crack and fall when the cement of love was removed in the increase of selfishness—increasing as it always doth by its own indulgence.

But oh how altered is the feeling with which the world is regarded when lighted by the star that rose in Bethlehem, and never sets, and never is clouded to the Christian's eye. The first time his faith has become strong enough to rule his practice is to him such an hour as we considered above, when new evidence

---

4. Cf. Judges 5:20.

5. Apparently Emerson's free translation of Persius ("Carpamus dulcia, nostrum est, / Quod vivis, cinis, & manes, & fabula fies") as quoted by Montaigne in "Of Solitude," in *Essays of Michael Seigneur de Montaigne . . .* , trans. Charles Cotton (London, 1693), 1:389. See also *JMN* 6:19.

6. Compare the quotation attributed to Andrew Marvell in *JMN* 6:87: "The froth of the town & the scum of the university."

comes in of the spiritual world. For then he says, 'I am arrived in life: I am associated by God to his infinite family of intelligent children. In this spot of earth my career is begun, which ages shall not measure nor worlds confine. My fate is in my own hands. Let me carry up my actions to the high level of my destiny. What can I not perform? what can I not know? no pitch of virtue is beyond my reach. Hasten, oh my soul, every event is an opportunity, a step to mount by; every moment contains a virtue. Awake, and live and ascend forever and ever.'

Let us consider, brethren, that if the presumption were very small, that we should live again, the plainest reason would enjoin us to lead lives of preparation for the future, but now that all the hints and tendencies of nature and the soul's own desire are confirmed by express communication from the spiritual world, let us faithfully perform the duties of this our first stage of being and always act with the dignity and forethought of eternal agents. I am afraid if our actions were studied closely it would not appear that we believed ourselves immortal. The horse and the dog, let them eat their food and seek their pleasure—it is their all. But man, with the sense of eternity dwelling in him, let him not eat and drink and sin as his perishing body shall tempt him, but let the love of God and the name of Christ prevail with him to carry up his life to his faith.

XXXV

We should live soberly, righteously, and godly in this present world.

Titus 2:12

It is my design in the present discourse to invite your attention to some considerations on the third topic of this comprehensive text. On a former occasion I offered to your consideration some remarks upon the three classes of duties to which the apostle alludes in enjoining men to live soberly, righteously, and godly.

The view I had proposed to take of our duties to God was then left imperfect. The affections were considered in relation to their excellent nature, their strength, and their true objects, and some description was attempted of the manner in which God fixes our attachment upon his perfections by means of our love of human virtues.

It is proposed at present to push still farther the inquiry concerning the full meaning of 'living godly,' that is, of giving our affections to God; and to give some idea, however imperfect, of the great truths that lie like unfathomable mines, (how little explored) in this region of thought.

The next fact to which I wish to call your attention on this inquiry, is this, that the affections can be cultivated. I cannot say, says one, that I love God. When I sift my thoughts and dispositions I do not find that I relish those employments which the love of God might dictate. I do not go to Church with the same eager pleasure that I often find in going to my place of business. I must confess I go much from motives of decency rather than of devotion. I have a reluctance to engage in prayer—and all this—to speak frankly, what can it be but a certain repulsion from God? It cannot spring from his love. And yet I am esteemed an innocent and good citizen, an industrious farmer, an upright merchant, a skilful mechanic; I am not a bad man. I do not see then how I am to blame if I do not love God.

Preached seven times: May 3, 1829, at the Second Church, Boston; September 24, again at the Second Church (Thursday Lecture); September 27 at the Harvard College Chapel; July 11, 1830, in New Bedford; September 5 at the Second Church, Boston; September 16, 1832, again at the Second Church; and August 28, 1836, in East Lexington. Emerson here continues the subject of Sermon XXVI, producing the fourth and final part of a series including Sermons XXIV–XXVI. A heavily revised early version is given in the Textual and Manuscript Notes. The sermon has its origin in notes written in December, 1828; see *JMN* 3:146–47.

Now the answer to this excuse of a worldly mind lies in the fact just now stated, that the affections can be *cultivated*. It is a great law of the affections that they grow by their own exercise. Habit comes in to the aid of inclination. All proverbs in all tongues attest it. Do what is right and use shall make it pleasant. Consider a moment what you must sometimes have perceived to be the main secrets of the human organization: that whatsoever we do we do with more ease the second time than the first; that things long reckoned impossible, a steady perseverance will perform; that whatsoever postures or expressions of countenance we assume we immediately become sensible of some degree of those emotions of the mind, those passions whose expression we have thus arbitrarily taken; and much more if we do with any steadiness for any long period, certain actions, virtuous or vicious, certain good or evil offices to any person, we inevitably acquire with great degrees of strength the feeling of which those actions are the proper expression. If you hang a bar of steel, for a long time, in the direction of the magnetic poles, it becomes a magnet itself; and just as surely if you do the actions prescribed by one state of mind they will make that state of mind habitual to you. Thus if there be any person against whom you nourish without reason a strong dislike, and sensible that this aversion is at war with Christian principles, you should now treat that person with studied kindness, should eagerly watch every secret and open way to promote his advantage; by every benefit you confer upon him you shall find your own benevolence to him increased, until your prejudices have given place to the most sincere kindness.

So also may the affections be directed to their divine object—be given to God by an act of the Will, when of themselves they do not go thither. "If ye do my commandments ye shall abide in my love."[1] The experience of all good men conspires in one testimony, that precisely in the same proportion as we advance in virtue, precisely in the same proportion does the great Idea of God discover itself and shine within the mind. Say not therefore, 'I am good, but I do not love God.' You are not good, think again; some deadly sin, some fatal bar, lies in your way, and keeps you out from heaven. Be humble, be just, be true, be temperate, be chaste, be merciful,—and you shall learn the love of God.

I do not think there is any aspect under which human nature is so respectable as in view of its affections. We delight to talk of ourselves as very powerful beings, but there is the seat of our power. Without them our pretensions to any real efficiency are exceeding feeble. By them our strength is all but omnipotent; for it touches the Omnipotent himself. Let me go a little into the particulars of this proposition. It is the property of the affections to awaken correspondent feeling in their objects. The love, deep and steadfast, which you bear to another being, let that other be of what degree or nature soever, will extort a mutual regard from him. (I now state the general law without stopping to explain what may seem to be exceptions.) And this statement is true, because the fact that we entertain a strong inclination for any object, at once proves us capable of appre-

1. John 15:10.

ciating the nature of that object, and so of being an object of sympathy to it,—our knowledge being necessarily the foundation of our regard.

There is no exception to this in the fondness of the lower animals for man. Among the lower degrees of intelligence, in the brute creation, each animal attaches itself to those of its own kind, and the regard which the domestic animals manifest for man, is something very different from the regard of man to man, is always the leaning on a superior nature for protection, and never that feeling into which some perception of equality must always enter—the feeling of *love*.

As in all our analysis of the affections in their aspect toward God, we necessarily use the analogy of the affections we bear to men, it seems proper to say that I use the word *love*, to denominate such a relation as is the most near and generous friendship that can subsist between two virtuous men. For in attachments between the sexes, nature has ordained a certain exclusiveness, giving rise to the passion of jealousy, which has no archetype in the Divine love. And when I say that love can extort love, I speak of no casual kindness, but I speak of the abiding sentiment that the spectacle of the virtues of one mind, must awaken in another healthy mind that beholds them.

Suppose there be a man whose actions have exhibited a certain heroic virtue, and some individual, drawn by this spectacle, conceives a strong regard for him, and does keenly relish and approve the beauty of his life and all the finish of his character; this very approbation and honour he pays him, shows himself to be capable of equal degrees of virtue, and therefore to be a mind with which that other cannot fail to sympathize. And as the first perceives by every mark of kindness that this man does entirely love him, he cannot help feeling within himself the growth of mutual regard.

Now, brethren, see how hence is seen in the affections, the mighty force of human beings. Since it is the law of all mind, that love can extort love, and since we are made capable of cultivating the regard of God, it follows, that we, out of the dust and meanness of the earth, are yet able to compel—I say it with reverence—by our love of God, new measures of God's love to us. And to confirm this position, I appeal, brethren, to your own experience, whether, with each new conquest that you have made over temptation, you do not feel as sure of an increased favour of God, as you do of your own?

And hence we are led to another general and important remark, that love has a certain power to equalize whom it unites.

It is an important consideration to be borne in mind in these speculations, that we use the name *love* to denominate very different relations. The love of the parent to its offspring is only an animal instinct and no wise founded in the perception of qualities that excite approbation and attachment in mature minds. But when the child grows up to the power of thought, to the exercise of the affections, and the formation of character, then the relation of the parent changes from the instinct, from protection and patronage, to friendship. If, however, the child as he grows old, becomes corrupt, and injures and hates his parent, this relation of love properly so called can never exist between them. The disappointed yet surviving hope of a parent, the remains of instinctive fondness, will be added in his bosom to the pity of an impartial spectator, but continual hatred on the part of the child it is likely in time would obliterate every remembrance of affection.

Now do we not all feel that God's love to men, must be very closely analogous in its workings to this familiar relation? He has made us. It is his pleasure that we should exist in this state of discipline, capable of learning by slow degrees, the laws of his universe, and that we should stand amidst this balance of motives and pleasures and advantages with the power to make ourselves good or bad, with the power to act or to counteract his will.

But whilst he has imparted to *all* of us these infinite capacities of happiness, it would be idle to say that his benevolence is *indiscriminate;* or if you have a mind to say, that his benevolence is universal, it is not so with his *love*. There is, I believe, the firmest foundation in nature for the doctrine of Election—not, surely, in the absurd way in which that doctrine has been taught, but for the sentiment out of which it doubtless grew—the sense that God doth love one, and doth not love another of his children. His regard for us must always depend entirely on us,—on our regard for him. The all wise, the all pure spirit cannot sympathize, surely, with ignorance, and brutish lust, and brutish cruelty. He may, however, afford light and good motives to the darkened mind: He may send revelations of his will to such a mind, by Jesus Christ; and, as the sinner departs from sin, as a man becomes better and wiser, and learns to love God, and is by that love ennobled, and continually prompted to efforts to serve and please him, he also changes the relation of God to himself. For, as God has made him free, he has made him able to deserve his esteem, and so, as he more and more deserves it, the relation of Parent merges continually into the relation of Friend. And, therefore, observe how naturally all wise and good men, as they have made proficiency in goodness, have imperceptibly changed the style of their addresses to God and have come to speak of him as their Companion and Friend, who having the good of the Universe at heart, as also they had, they felt with his feeling and saw as with the Divine Eye.

Such is the language of some of the noble teachers of the sect of the Stoics— those forerunners of the Christian religion. Such is the language of David in the best of his Psalms. Such is ever the language of our Lord and from this beautiful connexion, which as he felt he expressed, this identification of himself, his whole being with the Father, has very naturally arisen that misinterpretation of the nature of his union with God, which has so unhappily divided the Christian world. I should think he had sufficiently explained himself in promising to make his disciples one with him, as he was one with the Father.[2]—And, as such was the language of our Lord, such also has been the language of every true disciple of Christ, as the conquest of the mind over the body became more and more complete, as the principle of benevolence unfolding within him con-

2. John 17:21–23.

tinually took a wider range, embracing friends, neighbours, country, and man-kind. I said that love was powerful—and is it not? affecting, as it would, the Father on his Throne. It would change the complexion of his will to us. It would change the complexion of events to us. If the order of events without us, be, as I believe it is, always delicately adjusted to the spiritual world within us,—an entire change of heart in us, would beget a change also in our outward condition. But if this be thought unreasonable, it does not at all affect the argument, for the same events, to an altered mind, would speak an altered language. To such a mind, there is no adversity, there is no evil, there is no temptation. For as in all things the will of God is done, so is its own.

Once more: Love equalizes. If you devote yourself to things low and base, you shall be degraded to them; if you love what is grand and pure, you also shall be raised and purified: for what is love but the adoption of the feelings and interests of the being that is beloved and making yourself one with that being? Therefore if you love God and adopt his interests and make yourself one with him—you shall part with sin, you shall part with imperfection and pain and mortality, you shall grow divine. Adopt his Interests! make yourself one with Him! What doth it mean? the Interests of all beings that exist, the Infinite good of the immeasureable Creation!

My brethren, do you think there is anything of extravagance in these views of the connexion of the human soul with the divine? It will be said, perhaps, that we forget the habitual lowness of man when we suppose him capable of enter-ing into these intimate and majestic relations with God. Man! Why the streets are full of men, and the men are full of vices and littlenesses; they are drudging all the year round for a little meat by day and a warm bed by night. They are servants to such paltry necessities, and are such as they to influence the Mind that quickens all being? to stand in relations to it, so near as you represent?

I know it appears strange: the contrast between what we see and what we desire seems too bold, the hope too glorious, for truth. But is not that the very paradox in man with which we are familiar? Is it not the very history of human nature, the mode in which it does really exist, this *sympathetic character*, by which it can appear equally at home in the highest and in the lowest, and in every part of a mighty range of existence,—from the clod in which is its root, to the heaven in which the bright blossoms of its hope are flourishing? If God has chosen to liken and unite it by its house of flesh to the worms among which now it resides, and with whom shortly it shall leave its body,—has he not also by its infinite soul made it the peer of angels and spirits and capable of finding all joy and all pain in a spiritual world? Has he not endowed us with the wonderful power of continually changing ourselves from that which we are to that which we wish to be—of becoming what we admire, of growing by knowledge?

The old philosophers called man a microcosm,[3] that is, the *Universe in mini-*

---

3. Emerson mistakenly attributes the definition to Aristotle in *JMN* 6:102. George Perrigo Conger, in *Theories of Microcosms and Macrocosms* (New York, 1922), 28, discovers no definite

ature. In the Scriptures, to the same intent, he is called the Image of God.[4] He is both. He is the Image of God, inasmuch as he is the perceiver of all his works, the perceiver of the harmony and design of all; inasmuch as the clearer his eye becomes, his conviction grows stronger, that right is always beautiful, and wrong is always deformed; that the interests of God and of man are one; and that then has he reached the perfection of his being, when his own selflove is swallowed up in his devotion to the cause of the Universe, and to God the Father.

---

formulation of the idea earlier than Philo Judaeus (30 B.C.–45 A.D.); it is thereafter a philosophical commonplace. See, for example, *The Advancement of Learning* in *The Works of Francis Bacon*, ed. James Spedding et al. (London, 1857–1874), 4:380.

4. Cf. Genesis 1:26–27.

XXXVI

And, besides this, giving all diligence, add to your faith, virtue; and to virtue, knowledge.

II PETER 1:5

I wish to ask your attention to some remarks upon the duty of cultivating the mind. The duty of acquiring knowledge, of cultivating the mind, is not much insisted on in the common course of subjects of pulpit discussion. I see no reason why it should be omitted. I see the strongest reasons why it should be strenuously urged. The patriot presses it on his fellow citizens in earnest and monitory tones. The father and the mother urge it on their children, at school with affectionate and anxious emphasis. All people who think at all, think alike on this subject of the priceless value of wisdom, that houses and lands, that gold and silver, cannot equal it, yet men abstain from adding to this great cause the authority of religion. Now to my mind the whole value of religion consists in its being a rule of life. Whatever is essential to a good life it seems to me to enjoin, and it enjoins few things with more energy than the cultivation of the mind, because it is necessary to know much in order to think well.

But you may see men look grave when the duty of cultivating the mind was strongly pressed and men were commended for their intellectual gifts, and say, 'Yes, 'tis very well to be learned, but there are much more important things to be attended to; and Jesus Christ was not brought up in schools, neither did he, in any of his conversations that have come down to us, urge on men the importance of learning.'

In answer to these two objections from the example and from the silence of our Saviour, I observe in the first place, that his example is of no use to us in that particular, unless we, like him, had received spiritual direction, a miraculous influx of light into the soul to supersede the necessity of a painful progress from the elements of knowledge.

In the second place it may be remarked that there are many things which it seems right to enjoin on men which are not directly enjoined by revelation among our duties, at least not with that degree of force which they appear to deserve. The recommendation must be got by implication, if it is got at all. Such

---

Manuscript dated May 9, 1829, at Chardon Street. Preached twice: May 10, 1829, and January 8, 1832, on both occasions at the Second Church, Boston.

a duty is the improvement of the mind. The obligation from natural religion to the cultivation of all our powers is obvious and conclusive. The motives that urge it are paramount and infinitely worthy. Now is this important ground to be abandoned for lack of a text? Because of the silence of revelation shall we not beseech men to observe this primal duty? To these questions it seems to me the answer is plain, and no objection can lie against revelation on account of the omission, and no doubt can be felt of the obligation. This duty is one which follows inevitably, legitimately, from the positions of the Christian religion.

Christianity corrects the distortions of the mind, heals the plague that has corrupted the moral nature of man. It takes off the film that had got on the human eye. But when health is once restored to the intellectual functions, we see at once without a teacher, the obvious interest and duty of cultivating the mind. It had been superfluous then in Christianity, to enjoin what reason would teach as soon as by its means reason could have its perfect work. Shall we say that Christ neglected the improvement of the intellect? Shall we say that the oculist did not wish the blind man to see the sun, or the face of his father and mother, because he only removed the film, and left him no directions what to do with his eyes?[1]

Yes, my brethren, this duty is a strict deduction from the discoveries of Christianity. What we continually recur to that dispensation for, is the revelation that it brings us of the immortality of the soul. Now if the soul is really immortal then the business of life is clear and distinct, to give our whole attention to increase its force, to refine its desires, to multiply its means of action and happiness, which is done in two ways: by increasing our virtue, and our knowledge.

I am afraid that some minds shall be disturbed hereafter by the discovery that the spiritual world does not differ so much from this, as we are apt to imagine. The gift of simple existence is of doubtful value. To the vacant mind eternal life, I am afraid, would be eternal sorrow. I do not wonder that people ask with some curiosity what shall be the employments of heaven when their work is done. A few hours hang very heavy on their hands and they are with reason a good deal alarmed with the prospect of ages. But this darkness is cleared up into a noonday brightness to the mind that has tasted the enjoyment of exploring and discovering truth.

A further reason why as religious beings we are bound to every effort to cultivate our minds, is, that the more we know, the clearer our convictions become of the infinite value of religion. A man who has only half a dozen ideas and clings strongly to his faith does not know what might be the effect of an infinite multiplication of thoughts in his mind; and he is shaken by the skepticism of one, whom he supposes much better informed. He thinks that possibly this man may see so far, as to *see behind his faith*, and may perceive human causes sufficient to account for what he reverences as the manifest work of a

---

1. "In the second place . . . his eyes?": see *JMN* 3:100–101.

Divine Cause. And it is only an acquaintance with history, and with the speculations of reflecting men that can convince him that it is not what men know
that makes them unbelievers, but a wrong state of feeling, and that an unsubdued self love; if the mind is in a sound state, if the principles are good, every
new fact that is learned adds new evidence to faith. All study, all attempts to
acquire knowledge, it will be understood, are efforts to acquire truth; and truth
is the mind's home. All that we want to know is What is true? and no man need
ever fear that his virtuous character can suffer or can fail to be improved by new
acquisitions of truth. "There is no sympathy so intimate," says the prince of
modern philosophers, "as that between truth and goodness. They are seal and
print."[2]

I think the fact deserves great attention which is drawn from the records of
our courts, that men of education are never or in extremely rare cases brought
to trial for felonious offences. So, our own community, in which the means of
knowledge are widest diffused, is a more moral community than any other. In
like manner, it has been well observed that wherever the *love of reading* can be
created, it seems to be an effectual antidote for two vices, indolence and intemperance. This statement, no doubt, must be qualified; yet that it can, in any
great degree, be true, is a fact of the greatest value.

Therefore, brethren, I hold it to be my duty as a minister of Jesus Christ to
exhort all, if any be grown old among you, to offer them my anxious wishes,
and if any are young among you, my earnest request, that they should never lose
sight of this great and respectable purpose, the improvement of the mind, the
increase of knowledge, that *you should never lose sight of it*—this is the essential precept; for to gain knowledge it only needs to keep oneself in the disposition to receive it, for there is no employment, no condition, no place, no
company, where one will not grow wiser, if he has the will to grow wiser. Say
not, who shall go up to heaven, or down into the abyss, to fetch it to us? for,
here it is by your side, around you, within you. Knowledge is in books, and in
conversation, and in business, and in meditation. Knowledge is abundant
enough, accessible enough; it is the *eye* that is defective. In your mind you have
an eye which now is dim by disuse, and can see but a few inches around you; but
you can train that organ till it shall be a telescope in power and bring in floods
of light and multitudes of facts from all the universe. And this, brethren, is all
your part, to use the organ. God will provide knowledge enough if you will only
keep your eye open.

Indeed so distinct an object of our existence does the acquisition of knowledge seem to have been in the design of the Former of our being that nothing
seems to have been so much consulted. In some sort you become wise perforce
by the progress of life. You strive to be happy but often in vain. You often
traverse your happiness by your own efforts to increase it. But every hour and

2. Possibly paraphrased from Francis Bacon, *The Advancement of Learning* in *The Works of
Francis Bacon*, ed. James Spedding et al. (London 1858–1874), 4:405. See *JMN* 1:261, 6:89, 6:301,
9:346; used in "Swedenborg," *CW* 4:66.

every event, fortunate or unfortunate, contributes something to your experience. He therefore that would know how to be always pleased—glad of success and glad of disappointment—should accustom himself to reflect that every event, of whatever complexion, increases his knowledge, and in consequence his power. But let it be remembered that this beautiful law can only hold whilst the mind is kept in a healthy state, for when the attention is habitually drowsy the faculties become obstructed, and fail to perform their office. I shall not stop to go into the wonderful relations of the mind to truth, and the wonderful relation of truths to each other, which so facilitate its acquisition, but for the sake of coming sooner and straighter to our practical conclusions, I pass them by. Suffice it to mention that the law of acquiring is this, that the value of every new fact to the mind is increased by the number of facts it already possesses.

To put the matter out of the reach of objection, I will only ask if there is a single fact you know, if there is a single idea in your mind, that has never been of use to you—one that you can as well spare as not? I believe there is none. I never knew a serious man who had any—the least particle of knowledge—that he did not feel to be valuable.3 We have a vulgar proverb which says, "Keep a thing by you seven years, and it will come in use."4 I am sure it is true of the virtuous mind. There is no fact or shade of experience that is in your memory but the chances of conversation and turn of events will at some time make valuable to you as illustration or as evidence. The most insignificant fact within your observation, your acquaintance with the colour of a pebble, the shape of a blade of grass, is not without its use; if it has not a specific distinct value of its own, yet it contributes somewhere to strengthen some general conviction. (And though this may seem a paradox I am confident it is none.) Now if all the knowledge you have is thus valuable to you, even to the last tittle, do you not suppose that you would be as unwilling to part with whatever more you should acquire?

But one says, I am content, I know that my powers were not given to be neglected. I desire to fulfil this duty and to acquire knowledge. What am I to do? Use the means within your reach. The disposition to neglect common blessings can hardly be more palpable any where than it is here. The facilities for the communication of truth are numberless. The art of writing and now the art of printing has enabled any one man now alive to come at all the truth that all men in all the past have disclosed upon any one department of knowledge. Go into any large library and you have within your reach the history of the human race. You have all the facts, collected and arranged, that generations of inquirers have accumulated in each science. You have the history of human opinions; the inquiries of great geniuses into the laws of the human mind, the anatomy of the faculties and of the affections—so that on any one subject in a few hours you can become possessed of knowledge which it cost centuries to gain.

3. "And there is no knowledge which is not valuable": attributed to Edmund Burke in *JMN* 1:192.
4. See *JMN* 3:139, 9:268.

I only am anxious you should feel your interest on this matter with sufficient force to begin. For once get a little into the habit of reading valuable books, get a taste of that surpassing pleasure, the acquisition of new thoughts, and there need be no fear that you will ever lose it. Every one has or can obtain information concerning what books are good and what are not. Every body knows what are our most valuable English histories—then there are good books of travels into every country, on the globe; and there are biographies of great and good men, and of bad men, by which you can hardly help being made better; as the Life of Franklin, of Howard, of Wesley, of Dr. Johnson, of Washington, and of Napoleon. Then there are the richest thoughts of best men upon the conduct of life and the formation of the character. There is Thomas à Kempis and Taylor and Fénelon and Scougal and William Penn.5 There are the Scriptures. Above all remember that for the improvement of the mind it is not how many books we read but how well.6 Compare every sentence with your own thought.

Now here, brethren, is a plain practicable advantage proposed to you, which, the more attention you will bestow upon it, the more inestimable will it show itself, and which I hope will obtain your attention. If you consider that with every new idea you are a more powerful being, and farther removed from the savage and the brute—if you consider the immense difference there is between your present state of mind and the highest cultivation of which your powers are capable—you will feel how far you are responsible to God for the neglect of his gifts—but there are innumerable advantages that will continually disclose themselves not obvious at first.

To name one, it has a continual tendency to create a tranquil, thoughtful habit; it begets an useful self respect in the student himself. The reason why sometimes you are petulant in your family is that you are out of humour with yourself. You have been idle not with your hands only but with the head. The mind has found nothing to rest on; no home of sacred and pleasant thoughts within itself, (which the use of books creates) and as soon as the hands were idle and you eat and drink freely, you grew wanton and quarrelsome. Well now, if, in the intervals of business you had taken a book and had only read a few pages of the histories of Plutarch or of Robertson,7 had only caught some one heroic trait of Aristides, Luther or of Washington, you would feel very differently, and incomparably better. You would feel at ease with yourself and others—a quiet sense of having done well. The mind would be at rest, not spying malignantly about to observe upon the faults or the advantages of others, but occupied with dignity at home, upon grave and tranquillizing images, upon states and cities,

5. Emerson owned James Boswell, *The Life of Samuel Johnson* (London, 1827); Thomas à Kempis, *On the Imitation of Christ* (London, 1797); Jeremy Taylor, *The Rule and Exercise of Holy Dying* (Glasgow, 1820); several titles by François de Selignac de la Mothe-Fénelon, including *Télémaque* and *Dialogues of the Dead* (London, 1797); and Henry Scougal, *Life of God in the Soul of Man* (Boston, 1823).

6. Aquinas. [Emerson's note]. Cf. *JMN* 6:82.

7. William Robertson, author of *The History of America*, 2 vols. (London, 1777).

and great virtues, upon good lives and noble deaths, and the economy of Providence.

Consider, brethren, in these remarks, I recommend nothing impracticable. There is no man whose life is so wholly engrossed by business that he cannot dedicate a little time of every day to useful reading, and there is no business so engrossing that will not leave a good deal of time when the thoughts can be occupied upon that reading. And further, there is no young man or young woman who cannot if they will form their habits to a practice which will surely lead to both the others, and give to them both a new value,—the practice of keeping in writing some journal, however imperfect, of their thoughts, especially of their religious thoughts, where their resolutions may be registered and their plans of action and of study recorded, which may be an enduring picture of the mind, by which the past state of feeling may be compared with the present. Here in this blessed land of New England, where the system of public education sends its searching light through the whole range of society; where books abound, and can always be got by any one who really wants to read; and where merit in any kind is so freely recognized,—I do not see what should prevent men and women in every class, not only the merchant and thriving mechanic, but the poor man and poor woman, who gain their daily bread by daily labor, from saving yet a few precious hours in the week for honourable and elevating efforts at self improvement. You may say it is romantic: it is not romantic; it is reasonable; it is Christian; it is human desire. Shall it be thought reasonable that the humblest wretch that wears the human form should be instructed to aim and to hope to become perfect as God the Father is perfect and at the same time reckoned quixotic that we ask the labourer to read and to write?[8]

Therefore do I commend and honour the institution of Sunday Schools, with their libraries, believing there is no more real and effectual charity than is done by a judicious teacher in these useful schools.

But we are all ignorant. "What we know is a point to what we don't know."[9] We were made for this perception and therefore what we acquire in this way enters into the substance of the soul and like virtue is ineradicable. Your property, which you toil so hard to get, you may presently lose it all. Every day we hear of new disasters in the manufacturing and commercial interests. It is true if we wait for a few months this evil will be overpast and new enterprize will be attended with new success, but there will always be this uncertainty, this peril of commercial ruin. Why not then try to get property which no accident will reach, bags of treasure which wax not old.[10] It is recorded of Paulinus, the wise bishop of Nola, that having lost all his effects when the city of Nola was sacked

8. Cf. Matthew 5:48.

9. B[isho]p. [Joseph] Butler. [Emerson's note]. Quoted from Robert Plummer Ward, *Tremaine* (Philadelphia, 1825), 3:125-26. See *JMN* 6:64; used in "General Views," *EL* 2:358, in *Nature*, *CW* 1:25, and in "Immortality," *W* 8:341.

10. Luke 12:33.

by the barbarians, he prayed that he might be defended from being sensible of such a loss, "for, they have touched nothing," he said, "which I could call mine"; "the riches (of knowledge) that made him rich, and the goods (of virtue) that made him good, remaining to him entire," (says Montaigne).[11]

There is one important consideration to be held in view to guard these remarks, that they are addressed to those who mean to live well. Knowledge makes the good man better but it makes the bad man worse. Knowledge in a well-ordered mind is the perception of the material and moral works of God, for He is in all things and all things exist by him. If the mind is so disordered that it does not discern him, knowledge availeth not. But to the mind that is filled with his love, all things speak of him. Let his presence go with you and all your study shall be the exploring of your Father's house. He that underrates knowledge has no just view of the generous nature of religion. A good man is never in a more religious frame than when his whole soul is excited by the discovery of new truth. There can be no acknowledgment more grateful to God than the strong and sincere joy that is then felt in its own being and powers by a pious mind. To use his gifts well, to use them according to their manifest design, and to use them for the good of all others, is surely the most acceptable tribute we can pay. And so, brethren, let us as we have opportunity get wisdom.[12] Let us save, in the week we have begun, one hour from schemes of gain, let us rob our passions of some indulgences, let us snatch some hour from the pleasant waste of idle conversation, to fence in and cultivate some spot of this domain that lies barren within us; to add one more unit to our little stock of eternal truths; to gain new and juster views of God and of his Creation.

11. "Of Solitude," in *Essays of Michael Seigneur de Montaigne* . . . , trans. Charles Cotton (London, 1693), 1:377–78; paraphrased in *JMN* 6:19.
12. Cf. Proverbs 4:7.

_____

Our conversation is in heaven.

We are all, in obedience to a law of our nature, seeking for heaven. The word was not new, the idea was not new to man when Christ brought it from God. The germ of the good he revealed lay before in the human breast. If no revelation had ever come, heaven would not the less be the desire of the soul. For, before it came, the reason of the wise and the imagination of the ignorant had concurred in this—to suggest the image of a purer existence from which hope excluded all that makes this life painful. Though there was abundance of grossness in the vulgar view, the purer minds of every nation had framed to themselves much the same vision of the state of reward—a land of unmixed love, of unfaltering virtue, of unclouded knowledge.

But the simplest account of this belief may be seen in the fact which is the origin of all these glowing pictures of future life that had been drawn—the simple hope on which these systems of hope are reared, which is shortly this; *all men do here and now from moment to moment expect to better their condition.* Every one that is born of woman beareth about with him in every hour, in all companies, in every degree of enlarged knowledge and growing virtue,—this desire (which is the element of the hope of heaven,) this desire and expectation of something better in the next hour, in the next month, in the next year, in the next life. There is in human nature this onward look;[1] and let it grow as wise as it will, it cannot outgrow the habit. You may reason with it—you cannot reason it down. Children hope; men hope; and hoary heads hope. It cleaves to the soul as a part of itself; and so it is. The mind is always looking forward and the next moment is the heaven of the present moment, as the next life is to be the heaven of this.

The first fruit of this universal desire is action, progress.

Completed May 23, 1829, at the Chardon Street house. Preached eight times: May 24, 1829, at the Second Church, Boston; November 26, 1830, again at the Second Church (Friday Lecture); December 6, 1835, in East Lexington; December 13 in Waltham; September 11, 1836, in Concord, Mass.; October 15, 1837, in Billerica; November 26 in Weston; and April 29, 1838, in Waltham. A heavily revised early version is given in the Textual and Manuscript Notes.

1. Cf. *JMN* 6:97, where the quotation is perhaps an adaptation or reminiscence of Coleridge's translation of *The Piccolomini; or the First Part of Wallenstein*, IV, iv, 54 (see Coleridge's *Works*, 1884, 7:500, and *JMN* 6:79).

The constant expectation of something better than we have, produces a constant effort to obtain it; and hence the continual enlargement of our possessions and our powers. This is its action in each moment.

The next result of this principle, is, its comprehensive view of the whole future,—is, the theory of a *better world*, which in every nation has prevailed, and always deriving its colour and form from the character of the believer. The heaven of every country has only been a mirror of that country, in which the disagreeable parts of life were left out, and the agreeable parts heightened. The idea of heaven entertained by any people is always simply a glorification of the state of society that really exists among them. In the books of the Greeks and Romans we find their Elysium described. It was a refined, a wellborn, a martial, a rich, a selfish heaven that filled their imaginations. The other world recognized the distinctions of this. The Greeks believed in a wild and partial Providence which they called Destiny, which delighted to raise and sustain the prosperity of a single family such as that of Pisistratus or Cadmus.[2] This disdain of the general rights in the selection of a few, this unfounded favouritism which they charged upon the gods, they transferred also to the other world. It was the spacious and pleasant domain of these lordly heroes, where they exercised themselves in warlike games, where illustrious kings, and sages, and poets wandered at will in beautiful meadows, and drank nectar, and were associated with the gods. But no place was there for the poor, for obscure virtue, for lowborn wisdom, for persecuted patience, for the rags and scum of life nobly borne. There were no laurels for charity. No trumpet sang the praises of humility.

But that dream of the human mind departed, when the fierce savages of Asia overran the Roman Empire. They too had their mythology, they had a *warlike* heaven, a paradise of the strong,—a glorified gymnasium; and it is pitiful to see of what cheap materials their highest visions of happiness were composed. Fresh air, fine horses, robust health, and good game filled up to the brim all their conception of well being. Yet even in this humiliating expectation is something more respectable than the notions of happiness that prevail in the East, the wretched schemes of the Turkish and Persian perfection. These asked for nothing but the lowest pleasures of sense. They would make corruption and sensuality immortal. Away with the trumpet of war—away with the chase—with labor—with abstinence. To puff smoke with a pipe—to dwell in a heaven of opium, of coffee, of debauchery as of beasts, was all they desired of their maker—was the top of their miserable ambition.[3]

Alas, my brethren, I hardly know where we should go for a more melancholy picture of man than is found in these, his famous dreams,—the dreams of centuries and of mighty nations—of a future state. These are not occasional outbreaks of passion—not the momentary paroxysm that bereaves him of his

2. "It was . . . Cadmus": see *JMN* 3:147. Pisistratus (c. 600–527 B.C.) was tyrant of Athens; Cadmus was the legendary founder of Thebes.

3. "But no place . . . ambition": see *JMN* 3:147–48.

reason, and produces falsehood or rapine or adultery or murder—no, that could have been borne in the view of the compensation of all his virtues, and the elevation of his ordinary motives; but these are the ordinary motives themselves; these are his grave and solemn hopes for the employment of all his powers during all his existence. These were his theories of the purpose for which the Almighty Maker of the Universe had created and endowed him, these were his ideas of the best things God could do for him. The most melancholy aspect of all, is when we contemplate them in view of their inevitable effect upon the characters of the believers. Such a belief would act with a steady force to degrade the soul.

But I must stop here to say that I do not believe that these gross superstitions ever possessed the weight they are supposed to have had in the communities where they existed. History gives her accounts by the gross, and never stops to record the exceptions. Every man's experience furnishes him with grounds for believing that there is in every country, how ignorant or savage soever, a minority of scrupulous contemplative minds who in every extreme of public madness retreat upon the eternal principles of truth and never give in to the revolting superstitions of the vulgar bigot. And we know that many a pious mind among the ancients was uplifted by true conceptions of God and juster hopes.

But these and such as these have been the views of future happiness entertained by the bulk of mankind, and these views it pleased God to correct by the revelation of Christ. That opened another heaven. It said to the astonished soul—'*The kingdom of God is within you.*'[4] Stop this mistaken career. Is wealth and carnal pleasure thy chief good? Behold, thou art poor with all thy treasures, thou art sorry in the midst of all thy delights. Outward things are thine instructors, thy school, and not thine home. Thou art made sufficient to thyself. Thy joy, and thy glory, and thy punishment, thy heaven, and thy hell are within thee. There is the heavenly host; there is the eye of God. The heaven thou seekest thou shalt not find. Eternal mansions, streets of pearl, and streams of amber, and trees of life, and the music of innumerable harps praising God— these are but the types—the outward representatives whereby to mortal ears the secrets of spiritual joy are faintly shadowed forth. Heaven is not a place, but a state of the mind. *Hell* is Vice, the rebellion of the Passions, the army of cares, the night of selfmade ignorance, the stings of self accusation. *Heaven* is the well ordered, informed, benevolent, self devoted mind when it adopts God's will for its own.

Whoever patiently considers what materials of happiness he already possesses, may satisfy himself that they are of an infinite nature, and so if wisely used, may produce infinite wellbeing.

Let me suggest three chief sources of happiness that are common to all men.

1. Consider the power you have of acquiring knowledge, and the great delight that belongs to the exercise of the faculties of the intellect.

4. Luke 17:21.

When first the mind perceives a new and important truth, when the intellect is quickened into rapid and powerful action, it becomes conscious of a delight which far exceeds all ordinary pleasures. In that hour the man wonders how he could ever have spent any leisure upon meaner occupations. I have seen in a French writer a description of that period of excitement which every one who has much accustomed himself to the labor of thought will recognize. "On many occasions," says he, "my soul seems to know more than it can say, and to be endowed with a mind by itself, far superior to the mind I really have."[5] Every contemplative man can recall seasons in his life when by some happy conversation, or public discourse, or private study, he had arrived at one of those general ideas which not only epitomize whole trains of thought, but cast a flood of light upon things inscrutable before. It seemed to him as if after waiting months in the vestibule of that inner temple, he had picked up unawares the master key whose touch opens every door, and the pleased adventurer goes on astonished from cell to cell, and from chamber to chamber, gratified but overawed at the unexplored extent and opulence of his own possessions.

Now these seasons may in some sort, by steady effort, be made frequent familiars. All of us have the same faculties.

2. Consider how much enjoyment belongs to the decisions of the moral sense. When you have bravely resisted an old temptation, when you have manfully given up a pleasure that was dear to you, for duty that was dearer, when you have entered heart and hand into a good cause, and feel that this day you have discharged your duty, and listen, in the silence of the passions, to the incorruptible praise of your own thoughts, with the conviction that you have endeared yourself to God, that you are recognized a good citizen of his creation, and have caused many to rejoice and not one to regret your existence,—will no serenity smooth your brow? Will no new joy light your eye? Will the meditations of that day be as the meditations of a day of sin?

3. Consider the power of the affections. Have you a friend? Have you a husband? Have you a wife? Have you a child? Have you a parent? Then I need not enlarge upon the unmeasured enjoyment God has connected with the indulgence of these powers. For there is that in every heart will vibrate to these simple names. The goodness of God is not known, the powers of the human mind are not known, until these deep and holy affections have kindled their fire therein. What work of God is so beautiful as this fellowship he has established among his creatures, this mutual relation of man to man? We speak and are understood, heart to heart, and find our attachments knit closer in proportion to the measure of virtue, and so are drawn onward to the love of God by admiring the fragments of his perfections that appear in men.

But neither is this pleasure perfect until that consecration of the affections is made when the Soul has learned to love God supremely, to regard all things as

---

5. Marivaux [Emerson's note]. See *JMN* 6:73, where the sentence is quoted from Isaac D'Israeli, *The Literary Character; or the History of Men of Genius, Drawn from their own Feelings and Confessions* (London, 1818), ch. 15.

only the manifestations of his love to it and so becomes reconciled to adversity and finds a pleasure in the darkest events, because in them God's will is done.

But these felicities of which I have spoken are open to all. We all have minds; we all have a conscience; we all have hearts; and God is the Father of us all.

Brethren, I wish to represent to you the heaven of common life. I wish you to feel that the materials of a felicity which no man attains, are yet cheap. I wish it to be felt that in the low, damp, unclean chamber of an almshouse, a joy may shine that is a stranger to houses of granite and marble. Have you dispositions that can be cultivated? Have you a mind that can be trained? Have you books that you can read? Have you friends that you can love? Have you a fellowbeing that you can benefit? Have you knowledge of God? Then heaven is before you, is around you, and when you will you may cross its threshold, and enter the everlasting doors.

For, since such is the heaven we are to look for, it immediately becomes evident that it is not postponed, that its enjoyments do not depend upon remote contingences, upon great changes that may take place in the universe, upon life or death, but that it may be entered now, that the gates of the paradise of God stand open night and day.[6]

Why do you wait? Do you wish to be happy hereafter, thirty or forty years hence? Why do you put a value upon happiness *then*, and neglect the present hour? Five minutes of this day are as much a part of my being, and the enjoyment of that space of time as important to me, as the enjoyment of five minutes a million of years hence.[7]

But, says the voluptuary, I also say the same thing, and because present pleasure is as good as future pleasure, and more good in as much as it is more secure,—it is unwise to practise the self denial that religion demands.

The answer to this cavil is plain. Whilst the enjoyment of the present is valuable to me so is the enjoyment of the future. I will therefore choose such pleasures now as shall not prejudice my happiness hereafter.[8] I find there are such pleasures. Upon trial I find there is a wonderful difference between their *end* and the end of others. I find the pleasures of sense change their character the moment they are past and appear to me flat and foolish when they are no worse. But these have no base conclusion—no deformed old age. These pleasures are not dead. They live and add to the amount of my happiness after they are acted. They are medicines and solaces and motives.

I do not, my friends, undervalue the scene that revelation has promised to good men when this life closes because I believe you may anticipate its bliss. I believe a magnificent scene shall open upon the soul equal to its enlarged powers. The body is here a constant obstruction to the energies of the mind. Its obstructions, its temptations, its diseases, shall be dropt with it. If the mind can

6. Cf. Revelation 2:7.
7. Cf. *JMN* 9:56.
8. Emerson's adaptation of Epicurus; see *JMN* 6:157.

only act with as much freedom as we can imagine, the gain of that loss will be immense. But I believe its good then, will be of the same nature as its good now.

It is not that I wish to lower your views of the future, but that I would exalt your views of what may be done in the present. I would to God I might awaken the attention of every torpid hearer till he had measured with his eye the scope of his powers; till he saw how glorious this low life that we lead might be made; till he saw how much knowledge the faithful use of every moment might collect; till he saw to what colossal proportions of wisdom that knowledge would swell the soul; till he saw what degrees of self-command a human soul may attain; till he apprehended the depth of the affections and the majesty of truth; till he apprehended the intimate connexion which can subsist between himself and God, when his own heart shall beat pulse for pulse in harmony with the universal whole and by assimilating to the character, begins to enjoy the beatitudes, of the Divinity.

Whoso can carry out these views to a just extent will find that there is heaven enough in man to satisfy the sublimest hopes; that there is nothing injurious to our expectations in the doctrine that our richest enjoyments are already ripe and wait to be gathered; there is nothing injurious—because the more deeply you drink at these fountains the more happiness they will yield.

Therefore, let our conversation be in heaven. Now, whilst yet these pleasures are in our power; now whilst yet is the accepted time;[9] that when death comes to us which is every day bereaving us of our friends, we may already have made proficiency in the language, and the spirit, and the customs of that better country to which God has called us.[10]

9. II Corinthians 6:2.
10. Cf. Hebrews 11:16.

XXXVIII

*Be ye therefore perfect, even as your father
who is in heaven is perfect.*

MATTHEW 5:48

The alarming amount of moral evil excites a general concern, and gives rise to numberless plans to counteract and remove it. Societies are formed, and sermons preached, and contributions levied, and tracts distributed with this intent; and when all is done, good men often sigh with despondency because after all this costly apparatus of means has been exhausted, there stands the monumental evil as strong and as threatening as ever. What is the reason of this? Can we do nothing to lessen this putrefying mass whose poisonous vapor ascendeth forever and ever?[1] If not, we are lost, for the very reason of our interest is that it is full of contagion and menaces our health and peace and that of the human family. What is the defect in our remedies?

The fault seems to be in the disposition of men to regard virtue and vice as *things of the world*, in which we had not a first concern. We forget that *we* are the world; that the reason why society is sensual or dishonest or illiberal or malignant or calumnious is that we are so. The member of the *society for suppressing intemperence* is himself to a certain degree intemperate; he eats and drinks too delicately and too much. The member of the *Peace Society* is petulant in his family, and is hard in a bargain with his neighbour—and these things are the very causes of war. The member of the *Howard Benevolent Society*[2] is an indolent man or he brings up his children in expensive habits, and forgets that thus he is doing far more as a member of the community to increase the objects of charity twenty years hence than he is doing as a member of the society to relieve what misery now exists. The member of the *Bible society* does not govern his own life by the book which he would have translated into all languages, and of the *Missionary Society* is apt to forget in his conversation that charity begins at home.

A man hardly excuses himself if he have lent his aid and countenance to no one of these numerous benevolent efforts; and when he has done this, he com-

---

Manuscript dated May 30, 1829, at Chardon Street. Preached twice: May 31, 1829, at the Second Church, Boston, and June 27 in Concord, N.H.

1. Cf. Revelation 14:11.
2. A Boston Unitarian charity to aid the poor, founded in 1812.

placently congratulates himself upon the efficiency of the means whereby we act on others;—*to act on others*—that is the word—as if it would do any good to act on others without first acting on yourself.

Brethren, here is the sin on which I wish to fix your attention, that we are living without sufficient elevation of purpose. Is it not true that men, or that each individual man, having within him *reason*, the light which the Almighty has given him, yet lives without using it? Is it not true that we live, (to use the vulgar expression) from hand to mouth,—we live by accident, and not by foresight. We do not move by system but by chance. It would not be guessed from our actions that we are children of God who are offered an unmeasured spiritual benefit as the reward of the exertions we shall make. We are slovens on Providence. No man does all the good he can, or measures the extent of his ability; but is pushed up by chance into influence and place. You are well acquainted with the way of life and manner of thinking of fifty or a hundred persons. How many of them do you suppose bring all their habits to the bar of reason?

Men measure what is expected of them by what they see without, and not by what they feel within. Is it not true that for the most part each man does with the least amount of virtue that will pass? They avail themselves of bad customs as a plea for their own delinquency. They forget that they are the very persons who should *originate* customs, bring severe virtue, lofty action into use. Indeed they who know best do sometimes seem to connive at a low standard that inconvenient exertions and sacrifices may not be expected from them.

Men are content with the creditable not the possible measure of truth and goodness, and desire to be as well-informed and as temperate and as honest and as bountiful as others, and not as much so as they can.

Hence all the ridicule which the satire of every age has thrown, and justly thrown, on the tyranny of custom, whereby men habitually permit themselves to descend from the dignity of humanity to be led as a flock of sheep to the slaughter house of every passion and every vanity. There is a regard prevailing among us to the usage of society in evil things, that is a proper superstition. We have a reverence for society in the aggregate, that we have not for it in detail. We have many neighbours and friends—some of them wise and good men—but when we consider the character of each of them apart we find in it many defects—much that is wrong and much that is only ridiculous. Each of them however falls far short, in our judgment, of the perfection of his nature. He is only a common man and in no wise fit to be the keeper for our conscience. But the moment you put them together and they appear as Society—though the characters are the same in the multitude that they were alone; though 'tis nothing as before but a great many disagreeing, imperfect, passionate persons, yet the eye is vanquished, and the reason prostrated. Now we are willing to surrender our freedom. Now we *must* do as they do. Their opinion begins to look to us like truth, and their act like virtue, fashion for Virtue. And so it happens that a thousand base and injurious falsehoods in religion, in politics, and in education, that have been palmed on the world, maintain their ground like truths and nature, by reason of the reverence men give to "the hoary head and wicked face of ancient Use."[3]

The design of the gospel of Christ, the object of every admonition God sends to the soul of man from without or from within, is, to break this evil yoke, divorce you from these relations to others, and to make you free, to make you solitary. Man! Woman! in the relations you sustain to God, no other creature in the universe can partake. You exist to him and He exists to you in a regard that excludes all other fellowship. The gospel teaches you to act for yourself, to act as if there was none but yourself in the world to give account of his actions, for, in this regard, the creation is clean swept of all existences beside; there are no sympathies to support, no intercession that can avail you. It teaches you to cease from this poor shuffling to shift your responsibility to any other shoulders. It cannot be done. To each moral agent whom God has made, is a relation independent, lonely, peculiar; a solitary law; a several universe. As the times, parentage, talents, national religion, health, and so forth, of every individual varies from those of every other, so to each must justice be administered with a compound regard to all these circumstances. The believer of the Koran must be judged by one law, and he to whom the light of Christianity has come, by another.

In this great operation of Christianity, its separation of each from all, it does not address classes but individuals; it does not speak to kings, or to gentlemen and to heads of families, to the old or to the young; it marks not out invidiously a middle interest; there is no lower class inferior in this wide republic of moral being. It addresses itself with a directness and application to each soul from which none may shelter or withdraw. It calls upon every one that is among you to cleanse and exalt the motives of your action; to obey the scripture which God has writ within you, which the divine word in our text echoes; to be satisfied with no imperfect attainments; to leave your leanings upon all other beings and faithfully obey, for yourself, every commandment of God.

It declares to you that God has marked you with an immutable distinction from his other works, that is, by *Understanding*. Now, inasmuch as an animal is of more value than a machine, so is an independent mind more excellent than a dependent one. Nay this is only half the truth, for, the very nature and use of mind, is *intelligence, sight;* but if the mind will not see, but takes report from the eyes of others and forgoes its own faculties to borrow theirs, it does deny, it does unmake itself, it does what it can, to lay down all its title to the unutterable glory God has formed it to enjoy. It holds cheap the gift of God. It is spiritual suicide, and if any thing shall move the Author of our Being to quench the spark he hath imparted, one would think it would be this ungrateful stupidity. Fear thou that which shall kill the soul.[4] You are made capable of independent action, and you are called to it.

3. Montaigne [Emerson's note]. See "Of Custom," in *Essays of Michael Seigneur de Montaigne* . . . , trans. Charles Cotton (London, 1693), 1:161–62.
4. Cf. Matthew 10:28.

"The delivery of the talent is the call."[5]

Forbear then this treacherous habit of appealing from yourself—from the eternal man within your own breast[6]—to the judgements of others, whenever you would speak or act. Forbear that inquiring look into others' eyes. It marks a submission both disgraceful and dangerous. Read, study and know yourself. Believe God will never be wanting to you if you are not wanting to yourself. And sleep out no more time in a stationary religion. Wake to the truth that no moment of your life is without consequences, for yourself is improved or injured every day. Set your eye in performing a good action on the true reward, and not on a false one. When you are going to make a sacrifice, do not propose to yourself *praise*, even the most private, not the praise of your wife, or your brother, or of the obscurest child of indigence you visit and relieve, but the virtue itself. Sublimity of character must proceed from sublimity of motive.[7] Scorn every motive that presents itself but the highest one.

It is one mark of real elevation of mind, if you are content to notice, on any occasion, your own superiority in knowledge, or in manners, or in strength and severity of virtuous feeling, with gratitude to God and desire to increase it without calling the notice of others to the same, or permitting yourself to wish for the observation of it by others; for, the moment you do hunger for that praise, you descend from your elevation.

And fear not that when your secret good deed escapes the knowledge and so loses the approbation of those who are nearest to you or of those whom it benefits, fear not that its advantage is, in any the least particle, lost to yourself. Every such action, whatever else it may do, does one thing—elevates, ennobles the doer, makes you a more powerful being, and by and by you shall feel its effect in the increased esteem of all other minds, and in the augmented vigor of your own. For do you suppose that you could long govern yourself by this lofty regard to the perfection of your being, without the most sensible effect? It would appear in your countenance, it would appear in your manners, in your carriage; if an angel was within, the body could not disguise its inmate. Love and honour and the imitation of all ingenuous minds could not fail to follow you. So should the declaration of the apostle take effect, that godliness hath the promise of the life that now is, and of the life that is to come.[8]

And now, my brother, consider that every place is a theatre of trial and, if you choose, a theatre of triumph. Wherever man exists—wherever your vocation lies—is duty to be done and perfection to be sought. In the parlor, shop, court house, church, these objects may be attained. When you go to the family board

5. See *JMN* 3:223, where the sentence is attributed to Abraham Tucker (pseud. "Edward Search"), author of *The Light of Nature Pursued*, 7 vols. (London, 1768-1777). Used in "Ethics," *EL* 2:147 and in "Spiritual Laws," *CW* 2:82.

6. See Sermon I, n. 15.

7. This sentence is a quotation from Mary Moody Emerson. See *JMN* 1:340, 2:260, 3:4, 3:26; used in "Mary Moody Emerson," *W* 10:406.

8. I Timothy 4:8.

consider it as a place where these highest motives are to come in, that there are the temptations with which you must strive; there are the companions with whom God appoints you should pass your life; there are the means of strengthening your self command, and nourishing your virtues. O then carry yourself cautiously, keep reason master of the appetites. In all your conversation, set a sleepless watch over your tongue, that you utter no slander, that you utter no falsehood, that you vent no intemperate illnatured expression, that there and everywhere, in every moment, you carry into execution the faintest whispers of the conscience.

My brethren, the great heights of perfect obedience, which as far as they are within your reach are within the command of your duty, your religion, are not to be attained without the love of God, without the acknowledgment of him by prayer, and by praise; without living in a stricter connexion with him than the naming his name, and coming up to his churches. The sense of his presence and providence must never desert you. But consider, every effort in one kind is an effort in the other. When you come to strict truth, there is no ground for the distinction that is continually made between religion and morality. All good feelings are related to each other. All good works are of God, and lead directly to him. By every virtue that you practise *in the spirit of a virtue*, that is, not for ostentation or pride, or some mean purpose, but for virtue's sake, you shall find you love God better, and more clearly behold him; so also by every act of genuine worship to God, you shall find you more easily desire and practise the virtues.

Finally, let it cheer you in every attempt you make to attain the perfection of your being that by each act you are answering in the only effectual way the purposes of reforming the world which men are now essaying with such feeble success. For when it is directed at your own character, not a single effort is without effect. That is the true way to act on others. You compel people to be better, by being better yourself. For you do something to raise the standard of virtue in the world which is always the average of the virtue of individuals. *Be ye therefore perfect even as your Father in heaven is perfect.*

XXXIX

The day is thine, the night also is thine: thou hast prepared the light, and the sun. Thou hast set all the borders of the earth, thou hast made summer.

PSALMS 74:16–17

In this grateful season, the most careless eye is caught by the beauty of the external world. The most devoted of the sons of gain cannot help feeling that there is pleasure in the blowing of the southwest wind; that the green tree with its redundant foliage and its fragrant blossoms shows fairer than it did a few weeks since when its arms were naked and its trunk was sapless. The inhabitants of cities pay a high tax for their social advantages, their increased civilization, in their exclusion from the sight of the unlimited glory of the earth. Imprisoned in streets of brick and stone, in tainted air and hot and dusty corners they only get glimpses of the glorious sun, of the ever changing glory of the clouds, of the firmament, and of the face of the green pastoral earth which the great Father of all is now adorning with matchless beauty as one wide garden. Still something of the mighty process of vegetation forces itself on every human eye. The grass springs up between the pavements at our feet and the poplar and the elm send out as vigorous and as graceful branches to shade and to fan the town as in their native forest.

Those who yield themselves to these pleasant influences behold in the activity of vegetation a new expression from moment to moment of the Divine power and goodness. They know that this excellent order did not come of itself, that this organized creation of every new year indicates the presence of God.

We are confident children, confident in God's goodness. Though we all of us know that the year's subsistence to us depends on the fidelity with which rain and sun shall act on the seed, we never doubt the permanence of the Order. We do not refer our own subsistence, especially in cities, to the rain and the sun and the soil. We do not refer the loaf in our basket, or the meats that smoke on our board to the last harvest. And when we do, we fail often to derive from the

---

Manuscript dated June 13, 1829, at Chardon Street. Preached three times: June 14, 1829, at the Second Church, Boston; June 19, 1831, again at the Second Church; and July 16, 1837, in East Lexington.

296

changes of nature that lesson which to a pious, to a Christian, mind, they ought to convey.

My brethren, all nature is a book on which one lesson is written, and blessed are the eyes that can read it. On the glorious sky it is writ in characters of fire; on earth it is writ in the majesty of the green ocean; it is writ on the volcanoes of the south, and the icebergs of the polar sea; on the storm, in winter; in summer on every trembling leaf; on man in the motion of the limbs, and the changing expression of the face, in all his dealings, in all his language it is seen, and may be read and pondered and practised in all. This lesson is the omnipresence of God—the presence of a love that is tender and boundless. Yet man shuts his eyes to this sovereign goodness, thinks little of the evidence that comes from nature, and looks upon the great system of the world only in parcels as its order happens to affect his petty interest. In the seasons he thinks only whether a rain or sunshine will suit his convenience. In the regions of the world he thinks only of his farm or his town. Let us lift up our eyes to a more generous and thankful view of the earth and the Seasons.

Do they not come from Heaven and go like Angels round the globe scattering hope and pleasant toil and recompense and rest? Each righting the seeming disorders, supplying the defects which the former left; converting its refuse into commodity and drawing out of the ancient earth new treasures to swell the capital of human comfort. Each fulfils the errand on which it was sent. The faintness and despondence of a spring that never opened into summer; the languor of a constant summer; the satiety of an unceasing harvest; the torpor or the terror of a fourfold winter are not only prevented by the ordination of Providence, but they are not feared; and emotions of an opposite character are called forth as we hail the annual visits of these friendly changes at once too familiar to surprize and too distinct and distant to weary us. It is in these as they come and go, that we may recognize the steps of our heavenly Father. We may accustom our minds to discern his power and benevolence in the profusion and the beauty of his common gifts, as the wheat and the vine. Nor do these seem sufficiently appreciated. We look at the works of human art—a pyramid, a stately church, and do not conceal our pleasure and surprise at the skill and force of men to lift such masses and to create such magnificent forms, which skill after all does but remove, combine, and shape the works of God. For the granite, and the marble, and the hands that hewed them from the quarry, are his work. But after they are builded, and the scaffolding is thrown down, and they stand in strength and beauty, there is more exquisite art goes to the formation of a strawberry than is in the costliest palace that human pride has ever reared. In the constitution of that small fruit is an art that eagle eyed science cannot explore, but sits down baffled. It cannot detect how the odour is formed and lodged in these minute vessels, or where the delicate life of the fruit resides.

Our patient science explores, as it can, every process, opens its microscopes upon every fibre, and hunts every globule of sap that ascends in the stem, but it never has detected the secret it seeks. It cannot restore the vegetable it has dissected and analyzed. Where should we go for an ear of corn if the earth refused her increase? With all our botany how should we transform a seed into an ear, or make from the grain of one stalk the green promise and the full harvest that covers acres with its sheaves. The frequency of occurrence makes it expected that a little kernel, properly sowed, will become at harvest time a great number of kernels. Because we have observed the same result on many trials, this multiplication is expected. But explain to me, man of learning! any part of this productiveness. There is no tale of metamorphosis in poetry, no fabulous transformation that children read in the Arabian Tales more unaccountable, none so benevolent, as this constant natural process which is going on at this moment in every garden, in every foot of vacant land in three zones of the globe.

Go out into a garden and examine a seed; examine the same plant in the bud and in the fruit, and you must confess the whole process a miracle, a perpetual miracle. Take it at any period, make yourself as familiar with all the facts as you can, at each period, and in each explanation, there will be some step or appearance to be referred directly to the great Creator; something not the effect of the sower's deposit, nor of the waterer's hope. It is not the loam, nor the gravel, it is not the furrow of the ploughshare nor the glare of the sun that calls greenness from the dust, it is the present power of Him who said 'Seedtime and harvest shall not fail.'[1] Needs there, my brethren, any other book than this returning summer that reminds us of the first creation to suggest the presence of God? Shall we indulge our querulous temper in this earth where nature is fragrant with healthful odours and glowing with every pleasant colour? Man marks with emphatic pleasure or complaint the pleasant and the unpleasant days, as if he forgot the uses of the storm, the masses of vapour it collects and scatters over thirsty soils and the plants that were hardened or moistened by the rough weather, forgot the ships that were borne homeward by the breeze that chills him, or in short, as if he forgot that our Father is in Heaven, and the winds and the seas obey him.[2]

We have been looking at nature as an exhibition of God's benevolence. It will be felt the more to be so when it is considered that *the same results might have been brought about without this beauty*. The earth contains abundant materials for the nourishment of the human stomach, but they do not exist there in a state proper for our use. Now the tree, the vegetable, may be properly considered as a machine by which the nutritious matter is separated from other elements, is taken up out of chalk, and clay, and manures, and prepared as by a culinary process into grateful forms and delicious flavours for the pleasure of our taste and for our sustenance. The little seed of the apple does not contain the large tree that shall spring from it; it is merely an assimilating engine which has the power to take from the ground whatever particles of water or manure it needs, and turn them to its own substance and give them its own arrangement.

1. Genesis 8:22.
2. Matthew 8:27, Mark 4:41, Luke 8:25.

For the nourishment of animal life this process goes on, and to such incom-
putable activity and extent, not in one spot, not in one land, but on the whole
surface of the globe. Each soil is finishing its own, and each a different fruit.
Not only on the hard soil of New England, the oak, the potato and the corn are
swelling their fruit, but on the shores of the Red Sea the coffee tree is ripening its
berries; on the hills of France and Spain the grape is gathering sweetness. The
West Indies are covered with the green canes and the East with spices—and the
mulberries for the silk worm. The cotton plant is bursting its pod in the warm
plantations of the south, and the orange and the fig bloom in the mediterranean
islands.

But all this food might have been prepared as well without this glorious show.
To what end this unmeasured magnificence? It is for the soul of man. For his eye
the harvest waves, for him the landscape wears this glorious show. For to what
end else can it be! Can the wheat admire its own tasselled top? or the oak in
autumn its crimson foliage, or the rose and the lily their embroidery? If there
were no mind in the Universe, to what purpose this profusion of design? It is
adapted to give pleasure to us. I cannot behold the cheering beauty of a country
landscape at this season without believing that it was intended that I should
derive from it this pleasure. It is for the same reason as the rainbow is beautiful
and the sun is bright.

But there is more in nature than beauty; there is more to be seen than the
outward eye perceives; there is more to be heard than the pleasant rustle of the
corn. There is the language of its everlasting analogies by which it seems to be
the prophet and the monitor of the race of man. The Scripture is always appealing to the tree and the flower and the grass as the emblems of our mortal estate.
It was the history of man in the beginning, and it is the history of man now.
Man is like the flower of the field. In the morning he is like grass that groweth
up; in the Evening he is cut down and withereth.[3] There is nothing in external
nature but is an emblem, a hieroglyphic of some thing in us. Youth is the
Spring, and manhood the Summer, and age the Autumn, and Death the Winter
of Man. My brethren, do you say these things are old and trite? that is their very
value and warning; so is the harvest old—the apple that hangs on your tree, six
thousand times has shown its white bloom, its green germ, and its ripening
yellow since our period of the world begins. And this day, as the fruit is as fresh,
so is its moral as fresh and significant to us as it was to Adam in the garden.

I have spoken of the great system of external nature as exciting in our minds
the perception of the benevolence of God by the wonderful contrivance their
fruits exhibit; by the food they furnish us, and by the beauty that is added to
them; and now, of the admonition they seem intended to convey of our short
life.

But there is yet a louder and more solemn admonition which they convey to
my mind as they do from year to year their appointed work. They speak to man

3. Psalms 90:5–6.

as a moral being, and reproach his lassitude by their brute fidelity. Here we sit waiting the growing of the grain, with an undoubting reliance. If it is blasted in one field, we are sure it will thrive in another. Yet we know that if one harvest of the earth fails, the race must perish from the face of the earth. We have an expectation always of the proper performance of the vegetable functions that would not be increased if one rose from the dead.

Well, now, whilst thus directly we depend on this process on the punctuality of the sun, on the timely action of saps and seed vessels, and rivers and rains, *are we as punctual to our orbit?* Are we as trustworthy as the weed at our feet? Yet is that a poor machine—and I, besides the animal machinery that is given me, have been entrusted with a portion of the spirit that governs the material Creation, that made and directs the machinery.—Are ye not much better than they?

Shall we to whom the light of the Almighty has been given, shall we who have been raised in the scale of the Creation to the power of self government, not govern ourselves? shall the flower of the field reprove us and make it clear that it had been better for us to have wanted than to have received intelligence?

My friends, let us accustom ourselves thus to look at the fruits of the earth and the seasons of the year. Let all that we see without, only turn our attention with stricter scrutiny on all that is within us. In the beautiful order of the world, shall man alone, the highly endowed inhabitant, present a spectacle of disorder, the misrule of the passions, and rebellion against the laws of his Maker? Let us learn also the lesson they are appointed to teach of trust in God; that he will provide for us if we do his will; remembering the words of the Lord Jesus, who said—"If God so clothe the grass of the field, which today is and tomorrow is cast into the oven, will he not much more care for you, o ye of little faith!"[4]

4. Matthew 6:30 and Luke 12:28.

XL

And above all things have fervent charity among yourselves, for charity shall cover the multitude of sins.

I Peter 4:8

The season has arrived, as you were notified the last Sabbath, when it is usual to call upon you for a contribution to the Evangelical Treasury. It is pleasant to me to plead its cause. I cannot let the occasion pass without offering to your consideration some remarks that have a wider scope than the recommending to your notice our small but useful fund—I mean in general but briefly to urge the duty of Charity.

The social duties, at least when they get out of one's own household, do not seem to be allowed their full claim. In transactions with government, in paying the price of protection and reasonable independence, men are apt to take a latitude which they would severely condemn in themselves in their private dealings. Yet it can easily be shown that by their tax, or their duties on merchandize, they do purchase real advantages which they could not do without and therefore are guilty of as culpable frauds in evading them as if they had been dishonest in a private bargain.

So in regard to those general duties which a man owes to the community, his concurrence and aid in designs of common utility, his adhesion to a political party, his duty of not only guarding but giving his suffrage in elections, his patronage of good schools, of libraries, of lyceums, and the like—men seem to do what they do out of courtesy and not as if they felt any strain of obligation. I should rather men would do it out of good will than because they were bound, but those who leave this duty undone ought to feel that whilst these duties are from their very nature very indefinite, very little specific, and have a different demand on every individual varying with his means, age, talents, condition, yet is their obligation always to do something and the obligation is always demonstrable.

So is it with Charity. God does not enjoin the giving a farm, a purse of gold, a

---

Preached once: June 14, 1829, at the Second Church, Boston. The minister of the Second Church was responsible for reporting annually to the congregation on the distribution of funds from the Evangelical Treasury. Emerson took the opportunity to preach on Charity.

301

tithe or an hundredth of your estate; he writes no positive law, no arithmetic, but he says, give all.[1] Hold all with that state of mind which feels all is only a trust held during God's good pleasure. He says to the rich man, and every man in some way is rich, Be my steward. Use my gifts for the benefit of my children, thy fellow men. He does not stipulate in words. It is not God's way. But he sends to your door a ragged beggar to receive the divine rents. He casts into your sight or hearing the account of a suffering family. Some friend brings you the Report of the Fragment Society or of a Charity School. Some unfortunate person on whom the world puts affronts or a freezing neglect is thrown in your way who needs consolation and attentions which at the moment it may require a considerable sacrifice of time or inclination for you to bestow.

A man who holds strange and bigoted views of religion is reviled in your presence, but you know some good of him, have reason to believe that he is at bottom a good man. This is the call that God makes on you. These are all charities. For Charity does not depend on the amount of treasure: remember the widow's mite.[2] There is sometimes more hospitality in a smile than in sumptuous entertainments. The gospel deals with principles and only desires to bring out the will, for the same will that prompts the cordial smile now would prompt the devotion of property or of life on the proper occasion. But in all, the duty is not to be embraced within general rules—is new and peculiar in each new case and yet in each is solemn and binding.

The Gospel whose servants we are does not leave us in the solitary state. It separates men to bear each his own responsibility to God, but it joins men together for affection and mutual help. It animates to a greatness of charity, to an expansion of the heart, that we are very slow of attaining. The sublime theory we have learned from the Bible, is that man is made in the image of God and we are taught to feel this conviction and to carry ourselves worthily of it and to aim to be like him,[3] to be satisfied with no grandeur of character less than the grandeur of those affections that embrace the whole system of Being in their omnipresent force. We are to be fellow workers with God and every moment of life and every power we have is to be spent in the effort to add to the vast amount of well being of the whole. Well, brethren, this is the theory, and how stands the fact? I am almost disheartened at pursuing in words the contrast which the mind of every one reads in an instant. Yet I will say it. Will the desire of the imitation of your Father in Heaven let you be content when you have paid for your bread and paid for your clothes and paid for your comforts with as many dollars as would buy them; when you have bought your protection, your pleasures, your distinctions, and all that Society could give you, with just that pittance that would procure them and not a cent more, and now do you say, 'I have defrauded nobody; the world and I are square'? And thus do you imitate God?

1. Cf. Matthew 19:21, Mark 10:21, and Luke 12:33, 18:22.
2. Mark 12:42–44 and Luke 21:2–4.
3. Cf. Genesis 1:26–27.

But in detail. Think again. You have earned your own estate by your own labour. But whence had you the powers of successful and self improving action? Have you paid a price for the simple enjoyments of being, of thinking, of acting, of loving? Have you paid for the hope of immortal life? I am afraid there are blessings for which you have forgotten to thank God. I thank God there are blessings for which you can never pay the price.

But yet, says the selfish man—I take care of my own household; if every one will do as much there is no need of suffering.—Aye, but God takes care of this forlorn family by giving you more than enough for the support of your own.

Yet the selfish man says,—all charity is a bounty to vice. There was mismanagement somewhere or there never would be misery. I am sorry they suffer, but follow it up, and you shall find it was their own fault.—But is it for you to punish? Do you desire the office of the executioner by your avarice and hardness of heart—of the divine chastisements?

And whom in this do you say you imitate? Not Him surely who sendeth his rain on those who serve him and those who serve him not;[4] not Him who asks no return of his boundless beneficence save poor good will alone; who whilst the objects of his bounty are nothing, are atoms, emmets on the ground, never a moment relaxes the energy and profusion of his overflowing bounty; not Him who adds comfort to the bare necessaries of life and joy to comfort and majesty to joy and goes on endowing with endless duration and infinite enlargement the powers that lie folded up in the soul of man. Him who has lit up the Universe with this splendid congregation of suns and systems, wherein the earth we inhabit is an unseen speck, and now speaks to the mind of each of you in his word to assure you that all this glory is dull and base to the immortal endowments with which he has clothed you to live in communion with Him forevermore.

My brethren, besides this comprehensive doctrine of the imitation of a perfect being which our religion teaches—it is a beautiful distinction of Christianity that it ever inculcates with great force this law of love, that it teaches charity. And its effect has been to create throughout Christendom charitable institutions, with every variety of pious object that human want could suggest. Then it has made *charitable men*. These are its true trophies, these are the redeemers of the race. Amid all the depravity we see and feel, amid all the anecdotes of sensuality and selfishness that pain our ears, let us rejoice that Charity is no unreal fabulous virtue. There is hope for the race while the servants of this grace survive. We know there are men who feel and act habitually from this godlike impulse, who, in the community which they bless, are honoured contributors to human happiness—men whose hearts are the asylums of the land—where the wretched find a solace and a home, the men to whose ears every tale of sorrow, every kind and useful project, finds its unerring way—pick

---

4. Cf. Matthew 5:45.

them out by instinct—and whose hands are swift and skilful in the work of deliverance.

Nor will I leave this most grateful topic until I have uttered my tribute of respect to one form which this virtue takes and which impresses my mind with peculiar force: I refer to those instances which are continually brought to light of donations to good objects, of benefactors whose name no tongue repeats, only one breast in the wide earth knoweth. I do reverence and honour with all my heart, that elevated mind who needs no praise but his own, who has trusted the secret of his bounty with God alone. It is one of the most beautiful acts of which man is capable. It is a contract with his maker. He has trusted himself to principles which the future shall justify. He has cast his bread upon the waters, upon the waters of God's Providence, and surely it shall come back to his bosom in mighty increase.[5]

But it is time to bring before you the subject which gave occasion to these remarks. As the institution denominated the Evangelical Treasury is designed to be and has been the Almoner of this religious Society, it seems perfectly reasonable that you should be informed of what it has done and what it has desired to do. As all who hear me may not be acquainted with it, I may mention the Evangelical Treasury is a charitable association of this parish. As we are united as a Christian Society, we feel it to be our duty to comply with Christianity's great requisition—to do good; and as more efficiency can be gained by an independent body than by the society at large, a large number of individuals associated themselves five years ago in a benevolent institution to consider and act upon any charitable objects, especially those that arise within our own church, or the schools, or other benevolent interests related to it. Each member subscribed one dollar a year, and by leave of the standing Committee, it was agreed to collect an annual contribution. Not more than $200, I believe, has been raised in any year. A few objects have always demanded and received steady attention of the Directors. An annual appropriation has been made to a committee of which the Pastor has been one, for the relief of the sick and indigent in the Society, and has been applied to the purchase of wood, the payment of rent, and other uses, as their discretion dictated in individual cases.

The annual appropriation of twenty five dollars is made to the Church Library. Other appropriations have been to the Sunday Schools; to the Evangelical Missionary Society; and to the instruction of the poor in this city, and to other claims appearing to have the same commanding importance.

On account of the absence of the Pastor the last June,[6] it is now two years since any report has been made. I briefly state in behalf of the Directors what has been done. About $350.00 have been expended in these two years.

In May, 1827, the attention of the Directors was called by the Pastor to the

5. Cf. Ecclesiastes 11:1.
6. Henry Ware, Jr.

wants of the Society of Christians in the city of New York, and the sum of fifty dollars was voted to aid them in building a house of public worship.

The claims of the Evangelical Missionary Society, a very useful society which provides for the preaching of the gospel in destitute places, have been felt and the amount of $100.00 has been given them, fifty dollars each year.

The Hancock Sabbath School has received at different times the sum of $45.00. With the interests and successful operation of this school I rejoice that you are well acquainted.

The Church Library has received only twenty dollars each year of the two last instead of the former appropriation of $25. I sincerely hope the means of the Treasury may be so enlarged in the present year that this important object may have its full share. This is a charity which begins at home. It is the interest and the duty of every family and every individual to give the greatest activity of circulation to good books of every kind, those seeds of civilization, those silent benefactors, those modest missionaries that carry light and truth and virtue from one generation to another.

The Sick and Indigent, and particularly those in our own society, have drawn the attention of the Directors. It was the dictate of common humanity to find out and to help these unhappy sufferers. We live in a fair city. It is full of commodious and of spacious mansions. But the eye that sees the morning sun shine on long streets of decorated dwellings is apt to forget how many obscure garrets, how many damp basements, are here and there found amid this magnificence that contain victims of real suffering, poor men and women reduced by consumptions or bedridden with rheumatisms, or worn with fruitless labors to meet demands the quarter day. The Committee, chiefly by their organ, the Pastor, have aided according to their means in giving very limited but, as it is believed, valuable assistance in these cases, by sending fuel, and small sums towards the payment of rent.

On these objects they have in the two years expended the sum of $85.17.

It is well known that within a few years past a very considerable attention has been paid to the subject of the Free Religious Instruction of the Poor. It was ascertained that this city contained 13,000 families, and that between 3 and 4000 families were left without the reach of religious instruction. Anxious, the Directors gave fifty dollars to aid in erecting the Chapel in Friend St. They did what they could and regretted it was no more. And at this moment a new application is before one of their committees for a yet more urgent exigency of the same cause. $2.50 have been paid for incidental expenses.

My friends, I have laid these facts before you, our little labours for great objects. I bring this petition in my hand. I heartily beg you to enlarge our means. In making this request, bear me witness, brethren, I have not a desire to push it an inch beyond its merits. I would not if I could make a demand on your good feelings, which reason would not support me in making.

No, and therefore I do not make it to all. There are always some in every congregation who need charity themselves to meet their own just obligations.

To such I say, We ask nothing but your good will. You have no right to be charitable. God has seen fit to deny to you, the luxury of doing good, at least in this way. But if there be any whom he has blest in your basket and your store, whose children are rising around you under the smile of his Providence, whose friends regard you with deference and love, and congratulate you on your growing prospects of usefulness and good repute in the community, any to whom health and power of an active mind, the means of knowledge and troops of friends and spiritual gifts,[7] the gospel of Christ and the hope of everlasting life have been given to them, I say, show now your title to the blessings you enjoy by doing what you can to impart them.

My brethren, I hope you do not think that I am disposed to overrate the importance of this Charity. I think these claims are serious and strong, but it is not so much this particular claim that I value but that in every instance where a proper call is made the cold restraints of an extreme prudence, the low calculations we are all prone to make, should be accustomed to give way, that we should feel there is something better than being rich, and that our hearts should be habituated to expand to a wide, a divine benevolence.

Do you say this is a slight occasion? Life is made up of slight occasions. These humble appeals of humble men are in the course of Providence the very strongest calls God chooses to make on those affections that belong to your highest nature and must be brought out or you are lost. And the day will come when this hour and this hour's admonitions will be remembered with great distinctness and the event of this appeal will lie in your memory. It was written on the tomb of the benevolent man "What I have given away is all I now possess."[8] The day will shortly come to close the mortal account of all, the day which takes all we have out of our hand. Our earthly comforts, the pleasures and luxuries which money can buy—can please us but a few months or a few days; hold on them as you will they are slipping out of your hands; but by their sacrifice the character which we carry out of this world shall be enriched. Thus has God put it into our power with our earthly wealth to buy us bags of treasure which wax not old, a treasure in the heavens that shall forever accumulate.[9] Verily I say unto you, said our Lord, He that has given unto the least of these, my brethren, a cup of water, shall in no wise lose his reward.[10]

7. Cf. Shakespeare, *Macbeth*, V, iii, 25.
8. The many variant forms of this sentence are traceable to a line by the Latin poet Rabirius ("Hoc habeo quodcunque dedi") quoted by Seneca in *De Beneficiis*, VI, iii, 1.
9. Luke 12:33.
10. Cf. Matthew 10:42 and Mark 9:41.

XLI

Though I walk through the valley of the shadow of death I will fear no evil for Thou art with me.

PSALMS 23:4

My friends, we come up to this holy place once in seven days and what we do often, we are prone to do thoughtlessly. We grow familiar with the sight of a house of worshippers, and the scene loses something of its solemn interest. Let us not come up hither to sleep, and let us not come with torpid souls. Here at least, in professed worship of the Author of the mind, let the mind awake. It is good to fix our attention upon those latent but living relations that always subsist in an assembly gathered for such a purpose as ours; to stimulate our drowsy interest by frequent inquiries of the object we seek, the manner in which we seek it; the sympathies that unite us, the likeness and the difference that is between us. The same varieties of condition that are collected in a church are found in any mixed assembly; but the church is the corrector of distorted views. The pious mind which views them there, overlooks very great inequalities in condition, in its regard to more momentous inequalities in character. For in the church, those tests of character and those scenes of action and those great changes in God's Providence, are suggested to the mind which are of that spiritual and enduring dignity that puts down all other distinctions into the rank of trifles. In the church, if any where, we feel our faith. Men that are believers in general are very apt to be infidels in detail, that is, they assent to Christianity, when its evidence is stated, but each day they live as if this world was all. But in the church, at least, Christianity affects all our speculations, disciplines our pride, orders our prayers, and draws the moral from our views of life. In the church we cannot keep it down—the memory of death, the belief of divine Providence and of a future state, and these views have a wonderful effect upon all our observations on man. Here we cannot help applying them to the striking contrasts of external condition that a congregation usually exhibits, where are commonly met every variety of fortune, of profession, of character. What disparity of tastes, of ages, of success, and of expectations! There are

Manuscript dated July 2, 1829, at Chardon Street. Preached three times: July 5, 1829, at the Second Church, Boston; September 4, 1831, again at the Second Church; and July 30, 1837, in East Lexington.

some who by their talents or their wealth or their office exercise a great amount of power, and some who hardly earn their bread. Here are the young who as yet have almost no guess what part is appointed and what success prepared for them. There are some perhaps to whose juvenile ear ambition is yet an unmeaning name and yet not many years will go by before this whole nation may watch with alarm their dangerous greatness. And some perhaps are here, the children of good men, or born perhaps in the lap of affluence, who when they come to man's estate, shall experience uncommon degrees of suffering; shall wear out long winters of squalid poverty, who shall people the hospitals and carry thither new and nameless forms of excruciating pain. Some are here who listen with impatience to the dirges of experience, whilst their breasts are cheered by brilliant hope, who are waited for a little farther on, by hideous disappointments. And many that are now timorous and unhappy, perhaps the sons of unfortunate men, shall presently find a new turn in their affairs, and shall be swoln perchance with worldly pride, and consume their life in decorated chambers— in luxury and to full age. And here are some—here are a few—among all that I now behold God grant there may be some—who shall so sternly train their passions, and so piously educate their virtues, that they shall be adorners of their race, examples of Society, the strenuous assertors by speech and by action, of truth and right at every hazard, meek and holy lovers of God and Christ, to the last hour of a spotless life.

Here are the votaries of all pursuits—some who shall delight in the entertainments of piety and some in the fields of war; some in sloth; some in debauchery; some in adventure; some in science; some in bodily prowess and accomplishments; some in political address.

The years that are coming are bringing on their wings beauty for one, and eloquence for another, and grace and disgrace and power and learning and madness and sorrow.

But why go on with these dubious anticipations? To each of us, we know, is a different measure and manner and term of being. We live in different houses, in different company, with different opportunities, and different deserts. Each must weave his own web to a solitary texture and pattern. No two shall walk side by side with even character and even fortune.

Well, now, what method, what likeness, what end to these wide diversities?

These inequalities shall come to an end. These dissevered and particoloured threads again unite; these sundered paths all run to one place; we all shall taste of death.

We are each of us to be sick. Fever or Consumption or palsy will come in turn to each. Cold shaking rheumatism or frightful convulsions, and a bed will be made for each in the bosom of the ground. In seventy or eighty years, all these restless limbs will be still enough, the dismembering clay will have lost its form and long ere that, most of us shall be gathered in dust. Soon the eye shall lose its nimble expression, and the porches of the ear shall be stopped to the voice of reproof and the sound of flattery.[1] The worm already reckons on his banquet. In some of us at this moment the seeds of disease are ripening in our frames. No strength of constitution, no energy of purpose, no unrivalled advantages of condition, can save you. A little longer or a little shorter term, an inch more or less on this span of life, makes all the difference.

My friends, do you ask to what good end are these old shades? The idea of death is a wholesome check. Yet if this were all, if death were the end of things, I would not repeat these ancient knells. Yet it is not without reason that, in every age of the world, these gloomy pictures have been presented by the wise. This is the way in which preachers of both dispensations, the New and the Old, have discoursed on death, this the train of images to which the poet or the moralist would have recourse whenever they would chill the young or startle the mature sinner, or convert grey hairs to holy living. Herses and palls and funeral trains; the poor corruption that takes the place of healthy complexion and proportioned form, the bells that toll and the tears that are wept for us and that frigid feeling of vacancy we all understand so well, in the sad words of Solomon, that the dead have no part in all that is done under the sun[2]—these are the dismal pageantry that have been hung up by the wise in holy places as monitors of appetite and passion, the shadowy curtain by which the future is shrouded.

This *has been*. But it is said that to many minds, if not to all, these commonplaces have lost their force. I am afraid they will not avail to stop the heady career of ambition; nor take one scornful glance from pride; nor prevail with intemperance to forbear a single cup; nor with avarice to forgive a debt. The terror of death will not shut one shop in the street nor stop a dance in your houses nor abate the colour in any cheek nor still the mirth of an idle song.

My brethren, if these terrors are ineffectual let us do without them. Let us find some new check upon sin. If we have got above these let us adopt those that are suited to our state.

Let us own that after the light of Christianity has entered us we see it to be an error, a great and pernicious error, the gloomy aspect under which death has always been presented to us. We say nature shudders at the thought. Is it not rather the effect of our own sinfulness? We feel the great inconvenience and unhappiness of losing the society of our friends. We put on black garments and encourage each other in the indulgence of the most miserable sorrow. My brethren, what has this to do with death? How does all this misery consist with the faith we confess? My friends, we are pagans when we put the mortal remains of our friends in the ground with these unutterable regrets. We are pagans when we contemplate our own end with this sinking spirit and shuddering nerves. We are not Christians. For a Christian believes that this world is only a porch and a threshold and not itself the temple of the divine glory. He believes he is here merely to be trained—here at school to learn how to act and suffer;

1. Cf. Shakespeare, *Hamlet*, I, V, 63.
2. Ecclesiastes 9:5–6.

that the Universe has a great many more worlds than this ball of earth which has been shown to him; that God has a great many more passages of life and action for him than the little part which he has practised here. He believes that when he leaves this world he drops the impediments of a finite nature, and continues to exist with new and infinite powers. He perceives the twofold nature of the body and the mind. He sensibly feels the numberless inconveniences and imperfections that in this world block up the path of knowledge to his inquisitive soul, the low necessities of the body, its limited powers of locomotion; he can walk but a step at a time; he is hungry; he is athirst; he is sick; he is fatigued. He finds that it is very hard to preserve from day to day this animal life. It must be sustained by bread and flesh, and invigorated by exercise. It is disordered with all our care by some trifling exposure to cold or heat; and all lands must be ransacked for juleps and tonics to recover its tone, and after all is done its health is seldom perfect for twenty four hours.—But the mind is of another constitution. It is of that nature that years and generations and centuries bring no wrinkle, no decrepitude to it. It is infinite.³ Well, now, shall it look at that event as dark which severs its spiritual energies from the clay which cripples them?

God has admonished him by Jesus Christ of the future state, and offered him eternal happiness as the reward of obedience. That revelation changes his view of this life. It was the whole; now it is a part and a very small part. It was the fruit, now it is only a seed. It was full of desirable objects. But now his eye has caught a glimpse of what is vast and bright, and these tinsel attractions are tawdry and vile. He becomes reconciled to death as a process of nature as essential as birth, and indeed as it is a second birth the separation of the spirit from the body as the first was a separation of the body from its parent body. *He becomes reconciled to death.* Then as his faith grows more practical, as his experience of the unsatisfactoriness of this world increases, as his thoughts dwell more habitually on the advantages of another, *he becomes desirous of death.* He thirsts with a divine curiosity for its awful revelations. He contrasts what reason and scripture inform him of that state of the soul with the present. He laments here the difficulties which the barriers of society and distance and the grave put in his way. I would enjoy the instructions of a wise man who I am told has given years of noble thought to the particular truths on which I wish light. But that man is not of my acquaintance and has his own vocation to attend, or he lives in Europe, or he is dead; and I cannot get access to him. Well, now, what is the hope that the Spiritual world holds out? Has God in his goodness prepared for my mind an uninterrupted intercourse with the majestic society of all souls? Can I borrow the aid of the sublime understandings that in the elder ages or in the later have borne testimony among men to God and to all truth and now have been widening their vision and taxing their powers in the presence of God? Shall the powers of Socrates, of Newton, be my willing teach-

3. "He finds that . . . infinite": see *JMN* 6:71.

ers? Shall I dwell in the beatitude of this flood of social illumination? Then shall I mourn the event that releases me from the prison and sends me to this society? to the presence of all that is holy and ravishing in moral beauty, to the presence of Christ—to the vivid perception of the character and operation of God himself,—shall I mourn an event that shall carry these anxious affections where distrust and change and human accidents can no longer interrupt their blissful exercise?

But Jesus Christ our Lord hath risen from the dead, hath taught us how we may make death thus joyful and good to us. He is the resurrection and the life. If ye do my commandments ye shall never die.[4]

Well, now, if this be death—if it is not the suspension but the prolonging and magnificent enlargement of life, if the same laws that rule us here, shall reach and rule us there, undisturbed by the imperfections that cross them now, then let this be the check upon sin. Let this mighty hope for which God has opened the heavens and sent his messenger to tell—let this be the check upon sin. Away with these fears, these forebodings, these downcast eyes, these sable weeds and sullen death bells.—Let us bless God we can die, or rather bless him that we cannot die, and open every affection and watch every moment that that hour may find us ready when ever it shall please God through the valley of death to call us home.

4. John 11:25-26. Cf. John 8:51.

XLII

Where the Spirit of the Lord is, there is liberty.
II CORINTHIANS 3:17

It has pleased God in his providence to distinguish our country in great and important respects. Fifty three prosperous years have elapsed since the Declaration of American Independence. The pleasant sounds of that anniversary have hardly ceased. It is a just subject of national congratulation. And the Christian has peculiar reason to rejoice in an event that he can't help regarding as the fruit of Christianity. Whilst the public festivals of other parts of the world are celebrations or commemorations of frivolous things, whilst the Eastern nations lavish all the ostentation of barbaric magnificence upon the coronation or the worship of an imbecile child, or in the provinces of Orissa and Bengal dragging that infamous idol-chariot over the victims that block its way:[1] whilst in Europe, the holidays of polished nations are the monuments of gross superstition or of fawning adulation—I cannot but rejoice that one people celebrates a manly event, that whilst other nations hang out their banners as if to hide their shame and fill the air with roaring of cannon as if to outspeak in their own ears the secret whisper of contempt, whilst they march in the processions of despotism and swell the pomp of a crowned wretch whom they despise, I cannot but rejoice that our anniversary is full of honour, is the memorial of virtue of a self-devoted Christian struggle, where a whole people sympathized and suffered, and many a noble martyr gave up the ghost—*for a principle*. It is a passage of human affairs that good men cannot contemplate without emotion. Let us not be backward to indulge our joy: there is sorrow and sin enough; enough dark lines in every past and present aspect of public affairs to make us welcome every innocent, and much more every splendid occasion of public congratulation. It has come; it has past. Throughout our extensive country, through all its crowded maritime cities, through all the youthful nations that are building their towns in the depths of the falling western forests—the signs of this joy have been shown. The din of business has given way to the public acclamations. The voice of eulogy has been heard; the names of the revolution

---

Manuscript dated July 4, 1829, at Chardon Street. Preached once: July 5, 1829, at the Second Church, Boston.
1. See Sermon XIV, n. 4.

have been named; all classes, all ages, have partaken in some degree of the general joy until the sun went down and night shut in over the exulting land.

I see in this a reasonable topic of gratitude. Let us thank the Father of all men for the signal gift he has imparted to us. And let us be careful that we have right views of the blessing and sure conviction that we partake in it. There are many men who talk of freedom, who are not free. There are nations that boast of their independence, long after their independence is gone. For the forms of a free government do not make a free state. This freedom is a very volatile principle which no forms can long confine. It does not exist in the order or numbers of a legislature much less in the names of offices or of public buildings or in volumes of laws. To exist in the Community it must exist in the heart of the citizen. The independence of the state is the independence of individual men, and when that is gone—though the forms of a free government survive, and hold sway over a degenerate race, it is but a reptile crept into the skeleton of a giant, and the more despicable from the contrast of its pretensions with its nature.

This Freedom is a real and precious good, a precious part of God's endowment of man, but like all the rest of his best gifts offered to our exertions, not dropped into idle hands. Many men are apt to think that the duties of these days are done when a sympathy has been felt in the exultation of the Community, and so it is often asked to what end this vapouring about liberty? And often the question is pertinent enough. Not many men know its value, not many men feel the dignity of the distinction. Our sympathies are very cheap, easily excited. It is easier to shout with a crowd than to forbear on any stirring occasion. But a few men always do understand the worth of this birthright and hold it with religious awe. And oh, my friends, the awful voices that in this country, from time to time, have warned you of your public duty, have indeed pleaded in vain, have wasted their lofty genius in a most idle declamation, if you have been led to believe that that duty ended in a simple sympathy. It was not for this, be assured, it was not for this that the ardent leaders of public opinion half a century since poured forth the flood of anxious eloquence to soothe the sorrow and stir up the principles of irresistible right in the bosom of the community. It was not the clamorous burden of a national song, a boyish exultation in a victory gained by a countryman one does not know over enemies we do not fear on distant seas or in other continents, the joy of little men over little things. It was not this that was the object of their study by night, their argument by day, their moving exhortation in the hall; of their action in the city, or in the tented field. Nor was it for this, that the patriots since of whom we have been so fond or proud, have on days of high event, or burning recollection, impelled anew the stream of benevolent and elevating affections and shut up the channels of private interest to give freer vent, and greater volume to the swallowing tide. It was for no small or puerile or casual purpose—not for an acclamation, not for a clapping of the hands. For the truly wise in all times, in all cases, have common ends. The moral energy that rises anywhere in man to sublime thought and action must always rest on sublime motive. And true greatness under whatever form exhibited, in whatever disparity of condition, consents to itself across a thousand years, across the face of the globe. It is always bottomed on truth and goodness.[2]

What is Freedom which they sought? What is that inestimable gift for which the highest minds have endured so much? Let us further explore and try to define this feeling so exhilarating that it communicates electricity at the very naming. There is something in it so dear to man that you can hardly hear a sincere expression of the sentiment but the nerves tingle in them that hear. Yet all who honour it do not possess the blessing. I said it was not common. When a band of patriots breaks up, let us follow the departing individuals to their houses. Here is one who was loud in his applause of every generous sentiment. I attend him to his house. I observe him in his dealings. I find that he rises early and sits up late, and that he is wholly intent on increasing his wealth. I find him the intense observer of all the persons and ways by which his interest can be promoted. Whatever cause he espouses, he gives up, when it interferes with this. Truth is not so dear to him but he treads on it for this. His friendship is hollow, where his property is staked; his word is no warrant, his affections are unstable; pleasure is no bribe; Religion is no guard; honour no defence; Interest—hard, sordid, unrelenting desire of gain—will buy him body and soul. That man is not free. The declaration of assembled nations cannot make him so. He is the prisoner of his own avarice. He cannot go, he cannot come, he cannot take his own rest or pleasure, but as that bids him.

But I mark out another who retires late and unwilling from the festival. I watch his fresh complexion and rolling eye. I find him delicate in his meats and drinks, curious in the relish of meats and the flavour of wines. His means are limited but his appetites are not. He has not a cent for charity, but he will pawn his clothes for his luxury. I find him devising contemptible stratagems for the gratification of this diseased craving. I find him giving time and ingenuity and character for these gratifications. He will walk miles for a cup of wine. There his eye rests, there his debased affections grovel. Neither is this man free. He is the servant of his belly.

Another rises early, to work, as he says, for the public. He writes and talks and contrives for a political party to which he attaches himself with the same zeal with which others toil in their private affairs. But I ask him if he loves this man—he does not know—he will ask his party. Will you give your influence to aid this great object for the good of the city or the state?—He says, he thinks it will be of manifest advantage, but he must ask his party. Once more, will you come to church and listen to interpretations of Scripture which you approve—I cannot come, for this venomous party spirit has invaded the spiritual world with the wretched chances of human hatred, rancour, and patronage, I cannot

2. "And oh, my friends, . . . goodness": see *JMN* 3:30–31.

come on account of my party. Is he who is thus bound hand and foot and cast into the sevenfold heats of the furnace of party, is he a free man?[3]

Alas, my brethren, if thus we go up and down sifting the pretensions we meet in society, the army of freemen will be thinned of many a boastful champion. Some men are the slaves of pride and will do and suffer a great deal to win some small courtesy from those who are called fashionable, and some are the slaves of their affections and will be prevailed with by a foolish child to gratify its caprices at the risk of its own present and future good, and some are the slaves of malignant passions and will encounter every risk to feed their resentment.

Who then is free? Is it not plain that multitudes of men born in this land to the blessed heritage of civil and religious independence have yet reduced themselves to a thraldom of one or another kind that is as effectual in crippling their powers of action as if the irons of a gaol were actually used to restrain them?

Let us go to the word of God by Jesus Christ for an answer to this question. It is written in the gospel of John that Jesus said to those Jews who believed on him, "If ye continue in my word then are ye my disciples indeed. And ye shall know the truth and the truth shall make you free." They answered him (as the proud American would answer to the insinuation that he was a slave)—"We be Abraham's seed, and were never in bondage to any man. How sayest thou Ye shall be made free? Jesus answered them, Verily verily I say unto you, Whosoever committeth sin is the servant of sin." Then said he—"And the servant abideth not in the house forever, but the Son abideth forever," that is, from the house of God, from the Universe of good beings, the evil servant shall be cast forth, but the Son and the glorious system of truth of which he is the revealer, these abide.—If the Son therefore, he added, if the Son shall make you free, ye shall be free indeed.[4] Here then brethren is a full and satisfactory answer.

He and he alone is free whose whole soul no inducement on earth can reach but his own decisions of right and wrong, who feels that in the wide Universe he is accountable to God alone, who sternly and immoveably seeks the truth, who governs himself by the commandments that God has written in his own mind and confirmed and sanctioned in the written revelations of his will, who is placed by his love of God and of Christ out of the reach of earthly motive, who is incapable of fear, cold to pleasure, deaf to flattery, master of himself. How many men are free, my brethren?

It is only in proportion to men's advances toward this enfranchisement, this being freemen of the City of God, that the prosperity and permanence of civil distinctions can be secured. Our prejudices, our fears, our affections, entangle us and abridge our liberty. No man is perfect; no man is wholly free. All virtuous action, all religious character, is a perpetual approximation to this freedom with which Jesus Christ our master hath made us free.[5]

3. Cf. Daniel 3:19-21.
4. John 8:31-36.
5. Galatians 5:1.

It is to a virtuous community, to a community in which existed a strong degree of this freedom which Jesus gives, that we owe the great result which yesterday we celebrated. As I listened to the peal of bells as the sun went down I could not help thinking how that freedom is local and temporary. It is confined within some hundred miles of seacoast, and bounded by rivers and mountains. It is precarious. It belongs to this generation. Another generation or even our own may bereave itself of it, and if it should last, we ourselves can rejoice in it but a few anniversaries more; but as the minister of Christ I speak of a freedom that hath no bounds—the liberty with which Christ makes you free, is not measured by periods of time or limits of territory, is perfect, and infinite, and everlasting;—The passions are the tyrants from which it releases you. Every temptation that you overcome, every virtuous act you do, is a Marathon of the soul, is a progress to a mightier independence. The habit of holy action, the spirit of God in your spirit, shall be your charter. Fear and lust and pride and sloth and wrath shall be trodden under feet. To what world soever you shall go, in what society, in what scene soever, you shall act, through all time, through all space, wheresoever the spirit of the Lord shall guide you, there the soul shall walk forth erect and sublime in the liberty of his love.

Textual and Manuscript Notes

In these notes, a physical description of the sermon manuscript is followed by a record, keyed to the text by page and line number, of all of Emerson's insertions, cancellations, variant passages, and transpositions, as well as all editorial changes not covered in the categories of silent emendations outlined in the Textual Introduction. The text given here is a literal genetic transcription of the manuscript and therefore differs in some respects from the edited version above. Editorial matter is enclosed in square brackets, while Emerson's brackets are represented as curved. All inscription is in ink unless otherwise noted.

The symbols used in these notes are explained in the list below. Matter that immediately follows a cancellation without a space or symbol of insertion, as in "⟨i⟩It" or "⟨we⟩you," should be understood as having been written directly over the canceled matter.

Symbols

⟨ ⟩	Cancellation
↑↓	Insertion
/ / /	Variant
[ ]	Editorial insertion
{ }	Emerson's square brackets
¶	Paragraph

Sermon I

Manuscript: Five sheets folded to make four pages each; folios stacked and cross-stitched with white thread around left edge; pages measure 24.5 x 19.8 cm. A strip (18 x 3 cm) tipped to verso of first leaf; a leaf (20 x 19.5 cm) containing variant opening (dated "3 April 1828") attached to recto of leaf 2 with red sealing wax and included in the sewing; a strip (20 x 5 cm) attached to the verso of leaf 5 and another (18.5 x 6.5 cm) to the recto of leaf 7.

Lines	*Page 55*
3–5	works. ⟨Because⟩ ↑Since↓ we . . . assign ↑↑for . . . neighbor↓ . . . those↓ motives ⟨in any respect differing from the most natural connexions we have observed, in our own person, to join important actions.⟩ ↑which . . . circumstance[ms. torn] to guide our own↓
6	tho't, ⟨ & can hardly discourse with confidence after we have passed the boundary of material science,⟩ ↑to . . . soul—↓
8–9	mind⟨s⟩ . . . as prop[ms. torn]ly, as the ⟨motion⟩ sounds . . . or the mo[ms. torn] of

317

10   to ⟨with confidence⟩ on
11   not ⟨often⟩ appeared
13–16   with. ¶ ⟨It is a portion of moral science which tis⟩ ↑It ought . . .
                other;↓ ⟨i⟩It [addition on a strip of paper attached with red sealing
                wax to the left margin; verso blank]
19–21   him↑.↓ ⟨wh.⟩ ↑The world↓ ⟨h⟩He . . . ↑enough↓ . . . but ⟨wh⟩it
24   & ⟨permanence⟩ ↑certainty↓

                                    Page 56
1   hardly re[ms. torn]ind you
2   not [ms. torn]k you
8   faculties ⟨of⟩ &
10   eagerly ⟨chiefly⟩ intent to study ⟨ & learn⟩ the
12   that ⟨all the great interests of life, & not those only, (which cannot be
                reproached, for so much grows necessarily out of our humble condi-
                tion,) but⟩ almost
16   ↑and↓ our houses, ↑and↓
17   [The following alternate introduction, written on one side of a single
                sheet, was attached by red sealing wax in the left margin before the
                fascicle was sewn. It was affixed where the original text resumes:
                "This is the great error . . ."]

                ↑Fast Day   3 April 1828
                    Pray without ceasing. I Thess. Ch. V.17.

                ⟨I shall think it no violation of the duties appropriate to this
                occasion to⟩ ↑↑The duty [ms. torn] prayer is one of those most
                insisted on in the enumeration of our duties. [ms. torn] it is always
                appropriate.↓ I shall need no apology for↓ invit⟨e⟩↑ing↓ yr. attention
                to the consideration of prayer; of prayer, as it is a state of mind, a state
                of continued preparation for the duties of life.
                    There is a ↑previous↓ consideration of great importance ↑to↓
                which w⟨h⟩e must attend. It is this, that tho' we have no faculties by
                which we can see the thoughts of men, & are always obliged to judge
                of ↑men's↓ thoughts by ⟨men's⟩ ↑their↓ words & actions yet it would
                be foolish in us to suppose that no beings have such faculties. On the
                contrary—as God sees the soul—so it is probable that the thoughts
                which are now passing in our minds are percieved by some beings, as
                properly as the sound↑s↓ of the voice or the motions of the hand are
                by us. Now this is very little remembered by us. We give heed to the
                body & not to the mind. We are absorbed in the contemplation & the
                pursuits of outward things of bread & wine & dress of houses &
                furnitur[ms. torn] ↑This is the great error which the strong feeling,
                &c &c.↓↓
19   th⟨e⟩is
22   are /integral/so many/ [The word "integral" is circled in ink;
                possibly the intended reading is "so many integral parts."]

26–28	natures↑, the spirits . . . everlasting,↓ open⟨s its⟩ ↑their↓ . . . specu-late⟨s⟩
32	↑Every . . . prayer↓
33	of ⟨prayer⟩ ↑devotion↓. [emendations in pencil]
38	& ⟨a⟩the
43-(57)1	that ⟨we⟩you ↑would↓ disguise from ↑y↓ourselves

Page 57

4–5	know⟨,⟩ that . . . perfec[ms. torn]
26	² wit, or ¹ beauty, . . . desireable
30	↑proper↓ sense ⟨that can be truly put upon the word⟩, ⟨it⟩ ↑the position↓
40-(58)8	↑For is . . . after?↓ [addition on a strip of paper attached to the left margin with red sealing wax; verso blank] ¶ For i⟨s⟩t i⟨t⟩s ⟨not⟩ the . . . that ⟨he is⟩ ↑we are↓ . . . *within* ⟨*his*⟩ ↑*our*↓ *reach;* and ↑⟨he has⟩ that we have↓ . . . bring ⟨him⟩ ↑us↓ to ⟨their⟩ ↑⟨his⟩ our↓ ends; that ⟨he is⟩ ↑we are↓ . . . and ⟨does not his⟩ ↑our↓ free agency consist↑s↓ in this, that ⟨he is⟩ ↑we are↓ able . . . which ⟨his⟩ ↑our↓ election falls⟨?⟩. And

Page 58

20	↑Assuredly he will.↓
29–30	man, {a pre-[end of line] existent . . . things}
35	⟨wa⟩is
39	crowds, ⟨but⟩ and

Page 59

10–15	↑Let . . . privilege . . . life↓ [on a small slip of paper attached at this point; verso blank]
23–24	with {adverting to its ⟨general⟩ value ["hasten" in pencil above the penciled bracket]
35	soul that

Page 60

10	things ⟨absolutely⟩ actually
16–19	blood. ⟨They like you are uttering deep ejaculations of good or evil to the God & Father of us all, and theirs, like yours, are registered in heaven.⟩ ¶ ↑My friends ↑in . . . made↓ I have already ↑in part↓ . . . Heaven.↓
20–21	be ⟨little⟩ ↑of limited↓ worth⟨,⟩ if
25	stated ⟨I⟩you come to ⟨my⟩your
37	decent ⟨competence⟩ comforts,

Page 61

1	friend↑s↓,
19	place ⟨of every place⟩ of
21–22	these ⟨nauseous vermin⟩ ↑pampered appetites↓
25	that {these appetites ⟨{that have been pampered into tyrant habits &

find now no scope for indulgence, must}⟩ ↑will↓ [all three brackets in
pencil; "will" in ink over pencil]
29-(62)12   man. ¶ {Of this . . . unlimited happiness.}
37   from ⟨every⟩ temptation

Page 62

19–20   what ⟨God⟩ Conscience,
29   all ⟨open⟩ ↑fasten↓

Sermon II

Manuscript: Five sheets folded to make four pages each; folios stacked and sewn (thread
now missing); pages measure 24.5 x 20.5 cm.

Lines   Page 63
21–22   the ⟨prevalent⟩ ↑mark of the superior↓ . . . evidence ⟨there⟩ ↑that↓
                   is in man, [last four words underscored in pencil]

Page 64

15–16   of m⟨a⟩en,
34   absence ⟨is⟩of

Page 65

11   down ⟨in⟩and
23   ↑uneasy↓
41   us,—⟨this⟩ created
43–44   {that . . . nature.}

Page 66

2   learn- [end of line] of
12–13   experience ⟨enable us to judge⟩ can
19   unhappiness ⟨tends to⟩ ↑is designed for↓
21   are are all
38-(67)16   {Herein . . . made.}

Page 67

16   excuse⟨s⟩,
19   virtue↑s↓
21   a ⟨light & sloven⟩ ↑lazy↓
29   ↑contentment↓
33   of ⟨alterable⟩ events ↑over . . . power↓

Page 68

8   inexcuseable
19–33   {Some . . . posterity.}
24   & [end of line] & disease, . . . be, ⟨consigned⟩ by
31   in [end of page] in the

Page 69

4	ha⟨d⟩s
5–8	{In . . . the ⟨shame⟩ ↑cross↓ . . . the ⟨cross⟩ ↑shame↓.} [emendations in pencil]
9–12	{It . . . ↑that . . . example;↓ . . . repining.}
14–15	evils ⟨to⟩ which embarass
16	the /hands/guideboards/
19–20	{brushes . . . sensuality} [brackets in pencil]
31	to ⟨struggle⟩ ↑wrestle↓; . . . in ⟨h⟩Heaven,
33	is ⟨sorrow⟩ with

Sermon III

Manuscript: Five sheets folded to make four pages each; folios stacked and sewn with white thread; pages measure 24.5 x 19.5 cm (folios 1–2) and 24.5 x 18.8 cm (folios 3–5).

Lines	*Page 70*
3	for ⟨his⟩ ↑our↓
8–10	It . . . happiness. [struck through once diagonally in light pencil, perhaps to cancel the sentence]
13–14	↑We . . . nearer↓
17–18	↑can↓ see & ⟨hear⟩ ↑feel↓.
19–20	obedience ⟨more⟩ ↑very much↓ . . . example ⟨than the precept⟩ of . . . us. ⟨And tho' the admonitions wh come to ⟨man⟩ ↑us↓ as the creatures of God ought to be sufficient, he would do great injustice to the condition of man who should leave out of the account the immense force ⟨in⟩ ↑by wh.↓ his social relations ⟨by which he is⟩ draw⟨n⟩ to ↑him↓ evil & to good.⟩ [sentence canceled in pencil] The
24	↑I am . . . it↓

	Page 71
2–4	involves ¶ ⟨Let us⟩It is ⟨then look for a moment at the vast advantage which is derived from our connexion with other men to our power & happiness⟩ ↑almost . . . social↓.
6	social. ⟨When we came⟩ All
12–13	is /shut/barred/? [variant in pencil] . . . o⟨ur⟩f ⟨our⟩ ↑his own↓
15	alien ⟨from⟩ to
23	run⟨d⟩s
25–26	↑The prosperity . . . you↓
27–28	↑standing . . . Concord)↓ if ⟨the b⟩ your
31–33	but ⟨we⟩it . . . ↑for a time↓
35	as ⟨the light of day.⟩ ↑they are grand↓
39–40	↑wondrous↓ . . . with ⟨those⟩ ↑the unprovided rock↓

	Page 72
2	ignorance, his
10–22	{Consider . . . society?} [brackets in pencil]
18–19	laws, ⟨decorated⟩ ↑enriched . . . arts,↓
22	joint ⟨mutual⟩ ↑human↓ exertion ⟨of men⟩;

25   th⟨ey⟩is ⟨ha⟩ condition
26–27   ↑This world . . . heaven.↓
28–32   virtue. ↑& our happiness↓ ↑{Insert A} A ⟨This social system has its
            evident advantages to ⟨our happiness.⟩⟩ Our . . . of ⟨our friends⟩
            those . . . much ⟨we enjoy their applause⟩ our . . . approbation.↓
33   influence, of
36   the ⟨same⟩ ↑more↓
39–40   ↑Almost↓ Before . . . we ⟨lisped⟩ ↑uttered↓
43   forever ⟨preserve⟩ ↑retain↓.

                                   Page 73
1–2   how ⟨perilous⟩ ↑burdensome↓
7   invironed
9–10   ↑to . . . example↓
14   to ⟨countenance⟩ sanction
18   to ⟨learn⟩ ↑copy↓
22   tho't↑s↓,
25–26   ↑of those↓ member↑s↓ of who make up society. It ⟨belongs⟩ to
            ↑depends on↓ ["to" accidentally uncanceled] . . . of ⟨virtue⟩
            ↑religion↓
28   ↑the . . . of↓
34   you ⟨produce⟩ ↑exert↓
35   ↑the issues of↓

                                   Page 74
2   little ⟨a⟩ matter
16   to ⟨that⟩ ↑another↓
21   calamities. ⟨Beware then whilst it is in your power that you be
            blameless in your high vocation.⟩ [canceled in pencil] Your
25–26   to ⟨make⟩ cooperate with God ⟨by⟩ in
27–33   men. ⟨Remember also that it is in vain you appeal to an imperfect
            example & say I have done good yesterday I have given to the poor
            today & my example was not copied It is because men had learned⟩
            ↑Why . . . trustworthy.↓
38   not↑,↓ ⟨ascribe⟩ ↑for↓
39   ↑I lament . . . feebleness.↓

                                   Page 75
5–6   sinful ⟨competition⟩ ↑emulation↓ . . . emulation ⟨in⟩wherein
9   ↑not↓
12   worlds ⟨kings & conquerors⟩ ↑greatness↓
13–14   ↑glorious↓ . . . ↑"a form↓
34   great ⟨men⟩things
39   {the laurels . . . light} {The glory [brackets in pencil; the last lacks a
            companion]

Page 76

1	ago ⟨was⟩ the
2–5	↑It has . . . world↓ . . . latter⟨s⟩ . . . ↑on . . . servants↓
15	happiness ⟨is⟩ ↑are↓ incalculably ⟨increased⟩ ↑augmented↓
17	to ⟨do right⟩ cease
19	in ⟨virtue⟩ ↑a religious life↓
34	unseen ⟨congregation⟩ ↑assembly↓

Sermon IV

Manuscript: A sewn gathering cross-stitched in white thread around the left margin, consisting of one sheet folded to make four pages (each measuring 23 x 18.8 cm), a single leaf (21 x 15 cm), three sheets folded to make four pages each (pages measuring 25 x 20.5 cm), and one sheet folded to make four pages (each measuring 23 x 19 cm). A leaf (19 x 14.5 cm) is attached to the recto of leaf 9.

Lines	*Page 77*
Bible Text	mocked; ⟨that which⟩ ↑for whatsoever↓
1–2	upon ⟨civilized⟩ society . . . interest ⟨& as matter of abundant speculation⟩ in
3	b⟨y⟩ut
4	↑We . . . property.↓
7–8	into ⟨a⟩ connexion↑s↓ . . . connexions ⟨increase⟩ ↑multiply↓
8–9	is ⟨not⟩ ↑more than↓ a ⟨mere⟩ necessity
11	friends. ⟨These⟩ ↑Such↓ are the first ⟨necessities⟩ ↑reasons↓
16–17	It ⟨becomes⟩ is . . . power. ⟨He that in the⟩ ↑Civil . . . a↓ very . . . goods, ⟨that civil society produces⟩ ↑and he that↓
25	is ⟨moved⟩ ↑shaken↓

	Page 78
2	priveleges
4–6	diligent ⟨pursuit⟩ desire . . . savage ⟨misery⟩ ↑want↓
9–10	↑the hourly↓
12	the ⟨im⟩ excess of ⟨this⟩ ↑the↓
14	the ⟨philosopher⟩ ↑good↓ & ⟨the⟩ ↑wise↓
18–20	↑its↓ importance ⟨of⟩ as . . . ↑upon . . . it↓
21–22	moment. ¶ ⟨It is hardly possible to live long in the world ⟨without⟩ & extend our observation beyond our first & grossest wants without becoming sometimes sensible of that strange system of compensations that is carried on. All things are double one against another Every defeat in one manner is made up in another Every suffering is rewarded every sacrifice is made up every debt is paid. ¶ The history of retributions is a strange & awful story. It will confirm the faith that wavers & more than any other moral phenomenon offers itself to examination & analysis & is more than any other fit to establish the doctrine of divine Providence.⟩ ¶ ⟨It is hardly possible to live long in the world without becoming sometimes sensible⟩ ↑I . . . deserves↓

25–30   ↑Since . . . life↓ All . . . known ⟨refer⟩ to . . . disclosed. ↑& there
. . . whole ex. here & hereaf. perfect . . . all.↓ But I am ⟨prepared⟩
↑disposed↓ to ⟨assert⟩ ↑⟨believe⟩ think↓ that there are
⟨nevertheless⟩ strong

40–41   decays; these ↑↑These & similar↓ remarkable compensations↓ & all
⟨this most important class of facts ↑yᵗ we see↓⟩ ↑which we see↓

41–(79)1   attributes. ¶ ⟨It is a⟩ ↑⟨This⟩ ↑And it↓ makes the the great value of
this↓ class of facts ⟨which have great value in⟩ the

Page 79

2–6   {No man . . . result ⟨can doubt⟩ ↑but has . . . his soul↓ . . . mens
⟨are⟩ behold . . . of them.} ¶ ↑But↓ This . . . embarassing

11   I ⟨proceed then to say⟩ ↑believe . . . felt↓

14–18   ↑This . . . see ⟨how⟩ ↑whether↓ . . . hold.↓ ¶ ⟨Our nature has a
twofold aspect towards *self*, & towards *society*, and⟩ ↑There are 2
ways in which ⟨in⟩↓ the . . . evil, ↑&↓ . . . measured ⟨of course by
its relation to these two⟩ ↑as . . . these 2 respects.↓

19   I. ↑Let . . . men↓ And in the ⟨first⟩ view

24–25   ↑In . . . judgment↓ Am . . . m⟨e⟩an

28   recieved

36   the ⟨pelf⟩ ↑property↓

Page 80

8–9   be ⟨counterfeited. We have we trust made it apparent⟩ ↑fraudulently
. . . all↓

11–12   sound. ↑That . . . acquired↓

14   nature↑, i.e., . . . end.↓.

19   of ⟨his⟩ ↑a man's↓

27–28   ↑It . . . firm↓

28   the ⟨sorry⟩ ↑ill↓

33   ↑that mortal wit↓

34–(81)2   {Perhaps . . . do. ⟨↑On account of the stern equality which pervades
the intellectual endowments of all nations, no mind was ever created
of such towering greatness but that it can easily be matched with a
level mind.↓⟩ The . . . reveal.} [The added passage, supplied at the
bottom of the page below a rule, is keyed with asterisks to two
locations: the one indicated and probably erroneously after the word
"case." Both of the asterisks and the added passage are canceled.]

Page 81

3   ¶ But ⟨supposing⟩ ↑granting↓

6   such ⟨mis⟩apprehension↑s↓

8   ↑My . . . hid↓

14   manner he ⟨who breaks over the virginity of his virtue⟩ ↑that . . . he↓

20–21   ↑to . . . Hell.↓.

28–30   ↑unless . . . mischief↓ . . . his ⟨dreadful⟩ ↑downward↓ . . . fallen.
⟨Man will⟩ For

36   wonderful /in/in the view of/

38-(82)8   all / in some manner laboring to become rich / have the same wants /
[variant in pencil; incomplete emendation] it is ⟨very in⟩ ↑of much↓
. . . that / wealth and even honor are not happiness / the means of
happiness are not happiness unless the mind consents / [variant in
pencil] ⟨↑It is an old saying that riches alone cant give happiness. But↓
I will not deny that riches can add great means of comfort to a healthy
man. But it is as undeniable that there are⟩ ¶ ⟨↑It is an old saying that
riches alone can never confer happiness. But from many causes wh.
we must not now attempt to trace it is little believed but is set down to
the account of envy or hypocrisy. Yet it is inscribed by God in lines of
fire on the face of society.⟩ [canceled in pencil] ⟨Riches⟩ It is . . .
man. ↑{Insert X} X {Our . . . conditions ⟨the gospel⟩ which . . .
satisfaction}↓ But . . . happy.↓ victims

Page 82

14-15   moralist. ⟨I have seen, all men in the common circumstances of life
may see⟩ ↑Who has not seen↓

19   they ⟨shall⟩ ↑have↓ receive↑d↓ [emendations in pencil]

32-34   overcome↑,↓ [addition in pencil] . . . ground. ⟨God pun⟩ But these
⟨sinners⟩ have . . . Maker. ⟨God punishes them with⟩ ignorance ↑is
theirs↓ [emendations in pencil except the first cancellation]

37-38   adding ⟨new⟩ to . . . the ⟨p⟩ means . . . cause↑,↓ [addition in
pencil]

Page 83

2-3   within. ⟨The maladies whose seeds are sown in all our frames shall
plague them shall fasten on their souls when they torment their
bodies. When these visit the Christian philosopher whose mind is
balanced by the contemplation of his faith, he freely bids them try
their worst on his body, for he knows that it is clay, he knows that it is
not himself. He exults in the harmony & health of his inner existence
when the outer is torn by pain or broken by age. The ⟨Stoic⟩ ↑wise
man↓ the Christian gathers himself unhurt within. But these have no
divine antidote to the poison of mortality "Their soul can scarce
ferment its mass of clay" They say to the Worm thou art my brother:
to corruption "My sister & my mother."⟩ [passage is canceled lightly
in pencil] ¶ My . . . have ⟨labored⟩ ↑attempted↓

6   right; ⟨that⟩ ↑because↓ . . . ↑long↓

7-17   society. ↑Insert A A {Let . . . ↑that . . . estate↓. You . . . equivalent.
ᵇ{But . . . is ⟨almost⟩ [canceled in pencil] indispensable . . . Lord.
ᵃ{Many . . . lost?} ⟨Or will any repine that his lot in life is straitened
whilst the ⟨offenders⟩ oppressor that has grown rich at his expense is
prospered in his dealings, meets no reverses, is adding new acres to his
broad lands new tenements to his decorated dwelling. Fret not thyself
because of the evil doer, tho' you are disquieted God is not mocked.
Leave them to their riches Let them get from them what comfort they
can. Truly they need it all; all the consolation they can glean from
saying I have riches if I cannot enjoy them.}⟩ [canceled in pencil] ⟨Be

not deceived God is not mocked Whatsoever a man soweth that shall he also reap.⟩↓ ¶ But

22–23	God ⟨in⟩ ↑running thro'↓
35	lo⟨o⟩se
40	↑will↓

Page 84

1–2	not ⟨walk⟩ ↑pass↓ . . . beseige every road ⟨in⟩wherein we walk. ↑Let us↓ Beware

[The following is inscribed on a sheet of blue paper inserted at the end of the sermon:]

We are a perpetual wonder to ourselves. Ther[e] is no riddle so high & hard to solve by man as man. We are so great & so little; we have powers so gigantic & spend them on such petty things; we are so strangely allied on one side to all that our imagination can body forth most grand & enduring & on the other are so nearly like to beasts & worms; the same individual acts at one time upon principles so lofty that it seems inspiration and at another from views the most contemptible,—that we find it hard to reconcile our hopes with our experience, or our experience with itself.

[The following notes are inscribed on a blank page at the end of the sermon:]

Plenty of Compensations may be seen every day. It wd. be good to make a Baconian list of particulars. e.g.

I ⟨get⟩ ↑commit↓ a new composition accurately to memory. It crowds out what is worth as much. I have to pay somehow for every accommodation albeit small. I was glad to find old gloves in the house to dig with. Two days after it was complained yᵗ yᵉ gloves were torn

"Harm watch: harm catch", an old English proverb, so the Latin; Sibi parat malum qui alteri parat. To this subject eminently belongs the story of the young man killed by the fall of the statue he was pulling down.

Leave no arrears for thy posterity to pay. Jeremy Taylor. Jesus answered & said Verily verily whoso committeth sin is the servant of sin. St John VIII 34

Sermon V

Manuscript: Five sheets folded to make four pages each; folios stacked and sewn with white thread along left margin; pages measure 24.5 x 20.5 cm (folios 1–4) and 23 x 19 cm (folio 5).

Lines	*Page 85*
9	heard ⟨in⟩ ↑amid↓
18	age. ⟨I desire⟩ ↑I . . . attempting↓
21	cheerfully ⟨reciprocated⟩ ↑exchanged↓

	Page 86
1	world; ⟨and⟩ ↑he rejoices that↓
7	↑abstemious↓
8–10	& ⟨commendable⟩ reasonable . . . priv⟨e⟩ileges, to the ↑suffering↓
16–20	Christ. ¶ ↑It . . .sin.↓
21–22	pourtrayed

24	question, ⟨a being whose influence upon the world is now I had almost said but beginning to be felt,⟩ one
28–35	ridiculous; ⟨He was⟩ one whose ⟨influence⟩ ↑effect↓ . . . impulse / that ever acted thereon / of those yᵗ ever wore the human form / . . . ↑on↓ . . . ↑have↓ . . . admiration. ⟨{And who was this sinless martyr & where was this lofty spectacle of God's goodness disclosed? He was a despised Hebrew among men reputed a carpenter's son, a lowly man, not born in the lap of grandeur nor acquiring by deeds of violence & hands bathed in blood a throne firmly founded on the fears of his people & transmitted when he had fu⟨f⟩lfilled his ⟨course of passion⟩ ↑appetite of↓ pleasure & power & gone down to the tomb amid the panegyric & funeral ostentation of a whole people to his posterity. None of all this, none of the men of mire & blood was this man but a sufferer

The man who was crowned with thorns
The man who on Calvary died
The man who bore scourging & scorns
Whom sinners agreed to deride.}⟩
¶ The remark |
| 38 | not ⟨seconded⟩ ↑supported↓ |

Page 87

4	↑men say↓
7	religion ⟨there⟩ it
12	they ⟨are the natural fruit⟩ ↑grow . . . soil↓
16–19	passion.' (J.T.) ↑Who . . . God ↑when . . . servt↓ . . . theirs.↓ ¶ ⟨And now,⟩ my
20–22	↑Was he like . . . blood↓
22–25	Caesars, ⟨nourished on the⟩ cushion⟨,⟩ed ↑on the soft embroidery↓ . . . & ⟨bro't⟩ ↑nourished↓ . . . gold⟨?⟩ like
26	by ⟨conquest⟩ ↑military fame↓
35–36	these ⟨men of mire & blood⟩ whom . . . ↑in . . . men↓

Page 88

11–12	was ⟨given⟩ ↑added↓
13–14	tidings. ¶ ⟨But come let us repair to the mount of Crucifixion.⟩ Pilate
17	↑But↓ They
19	↑fortune↓ & good ²{are accidents} ¹{to which . . . men}
20–21	it↑s composure↓. It sleeps ⟨in a vision⟩ ↑to them↓
24–28	↑Let . . . suffer" ⟨Yet at the foot of his Cross in the hour of his passion ⟨the Centurion⟩ ↑one of those who beheld him↓ exclaimed Truly this was the son of God.⟩ And . . . many.↓
31	insane ⟨ferocity⟩ ↑vindictiveness↓ [emendation in ink over pencil] . . . blood ⟨{when no eye was found to pity & no arm to save,}⟩ the

Page 89

1	w⟨ho⟩as
4–5	↑the . . . forgot↓ . . . of ⟨the⟩ ↑his↓ ghastly cross ⟨forgot himself⟩ in

³{↑of↓ his benevolen⟨t⟩ce} ²{↑the↓} ¹{impulse}. [incorrectly marked for transposition]

7   forward ⟨& pierced⟩ ↑to the↓ the

11   despair, ⟨they should ren⟩ heedless

12   ↑in their streets;↓

13–15 ↑the↓ mothers ↑of Judaea,↓ . . . at ⟨her⟩the

16   of [end of page] rusalem

29–31 ↑He has borne . . . to do↓

33–34 ↑There . . . him↓

Page 90

22–23 in ⟨savage⟩ ↑daring↓ [emendation in ink over pencil] irony; ↑They . . . heads↓

28–35 twain. ²{These . . . ↑his↓ . . . & ⟨at⟩ ↑with↓ . . . came.} ¹{He— . . . them}↓

36–37 a ⟨noticeable fact⟩ ↑memorable answer↓ & ⟨reads⟩ ↑exhibits↓ . . . recorded ⟨of the⟩ by

Page 91

5–6   watch↑;↓ go your way↑,↓ Make

25–27 unseen ⟨congregation⟩ ↑society↓ . . . or ⟨topics⟩ ↑reasons↓

31–32 ↑after the Resurrection↓ on the Mount↑ains↓ ⟨of Olives⟩ ↑of Galilee↓—

34   ↑He . . . men↓

Page 92

3   spirit ↑⟨is near you⟩ commends you; he↓ . . . ackn-[end of line]nowledge

[The following stray note appears after the end of the sermon:] Faith in hi⟨s⟩m ⟨death⟩ is a duty & you make vain his death by neglecting to assure yourselves of the truth.

Sermon VI

Manuscript: Four sheets folded to make four pages each; folios stacked and sewn with white thread along left margin; pages measure 25 x 20 cm.

Lines	*Page 93*
Bible Text	⟨thy⟩your . . . ⟨thou⟩you
1	¶ ⟨We are the changing inhabitants of a changing world.⟩ ↑We . . . world. ⟨We derive a melan an [illegible]ing fear, a melancholy forboding, from the uninterrupted motion that goes on around us. Nothing is firm. Nothing in nature gives us the comforting idea of indestructible strength or permanent repose.⟩↓ The
3	waning ⟨of the⟩ moon . . . & ⟨th⟩ reflux . . . arts & ↑of the↓
18	frame. ⟨{Age the imperceptible destroyer is invading the organs of sense. The eye has ceased to trace with swift recognition the faces of our friends has ceased to pore with unsparing diligence from morn till

midnight over the writings of the wise it sinks already within its socket & complains of the light of the sun. Age too has choked up the fine channels of sounds & the ear forgets the voice ⟨familiar to former⟩ ↑that sounded so sweet in earlier↓ days, the melodies of nature & the harmonies of music. The touch the taste the smell are grown obtuse & unfaithful. None have been exempt from these changes in the past but none apprehend them in the future.}⟩ Beautiful

21–23   {Love . . . long.} [brackets in light pencil]

Page 94

3   this ⟨tremendous⟩ ↑universal↓ [addition in ink over pencil]
4   ↑the well . . . unknown↓
5–7   ↑There . . . us.↓
8   We ⟨regret⟩ ↑dislike↓
14   halts; ⟨and⟩ already,
17–18   tomb. ¶ ⟨It is a question which arises with great force in our minds whenever we turn our thoughts to these melancholy images of change & ruin, Whither we shall go for refuge What race what rampart is left behind which we may retire & feel safe What is the proper relief that man possesses to keep him from growing giddy whilst he gazes on the turning wheels of human fortune.⟩ ¶ Is
21   ↑& lighted↓
24–25   show to ² our ghastly enemies, ¹ Pain & ⟨d⟩Death? Shall
26   ↑be↓
28   ↑the next↓ twenty years. ⟨Twenty years⟩ ↑It↓ [emendation in pencil]
30   ↑up↓ ⟨as⟩to
32   He ⟨wi⟩shall
39–(95)2 the ⟨s⟩dance . . . /to some of these/to some of the young/ . . . the⟨se⟩↑m↓

Page 95

8   have ⟨changed⟩ ↑blasted↓
9   un⟨expected⟩↑looked for↓ & all undesired ⟨changes⟩ ↑alterations↓
11–12   pleas⟨ant⟩↑ing↓ . . . ⟨you⟩they
14–19   {Each . . . countenance; ⟨another break the spirits⟩ another . . . the ⟨re[v]olving⟩ ↑loitering↓ . . .wings.} [brackets in pencil] These are the ↑⟨physical⟩ outward↓
22–24   who ⟨have grown up, & grown old; & gone into other places, or other lands; or are confined at home ⟨to⟩ in sick chambers; & will fail to recognize many whose faces & forms are changed by the good & evil events of life; but there will many be absent who⟩ are . . . or ⟨i⟩on . . . who⟨se sp⟩ have
26   of ⟨sp⟩ souls,
29–30   ears⟨.⟩, ↑will . . . Providence.↓
31   whose ⟨doom is sealed⟩ ↑days are numbered↓
36–37   vice⟨.⟩; ⟨Twenty years⟩ shall . . . suffering ⟨ & horror.⟩↑.↓ ["& horror." canceled and the period restored in pencil]

39	The ⟨changes⟩ ↑vicissitudes↓
40–41	↑all↓ the ⟨whole⟩ inhabitants . . . part⟨, all over the globe.⟩↑.↓

Page 96

1–4	{The . . . ↑far &↓ . . . night.}
5–11	himself ⟨tossed like the leaves that are scattered on the autumn wind blown in a perpetual eddy till he is resolved again into dust⟩ ↑afflicted . . . of ⟨change &⟩ ↑progressive↓ . . . nature?↓
12	one ⟨unchanging⟩ ↑immoveable↓
14–16	↑of↓ . . . change, ⟨His h⟩ ↑whilst . . . world↓
18–19	of ⟨unchangeable⟩ ↑immutable↓ perfections, ⟨by⟩ who
24–25	who ⟨set up⟩ upholds . . . {some . . . glory,} [brackets in pencil]
28	↑in literal truth,↓
34–36	{Despite . . . temper} . . . ↑of nature↓ . . . workmanship ⟨ever⟩ to [brackets in pencil]
37	↑of a God↓

Page 97

5–9	bright ⟨memory⟩ intelligence . . . some ⟨intimations more or less obscure⟩ ↑knowledge↓ [emendation in pencil] . . . {some . . . name}. ⟨in proof of⟩ ↑Somewhere we shall meet↓
12–13	wrong. ¶ ⟨My friends⟩ ↑And . . . God↓
16	in the ⟨image &⟩ likeness
23	to ⟨these⟩ ↑its↓
26–27	sublime ⟨consolation⟩ ↑⟨doctrin⟩ character↓,
29	because ↑#↓ time [caret in ink; "#" in pencil]
33	you, ⟨my friends⟩ ↑then↓,
35	↑your↓
39–(98)2	to ⟨the⟩ ↑the pursuit of↓ . . . pleasure↑s↓, to dust & ashes or ↑⟨whether turn away from these ⟨poor⟩ ↑wretched↓⟩ ↑whether . . . these↓ shadows & join yourself↓ . . . ↑form . . . duty↓ [carets after both "ashes" and "or"]

Page 98

5	you ⟨walk⟩ go
7	↑shall↓ have ⟨linked⟩ ↑united↓
10	render ⟨nearer &⟩ more
20–22	Angel . . . him not, [marked by an ink line in left margin] who is ⟨too great & too glorious for our eyes to bear⟩ not
23	is ⟨o⟩One
28	here? ⟨Does not th⟩ He,
35	↑first faint↓

Page 99

4–5	to ⟨show⟩ ↑⟨exhibit⟩ show↓ . . . shall ⟨show⟩ ↑teach↓

[Following the end of the sermon, the notation in pencil:] 30 minutes

Sermon VII

Manuscript: A gathering sewn with white thread along left margin, consisting of one sheet folded around two stacked folios, followed by a single folio; pages measure 24.8 x 20.4 cm. A leaf (13 x 19.5 cm) once attached to the recto of leaf 2 with red sealing wax is now detached.

Lines	*Page 100*
5	came. ↑It is pleas. to reflect yᵗ yᵉ cloud whose snows have hindered our families covers but a little district↓ Nor [added in pencil, evidently in October, 1827]
12	custom⟨ary⟩
17	doubt as to the justness [end of line] ⟨ & truth of the views entertained on this⟩ ↑whether a just value of this sacred day is↓ subject by [end of line] his [Because the evidence equally supports a number of possibly intended readings, all of which are speculative, the emendation is rejected.]
25	the /conventional/received/

	Page 101
1	shou⟨d⟩ld bind men ↑(let me say)↓
4–15	church. ¶ /{My friends the obligation of the observance of the [S]abbath [letter obscured by the red sealing wax] has been ⟨often⟩ ↑sometimes↓ controverted. It is admitted that it was binding on the Jews as a part of their ceremonial Law. It is doubted whether it is also binding on us; whether it was not abrogated with the rest of that antiquated ritual when Jesus Christ brought into the world a purer faith suited to the exigencies of more enlightened ages and was declared among other offices of dignity, Lord also of the Sabbath. My friends, ⟨I am ⟨fain⟩ to⟩ believe it binding also on us, as a ceremonial institution. But, waving at present this discussion, I am desirous to present it to you on the broad ground of moral obligation, ⟨which we cannot if we would dispute.⟩ ↑where it cannot be overturned.↓} I conceive, that, if its cause were faithfully pleaded, /[inserted half leaf attached to ms. p. 3 by red sealing wax; verso blank] ↑It is . . . of↓ The . . . dates; the day ⟨from which eternity⟩ on . . . pleaded, &c/ only
16	could ⟨evade⟩ ↑escape↓
19	↑now↓ . . . ↑written↓ Law but ↑I speak as to↓
20–22	children. ⟨I invite your attention to those words of our benevolent master, when he permitted on this day the indulgence of necessary appetite "The Sabbath was ⟨not⟩ made for Man."⟩ ↑I desire ⟨your att⟩ to . . . those ⟨relations⟩ ↑particulars↓ . . . Man.↓
24	"thou ⟨the⟩ shalt
27	be ⟨expanded⟩ ↑discussed↓
30	to ⟨car⟩ invade
31–34	Indeed ⟨in⟩even . . . to ⟨b⟩ make . . . ↑but an advantage↓. ↑I . . . consideration.↓

35   man ⟨f⟩ as
38   Or ⟨are⟩have

Page 102

1   chiefly ⟨subserve⟩ ↑seem to regard↓.
8–20   this. [added at the bottom of the page and keyed by Emerson's
          asterisk:] ↑Here insert the following—I know . . . of ⟨morality⟩
          ↑religion↓ . . . spirit of ⟨humanity⟩ in . . . heaven.↓
21   to ⟨fit⟩ ↑train↓
22–23   still ⟨celebrate⟩ cultivate . . . of ⟨humanity⟩ ↑men↓
25–26   ↑moral↓ inferiority in ⟨the state⟩ ↑society↓ . . . the⟨se⟩ ↑other↓
28–29   free." ¶ ⟨I think i⟩It
31   which ⟨the⟩ Religion
36–37   ¶ ↑III. . . . *week*.↓

Page 103

5   association, ⟨upon⟩ the
18   treating ⟨↑& one which has great advantages in its place↓⟩ becomes,
19   ↑then↓
23   an /absorbing/⟨engrossing⟩/
23–24   ↑As Timothy Alden . . . Epitaphs.↓ [at the bottom of page, keyed
          with an asterisk]
28–31   insanity, ⟨in⟩ ↑the↓ . . . round; ⟨in⟩ ↑the↓ . . . nature; ⟨in⟩ ↑the↓
33   a ⟨ductile⟩ force
35–36   ↑growing . . . itself↓

Page 104

3   to ⟨purs⟩ services
4   in ⟨one⟩ ↑a single↓
5   It ⟨summoned off⟩ ↑found↓
14–20   objects. ⟨My brethren⟩ It . . . ground⟨s⟩ . . . ↑e↓lev⟨el⟩↑ation↓,
          [last emendation in pencil] . . . widielying ⟨prospect⟩ ↑landscape↓
          . . . valley ⟨in⟩ wherein . . . of other world⟨s⟩ [last cancellation in
          pencil; Emerson may have attempted to restore the "s" by canceling
          the cancellation] ↑20 minutes↓ [in pencil]
22–23   ¶ ↑{I trust . . . breasts}↓ My brethren, ↑I trust that we↓ have ⟨you
          never⟩ ↑all at some time↓
29   you⟨r spirit⟩ in ↑yᵉ ↓
33   memory ⟨strongly dwelt on⟩ ↑found . . . in↓
34   not ⟨hope⟩ conscience ⟨challenged⟩ ↑called↓
38   care, ⟨less absorbing⟩ have
40–41   men, ⟨in the ⟨view⟩ ⟨↑aspect↓⟩ of⟩ /appearing/in the . . . God/
          means & not *ends*, ⟨in the ⟨view⟩ ↑aspect↓ of⟩ ↑appearing↓

Page 105

6   now ⟨choke⟩ ↑deafen to men↓
12   ages ⟨when civil law uttered a feeble voice⟩ when . . . the ⟨civil⟩
          laws

15–22	monastery. ↑It . . . theology (Insert X) X It has . . . Melancthon.↓
24	tone ⟨with⟩ ↑to . . . of↓ . . . Their ⟨sound⟩ ↑peal↓ is not ↑now↓
33	the ⟨welcome⟩ music ↑of Revelation↓ thro centuries ⟨{in the ear of devout & wise},⟩ in

Page 106

1	land ⟨shall⟩let
4	their ⟨Sabbath⟩ ↑sacred↓
4–7	The⟨y were⟩ men from ↑whom↓ . . . descend ↑were↓ men of no ⟨fug⟨a⟩itive⟩ ↑fading↓ . . . self-denying ⟨pilgrims⟩ ↑Christian⟨s⟩↓ who ↑knew that they↓
12	degenerate ⟨excuses⟩ effeminacy . . . excuses ⟨itself⟩ ↑healthy men↓
19	their ⟨posterity⟩. childrens
28	your ⟨fore⟩fathers
31–32	↑be . . . you↓

[Following the end of the sermon, the notation in pencil:] 30 minutes

Sermon VIII

Manuscript: Four sheets folded to make four pages each; folios stacked and sewn with white thread along the left margin; pages measure 20.8 x 17 cm.

Lines	*Page 107*
1	religion⟨,⟩. ⟨that i⟩It
4	several ⟨prejudices⟩ conditions
6–9	world↑.↓ ⟨a⟩And ⟨as⟩ ↑when↓ . . . resurrection the /cearments/ graveclothes/ [variant in pencil] . . . ⟨h⟩it
12	↑with↓
21–22	↑that . . . expressed↓ . . . the ⟨people⟩ ↑times↓
25	↑has↓ cast⟨s⟩ a ↑mist of↓ deformity ⟨on⟩ ↑around↓
27	↑has↓ shroud⟨s⟩ed
28	charge⟨s⟩d

Page 108

1	clothe⟨s⟩d
3	↑Every . . . errors↓ [in pencil]
10	↑Christian↓
11–13	↑(↓It [addition in ink over pencil] . . . to ⟨be⟩ their beauty.↑)↓
15–16	attractive. ⟨We can explore t⟩The cause of it ⟨in part⟩ ↑is to be explored↓ . . . ↑& mainly in yᵉ incor. views of God↓ that ⟨are popular.↑⟩↓⟩ ↑prevail in the world.↓ [parenthesis in pencil]
17	God, ⟨that idea wh.⟩ ↑which↓
20	↑felt↓
21	It ⟨curbs⟩ ↑arrests↓
40	the⟨se⟩ senses,

Page 109

3–4	this ⟨fine⟩ ↑delicate↓ . . . to ⟨melody⟩ music
7–8	↑brooding in ⟨fearful⟩ ↑the↓ solitude [Emerson inserted a caret here without adding text] over . . . inflict↓?
11–15	↑who . . . toil↓ . . . ↑refreshing↓ . . . should ⟨be⟩ every . . . ↑indeed↓ . . . terror. ¶ ⟨Or⟩ ↑Again. Consider↓
22	↑too↓ exhausted ↑expenditure of the ⟨two⟩↓
28	mountains ⟨round⟩ with
29	takes ⟨the⟩ off
32	should ²love or should ¹⟨fear⟩ ↑dread↓
36	Mind. [in print-writing]
37	not ⟨harbingered⟩ charioted
39–40	Thus ↑Even . . . Bethlehem ⟨speaks⟩↓ men ⟨were taught⟩ [end of line] ↑is taught↓ that . . . to their welfare

Page 110

2–3	mind. ⟨The Son of Man came⟩ This . . . the ⟨outset⟩ ↑advent↓.
6–7	good. [added passage marked "A," used below] ¶ But
8–12	love? ↑Insert A↓ [above, marked "A":] ↑{Is . . . Vengeance"}↓ ↑("Perfect . . . fear")↓
16	such ⟨is⟩ must
36	Wilder↑n↓ess

Page 111

2	friends ⟨did⟩ ↑does↓
7	↑of sacrifice↓
9	↑wh. have . . . opinion↓
12	demand⟨.⟩s.
15–20	attain. ↑Insert A↓ [at bottom of page, marked "A":] ↑{Be not decieved . . . man.}↓ ↑God . . . end.↓ ¶ ⟨Thus is it that according to the language of our text the ways of religion are ways of pleasantness & all her paths are peace.⟩ ¶ But
27–28	the ⟨just⟩ full . . . ↑God & of↓
29	history. ⟨{⟩There
31–32	{Such an epoch ⟨was⟩ ↑has been↓ . . . & ⟨there exists a⟩ ↑has . . . the↓ tendenc⟨y⟩ies ⟨towards it in⟩ of
34–(112)1	this ⟨happy⟩ ↑soaring↓ . . . world ⟨notwithstanding⟩. ↑I have not forgotten,↓ ↑I remember with grief↓ [last addition in ink over pencil]. . . ignorance ⟨notwithstanding⟩ ↑I remember↓ . . . the ⟨bosom⟩ ↑⟨centre⟩ heart↓ of Christendom; ⟨& & tho we have to⟩ ↑I know and I↓ . . . ↑do yet↓ . . . God; ⟨yet there is a⟩ ↑& which . . . that↓ . . . ↑wholly↓

Page 112

2	thought ⟨that a purer age shall come⟩ ↑that↓
13–14	↑all↓ . . . wealth. ⟨& pleasure.⟩ When
17	greatest ⟨amount⟩ ↑aggregate↓
19–30	¶ {Let . . faith? ⟨The⟩ Its . . . feel.}

32–33	Millenium . . . hopes of ⟨romantic⟩ ↑pious↓
34	↑great↓

Page 113

1–2	↑the service of↓
5	the ⟨end⟩ ages

Sermon IX

Manuscript: Four sheets folded to make four pages each; folios stacked and sewn along left margin (thread now missing); pages measure 25 x 20 cm. Two strips (7 x 19 cm and 9.5 x 20 cm) are attached with red sealing wax to the recto of leaf 5; the second of these contains Insert "X."

Lines

Page 114

4	minstrel ⟨of Judah's line⟩ after
21	a⟨l⟩lthough
26	of ⟨what power⟩ what ⟨action⟩ ↑agency↓
27–(115)4	↑What is man . . . God?↓ ↑Insert A↓ [On next page, marked "A":] ¶ ↑{It . . . him.}↓

Page 115

11	to ⟨rest⟩ dust.
14–17	↑He . . . race.↓
18	where lies
20	talk, ⟨&⟩think,
22	↑No . . . lot.↓
26	the ⟨highest⟩ deepest
31–32	of ⟨reason⟩ experience
38–39	the ↑⟨circle⟩ ↑equipment↓ of↓

Page 116

1	the ⟨imperfect⟩ ↑⟨un⟩folded up↓ . . . th⟨ese⟩is
2	↑ourselves↓ [in pencil] to ⟨acquire the⟩ bring them ⟨from⟩ ↑out of↓
5–6	↑& mark how↓
8–9	↑in succession↓ one motive one ²group ↑of objects↓ one ¹desire. . . several ⟨objects⟩ ↑ends↓
13–16	purposes↑,↓ ⟨of⟩ to . . . & ⟨physical⟩ ↑bodily↓ [cancellation in pencil; addition in ink over pencil] . . . larger ⟨scenes⟩ opportunities,
21–26	joy. ↑Insert B ⟨{B⟩ ↑B My . . . nature↓ We . . . us. ⟨Our own nature, my friends, contains wonders which we are very apt to overlook.⟩ Man . . . fate. We ⟨are heedl⟩ disregard . . . which ⟨if it stood alone⟩ would . . . alone.↓ ⟨In t⟩The
29	desireable
30	the ⟨capacious⟩ memory,
38–39	powers, ⟨which⟩ ↑since↓ . . . that ⟨daily⟩ standing . . . to ⟨show⟩ ↑see↓
40–41	these ⟨marshalled powers⟩ ↑collected energies↓
42–(117)1	that ⟨adds⟩ gives

Page 117

8–15	¶ ↑↑To . . . preached↓ The . . . evil.—Rom II↓
16–24	these ⟨indications⟩ ↑observations↓ . . . which ⟨is sanctioned by the Scripture⟩ ↑reason . . . sanction↓ [emendation in ink over pencil] . . . the ⟨reason⟩ ↑account↓ [emendation in pencil] . . . ↑which each ⟨man⟩ of . . . himself,↓ . . . which ⟨he⟩ ↑we↓ ha⟨s⟩ve [emendation in pencil] . . . before ⟨him⟩ ↑each of us↓ [emendation in pencil] for ⟨his⟩ ↑our↓ . . . /him/us/ [variant in pencil] . . . into ⟨his⟩ neighborhood ↑of each↓ [emendations in pencil] . . . be ⟨his⟩ ↑our↓ [emendation in pencil] . . . ⟨h⟩we [emendation in pencil]
25–32	disclosed. ↑Insert X ¶ X My . . . considerations [ms. torn] us . . . our na[ms. torn] not. . . the las[ms. torn] feeling . . . endowme[ms. torn] & . . . comparing ⟨w⟩ the greatness of ou[ms. torn] makers. . . us hum[ms. torn] may . . . better.↓ [right margin of inserted quarter-leaf torn]
33	purpose, ⟨my friends⟩ does
36–37	↑when . . . close↓ . . . ⟨w⟩that . . . obedience ⟨find⟩ has
40	imagine, of

Page 118

6	science⟨,⟩ were
12	antichamber
17–18	↑Youll . . . this.↓
32	acheivement

Page 119

1	friends ⟨the⟩ what
3	↑bloated & terrible↓ . . . a ⟨consuming⟩ pestilence
6	bal⟨m⟩sam is in Gilead ⟨for this⟩ to
17–19	need ⟨not⟩ hardly . . . you, ⟨that⟩ if . . . of ⟨age &⟩ disease
20–23	↑chronic &↓ . . . all ⟨our⟩ ↑this↓ . . . made ⟨our⟩ ↑this↓ . . . to ⟨our⟩ ↑this↓ . . . to ⟨us⟩ ↑him,↓ . . . when ⟨you⟩ ↑the↓ . . . filled ⟨your⟩ ↑this↓
27	↑in . . . soul.↓
28	this ⟨malady⟩ pest
31–33	↑shedding↓ . . . understanding ⟨adds a new impulse to⟩ ↑impels like a torrent↓
40–41	candidates ⟨of⟩ ↑for↓

Sermon X

Manuscript: A gathering sewn with white thread along the left margin, consisting of one sheet folded around two stacked folios, followed by three stacked folios; pages measure 25.3 x 20.4 cm.

Lines	*Page 120*
Bible Text	them ²first ¹learn
1–2	eminence of /the actors in our/men in forming our/ [variant in pencil] . . . ↑A . . . telling.↓
3–4	↑degree of↓
6	↑the exhibition of↓ [in ink over pencil]

	Page 121
3	concerted ⟨resoluti⟩ signal of ⟨my⟩ a
4–5	to /see in ⟨reverted⟩ vision/go back & see/ [variant in pencil] . . . ↑precisely . . . seen↓
15	faith. ⟨The⟩ Less
17	Home /is/are/
18–22	↑Our . . . whatsoever↓ [in pencil] . . . petulent . . . another ⟨the least of these⟩ even . . . ↑humble↓ worth ↑the least of these↓
27	regard of of religion
28–29	home. ¶ ⟨Again, if it be said⟩ ↑It . . . intimated↓
33–34	to ⟨be religious⟩ love . . . ↑in . . . another↓
37–40	whole? ²{Must . . . strength?} ¹{Provided . . . ↑in the street↓ . . . house?} [The transposition makes nonsense of the sentence that follows, which has therefore been omitted from the text:] No; nothing of all this.

	Page 122
1	they ⟨bear⟩ contain
4–5	dec⟨ie⟩eive themselves ⟨with⟩ ↑by pushing forward↓ any substitute ⟨for⟩ ↑in the place of↓
11–12	↑when the . . . drawn↓
14–16	grows ⟨wayward⟩ ↑silent↓ & splenetic ↑he . . . praise.↓.
21	a ⟨conspicuous arena⟩ ↑great occasion↓ [emendation in ink over pencil]
28	on ⟨the⟩ piety
29	¶ ↑Let . . . that↓ ⟨I⟩it
42–43	↑and . . . it,↓

	Page 123
3–4	pleasures of the [end of page] of the . . . of ⟨self⟩ ↑property↓
11	of /fashion, {high titles,} /people in higher rank/ [brackets in pencil]
15	letter ⟨that⟩ and
20–21	for a [time?] to [word omitted at end of page] . . . of ⟨virtue⟩ ↑religion↓
33–35	↑Did . . . man↓ [in pencil]
37	↑eye↓

	Page 124
1–2	↑learned . . . you↓ kept ⟨the purity⟩ the
3–4	↑prayer . . . on↓ . . . God ⟨therein has been duly served night &⟩ morning
11	you /shrink from/are afraid to give/ [variant in pencil]

13–14	↑pernicious↓
19–(*125*)7	¶ {III. . . . {My friends, . . . world?}
29	↑Let . . . burdens↓
30–33	emergencies. ⟨In distant⟩ ↑When . . . into ⟨far &⟩ foreign↓ . . . ↑of affection↓ . . . ↑from afar,↓ . . . & ⟨call⟩ . . . come ⟨back upon⟩ ↑over↓
35	severed, ⟨ever⟩ for

Page 125

8	yet ⟨bears⟩ shines
10	that ⟨prevent us⟩ ↑stand in the way↓.
11–13	efforts. ⟨We aim to spend a⟩ ↑What . . . Sabbath.↓ ↑Men↓ Come . . . & ⟨are⟩ struck . . . presented, ⟨our⟩ their . . . witness ⟨we⟩ they
18	↑Now . . . less↓ [in pencil]
21	spend ⟨a⟩ one
28–29	↑that . . . accident↓
40–41	↑no matter how . . . blows,↓

Page 126

2	that ⟨hour⟩ ↑day↓

[Following the end of the sermon, the notation in pencil:] 27'

[On the otherwise blank page opposite the end of the sermon, the notation in pencil:] Heb 12. 22

Sermon XI

Manuscript: Four sheets folded to make four pages each; folios stacked and sewn with white thread along the left margin; pages measure 25.4 x 20.4 cm. A strip (3 x 15 cm) containing Insert "X" is affixed with red sealing wax to the recto of leaf 6.

Lines	Page 127
3	melancholy ⟨&⟩ or
7	events↑,↓ [addition in pencil]
7–8	They ⟨want⟩ ↑speak as if their↓ their days ⟨to⟩ ↑shd↓ [emendations in pencil]
11–12	It /is tho't/ seems/ [variant in pencil] . . . ⟨a⟩ occupy
14	this ⟨is said⟩ in [cancellation in pencil]
28–29	an ⟨eloquence⟩ ↑intense interest↓ [emendation in pencil]

Page 128

1	wh⟨y⟩ence
9–11	contracted ⟨i⟩ on . . . with which which we
15	to ⟨bury⟩ ↑let↓
18–19	{of using . . . that} ⟨it needs not the light of revelation to make it felt.⟩ The
26–27	it, ⟨with the⟩ ↑when . . . of↓

32   need ⟨wander⟩ ↑go↓ [emendation in pencil]
36   ↑not alone↓

Page 129

1–3   agents↑,↓ . . . about↑,↓ [additions in pencil]
7   called↑,↓ [addition in pencil]
11   ↑d↓o⟨p⟩minion
15   & ⟨spurning⟩ ↑wisely despising↓
20–23   structure↑s↓ {He . . . waters. ⟨A bauble, a particle on the interminable waste I see it mount the ridges, & sink into the vallies of the ocean; but the understanding of him that guides it, ↑which is the gift of God↓ se⟨e⟩ts ⟨re⟩sovereign of its course Its curious furniture of helm & sail & compass lead the little adventurer on in safety, & tho the whirlwind from heaven sweep across ⟨its⟩his path, & the tempest tear his canvass as in sport, he contends with the elements, & rides out the storm, and comes at last over nearly a straight line of thousands of leagues of water to visit the farthest corners of the world. When the message of another nation is delivered here, & the fruits of the tropics are bartered for those of the pole, when the character, language & country has been scrutinized by the eyes of the stranger he sets his sail anew & flees over the deep, to enrich the science of his own land with his strange tidings, & its wealth with those gifts of Providence which are denied to its soil.}⟩ ¶ ⟨This is but a small part of⟩ ↑These . . . in↓
32   enumerate ⟨the⟩ ↑this↓ endless ⟨↑catalogue of↓⟩ inventions ⟨by which civilization is supported.⟩. The
37–39   the ⟨summits⟩ summits . . . of ⟨the⟩ nature

Page 130

6–8   ↑use &↓ . . . triumphs, a
23–25   & ⟨g⟩satisfy. ⟨But we do not⟩ ↑Shall we then↓ [emendation in ink over pencil] . . . fault⟨.⟩? [ink over pencil] ↑Not in the least;↓ [over ↑Not a jot↓ in pencil] we ↑are↓ only ↑to↓ [additions in pencil]
29   There ⟨is that⟩ ↑are the↓ endless & wonderful ⟨catalogue of⟩ contrivances
31–32   divine ⟨retributions⟩ ↑compensations↓; [emendation in ink over pencil] . . . of ⟨compensation⟩ ↑retribution↓
33–34   confederated ⟨final⟩ causes, ↑the manifestations of design↓ [emendation in ink over pencil]
37   human ⟨soul⟩ ↑heart↓ . . . exists↑,↓ [emendations in pencil]
39–(131)2   idea ⟨these & the all unexplained "mysteries of the human mind ↑that investigates them all↓⟩ ↑{Insert X} X and . . . furnish &c↓ may furnish [insert on slip attached to ms. at this point; verso blank] . . . to ⟨y⟩ the

Page 131

2–18   curiosity. ↑Insert A ¶ {A Is there . . . the⟨se⟩ study . . . affairs, ⟨&⟩wherein . . . Or↑,↓ ⟨my friends, at least you may⟩ ↑can you not↓ . . . ↑for our sin↓ [addition in pencil] . . . cross.}↓

20   have ⟨begun⟩ ↑entered↓ . . . ↑absorbing↓
21   Yes, ⟨my friends,⟩ before
31   there ⟨is⟩yet
33   wisdom ⟨issuing in⟩ of
36   ↑most↓

Page 132

4   ↑And . . . works?↓
5–6   ↑that . . . wisdom↓ [ink over pencil]
20–21   ↑"The good . . . glorify"↓
23   Happier ⟨than⟩ in

[The following is inscribed in pencil on the page following the end of the sermon and opposite the ink version:]

> —"The good man wears
> Disaster as the angel⟨s⟩ wear↑s↓ his wings
> To elevate & glorify."

Sermon XII

Manuscript: A gathering sewn with brown thread along the left margin, consisting of five sheets folded to make four pages each, followed by four single leaves and one folio; pages measure 25 x 20.4 cm.

Lines   *Page 133*
7–9   voice ⟨voice⟩ of . . . has ⟨from⟩ ↑ever since↓ the beginning ⟨↑hath↓⟩ ascended

Page 134

4   others;" ⟨it is⟩ who
12–16   blessings. ↑{Insert A}↓ [On the previous page, marked "A":] ↑Others . . . desire.↓
21   No, ↑{Insert X}↓ [On the previous page, marked "X":] ⟨↑{if we cannot hear the voice of events that say it to us, let us repeat it to ourselves↓⟩ we
23–24   exposure. ignorant,
26–27   ↑It . . . that↓ Whom . . . chasteneth, ⟨saith the scripture.⟩ It
30–31   hardy ⟨north⟩ alpine . . . corrupts ⟨d⟩&
33   ↑in the sugar islands↓
37   that ⟨⟨when⟩the⟩ ↑the↓

Page 135

3–4   ↑This . . . Providenc[inscription runs off the edge of the page]↓
7–8   inference ⟨of⟩from . . . reflexions? ↑{Insert X}↓ [On the previous page, marked "X":] ↑{Ought . . . misfortune?}↓
12–13   human ⟨happiness⟩ ↑felicity↓.
19   receive ⟨g⟩God's
22   the⟨y⟩se ↑blessings↓

23–24   But↑, it is said,↓ . . . ⟨h⟩Him, . . . nothing ⟨we reptiles⟩ ↑which . . . are↓

30   no⟨thing⟩ ↑gift↓

30–31   will ⟨offering⟩ effort, . . . which ⟨if you choose to withhold cannot be compelled⟩ God

37   action. ⟨↑I am overawed.↓⟩ It

39   is [canceled caret] an eternal ↑⟨a⟩ brotherhood [end of line] a perfect↓

Page 136

2–4   to ⟨be ready⟩ ⟨to bestow what he feels he has received.⟩ ↑to . . . experienced.↓ [addition in ink over pencil] [end of page] ¶ ⟨{Is it such a jubilee as that Babylonian ⟨p⟩holiday of old when a haughty lord of half the East had set up a golden image on the plain of Dura & all people & nations & languages were summoned at the sound of music to worship it on pain of death and a nation of men prostrated themselves before a block of gold? The harp & the dulcimer sounded indeed but the roaring of the furnace of fire was less harsh & dreadful in the ear of virtue & freedom.}⟩ [end of page] ¶ And

8   its ⟨force⟩ ↑poison↓,

11   restores ⟨a⟩ peace.

12   festival ⟨when thei⟩ for . . . when ⟨their⟩ a

15–16   ↑the↓ musket⟨s⟩ ⟨in⟩ at their ⟨hands⟩ ↑shoulder,↓

21–26   afraid. ⟨We⟩ [end of page] ↑We . . . venerable ⟨inst⟩ custom ⟨of our⟩ sanctioned . . . centuries ⟨whereby⟩ ⟨& . . . come to quote, &c.↓ [end of page] come to quote,

29–30   ↑in . . . hands,↓

37   ↑recorded↓

39–40   ↑with . . . spirit,↓

Page 137

2–4   praise. ⟨I need not point⟩ [end of page] ↑Within . . . progress↓ [addition in pencil]

6–7   the ⟨eyes⟩ ↑view↓ of all ⟨the world,⟩ ↑mankind,↓

11–13   ↑or . . . others↓ [addition in ink over pencil] . . . increases ⟨the⟩ pleasures ⟨of life⟩ &

14–(138)13   We . . . praise. [struck through lightly in pencil]

15   ↑progress . . . the↓

25   him [canceled caret] that guides it, ↑which . . . God↓

35   & ⟨th⟩its

Page 138

3   kingdom⟨s⟩

7   whe⟨re⟩↑nce↓

10   traverses ↑the↓

12–13   ↑And . . . praise?↓

17   source↑s↓ . . . reason↑s↓

21   whose ⟨depths⟩ wastes

22–24   ⟨a⟩Art; . . . the ⟨printing⟩ presses, . . . mountain↑s↓ & lake↑s↓
29   cities ⟨or they may be rent by the force of subterranean fire⟩. All
30   fondest ⟨pa⟩ affection,
37   immortal ⟨beau⟩ youth
38   those ⟨pure⟩ affections

Page 139

2–3   {& . . . life.}
4–11   praise. ↑Insert X↓ ¶ ↑X {There . . . remain.}↓
11–12   the ⟨light⟩ ↑passing↓ [addition in pencil]
16–25   ¶ ↑In . . . depends.↓
34–35   to ⟨copy⟩ ↑take a lesson↓
40–(140)1 them ⟨to the uses⟩ devote . . . ↑sovereign↓

Page 140

3   away ⟨your⟩ his
5–7   {We . . . pensioners.}
8   pay ⟨the⟩ ↑a↓

Sermon XIII

Manuscript: A gathering sewn along the left margin (thread now missing), consisting of a single folio, two nested folios, and three stacked folios; pages measure 21 x 17 cm. A sheet once attached with red sealing wax to the recto of the first leaf is now missing; a sheet (12.4 x 16.5 cm) affixed with red sealing wax to the verso of leaf 5 covers the lower two-thirds of the page; a sheet folded to make four pages (each measuring 20 x 12.4 cm) contains Insert "X" and is tipped with red sealing wax to the recto of leaf 6; an irregular scrap containing Insert "A" is tipped with red sealing wax to the recto of leaf 8; a sheet folded to make four pages (each measuring 20 x 12.5 cm) contains Insert "B" and is tipped with red sealing wax to the recto of leaf 9.

Lines   Page 141
1–4   ¶ {We . . . day.} [brackets in pencil]
7–8   ↑out . . . came↓ . . . & cruel [circled in ink] . . . Puritans↑,↓ [comma in pencil]
11   apprehensions. ⟨The⟩ Two
16–17   the ⟨improper⟩ ↑usurping↓ [emendation in pencil]

Page 142

1–3   priveleges . . . ↑to God,↓
10   other ⟨occasions⟩ ↑seasons↓ . . . joy, ⟨there is in⟩ this [cancellations in ink over pencil; addition in pencil]
13–14   ↑Can . . . hour?↓ [in ink over pencil; pencil inscription reads "Can . . . master one hour"]
21–22   world. ⟨{It is pleasant to reflect that we are not alone in our service. Besides the vast numbers of Xns that in our own land ascribe peculiar solemnity to this day, the Spanish Church throughout the Mexican territory and thro' all the civilized portion of South America along the

shores of the Amazon & on the sides of the Andes this day exhibits its
religious pomp. Across the seas ↑there is joy in↓ the land of our
fathers↑.↓ by an immemorial custom /in/thro/ all ⟨the forms of joy⟩
↑its classes↓ celebrates this day the chief feast of the year In the
sumptuous cathedrals of all Catholic Europe the high mass is said &
the Greek Church /all /over Russia/on the shores of the Mediterran-
nean/ resounds with solemn joy.}⟩ [end of page] ¶ In [all emendations
in pencil; passage canceled in pencil]

22	of ⟨joy⟩ ↑/gratitude/gladness/↓
24	↑what was once↓
28–30	evil↑:↓ . . . God↑:↓ . . . happiness↑:↓ . . . sin↑:↓ [additions in pencil]
33–34	↑peculiar . . . the↓ . . . event /{we meet to celebrate}/this season commemorates/. [brackets and variant in pencil] ⟨It is a singular & very⟩ ↑You . . . the↓

Page 143

9	↑in expectant silence↓
10–17	/{There . . . ↑by the wisest↓ in Greece} ⟨there seems also to be some evidence that in⟩/↑Beside certain remarkable passages that indicate this anticipation in Greece↓/ ↑it . . . in↓ [variant in pencil]
18	Sybilline ⟨oracles⟩ prophecies,
20–21	he ⟨predicts⟩ foretells
22–23	↑for the . . . hundred y.↓ . . . ↑universal↓
30–(144)31	therein. ⟨↑{Insert X}↓⟩ ⟨⟨{He walked on the Earth but there was no voice of God. he explored the stars but they were silent in their courses He looked impatient for some light to break that should show him why he was made & what was to become of him in the immense futurity before him.⟩ He waited not in vain. In the sky of the East a star arose. On the midnight heaven the silver accents were heard of the heavenly host praising God & saying Glory to God in the highest & on earth peace & good will to men This day is born in the city of David a Saviour which is Christ the Lord.⟩ [The entire passage is canceled by being pasted over with the half leaf containing the following substituted paragraph:] ¶ ↑↑Man . . . for ⟨presenting⟩ ↑dwelling upon it↓ it ↑a moment↓ in this connexion. {Insert X}↓ [On an insert, folded to make four pages and attached to the ms. with red sealing wax, a passage marked "X":] ¶ {⟨Men felt whilst God was not clearly made known what all men now feel when they live without ⟨acknowledg⟩ment of God—a strange disproportion between his desires & his condition. So noble in his powers & so lowly in his necessities, that there needed ⟨the solution of⟩ another world ↑to explain the difficulties of this.↓⟩ Though . . . Lord.↓

Page 144

8	talk ⟨&⟩ to
9–10	adorned. ⟨The⟩ Let . . . ↑yᵉ sky↓
13–15	know [space at end of line] he . . . ↑the . . . appetites;↓ . . . some ⟨lit⟩ minute

26   should / reveal / show /
28–29   accents ⟨aros⟩ were
43   would ⟨lead⟩ ↑invite↓ [emendation in pencil]

Page 145

17–21   wander. ↑{Insert A}↓ [On a slip of paper attached with red sealing
              wax (verso blank), a passage marked "A":] ↑The . . . God.↓
23   it ⟨to acquire & carry⟩ for
26–28   them↑,↓ . . . have↑,↓ . . . God↑,↓ . . . man↑,↓ . . . God↑—↓ [addi-
              tions in pencil]
31–33   sting. ⟨They⟩ In . . . service↑,↓ [emendations in pencil]
36   them ⟨better⟩ ↑their error↓. [emendation in pencil]
37   in ⟨such⟩ ↑a↓ [emendation in pencil]
38   Cherubim, ⟨But⟩ for

Page 146

1   the ⟨div⟩ ⟨virtues⟩ divine
2   decrees. ⟨a⟩And
10–11   is is better . . . paganism ⟨T⟩ He↑r votary↓ . . . stainless ⟨& the⟩
              benevolent;
12–14   the ⟨face that we have of the Virgin from the imagination⟩
              ↑countenance which the genius of↓ of . . . ↑has . . . virgin↓ ⟨is⟩has
              . . . different [incomplete caret in pencil] ⟨from⟩ ↑↑& . . . attrac-
              tive↓ than↓ [emendations in ink over pencil, except canceled "from"
              and inserted "than," which are in ink only]
19–(147)1   men. ⟨↑And this was the design of Xty.↓⟩ [addition in ink over pencil]
              ↑Insert B↓ [On an insert, folded to make four pages and attached to
              the ms. with red sealing wax, a passage marked "B":] ↑{The . . . To
              show himself↓ To show himself
20–21   great ↑internal↓ . . . of ⟨this⟩ ⟨r⟩Revelation ↑we receive↓ . . . only
              ⟨one⟩ ↑account↓ that has ⟨revealed a⟩ ↑disclosed a character of↓
23–24   elevated, ⟨obtruded⟩ ↑distorted . . . with↓ . . . features ⟨upon the
              soul.⟩. Something
26–27   as ⟨like ourselves We are assured⟩ ↑the . . . us↓ . . . ↑moral↓
29   humblest ⟨wretch⟩ ↑outcast↓
31–34   Universe. ¶ ⟨God is⟩ We . . . minds ⟨We are made to enter into a
              sublime sympathy with him, ↑to speak to him day by day, to act with
              him & from him↓ are set forward on a progress in the effort to bring
              ourselves into his likeness—⟩ ¶ We

Page 147

20   that ⟨eventful⟩ ↑joyful↓ [emendation in pencil]
24–25   humanity. These [end of line] ↑When . . . institution↓ great
34   & ⟨pi⟩ inspired,
36–37   despair; . . . ↑to . . . man↓
39–40   & ⟨i⟩trace . . . am ⟨content to add my humble voice to swell the note
              of joy & praise⟩ overawed

Page 148

8–13	own. {⟨But⟩ And . . . heaven} [passage circled in pencil]
21	↑faithful↓
24	↑prevailing↓
28	as opportunity
33	his ⟨laws⟩ temper

Sermon XIV

Manuscript: Four sheets folded to make four pages each; folios stacked and sewn with white thread along the left margin; pages measure 25.2 x 20.4 cm.

Lines   *Page 149*

11	↑precept . . . the↓
15	pre⟨dominate⟩↑ponderate↓?
15–16	ask ⟨if⟩ ↑whether↓
18–23	↑man a↓ . . . despot ⟨if⟩ ↑whether↓ this ⟨be not better⟩ government, ⟨where there is⟩ ↑which secures↓ . . . virtue ⟨without⟩ hope, ⟨if this⟩ be . . . course of /indolence/impolicy/
24–25	which ⟨murders every man⟩ ↑takes . . . him↓

Page 150

2	superstition ⟨on the part of the vulgar & the silence of terror mixed with contempt on the part of the better informed⟩ be not more desireable
5	↑of the SS.↓
9	In ⟨the⟩ our
13	blessings ⟨amply⟩ worth
25–26	↑Every . . . congratulation↓
27	of ⟨public⟩ religious
30	sincere /congratulation/pleasure/.

Page 151

1	to exchange /what/the truth/ . . . for /what/the prejudice/ [variants in pencil]
13	civil ⟨& religiou⟩ institutions
18	by ⟨prejudice⟩ ↑ignorance↓
20	& ⟨b⟩ recovery
24	kindred (⟨who sincerely honour God⟩) rejoice
25	who ⟨rejoice⟩ ↑have joy↓
36–38	gods /by plunging his child into ⟨{the foaming flood of}⟩ the Ganges/by mutilating his form/ or follows {with gloomy countenance} [brackets in pencil] . . . lands: ⟨{or from the foolish & odious idolatry of China & Japan.}⟩ But

Page 152

4–5	by ⟨Er⟩ Wicliffe
14	those ⟨bewildering evils⟩ ↑high charges of↓

15–16   ↑the lessons of↓
19–20   horror. ⟨We have learned to reject⟩ ↑We . . . admit↓ that
23–25   ↑to give . . . revelation↓ . . . for ⟨immortal⟩ ↑endless↓
31–33   mark of /excellence/truth/ . . . of ⟨God⟩ the
39   ↑make our own, to↓
41–42   ↑yourselves↓ . . . pride⟨.⟩; ⟨Let none⟩ ↑& . . . others to↓
44   to ⟨vindicate our faith⟩ to use

Page 153
6   friends, ⟨without⟩ ↑unless↓
15   la⟨y⟩w
20   best ⟨ca⟩ promote,
22   the the things
38   ↑we perceive↓

Page 154
4–5   ↑Perhaps . . . embraced↓
7–8   Because ⟨we⟩ ↑you↓ have altered ↑y↓our . . . Because ⟨we⟩ ↑you↓
9   this ⟨should be the case⟩ ↑delusion . . . minds↓
12–13   and ⟨have rejected⟩ do . . . of ⟨Athanasius or Calvin⟩ ↑the . . .
             church↓, [last emendation in ink over pencil]
27–28   ↑(God grant we may!)↓
31   the ⟨time⟩hour

Sermon XV
Manuscript: Four sheets folded to make four pages each; folios stacked and sewn with
white thread along left margin; pages measure 22.5 x 20.4 cm.

Lines   Page 155
1–2   We /{are assembled once more, my brethren, for religious worship.
             The light of another Sabbath has brought us up}/return/ [brackets
             and variant in light pencil; rejected as a probable late revision] . . .
             our ⟨duties⟩ ↑hopes↓
5–6   We ⟨have dismissed⟩ ↑This day has begun↓ another week↑.↓ ⟨{of our
             short life into the eternity of the past.}⟩ Again [emendation in light
             pencil; rejected as a probable late revision]
11   ↑final↓
17   th⟨is⟩e
21–22   gifts ⟨to⟩ ↑on↓ . . . ↑he causes↓ some ↑to↓ . . . ↑to↓
24–25   please. ⟨No⟩ This ⟨abstraction⟩ ↑possession↓

Page 156
15–19   of ⟨our⟩ God's . . . life. ⟨And i⟩It . . . consideration. ¶ ⟨Farther⟩
             ↑But↓ ⟨the⟩let
21   ↑he↓
33   brethren ⟨& wherein did that d⟩? It

Page 157

8	that ⟨business cannot be⟩ just
11	that time that time
12–14	↑What . . . political ⟨distinction⟩ ↑power↓ . . . ↑honor↓ . . . fame. ↑science↓↓
28	of ⟨time⟩ ↑age↓,
34–36	devotion; ⟨of⟩ the . . . hope, the

Page 158

2–3	we ⟨forget⟩ refuse
7	th⟨is⟩e
9	your ⟨own⟩ unwillingness
15	↑not . . . but↓
17	↑evils↓
18–19	man. ¶ ⟨Let us⟩ ↑If we↓ . . . day ⟨of our lives⟩ we
23	thoughts. ⟨Or I will go further and ask if there is within these walls that holy man who bears on his memory a single day in which he lived as he ought in which he wasted no one moment in which there was no unlawful act, no selfishness no sensual indulgence no sinful desire. If it be so, then I say, blessed, for his sake, is this place, & this people!⟩ It ⟨does appear⟩ ↑seems↓
25	↑us↓ all ⟨who hear me.⟩. Have
29	curious / vase / vessel /
32	for ⟨its⟩ the
35–37	wea⟨l⟩lth . . . ingots ⟨of price⟩ ↑& diamonds↓, ↑precisely↓ in proportion / as it is wrought / to the labor / ?
42	desire? ⟨If it be so then⟩ I say Blessed, / for his sake, / among all that are born of women / [variant in light pencil; rejected as a probable late revision]

Page 159

5	↑a cement of↓
12–15	Lord." ⟨Is not this man then⟩ ↑Shall . . . to↓ . . . he ⟨will soon return⟩ ↑is shortly bound↓?
16–17	confidence ⟨in the event.⟩. ¶ Will
20	How ⟨much⟩ shall

Page 160

3–4	the ⟨last⟩ ↑extreme↓ . . . & of / sublime / divine /
20	↑a↓
30–31	This / day / year / [variant in light pencil; rejected as a probable late revision] . . . ↑irrevocable↓
32	tablets. ⟨Yonder⟩ ↑The↓ sun ↑of this commencing day↓ [emendation in light pencil; rejected as a probable late revision]
33	vow ⟨this day⟩ ↑in this term↓ [emendation in light pencil; rejected as a probable late revision]

Sermon XVI

Manuscript: Four sheets folded to make four pages each; folios stacked and sewn with white thread along the left margin; pages measure 25 x 20.4 cm.

Lines	*Page 161*
Bible Text	their's
1	spirit ⟨to⟩ ↑on↓
13	their's
24	whether ⟨covered⟩ ↑laid↓

Page 162

2   & ⟨inevitable⟩ ↑unsharing↓ distemper. ⟨{This it is, which, showing itself under a thousand forms, gave colour & currency to that melancholy creed that man came into the world poisoned with hereditary depravity.}⟩ And [emendation and cancellation in pencil; see James Elliot Cabot, *A Memoir of Ralph Waldo Emerson* (Boston, 1887), 1:44]

11   calls ⟨the⟩ *poor*

12–17   who ⟨do not⟩ ↑fail to↓ . . . world ⟨for⟩ ↑because they↓ want ⟨of⟩ courage . . . higher⟨.⟩: ⟨They have no admirat⟩ not . . . things ⟨which men usually covet⟩, now . . . own ⟨immeasurable inferiority⟩ deficiencies.—

22   disgrace." ⟨It⟩ All

28   that ⟨in⟩to

30–34   of ⟨that⟩ ↑the same↓ . . . as ⟨many⟩ ↑the more odious↓ . . . in ⟨heinousness⟩ ↑enormity↓, . . . mischief, ⟨to wit⟩ ↑I mean↓,

34–35   this ⟨feature which other vices have not,⟩ ↑aggravation,↓ . . . that ⟨men⟩ its

37–39   pride. ⟨It seems to me we shall perform an useful labor if we establish against this grand enemy these charges:⟩ ↑We . . . I ⟨am going to⟩ ↑shall↓ . . . things↓

Page 163

3   their ⟨array⟩ ↑strength↓? [emendation in pencil]

5–7   when ⟨the explosion of⟩ a . . . ↑or . . . worm↓ ⟨is⟩has . . . ↑the↓ . . . ↑& the . . . earth↓ & shake

9–11   shall ⟨bring down⟩ ↑burst↓ . . . ↑a . . . spent,↓

13–14   What ⟨pencil hath ever painted such amazing⟩ ↑more↓ absurd⟨ity as⟩ ↑than that↓ . . . ↑as he is↓ . . . him; /bowed/ ⟨weighed down⟩/

17–18   & ⟨toss his head⟩ ↑be uplifted↓ . . . ↑he says that↓

20   the ⟨horrible⟩ ↑dismaying↓ [emendation in pencil]

32   is our /perception/discovery/

36–37   ↑man↓ . . . ↑reveres↓

Page 164

2   things ⟨that⟩ whose

14–15   inferior, ⟨then they⟩ ↑are ready to↓ . . . pride, ⟨they⟩ ↑and↓

18	make ⟨men⟩ ↑us↓
23	at ⟨that enrapturing vision⟩ ↑the true nature↓
26	An ⟨a⟩ Arab
33–35	↑Is . . . spirit↓ [in pencil]

Page 165

12	↑shows↓
17–18	↑& . . . him.↓.
34–35	↑1.↓ the ⟨three facts⟩ unsuitableness . . . the ⟨human⟩ condition
43	heart:"

Page 166

4	the ⟨sources⟩ ↑occasions↓
6	↑there↓
13	us ⟨feel that⟩ be
16–17	↑we . . . proud;↓

Sermon XVII

Manuscript: Four sheets folded to make four pages each; folios stacked and sewn with white thread along the left margin; pages measure 24.8 x 20.2 cm.

Lines   Page 167

15	by ⟨the⟩ any
23	↑nature &↓

Page 168

1	↑to↓ nations,
6	perhaps ⟨b⟩ have
12–14	The ⟨tremendous⟩ ↑great↓ [emendation in ink over pencil] . . . suffer↑,↓ . . . time↑,↓ [commas in pencil]
27	so /mighty/decided/
30	in ↑the↓
39	at ⟨concord⟩ ↑agreement side by side↓

Page 169

3–4	from ⟨a⟩ violent priest⟨hood⟩↑s↓
5–6	came ⟨out from the roar of crowded cities⟩ forth ⟨upright men⟩ from the ↑persecuting↓ roar & ⟨the⟩ hiss
26	↑earthquake↓
28	If ⟨it⟩ ↑such should↓ be the ⟨will⟩ order
30–31	a ⟨barren⟩ heap . . . scarce↑ly↓
33	ha⟨s⟩ve the ⟨storm⟩ ↑winds,↓
39	↑up↓ the ⟨angry ocean⟩ ↑sea↓

Page 170

2	↑in . . . tide.↓. [the date "1430" in the margin]
3	beneath ⟨the⟩ his

6–7	hills? ¶ ⟨The earthquake at Lisbon in [space left] destroyed⟩ ¶ I see
9–10	omnipotence. ¶ ⟨We see, then, that⟩ man . . . & ⟨that⟩ the
14	hint⟨s⟩
16	God ⟨which by a⟩ ↑in the↓
18	la⟨y⟩id . . . of ⟨of⟩ our
19	↑When . . . nations↓
24	was ⟨faint⟩ ⟨putrid⟩ ⟨corrupt.⟩ ↑rotten.↓
26	has ⟨had⟩ ↑begun to have↓
31	state; ↑{Insert X}↓ [At the bottom of the page, a passage marked "X":] ↑something . . . of ⟨embittered⟩ religious controversy,↓
32–35	of ⟨corrupting⟩ vices,— . . . our ⟨spacious domain.⟩ ↑land.↓ [last cancellation in ink over pencil] ¶ Hence ⟨the⟩ arises
39	deliverance. [Here follows one line of undeciphered shorthand.]

Page 171

1	with ⟨the most⟩ religious
3	↑If it be so↓ To
13–16	be⟨moan⟩↑wail↓. ⟨{On a former occasion I took an opportunity to invite the attention of this congregation⟩ ↑God calls your attention ⟨to⟩↓ to the immense importance of their conduct when considered as *example*.⟨}⟩ ⟨That consideration returns upon our minds with all its force in this connexion.}⟩ For [Except for "bewail" the emendation is rejected as a late revision.]
16	For ⟨why⟩ ↑how↓
25–26	of ⟨his⟩ that . . . sin↑, would . . . down,↓
29–30	public /virtue/sentiment/, . . . for ⟨punishment⟩ judgment.
37	to ↑the↓

Page 172

4	compl⟨y⟩iance
5–6	the ⟨lapse⟩ ↑passage↓ . . . ↑so many↓
8–9	to ⟨g⟩ afford
12	is ⟨set down to his account⟩ written
12–13	↑Let . . . country.↓
15	shall ⟨be⟩ ↑come to him↓

[On the last manuscript page are three lines of undeciphered shorthand.]

Sermon XVIII

Manuscript: A gathering sewn with white thread along the left margin, consisting of a sheet folded to make four pages and another folded around two stacked folios; these are followed by a single half-leaf not included in the sewing. The pages measure 25.2 x 20.4 cm. A sheet (also 25.2 x 20.4 cm) is tipped with black sealing wax to the recto of leaf 2.

[Below the Bible text is Emerson's note:] ↑St Augustine says in reference to this passage I find many [space left] but I no where find Come unto me all It has peculiar interest from the circumstances.↓

Lines   *Page 173*

1   the ⟨p⟩burdensome
8   ↑through ⟨them⟩↓
12   ¶ I⟨t⟩s i⟨s⟩t ↑not↓ strange ⟨enough⟩ that
15–18   has ⟨prevented⟩ mankind ↑stood . . . pride↓ . . . obedience? ⟨Yet so
                     it is. Every cruel rule that has usurped the name of religion in the
                     world, that has enjoined an infinite multiplication of empty forms,
                     that has commanded men to abstain from lawful pleasure, to fast, or
                     to whip, to torture to slay themselves to burn or to drown their
                     children—every one that has bid them do thus in the name of God—
                     for the sake of their souls, has been sure of success. It has had no lack
                     of votaries, and its votaries have had no lack of zeal. It has taken up in
                     its turn the axe of persecution & has hunted its victims. I know I am
                     speaking of well known things. It is melancholy to me to think how
                     trite is this topic. I know how often ⟨the sacred teacher⟩ your
                     preachers have bid you mark the astonishing severity of Asiatic
                     superstition whether under the iron ⟨rod⟩ ↑rule↓ of the Bramins or
                     the milder ⟨rule⟩ ↑law↓ of Mahomet. But connected as it is with the
                     most solemn interests of man; being, as it is, in that country only a
                     more striking instance of an error that prevails almost to an equal
                     extent among us I know not how to be silent. I cannot but quote it to
                     you. The Pulpit must repeat & repeat the charge till the evil (which
                     God grant) shall cease to exist.
                          God has given to men a clear and simple law. Man has always
                     perverted it. And it is hard to recognize in any of the systems of
                     human faith the features of that primitive religion which man received
                     of his maker. God requires *principles;* but man all the world over,
                     pretending authority from his maker, insists on *opinions.* In one
                     nation a body of priests loads the votary with a thousand foolish rites
                     & wastes his life in an endless variety⟩ ¶ Let

18   [The following passage, inscribed on both sides of a leaf attached to
                     the manuscript with black sealing wax, was written for a later
                     delivery, most probably for the last delivery of the sermon in an
                     evening service, March 20, 1831, at the Friend Street Chapel; it was
                     apparently meant to substitute for two paragraphs ("Let us consider
                     . . . passions?") in the original:] ↑Let us try this evening my friends to
                     understand what Jesus meant by this declaration. *My yoke is easy &
                     my burden is light.* I have thought that there were three yokes at least
                     under which men bring themselves (and each of us is probably in
                     some degree under one of them) that might be in his mind, when he
                     spoke these words. 'My yoke is easy' compared with the yoke of
                     ⟨passion⟩ bad passions, or with the dominion of human opinions or
                     with the yoke of false religion all which oppose the authority of
                     Christ.
                          ↑Now↓ ⟨L⟩let us consider a few moments each of these yokes or
                     burdens.
                          I. The yoke of the passions is harder to be borne. Our passions will
                     always be either servants or masters. If we do not govern them they

will govern us There's no middle way. But they are very artful tempters. They never show you at first where they are going to lead you. But it seems to you as if you were only seeking a little gratification that lies in your [end of page] and if you do not like it why the next time you ⟨ca⟩ need not take it. You ⟨are⟩ give way some times to anger. You cannot help throwing out a hard word in return for a hard word & it seems ⟨a⟩ no great affair; but it is throwing oil on fire, for your neighbor grows more angry, you provoke each other more & more until you have become without knowing it two roaring madmen possessed by a devil.

Is it any better with the wretched man or woman who has given up his or her reason to the love of liquor. A sweet or a strong taste led them first to sip the glass & now it has sucked out their brains.

Is it any better with those more wretched men & women who have polluted their body this ⟨wonderful⟩ frame so fearfully & wonderfully made to be the filthy vessel of their lusts ⟨killin⟩ destroying the body with disease, & the soul with sin↓

19–20	↑own . . . religion,↓
24	us. ⟨They are uneasy companions.⟩ ↑There's no middle way↓
27	can ⟨straightway⟩ refuse
27-(174)1	ambush ⟨for our easy unguarded hours⟩ to . . . ↑at↓ eas⟨y⟩e,

Page 174

3–5	he ⟨sees not⟩ ↑does not see↓ . . . ↑does not↓ hear⟨s not⟩ the . . . ↑this↓ . . . fast, ⟨he⟩ you . . . path ⟨↑wh. he tells you↓⟩ he ⟨condemns.⟩ ↑shudders to tread.↓ ↑which . . . tread.↓
8–16	seen ⟨a⟩ ↑notorious↓ malefactor↑s↓ . . . end, ⟨that t⟩ what . . . exhausted ⟨the⟩ the . . . ↑to roll . . . but↓ . . . freedom ⟨of⟩ ↑from↓ . . . ↑squalid &↓ . . . in ⟨the most uncomfortable⟩ ↑forlorn & frightful↓ . . . metropolis; ⟨& that⟩ ↑whilst↓ . . . exhibited ⟨for these⟩ ↑with this↓ wretched ⟨purposes⟩ ↑success↓ . . . ↑honest↓
21–22	The ⟨Chr⟩ gospel
24–25	have ⟨deformed⟩ ↑disguised↓ ⟨its ⟨beauty⟩ simplicity & in their⟩ ↑gentle spirit of his gospel under their↓ . . . have ⟨insisted⟩ ↑sat in judgment↓
27	↑they↓
28–29	↑authority,↓ . . . spirit ⟨⟨& bewilder mankind⟩ the ⟨mind⟩ understanding.⟩ ↑and . . . truth.↓
31–33	religion. /I need hardly repeat/It is only necessary to remind you of/ what ⟨the pulpit has spoken so often⟩ ↑been . . . shown↓ . . . ↑Indostan . . . islands↓
34–35	no⟨thing⟩ ↑abomination↓ . . . ↑sometime or somewhere↓
36–38	has ⟨commanded⟩ ↑enjoined↓ . . . fast; . . . torture;
41–42	persecution⟨.⟩, ↑& . . . victims⟨.↓⟩, ↑among . . . wise.↓

Page 175

4–5	↑thing↓ . . . world↑; and . . . requires.↓ ¶ ⟨But t⟩The
6	↑existed and↓

8	demands. ⟨Consider⟩ ↑Think↓
9–10	nature ⟨It⟩ ↑nor↓ throws ⟨no⟩ dangers . . . pale ⟨It⟩ nor
13	single ⟨thing⟩ ↑duty↓
14	↑To do↓ This↑,↓ ⟨it⟩ is
16–17	momentous ⟨matter.⟩ ↑law.↓ I am ↑very↓ . . . of ⟨this great law.⟩ ↑the . . . plead.↓
22–23	↑roving↓ thoughts. ↑Wd. you . . . one ⟨choice.⟩ thing to do.↓
25–27	↑At one instant↓ The . . . themselves ⟨at the moment⟩ to your mind. ↑There . . . done.↓
29	of ⟨nature⟩ ↑hunger↓
29–30	In ⟨the⟩ ↑a particular↓
31	↑There . . . done.↓
37	events, ⟨that may befall us⟩ &
41–42	finger. ⟨↑Sin, on yᵉ contrary↓⟩ ¶ Such

Page 176

3–4	lighter. ¶ ⟨Sin, on the contrary, consists in choosing the wrong thing in each moment.⟩ ¶ And
6–7	↑Can . . . moment?↓
8	↑err in↓ contemplat⟨e⟩ing
11–15	{I . . . well} [Emerson's note, preceded by an asterisk, follows this paragraph at the bottom of the page, but there is no corresponding asterisk in the text:] {always the alternative to act in reference to God or to act from a low self-love.}
17	↑the substance of↓
33–34	of ⟨Palestine⟩ ↑Samaria↓ . . . the ⟨street⟩ ⟨↑Gilgal↓⟩ ↑village↓,
36	messenger, ⟨bidding⟩ directing

Page 177

3	with /power/prayer/
17–18	↑It . . . ourselves.—↓
28	be ⟨cured.⟩ ↑healed.↓

Page 178

1–2	Naaman, ⟨If the prophet of God had bid thee do some great thing, wouldst not thou have done it, how much more when he saith to thee, wash & be clean.⟩ At . . . this ⟨religion⟩ ↑divine . . . revelation↓
4	↑It . . . virtue.↓

[The following occurs on a loose leaf laid in at the end of the sermon:] ⟨At⟩ You have accustomed to hear without pain & to use without remorse the name of God in vain. The occasions are now coming—every hour shall bring them which shall give you opportunity to indulge or to resist that sinful habit. Look well to the temptation & make your choice when the moment comes whether you will honour or dishonour your Maker's name.

Or you are a man constitutionally liable, you say, to faults of temper. Every little vexation throws you off your guard and you cannot help being very angry about very little things. But when you see that all this ill nature punishes itself, that it curdles your own blood, sours your own peace injures your children by the example it gives,—will you not think it wiser the next time you are vexed to seal your lips

Sermon XIX

Manuscript: Three sheets folded to make four pages each; folios stacked and sewn with white thread; pages measure 25.2 x 20 cm. Two strips (9 x 20 cm and 6 x 15 cm) containing Inserts "A" and "B" are tipped with red sealing wax to the recto of leaf 4; a strip (9 x 19.5 cm) containing the canceled Insert "X" is tipped with red sealing wax to the recto of leaf 5; a strip (4 x 19.5 cm) is attached with red sealing wax at the right and left margins across the middle of the recto of leaf 6 (now loosened at the right).

Lines	*Page 179*
5	↑of the gospel↓
6–7	↑We find that↓ It
8	gospel ⟨breathes⟩ ↑breathes . . . always↓
10	tha⟨n⟩t
17–19	regarded. ⟨And i⟩It is to ⟨this⟩ some . . . actions ⟨are unimportant⟩ ↑have . . . principle↓,

	Page 180
1	your ⟨grave⟩ ↑solemn
2	but ⟨th⟩ in
9–10	↑to . . . poverty↓
13–14	↑you↓ . . . his ⟨frozen⟩ ↑frosty↓ . . . covered ⟨his bed⟩ ↑the . . . lies↓
16	↑to↓
17–19	↑The performance of↓ ⟨T⟩that . . . increase ⟨the⟩ ↑a↓
1–32	have ⟨told⟩ ↑uttered↓
35	words. / You are / One man is / [variant in pencil]
39	for ⟨the⟩ ↑an↓
44	to ⟨the universe⟩ ↑your nature↓ . . . ↑for↓

	Page 181
1–2	tremendous⟨.⟩, ↑in . . . things.↓
3–4	Temperance ⟨by one⟩. The . . . may ⟨not do but⟩ ↑be very↓ little ⟨injury⟩ to
5	The ⟨ignominious⟩ ↑shameful↓
7	b⟨ell⟩ody.
7–10	your ⟨destiny⟩ ↑life,↓ . . . ↑of your↓ . . . a ⟨beastly instinct⟩ ↑base appetite↓. ↑You . . . self degradation ⟨& ruin⟩ ↑this . . . man↓ wh. . . . deplored.↓
12	↑effect of the↓ . . . dictate, ⟨but⟩ that
15	↑There . . . history.↓
16	fathers ⟨refused to⟩ associated
21	↑practical↓
24–25	to ⟨say⟩ ↑deny↓ . . . are ⟨not⟩ of ⟨the⟩ great⟨est⟩ importance, ⟨but that they are so,⟩ ↑for they surely are ↑of the greatest↓; but ⟨it⟩I ↑w↓is↑h↓ . . . is↓

27   world. ⟨Men of a⟩ The
30–32   ↑In a moral view↓ The ⟨p⟩ action ↑the . . . conviction↓ . . . ↑in both
            cases↓
35–42   country. ↑{Insert A}↓ [On a slip of paper attached to the page with
            red sealing wax, a passage marked "A":] ↑They . . . to this [ms. torn]
            that . . . activity.}↓

Page 182

6–14   the ⟨Universe⟩ ↑moral . . . creation↓ . . . character. ↑{Insert B}↓ [On
            a slip of paper attached to the page with red sealing wax, a passage
            marked "B":] ↑Do . . . ↑of↓ . . . cause.↓
18–19   you. ⟨I pity thy⟩ ↑Alas for thy↓ . . . ⟨h⟩He,
20–21   Himself?— ¶ ↑{Insert X}↓ [On a slip of paper attached to the
            following page, a passage marked "X":] ⟨↑Let us consider that the
            true reason which each one of us must give to himself of all the
            persons & events with which he has been associated is this that God is
            unrolling the ⟨Universe⟩ ↑world↓ before me for my particular
            instruction: is bringing into my neighbourhood now one & now
            another mind or group of minds in exact adaptation to what he sees to
            be my peculiar exigences at the moment, until by just degrees I shall
            be fitted in each immortal fibre for the scenes of action & thought
            that are presently to be disclosed. ⟨in another world.↓⟩⟩ [passage is
            canceled in pencil and ink] ¶ The . . . for ⟨these⟩ ↑all↓
26–27   shall /live/⟨reside⟩/; . . . inferiour ⟨questions⟩ ↑considerations↓,
            . . . ↑in↓ . . . shall ⟨live in⟩ ↑reside↓?
38–41   is ⟨forgotten⟩ no . . . when↑,↓ [addition in pencil]. . . hosts, ⟨&
            marshalled them on high,⟩ they

Page 183

3–4   ↑the scenes . . . &↓
13   duration—⟨they are⟩ ↑in↓ immortal ↑youth↓. [emendation in pencil]
18   minds↑,—↓ [addition in pencil]
19–22   hour.— ↑Insert D↓ ↑It . . . ↑of↓ . . . God."↓ [Insert "D" is in pencil.]
31–42   by /heaven/⟨star⟩/-born . . . within: ⟨in h⟩ ↑in . . . is↓ . . . by
            ⟨observing⟩ obeying . . . observes. ⟨⟨It is the most venerable glory
            permitted to human nature to value these unseen thoughts which
            make the charm of life more than life itself and whenever they are put
            by the violence of man in competition cheerfully to sacrifice life for
            their sake.⟩ To be governed by⟩ ↑I . . . in↑to↓ . . . ↑the authority of↓
            those ⟨stupendous⟩ ↑majestic↓ . . . of ⟨my nature⟩ ↑humanity↓ .
            . . . I ⟨am backed by⟩ ↑hear . . . from↓ . . . by↓

Page 184

4   the ⟨theatre⟩ ↑occasion↓
5–7   no ⟨circumstances are⟩ ↑place is↓ . . . but ⟨they⟩ ↑it↓ . . . ↑no . . .
            venerable;↓ . . . ↑ever↓ be mean, ⟨↑in the shop, in the farm, in the
            parlour, in the senate, on the sea,↓⟩ &

[On the otherwise blank last page are the following notes; all but the hymn citations in pencil:]
Dabney 3ᵈ Edit

  H 241
    169
    102

↑For example↓ You are a son & such & such conduct you perceive to belong to you in that relation

You are a brother & such & such—

You are a merchᵗ

You belong to this city & such & such are the duties which make up a make up your virtue or your ⟨vice⟩ ⟨vice⟩ sin as ⟨a cit⟩ [canceled in ink] in your character as citizen

One step further, you belong to this country as an ⟨Un⟩ Confederacy of States & thence come other duties &c.

Farther still you belong to mankind & as a man therefore &c &c

But is this all?—You belong to one still ⟨f⟩ more extensive family—brotherhood—community—&c &c— [cf. *JMN* 3:138]

Sermon XX

Manuscript: Four sheets folded to make four pages each; folios stacked and sewn with white thread along the left margin; pages measure 25.2 x 20 cm (leaves 1–2 and 5–6), 25.2 x 18.5 (leaf 3, containing Inserts "A" and "B"; cognate leaf 4 cut off, leaving a stub), and 24 x 20 cm (leaves 7–8). A strip apparently containing Insert "A" and once attached with red sealing wax to the recto of leaf 1 is missing. (Since there is a second Insert "A," this may have been removed by Emerson.)

Lines	Page 185
3	and ↑which↓
4–5	neighbour. ↑{Insert A}↓ I [see manuscript note above]
7	{peace &}
8	daylight; ⟨but⟩ what
17–18	them; ¶ ⟨I.⟩ ↑And chiefly↓ The
21	which fall to
23–24	↑with . . . individual↓

	Page 186
1	our ⟨might.⟩ ↑strength↓
3–4	cannot ⟨take away the principle⟩ ↑touch↓
8	↑of course↓
13	by ⟨uttering⟩ ↑relating↓
15	that ⟨momentary⟩ pulse of ⟨merriment⟩ ↑momentary mirth↓
16–17	Remember ⟨how dear how much dearer⟩ ↑at . . . higher↓ . . . life ⟨is⟩ ↑he holds↓
26–(187)12	forbear. ↑{Insert A}↓ ¶ [On both sides of the following leaf (which is included in the sewing), a passage marked "A":] ↑{In . . . them."}↓
29–30	↑and . . . it.↓.
32	nothing. ⟨It⟩ ↑The mind↓

35	↑above all↓
40–41	↑the . . . Athens↓ . . . not ⟨throw down⟩ overthrow

Page 187

1	↑sentiment↓
2–9	us. ⟨Besides⟩ ⟨↑We may make good out of evil;↓⟩ ↑{Insert B}↓ [At the bottom of the page, a passage marked "B":] ↑{You . . . you ⟨belong⟩ ↑adhere↓ . . . ↑great . . . heaven↓ . . . evil.}↓ ⟨w⟩When
11	matter," ⟨said he⟩ ↑he replied↓
12–13	them."}↓ ¶ ↑We . . . possessor↓
17	{and . . . it.}
18	↑to . . . farmhouse,↓
22–23	and has [catchword at the bottom of the page:] has
25	name ⟨by⟩ ↑in . . . of↓
29	↑longer↓.
32–33	which / ascribe/ found/ all virtue /to/upon/ a ↑creeping↓
34–35	↑Besides . . . hours↓ We

Page 188

3	↑friends↓
10	brings ⟨them⟩ up ↑their images↓
12–13	↑firstly↓ . . . ↑secondly↓
16	↑it may be↓ regard ⟨perhaps⟩ the
17	our ⟨hands⟩ ↑aid↓
22	think ⟨also⟩ ↑perhaps↓
23–24	But ⟨remember⟩ ↑consider ⟨that⟩↓ that ↑this↓
27	who⟨m⟩se ↑ear↓
35	better↑,↓ ⟨than other men⟩ hath . . . finding ⟨that they⟩ ↑wherein others↓
36	to ⟨this⟩ evil
40	motives. [At the bottom of the page, below a rule, keyed to an asterisk, Emerson's note:] ⟨Mens failings live in brass / We write their virtues in water.—"⟩

Page 189

4–5	played ⟨the jackal⟩ a . . . minds. also
19	of ⟨punishing⟩ ↑stigmatizing↓
20–21	be ⟨pursued⟩ ↑exposed↓
24–25	↑Here . . . water.↓
27–28	man. ⟨↑For this is the evil side of our nature. It is an old observation of too much truth yᵗ "Mens failings live in brass, &c"↓⟩ ¶ On
30–31	better ⟨a⟩ since / {there is} /the world is shaken by/ . . . calumny↑,↓ {in the world} ["there is" and "in the world" circled in ink to indicate coordinate parts of the variant]
39	good ⟨they could⟩ ↑word or action ⟨be⟩ one could↓ remember⟨ed⟩ of ⟨each⟩ ↑another↓.

Page 190

2–5   dreadful. ⟨{We drive out of society we persecute to the death the wretch who spills the blood of man. How much more infamous should he be held who touches not the mortal life but strikes at the immortal life of man, the murderer of character. Mark him} as he goes}⟩ [second bracket in pencil; the first and third in pencil and ink] ↑to . . . whisperer;↓ [addition in ink over pencil] . . . of ⟨his species⟩ ↑others↓; . . . of ⟨their⟩ every ⟨foible⟩ ↑crime↓; . . . infamy! ⟨{He sows the wind with libels}⟩ [brackets in pencil] ¶ But . . . the ⟨hand⟩ arm . . . retribution ⟨has found him out⟩ ↑overtakes the offender↓. ["overtakes" in ink over pencil]

7–8   {If . . . him.} [brackets in pencil]

Sermon XXI

Manuscript: Four sheets folded to make four pages each; folios nested and sewn with white thread along the left margin; pages measure 24 x 20.4 cm.

Lines   Page 191

1   ¶ ⟨It⟩ ↑In . . . it↓

3–4   Conscience⟨,⟩ ↑↑to . . . relates;↓ to . . . lastly↓

17   ↑to↓

23   another ⟨shorter⟩ ↑less,↓

                   Page 192

6–7   & ⟨the⟩ morals . . . developement

9   the ⟨young⟩ ↑infant↓

11   a⟨n⟩ ↑particular↓

12   judges / wrong/ at random/

16   virtue ⟨&⟩or

31   had ⟨c⟩ bid him / teach/ speak/

                   Page 193

5–7   ↑I . . . & ⟨f⟩as fully . . . us.↓

10   no ⟨misc⟩ ignorance,

10–11   ↑Its ⟨power⟩ ↑force↓ . . . race.↓

16   ↑It . . . laws.↓

28   No ⟨distant &⟩ ↑precarious or↓

35–37   ↑in . . . mankind↓ . . . blame ⟨I defy⟩ &

38   ↑to . . . ancient,↓

                   Page 194

4–5   victim. ¶ ⟨Is there one whose fame is fair, & whose good nature & good life have always secured his peace of mind? & does he imagine that he is so much his own master, that in any event he can still hold the reins of his own mind?⟩ Let ⟨him go out now, & commit a deadly crime, & then,⟩ ↑the . . . firm↓ . . . ↑to↓

8   it⟨s⟩

9	& ⟨go⟩ quicken
15	face ⟨f⟩or
33–34	& ↑in . . . all↓ . . . darkest / details / mysteries / passages / [variants in pencil]
41	speech ⟨when he should be mild.⟩. Has

Page 195

3	this ⟨uneasy⟩ ↑changing↓ [addition in pencil]
17	law ⟨is the⟩ so
18	that ⟨mu⟩keep
20–22	element: ⟨upon⟩after . . . ↑at↓ which ⟨the⟩ ↑moral↓ . . . ↑viz.↓
25–36	to ⟨obviate⟩ elude . . . dominion. ↑{Insert X}↓ ¶ [On the last inscribed page, following the end of the sermon, a passage marked "X":] ↑{⟨There are some Christians who find⟩ ↑It is↓ matter of ↑lamentation &↓ offence in ↑to many↓ the fact that ⟨a⟩ ↑the↓ . . . the ⟨bible⟩ ↑scriptures↓ . . . . But ⟨it seems to me⟩ ↑I apprehend↓ . . . infinite ⟨power⟩ ↑force↓ . . . it ⟨never fails⟩ to follow↑s↓ up transgression ↑⟨no⟩ [originally added after "feel"; canceled in pencil] . . . ↑↑can . . . to↓ doubt ⟨not⟩ the reality of ⟨the suffering of sin⟩ future retribution↓ ↑He . . . he will &c↓↓ will . . . that ⟨a⟩wait o⟨ur⟩n iniquit⟨ies⟩y.}↓
41	↑on earth↓,

Page 196

4–5	↑I have . . . . ↑But↓↓ There ["But" in pencil]
15	end. ⟨I perceive⟩ I
26–30	us. ↑{Insert Y}↓ [On the last inscribed page, below the passage marked "X," a passage marked "Y":] ↑{↑There . . . wh.↓ Every man must judge ⟨of these questions⟩ wholly . . . I ⟨fully believe⟩ ↑for one am satisfied↓ that ↑in this life only↓, . . . Conscience.}↓
32	it, ⟨a⟩our good or ⟨an⟩our
34–36	the ⟨joy⟩bliss . . . hell. ↑{Insert ¶}↓ [At the bottom of the page, a passage marked "¶":] ↑{Let . . . is ⟨the⟩ ↑a↓ law ⟨not only⟩ if . . . life.↓

Sermon XXII

Manuscript: Four sheets folded to make four pages each; folios nested and sewn with white thread along the left margin; pages measure 24 x 20.4 cm. A strip (5.5 x 12.4 cm) containing Insert "A" is tipped with red sealing wax to the recto of leaf 7.

[Written lengthwise in the left margin of the first page:] ⟨R. W. Emerson, Divinity Hall, No 14⟩

Lines	Page 197
7	valuations ⟨of⟩by
12	feeble ⟨ought to be forborne⟩ ↑can wholly fail↓
19	between ⟨truth & falsehood.⟩ ↑what . . . not.↓

Page 198

5	of /equivocation/fraud/ [variant in pencil]
12	↑perhaps, shall↓ discover⟨s⟩
16–17	are ⟨thwarted⟩ ↑confounded↓ . . . & ↑those↓ unembarassed ⟨speech⟩ ↑words↓,
21	done. /{It is a true nobility of minds, whose badge is the love of truth.}/{It . . . minds}/
22	pleasing ⟨b⟩ &
23–27	peer ⟨↑in a court of justice⟩ ↑when . . . judgment↓↓ . . . of ⟨an oath⟩ ↑swearing,↓ & ⟨consid⟩ accepts his ⟨bare⟩ affirmation, . . . as to ⟨a⟩ ↑the guilt of↓ falsehood. ¶ ⟨Truth⟩ ↑This principle↓
28	No↑ne↓ ⟨lie⟩ can ⟨be⟩ ↑weave a lie↓ so well↑,↓ ⟨woven⟩ that
31	daily /dealings/intercourse/,
37	a⟨n⟩ ↑vacant↓
38	you ⟨will have to⟩ ↑must↓

Page 199

6	& ⟨all⟩ quarrels
10	↑Thus,↓ It
12	both ⟨of a⟩ public ⟨or⟩ &
15	of ⟨property⟩ ↑wealth↓
18–24	↑all animal↓ . . . that ⟨it has found that every⟩ ↑when . . . each↓ . . . gratification ⟨of appetite⟩ to ↑have↓ be↑en↓ . . . seemed ⟨it⟩ to . . . but ⟨th⟩ it was ↑found to be↓ . . . of ⟨him that sinneth⟩ ↑man↓ . . . every ⟨crime⟩ ↑moral delinquincy,↓ . . . {a . . . frightful↑,↓ . . . it ⟨loses⟩ ↑seems to lose↓ . . . departure.} [brackets and added comma in pencil]
33–34	↑let . . . if↓ should we not ⟨be forced to⟩ think . . . differently? ⟨Then are we wrong now.⟩ Let
37–38	you ⟨never⟩ accepted . . . deserve? ⟨This was to depart from truth.⟩ Have you ⟨not⟩ excited
38	you ⟨not⟩ awakened
41–42	you ⟨not⟩ pretended, . . . is ⟨far⟩ ↑much↓
43–44	you ⟨not⟩ oppressed

Page 200

1–3	you ⟨not yourself⟩ been . . . the ⟨fear of⟩ ↑fear of↓ derision, ⟨{of fools}⟩ the . . . your ⟨own⟩ opinions, [brackets in pencil]
7–10	all?—¶ ⟨But⟩ ⟨I would lead you to consider⟩ ↑It . . . with↓
15–16	pretended ⟨admiration⟩ ↑wonder↓ . . . it, ⟨though⟩ ↑which↓ . . . . value ⟨it⟩ at
37–38	feelings; ⟨&⟩ ↑a man who ⟨has no privacy &⟩ derives . . . observation,↓
39–(201)1	seen. ↑{Insert A}↓ [On a slip of paper attached by red sealing wax to the following page, a passage marked "A":] ↑Other . . . & ⟨fears⟩ suspicions. . . . privacy.↓ [verso inscribed in an unidentified hand: "⟨Mʳ R. Waldo Emerson / Divinity Hall / Cambridge⟩"]

Page 201

4	↑says his Biographer,↓
10–11	which ⟨reason⟩ ↑experience should↓ win⟨s⟩ . . . the /heart/reason/
14	a ⟨very⟩ ↑most↓
15	said, ⟨of⟩ in
17–20	↑The . . . our ⟨secret⟩ ↑innermost↓ . . . world. ↑{Insert X}↓ [Following the end of the sermon, a passage marked "X":] ↑{↑In . . . (Luke X.2.)↓↓ . . . known.'↓↓
24	men↑, . . . God,↓
26–31	¶ ↑My . . . & ⟨truth⟩ discovery. . . . loves.↓ ¶ ⟨My brethren l⟩Let
33–34	↑There . . . glorious↓ [addition in pencil]
39	however ⟨trifling⟩ ↑insignificant↓

Page 202

1	us ⟨make⟩ ↑bring↓
5–6	↑"Stand, . . . truth.—↓

[The following note appears after the conclusion of the sermon:] {When Aristotle was asked "what a man could gain by uttering falsehoods?" he replied, "not to be credited when he shall tell the truth"

Sermon XXIII

Manuscript: Four sheets folded to make four pages each; folios nested and sewn with white thread along the left margin; pages measure 24 x 20.4 cm. A leaf now missing, evidently bearing a variant opening, was once affixed by red sealing wax to the recto of leaf 1, where it covered all the inscription below the biblical text; a strip now missing was once tipped with red sealing wax to the verso of leaf 4.

Lines	*Page 203*
3–4	↑A . . . but↓ The
10–11	[wo]ndrous [letters obscured by sealing wax] . . . th⟨is⟩e
22	his ⟨race⟩ ↑species↓, [emendation in pencil; rejected as a late revision]

	Page 204
1–2	↑On . . . Deity.↓
3–4	k[ms. torn]ledge . . . will ⟨make itself felt.⟩ ↑work out great effects.↓
12	for ⟨g⟩ bread,
14–15	⟨i⟩on . . . the /woods/tribes/ [variant in pencil] . . . ↑beyond the Caucasus↓
23–27	skill; ⟨and flaming with metals & gems;⟩ or . . . idea ⟨by⟩ which
29	race ⟨and⟩ (to which ↑fact,↓
34	th⟨is⟩e
38	accessible ⟨they⟩ are
40–41	not ⟨aim to convince atheists: ⟨I⟩it may be doubted, whether a proper atheist can be found among intelligent minds;⟩ ↑ask . . . atheism,↓

Page 205

4–5	↑& what is gravity?↓ . . . answer—⟨God.—⟩↑the . . . God.↓
10	thought; ⟨the⟩ its
17	in ⟨himself⟩ his
21	harmonious ⟨tribes⟩ sympathies
23	⟨occ⟩that

Page 206

1–2	↑the form of↓ Youth is yet ⟨beautiful⟩ ↑comely↓; . . . ↑yet↓
7–9	ourselves, ⟨in whose eyes⟩ ↑to whose healthy mind↓ . . . if ⟨the⟩ ever
14	lost ⟨a⟩ its
24–25	& ⟨P⟩ government
26	the ⟨evidence⟩ conclusion.
30	↑last↓
32–33	is ⟨at⟩ the . . . not ↑of↓ . . . ↑that↓ respect⟨ing⟩
34–35	best ⟨evidence of⟩ ↑testimony to↓
35	We ⟨must⟩ ought
37	↑neglecting↓
42-(207)1	explored. ¶ ⟨It was my intention in introducing this subject for our⟩ ↑The . . . these↓ . . . ↑is↓ . . . soul. ⟨But this is ↑a↓ great & absorbing object, & must now be postponed. ⟨↑We shall have opportunity to enter on↓⟩⟩ ["We . . . on" added and canceled in pencil] That

Page 207

4	↑order &↓
10–11	reflexions. [The following was added in pencil, probably for the December 21, 1828, delivery in Concord, New Hampshire:] ↑we shall have an opportunity this evg. to enter on this topic which forms the proper sequel to the personal & social duties↓

Sermon XXIV

Manuscript: Four sheets folded to make four pages each; folios nested and sewn with white thread along the left margin; pages measure 24 x 20.4 cm. Between leaves 2 and 3 is a single inserted leaf (24 x 20 cm), which is not included in the sewing; leaf 7 is cut off, leaving a 2-cm stub bearing evidence of a draft version of the insert.

[Written lengthwise in the left margin of the first page:] R. W. Emerson Divinity Hall No 14

Lines	*Page 208*
12	to ⟨you⟩ ↑us↓, though ⟨you⟩ ↑we↓
18–19	felt ⟨the connexion that exists between the visible & the invisible world?⟩ ↑how . . . below?↓

Page 209

13	the ⟨Lord⟩ great
15-(210)21	works." ¶ ⟨We should live soberly, righteously, & godly. It is thought

that all human duties are comprized under this precept. To live soberly, is to perform our duties to ourselves, to live righteously—our duties to others; & godly—our duties to God. I ↑design to↓ ask your attention to ⟨a few⟩ ↑some↓ remarks upon each of these classes. ↑In the present discourse we shall confine our attention to the first.↓⟩ ↑Herein . . . wants.↓ [The last three paragraphs of this added passage occupy both sides of a single leaf laid in between pp. 4 and 5; see the last note, below.]

15–16   relations; ⟨and⟩ its . . . which ⟨it discloses, made known⟩ God . . . performance, ⟨is intimated⟩ made

26   the ⟨ancient⟩ ↑{old}↓ [brackets in pencil]

30   ↑& most extended↓

34   & ⟨enormous⟩ ↑gross↓

36   or ⟨power⟩ influence,

40   ↑Diligence . . . for↓ ⟨T⟩this

Page 210

5–6   reference [end of page] temptation . . . ↑by strong effort↓ . . . itself, ⟨by strong effort⟩ to

7–10   ↑disobedient↓ . . . ↑I . . . think↓ . . . immoveable ⟨resolution⟩ ↑determination↓

12   ↑comprised↓

14   the ⟨pre⟩ foolish

14–15   is ⟨lowly⟩ humble.

22   ¶ ⟨We⟩ ↑II. That we↓ . . . ↑implies . . . command.↓

23–24   ↑original↓ . . . ↑peculiarly↓ . . . self ⟨command;⟩ ↑restraint;↓

32   steep [end of page] steep

39   ↑out↓

Page 211

9–10   good ⟨the gods⟩ ↑nature↓ have provided [emendation in pencil]

16   repentance ⟨reflection⟩ comes,

29   from ⟨ourselv⟩ others,

35   ↑with↓

40–42   {for a time,} . . . bount⟨eous⟩ifully . . . {& sleep long,} [brackets in pencil]

Page 212

1–2   ↑The . . . idle↓ [addition in pencil]

5–6   & ⟨triflings out of tune.⟩ ↑is most unseasonable↓

6   affect ⟨today⟩ at

13–16   ¶ {This . . . himself.} [brackets in pencil]

23   ↑His private retirement,↓ His

28–29   ↑when↓ . . . of ⟨passion⟩ ↑compliance↓ . . . ↑to temptation↓

33   years ⟨in⟩ deploring

36   ↑as↓ under ⟨an iron check⟩ ↑bars of steel↓

Page 213

5   mislead ↑us↓;

[The stub of the leaf bearing pp. 13–14 contains the following words and partial words, which can be identified as a partial draft, struck through in ink, of the five-paragraph addition beginning on p. 4 of the ms.:]

    [p. 13:] post / duti / reg / us / wit / or / becom / God / It / with / This / ⟨It does⟩ / day / has g / their / ⟨the⟩ / grace / not sc / than / it in / what

    [p. 14:] cient / pects: / Com- / ch

Sermon XXV

Manuscript: The original fascicle consists of three stacked folios sewn with black thread through the center fold; pages measure 24 x 20 cm. The fascicle is laid inside a folio containing a variant opening on its first page (the others are blank). A leaf (20.5 x 12 cm) containing Insert "A" is tipped with red sealing wax to the recto of fascicle leaf 2; a leaf (20 x 16.8 cm) containing Inserts "X" (recto) and "Y" (verso) is tipped with red sealing wax to the recto of fascicle leaf 4.

[The following variant opening was to replace the original Bible text and first paragraph, which are bracketed in ink:]
We shd live righteously in this present world Titus 2. 12.

We stand in such close connexion man to man that every day gives a fresh interest to discussions of social right. The Gospel is not a contemplative but a practical system & would be of little value to us if it overlooked our social condition. It assuredly does not. It abhors selfishness. It is a law of ↑domestic love enjoining yᵉ duties of husband & w. father & son master & servt↓ love. It is a law of neighborhood. It is a law recognizing the relations of Rulers & ruled. It is a law of yet wider benevolence which / contemns/ frowns down/ the ⟨jealous⟩ ↑exclusive↓ spirit of party, ↑the jealousies of nations↓ & joins all men together as the family of God. In the present discourse I wish from the words of my text to invite y⟨r⟩our attention to yᵉ full import of yᵉ command yᵗ we shd. live righteously.

[Written lengthwise in the left margin of the first page of the sewn fascicle:] R. W. Emerson. Divinity Hall. No 14

Lines	
	Page 214
1–2	{In . . . that} [brackets in pencil]
5–7	{It . . . injunction.} [brackets in pencil]
7–8	discourse / {let us consider} . . . command/I wish to invite yr attention only to some considerations upon yᵉ 2d pt. of yᵉ precept/ [brackets and variant in pencil; variant rejected as a probable late revision, preliminary to the variant opening]
12	↑the consideration of righteousness in↓
16–17	in ⟨the world⟩ ↑it,↓ . . . uti⟨l⟩lity
19	world. ⟨↑{Insert A}↓⟩ We
21	constant ⟨discipline⟩ ↑exercise↓, /a school-master/an education/,
22–(215)2	powers. ⟨My brethren, I hope I am understood. I mean to say that ↑though↓ as long as we live in the body, property ⟨will⟩ ↑must↓ be valuable to us, as it increases the bodily comforts, ⟨but⟩ ↑yet↓ that to

the soul, to ourselves, it has no value at all, except that of discipline↑.↓ ⟨that just as⟩⟩ ↑To use a familiar illustration↓ ↑{Insert A}↓ [On a slip of paper attached to the following page with red sealing wax, a passage marked "A":] ↑⟨It is⟩ ↑I . . . sufficiently↓ plain ⟨at first sight⟩ that . . . are ⟨eating drinking ↑creat↓⟩ now tenants of a ⟨frame⟩ ↑body↓ . . . ↑all↓ . . . no ⟨acre of our⟩ reversion . . . world ⟨We occupy of all⟩ He . . . {& not long ⟨the changes of nature⟩ ↑ere . . . nothing↓ will ⟨consume⟩ ↑change↓ . . . life.} . . . /to the soul/ to our eternal self/,— . . . a ⟨discipline⟩ means of instruction.—↓ ⟨i⟩In

Page 215

3–7	is ↑to↓ . . . ↑greatest↓ . . . vigor, ⟨certain⟩ ↑the frames and↓ . . . ↑which↓ . . . ↑found there &↓ . . . exercises, ⟨and are⟩have ⟨valued not for ↑of little or⟩ no worth in↓ themselves ⟨as so much⟩ ↑in . . . there; ⟨beyond other blocks of⟩ they . . . of↓ wood . . . but ⟨only for this use,⟩ ↑in . . . value, ⟨in⟩↓ as ↑being↓
8–9	chest. ⟨So is⟩ ↑Now . . . of↓ Property, ⟨to be esteemed⟩ as
13	live ⟨by it⟩ righteously'
24–25	having ⟨stolen from⟩ ↑robbed↓ . . . ↑who↓ will
25–28	↑That . . . labour ⟨&⟩ ↑& . . . or↓ . . . ↑period of↓ . . . the ⟨day of payment⟩ ⟨settlement of his account⟩ ↑payment of a debt↓ . . . those ⟨who shd. receive it.⟩ ↑from . . . withheld.↓↓
31–32	beside. ⟨It is true,⟩ ↑I know↓ . . . ↑sometimes↓
34	↑a↓ political ⟨events⟩ ↑cris⟨e⟩is↓; . . . your /warehouses/factories/; [variant in pencil]
36	↑these↓ . . . the ⟨frequent⟩ ↑ordinary↓
40	the ⟨fruitful ↑ordinary↓⟩ ↑usual↓
43	Or, ⟨you⟩ it

Page 216

4	as ↑in↓
6–8	↑have↓ attained its ⟨true⟩ ↑just↓ . . . ⟨a⟩one
10	are ⟨crowned⟩ ↑visited . . . perhaps,⟩↓ . . . ↑& undeserved↓
13	have ⟨not⟩ made
16	¶ ↑My brethren,↓ We
18–29	ridiculous. ↑{Insert X}↓ [On a leaf attached by red sealing wax to the following page, a passage marked "X":] ↑{Men . . . ⟨k⟩feel . . . own.↓ [For an earlier draft of this passage, see the last note, below.]
32	↑early↓
34	impart th⟨is⟩e
37–38	(& ↑⟨⟩alas! . . . country⟨⟩)↓ . . . liberty) ⟨are⟩ ↑⟨as⟩ is↓
39–40	²{if . . . word,} ¹{and call him righteous}

Page 217

4–13	man. ↑{Insert Y}↓ [On the verso of the leaf (see above) containing Insert "X" on the recto, a passage marked "Y":] ↑{I . . . But, ↑I↓ . . .

⟨br⟩give . . . imperative↓ [For an earlier draft of this passage, see the last note.]

15–16   ↑Thus,↓ If . . . punctuality ⟨through⟩ ↑in . . . of↓

18–19   a ⟨fellow man⟩ ↑wretched beggar↓ . . . ↑most imperious↓

23   yourself⟨—⟨tho⟩ even though the laws are silent on ↑all↓ these offences?⟩?

24–25   of ⟨yo⟩the . . . have [a] right [word obscured by sealing wax]

26–27   ↑Yet . . . hearts.↓

28   ↑that↓ punctuality ⟨in the⟩ ↑which↓ fulfil⟨ment⟩s even ⟨of⟩ trivial

38–(218)2   ↑that . . . reward↓ . . . the ⟨happ⟩ advantage of others. ↑{Insert XB}↓ [At the bottom of the page, a passage marked "X":] We . . . every ⟨hour⟩ day, . . . sun.↓

Page 218

3   itself ⟨to⟩ ↑that it may↓

8   some ⟨petty⟩ ↑trivial↓

10   for ⟨themselves.⟩ ↑their own.↓

14–15   false ⟨enthusiasm⟩ ↑spirit↓ . . . true ⟨enthusiasm⟩ ↑obedience . . . charity,↓

19   has ⟨atoned⟩ ↑compensated↓

21–23   sacrifice, ↑n↓or . . . nor ⟨splendid⟩ achievements ↑of valour,↓ . . . is ⟨a⟩ more

26   of [end of page] of virtue

27–30   the ⟨distinctions⟩ ↑inequalities↓ . . . away. ⟨↑But the righteous shall shine as the sun forever.↓⟩ [cf. Matthew 13:43] ↑But, . . . still.'↓

31   the ⟨life⟩ ↑example↓

33   of ⟨ac⟩ a

37   & ⟨respect⟩ ↑consideration↓

[Following the end of the sermon, Emerson wrote:]

———

Under this division of duty comes the obligation of kind treatment of animals.

———

Our public duties as citizens ought to be insisted on: particularly that slipperiness sanctioned by Custom (quae fuerunt vitia sunt mores) [Seneca, *Lucilium Epistulae Morales*, XXXIX, 6; cf. *JMN* 2:282] shd. be strongly condemned, which suffers reputable men to lie & perjure themselves, concerning the amount of their property, to the Collectors of taxes.

⟨⟨X {Men ↑whose fortunes are not equal to their own necessities↓ are solicited to give their names to this subscription for a new book, or a public work or for some scheme of social enjoyment They are pushed on to expenses they cannot meet by the fear of being esteemed meanspirited, when they ought to feel that it is a meanness of spirit that prevents them from saying *No*. And, sometimes, there appears a greater apology for unlawful expense, when a demand is made on your charity. But consider that you have no right to be charitable, whilst your just obligations are not redeemed. For in yielding to what you call an impulse of generosity you are giving away the bread of another. The merit of all charity must be commensurate with the sacrifice: but you sacrifice what is not your own.⟩

⟨Y {I hope yᵗ in yᵉ remarks I just now made I shall not be misunderstood as in yᵉ smallest degree aiming to weaken yᵉ spirit of benevolence. Those remarks are strictly limited to cases where the will outruns the means. But I consider yᵗ in its fullest the law of righteousness enjoins the benefits generosity sacrifices. The righteous man will not only give to the poor but he will freely contribute his part to keep ↑up↓ the good action & enterprize of society; will feel the claim of useful and of elegant institutions upon his countenance & aid. Besides there are in daily life & conversation ⟨the⟩ occasions that cannot be specified where the duty is imperative.—}⟩⟩

Sermon XXVI

Manuscript: Four sheets folded to make four pages each; folios nested and sewn with black thread through the center fold; pages measure 24 x 20.4 cm. On the recto of leaf 1, traces of red sealing wax over traces of blue sealing wax offer evidence of one or more lost variant openings, which undoubtedly corresponded to the bracketed matter in the first paragraph of the text. A leaf (22 x 20 cm) tipped with red sealing wax to the recto of leaf 8 contains Insert "X."

[The following is written lengthwise in the left margin of the first page:] ⟨R. W. Emerson No 14 Divinity Hall⟩

Lines	
	Page 219
1–6	{We have/, in two former discourses upon this text, considered/ recently considered/ [The variant, in pencil, is rejected as a late revision, probably belonging to the delivery in Concord, N. H., December 21, 1828.] . . . taken.} Nevertheless} [bracket in pencil] . . . ↑alone↓, ↑&. . . idea↓ . . . to ⟨erect⟩ ↑build↓
10–11	a ⟨perfect theory⟩ ⟨of duty⟩ ↑complete system,↓ . . . personal⟨,⟩ ↑obligations,↓
12–13	feel ⟨them⟩ & . . . feel ⟨them.⟩ ↑their obligation.↓
19–22	But /{now we come to put}/in . . . puts/ . . . sovere↑i↓gn . . . would ⟨erect⟩ ⟨rear⟩ ↑erect↓
26–(220)1	pleasure, o⟨f⟩r . . . your ⟨th⟩ mind . . . ↑outwardly↓

	Page 220
3–9	↑says . . . trade.↓ ²{I say . . . stated ⟨charities⟩ quarterly . . . charities.} ¹{I . . . profane;}
9	give⟨,⟩
10–11	↑Religion . . . all,↓
18–21	calculation. ⟨Here is a man⟩ You . . . whose ⟨c⟩ happiness
25–27	for ⟨the⟩ opinion, . . . of ⟨the parent⟩ ↑her↓ . . . ⟨his⟩that
28–30	↑by↓ . . . ↑of duty↓
33	the ⟨being⟩ ↑habits↓
38–40	↑in so doing↓ he is ⟨doing⟩ ↑performing↓ . . . ↑(which was mean before)↓ becomes ⟨dignified⟩ ↑elevated↓
43	↑own↓

Page 221

1–6   farther. ⟨Even⟩ ↑For↓ . . . in the⟨ir⟩ . . . ↑of animals↓. . . . in ⟨an old⟩ ↑the↓ . . . ↑white↓ . . . ice⟨,⟩ ↑fields↓ /under/of/ ⟨the⟩ ⟨↑a↓⟩ polar ⟨sky⟩ ↑circle↓, . . . sailors ⟨shot her⟩ ↑put . . . life↓

7–11   as ⟨be⟩ pecking her ⟨own⟩ breast & ⟨feeding⟩ ↑nourishing↓ . . . with ⟨her own blood.⟩ ↑the . . . veins.↓ . . . make ⟨it⟩ more . . . affections ⟨never⟩ ↑nowhere↓ . . . that ⟨concerns them.⟩ ↑they touch.↓ ¶ ↑II.↓ I beg you, ⟨also⟩ ↑in . . . place,↓

12–13 ↑seem to↓

15–18 force. ⟨Here is a⟩ ↑Observe this↓ . . . city, ⟨who is⟩ oppressed by fortune, ⟨who is⟩ ↑hindered by↓ . . . no ⟨hope or heart⟩ portion

19–20 ↑I see that↓

27   the ⟨beauty⟩ ↑excellence↓ . . . *strength* ⟨I c⟩ of

29–33 ¶ ↑III.↓ . . . society ⟨he⟩ ↑we↓ seek⟨s⟩ . . . {whose . . . ↑only↓ . . . not ↑have↓ perished . . . remediless.}

34–35 sometimes ⟨makes⟩ ↑proposes as↓ . . . exertions. ⟨Well n⟩Now, . . . that ⟨we⟩ ↑you↓

36–37 ⟨y⟩our friend? . . . if ⟨it were instead of acts of kindness⟩ your

41   if ⟨now⟩ he

Page 222

3   the ⟨vessel⟩ vehicle,

5–8   ↑that . . . object↓ . . . perfection↑.↓ ⟨to satisfy them.⟩ ¶ What

12–14 wisdom? ⟨Is it not true that⟩ What . . . a ⟨parent⟩ ↑mother,↓ . . . *affections?* ⟨Is it not true that⟩ Why

18–19 it ⟨quits⟩ ↑recoils from↓

26–29 to ⟨carry on⟩ ↑push↓ . . . into ⟨⟨his⟩ ↑your↓ path⟩ ↑this↓

31–33 a ⟨nearer⟩ longer . . . the ⟨goods of the⟩ Universe . . . bribe, ⟨nor all its terrors shake;⟩ a

40–41 would ⟨yo⟩ not . . . devot⟨ion⟩↑edness↓

Page 223

1–6   ↑that . . . glorious↓ . . . Infinite ⟨Being;⟩ ↑Mind;↓ . . . ⟨a⟩thus

10   the ⟨hope⟩ ↑desire↓

12   ¶ ↑My friends,↓ Do . . . ↑a far fetched↓ an↑d↓

13   ↑thus↓

23   mind⟨;⟩?

30–(224)3   Himself. ¶ ⟨⟨This subject expands before us, as we go on. We must omit the consideration of many important truths that offer themselves to our notice—& hasten to our conclusion.⟩

       {Whilst the time admonishes me to conclude, I see well that I have only opened the great duty of which I proposed to treat. It expands before us as we go on. It is a subject too vast for me now to introduce, the manner in which the affections are to be trained to their great object; the manner in which the soul unites itself to God. I hasten in a few words to bring these remarks to a close.— }⟩

       ⟨↑{Whilst I see that the remarks yᵗ have been made are hardly more than an introduction to this expanding subject yᵉ time admonishes me}↓⟩

↑Insert X [On a leaf attached with red sealing wax to the following page, a passage marked "X":] {Whilst . . . approve.}

39   knowing (⟨that⟩ according to the ↑consenting↓ [For an earlier draft of this paragraph, see the final note below.]

Page 224

2-3   we ⟨are to obtain the love of God by ⟨ob⟩doing those things which we know he will approve.

{In particular there are methods especially adapted to this end, namely what we call religious observances those of prayer of public worship the regard of the Sabbath ↑& now under the Xn dispensation, the use of the ordinances—↓ & ⟨↑{mainly, as the soil out of wh. all yᵉ rest will grow}↓⟩ that devotional frame of mind which at all times & in all places judges itself by secret reference to the Divine Will.} [brackets in pencil]

These remarks are already far extended, I hasten in a few words to bring them to a close.⟩ ↑are . . . approve.}↓↓

9   was ⟨hi⟨s⟩mself⟩ ↑Himself↓
11   righteously ⟨& godly.⟩. Let
12-13   finish- [end of page] this
14-16   also. ↑m.f. the Apostle ⟨John⟩ ↑Paul↓ saith ⟨The whole law is made perfect by love⟩ ↑love . . . law↓: . . . all.↓
20   earth." ⟨My brethren, the apostle John saith unto us, that "the whole law is made perfect by love." If we will discharge this highest duty, ↑you cannot fail in duty to yrselves & to men; it includes yᵐ all.↓⟩ fear

[The following passage, an earlier draft of the second paragraph of Insert "X" above, follows the end of the sermon; some words and parts of words are obscured by the sealing wax used to affix Insert "X" to the page:] ⟨⟨{What is the inference from these reflexions? What but this? that we are to learn the love of God by cultivating with tender care our reverence for virtue wherever [it a]ppears knowing that this is his nature & the law of his being knowing [that] precisely in proportion as our regard to goodness increases so will the idea of God reveal itself to the eye of our mind.⟩

Sermon XXVII

Manuscript: Four sheets folded to make four pages each; folios nested and sewn with black thread through the center fold; pages measure 24 x 20.4 cm.

[Above the Bible text:] {This discourse is intended as a sequel to the XXIV.}

[Lengthwise in the left margin of the first page:] R. W. Emerson. No. 14. Divinity Hall.

Lines   *Page 225*
1   his ⟨second⟩ [cancellation in pencil and ink] ↑first↓
5   because ⟨he⟩ ↑himself↓ . . . Paul⟨, & another contemned Paul, to ⟨extol⟩ praise Apollos.⟩. But

12   expression. [The following was added for the second delivery,
            December 14, 1828, at Concord, N. H.:] ↑{The remarks I have to
            offer—seem to me a proper sequel to the reflections we pursued in the
            morning from the precept that commands us to live soberly—and in
            order to offer them at this time I postpone the consideration of the
            social duties which are next in order.}↓
14   is ⟨plainly⟩ ↑only↓
15–18   when ⟨their⟩your . . . & ⟨their⟩your . . . ↑& so precarious,↓ . . .
            illness↑,↓ bereav⟨ed⟩ing . . . ↑appear↓ . . . some ⟨violence⟩ danger
21–23   ↑to simple self love,↓ . . . befriend; ⟨I appeal to yourselves if you⟩
            have ↑you↓

Page 226

6–13   ¶ ↑There . . . many ⟨thots⟩ ↑words↓ . . . little ⟨life⟩ ↑spark↓ . . .
            cause, ⟨that⟩ viz. . . . possessions↓
14   ↑the spiritual↓
18   ↑virgin↓
26   cheap. ⟨I⟩ ↑We↓
29–30   are, ⟨because⟩ ↑if↓ . . . circumstances, ⟨over the outward world,⟩ &
32–33   to ⟨use as well as⟩ ↑make the best use↓ we can ↑of↓
40–(227)2   ↑of consideration;↓ . . . ↑proper↓ object of all ⟨learning⟩
            ↑knowledge↓ . . . {that, . . . ours.}

Page 227

6–7   ↑let . . . page⟨s⟩?↓
16   ↑or ⟨object⟩ instruments . . . ⟨y⟩our own virtues.↓.
21–22   that ⟨th⟩my . . . torment ⟨that will not destroy the life of⟩ ↑which↓
            the body⟨.⟩ ↑can bear & live.↓
25   ↑& arts↓
29   than ⟨to⟩ ascertain
29–31   ↑Because, . . . appear?↓
34–35   ↑till . . . land;↓ . . . laws; {till the earth;} these [additions and
            brackets in pencil]
37   ↑&↓

Page 228

1   ↑once↓
3   of ⟨others⟩ ↑their fellowmen↓;
6–7   timidly ⟨pr⟩ wish . . . you ⟨timidly⟩ anticipate ↑with a faint heart↓
            . . . suffer, ⟨in the company⟩ at . . . of ⟨as⟩ business
16   /social entertainment/⟨party⟩/,
18   of the /party/company/,
36–38   And ⟨that if they can only obtain an advantageous situation in a
            foreign country⟩ ↑they . . . unknown↓
40   ↑the↓ disease
41   ↑England in the↓ Indi⟨a⟩es as ⟨in New England⟩ ↑at home↓ if you↑r
            hands↓
44–(229)1   I ⟨believe it may be shown⟩ ↑will . . . think↓

Page 229

3   ↑It may be↓ The . . . come ⟨when ↑perhaps↓⟩ to
5–7   ↑if↓ . . . was ↑not↓ . . . was ↑not↓ . . . ↑yet . . . mind,↓ [The longer
         addition (which seems to complete the sense of the shorter additions)
         is added at the bottom of the page without the usual indication of
         placement.]
11   these ⟨views⟩ ↑truths,↓
17–19   life. ⟨In your own observation you have met with⟩ ↑Here is↓ . . . &
         ⟨re⟩ who ⟨ev⟩ ↑{knows . . . by}↓ manifest⟨ed⟩s
20–21   borrows /his/the/ key . . . those ⟨with⟩ whom he ⟨converses⟩
         thinks
36–42   yours. ↑{Insert X}↓ [On the next page, a passage marked "X":] ↑{Let
         . . . us.} ↑and . . . responsibility.}↓↓

Page 230

2   just ⟨{& righteous}⟩ &
9   ↑also↓

[The following is inscribed below the end of the sermon:] God, saith Solomon, hath
made every thing in beauty according to ⟨its⟩ season; also he hath set the world in man's
heart, yet can he not find out the work which God worketh from the beginning to the
end. [Cf. Ecclesiastes 3:11]

Sermon XXVIII

Manuscript: A gathering of four nested folios sewn through the center fold with black
thread followed by a single folio attached by cross-stitching with white thread around
the left edge of the entire fascicle. Pages measure 24 x 20 cm, except those of the last
folio, which measure 24.8 x 20 cm.

Lines   *Page 231*
2   I⟨t⟩n
4   all /manner/⟨(shapes)⟩ terror ⟨& a⟩/ [variant in pencil; all but
         "terror" erased]
6   mortifications ⟨serenely⟩ ↑to be↓
9   not ⟨this⟩ alone,
16–18   ↑{"odio . . . martyrdom.}↓
21   ↑this↓
22   Rome ⟨in the time of Nero⟩ his

Page 232

4   word ⟨the⟩ what
9   brethren, /it needs little heroism now to/if . . . P. it is easy to/
13   ragged ⟨face⟩ ↑front↓
22   I ⟨th⟩ believe that ⟨the⟩ many
25   men ⟨regard⟩ ↑esteem↓
29–31   ↑I . . . ↑& to affirm↓ . . . sentiment.↓ . . . the ⟨violent & the
         proud—⟩ ↑great . . . world—↓

Page 233

5–6	him⟨self & ⟨th⟩ upon the people of his charge.⟩. ¶ The
11	these ⟨duties⟩ offices,
17	↑soothe &↓
20	in ⟨the⟩ producing
21–25	who ⟨acts⟩ studies . . . ↑the↓ . . . sentiments ⟨beyond the reach of rhetoric⟩ that
30	↑the↓ conviction
32–36	↑t↓his . . . dismiss⟨ing⟩↑es↓ . . . offensive ⟨word⟩ syllable,

Page 234

8	apprehensions ⟨the⟩ which
10–11	eloquence. ⟨Which⟩ ↑I . . . one↓ . . . brethren, ⟨of⟩ whose
13	mind⟨,⟩ ↑& . . . interest,↓
22–23	principles ⟨seeds⟩ of . . . he ⟨wishes⟩ ↑lives↓
25	↑God . . . indifference↓
31	↑the↓ priest↑hood↓
32	when ⟨well borne⟩ ↑its . . . discharged↓
33–35	worthily ⟨borne⟩ ↑filled↓— . . . & ⟨natural⟩ ↑free↓
36–37	↑has found↓ . . . ↑a defect↓ . . . ↑a defect↓
40	no ⟨man⟩body

Page 235

1	copy ⟨caricature⟩ which
4	& ⟨ill⟩ evil
5	strings ⟨& does not make⟩. It
15–17	Yes . . . return. [marked by an ink line in the margin]
27	↑which↓
29–30	↑wretched↓ . . . ⟨earth⟩globe,
45-(236)1	me ⟨that⟩ the . . . of ⟨dignity⟩ solemnity . . . remind ⟨th⟩ him, . . . ↑of Scripture↓

Page 236

10	steam, ↑& of gas↓
11–14	nation? ¶ ⟨In fine⟩ ↑It . . . that↓ . . . mind ⟨all⟩ the ↑highest↓ cultivation↑, & . . . kind↓
23	vine ⟨to⟩&
26	congratulate ⟨each other⟩ ↑themselves↓
28	Bel⟨ei⟩ieve
30	↑friendly↓

Sermon XXIX

Manuscript: Four sheets folded to make four pages each; folios nested and sewn with black thread through the center fold; pages measure 25 x 20.5 cm.

[Above Bible text:] Sermon after Ordination 1829

Lines   *Page 238*

Bible Text   ⟨Now then we are ambassadors ⟨o⟩for Christ as though God did
                  beseech you by us. We pray you in Christs stead, be ye reconciled unto
                  God II Cor V. 20⟩ ↑But . . . ourselves but . . . Lord & . . . Jesus sake
                  II Cor IV. 5.↓

3   ↑of matrimony,↓ of baptism↑,↓

4–6   ↑brief↓ . . . duties, ⟨with regard⟩ of sympathy & ⟨support⟩
                  ↑cooperation↓

8–11   ¶ ↑He . . . ↑& order↓ . . . union.↓

14   in⟨different⟩↑significant↓ . . . & ⟨the⟩ baptism

20–21   parents ⟨joy,⟩ ↑gladness,↓ . . . ⟨h⟩His

                           Page 239

2   wear⟨s⟩.

6   no ⟨correspondent⟩ archetypes

9–10   ↑marriage of↓ . . . ↑of↓ . . . to ⟨yet more⟩ affectionate & ⟨intimate⟩
                  ↑⟨&⟩ *domestic*↓

11–12   ↑Whilst . . . myself↓

14   limit ⟨that⟩ ↑of↓ my powers⟨, will warrant me in marking as within
                  my reach⟩. But

16   the ⟨ground⟩ ↑scene↓

18–23   light. ⟨I⟩ ¶ It . . . is ⟨regarded⟩ ↑eyed↓ . . . strikes ⟨the young⟩
                  ↑prattling childhood↓ . . . disgusts ⟨the⟩ light hearted ↑youth↓;

25–26   joy. ↑that . . . men.↓

27   is regarded [The stray notation "⟨dialogues⟩" appears above these
                  words.]

29–31   meet↑; whose . . . only ⟨remembered⟩ ↑grateful↓ . . . cloud↓ ¶ ⟨Nor
                  ⟨should he be regarded⟩ is it less injurious to his character ⟨when he
                  is to be a⟩ when he degrades his office to be a spy in the families of his
                  flock; nor less when he ⟨condescends to servility &⟩ ↑betrays his
                  cause to↓ flatters your vices & condescends to scandal in servility to
                  you⟩ ¶ Not

37–40   the ⟨mottled⟩ succession . . . your ⟨own⟩ good,

                           Page 240

1–3   {It will . . . to ⟨our⟩ ↑God's . . . call↓ [emendation in ink over pencil]
                  . . . ↑we↓ decay.}

11   releive. ⟨It is true to the outward eye⟩ ↑I say↓ you are ⟨not⟩ alone; ↑it
                  is true↓

12   They ⟨visit⟩ ↑knock at↓

13   my ⟨brethren⟩ ↑brother,↓

17   ↑Can . . . back?↓

22   ↑has↓ . . . that [end of page] ⟨into⟩ darkness

23–25   Yes brethren ⟨if⟩ ↑when↓ God ⟨shall⟩ enable↑s↓ ⟨me⟩ ↑him↓ . . . of
                  ⟨my⟩ ↑his↓ blameless ambition ⟨I hope to⟩ ↑the . . . may↓ . . .
                  ↑trifles . . . &↓ [passage marked in the margin with a line in ink]

29	↑endeavour to↓
36	so ⟨much feared⟩ ↑long dreaded↓

Page 241

2	of ⟨pastors⟩ ↑a clergy↓
14–15	duty. ⟨And there is a general remark of great importance that may be made with regard to them ⟨{or}⟩ which may serve to show their importance.⟩ /It is/And . . . importance/
17–19	that ⟨any⟩ ↑a↓ . . . ↑with any accuracy↓ . . . from ⟨only⟩ such . . . as ⟨ordinary⟩ ↑most↓ . . traits ⟨of character⟩ ↑& dispositions↓
20–21	↑When . . . yours.↓
23	people. ⟨When⟩ He
29–32	hearts ↑he . . . motive↓ . . . ↑to↓
34	Besides ⟨he⟩ when
40	It ⟨it⟩ is

Page 242

1	excused ⟨because in the past week those duties were plainly & feelingly opened by one who is no stranger to the pastoral work Moreover⟩ ↑because↓
8–14	m⟨e⟩y ↑inexperience↓ . . . your ⟨clergyman⟩ minister. ⟨It will not be⟩ ↑I cannot ⟨pass by⟩ ↑leave↓ . . . am↓ permitted ⟨me at this hour to express how much I venerate his worth. I shall emulate his example.⟩ ↑to . . . ours.↓
19	a ⟨re⟩ ⟨good reason⟩ ↑a palliation↓
21	me ⟨it should⟩ no
22	received ⟨without ceremony⟩ on
24–36	↑Let . . . God.↓
27	↑mistimed↓
29	an⟨d⟩y doubt ⟨of the⟩ any
33–36	your ⟨reverence⟩ interest . . . work. ↑remembering that↓ We . . . us⟨.⟩; ↑that↓ We . . . ⟨'⟩Be

Page 243

3	↑a youth &↓
4	↑to↓

Sermon XXX

Manuscript: Four sheets folded to make four pages each; folios nested and sewn with black thread through the center fold; pages measure 25 x 20.5 cm.

Lines	*Page 244*
Bible Text	↑While we↓ Look⟨ing⟩ ↑not↓ at the things ⟨unseen⟩ which
3–6	infant. ⟨These material⟩ ↑As . . . infinite ⟨lesson⟩ ↑work↓ . . . the⟨se material⟩ ↑world . . . live↓↓ objects ↑of sense↓ are ⟨to be⟩ our tools of art ⟨the books, as it were ⟨on which⟩ we are to learn

afterwards, the lessons of thought & duty, which is our main business⟩ ↑& our materials↓,

10   of ⟨use⟩ ↑utility↓.

12–13   child ⟨esteems⟩ ↑values↓ . . . apple ⟨of more value than the⟩ ↑above a↓ kingdom ⟨of England.⟩. As

14–17   begin to / guess that more exists than the eye perceives, / catch . . . in world . . . bodies / . . . is, ⟨live⟩ to

19–22   ¶ ↑We . . . scene↑. The . . . toils.↓↓ ["The . . . toils." and the preceding period are in pencil. The entire paragraph was written around (and therefore added after) "Insert X" (see below).]

24   ↑we↓

Page 245

3–8   ↑In . . . time. ↑Insert X↓ [On the previous page, a passage marked "X":] ↑{And . . . habits.}↓↓

14   he ⟨designs⟩ ↑means↓

18   ↑round piece of↓ silver ⟨dollar⟩ &

20–21   one ⟨d⟩ are . . . ↑tho' . . . all↓

23–26   it ⟨is past a doubt that⟩ ↑may . . . sense↓ . . . ↑than in the visible↓ . . . now ⟨present⟩ before

29   of a ⟨few chairs⟩ ↑certain articles of furniture↓, a ⟨certain⟩ picture

33–(246)6 {There . . . unfolds.}

33–39   difference ⟨of⟩ ↑in↓ . . . to ⟨one⟩ ↑the instructed↓ . . . another ⟨I know you will excuse me brethren if I detail in part the train of thought which was lately forced on my mind⟩ ↑In every ⟨assembly of a⟩ large . . . any ⟨ey⟩ mind . . . all.↓ ⟨w⟩When ↑lately↓ . . . differen⟨t⟩ce ⟨eye with which my brother saw you & I saw you⟩ ↑⟨ & the instructed⟩ of . . . mine↓.

40   ↑which . . . curiosity↓

Page 246

2   ↑changes &↓

3–6   fate ⟨There is as much⟩ The . . . contains ⟨as much⟩ ↑the same↓ . . . empire. ⟨But a⟩ ↑And the↓ . . . ↑more↓ intimate ↑the↓ . . . it ⟨is necessary⟩ the

7–8   ↑is,↓ . . . *unseen* ⟨*world*⟩ *part;*

13–18   ¶ ↑{I . . . For ⟨the sensualist⟩ the ↑most↓ . . . senses.}↓

25   ↑generous↓

27–28   ↑upon ⟨a⟩ tho'↑s↓ than upon ⟨a⟩ thing↑s↓↓ upon the ⟨thoughts⟩ ideas [emendations within the addition are in pencil]

30–36   faggot; ⟨& more than the martyr whose flames⟩ ↑and . . . for ⟨his⟩ the . . . torture↓ . . . populace↑.↓ ⟨the⟩ ↑But there are ⟨some⟩ ↑sufferers↓ . . . There is↓ many a ⟨poor⟩ ↑pious↓ [emendation in pencil] . . . age ⟨↑& who↓⟩ ↑& who↓ wast⟨ing⟩es ↑her years↓ . . . ↑without one petulant syllable↓

39–41   ↑Many . . . erect.↓ [addition in pencil]

1   unseen [Here follows an incomplete addition in pencil:] ↑This is yᵉ
     meaning yᵗ beams in every page of the history of Xt ⟨wh⟩ the appeal
     yᵉ mind makes from a mean outside to a sublime &c.↓

3–4   the ⟨sense &⟩ sentiments . . . the ⟨ef⟩ appearance

17   ↑the sum of↓

24   is ⟨great⟩ done

29–32   hour the . . . being ↑Insert A↓ [At the bottom of the following page,
     below a rule, a passage marked "A":] ↑This . . . ↑enters . . . vail↓ . . .
     saved.↓

33–(248)5 {↑Hence . . . ordinances↓ . . . ↑What . . . know.↓ . . . if↑,↓ ⟨we
     pour out the cup⟩ when . . . hither.}

6   are ⟨un⟩seen,

13   yet ⟨y⟩ they

15   into ⟨a⟩ ↑a↓nother

24–32   ↑Do . . . ↑that↓ ⟨an⟩other life↓

33   into ⟨yo⟩ every

36   opening ⟨your⟩ the

40   ↑(if need be) of↓

[On the page following the end of the sermon:]
 {The man who acts with this elevation is like those who were fabled to have their eyes
anointed so that they cd. see the agents of ⟨the⟩ another world fairies & goodmen
walking & acting among men unperceived by men. So does he yet walk among his
departed friends when the godly man ceaseth & the faithful fail,—to him they do not
cease, to *him* they do not fail.}
 "Darken five windows that the house may shine," says an Arabian proverb. [quoted
from William de Britaine, *Human Prudence*, 1806, 73; see *JMN* 6:90]

Sermon XXXI

Manuscript: Four sheets folded to make four pages each; folios nested and sewn with
black thread through the center fold; pages measure 25 x 20.2 cm. A leaf once tipped
with red sealing wax to the recto of leaf 1 is missing.

Lines   *Page 250*

10–11   ↑you . . . and↓

14–17   young & /aspiring/hopeful/, [variant in pencil] . . . ⟨p⟩hope . . .
     {whose . . . meat} . . . ↑a . . . pleasure↓

21   How /beautiful/excellent/

23–24   praise ¶ ⟨↑None can know better than those I now address the reach
     of the arts. Most of those I address have ⟨seen the⟩ your dwelling in
     that greatest work of the arts. He descends to yᵉ margin of yᵉ sea &
     launches his little bark on its unfathomable waters. A bauble a
     particle on yᵉ interminable waste I see it mount yᵉ ridges & sink into
     yᵉ vallies of yᵉ ocean but yᵉ understanding of him yᵗ guides it sits

sovereign of its course. Its curious furniture of helm & sail & compass lead yᵉ little adventurer on in safety & tho' the whirlwind from heaven sweep across his path & yᵉ tempest tear his canvass as in sport he contends with the elements & rides out yᵉ storm⟩ overflowed on all around the↓ ¶ ⟨a⟩ And

Page 251

8	by ⟨&⟩ the
12	mean. ⟨You⟩ [end of page] yourselves
15	in ⟨the⟩ ↑every↓ experience↑,↓ ⟨of each of us⟩ to
19	sentiments ⟨w⟩ concerning
20	the house [Above these words the phrase in pencil:] world is yᵉ house
22	given ⟨for frolic⟩ ↑without . . . end↓. [emendation in pencil]
25	What⟨s the⟩ is this
27–28	certainly ⟨is not⟩ ↑does not appear↓ . . . first ⟨appearance⟩ sight
30	beleive
31	irreconcileable ⟨opposition⟩ contradiction
39	But ⟨true⟩ goodness
40	And ⟨I believe⟩ if

Page 252

5–12	employment. ↑Here are two men who dwell side by side with what unlike life One of them↓ [uncanceled false start in pencil of the variant passage, marked "A," inscribed on the preceding blank page] /Tomorrow if you traverse the /streets/roads/ [variant in pencil] of the town you shall find thousands of men occupied in /mechanical toil/⟨of⟩ manual labor/, [variant in pencil] the largest part of whom have no leisure for books and only go from the shop ↑or the field↓ [addition in pencil] to their meals and to their beds. Thus they do day by day for thirty or forty years. ⟨And a few miles⟩ /Continue your walk a few miles/Go to one of the towns of our seminaries of learning/ [variant in pencil] and you shall find a hundred men who never lay their hand upon the ↑plough↓ [addition in pencil] chisel or the axe but who spend their whole time in literary and scientific speculation./A Now . . . ↑from . . . sunset↓ . . . ↑farm or his↓ . . . numbers./
17–20	↑(↓which . . . observation↑)↓ [additions in pencil] . . . religion, /makes the poor argument of the skeptic/has . . . religion/ . . . ↑in apology↓ . . . /who/& . . . business/ [variants in pencil]
23–24	shroud ⟨to⟩ ↑from↓ . . . ↑town↓
31	bed ↑⟨without⟩ until he has uttered↓
32–33	torment ⟨which foot to put down on the floor & how often & in what manner to raise his hand;⟩ ↑what . . . food↓
33–36	nor ⟨rinse his teeth⟩ ↑his lips↓ . . . wearisome ⟨nonsense⟩ ↑folly↓ . . . ↑if . . . laws↓
39	not ⟨enjoin⟩ lay

Page 253

11-12   is ⟨way⟩ ↑mode↓ . . . of ⟨our⟩the . . . at ⟨dinner⟩ ↑recreation↓

14-15   learn. ²{I can never too much insist,} ¹{in obedience to my own convictions,}

16   not ↑⟨to⟩ being↓

21-22   good. ¶ ⟨Whats⟩ There

24-27   duty, ↑by↓ . . . into ⟨a⟩ ↑the natural, the↓ . . . into ⟨a better⟩ another world. And ⟨this⟩ to

28-29   famous. ⟨Each of us has got to discover for himself certain moral facts which no one ever did take on credit: he has got to find out for example that all that he does out of goodwill is not thrown away, but is safe—every atom,—is bro't back in full store of happiness to his own bosom. He has got to find out that when he wrongs his neighbour, he wrongs himself, plunders his own felicity. Now there is no course or manner of life in which these truths do not discover themselves. In the lowest trades & in the largest transactions, {in a bargain between boys, & in a treaty between empires,} the same principles appear.⟩ [canceled in pencil] ¶ What

32-33   is ⟨with⟩ out

34   ↑This . . . Christ.↓

35-38   a ⟨creed⟩ ↑doctrine↓ . . . difficult ⟨duty⟩ ↑ways↓ not in ⟨far⟩ strange . . . th⟨e⟩at

39-(254)4 lies. ↑{Insert X}↓ [On the previous page, a passage marked "X":] ↑{There . . . ↑yet↓ . . . a ⟨little⟩ fleeting . . . minds.}↓

Page 254

7   appoints ⟨th⟩ our . . . ↑parentage↓

9-10   life by whatever / compliments flattered / men say of it / by / whatever adoration of the crowd regarded / how . . . envied / [variants in pencil]

11   names, ⟨the⟩ ↑and all↓

14   ⟨y⟩life

[The following occupies the top of the page after the end of the sermon:] ⟨The hour is not far off when all of us who ⟨now⟩ ↑now↓ are here so full of life & strength shall be cold in⟩ death. ⟨Some of us the sea shall cover with its dreary roaring waves & some of us lie in graveyards on the shore. Then shall perish our strength, our wealth, our pleasures our pride—but then our virtues & the reward of ⟨our⟩ all the good works we have done shall survive & last forever.⟩

Sermon XXXII

Manuscript: Four sheets folded to make four pages each; folios nested and sewn with white thread through the center fold; pages measure 25 x 20.2 cm. A leaf (19 x 15 cm) containing Insert "A" is tipped with red sealing wax to the recto of leaf 6.

Lines	Page 255
Bible Text	our ⟨sins.⟩ debts.
6–8	↑uncovered,↓ . . . ↑with our skepticism,↓ when th⟨at⟩e . . . ↑us↓.
12	with ⟨the stars for his book,⟩ the . . . ↑for his book,↓
18–21	solitary ⟨rapture⟩ faith ⟨supported⟩ shared . . . fortune ⟨suitable⟩ to ↑worthy of↓ the idea ⟨a suitable celebration, in⟩ ↑would not↓ . . . ↑seem . . . way↓
23–24	a ↑/There is this universal consent to God's existence/There . . . stops./↓ [The shorter, preliminary version is in pencil.]
27–28	the⟨ir⟩ Idea ↑that is entertained↓ . . . Universe. ⟨In⟩To every mind ↑also↓ is ⟨the same⟩ ↑an↓

	Page 256
4	↑the botanist . . . physician,↓
7–8	knowledge. ⟨The⟩ ↑A↓ . . . me ⟨a sinner.⟩. The
11	↑has↓
12	This ⟨feeling⟩ ↑observation↓
15–16	prayer & [end of line] & I . . . plain ⟨&⟩ manner . . . of ⟨this⟩ ↑the↓
18–21	between ⟨of⟩ forgiveness . . . ↑a . . . faith↓ . . . ↑from . . . comes↓
22–23	is ⟨properly⟩ ↑the proper & perfect↓
24–25	but ⟨bring⟩ the [end of line] ⟨will into⟩ ↑the last . . . into↓
29–33	him. ⟨Perhaps⟩ ↑It may be↓ ⟨b⟩By . . . your ⟨own⟩ honour, . . . has ⟨uttered against you⟩ ↑aimed . . . character↓
36	↑can↓
39	↑whilst . . . power,↓

	Page 257
1–2	two ⟨savages⟩ ↑strangers↓ ⟨meet in company they⟩ ↑are introduced ⟨to⟩in society . . . &↓
4–6	are ⟨a good man⟩ ↑of a sound mind↓ . . . ↑to you↓.
6	enmity ⟨to⟩ ↑towards↓
11–16	be ⟨the⟩ of . . . good ⟨with⟩ ↑by↓ . . . benevolence ⟨of⟩ ↑on↓ his ↑part↓, . . . your ⟨hatred⟩ vengeance; . . . cannot ⟨help⟩ ↑fail to↓ effect⟨ing⟩
17–18	him? ¶ ⟨For what is⟩ It
19–21	discovers. ⟨If a tree⟩ A . . . broken ⟨a⟩ ↑one of your↓ limb⟨.⟩s. ↑You cannot repress ⟨your⟩ the . . . anger.↓
22–24	the ⟨injury⟩ harm . . . ↑that . . . mind,↓ [addition in ink over pencil] . . . ↑be↓
25–26	You ⟨have⟩ are conscious ↑by . . . ill-nature↓
27–29	↑In . . . you:↓ You . . . with ⟨extreme⟩ ↑yet more↓
31	and ⟨now⟩ y⟨ou⟩et
33	↑some remains of↓
34–35	you ⟨ask why⟩ feel . . . ↑& is wholly unjust↓;
37	↑Not . . . but↓ That
42	them↑,↓ ⟨yourself,⟩ do

Page 258

1–3   brethren, ⟨carry⟩ ↑with↓ . . . ↑let . . . inquiry↓ . . . consider ⟨it in relation⟩ ↑the . . . made↓ to God. ⟨Our⟩ The

6   ↑by us↓

13   ↑when . . . fellow,↓

15–16   are ⟨led⟩ ↑brought↓. Here ⟨is⟩lies

22–29   moment ⟨he uttered⟩ it ↑of utterance↓, . . . prayer ⟨was⟩ ↑is↓ granted. ¶ ↑{Insert A}↓ [On a slip of paper attached to the next page with red sealing wax, the following:] ⟨↑How far it is in accordance with what we know of human nature we have already seen, and how far it accords with Xn doctrine may be seen in every page of N. T. which represents wholly a spiritual service. ⟨What⟩ It is said by Paul, The spirit itself beareth witness by our spirit y^t we are ye children of God & what else is ye meaning of those remarkable words of our Lord Whatsoever things ye desire when ye pray believe that ye receive y^m & ye shall have y^m .⟩ [cf. the last note below]
     {A} If . . . you ⟨a new⟩ ↑the old↓ . . . vain↓

32–33   ↑It . . . Christ.↓

33–34   ↑that when↓ . . . [co]nsequences [letters obscured by sealing wax attaching "Insert A"]

40–41   of ⟨devils⟩ the spirits of hell. ¶ ⟨↑Ponder well then the meaning of the prayer, & examine yourself if then you truly repent & truly resolve to offend no more then God hears you↓⟩ [canceled in pencil and ink] ¶ So

Page 259

1–4   do ⟨as⟩ what . . . prayer ⟨forgive other⟩ ↑abstain from injuring↓ . . . thus ⟨see⟩ ↑look↓ . . . ↑& as God sees it,↓ . . . you ⟨hate⟩ do

[The following notes appear below the end of the sermon:]

_____   Lect.

The Spirit itself beareth witness with our spirit that we are the children of God. Rom. VIII. 16   .

_____

Therefore I say unto you What things soever ye desire when ye pray believe that ye receive them & ye shall have them. Mark XI 24

_____

Sermon XXXIII

Manuscript: Four sheets folded to make four pages each; folios nested and sewn with white thread through the center fold; pages measure 24 x 20.5 cm. A leaf (10 x 8.5 cm) containing Insert "B" is tipped with red sealing wax to the verso of leaf 1.

Lines		
Bible Text	*Page 260*	
Bible Text	is, ⟨first,⟩—	
6	affairs, . . . a ⟨great⟩good	
7	to our ⟨condition⟩ ↑the state of man↓.	
22–23	is, ⟨first,⟩ gentle."	

Page 261

6   value. ↑when . . . others.↓
12   tho' ⟨infirm⟩ of
14   the ⟨Church⟩ church
18–24   heroes. ⟨It is remarked that in difficult & disastrous times⟩ ↑{Insert
             B}↓ [On a slip of paper attached with red sealing wax to the previous
             page, a passage marked "B":] ↑{Now . . . disastrous times, &c—↓
             . . . not ⟨scares⟩ ↑shakes,↓
39   time ⟨set aside⟩ suspended,

Page 262

1–2   ↑They . . . forever.↓
3   no ⟨instance recorded⟩ ↑character↓
5–7   famous ⟨e⟩ sentence . . . ↑when . . . heresy↓
8–9   ↑He . . . not ⟨here⟩ be . . . sentiment↓
11   if↑,↓ ⟨he⟩ with
12   ↑not↓
18–23   thee." ⟨And it is written in the Evangelist of our Lord in whom the
             perfections of his Father & our Father in heaven were shown forth,
             that when he was reviled he reviled not again⟩ ↑{Insert A}↓ [At the
             bottom of the page, the following:] ⟨↑A {And the highest example of
             gentleness on record was reserved for the closing hour of the life of our
             Lord who said as he hung over his murderers Father, forgive them for
             they know not what they do.}⟩ A {But . . . when ⟨the⟩ all . . .
             them.}↓ & in
28–29   ↑(I . . . one.—)↓

Page 263

2   their ⟨good⟩ ↑sweetness↓.
10   averse ⟨frame⟩ inclination
13–17   yet /with/after/ . . . ↑domestic↓ delay ⟨embarrassment⟩ ⟨pricks⟩
             goads . . . their ⟨fireside⟩ ⟨↑town↓⟩ ↑family board↓
20   ↑sally of↓
22   of ⟨wonder⟩ ↑surprize↓
26   ↑very↓
27–28   fill ⟨him⟩ ↑the ill tempered man↓ . . . only ⟨the ⟨sp⟩ transient
             splendour of⟩ an
41   ↑of↓

Page 264

10   you ⟨th⟩ a
20   the /strength/might/
33   is ⟨first⟩ gentle.
34   oursel⟨f⟩ves
40–(265)3   And ⟨↑if↓⟩ the best ⟨rule that can be offered⟩ ↑way↓ ⟨t⟩of restrain-
             ↑ing↓ . . . ↑the habit of↓ Consideration. ↑And . . . this,↓ Accustom

Page 265

5   speak. what
8   is ⟨first⟩ *gentle*.—

Sermon XXXIV

Manuscript: Four sheets folded to make four pages each (only a stub remains of the second leaf of the innermost folio); folios nested and sewn with black thread through the center fold; pages measure 24.8 x 20.2 cm. A leaf (19.8 x 12.5 cm) containing Insert "B" (recto) and canceled Insert "C" (verso) is tipped with red sealing wax to the recto of leaf 5; a strip (6 x 12.5 cm) containing uncanceled Insert "C" is affixed with red sealing wax to the verso of leaf 5.

Lines	*Page 266*
1	↑by . . . life↓ that ⟨we⟩men
5–6	↑You . . . 2 or 3000 more.↓
7–8	true ⟨you will find much⟩ ↑a . . . you↓
12	↑some↓
22	universal ⟨growth⟩ ↑extension↓
24–27	patien⟨t⟩ce . . . untiring ⟨action⟩ activity, . . . got, ⟨no⟩ there . . . ↑provided, which↓
28	one / dazzling prize / high place /

Page 267

3	office, you ⟨fail⟩ lose
12–13	↑as long . . . life↓
17–20	¶ ↑It . . . / to teach / us / the mind even in pagan ignorance / to . . . reason / . . . some↑thing↓ better↑.↓ ⟨world.⟩ The . . . immortality.↓
21–23	¶ The ⟨↑hope⟩ ↑expectation↓ which is the↓ . . . nature, ⟨the hope⟩ that . . . ↑golden↓ . . . the ⟨hope⟩ ↑ / belief / doctrine / ↓
24	↑who . . . of human condition↓
26–30	choice, ⟨many men⟩ ↑some, I am persuaded,↓ . . . down ⟨& having⟩ ↑under↓ the ↑heavy↓ . . . grave ⟨thrown heavily on them.⟩. ¶ ↑↑On this account↓ All . . . yet↓ Men & women ⟨in⟩ within
34–35	mighty / diffuser of common sense / [diffus]ion of knowledge /, . . . nigh ⟨gone⟩ ↑vanished↓.
36	↑without miracle↓
38–39	& / horror / strong repugnance /
41	mind [Here Emerson wrote the initial "W" twice, and over that "Ellen L. Tucker"; all in pencil.]

Page 268

1–3	¶ ↑Granting the ↑re-↓appearance . . . possible,↓ . . . or ⟨hoped to have⟩ ↑laboured for↓ . . . ↑all acquirements all possessions↓
5–8	↑an↓ awful ⟨moment⟩ ↑season↓ . . . ever ⟨equal⟩ ↑supply↓, ↑the . . . observation↓
9–11	moment ⟨that my⟩ ↑in which the↓ . . . ↑was↓ communicat⟨ed⟩ing . . . to ⟨me⟩ ↑it↓ . . . death ⟨It seems to me it could be nothing else but⟩ ↑To . . . be↓ a ⟨time⟩ ↑rapture↓

12   The ⟨soul⟩ ↑mind↓

14   ↑seen↓

15–31   ↑assurance of↓ [addition in pencil] the prisoner ↑himself↓ [addition in
              pencil] come out ↑from his narrow cell↓ into the ⟨light⟩ ↑glory↓ of
              day ↑↑assurance that↓ [addition in pencil] The . . . poor ⟨body⟩
              ↑clay↓ . . . come ⟨out⟩ ↑forth↓ [emendation in pencil] . . . virtues.↓
              ¶ ⟨The future state the resurrection of the dead has always been the
              high point of speculation to men so desireable that it seemed too great
              a thing to hope. And it must always remain to mortal men the theme
              of ardent hope & dearest interest. For all the faculties of our nature
              are progressive, all have an onward look & tendency & the strongest
              argument from nature no doubt lies in this fixed on-look of the soul.⟩
              ¶ ↑{Insert B}↓ [On a slip of paper attached with red sealing wax to the
              following page, a passage marked "B":] ↑{It . . . immortality. ⟨I hope
              soon to be able to bring that subject before you with more⟩ {I . . .
              upon} . . . ↑& . . . you↓. . . desireableness . . . chief ⟨light⟩
              ↑evidence↓. . . . get.}↓ ¶ ⟨Let us, my brethren, consider what we do
              know of it.⟩ ↑↑Before Revelation↓ The . . . ⟨s⟩consolation . . . the
              perfect reasonableness↓ It is ⟨a⟩ strange ⟨fact⟩ and ⟨one⟩ of

42–(269)2   forming ⟨a faint⟩ ↑some↓ idea ↑though faint↓ of ↑the↓ . . . gone⟨?⟩
              and which [i]dea [letter obscured by sealing wax attaching "Insert B"]

                                    Page 269

3–8   [h]ave [letter obscured by sealing wax] no . . . things ⟨that⟩ ↑that
              . . . which↓ . . . affect. ↑{Insert C}↓ [On a slip of paper affixed with
              red sealing wax over the lengthy canceled passage given below, a
              passage marked "C":] ↑Clearly . . . duration↓ [An earlier draft of
              "Insert C" occurs, canceled, on the verso of Insert "B":] ⟨C {Clearly
              clearly do I see that there are thoughts in the soul which are
              independent of the changes of matter; ⟨that the feeling of duty is
              something very distinct from my mortal nature & must be eternal,⟩
              that there are some feelings agreeable to the child & to the man that
              cannot change if I should endure for endless duration.⟩

10–12   feeling ⟨you now make⟩ ↑↑&↓ . . . strong ⟨selfish⟩ purpose ↑of
              ⟨cruelty⟩ revenge↓ . . . to ⟨make a benevolent exertion which your
              conscience has required of you⟩ ↑instead . . . you↓. [Emerson origi-
              nally added "instead" after "make" and canceled the original wording
              (neglecting to cancel "to"), finally supplying the remainder of the
              addition.]

13–14   ↑granting . . . mind↓ . . . ↑memory of this↓

15–16   Church. ¶ ⟨↑Well now the reason why you cannot predict the↑se↓
              ⟨same things⟩ ↑yʳ existence↓ with the ⟨⟨same⟩⟩ ↑absolute↓
              assurance ⟨of your bodily person that you can of your spiritual self⟩ is
              the obvious one that we see our own bodies & all other matter
              continually de⟨ranging⟩caying, passing into new forms↓ ⟨For
              ↑But↓,⟩ ↑But you cannot help discerning that you are of a twofold
              nature, matter & spirit, and↓ you cannot fail to see that there are
              things which are spiritual that do as really & distinctly exist as brass

or stone↑,↓ & ⟨yet are⟩ ↑things that are moreover↓ eternal ↑as brass & stone are not↓ because they are what time cannot change, cannot touch. Do you not see [tha]t truth is good & falsehood evil as surely as honey [is s]weet or the water of the sea is salt? ⟨Brass & stone will rust & crumble, the changes of the atmosphere act on them & therefore time will consume them, but truth & falsehood are things that have no reference to sun & air & chemical changes, & which time therefore will never affect. And does not↑ ↑[Bu]t whatever other laws may govern water & honey,⟩ & w & h may ch[ange their na]ture & be governed by new laws but↓ /truth & falsehood/moral truth moral being/ will never alter are of unchangeable nature Therefore th[ere is] nothing unnatural that the soul will be thus thinking at that remote hour whilst it is unnatural to expect such continuance to the body Consider brethren if↓ this perception of the eternity of certain feelings which we partake ↑does not↓ afford strong presumption that we who feel them are eternal also?⟩ ¶ Well [The paragraph is circled and canceled; words and parts of words are obscured by the sealing wax attaching Insert "C."]

16–17   why ⟨↑from [illegible word]⟩ without revelation↓ . . . with the absolute assurance [space left] is

32   Now ⟨it is⟩ ↑brethren I rejoice in↓ this ⟨fact of the⟩ perfect

37–40   that ⟨I suppose no⟩ ↑it . . . any↓ . . . man ⟨will dispute⟩. ↑I . . . to ⟨this⟩ Xty . . . doctrine↓

41   is ⟨comparatively⟩ ↑utterly↓

42   or ↑whether we↓

Page 270

1   ↑is it↓

2–18   all? ¶ ↑{Insert X} [Two pages later, occupying the entire page, a passage marked "X":] ↑{If . . . fail.—↓ . . . ages ⟨that impend⟩ ↑that . . . intercourse↓ . . . tho↑u↓ght . . . But ⟨shake⟩ ↑strike↓ . . . seriously.}↓

20–22   that ⟨measureless⟩ ↑illimitable↓ . . . ↑& . . . there↓ . . . immeasureable ⟨extent⟩ solitudes, . . . ↑cheerful↓

23   is ⟨a⟩my

24   shall ⟨utter⟩ ↑take up↓

26–29   f⟨in⟩rom . . . ↑unless for amusement↓ . . . what was the opinion↑s↓ ⟨of men⟩ about . . . men of

32   would ⟨sunder⟩ ↑crack↓

35   ↑& never is clouded↓

36-(271)1   ↑enough . . . practice↓ . . . ↑of . . . world↓.

Page 271

2–3   to ⟨the⟩ his . . . ²{My career is begun} ¹{in this spot of earth}

6–7   to ⟨ascend⟩ ↑mount by↓;

8–9   ever. ¶ ⟨It has been my aim in this discourse simply to show how desireable & how reasonable was the doctrine of our own immortality. I have not attempted to prove the immortality of the soul. I have reserved that subject for another occasion when I hope to be able to do more justice to that topic than now I could. In the meantime, I may say that ⟨I cannot⟩ after all the arguments that can be suggested from reason are offered, we ⟨can⟩ must depend on revelation for our chief light. We cannot afford to do without. The ⟨subject⟩ ↑truth↓ is too important to us, to ⟨lac⟩ let it lack any light we can get.⟩ ¶ Let

[Following the end of the sermon:] 26 minutes

Sermon XXXV

Manuscript A (earlier version): Four sheets folded to make four pages each; folios nested and sewn with black thread through the center fold; pages measure 25 x 17.5 cm. A leaf (20 x 16 cm) containing Insert "A" is tipped with red sealing wax to the recto of leaf 4.

[The text of the earlier version follows:]

XXXV.

We should live soberly, righteously, & godly, in this present world. Titus, II. 12.
{Fourth Part.}

On a former occasion, I offered to your consideration some remarks upon the three classes of duties ⟨to ourselves⟩ personal, social, & divine, ↑to↓ which the apostle alludes in enjoining men to live *soberly, righteously, & godly.*

The view I ha⟨p⟩d proposed to take of our duties to God was then left imperfect. ⟨The strength, the⟩ ↑The Affections were considered in relation to their↓ excel ⟨lence⟩↑lent nature↓, ↑their strength↓ & the↑ir↓ /natural/true/ objects ⟨of the Affections were successively considered⟩ & ↑some description was attempted of↓ the manner in which God fixes our attachment upon his perfections by means ↑of our love↓ of human virtues.

It is proposed at present to push still farther the inquiry concerning the full meaning of 'living godly,' that is, of giving our affections to God & to give some idea however imperfect of the great truths that lie like unfathomable mines (how little explored) in this region of thought.

The next fact to which I wish to call your attention on this inquiry, is this, that the affections can be cultivated. I cannot say, says one, that I love God. When I sift my thoughts & disposit⟨t⟩ions, I do not relish those employments that the love of God might dictate I do not go to church with the same eager pleasure that I often find in going to my business. I must confess I go for decency not from devotion. I have a reluctance to engage in prayer—And all this—what can it be but a certain repulsion from God? it cannot spring from his love. And yet I am esteemed an innocent & good citizen, ⟨a good⟩ ↑an industrious farmer, an upright↓ merchant, a skilful mechanic; I am not a bad man. I do not see, then, how I am to blame, if I do not love God.

Now the answer to this excuse of a worldly mind lies in the very important fact just now stated that the affections can be *cultivated.* It is a great law of the affections that they grow by their own exercise. Habit comes in to the aid of inclination. All our proverbs ↑in all tongues↓ attest it. Do what is right, & use shall make it pleasant. Consider a moment what you must sometimes have ⟨felt⟩ ↑perceived↓ to be the prime secrets of the human organization, that whatsoever we do, we do with more ease the second time than the first; that things long reckoned impossible,—a steady perseverance will perform. *I will* is a strong word that moves mountains; that whatsoever postures or expressions of countenance we assume we immediately become sensible of some degree of those emotions of the mind, those passions, whose expression is thus arbitrarily assumed; &, much more, if we do with any steadiness, for any long period certain actions, virtuous or vicious, certain good or evil offices to any person, we inevitably acquire with great degrees of strength, the feeling of which those actions are the proper expression. If you hang a bar of steel for a long time in the direction of the magnetic poles, it becomes a magnet itself, and just as surely if you do the actions prescribed by one state of mind, they will make that state of mind habitual to you. Thus if there be any person against whom you nourish, without reason, a strong dislike, and sensible that this aversion is at war with Christian principles you should now treat that person with studied kindness; should eagerly watch every secret & open way to promote his advantage; ⟨you shall find⟩ by every benefit you confer on him you shall find your own benevolence to him increased until your prejudices have given place to the most sincere kindness.

So also may the affections be directed to their divine ⟨Home⟩ ↑object↓ be given to God by an act of the Will, when of themselves they do not go thither. "If ye do my commandments ye shall abide in my love." The experience of all good men conspires in one testimony that precisely in the same proportion as we advance in virtue in the same proportion does the great Idea of God reveal itself more distinctly within the mind. Say not therefore I am good but I do not love God. You are not good. think again: some deadly sin, some fatal bar ⟨r⟩lies in your way & keeps you from heaven. Be humble, be just, be true, be temperate, ↑be chaste,↓ be merciful, & you shall learn the love of God.

I do not think that there is any aspect under which human nature is so respectable as in view of its affections. We delight to talk of ourselves as very powerful beings, but there is the ⟨secret⟩ ↑seat↓ of our power. Without them our pretensions to ⟨dura[tion]⟩ ↑any real efficiency↓ are exceeding feeble. By them, our strength is all but omnipotent. For it touches the Omnipotent himself. ⟨And thus it is.⟩ ↑And this position I think it is easy to establish↓ It is the property of the affections to awaken correspondent feeling in their objects. The regard deep & steadfast which you bear to another being, let that other be of what degree or nature soever will extort a mutual regard from him. I now state the general law, ↑without stopping to explain↓ & by & by we may attend to the exceptions or what seem to be so And this statement is true, because, the fact that we entertain a strong inclination for any object at once /proves/argues/ [variant in ink over pencil] us capable of appreciating the nature of that object, our knowledge being the foundation of our regard.

↑There is no exception to this in the fondness of the lower animals for man↓ Among the lower degrees of intelligence, in the brute creation, each animal attaches itself to those of its own kind, & the regard which the domestic animals manifest for man ↑something very different from the regard of man to man↓ is always the leaning on a superior nature for protection & never that feeling into which ⟨some feeling⟩ ↑⟨the⟩ perception↓ of equality must always enter, the feeling of love.

↑{Insert A} A {As in all our analysis of the affections in their aspect toward God we necessarily use the analogy of the affections we bear to men, it seems proper to say I use the wor⟨l⟩d *love* to denominate ↑such a relation as is↓ the ⟨dearest⟩ ↑⟨the⟩ most near & generous↓ friendship that can subsist between two virtuous men. For in attachments between the sexes ⟨in our limited⟩ nature ⟨there is⟩ ↑has ordained↓ a certain exclusiveness giving rise to the passion of Jealousy, which has no archetype in the Divine love.

⟨↑And when I say love can compel love↓ I speak of no casual fancies by this sacred name, I speak of an abiding sentiment that unites one healthy mind to another growing out of the moral approbation of the virtues of the soul.⟩

And when I say that love can extort love I speak of no casual ⟨ca⟩ /fancy/inclination/ but I speak of an abiding sentiment that the spectacle of the virtues of ⟨a healthy⟩ ↑one↓ mind ↑must↓ awaken⟨s⟩ in another healthy mind which beholds them.}↓

⟨⟨And⟩But if among men, one ⟨man⟩ ↑individual↓⟩ ↑⟨I speak of no casual fancies⟩ ↑Suppose there be a man whose action↑s↓ ha⟨s⟩ve exhibited a certain heroic virtue & ⟨an⟩some individual drawn by this spectacle↓ ↓conceives a strong regard for ⟨another man⟩ ↑him,↓ & does keenly relish & approve the beauty of his life, & all the finish of his character; this very approbation & honour he pays him, shows him↑self↓ capable of equal degrees of virtue, & therefore to be a mind with which that other cannot fail to sympathize. And ⟨if he knows⟩ ↑as the first perceives by every mark of kindness↓ that this man does entirely love him, he cannot help feeling within himself the growth of a mutual regard.

⟨Well⟩ now brethren see how hence is seen in the affections the mighty force of human beings. Since it is the law of all mind that love can extort love, & since we are made capable of cultivating the regard of God, it follows, that we, in the dust & weakness of the earth are yet able to compel, I say it with reverence, by our love of God, new measures of God's love to us. ⟨Our regard to him must determine the nature & degree of his regard to us⟩ [canceled in pencil and ink] ↑I appeal to your own experience to confirm the remark Do you not feel as sure ⟨whe⟩ with each new conquest of your virtue over temptation of an increased favor from God as you do of your own?↓ And hence we are led to ⟨the⟩ ↑another↓ general & important remark that Love ↑has a certain power to↓ equalize⟨s⟩ whom it unites.

It is an important consideration to be borne in mind in these speculations that we ⟨call by⟩ use the same name *love* to denominate very different relations. The love of the parent to its offspring is only an animal instinct, & no wise founded in the perception of qualities that excite approbation & attachment in mature minds. But when the child grows up to the power of thought, to the exercise of the affections, & to the formation of a character, then the relation of the parent changes from the instinct, from protection & patronage, to friendship. If however the child as he grows old becomes corrupt, & injures & hates his parent, this relation of love, properly so called can never ⟨sp⟩ ↑exist↓ between them. The disappointed yet surviving hope of a parent, the remains of instinctive fondness will be added in his bosom to the pity of an impartial spectator, but continual hatred on the part of the child it is likely in time would obliterate every remembrance of affection.

Now do we not all feel that ⟨the relations which we call⟩ God's love to men must be very closely analogous ↑in its workings↓ to this familiar relation?

He has made us, It is his pleasure that we should exist in this state of discipline, capable of learning by slow degrees, the laws of his universe, & that we should stand ⟨in⟩ ↑amid↓ this balance of motives & pleasures & advantages with the power to make ourselves good or bad, with the power to act or to counteract his will.

But whilst he has imparted to all of us these infinite capabilities of happiness, it would be idle to say, that, his benevolence is indiscriminate. Or if you have a mind to say that his benevolence is universal, it is not so with his *love*. There is I believe the firmest foundation in nature for the doctrine of Election; not surely in the absurd way in which that doctrine has been taught, but, ↑in the sentiment out of wh. it doubtless grew↓ in the sense that God doth love one, & doth not love another of his children. His regard for us must always depend entirely on us, on our regard to him. The all wise, the the all pure Spirit cannot sympathize surely with ignorance, & brutish cruelty & brutish lust.

⟨As the relation altered from fondness to friendship between a father & his son so now let us come to the divine Being⟩ ↑He may afford light & ↑good↓ motives to the darkened mind: he may send revelations of his will to such mind by Jesus Christ. And as the sinner departs from sin↓ As a man becomes better & wiser & learns to love God, & is by that love ennobled, & continually prompted to efforts to serve & please him, he also changes the relation of God to himself. For as God has made him free, he has made him able to deserve his esteem, and so ↑as he more & more deserves it↓ the relation of parent merges continually into the relation of Friend. And therefore observe how naturally all wise & good men, as they have made proficiency in goodness, have imperceptibly & inevitably changed the style of their addresses to God, & have come to speak of him as their companion & friend, who having the good of the Universe at heart, as also they had, they felt with his feeling, & saw with the divine Eye.

Such is the language ↑some↓ of the noble teachers of the sect of the Stoics, those forerunners of the Christian religion. Such is ever the language of our Lord and from this beautiful connexion which as he felt he expressed, this identification of himself his whole being with the Father has very naturally arisen that misinterpretation of the nature of his union with God, that has so unhappily divided the Christian world. ⟨One would⟩ ↑I should↓ think he had sufficiently explained himself in ↑promising to↓ mak⟨ing⟩e his disciples one with him, as he was one with the Father. ⟨And⟩ ↑And as such was the language of our Lord,↓ such has been the language of every true disciple of Christ, as the conquest of the mind over the body became more & more complete, as the principle of benevolence unfolding within him, continually took a wider range, embracing friends, neighbours, country, & mankind. ↑I said↓ That love ⟨would indeed be⟩ ↑was↓ powerful⟨,⟩; ↑and is it not?↓—affecting, as it would, the Father on his throne. It would change the conplexion of his Will ↑to us↓. It would change the complexion of events ↑to us↓. If the order of events without us, be, as I believe it is, always delicately adjusted to the spiritual world within us, an entire change of heart in us would beget a change also in our outward condition. But if this be tho't unreasonable, it does not at all affect the argument; for, the same events to an altered mind would speak ⟨a new⟩ an altered language. To such a mind, there is no adversity, there is no evil, there is no temptation. For as in all things the will of God is done, so is its own.

↑Once more.↓ Love equalizes. If you devote yourself to things low & base, you shall be degraded to them; if you love what is grand & pure, you also shall be raised & purified: for, what is love, but the adoption of the feelings & interests of the being beloved, & the making yourself one with that being? Therefore if you love God, & adopt his interests, & make yourself one with him, you shall part with sin, you shall part with imperfection, & pain, & mortality, you shall grow divine. Adopt his Interests! Make yourself one with Him? What doth it mean? the Interests of all beings that exist, the Infinite Good of the immeasureable ⟨universe⟩ ↑creation↓!

[The following is inscribed at this point in the text at the bottom of the page, below a rule:] Note. What else was meant by that ancient theory that the human soul was an emanation from the soul of the World, & at death returned into it which was illustrated by the figure of a phial of water broken in the ocean. Every view of the relation of man to

God that ever had currency is valuable. [end of note]

My brethren, do you think there is anything of extravagance in these views of the connexion of the human soul with the divine? It will be said perhaps that we forget the habitual lowness of the human mind when we suppose it capable of entering into these intimate & majestic relations with God. Man—why the streets are full of men & the men are full of vices & littlenesses; they are drudging all the year round for a little meat by day & a warm bed by night they are servants to such paltry necessities and are such as they to influence the Mind that quickens all being? to stand in relations to it so near as you represent?

I know it appears strange: the contrast between what we see & what we desire seems too bold the hope too glorious for truth. But is not that the very paradox in man with which we are familiar? Is it not the very ⟨wonder⟩ ↑history↓ of human nature—⟨what we find⟩ ↑the mode in which it↓ does really exist—this *sympathetic character*, by which it can appear equally at home in the highest & in the lowest & in every part of a mighty range of existence ↑from the clod in which is its root, to the heaven ⟨fro⟩ in which ⟨is its hope⟩ the bright blossoms of its hope are flourishing↓. If God has chosen to liken & unite it by its house of flesh to the worms among which now it resides, & with which shortly it shall leave its body,—has he not also by its infinite soul, made it the peer of angels & spirits, and capable of finding all joy & all pain in a spiritual world?

Has he not endowed us with the wonderful power of continually changing ourselves from that which we are to that which we wish to be, of becoming what we admire of growing by knowledge

The old philosophers called man a microcosm that is ⟨a little world⟩ the universe in miniature. ⟨He is the Image⟩ In the Scriptures he is called the Image of God He is the Image of God, inasmuch as he is the perceiver of all his works, the perceiver of the harmony & design of all; inasmuch ↑as↓ the clearer his eye becomes, his conviction grows stronger, that right is always beautiful & wrong always deformed; that the interests of God & of man are one; & that then has he reached the perfection of his being, when his own self love identity is swallowed up in his devotion to the Cause of the universe & to God the Father.—

Manuscript (revised version): Seven sheets folded to make four pages each; folios stacked and sewn with black thread along the left margin; pages measure 25 x 20.5 cm. A leaf (25 x 20.5 cm) is tipped with red sealing wax to the verso of leaf 1.

[Emerson wrote a variant opening for the revised version of sermon XXXV, which was meant to replace the original sermon text and the first three paragraphs. A draft of this variant opening was inscribed in pencil on the verso of the first leaf:]

⟨This text has been regarded as a compend of human duty. To live soberly is to discharge our duties to ourselves; to live ⟨god⟩ righteously,
    to live godly
    Our ⟨duties⟩ to relation to God is the highest we can sustain. A discharge of the duties it imposes will comprehend the faithful fulfilment of all duty. It is my design in yᵉ present discourse to some considerations upon the nature of this relation to push the inquiry concerning ye meaning of living godly ie of giving yᵉ affections to God⟩

[The revised, final version of the variant opening is inscribed on a leaf (verso blank) attached to the manuscript by red sealing wax and covering the pencil draft:]

↑Thou shalt love the Lord thy God with all thy heart. Matt. 22. 37.

Our relation to God is the highest we can sustain. A discharge of the duties it imposes will comprehend the faithful fulfilment of all duty. It is not inconsistent in any manner with the purest affections borne to our fellow creatures. It justifies & strengthens them. It is my design in the present discourse to invite your attention to some considerations upon the nature of this relation, to explain the meaning of the command in our text & to touch some of the great truths / which lie like unfathomable mines in this region of tho't / affecting yᵉ whole nature of man / . ↓ [variant in pencil]

[Below the Bible text:] (Fourth Part.)

Lines	Page 272
1–2	↑It . . . text.—↓ [addition in pencil]
15	¶ The / next / main / [The penciled "main" is rejected here as a revision probably done in conjunction with the later, variant opening]
16	say↑,↓ says one↑,↓ [additions in pencil]

	Page 273
8	perform; ⟨↑(↓I *will* is a strong word that moves mountains;↑)↓⟩ that [emendation in pencil; cf. Matthew 17:20]
15	of ⟨the magnetic poles⟩ the
27–28	God / reveal / discover / itself / {more distinctly} / & shine / [brackets and variants in pencil]
34–35	{Without . . . ↑exceeding feeble.↓} [brackets and the addition (inscribed in a space left for it) in pencil]
36–37	himself. ⟨And ↑to make good↓ [addition in pencil] this position I think it is easy to establish⟩ ↑Let . . . proposition↓.
38	The ⟨regard⟩ ↑love↓

	Page 274
1	↑& . . . it↓
10–12	God↑,↓ . . . men↑,↓ . . . *love*↑,↓ [additions in pencil]
16–17	casual ⟨fancy⟩ ↑kindness↓, [addition in ink over the same word in erased pencil] . . . mind↑,↓ [addition in ink over pencil]
19–20	virtue↑,↓ . . . individual↑,↓ . . . spectacle↑,↓ . . . him↑,↓ [additions in pencil]
24	first ⟨man⟩ perceives
27	¶ Now↑,↓ brethren↑,↓ . . . affections↑,↓ [additions in pencil]
29–30	we / in the / out of the / dust & / ⟨weak⟩↑low↓ / mean / ness [variants in pencil]
33	you⟨r virtue makes⟩ ↑have made↓ . . . sure ⟨as⟩of
44–(275)1	old↑,↓ . . . corrupt↑,↓ . . . parent↑,↓ [additions in pencil]

	Page 275
2	parent↑,↓ [addition in pencil]
9	universe↑,↓ [addition in pencil]
16–17	⟨in⟩for . . . grew—⟨in⟩ the

20	with ⟨brutish lust⟩ ignorance,
23	↑better &↓
29–32	imperceptibly ⟨& inevitably⟩ changed . . . saw ↑as↓ [addition in pencil]
43-(276)1	body, became . . . him, continually

Page 276

3	of ⟨ev⟩ his
4–6	events ⟨be, as⟩ without . . . beget ⟨also⟩ a
29	too ⟨strong⟩ bold

Page 277

4	becomes, ⟨the⟩ his

Sermon XXXVI

Manuscript: Four sheets folded to make four pages each; folios nested and sewn with white thread through the center fold; pages measure 25 x 20.5 cm. A leaf (12 x 9.4 cm) is inserted between leaves 5 and 6.

Lines	*Page 278*
Bible Text	⟨Get wisdom, & with all thy gettings get understanding. Prov.⟩ ↑/ And, besides this, giving all diligence, add to your faith, virtue; & to virtue, knowledge. II Peter. I. 5./And it is not good yᵗ yᵉ soul be without knowledge Prov. 19. 2./↓ [Since the sermon was given twice, it is probable that the text from Peter pertains to the first delivery.]
9	it, ⟨&⟩ yet ⟨with proper human inconsistency the pulpit is silent.⟩ men
12–13	& ⟨nothing⟩ ↑it enjoins few things↓ . . . because because it
14–15	¶ But ⟨I have known⟩ ↑you may see↓ . . . pressed, ↑& men . . . gifts,↓
20–22	the ⟨precept⟩ ↑silence↓ . . . him, ⟨had the necessity of a painful progress from the elements of knowledge superseded by a miraculous influx of light into the soul.⟩ had
25	¶ ↑In . . . be ⟨obs⟩ remarked that↓ There
28	all. {e.g. There is no denunciation of suicide, ⟨there is no law to command "piety at home" except by a perversion of the obvious meaning of the verse in Tim.} Now s⟩Such

Page 279

3	infinitely ⟨noble⟩ ↑worthy↓.
5	to ⟨do⟩ ↑observe↓
7	↑& no . . . obligation↓.
19	duty ⟨flows⟩ is
22–25	distinct ⟨to fill up the soul with knowledge,⟩ to . . . ↑which . . . knowledge↓.
26–36	¶ {I am afraid ⟨we⟩ ↑that some minds↓ . . . ↑hereafter↓ . . . ↑when . . . done↓ . . . truth.} ¶ ⟨The ↑It is a⟩A further↓ . . . bound ⟨to⟩ to

↑every effort to↓ . . . minds, ⟨is,⟩ that

37–38   only ⟨half a dozen⟩ ideas . . . ↑strongly↓ to his faith ⟨with all his might⟩ does

Page 280

2–4   of ⟨learned⟩ ↑reflecting↓ . . . them ⟨atheists⟩ unbelievers, . . . ↑an unsubdued self love↓ . . . a ⟨healthy⟩ ↑sound↓ . . . the /morals/ principles/ [variant in pencil]

10–11   ↑"They . . . print"↓ [The paragraph that follows is in ink over an erased pencil draft; the only recoverable variation is in the last sentence:] I know that this statement . . . greatest worth.

14   community ⟨where⟩ ↑in which↓

16–17   ↑wherever↓ . . . ↑can be created, it↓

19–27   value. ¶ ⟨For these reasons⟩ ↑Therefore↓, brethren, ⟨I wish⟩ ↑I . . . Christ↓ . . . grown ⟨up⟩ ↑old↓ . . . anxious /desire/wishes/, [variant in pencil] . . . earnest ⟨recommendation⟩ ↑request↓, . . . not ⟨{augment his knowledge}⟩ grow

29–30   ↑Knowledge . . . meditation.↓

31–33   ↑In your mind↓ You . . . you; ⟨now⟩ ↑but↓ . . . ↑in power↓

34–35   all ⟨I ask of you⟩ ↑your part↓,

36–(281)8   open. ¶ ⟨My brethren, this subject {of the value of knowledge to every one of us is so full of matter that the difficulty lies in the choice of topics It} is an endless theme. I should gladly go with you into some considerations upon the nature of knowledge⟩ ¶ ↑{Insert A}↓ [On the following page, a passage marked "A":] ↑{Indeed . . . his ⟨stock of ideas⟩ knowledge, . . . office.}↓ ↑I . . . truth,↓

Page 281

11–12   by↑.↓ ⟨at present⟩ ↑Suffice . . . that ⟨every⟩ [cancellation in pencil] the . . . is /determined/increased/ [variant in pencil] . . . possesses.↓

18   & ⟨you⟩ it . . . {I am sure} . . . ↑virtuous↓

20   events ⟨sometimes⟩ ↑will . . . time↓

21–25   {The . . . observation, ⟨the⟩ your . . . confiden⟨ce⟩t . . . none.)} [The first part of this passage is inscribed over the following in pencil:] Most insignificant fact not without its own contribution

27–28   acquire. [Below this paragraph, centered on the page, is the word "Boston," and to the right are two short lines of ink inscription, heavily inked over and circumscribed in a cartouche; the last word of the first line may be "Adams"; the second line reads: "be a good girl?"] ¶ ⟨You say⟩ ↑But one says↓ . . . I ⟨see⟩ ↑know↓

30   do?— ↑Use . . . reach↓

31   be ⟨better shown⟩ ↑more . . . where↓

32   the ⟨tr⟩ communication

34   have ⟨succeed⟨ing⟩ed in ascertaining⟩ ↑disclosed↓

36   ↑You have↓ . . . facts ⟨recorded⟩ ↑collected & arranged↓

39–40   ↑on any one subject↓ . . . it ⟨took⟩ ↑cost↓

Page 282

1   feel ⟨the duty⟩ ↑your . . . matter↓

3–4   that ⟨sweetest of all⟩ ↑surpassing↓ pleasure⟨s⟩ . . . & ⟨I have⟩
              ↑there need be↓

4–9   it. ⟨I⟩ ↑Every . . . ²histories ⟨in⟩ ¹English ⟨those of Hume &
              Robertson⟩—then . . . ↑& of bad men↓ . . . Johnson, ⟨&⟩ of

10–14   ↑Then . . . ⟨it⟩for . . . well. Aquinas. Compare every ⟨thot⟩ sen-
              tence . . . thot.↓

[A stray leaf has been inserted in the manuscript at this point:]

If one young man of acuteness & independence should devote a few weeks or the
leisure of a few months to one of these questions—his opinion wd. ⟨be valuable⟩ have
great value as an original testimony to other young men of similar education, i.e. who
knew yᵗ he wd. look at yᵉ matter much as they would. It will be easily seen yᵗ if he did not
bring them to his own opinion the advantage wd. not be less.

If a society of twelve or twenty young men shd. conspire in such efforts, it is tho't a
very useful effect mt. result, to themselves & to many more than themselves. ↑Saturnals
of all yᵉ world when every man stands under yᵉ eaves of his own hat & sings what please
him↓ [in pencil except for the last sentence; followed by mathematical calculations
inscribed upside down in relation to the text]

17   I ⟨am anxious to press upon your⟩ ↑hope . . . your↓

18–21   & ⟨more⟩ ↑farther↓ . . . feel ⟨the⟩ how

3–24   first. ¶ ⟨↑Apart from the ↑actual↓ increase of our knowledge↓ The
              ⟨love of⟩ reading ↑of good books↓ has great uses.⟩ ↑To name one↓
              [addition in pencil; previous sentence canceled in pencil] It . . .
              tranquil ⟨pensive⟩ thoughtful

26   ↑sometimes↓

27   with your . . . head [underlined in pencil, with an "X" below on each
              of the two lines occupied by the passage]

30   {& you . . . freely,}

31–33   had ⟨you had⟩ ⟨snatched⟩ ↑taken↓ [the addition and the second
              cancellation are in pencil] . . . ↑the histories↓ . . . of ⟨Epaminondas⟩
              ↑Aristides Luther↓ or of Washington ⟨or of Wesley⟩ you

36–(283)4   about ⟨at⟩ to . . . ↑upon good . . . deaths,↓ . . . Providence. ¶ [The
              following paragraph was probably intended to replace the paragraph
              "Consider . . . write?" (which is scribbled over with the word
              "Boston") for the second delivery:] ↑{I ask of you nothing impractica-
              ble, I do not expect of men in active professions to emulate the
              attainments of those great wits who have barreled up knowledge
              month by ⟨f⟩month for seventy or eighty years of industrious,
              untiring, ever-grasping acquisition,—but do what you can.}↓ ¶
              ↑Consider brethren↓ In [addition in pencil] . . . whose ⟨time⟩ ↑life↓

Page 283

7–18   reading. ⟨L⟩ And . . . to ⟨the practice⟩ a . . . ↑of action & of study↓
              recorded ↑which . . . present↓. ⟨You may⟩ ⟨I do not see what⟩
              ↑Here↓ . . . England, ⟨should prevent⟩ where . . . merit ⟨of⟩ in . . .
              freely ⟨allowed⟩ recognized,— . . . ↑thriving↓

24-29 perfect ⟨&⟩ as . . . ask ⟨them⟩ ↑the labourer↓ . . . write?—
["Boston" is inscribed here in print-writing] ¶ ⟨But brethren what is
knowledge which thus earnestly we bid you seek? What is it but the
perception of the material & moral works of God? for He is in all
things & all exist by Him. To the mind therefore that is filled with his
love all things speak of Him. But if the mind is so disordered that it
does not discern him knowledge is but a tinkling cymbal. When then
you study history consider Let his presence go with you & all your
study shall be the exploring of your Fathers house. Enter⟩ ¶ Therefore
do I ⟨honour⟩ commend . . . by ⟨the⟩ ↑a↓ [Written over by this
sentence are a few stray words: "Siquidem," "Court," "Student,"
"Courtlin," and "Bybooks"]

30 ↑But . . . know"—Bp. Butler.↓

33 lose ⟨/in the present/Here is now a painful/ depression of trade
among us.⟩ ↑it all.↓

35 months & this

37 ruin. ⟨↑{Insert B}↓ [At the bottom of the page, a passage marked
"B":] {A fire like that mournful conflagration which has desolated one
of our cities and turned ⟨thousands⟩ ↑1500 persons↓ into the street,
↑for↓ whose wants your charity is today implored, some such accident
will fall upon you.↓⟩ Why

38 ↑of treasure↓

38-(284)8 ↑It . . . of↓ Paulinus ↑the wise↓ . . . ↑that having↓ lost all ⟨he had by
the sack of Nola⟩ ↑his ⟨property⟩ ↑effects↓ . . . Nola↓ . . . the↓ . . .
↑⟨of knowledge⟩↓ . . . ↑⟨of virtue⟩↓ . . . Montaigne⟩ ¶ ⟨But, brethren,
what is the knowledge which thus earnestly we bid you seek? What is
it but⟩ ↑There is one ⟨gr⟩ important . . . is the↓ the perception

Page 284

9-11 him. ²{↑But↓ To the mind ⟨therefore⟩ that . . . him.} ¹{⟨But i⟩ If . . .
not}

13 the ⟨obligations⟩ ↑generous nature↓

14-15 the ⟨fresh⟩ discovery

16 is ⟨thus⟩ ↑then↓

20-23 save ⟨from time⟩ ↑in . . . begun↓ ²{one. . . gain}, ¹{let . . . indul-
gences} . . . this ⟨barren⟩ domain ↑that lies barren↓ . . . add ⟨to⟩
one

[Following the end of the sermon, in pencil:] With ⟨om⟩ the omissions 26'

Sermon XXXVII

Manuscript A (earlier version): Four sheets folded to make four pages each and a single
leaf containing Insert "B" (verso), which is inserted between leaves 5 and 6 and included
in the sewing; folios nested and sewn with black thread and white thread along the left
margin; folio pages measure 25 x 20.5 cm and the single leaf measures 23.2 x 17 cm.
[The text of the earlier version follows:]
[Lengthwise along left margin of first page, in pencil:] Read to W.E.F, AF

XXXVII.

Our conversation is in heaven. Philippians III. 20.

↑{Insert A}↓ [Following the end of the sermon, on the last inscribed page, a passage marked "A":] ↑{In the passage from which the text is taken the Apostle speaks to the Philippians to this effect. There are many whose example you shd. not follow. There are many as I have told you often & now tell you weeping that are enemies of the Cross of Christ; whose end is the ruin of others; whose God is their belly; whose glory is in their shame; whose soul is in the earth. But we disciples of God's revelation we are citizens of heaven. We learn its language we obey its laws we do its will. Thence we expect our deliverer who when our time of leaving this ⟨world⟩ imperfect state shall come, will change this low bodily life of ours into a spiritual & glorious life like his own—}↓

We are all ⟨by the⟩ ↑in obedience to a law of our↓ nature ⟨of us⟩ seeking for heaven. The word was not new,— the idea was not new to man when Christ brot it from God. The germ of the good he revealed, lay before in the human breast. If no revelation had ever come, heaven would not the less be the desire of the soul. ↑For before it came↓ The reason of the wise ⟨pagan⟩ & the imagination of the ignorant had concurred in this,—to suggest the image of a purer existence from which hope excluded all that made this life painful. ↑Tho there was abundance of grossness in the vulgar view↓ The purer minds of every nation had framed to themselves much the same vision of the state of reward, a land of unmixed love, of unfaltering virtue, of unclouded ⟨perceptions.⟩ knowledge

But a ⟨yet⟩ ↑the↓ simple⟨r⟩st ⟨illustration⟩ ↑account↓ of this ⟨fact⟩ ↑belief↓ may be seen in the fact which is the ⟨foundation⟩ origin of all these glowing pictures ↑of future life that had been drawn—↓the simple hope on which these systems of hope are reared. *All men do here & now, from moment to moment, expect to better their condition.* Every one that is born of woman beareth about with him in every land in every time ⟨in disaster in disgrace ↑as well↓ in the extacy of success ↑as in yᵉ ashes of disaster & disgrace↓ in all companies⟩ ↑in all companies↓ in every degree of enlarged knowledge & growing virtue—⟨this⟩ ↑this desire wh. is the↓ element⟨ary⟩ ↑of the hope of↓ heaven this desire & expectation of something better in the next hour—in the next month—in the next year—in the next life. There is in human nature this onward-look, & let it grow as wise as it will, it cannot outgrow this hope You may reason with it you cannot reason it down. ⟨Boys⟩ ↑Children↓ hope, & men hope, & hoary heads hope. It cleaves to the soul as a part of itself; & so it is. ↑The mind is always looking forward.↓ And the next moment is the heaven of the present moment, ⟨&⟩as the next life is to be the heaven of this.

⟨Now t⟩The ↑first↓ fruit of this unquenchable desire of improvement is action, progress, ⟨insatiable hunger seeking for its food⟩

The constant expectation of something better than we have, produces a constant effort to obtain it, & hence the continual enlargement of our possessions & our powers. This is its action in each moment.

The next result of this principle ↑is its comprehensive view of the whole future,↓ is the ⟨view⟩ ↑theory↓ of *a better world*, which in every nation has prevailed & always deriv⟨ing⟩↑es↓ its colour & form from the character of the believer. The heaven of every /people/country has only been a mirror of /the earth/that country/ in which the disagreeable parts of life were left out, & the agreeable parts heightened. ⟨It⟩ ↑The idea of heaven of any people↓ is always simply a glorification of the state of society ↑that really exists↓ among them. In the books of the Greeks' & Romans we find their Elysium described. It was a refined, a well born, ↑a martial,↓ a rich, a selfish heaven, that filled their imaginations. The other world recognized the distinctions of this The Greeks believed in a wild & partial Providence which they called Destiny, which delighted to raise & sustain the prosperity of a single family, such as that of Pisistratus or the line of Cadmus (which was fabled to bear from generation to generation on the body of each infant of the race the mark of the head of a spear as the sign of command). This disdain of the general rights in the pampering of a few, this unfounded favouritism wh. they charged upon yᵉ Gods they transferred also to the other world. It was the spacious & pleasant domain of these lordly heroes where ↑they exercised themselves in warlike games↓ where the illustrious kings & sages & poets wandered at will in beautiful meadows, & drank nectar, & were associated with the gods.

but no place is there for the poor, for obscure virtue, for low born wisdom, for persecuted firmness, for the rags & scum of life nobly borne. There were no laurels for charity, no trumpet sang the praises of humility.

But that dream of the human mind departed—↑when↓ the f⟨ei⟩ierce savages of Asia /broke in upon Rome/overran the Roman empire/. They too had their mythology, they had a *warlike* heaven, a paradise of the strong,—a glorified gymnasium; & it is pitiful to see of what cheap materials their highest visions of happiness were composed. Fresh air, fine horses, robust health, & good game filled up to the brim all their conception of well-being. Yet even in this humiliating expectation is something more respectable than the notions of happiness that prevail in the East, the wretched schemes of the Turkish & Persian Perfection. They asked for nothing but the lowest pleasures of sense. They wd. make corruption & sensuality immortal. Away with the trumpet of war, away with the chase, with labour, with abstinence. To puff smoke with a pipe, ⟨for ages⟩—to dwell in a heaven of coffee of opium of ⟨hideous sensual ⟨love⟩⟩ debauchery ↑of beasts↓ was all they desired ↑of their maker↓—was the top of their ⟨godlike⟩ ↑miserable↓ ambition.

Alas, my brethren, I hardly know where we shd. go for a more melancholy picture of man than is found in these his famous dreams,—the dreams of ⟨na⟩ centuries & of mighty nations—of a future state. These are not occasional outbreaks of passion—not the momentary paroxysm that bereaves him of his reason, & produces falsehood or rapine ⟨or murder⟩, or adultery, or murder—no that could be borne in view of the compensation of all his virtues, & the elevation of his ordinary motives—⟨but⟩ ↑but these are the ordinary motives themselves↓ these are his grave & solemn hopes for the employment of all his powers during all his existence, these were his theories of the purpose for which the Almighty maker of the Universe had created & endowed him these were his ideas of the best things God could do for him. The most melancholy aspect of all is when we contemplate them in view of their inevitable effect upon the characters of the believers. Such a belief would act with a steady force to /pull down/ degrade/ the soul into the dust

But I must stop here to say that I do not believe that these gross superstitions ever possessed the weight they are supposed to have had in the Communities where they existed. History gives her accounts by the gross, & never stops to record the exceptions. Every man's experience furnishes him with grounds for believing that there is in every Country how ignorant or savage soever, a minority of scrupulous contemplative minds, who in every extreme of public madness retreat upon the eternal principles of ⟨common sense⟩ ↑truth↓ & never give in to the revolting superstitions of the vulgar bigot. And we know that many a pious mind among the ancients was uplifted by true conceptions of God & juster hopes.—

But these & such as these ⟨were⟩ ↑have been↓ the views of future happiness entertained by the bulk of mankind, and these views it pleased God to correct by the revelation of Christ. That opened another ⟨sort of⟩ heaven. It said to the astonished soul *The kingdom of God is within you.* Stop this mistaken career. ⟨What hast thou to do with⟩ ↑Is↓ wealth & carnal pleasure ↑thy chief good? behold,↓ thou are poor ⟨in⟩ with all thy treasures, thou art sorry in the midst of all thy delights. Outward things are thine instructors thy school & not thine home. Thou art made sufficient to thyself. Thy joy, & thy glory, & thy punishment, thy heaven, & thy hell are within thee. There is the heavenly host; there is the eye of God. The heaven thou seekest thou shalt not find. Eternal mansions streets of pearl & streams of amber, & trees of life & the music of innumerable harps praising God—these are but the types of outward imperfect representatives whereby to mortal ears the secrets of spiritual joy are faintly shadowed forth. Heaven is not a place, but a state of the mind. ²{Heaven is the well ordered, informed, benevolent, self devoted mind, when it adopts God's will for its own.} ¹{Hell is vice, the rebellion of the passions, the army of cares, & the sting of contrition.}

↑Whoever patiently↓ Consider↑s↓ what materials of happiness ⟨you⟩ ↑the already↓ possess↑es↓, ⟨& compare one with another the felicities you have already enjoyed Consider the faculties of the intellect & the unmixed & elevating satisfaction that always results from their exercise Consider the affections of the soul the purifying increasing / conquering/religious/ power of love⟩ ↑/ may satisfy himself that they are of an infinite nature & so if wisely used may produce infinite wellbeing/may satisfy himself that they are of an infinite nature, & so if wisely used may produce infinite well being. Let me suggest ⟨the⟩ three chief sources of happiness that are common to all men / ↓ [the variant occupies the recto of the leaf bearing "Insert B" on its verso (see below); the leaf is part of the sewn fascicle] Consider the power you have of acquiring knowledge, & the great delight that belongs to the exercise of the faculties of the intellect.

⟨Consider the moral sense

{I am sorry that all men cannot be expected to sympathize in a mention of the pleasures of study. A general attention ⟨When⟩of ["When" was on the page first, and is perhaps a false start of the next paragraph] all men of all professions to the cultivation of the mind is left for another age. But the future is full of hope for the present is full of progress.}⟩

When first the mind perceives a new & important truth when the intellect is quickened into rapid & powerful action it becomes conscious of a delight which disdains all other pleasures. In that hour the man wonders how the could ever have ⟨been won to⟩ ↑spent any leisure upon↓ meaner occupations. I have seen ⟨a⟩in a French writer a description of that period of excitement which every one who has much accustomed himself to the labour of thought will recognize. "On many occasions," says he "my soul seems to know more than it can say, & to be endowed with a mind by itself, far superior to the mind I really have." (Marivaux.) Every contemplative man can remember seasons in his life when by some happy conversation or ⟨lecture or⟩ ↑public discourse or private↓ study he had arrived at one of those general ideas which not only epitomize whole trains of tho't, but cast a flood of new light upon things inscrutable before. It seemed to him as if after waiting months in the vestibule of that inner temple he had picked up unawares the master key whose touch opens every door & the pleased adventurer goes on astonished from cell to cell from chamber to chamber gratified but overawed at the unexplored extent & opulence of his own possessions.

Now these may in some sort by steady effort be made habitual. All of us have minds.

Consider ⟨the effect of⟩ ↑how much enjoyment belongs to↓ the decisions of the moral sense. When you have bravely resisted an old temptation; when you have manfully given up ⟨your⟩ ↑a↓ pleasure that was dear to you, for duty that was dearer; when you have sacrificed yourself laboriously & wholly to a good cause; & feel that this day you have discharged your duty; & listen, in the silence of the passions, to the ↑incorruptible↓ praise of your own tho'ts, with the conviction that ⟨those praises are echoed back clear & musical by the walls of Heaven that⟩ you have endeared yourself to God, that you are ↑recognized↓ a good citizen of his creation, & have caused many to rejoice & not one to regret your existence—will no serenity smooth your brow? will no new joy light your eye? Will the the meditations of that day be as the meditations of a day of sin?

Consider the power of the affections. ⟨You have seen them trampled upon & depraved.⟩ Have you a friend Have you a husband? a wife? Have you a child Have you a parent? ⟨Then you have the means of a transcendant joy in your own hands. You have seen these powers trampled upon & depraved You have come out of a brawling house You have seen how wounded love can poison life You have⟩ ↑{Insert B}↓ [On the previous page, a passage marked "B":] ⟨↑{You have escaped from the suffering of his porcupine humour—when you have joined the hands of a pure friendship & have done what you could to cultivate these holy}⟩ I need not then enlarge upon the unmeasured enjoyment God has connected with the indulgence of these ⟨affections⟩ ↑powers↓. For there is that in every heart will vibrate to these simple names. The goodness of God is not known the powers of the human mind are not known until these deep & holy affections have kindled their fire therein, ⟨this beautiful relation⟩ ↑What work of God is so beautiful as this fellowship he has established among his creatures this mutual relation— ↓ of man to man. We speak & are understood heart to heart, & find our attachments strengthened precisely in proportion to the measure of virtue ⟨↑We know in our own souls that those attachments are immortal↓⟩ & so are drawn onward to the reverence & love of God by admiring his perfections as they are partially revealed to us here.

⟨And in ↑But all of us have hearts; all have kindred either of friendship or of blood.⟩ But neither is this pleasure perfect until—↓ that consecration of the affections ↑is made↓ when the soul has learned to love God supremely, to regard all things here only as the manifestations of his love to it & so becomes reconciled to adversity & finds a pleasure in the darkest events because in them Gods will is done.

But these felicities are open to all. We all have minds, we all have a conscience, we all have hearts, & God is the Father of us all.— [This sentence is in ink over the same in erased pencil.]

Brethren, I wish to represent to you the heaven of common life I wish you to feel that the materials of a felicity wh. no man attains are yet cheap. I wish it to be felt that in the low damp unclean chamber of an almshouse, a joy may shine that is a stranger to houses of granite & marble. Have you dispositions that can be cultivated? Have you a mind that can be trained Have you books that you can read? Have you friends that you can love? Have you a fellow being that you can benefit? Have you knowledge of God? then Heaven is ²{around you} is ¹{before you} & when you will you may cross its threshold & enter the everlasting doors. ↓[End of Insert "B"]

⟨Now brethren,⟩ ↑For↓ since such is the heaven we are to look ⟨for⟩ it immediately becomes evident that it is not postponed that its enjoyments do not depend upon remote contingences, upon great changes that may take place in the Universe ⟨but that⟩ upon life or death but that it may be entered now, that the gates of the Paradise of God stand open night & day

Why do you wait? Do you wish to be happy hereafter thirty or forty years hence? Why do you put a value upon happiness then, & neglect the present hour. Five minutes of this day are as much a part of my being & the enjoyment of ⟨them⟩ that space of time as important to me surely, as the enjoyment of five minutes of million of years hence.

But says the voluptuary I also say the same thing & because present pleasure is as good as future pleasure & more good in as far as it is more secure—it is unwise to practise the ↑self↓ denial that religion commands The answer to this cavil is plain. Whilst the enjoyment of the present is valuable to me, so is the enjoyment of the future. I will therefore choose such pleasures now, as shall not prejudice my happiness hereafter. I find there are such pleasures. Upon trial I find them of a more exquisite relish than any others that they throw contempt on all others. ⟨Precisel⟩ I find a wonderful difference between their *end* & the end of others. I find the pleasures of sense change their character the moment they are past, & appear to me flat & foolish when they are no worse. But these have no base conclusion, no deformed old age. These pleasures are not dead. They live & add to the amount of my happiness after they are acted. They are medicines, & solaces, & motives.

⟨Therefore⟩ brethren I do not undervalue the scene that revelation has promised to good men when this life closes, because, I believe you may anticipate its bliss. I believe a magnificent scene shall open upon the soul equal to its enlarged powers. The body is here a constant obstruction to the energies of the mind. Its obstructions, its temptations, its diseases shall cease. If the mind can ↑only↓ act then with as much freedom as we can imagine, the progress will be immense.

But I believe its good then will be of the same nature as its good now

It is not ⟨so much⟩ that I wish to lower your views of the future, as to exalt your views of what may be done in the present I would to God I might awaken the ⟨torpid⟩ attention of every ⟨one who hears me,⟩ ↑torpid soul↓ till ⟨his⟩he had measured with his eye the full extent of his capacity, till he saw how glorious this low life we lead, might be made; till he saw how much knowledge the patient use of every moment mt. accumulate; till he saw to what colossal proportions of wisdom that knowledge wd swell the soul; till he saw to what miraculous strength the soul mt. attain by unceasing efforts after self-command; till he conceived the enthusiasm of the affections, & the majesty of truth; till he apprehended the intimate connexion that may ⟨cons⟩ subsist between himself & God; till his own soul beats pulse for pulse in harmony with the universal whole, & by assimilating to the character does enjoy the beatitude⟨s⟩ of the Divinity Whoso can carry out these views to /the/a/ just extent will find there is heaven enough in man to satisfy the sublimest hopes; that there is nothing injurious to our ⟨hopes⟩ ↑expectations↓ in the [written over the following in pencil: "that there is nothing injurious to us in"] doctrine that our richest enjoyments are already ripe, ⟨will find matter of sweet & strong encouragement⟩ for follow them as far as we can they are infinite & reach beyond.

Therefore my brethren let our conversation be in heaven Now while yet these pleasures are in our power, now while yet the accepted time is here, that when ⟨the hour of⟩ [canceled in pencil and ink] death arrives ↑to us which is every day bereaving us of our friends↓ we may already have made proficiency in the language, & the spirit, & the customs of the spiritual ⟨world⟩ country, to which God hath called us.

    Chardon Street   29'
    May 23, 1829.

Manuscript (revised version): Five sheets folded to make four pages each; folios stacked and sewn with white thread along the left margin; pages measure 25 x 21.5 cm.

Lines	Page 285
13	hope ⟨had been⟩ are

	Page 286
7	every ⟨people⟩ ↑country↓
15	Cadmus ⟨⟨which was fabled to bear from generation to generation on the body of each infant of the race the mark of the head of a spear as the sign of command.⟩⟩ This
32	perfection. ⟨They asked for⟩ These
36	of ⟨coffee⟩ opium,

	Page 287
5	of ⟨what⟩ the
23	*you.* [Close quotes are supplied here at the end of a direct quotation from the Bible, but Emerson's actual intention is obscure.]
42	belongs to to the

	Page 288
5	of ⟨a⟩ ↑that↓
24	conviction ⟨that ⟨you⟩ those praises are echoed back in sweet music by the walls of heaven,⟩ that
37	attachments ⟨str⟩ knit

	Page 289
1	love ⟨for⟩ ↑to↓
14	to ⟨seek⟩ look
34	to ⟨m⟩the

	Page 290
4	God ⟨that⟩ I

Sermon XXXVIII

Manuscript: Five sheets folded to make four pages each; folios stacked and sewn with white thread along the left margin; pages measure 25.2 x 20.5 cm. A leaf (13 x 12.5 cm) containing Insert "A" is tipped with red sealing wax to the verso of leaf 3.

Lines	Page 291
Bible Text	["Matt. V. 48" over "Matt V Chap" in pencil]
1–2	¶ ⟨It seems to be generally agreed that there is a great deal ⟨that is⟩ of

folly & of wickedness in the world⟩ Th⟨is⟩e . . . evil ⟨th⟩ excites
. . . re⟨leive⟩↑move↓

4–6 despondency ⟨that when⟩ ↑because after↓ . . . as /mighty/strong/

7 poisonous ⟨stench⟩ ↑vapor↓ [emendation in ink over pencil]

8–10 lost, ⟨sin⟩for . . . interest ⟨lies in⟩ ⟨is that it⟩ ↑is . . . &↓ menaces
⟨death to us & ours⟩ ↑our . . . of yᵉ ⟨world⟩ ↑human family↓↓.

10–11 remedies? ¶ ⟨It⟩ ↑The fault↓ . . . ↑in↓ . . . regard ⟨the⟩ virtue

16 ↑too delicately &↓ too much. ⟨& too daintily.⟩ The

18 ↑very↓

20–22 ↑as . . . community↓ . . . ↑twenty years hence↓ . . . ↑misery↓

22–24 the ⟨Mis⟩ *Bible* . . . his ⟨house⟩ ↑conversation↓

27 benevolent ⟨institutions⟩ efforts [space] & when

Page 292

4–11 the ⟨whole sentiment to⟩ ↑sin on↓ . . . to ⟨ask⟩ ↑fix↓ . . . purpose.
⟨I complain ↑It is to be regretted↓⟩ ↑Is it not true↓ . . . ↑using↓ it? ⟨I
complain⟩ ↑Is it not true↓ that we live, ⟨⟨if the⟩ ↑to use the vulgar↓
expression ⟨be allowed me⟩⟩ from . . . not by ⟨liberal & enlightened
calculation⟩ ↑foresight.↓ We do not ⟨live by plan⟩ ↑move by system↓
. . . chance. ⟨We are not in⟩ ↑It . . . from↓ . . . ↑that we are↓ . . .
who ⟨have received⟩ ↑are offered↓ . . . spiritual ⟨store⟩ ↑benefit↓

13–16 ↑You . . . reason?↓

18 within. ⟨I am ⟨apt⟩ ↑prone↓ to think⟩ ↑Is it not true↓

19–20 ↑They . . . delinquency↓

20 very ⟨ones⟩ ↑persons↓

22–24 standard ⟨to save trouble &c⟩ that ⟨g⟩ inconvenient . . . them; ⟨as I
have known in a college a ridiculous agreement among the leaders of a
class that none shd. attempt in recitations ⟨aught⟩ ↑anything↓ [last
emendation in pencil] beyond a certain standard of merit.⟩ ¶ Men
. . . with ⟨a⟩ ↑the↓ . . . of ⟨knowledge⟩ ↑truth↓

27 which ⟨reason⟩ ↑the satire↓

31 ↑proper↓

32 the ⟨lump⟩ ↑aggregate↓,

34 ↑apart↓

37 & ⟨no⟩ ↑in . . . the↓

38–41 Society—⟨though tis nothing as before⟩ ↑though the characters ⟨the
persons⟩ are . . . before↓ but a great ⟨number of⟩ ↑many↓ . . . is
⟨dazzled⟩ ↑vanquished↓, & the reason /overcome/prostrated/.

44-(293)3 that ⟨all the⟩ ↑a thousand↓ . . . religion, ⟨&⟩ in . . . ↑& in
education↓ . . . ⟨u⟩Use."

Page 293

5–6 yoke, ⟨to disencumber you from this thralldom to society, these⟩
↑divorce . . . these↓ . . . others, ⟨this dependence,⟩ &

7–8 in ⟨the universe ↑this creation↓⟩ ↑universe↓

9–11 fellowship. ⟨It⟩ ↑The gospel↓ . . . the ⟨Universe⟩ ↑creation↓

13 from ⟨these foolish⟩ ↑this poor↓ shuffling⟨s & dodgings⟩ to shift
⟨the⟩ ↑your↓

14   moral / agent / ⟨god⟩ / [variant (or stray word) in pencil and canceled
            in pencil]

15-18   the ⟨situation⟩ ↑times,↓ . . . ↑compound↓ regard to ⟨every one of⟩
            ↑all↓

18   Koran ⟨or of the Talmud⟩ must

21-31   great ⟨property⟩ ↑operation↓ . . . classes ⟨& distinctions⟩ ↑but
            individuals↓ . . . ↑to kings, or↓ . . . ↑to the old or to the young↓ . . .
            ↑not↓ . . . class ⟨no servant⟩ inferior . . . being. ⟨And as ⟨its⟩ ↑the↓
            servant ↑of the gospel↓ I would speak to you in its spirit⟩ ↑It
            addresses itself↓ . . . shelter ⟨& hide⟩ ↑or withdraw↓ ↑{Insert A}↓
            [On a slip of paper attached with red sealing wax to the previous
            page, a passage marked "A":] ↑It calls upon ⟨you in the name of
            Christ to⟩ every. . . action. ⟨I call upon you⟩ to . . . you ⟨&⟩ which
            / sentiment / yᵉ divine w⟨d⟩ord in/ [variant in pencil] . . . ↑for
            yrself,↓ . . . God, ⟨to strive after perfection ⟨c⟩to carry out every
            faculty & every affection to its noblest end, ⟨in obedi⟩ as Christ
            enjoins, as the voice of God within you commands.⟩
                ⟨↑regard to consequences
            regard Hard to act with↓⟩↓ [last two lines in pencil and canceled in
            pencil] ¶ I↑t↓ ⟨say⟩ ↑declares↓

            [The following passage occurs on the verso of the slip containing
            Insert "A"; two words are obscured by sealing wax:] ⟨↑I dont speak
            to gentlemen nor to heads of families↓ [Ther]e is no middle interest
            no lower classes [no] inferior no servant in this republic of moral
            being. You are capable. In you lies the infinite world only rouse your
            attention consider the result of action as well as action & propose to
            yourself when you are going to do a sacrifice not the praise of your
            wife or your brother or the obscurest wretch but the virtue itself. Be
            content to notice your own superiority in knowledge or manners with
            gratitude to God without calling the notice of others or permitting
            yourself to wish for the observation of it by others, for the moment
            you do you descend & fear not
                Hard to act from dist mot.⟩

33   ↑of↓ more ⟨respectable⟩ ↑value↓ . . . more ⟨respectable⟩ ↑excellent↓

34-37   Nay ⟨it is more than this⟩ ↑this . . . truth↓, . . . & ⟨forgets⟩
            ↑forgoes↓ . . . can, ⟨↑the↓ paltering ⟨wretch⟩ ↑sinner↓, it does what
            it can,⟩ to

38-39   enjoy. ⟨↑It is spiritual suicide.⟩ It ⟨treads with swinish foot on
            omnipotent gifts⟩ ↑holds . . . God;↓ ↑It is spiritual suicide.↓,

42   are ⟨summoned⟩ ↑called↓

                            Page 294

2   then⟨—henceforth & forever forbear⟩ this ⟨grovelling⟩
            ↑treacherous↓

5-9   ↑Read . . . w. to yrself.↓ And ⟨do not⟩ sleep out ⟨your life⟩ ↑no more
            time↓ in ⟨this moral lethargy⟩ ↑a stationary religion↓. ⟨↑Christ says
            to your paralyzed soul as he said to the palsied Jew↓ Take up thy bed

	& walk. /Rouse/Wake/ your ↑drowsy↓ attention⟩ ↑Wake↓ to the ⟨perception⟩ ↑truth↓ that no ⟨passage⟩ ↑moment↓ of your life is ⟨indifferent or⟩ without consequences↑, . . . day.↓. ⟨Consider the *result* of action as well as action, & in doing right set⟩ ↑Set↓ your eye ↑in . . . action↓
10–12	↑do not↓ . . . yourself ⟨not the⟩ *praise*, . . . private, ⟨do⟩ not . . . or ↑of↓
13	of ⟨conduct⟩ ↑character↓
14–16	highest /motive/one/. ⟨And in each moment ⟨let⟩ ↑have↓ the ↑great↓ ambition ⟨be⟩ to do as well as you ⟨are capable of doing⟩ ↑can↓.⟩ ¶ It . . . notice↑, on any occasion,↓
21–23	deed ⟨misses⟩ ↑escapes↓ . . . ↑loses↓ . . . it ⟨blesses⟩ ↑benefits↓, fear not ⟨that it is lost, or⟩ that
24–26	action↑, whatever . . . do,↓ . . . the ⟨actor⟩ ↑doer↓, . . . increased ⟨regard⟩ ↑esteem↓ . . . augmented ⟨powers⟩ ↑vigor↓
27	long ⟨rule⟩ ↑govern↓
29	appear⟨,⟩
30–31	inmate. ⟨↑The↓⟩ Love . . . ↑the↓
32	should the /promise/declaration/
35–37	↑Wherever . . . the ⟨shop⟩ parlor shop ⟨senate⟩ ↑court house↓ . . . attained.↓
37	the ⟨/dinner table/family board/⟩ ↑family board↓

Page 295

2–4	↑with . . . strive↓; . . . companions ⟨of⟩ ↑with . . . pass↓ . . . your ⟨moral powers⟩ ↑self command↓,
6–8	watch ⟨of⟩ over . . . carry ⟨out⟩ into ⟨action⟩ ↑execution↓ the ⟨farthest dictates⟩ ↑faintest whispers↓
10–11	the⟨se⟩ great heights ↑of perfect obedience↓ which ⟨we show you⟩ ↑as . . . are↓ within your reach ⟨& therefore⟩ ↑are↓
16–17	other. ⟨/I hate the separation/I do not ⟨understand⟩ ↑consent↓ [emendation in pencil] the distinction/⟩ ↑When . . . distinction↓
19–27	↑By↓ Every . . . practise ⟨you⟩ *in* . . . ↑but for virtue's sake↓ . . . him; ⟨&⟩ ↑so also↓ . . . /perform your duties/practise the virtues/. [variant in pencil, though the final "s" is repaired in ink] ¶ ↑Finally,↓ Let it cheer you ⟨also⟩ in . . . now ⟨so vainly⟩ essaying ↑with such feeble success.↓ For ⟨in⟩ ↑when . . . at↓
28	↑That . . . others.↓
30	the ⟨individual⟩ virtue

[Following the end of the sermon are these notations:]
Si vis me flere flendum est

730

I love the golden day
I love the starry night
The one is grand & gay
The other hath its own delight

Each hath its own delight
God hath made nothing poor
Every sense is a treasury door
And all the world is running o'er
Into the infinite universe

Sermon XXXIX

Manuscript: Four sheets folded to make four pages each; folios nested and sewn with white thread along the left margin; pages measure 25 x 20.5 cm.

Lines	
	Page 296
1	this ⟨beautiful⟩ ↑/grateful/⟨fine⟩/↓ ["grateful" in ink over pencil; "fine" added and canceled in pencil]. . . the ⟨manifest⟩ beauty ⟨& glory⟩ of
2–4	The ⟨greediest⟩ ↑most devoted↓ [addition in ink over pencil] . . . blossoms ⟨is⟩ [cancellation in pencil] ↑shows↓
8–9	dusty ⟨w⟩ corners they /do not see the/only get/
19–20	th⟨ese⟩is . . . God. ⟨They see him in the small leaf in the wide meadow in the sea & the cloud⟩ ¶ We
24–25	loaf ⟨to the harvest nor the loaf to the harvest⟩ ↑in . . . the ⟨roasted flesh⟩ ↑meats↓ that smoke⟨s⟩ on . . . to↓
25–(297)1	the ⟨glorious⟩ changes
	Page 297
10	and ⟨mighty⟩ ↑boundless↓.
11–16	goodness, ⟨ever consulting his own advantage & never [word illegible] over the defeat of his own petty purpose↑.↓ [addition in pencil] If he have a little scheme afoot that a rain or a frost defeats he quarrels with the order of the year ↑& almost always is he ⟨care⟩ heedless of its evidences↓ Let us lift up our eyes ⟨wit⟩ to a more generous & thankful view of the world [one or two words illegible] & its revolving Seasons Why shd. men ever repine at the order of the year? the seasons in their round ↑Do they not come from heaven↓⟩ ["Do . . . heaven" added in pencil] ↑thinks . . . order ⟨af⟩ happens . . . Seasons.↓
17–34	{Do . . . ↑wh.↓ . . . con⟨s⟩verting . . . & ⟨with irresistible charity⟩ ⟨commanding⟩ ↑drawing↓ . . . not /disguise/conceal/ [variant in pencil] . . . men⟨}⟩ . . . ↑skill↓ [addition in ink over pencil]. . . God.}
37–39	art ⟨in⟩ ↑goes to↓ . . . ↑straw↓berry . . . reared, ↑In . . . o⟨n⟩f . . . is↓
40–41	↑formed &↓ . . . these ⟨delicate⟩ ↑minute↓
42–43	¶ Our ⟨arrogant⟩ ↑patient↓ [emendation in ink over pencil] . . . microscop⟨ic⟩es ⟨eye⟩ upon . . . ↑in the stem↓
	Page 298
1–11	{Where . . . ↑With all our botany↓ How . . . covers ⟨↑thousands of↓⟩ acres . . . process⟨}⟩ . . . ↑on↓ . . . globe.}

12–29	¶ {Go . . . period, ⟨account for it in any way⟩ ↑make . . . can↓, . . . gravel, ⟨manure⟩ [cancellation in pencil] it . . . we ⟨murmur & moan⟩ ↑indulge . . . temper↓ [added over "permit our querulous" in pencil] . . . colour. ⟨It seems to me it wd. be better if we abstained from repining at the East wind, as if it were not an instrument of mercy.⟩ Man . . . ↑the . . . soils↓ ²{forgot . . . him} ¹{& the . . . hardened ⟨&⟩ ↑or↓ moistened by th⟨at⟩e ·rough ⟨vapour⟩ ↑weather↓} . . . him.}
33	stomac⟨k⟩h,
34–37	vegetable ⟨is⟩may . . . ↑by↓ . . . & ⟨luscious⟩ ↑delicious↓ [emendation in ink over pencil]
40	↑particles of↓

Page 299

1	& ⟨with what⟩ ↑to such↓
4	↑the oak↓
7–10	& the East . . . islands. [Written over the following in pencil:] & the East with spices—& the mulberries for silkworms. Orange fig bloom in the Mediterranean islands & the Cotton plant ↑bursting its pod↓ clothes us from the warm South
11	↑as well↓
15	its /embroidered/crimson/ . . . their /colour & form/embroidery/? [variants in pencil]
19–20	↑It . . . bright↓ [addition in pencil]
21–22	↑to be seen↓ . . . is ⟨a⟩ more ⟨language⟩ ↑to be heard↓
34–35	↑as the . . . so is↓ . . . moral ⟨is i⟩as
36	the ⟨Seasons⟩ ↑great . . . nature↓

Page 300

12	↑Are . . . they?↓
13–15	↑shall we↓ who . . . shall ⟨we stand⟩ ↑the flower of the field↓ reprove⟨d⟩

[On the page following the end of the sermon:]
⟨Mem.⟩
Addenda. All students of natural science simple & amiable men; not petulant like men of letters. Effect of some facts upon the mind—as the angles of the cell of a beehive

Sermon XL

Manuscript: Four sheets folded to make four pages each; folios nested and sewn with white thread along the left margin; pages measure 25 x 20.5 cm.

Lines	*Page 301*
Bible Text	⟨To do good & communicate forget not⟩ ¶ And
5	↑but briefly↓
8–9	transactions . . . protection, [centered above the line: "courtesy"]
11–14	↑on merchandize↓ . . . purchase ⟨a⟩ real . . . cd. ⟨ill want⟩ ↑not do

without↓ . . . ↑them↓ as if they ⟨cheated⟩ ↑had been dishonest↓ [the last emendation is in pencil]

17   his ⟨performance⟩ duty of ↑not . . . but↓

22–24   ↑very little↓ ⟨un⟩specific . . . ↑to do↓ . . . ↑the obligation is↓ [emendations in pencil]

26   not ⟨ask⟩ enjoin the giving / an acre of land / a farm /

Page 302

3–4   ↑He . . . rich,↓ Be
7   the ⟨report⟩ ↑account↓
10   the ⟨time⟩ ↑moment↓
15–16   ↑For . . . mite↓
22   in ⟨this insulated⟩ ↑the solitary↓
40–(303)1   square.' ↑And . . . detail↓

Page 303

3–4   ↑of thinking↓ . . . loving ⟨of thinking⟩? Have
5   blessings⟨,⟩ ↑for . . . God↓
8   suffering.—↑Aye,↓ But
12–14   fault.—↑But . . . chastisements↓
21   ↑goes on↓
24–25   to ⟨yo⟩ the . . . ↑dull &↓
28–30   ¶ ↑{My brethren . . . th⟨is⟩e . . . teaches—↓It . . . love that
36–37   while ⟨its ornaments⟩ ↑the . . . grace↓
38–(304)1   honoured ⟨felt to be⟩ contributors . . . ↑every . . . project↓ . . . ↑unerring↓ . . . swift ⟨to set in action the means⟩ ↑& . . . work↓

Page 304

3–7   have ⟨paid⟩ ↑uttered↓ . . . ↑of respect↓ . . . ↑& . . . pecul. force↓ . . . ↑only . . . knoweth↓.
8   heart, ⟨the evening thots of⟩ that
9–10   ↑It . . . maker.↓
13–19   increase. ¶ ⟨It is now two years since any public Report has been read to you of the doings of the Evangelical Treasury.⟩ ↑But . . . remarks.↓ ⟨As⟩As ⟨it seems⟩ ↑↑the instit denom.↓ The Evang. Treasury↓ . . . and ⟨as it⟩ has . . . this / ↑religious↓ Society / ⟨parish⟩ / ⟨seeking no aid beyond our parish boundaries⟩ it . . . that ⟨the⟩ you . . . desired ⟨but failed⟩ to do↑.↓ ⟨from want of means. I may mention the circumstance a⟩As . . . ↑I may mention↓ the Evang. Treas.
19–27   we ⟨teach⟩ are . . . benev. ⟨assoc⟩ instit. . . . ↑other benev.↓ . . . it. ⟨They⟩ ↑Each member↓ subscribed ⟨each⟩ one . . . ↑it was agreed to↓ collect⟨ed a⟩ ↑an annual↓ contribution ⟨in June⟩ Not . . . ↑I believe↓
29–30   to ⟨the⟩ a . . . Pastor ⟨was⟩ ↑has been↓
34–37   Library. ⟨The o⟩Other . . . Evang Miss. Soc.; ⟨to the society of Christians in N. Y.;⟩ & to the ⟨purpose of the free religious⟩ instruction . . . city⟨.⟩, ↑& to other claims appearing to have the

same commanding importance.↓ ¶ ↑On . . . the ⟨sickness⟩ ↑absence↓ of the Pastor the last ⟨year⟩ ↑June↓↓ It

39   About ⟨three $377.00⟩ ↑$350.00↓

Page 305

1   ↑city of↓

12–16   share. ⟨It is a charity we owe ourselves to keep the greatest number of books in circulation to our own houses that we can.⟩ ↑This . . . another.↓

17–18   ↑& particularly those↓ in our ↑town↓ . . . the ⟨particular⟩ attention

18–19   to ⟨inquire⟩ ↑find out↓ . . . these ⟨crying⟩ ↑unhappy↓ suffer-⟨ings⟩ers.

22–25   magnificence ⟨who never share it who never see this⟩ ↑that . . . suffering↓ . . . ↑demands↓

26–28   ↑very↓ limited but ↑as it is believed↓ . . . cases↑,↓ [comma in pencil] by sending ⟨wood⟩ ↑fuel↓, [emendation in pencil] . . . rent &—

29–37 $85.17. [end of page] [Heading:] The Free Religious instruction of the poor. ¶ ⟨Fifty dollars have been expended by the Directors to aid in erecting the Chapel in Friend St. And now a new application has been made from the friends of th⟨at⟩ese efforts because the⟩ ↑It is . . . that ⟨four thousand families or at least⟩ between . . . ↑Anxious↓ [addition in pencil] The . . . to the ⟨purpose of building⟩ ↑aid in erecting↓ . . . And ⟨n⟩at . . . incidental expenses↓

38–39   b⟨r⟩efore you ↑our . . . objects.↓ . . . I ⟨ask you with all my heart⟩ ↑heartily beg you↓

41   beyond ⟨reason⟩ ↑its merits↓.

44   congregation / who ⟨find it difficult⟩ ↑are compelled to strain ⟨with⟩ all their means↓ / who need charity themselves / to ⟨pay⟩ ↑meet↓ their ↑town↓ just ⟨debts.⟩ ↑obligations.↓ [The first two cancellations are in pencil and ink.]

Page 306

1–2   ↑You . . . charitable.↓

7–9   ↑health . . . mind↓ . . . ↑spiritual gifts↓ . . . ↑have been given↓

12–17   I think . . . but↓ It is not ↑so much↓ this / instance / particular claim / [variant in pencil] . . . be ⟨overleaped⟩ ↑accustomed . . . way↓ ↑yᵗ . . . rich↓ [last addition in pencil] . . . expand. ↑to . . . benevolence.↓

21   out. ↑or you are lost.↓ . . . come ⟨to you & to me⟩ when

23   memory. ⟨Need I remind you of that ancient Christian sentiment that Alms never impoverish "The poor" said the illustrious ↑physician↓ Boerhaave ↑"I have always found the poor↓ are my best patients for God Almighty is their paymaster;" and⟩ it [cf. JMN 6:66]

24   man "⟨w⟩What

25–26   all. ↑the . . . hand.↓

27–28   buy—⟨Yet by their sacrifice⟩ can . . . ↑hold . . . hands↓

33   of ⟨cold⟩ water,

Sermon XLI

Manuscript: Four sheets folded to make four pages each; folios nested and sewn with white thread through the center fold; pages measure 25 x 20.5 cm. An additional folio (pp. 2-4 blank) inserted between leaves 3 and 4 is not included in the sewing.

[Above the Bible text:] The sting of death is sin x x but thanks be to God who giveth us the victory thro' our Lord Jesus Christ I Cor 15.—56 57 [in pencil]

Lines	*Page 307*
Bible Text	I ⟨pass⟩ ↑walk↓
2-3	a ⟨congregation⟩ ↑house↓ [emendation in pencil]
6-9	but ⟨true⟩ [cancellation in pencil] ↑living↓ . . . ours↑;↓ . . . it↑;↓ [semicolons added in pencil]
10-11	↑a church are found in↓ . . . assembly↑;↓ ⟨are found in a church,⟩ but
16-17	↑puts down↓ . . . distinctions ⟨shrink away into⟩ ↑into the rank of↓ trifles ⟨before them.⟩. In
18	be ⟨pagans⟩ ↑infidels↓
23	of ⟨and⟩ divine
24-26	man. ⟨And I like to⟩ ↑Here . . . help↓ apply↑ing↓ . . . where ⟨usually⟩ are ↑commonly↓

	Page 308
6	here↑,↓ [addition in pencil]
16-17	↑among . . . behold↓ . . . some ⟨one⟩—who
41-42	↑the . . . form↓ . . . that↑,↓ [comma added in pencil]
43-(309)1	↑porches of the↓ . . . the ⟨voice⟩ sound

	Page 309
2	↑In some of us↓ At
7-11	↑if death . . . things↓ . . . knells. ⟨This is the way in which preachers have discoursed on death—this the train⟩ ↑Yet . . . train↓
15-18	that ⟨ugly⟩ ↑frigid↓ . . . the ⟨freezing⟩ ↑sad↓ . . . ↑that have been↓
19-20	shrouded. ¶ ⟨To⟩ ↑This . . . to↓ many
21-25	force. ⟨⟨They⟩ I . . . song.⟩ [The cancellation is rejected as a late emendation. The substituted text (given below) occurs on a full sized sheet folded to make four pages, of which pp. 2-4 are blank; the folio is not included in the sewing:]

↑It is said that these are unsuitable to our faith, that they only speak half the truth, that they hide the great fact which being known makes them of no account—the immortality of man

I am aware that these do speak only to a part of mankind or rather to a part ⟨of⟩ of every man's nature. The worm without has sympathy with the worm within; ↑terrors of flesh with the functions of flesh↓ the spirit within contemns it. There are persons to whom the prospect of being disinterred is gloomy & terrible, ⟨to⟩ ↑others↓ who fear to lie in the grave as if what makes a person cd lie in a grave.

Be it so. We will then speak of these terrors to the body ⟨in its⟩

when it grows wanton ⟨to the skeptic when⟩ ↑to↓ the rioter in his cups ↑to the unbeliever when he blasphemes↓ but we will not forget the Christian in us, we will not insult the emancipated soul with childish scarecrows. We will consent to the voice of Reason & of Revelation and ⟨to⟩ not put clogs in the way of our own improvement

Come up now therefore to that higher platform whereon Jesus Christ has placed us↓

27–29 If / these views ⟨are false⟩ / we have got above these ⟨terrors⟩ / let us adopt ⟨the true.⟩ ↑those . . . state↓ ¶ ⟨Is it not then⟩ ↑Let us own that ⟨it is⟩ after . . . be↓

32 of ⟨a false education⟩ ↑our own sinfulness↓?

Page 310

3 part ⟨i⟩which
5–6 ↑He percieves . . . mind↓
16–18 ↑Well . . . dark ⟨inexorable⟩ which . . . them.↓
22 desireable
31 of ⟨its⟩ that
33 who⟨m⟩
35 man ⟨lives in Europe⟩ is

Page 311

4 ↑vivid↓
8 hath ⟨/ shown in an event / so faithfully related that it is / almost as clear to us as to those wh witnessed it⟩ taught
13 ↑& rule us↓ . . . them ⟨here⟩ ↑now↓
16 ↑these downcast eyes↓ these ⟨black cloths⟩ ↑sable weeds↓
17–19 ↑bless him↓ . . . cannot, ↑die↓ & ⟨strain⟩ ↑open↓ . . . ready ⟨for a peace this world cannot give,⟩ when

Sermon XLII

Manuscript: Four sheets folded to make four pages each; folios nested and sewn with white thread through the center fold; pages measure 25 x 20.5 cm.

Lines   *Page 312*
1–2 ¶ ↑It . . . respects.↓ Fifty ⟨four⟩three ↑prosperous↓
3–6 ↑The . . . ceased.↓ . . . ↑And . . . that ⟨is⟩ ↑the . . . as↓ the . . . Christianity.↓
9–17 imbecile ⟨infant⟩ child . . . ↑the . . . Bengal↓ [addition in pencil]. . . ↑idol-↓chariot . . . [The word "carnival" appears above "nations."] . . . are the / records / monuments / [variant in pencil]. . . outspeak ⟨the hiss⟩ in . . . ↑the . . . contempt↓ . . . crowned ⟨culprit⟩ ↑wretch↓ . . . the ⟨record⟩ ↑memorial↓
23–24 of ⟨joy⟩ ↑public congratulation↓. . . . our ⟨ample⟩ ↑extensive↓
28-(313)2 acclamations ⟨Men have feasted⟩ The voice of ⟨eloquence⟩ ↑eulogy↓ . . . some ⟨sort⟩ ↑degree↓ . . ↑& . . . in↓ over the ⟨prosperous⟩ ↑exulting↓

Page 313

3   ↑reasonable↓ topic of ⟨true⟩ gratitude.

4   us. ⟨But o⟩ ↑And↓

9–10   confine. ⟨It must exist in⟩ It . . . ⟨in⟩much . . . office⟨rs⟩s

11–12   laws. ²{It must exist in the heart⟨s⟩ of the citizen⟨s⟩ ¹{to exist in the
             Community. The ⟨soul⟩ ↑independence↓ . . . the ⟨soul⟩
             ↑independence↓

18   ↑best↓

19   hands. ⟨P⟩ Many

22–23   value, ⟨&⟩ ↑not many men↓ . . . distinction. ⟨T⟩Our . . . ↑cheap,↓

25–26   always ⟨wh⟩ do understand. ↑the . . . awe.↓

38   that ⟨all⟩ the

Page 314

6–8   much. ⟨What is there⟩ ↑Let . . . feeling↓ so exhilarating about that
             idea that it communicates electricity at the very naming.

8–9   that ⟨every⟩ ↑you . . . a↓ . . . sentiment ⟨will make⟩ ↑but↓

9–10   ↑Yet . . . ⟨it⟩the blessing.↓

18   no /dependance/ warrant/

21   ↑declaration of↓ assembled ⟨universe⟩ ↑nations↓

24   ↑& unwilling↓

31   grovel. ⟨This man⟩ Neither

33   ¶ Another / {goes home from this triumph of the public} / rises early /
             [brackets and variant in pencil]

35   toil ⟨for themselves⟩ ↑in . . . affairs↓.

36   ↑give . . . to↓

41   of ⟨its⟩ ↑human hatred↓ rancour & ⟨its⟩ patronage,

Page 315

4   ↑boastful↓

9   will ⟨run⟩ ↑encounter↓ . . . to ⟨indulge⟩ ↑feed↓

10–11   free? ⟨O⟩ Is . . . heritage of of

15   John ↑(VIII. 31)↓ . . . ↑Jews↓

17   free. They answered him" (as

32   sa⟨ct⟩nctioned

38–39   ↑Our . . . liberty↓

Page 316

1   ↑a community in wh. exist⟨s⟩ed↓

3–4   celebrated. ⟨But⟩ ↑As . . . a⟨t⟩s ⟨sunset yesterday⟩ ↑the sun went
             down↓ . . . how↓

5   with↑in↓

7–18   & ⟨at best⟩ ↑if it shd. last,↓ we ⟨have to⟩ ↑ourselves can↓ . . .
             more⟨.⟩; But ↑as . . . Christ↓ I speak ⟨to⟩ ↑of↓ . . . ↑is not . . .
             territory,↓ . . . you; ⟨↑Earn this charter, comply with the terms on
             which this is offered, and↓⟩ ↑Insert A↓ [At the bottom of the page, a
             passage marked "A":] ↑{Every . . . charter.}↓ fear . . . feet to . . .
             there ⟨shall you go⟩ ↑the . . . forth↓ . . . sublime ⟨spirit⟩ ⟨in his
             liberty.⟩ in

Index

411